Reforming Theology

Explorations in the Theological Traditions
of the United Reformed Church

David R Peel

For Pat, Andrew and Heidi

ISBN 0 85346 211 9
© The United Reformed Church, 2002

Published by The United Reformed Church
86 Tavistock Place, London WC1H 9RT

The
United
Reformed
Church

Produced by Communications and Editorial, Graphics Office

Printed by Healeys Printers, Unit 10, The Sterling Complex, Farthing Road, Ipswich, Suffolk IP1 5AP

Contents

Part 5

Part 6

PREFACE

THOSE who wish to learn about the United Reformed Church (URC) are fortunate to have access to David Cornick's, *Under God's Good Hand*,[1] which, as its title goes on to explain, is 'a history of the traditions which have come together in the United Reformed Church in the United Kingdom'. This book attempts to do for URC theology what David Cornick has so valuably done for its history. I hope that it will become a useful resource to be used alongside David's book by those who want to know more about the United Reformed Church's ethos and the theological stances of Reformed Christians. The book may be particularly useful to those preparing for designated ministries in the URC, but I also hope that it will be of interest to enquiring church members. A glossary of theological terms is provided to help explain the technical terms I have employed.

David Cornick first suggested that I should write this book. There have been times over the last three years when I doubted the wisdom of having responded positively to his suggestion. As the enormity of my task became clearer, opportunities to tackle it seemed to reduce as my responsibilities at Luther King House became all consuming. Now that the project has been completed, I am not only glad that David placed the idea for this book in my head, but I am grateful for those at Northern College – governors, staff and students – who encouraged me to press on to complete it.

I am thoroughly convinced that the real insights in this book belong to the theologians I discuss rather than to me. Where I manage some sound theological judgements, though, it will no doubt be due to my formative university teachers (David Pailin, Ronald Preston and Raymond Plant in Manchester, and Schubert Ogden and John Deschner in the USA), or to those whose work I have read (e.g. my 'reading' of Reformed theology has been shaped largely by the work of Brian Gerrish). I am also grateful for the practical advice of Graham Spicer, whose friendship I have valued since my college days. Maurice Husselbee, Alan Sell and Donald Whitehead provided me with helpful and encouraging comments on a late draft of the text, while Carol Rogers and Sara Foyle at Tavistock Place guided the project to completion. Also in my debt are those who found suitable photographs and graphics to illustrate the text, particularly Jill Thornton who has contributed some notable art work. Finally, my thanks are due to Pam Corbishley who typed the various drafts and, despite my handwriting and computer illiteracy, managed to prepare a final version for publication.

David R Peel
Manchester
October 2001

---

[1]   David Cornick, *Under God's Good Hand* (London: URC, 1998).

The theologian's task is not to divert the ears with chatter, but to strengthen consciences by teaching things true, sure, and profitable.

John Calvin[1]

Reformed theology is reforming theology . . . .
Tradition and innovation are one process.

Jürgen Moltmann[2]

---

[1]   John Calvin, *Institutes of Christian Religion* 1,14,4. All references to the *Institutes* are from the F L Battle (trans.) and J T McNeil (ed.) edition (Philadelphia: The Westminster Press, 1960). They are cited by reference to book, chapter and section.
[2]   Jürgen Moltmann, 'Theologia Reformata et Semper Reformanda', in David Willis and Michael Welker (eds.), *Towards The Future of Reformed Theology: Tasks, Topics, Traditions* (Grand Rapids, Michigan: William B Eerdmans Publishing Company, 1999), pp 120–121.

PART 1

Introduction

AS THIS book was written the twentieth century came to an end. For the mainstream churches in Western Europe it had not been a successful period. Rampant numerical decline cast a gloomy spectre over the ecclesiastical scene. The URC, for example, lost over half its members between 1972 and 1997, the first twenty-five years of its life. The Christian churches seem to have increasingly found it difficult to get their message over, perhaps due to their being perceived as no longer having appropriate and credible things to say. The church has lost its intellectual credibility in the eyes of many people, but if we do not have a credible belief system we will not cut ice in the modern world.

As the churches have lost ground, they have gone about trying to meet the situation by seeking remedies which either point out the disease more clearly or simply reflect an inadequate diagnosis. As if the problem facing Western Christianity at the end of the twentieth century was resolvable by simply jazzing up our worship here and there, or returning to the warm glow of Moody and Sankey singsongs, or pretending that what we believe can be put to one side as we seek to change society, or applying modern management techniques, or turning the church into a counselling service!

No, the seeds of the demise run much deeper. Our basic problem is that we do not have a witness of faith which is at one and the same time congruent with the early Christian witness to Jesus and credible in the modern world. We have lost our theological confidence, and without sound theology the church is speechless. When rank and file church members cannot present a convincing case for their faith the church's primary arm of mission seizes up. Everything boils down to having a message which is believable, and Christians having such basic confidence in that message that they quite naturally wish to share it with others. Serious and effective evangelism is grounded in appropriate and credible theology.

This book is written with two basic convictions: first, I think that there is a desperate need to return to a serious consideration of what we believe; and, secondly, I judge that the Reformed ethos offers us rich resources to carry out the task. Now, by way of introduction, we turn first to a more extensive discussion of the book's purpose. Then I will offer some reasons why the average Christian is suspicious of theology and, hopefully, say something in its favour. Finally, the Introduction closes with a consideration of some of the problems and possibilities presented for theology by a serious engagement with scripture.

CHAPTER 1

The Purpose of the Book

THE FIRST problem the writer and readers of this book face is that the evidence suggests that there is no such thing as *the* theology of the URC. We are confronted with a plurality of evidence and opinion. Such is the range of theological perspectives in the URC that all those who feared that the advent of the URC would bring a stifling uniformity now can celebrate a very rich and newly fashioned diversity. Others, of course, claim conversely that the theological spectrum in the URC is now so wide that the church has an acute identity crisis when it comes to the content of its belief, and the church policy and practices which flow from it. People more and more, it is alleged, simply believe what they like rather than feel obliged to follow a party line.

One way of interpreting the present theological situation in the URC is in terms of the changes which have taken place in Western culture towards the end of the twentieth century. We are undergoing a move from a modernist to a postmodernist culture. Just what this involves can be seen from Figure One, where the distinctive ethos of postmodern culture is placed in juxtaposition to that of the modern.

FIGURE ONE [1]	
MODERNISM	**POSTMODERNISM**
homogeneous	fragmented
society is functional, bureaucratic and uniform	society is pluralistic and diverse
reduces all to rational and centralized control	abandons control and promotes eclectic variety, even anarchy.
envisages a single, unified society	envisages only diverse societies
the Old Soviet Union	the post-Gorbachev Republic
Yugoslavia	warring ancient nationalisms
rational policy of nuclear deterrence based upon mutual assured destruction	unpredictable prospects of vertical and horizontal nuclear proliferation
secularization	resurgent, competing fundamentalisms
ignored or patronized the past	yearns for the past – or, rather, selected parts of it

---

[1]   The material in the table is based on the text of Robin Gill's *Moral Communities* (Exeter: Exeter University Press, 1992), pp 55–56.

The outlook of a church invariably mirrors to some extent the age and culture in which it finds itself, and those of us who have been members of the URC since its inauguration in 1972 may well see its development in part at least reflecting the wider cultural changes: a strong stress on the search for organic unity in the church has tended to give way to a more general acceptance to work federally and through ecumenical networks; the centralised power and authority of the General Assembly has increasingly been challenged by regional and synodical alternative ways of working; contentious and deeply polarized theological convictions were discovered in the URC on the occasion of the debate about human sexuality; and a deepening concern about URC ethos, history and identity seems to have emerged as the URC has grown older and we have realised that we are destined for greater permanence than was originally intended – it is interesting and noteworthy that it took the URC twenty-five years and more to publish books which covered its historical foundations and theological ethos!

The URC, however, does more than simply reflect the spirit of the age. Being a union of four churches it inevitably carries within it some of the distinctive outlooks of the Congregational, Presbyterian and Churches of Christ traditions that came together to form it. As one moves around the URC, therefore, one often encounters emphases which clearly reflect part of a particular and distinctive past. This is apparent for example when one compares the level of importance attached to Elders' Meeting and District Council with that granted to Church Meeting and Synod across the denomination. A further and arguably more obvious example centres upon the fact that both infant and adult baptism are practised in the URC, thus honouring the different practices of the Congregational and Presbyterian traditions, on the one hand, and those of the Churches of Christ on the other. Every congregation is expected to make both modes of baptism available but the evidence suggests that usually one or the other dominates in most congregations. When adult baptism seems to dominate, however, this will not necessarily reflect a congregation or minister from a Churches of Christ background, since a preference for adult baptism within the URC may well have emerged through congregations and ministers being influenced by renewal movements whose theology eschews the practice of infant baptism.

The roots of the URC's theological diversity, however, go back much further. Talk of Reformed theology often hides the rich diversity which is displayed in the theological convictions of the great sixteenth century reformers. While Calvin and Zwingli were agreed on a common theological project, they had their own emphases, and hence each needs considering in his own right. Any suggestion that a totally common theology flowed from these reformers into the Reformed churches in Europe can only be a gross simplification. And the situation became even more complex when liberal theology came on the scene in the nineteenth century due to the work of a Reformed pastor, Friedrich Schleiermacher, the so-called founder of modern theology.

Schleiermacher believed that the work of theology entails presenting at any given moment an account of the church's belief. He was acutely aware of the historical and cultural influence on all thought and, hence, he accepted that, while the essence of Christianity remains fixed, the church's tradition which bears witness to Christ is subject to change as the church responds to challenges from secular insight and knowledge. Many people, of course, assume that church doctrine is something to be handed on intact or, at a pinch, merely to be translated into more accessible language and concepts. Schleiermacher, however, started a tradition which allows for the possibility that received dogma might be in need of reformation, and hence the probability that some ancient doctrines will need abandoning if the church is to bear a credible gospel. He prepared the way for an influential approach to theology which recognizes that there are twin criteria by which to judge theological adequacy: not just the *internal* criterion of fidelity to scripture, but also the *external* criterion of credibility as defined by the current state of knowledge.

It is hotly debated whether the liberal theology inaugurated by Schleiermacher can correctly be referred to as a legitimate development of Reformed theology. Karl Barth and Emil Brunner, for example, launched a vitriolic polemic against liberal theology, accusing it of reducing the historically given faith of the church to what might happen to be believable at any one time. Rather than being a legitimate development of the Reformed tradition, in the eyes of neo-orthodox theologians liberal theology was an unacceptable mutation of it. While they at least verbally accepted that theology needed to take into account the new knowledge appearing from science and history, they nevertheless proclaimed vehemently that theology must not depart from being the articulation of God's Word to humankind revealed to us through our ongoing engagement with the Bible. In their opinion there is one criterion of theological adequacy not two; the divine Word revealed in scripture is not to be judged by human experience or knowledge.

The influence of the neo-orthodox critique of liberal theology has been so great that, in the eyes of many commentators, liberal theology is not regarded as a legitimate strand within Reformed theology. However, the work of Brian Gerrish ought to persuade us otherwise. He shows convincingly that the nineteenth century liberal theologians did not think that they were abandoning their Reformed heritage. Most of them actually saw themselves as traditionalists rather than rebels. If some of their theological formulations ended up being reductionist, it was the result of their laudable aim to make the Christian faith more accessible to contemporary people. Their motives were thoroughly evangelical. What they were doing was formally little different from Calvin's use of Luther. Gerrish reminds us that 'the true follower does not mimic the master's every gesture but puts what he receives in a form of his own', and he goes on to argue that 'Calvin's own claim of continuity with Luther was a claim, not of formal identity, but of legitimate development'.[2] And which faithful Protestant would ever deny that the circumstances in which we find ourselves may require us to abandon or revise the tradition handed down to us? To do so would be to maintain a personal commitment to a perceived orthodoxy at the expense of denying the major theological significance of the Protestant Reformation!

The liberal theologians discovered the true nature of tradition. It is quite open-ended, developmental and fluid, rather than static and unchangeable. Gerrish even ventures the question as to '. . . whether there was not something characteristically Protestant about [liberal] thinking exactly because they understood continuity as a kind of change'.[3] It seems perfectly clear that liberal theology has as much right as neo-orthodoxy to count as a legitimate development within Reformed theology. Indeed, a case can be made for viewing neo-orthodoxy as an important self-critical moment within the history of liberal theology.

Objection to liberal theology is not just limited to neo-orthodox thinkers. In American Presbyterian circles at the start of the twentieth century the polemic against liberalism was equally passionate but rather more reactionary. A somewhat wooden reading of Calvin's theology by Princeton theologians gave rise to the assertion that there are certain 'fundamentals' of belief which are essential for Christians to hold (Figure Two).

---

[2] Brian A Gerrish, *Tradition and the Modern World: Reformed Theology in the Nineteenth Century* (Chicago and London: The University of Chicago Press, 1978), p 46.

[3] Ibid., p 3.

FIGURE TWO

**THE FUNDAMENTALS OF FAITH AND EVANGELICAL
CHRISTIANITY AS DEFINED BY
THE NORTHERN PRESBYTERIAN CHURCH (USA)
IN 1910**

* THE INSPIRATION AND INFALLIBILITY OF SCRIPTURE

* THE DEITY OF CHRIST

* CHRIST'S VIRGIN BIRTH AND MIRACLES

* CHRIST'S PENAL DEATH FOR OUR SINS

* CHRIST'S PHYSICAL RESURRECTION AND PERSONAL RETURN

B B Warfield and others believed in the verbal inspiration of the Bible and its infallibility in doctrinal matters, along with a range of other doctrines generally associated with conservative evangelical Christians, including some within the URC. The movement became known as 'fundamentalism', but the term is not often used today by those who hold similar views, since 'fundamentalism' is now saddled with a perjorative meaning associated with obscurantist attitudes rooted in anti-scholarly and anti-intellectual approaches. The conservative evangelical Group for Evangelism and Renewal (GEAR) within the URC recently offered a defence of some of the 'fundamentals' drawn up in Princeton in 1909.[4]

The theological diversity in the URC clearly has roots which go back to the Reformers themselves, the liberal theological outlook which blossomed in the nineteenth century and the reactions to liberalism in the early and mid-years of the twentieth century. But, we might ask, has diversity not been one of the hall-marks of Christianity since the Apostles? In some ecumenical discussions a picture is painted which suggests that the ecumenical task is to repair a divided church. But this picture presupposes that there was once an organically united church. Given the preponderance of ecumenical theologians to authorize their conclusions by reference to scripture, it also paints a false picture of the New Testament church. A more critical use of scripture reveals evidence of not only continuity but also discontinuity between the early Christians and Jesus. Differing doctrinal views are present in the earliest traditions, prompting the conclusion of Ernst Käsemann that 'the New Testament canon does not, as such, constitute the foundation of the unity of the Church' but, instead, 'provides the basis for the multiplicity of the confessions'.[5] Indeed,

---

[4]   See *In Gear*, 57 (January 1993).

[5]   Ernst Käsemann, 'The Canon of the New Testament and the Unity of the Church' in *Essays on New Testament Themes* (London: SCM Press, 1964), p 103.

---

famous ecumenical councils later never managed fully to standardize Christian belief: the argument over circumcision and food laws rumbled on well after the Council of Jerusalem was supposed to have settled it; the search for a conceptual understanding of the Trinity has kept theologians occupied ever since the Council of Nicaea, despite Constantine's political manoeuvres to get the matter resolved by the bishops whom he drew together in such pomp and opulence; while Arianism continued unabated for several generations, and well after the orthodox understanding of how Jesus was both God and man was supposedly set in stone at Chalcedon. So, to put the matter briefly and starkly, there never was a time when all Christians believed the same things!

The theological diversity abroad in the URC inevitably means that it will not be possible to do full justice to our task of providing an outline of the traditions and emphases which make up the theological outlook of the URC. This survey is bound to be limited; but I trust that readers will discover what is meant when I say that the Reformed heritage includes Calvin *and* Schleiermacher, Forsyth *and* Oman, and, more recently, Newbigin *and* Hick. Hopefully, they will also be encouraged to read some of the more important theologians who have belonged to the Reformed ethos. We shall attempt to achieve both these objectives by commenting on each section of the Confession of Faith found in the URC Basis of Union (Figure Three).

FIGURE THREE [6]

We believe in the one living and true God, creator, preserver and ruler of all things in heaven and earth, Father, Son and Holy Spirit. Him alone we worship and in him we put our trust.

We believe that God, in his infinite love for men, gave his eternal Son, Jesus Christ our Lord, who became man, lived on earth in perfect love and obedience, died upon the cross for our sins, rose again from the dead and lives for evermore, saviour, judge and king.

We believe that, by the Holy Spirit, this glorious gospel is made effective so that through faith we receive the forgiveness of sins, newness of life as children of God and strength in this present world to do his will.

We believe in the one, holy, catholic, apostolic Church, in heaven and on earth, wherein by the same Spirit, the whole company of believers is made one Body of Christ, to worship God and serve him and all men in his kingdom of righteousness and love.

We rejoice in the gift of eternal life, and believe that, in the fullness of time, God will renew and gather in one all things in Christ, to whom, with the Father and the Holy Spirit, be glory and majesty, dominion and power, both now and for ever.

---

[6] URC *Basis of Union* 7, 17 found in David M Thompson (ed.), *Stating the Gospel: Formulations and Declarations of Faith from the heritage of the United Reformed Church* (Edinburgh: T & T Clark, 1990).

CHAPTER 2

Theology in the Church:
Deathknell or Wellspring?

I GET the impression that URC folk are far more likely to show an interest in their denomination's history than in its theology. After all we are living in an age which yearns for the past, or at least selected parts of it, with the growth of the heritage industry being a prominent feature. But, by and large, theology is not held in esteem in our churches. It is widely believed that it is best left alone, since it only complicates simple believing and undermines faith. The press enjoy depicting theologians as heretics attacking the Church from within – John Robinson in the 1960s and David Jenkins in the 1980s, and that image has become firmly lodged in many minds. Others, not so distrustful of theology, do not regard it as something which concerns them, since such heady matters are best left to the clergy and the professional theologians who work in universities and colleges. Almost completely absent is the idea that being a theologian might be an important ministry in the church. When I left a pastorate to become a tutor at Northern College I was made to feel by people in the church that I had left the ministry. Underneath all these negative attitudes towards theology and theologians of course lies an acute anti-intellectualism.

Whatever the attitudes of our church members might suggest, unwittingly they repeatedly engage in theology and make theological judgements. They think about their faith choosing to endorse or reject particular beliefs. Even if they are not very forthcoming when it comes to declaring their faith in public, perhaps having imbibed the dictum that prudent people do not go public on matters of sex, religion and politics, they have nevertheless worked out some kind of belief system on the basis of their personal exploration and involvement in a church. The issue is not whether Christians are engaged in theology, rather it is how adequate their theology is when measured against established criteria. But what are we talking about when we use the word 'theology', and why is theology so low on people's agenda?

Theology is defined by Maurice Wiles as 'reasoned discourse about God'.[1] But if theology is 'reasoned discourse about God' and as such is an activity in which all Christians share however sketchily and shallowly, why has it such a low profile in their minds and in the churches' lives? Three reasons might help us answer this question.

First, theology has become largely associated with the preparation of ordained ministers for the churches. As medicine is to the general practitioner, so theology is to the minister of religion. In other words, theology has become 'clericalized'. This state of affairs is hardly surprising when one remembers the influence of Friedrich Schleiermacher's, *Brief Outline of Theological Study* (1811) on subsequent understandings of theology in the West. Schleiermacher was instrumental in the creation of the University of Berlin, and it was his wish that the new university should offer ordination training on a professional level comparable to the way it would educate lawyers and

---

[1]   Maurice Wiles, *What is Theology?* (Oxford: Oxford University Press, 1976), p 1.

doctors. He drew up a syllabus to convince sceptical friends that theology could be studied in a scientific way. It took the form of three branches (practical, historical and philosophical) unified by the single aim of educating people for leadership in the church. So, under the influence of Scheiermacher's proposals, an activity which essentially belongs to the whole church became in danger of being associated solely with ministers and clergy. And, if my experience is to be trusted, there is now a subtle collusion in churches between ordained and lay which helps to keep theology in the seminary and away from the congregation.

Secondly, Schleiermacher's proposals became modified over the years, with his three-fold pattern taking on the further dimension of systematic theology. It was hardly surprising, then, that over a period of time what once was a single course of study with distinct branches tended to fragment into a series of separate, scientific disciplines. Each study developed its own methodology and professional standards were set by the respective learned societies. Schleiermacher's aim of theology being a unified science in the service of the church quickly broke down as theology became a scholarly field within which different sciences operate. This makes a holistic understanding of the theological task impossible even for the professionals who work in the various theological disciplines, let alone ministers and church members. The theological world is now such a mind-boggling mix of different intellectual pursuits that inter-disciplinary work inside its own field is difficult enough, never mind with other fields. It is quite easy to see why those outside universities and seminaries find this state of affairs totally overwhelming, since if this is what theology is all about, in what sense is it any concern of the average minister or church member? People vote with their feet when they see theology as a business promoting the research and teaching status of a university, rather than addressing the church's agenda. The 'professionalization' of theology has tended to take theology away from church members.

Thirdly, the professionalization of theology has led to its increasing 'secularization'. The theological disciplines and their sub-disciplines increasingly make use of the standards set, and methods followed, by secular, cognate disciplines. So, for example, the methodology and criteria of secular historiography come to control the way we study church history; the current literary theory becomes the guide to our reading of the Bible; the ethos of non-directive pastoral counselling starts to determine the way we understand pastoral care. This is to offer an observation, rather than to make a value judgement. If the parameters within which theology is conducted are increasingly set by those outside the church, though, is it totally surprising that church members wonder whether it has anything to do with them? And, some of them, not necessarily the more conservative, will wonder at what point the warning of scripture will apply: 'But as the heavens are higher than the earth, so are my ways higher than your ways and my thoughts than your thoughts' (Isaiah 55: 9).

We can understand the theological inertia which exists in our churches, therefore, in the light of what I have called theology's 'clericalization', 'professionalization' and 'secularization'. There is a role for the professional theologian - to suggest otherwise would be akin to sawing off the branch upon which I am sitting! And that role needs to be maintained, supported and valued, but not at the expense of undermining genuine theological activity within local churches and among believers. Theology must attend faith, rather than be perceived as opposed to it. Faith is our way of living before God and in the world. It involves placing our whole trust in God for our ultimate well-being, but it carries with it a knowledge of a practical kind. This knowledge, often largely unreflective, is fundamentally part of faith. When we bring it to greater degrees of sophistication through reflection, what we know as theology occurs. Edward Farley, to whom a great deal of this analysis is indebted, speaks of 'a cognitivity which attends faith itself' called 'insightfulness'.[2] When we reflect upon our 'insight', theological understanding occurs. This reflection is simply 'the understanding required by the life of faith in the world'.[3] And why is it required? Precisely so that we may fulfil the exhortation laid upon us by the writer of the first epistle of Peter: 'Always be ready to make your defence to anyone who demands from you an accounting for the hope that is in you' (1 Peter 3: 15). Only a thoughtful faith will satisfy the mission imperative; only a well-worked-out theology will stand up in our sophisticated world.

Some of the most exciting and influential theological developments in recent times have arguably come from the proponents and practitioners of the various liberation theologies. Liberation theology is firmly rooted in the work of practising Christians, resourced and empowered in their critical reflection upon their praxis by ordained professional theologians. In many ways, the work of the so-called 'base communities' in Latin America is formally similar to the way the Church Meeting functioned in the early Independent churches. Alan Sell argues that the Church Meeting is where 'those who have sat under the preaching of the Word and received the bread and wine at the Last Supper gather to do their contextual theology in fellowship, and by the Spirit through the Word'.[4] Liberation theology recalls us to the essential task of thinking through our personal, social and political commitments in the light of the Christian faith. Juan Luis Segundo's *The Liberation of Theology*[5] sets down many of the basic features of this way of doing theology, and various British applications have been made of it.[6] Liberation Theology is rooted in the use of the Bible as a major means of providing a critique of our life and work, as well as the norm by which all our commitments are to be judged, namely, the liberating God who has been re-presented to the world uniquely in the life and teaching of Jesus. So, with this brief reference to a movement which seeks to give theology back to the whole church, it is appropriate to move to our discussion of the Bible's role in the theology of the traditions which flow into the URC ethos.

2   Edward Farley, Theologia: *The Fragmentation and Unity of Theological Education* (Philadelphia: Fortress Press, 1983), p 157.
3   Ibid.
4   Alan P F Sell, *Commemorations: Studies in Christian Thought and History* (Aberystwyth: The University of Wales Press, 1993), p 353.
5   Juan Luis Segundo, *The Liberation of Theology* (Maryknoll, NY: Orbis Books 1976).
6   See Margaret Kane, *What Kind of God? Reflections on Working with People and Churches in North East England* (London: SCM Press, 1986), pp 81–101; and Laurie Green, *Let's Do Theology: A Pastoral Cycle Resource Book* (London: Mowbray, 1990).

CHAPTER 3

The Authority of the Bible

ON 16th November 1996 a service was held in Southwark Cathedral to celebrate twenty years of the Lesbian and Gay Christian Movement. It received extensive coverage in the media. *The Guardian* on the day of the service carried an eirenic dialogue between Bishop Derek Rawcliffe, who had recently been sacked for blessing a gay wedding, and Lance Pierson, a married writer firmly of the view that practising homosexuals are breaking divine law. Towards the end the bishop exclaimed: 'Our differences have boiled down to the interpretation of two or three verses in the Bible and it's got very scholarly'. I drew two conclusions from that observation.

First, when Christians engage in any serious discussion about matters of belief and practice, invariably they turn to the foundational documents of Christianity for guidance. But once 'scholarly' readers manage to read out of the same texts diametrically opposed meanings, it is hardly surprising that the average church member decides to sit rather more lightly on the idea of the Bible's authority than perhaps their church's theology might request. This leads on to the second observation, namely, that we do not serve the Bible well when we use it as a crude means of canonizing beliefs and practices to which we are committed but others are not. The Bible can be used – and, indeed, *has been* used – to legitimize doctrine and witness that with hindsight we now all recognize as sub-Christian. From apartheid and racism to slavery and sexism, from burning scientists at the stake to driving indigenous people off their lands, from ruthlessly raping the natural world to justifying minors working twelve hours per day in mines, the scale of misery, abuse and inhumanity which has been perpetuated by biblical authorization has beggared belief.

In theory, if not always in practice, the URC has the spirit of the Reformation running through its veins. It's very *raison d'être* was hewn out of the theological debates, ecclesiastical disagreements and political struggles of continental Europe in the sixteenth century, and, nearer to home, the latter part of the seventeenth century. We carry the marks not only of, 'reform' but also of 'dissent' and 'non-conformity'. And the role of the Bible in shaping our ethos cannot be overstated. The battle cry of the Reformation was *sola scriptura* (scripture alone), and on matters of authority it is often said that 'if the reformers dethroned the pope, they enthroned Scripture'.[1] But it would be a mistake to assume that the Medieval church had no place for Scripture, as if the Reformers had hit upon something new. Indeed, quite the reverse was the case.

The medieval church took over from the early church a view of Scripture which was partly rooted in a doctrine of biblical inspiration that in effect equated the words of the Bible with the Word of God. It believed that everything of importance for Christianity can be found in Scripture. However, this overt biblicism was tempered by the way they approached the matter of biblical interpretation. The early Alexandrian theological school had made extensive use of allegorical

---

[1]   Alister E McGrath, *Reformation Thought: An Introduction,* 2nd. ed. (Oxford: Basil Blackwell, 1993), p 134.

methods of exegesis, and, as Brian Gerrish remarks, these enabled 'a sufficiently astute theologian . . . without much difficulty' to 'find any of the church's beliefs hidden or symbolized in the most unlikely corners of both the Old and the New Testaments'.[2] The medievals took their lead from the Alexandrians, and, in putting forward the maxim of *sola scriptura* the Reformers were not so much asserting the authority of Scripture for the faith and conduct of Christians as in fact arguing for a particular approach to reading the Bible – the literal rather than allegorical reading of the text. This literal approach insisted that the Bible does not need an ecclesial or academic hierarchy to guarantee sound interpretation; rather the plain meaning of Scripture is capable of being grasped by any serious and devout reader. And, once the view had been adopted that authority in the church does not derive from the status of clerics or theologians but from the One they serve, it was quite natural to go on to recognize that the proper authority of the Bible does not reside in the words of a book but in the Word to whom Scripture bears witness.

An interesting way of understanding the development of the traditions which make up the URC ethos is to focus on the perennial controversy between those who, like the medieval theologians, tend to treat the Bible as a series of sacred oracles and those who view it as a witness to an authority beyond itself. We now turn to five theologians who reflect a range of views that are encountered not only historically but also currently in the Reformed churches.

John Calvin

Calvin maintains that, while everyone in principle is able to grasp a knowledge of God from reflection upon the natural world, in practice because of their sin they are like blind people groping in the dark. We are responsible for our failure to know God, so we are without excuse; but God graciously has provided us with the Bible – 'another and better help . . . to direct us aright to the very Creator of the universe'.[3] Calvin views the Bible akin to spectacles; it helps us to see the Truth clearly. Our sin is so debilitating that a natural knowledge of God's saving significance is completely impossible. In Scripture, though, God has provided the special means whereby that knowledge can be received by us.

At the heart of Calvin's theology lies his idea of 'accommodation'. This enables him to suggest how it is possible for the great gulf between God and sinful humanity to be overcome. God in Jesus has come down to our level; the Deity has come to where we are that we might understand who God is. The analogy of the skilful orator lies behind Calvin's thought. Like any effective communicator, God knows the audience and selects language appropriate for it. As with God's self-offering in human form in the incarnation, so it is with God's gift of Scripture to the church: God gives us a message in 'language' we can understand – the example of a human being like us, and words, pictures, images and stories that we can grasp.

Calvin argues that the Scriptures are to be regarded 'as having sprung from Heaven' and as the medium through which 'the living words of God' are heard.[4] He objected to the Roman Catholic view of his day which claimed that the church is responsible for deciding what weight is to be afforded to the Bible; it is the church that is grounded upon Scripture, not vice versa! The Bible

---

[2] Brian A Gerrish, *The Old Protestantism and the New: Essays on the Reformation Heritage* (Edinburgh: T & T Clark, 1982), p 52.

[3] Calvin, *Institutes,* 1,6,1.

[4] Ibid., 1,7,1.

carries within itself 'as clear evidence of its own truth as white and black things do of their color, or sweet and bitter things do of their taste'.[5]   Those who struggle to understand the Bible may find their eyes glazing over at this point, but Calvin would ask them to remember that we do not believe that the words of Scripture are the Word of God on the authority of the church, or on the basis of our own reason; rather we gain our understanding and confidence to believe from God, through 'the secret testimony of the Spirit'.[6]   The Holy Spirit enables us to be certain that we hear God's Word to us in the Bible as 'from the very mouth of God by the ministry of men'[7]

According to Calvin, the Scriptures contain all that is required for our belief and practice. His doctrine of 'the sufficiency of Scripture' is both negative and positive. He seems to prohibit looking outside Scripture for guidance, as well as insist that the Bible contains all that we need. Living in an age untutored by the historical-critical approach to the Bible, he finds it easy to claim that the Bible is not distorted by anything earthly, that its parts harmonize together perfectly, and that its authority has been confirmed repeatedly. Any distinction between the words of Scripture and the Word of God seems to have collapsed when Calvin talks of God having 'his Word set down and sealed in writing', and of the Old Testament being 'composed under the Holy Spirit's dictation'.[8]

Set in his historical context Calvin was clearly an innovative exegete who possessed an enlightened view of the authority of the Bible. Nevertheless some passages in his writings are open to the view that he understood the Bible to be the inspired and inerrant Word of God. Fundamentalism, after all, was the creation of one group of Calvin's disciples. However, the Bible was essentially sufficient according to belief and practice for Calvin because it contains all that is ultimately worth knowing, namely, God's saving love in Jesus Christ. As the Scriptures are read and proclaimed in preaching, Christ is offered by the work of the Holy Spirit. Christianity is not a religion of the book but a faith rooted in a saving encounter of believers with God's love in Jesus Christ. It was the christological rather than the literal meaning of 'Word' which was at the centre of Calvin's theology. The Word is 'the everlasting Wisdom, residing with God from which both all oracles and prophecies go forth', and it is 'the wellspring of all oracles'.[9]   Christians hear *that* Word speaking to them through the written words of the Bible and receive *that* Word in the preaching and sacraments of the church.

In many Reformed theologies, therefore, the Scriptures have taken on a sacramental character: they are a means of grace.   Whatever some of Calvin's followers may make him out to be, Calvin was never a narrow-minded biblicist. Like Luther his mentor, he held fast to *sola scriptura*. The Bible is indeed a means of knowing the redeeming and liberating Word of God; but the Words of Scripture are only of ultimate significance because *through* them we encounter Jesus Christ. John W de Grucy, a Reformed theologian from South Africa, correctly argues that 'Calvin's primary consideration was the witness of the Word and Spirit to God's redeeming grace in Jesus Christ', and he goes on to affirm that this became for Calvin 'the chief basis upon which he interpreted the whole of Scripture . . . , the way whereby Scripture interpreted itself'.[10]

[5]   Ibid., 1,7,2.
[6]   Ibid., 1,7,4.
[7]   Ibid., 1,7,5.
[8]   Ibid., 4,8,6.
[9]   Ibid., I,13,7.
[10]   John W de Grucy, *Liberating Reformed Theology: A South African Contribution to an Ecumenical Debate* (Grand Rapids, Michigan: William B Eerdmans Publishing Company, 1991), p 55.

Friedrich Schleiermacher

Schleiermacher's theology is an attempt to give an account of the Christian witness of faith which acknowledges our debt to the Bible at the same time as taking into account contemporary experience. He believed passionately that the Reformation is not simply an event in the past but also the bearer of a perennially important principle: the Church is forever to be reformed, after the standard of Christ and in the light of new and changed circumstances. This carries with it the view that Christian theology is subject to development. Schleiermacher's life had been profoundly shaped by a vivid pietism. Under that influence he sought to address 'the challenge of the Enlightenment' and to respond to 'the insights of Romanticism', with the result that there emerged what de Grucy has called 'Reformed theology in a new key'.[11]

One of Schleiermacher's concerns is to address the challenge posed to theology by biblical criticism. Whatever else it had achieved, biblical criticism had shown the all too human nature of the Bible: its diversity rather than its unity, its contradictions as well as its uniformity. Schleiermacher, therefore, found it impossible to view theology in the same way as Calvin, nor could he attach the same kind of authority to the Bible as the Genevan Reformer. The Bible might be said to define God's Word to and for humankind, but the divine Word is not *confined* to it. God is also known in common human experience outside the stream of consciousness which flows from Jesus. Schleiermacher maintains that everyone, simply because of being human, possesses a general awareness of God. This *original* revelation endows us all with a rudimentary God-consciousness. God's self-revelation in Jesus Christ determines what that God-consciousness is in a special way. It is a *special* revelation of what otherwise might be dimly and differently known through experience outside Christianity. The many religions, therefore, are distinctive ways of witnessing to a common awareness of God, what Schleiermacher famously called 'a feeling of absolute dependence'. The intuitive piety we possess in common is understood in different ways in the reflective belief of the different religions. Christian doctrine consequently is an understanding of *Christian* piety, and hence the distinctively *Christian* experience of salvation in Christ.

It follows, for Schleiermacher, that the Bible is useful and important insofar as it illuminates or confirms what is known from experience. All the statements of the past are to be judged by present knowledge. The biblical writers were theologians like us, and their work is to be treated no differently from what we will hand on for others to use and reform as they please. Gerrish sums up Schleiermacher's position as follows: 'We acknowledge no authoritative interpretation of the Scriptures and no final dogmatic formulas; we interpret the Scriptures for ourselves with a greater wealth of exegetical aids than was available at the time of the Reformation and with the support of the divine Spirit, who has not died out in the meantime'.[12] Schleiermacher's influence perhaps led to the understanding of the Reformed heritage as *reformata et semper reformanda* (reformed and always to be reformed). But there are those who will argue that this particular understanding can also be found in theologies more rooted in the Bible's power to refresh and renew.

---

[11]   Ibid., p 69.
[12]   Gerrish, *Old Protestantism and the New: Essays on the Reformation Heritage*, p 191.

Peter Taylor Forsyth

Liberal theology seeks to establish a *rapprochement* between the Christian witness of faith rooted in God's special revelation in Jesus Christ and common human experience and reason, and vice-versa.[13] At its best, liberalism shows how the Christian message and the contemporary context can be mutually enriching; but at its worst it can reduce the Christian message to what the context will allow to be believed. John de Grucy is right to warn that 'if we are to hear the Word that speaks to us in Scripture, then we have to discern a Word which not only confirms our experience, need, and perspective, but more often radically challenges us'.[14] Few theologians have hammered home that point more directly than P T Forsyth, who identified liberalism as a cancer eating away at the Congregational churches in the early part of the twentieth century. Forsyth maintained that what the churches needed was a re-acquaintance with the heart of the Christian faith, an encounter with God's redeeming work in Jesus Christ, and that in turn involved a return to the Bible.

Forsyth did not believe in the verbal inspiration of the Bible; on that issue he sides with the biblical critics,[15] as he does with his view that Gospels are 'homiletical biography, not psychological; . . . compiled on evangelical rather than critical principles'.[16] The Bible *per se* is not authoritative, but the gospel of which it is the medium carries absolute authority for men and women. In the gospel we are confronted by '. . . an authority which is not simply God, but God as He has bestowed Himself on man, God as actual to historic Humanity and its evil case, God in history, God holy in guilty history, God as He gives Himself for man's sin in the historic Gospel, God our external Redeemer in Christ'.[17] Christianity is the religion of this gospel, not the religion of a book. Indeed, Forsyth is all too familiar with the misuses to which the Bible can be put. At the risk of offending a potential North American readership he remarks: 'The Bible is like the United States . . . , the richest ground in the world for every variety of "crank"'.[18] But he bemoans the fact that Christians are not immersed in the Bible. Only by paying greater attention to it will they encounter the final authority in all things, namely, Jesus Christ the Redeemer.

Forsyth speaks of the Bible in sacramental terms: 'The Bible, like its preacher, is . . . the sacrament of God to the soul, of the living God to living men, of the gracious God to lost men'.[19] We again see operative the distinction between the Word of God and the words of the Bible, making possible a christocentric understanding of the importance of Scripture for Christian belief and practice. Many commentators regard Forsyth as having put forward the same response to liberal theology as Karl Barth – albeit a couple of generations earlier.

---

[13]   See Schubert M Ogden, 'Truth, Truthfulness and Secularity: A Critique of Theological Liberalism', *Christianity and Crisis*, xxi, 5 (April 5, 1971), p 56. My understanding of the nature of theology has been significantly influenced by Ogden's work. See also his *On Theology* (San Francisco: Harper Row, 1986) and *Doing Theology Today* (Valley Forge, Pennsylvania: Trinity Press International, 1996).

[14]   de Grucy, *Liberating Reformed Theology: A South African Contribution to an Ecumenical Debate*, p 70.

[15]   P T Forsyth, *Positive Preaching and the Modern Mind,* (London: Independent Press, 1907), pp 7–8.

[16]   Ibid., p 8.

[17]   P T Forsyth, *The Principle of Authority: In Relation to Certainty, Sanctity and Society* (London: Independent Press, 1952), pp 324–5.

[18]   Forsyth, *Positive Preaching and the Modern Mind,* p 21.

[19]   Ibid., p 12.

Karl Barth

Karl Barth's theology is grounded in his attempt to interpret what he called 'the strange world within the Bible'. It largely centres on his exegesis of the message of Paul. His commentary on Romans suggests that the apostle's theme was: God is God! This meant three things for Barth. First, we are driven to recognize what Kirkegaard called 'the infinite qualitiative distinction between time and eternity'. This possesses both negative as well as positive significance: 'God is in heaven, and thou art on earth'.[20] Secondly, Barth came to understand sin as the attempt by which human beings try to obscure this basic distinction through religious experience, mysticism or reason. And, thirdly, he concluded that the great chasm between God and human beings can only be bridged by God. This was not because he believed that the gap is so great that effort from the human side is futile; rather, it was because he did not believe that God was absent in the first place. As God became a human being in Jesus Christ, the difference between God and human beings was constituted as God's nearness. The heart of the matter for Barth, like Forsyth, lies in God's redeeming work in Jesus Christ.

The importance of the Bible for Barth is that it is a sign which points to *the* ultimate authority, the triune God. Scripture is the authoritative source of what is normative in Christianity. Once again we notice a familiar distinction being made between the Bible and the authority to which it points, between the words of a book and the Word of God. Barth argues that the Bible is 'a human expression of God's revelation'; but he goes on to suggest that 'what we hear in the witness itself is more than witness, what we hear in the human expression is more than a human expression', because in Scripture we are confronted with 'the very Word of God'.[21] This presents us with one of Barth's familiar paradoxes: the words of the Bible and the Word of God, at one and the same time, are both distinct and united. He likens it, as did Calvin, to the paradox of the incarnation. An ultra-sceptical person might regard this as an attempt to explain one imponderable by invoking an even greater one, but it goes some way towards explaining Barth's rather maverick approach to critical scholarship. He agrees that historical criticism needs applying to the Bible, but it only serves as a first step to understanding. Full understanding starts when all judgements about the human nature of the Bible are over, when 'the Word' has been exposed in the words – and, *then* the Word of God is its own interpreter. As the original and true witness of God's revelation, Scripture therefore becomes God's Word for us through the activity of the Holy Spirit.

Barth is fond of talking about the way the words of the Bible become the Word of God in terms of a supernatural event. He speaks of it as 'the miracle which has to take place if the Bible is to rise up and speak to us as the Word of God'.[22] The fallible words of human beings become the medium through which the infallible Word of God is encountered and known. This is an event which we cannot bring about, only God can make it happen. There are clear implications here for Barth's understanding of the inspiration of Scripture. With one eye on biblical criticism he can admit that 'verbal inspiration does not mean the infallibility of the biblical word in its linguistic, historical and theological character as a human word', before going on to assert its true meaning in terms of the human word being 'used by God', and then received and heard by us 'in spite of its human fallibility'.[23] In this 'miracle' the role of the Holy Spirit is crucial: 'By Him, it became Holy Scripture, by Him and only by Him it speaks as such'.[24]

---

[20]   Karl Barth, *Romans* (London: Oxford University Press, 1933), p 10.
[21]   Karl Barth, *Church Dogmatics*, 1,2 (Edinburgh: T & T Clark, 1956), p 473.
[22]   Ibid., p 512.
[23]   Ibid., p 533.
[24]   Ibid., p 538.

The Bible is the oldest extant record of the origins of the church, and as such it has greater authority than other Christian documents due to its primitive nature. When the Reformers asserted their doctrine of *sola scriptura* they wanted Jesus Christ to be known and acknowledged as Lord of the church. Therefore, they directed Christians' attention to the witness of the Apostles in the New Testament as the primary sign: '. . . if it would see Jesus Christ, it is directed and bound to His primary sign and therefore to the sign of this sign – if it would see Jesus Christ, it is directed and bound by Holy Scripture'.[25] It follows that a Christian is either an Apostle, or one who bears witness with the Apostles that Jesus Christ is the revelation of God.

Peter C Hodgson

Peter Hodgson is a revisionary theologian. In his opinion, '. . . theology requires a continual process of interpretation that constructs new visions of Christian faith and practice from resources provided by scripture, tradition, reason, and experience in the context of contemporary cultural challenges'.[26] While Forsyth and Barth blaze a theological trail largely mapped out for them by Calvin, Hodgson clearly belongs to the liberal or modernist wing of Reformed theology inaugurated by Schleiermacher. He claims that his work stands 'within the tradition of Reformed theology – a theology that at its best recognizes the need for continually reforming itself',[27] and he insists that there needs to be a radical revisioning of the Christian faith in the light of all the new questions, challenges and intellectual resources that are being thrown up by our postmodern society. Hodgson regards theology as a constructive activity, and describes it by using a sailing metaphor.

> Theology. . . is a kind of ship, which has no foundation other than itself and no secure port; it sails on the open seas and is subject to the force of highly fluid elements, drawn and driven by the winds of the Spirit. No theology can claim to escape the always incomplete task of interpretation by grasping at the anchor of an authoritative scripture or a special revelation. The method of theology is in this broad sense interpretation and nothing but interpretation. It requires a constant "revisioning" of Christian faith.[28]

Hodgson's understanding of truth tries to steer a firm course between the rock which is the world of absolute certainties and the hard place of utter relativism. Like David Tracy, a fellow North American theologian, he accepts that truth can only be known with 'relative adequacy'.[29]

In Hodgson's theology, Scripture is not a normative authority. It does not possess the status of a book to which we can appeal to settle matters of belief and practice in a hard and fast way; it is rather one of several resources to be used in theology: Bible, tradition, other religious traditions, cultural history and theology, cultural context and religious experience. None of these resources possesses what Hodgson calls 'metaphysical and/or juridical' authority.[30] Their authority is simply functional. So the Bible is important because it shapes 'new human identities' and transforms 'individual and communal life', functioning as an important source of understanding for theology – a classic text.[31]

---

[25]   Ibid., p 583.
[26]   Peter C Hodgson, *Winds of the Spirit: A Constructive Christian Theology* (London: SCM Press, 1994), p xi.
[27]   Ibid., p xii.
[28]   Ibid., p 7. See also pp 3, 13 where the same metaphor is developed.
[29]   David Tracy, *Plurality and Ambiguity: Hermeneutics, Religion and Hope* (London: SCM Press, 1987), p 28.
[30]   Hodgson, *Winds of the Spirit: A Constructive Christian Theology*, p 28.
[31]   Ibid., pp 28 & 29.

The *formal* norm for theology in Hodgson's opinion is not Scripture but 'the complex interplay' in the adventure of interpretation between 'root experiences' which possess 'the character of the revelation of ultimate reality', 'the expressions of such revelatory experience' which have 'the character of the language of faith', and the theologian who interprets that language.[32] At the moment, 'the winds of the Spirit' to which theology is subject are the various liberation struggles, the ecological crisis and the need for serious and ongoing dialogue with non-Christian faiths and ideologies. It comes as no surprise therefore that the *material* norm which Hodgson selects as the criterion by which the content of the various theological sources is to be interpreted is 'a construal of the "gospel" as "liberation"'.[33] The theological task is to present a constructive interpretation which pays attention to a variety of sources including the Bible, to the extent that they reflect that quest for freedom, love and wholeness which is ultimately rooted in the life of the triune God.

Confessions and Declarations of Faith

The *Basis of Union* upon which the URC's life and work is grounded did not come out of a vacuum. It builds upon the doctrinal statements found in the Presbyterian, Congregational and Churches of Christ heritages. What do they have to say about the authority of the Bible?

The Westminster Confession (1647)[34]

The authority of the holy Scripture . . . dependeth not upon the testimony of any man or church, but wholly upon God (who is truth itself), the Author thereof; and therefore it is to be received, because it is the Word of God . . .

The whole counsel of God, concerning all things necessary for his own glory, man's salvation, faith, and life, is either expressly set down in Scripture, or by good and necessary consequence may be deduced from Scripture: unto which nothing at any time is to be added, whether by new revelations of the Spirit, or traditions of men. Nevertheless we acknowledge the inward illumination of the Spirit of God to be necessary for the saving understanding of such things as are revealed in the Word . . .

The infallible rule of interpretation of Scripture is the Scripture itself; and therefore, when there is the question about the true and full sense of any scripture . . . , it must be searched and known by other places that speak more clearly . . .

The supreme judge, by which all controversies of religion are to be determined, and all decrees of councils, opinions of ancient writers, doctrines of men and private spirits, are to be examined, and in whose sentence we are to rest, can be no other but the Holy Spirit speaking in the Scripture.

The Westminster Confession (1647) and The Savoy Declaration (1658)[35] largely take their lead from Calvin. It quickly becomes clear from them that the central claims concerning biblical authority in the URC have an ancestry going back to the seventeenth century, and to a period prior to the historical-critical method for interpreting the Bible. A similar high view of biblical authority is found in the Churches of Christ heritage.

---

[32] Ibid., p 29 & 13.
[33] Ibid., p 28.
[34] The selections from the Westminster Confession are taken from David M Thompson (ed.), *Stating the Gospel*, pp 13-14.
[35] The Savoy Declaration is found in David M Thompson (ed.), *op. cit.*, pp 61-117.

Thomas Campbell's Declaration (1809)[36]

Our desire . . . for ourselves and for our brethren would be, that, rejecting human opinions and the inventions of men as of any authority, or as having any place in the Church of God, we might forever cease from further contentions about such things, returning to, and holding fast by, the original standard; taking the divine word alone for our rule; the Holy Spirit for our teacher and guide, to lead us into all truth; and Christ alone, as exhibited in the word, for our salvation . . .

The clear distinction (but never complete separation) between 'the words of the Bible' and 'the Word of God' that is so typical of a great deal of contemporary Reformed theology is anticipated by Thomas Campbell in his phrase 'and Christ alone, as exhibited in the word'. In the Presbyterian Church of England's, *A Statement of the Christian Faith* (1956), however, the 'supreme and final source of truth' in matters pertaining to our salvation is outrightly said to be 'the Lord Jesus Christ'. This 'saving truth' is known through 'the living tradition of the Christian church', God's dealings with people in society, but 'uniquely' in the Bible, which 'is the inspired record and interpretation of God's supreme act of self-giving and self-disclosure in Jesus Christ'. As we read the Bible, the Statement affirms, we are 'confronted afresh in every generation with Christ, the living Word', and we find God speaking to us in him.[37] As well as locating biblical authority in the story of salvation history of which the Bible is the unique 'record and interpretation' the Statement acknowledges that there are 'new truths' to be appropriated today since God, the source of all truth, is active here and now.

A DECLARATION OF FAITH (1967)[38]

. . . we draw out the truth that God reveals himself with infinite generosity even though there be no true discernment nor any true obedience. No limits can be set to his generosity; none therefore may claim to measure in advance how much knowledge of God may be reached from other than Christian grounds.

We acknowledge an obligation to attend to everything God may have to say to us through human religious aspirations and religious experience, not only in Christianity, but also in other religions practised in the world . . .

We believe that God has revealed himself through a course of history which had as its central event the life of God made man in Jesus of Nazareth. The revelation is clear and it is decisive. The irreplaceable records of that revelation, and our only access to it, are the documents bound together in the Old and New Testaments of the Bible. Through the Bible God continues to draw men and women into fellowship with himself and keeps them faithful. Faith born and nourished from this source by his Spirit grows clearer and more certain for those who offer themselves to God by worship, love and obedience, through Jesus Christ.

---

[36]   Ibid., p 121.
[37]   Ibid., p 186.
[38]   Ibid., pp 209–11.

In the Congregational Church in England and Wales's, *A Declaration of Faith* (1967), a broad picture is painted in which God's *special* revelation in Jesus Christ is set firmly in the context of God's *general* revelation to the world. There is divine revelation outside the Christ event, for example, in 'the structures of the universe and . . . its various components', and even 'in the other religions practised in the world'. Any response to what is called God's 'wider revelation', however, which does not then become grounded in the Christ event will be 'at best insecure and at worse perverse'. What might be seen dimly in God's general revelation has been made 'clear' and 'decisive' in 'a course of history which had as its central event the life of God made man in Jesus of Nazareth'. The Bible is of fundamental importance for Christians, therefore, because it provides them with 'the irreplaceable records of that revelation, and our only access to it'.

The formulations and declarations of faith mentioned in the URC *Basis of Union*, and to a great measure reflected in its statements, lead progressively away from an understanding of the Bible which equates the Word of God with the words of the biblical text. Any residual echo of the medieval view of the Bible as an external and formal authority seems to have been silenced by an approach which finds within the Bible the authoritative norm for all our life and work – the Word of God, the living voice of Christ, the One who meets us ever anew as we hear the witness of the early Christians proclaiming him as their Lord and Saviour from the pages of the New Testament.

Conclusions and Observations

At the end of our discussion about the role the Bible plays in the URC, what conclusions have emerged?

1.   The great theological diversity present in the URC is underpinned by a basic disagreement concerning our approach to scripture. The *Basis of Union* largely reflects the neo-orthodox position by making a clear distinction between "the words" and "the Word". At every Ordination and Induction Service the following is stated:

> The highest authority
> for what we believe and do
> is God's Word in the Bible
> alive for his people today
> through the help of the Spirit.

and the members of the URC make their response:

> We respond to this Word,
> whose servants we are
> with all God's people
> through the years.

GEAR would like the Basis of Union to be amended to read, '. . . the Bible is His written Word', thus significantly collapsing the words/Word distinction.[39] The more liberal wing of the URC, on the other hand, question the status of the term 'the highest authority' when the Bible at many points

---

[39]   See *In Gear*, 67 (January 1993).

undermines what they now feel should be our view on significant issues, e.g. the role of women or human sexuality. Have we not things to learn from Christian traditions outside the canon of Scripture, our human experience and also reason? In actual fact, the liberal wing often operates with a view of authority which is more Anglican or Methodist than classically Reformed, allowing for authorities other than the Bible to be used in Christian decision-making: either Scripture, Tradition and Reason (Anglican) or Scripture, Tradition, Experience and Reason (Methodist). An ongoing task for the URC is to hold this diversity of view together in a creative and fruitful tension. This will not be easy since, in the words of one of the doyens of British conservative-evangelicalism, '. . . the cause of the division is . . . the deepest doctrinal divergence of all – disagreement as to the principle of authority'.[40]

2.   Experience suggests that people do hear the Word of God, or the living voice of Christ, when they engage with the Scriptures as they are read or expounded in preaching. The event whereby the human words of a book or a preacher become the vehicle for God's gracious promises to be heard is attested by far too many to be denied. What Barth called a 'miracle' does sometimes take place. And, yes, we can see what Forsyth is getting at when he talks of the Bible in sacramental terms. Our involvement with Scripture leads to 'disclosure situations' in our lives.[41] They cannot be manufactured by us, but they do reveal a clear assurance of God's liberating love. Through the work of the Spirit we can be confronted with the over-against-ness of God, the One who relativizes all our thought and activity, including the Scriptures. Therefore, as Gordon Kaufman has pointed out, 'the recognition that absoluteness belongs ultimately to God alone tends . . . to undermine every other alleged – authority' with the result that 'belief in God has, in the long run, worked to weaken the Bible's authority rather than support it'.[42] Overtly confident and dogmatic views of biblical authority regrettably are often found teetering on the edge of idolatry.

3.   Classical views of biblical authority have been challenged and damaged by biblical scholarship: an increased awareness of the Bible's diversity threatens the sense of its unity presupposed by classical views, while a developing realization that important events and discourses have been 'shaped' by the communities within which they took place, the oral traditions which preserved them and the writers who eventually recorded them, has questioned confidence concerning the Bible's historical reliability. When biblical scholars make a living disputing biblical interpretation, the lay-person is at best confused and at worst disillusioned! Acute problems are posed to biblical authority when the same texts are made to mean different things. The hermeneutical ingenuity of Bible readers is hardly new, though it seems to have been given a measure of respectability within biblical scholarship that is quite breathtaking. I am told that Mark Twain once likened the Bible to a drug store, and then observed that while its contents remain the same, the medical practice always seems to be changing! Nowadays, it is popular, for example, to set to one side the once common belief that the meaning of a text is the one intended by its author. We are asked instead to recognize that the different standpoints of readers invite multiple readings of the same text, so we hear talk of feminist, liberationist or gay readings of scripture. Who we are and the context we are in, the theory goes, will determine what we find in a text, but if the text can legitimately be interpreted in different ways, in what sense can it carry universal authority? It would seem that attempts to base faith and belief upon the *plain* teaching of Scripture face insurmountable problems.

---

[40]   J I Packer, *'Fundamentalism' and the Word of God* (Grand Rapids, Michigan: Wm B Eerdmans, 1958), p 17.

[41]   For the term 'disclosure situation' see Ian T Ramsay, *Models for Divine Activity* (London: SCM Press, 1973).

[42]   Gordon Kaufman, *In the Face of Mystery: A Constructive Theology* (Cambridge, Mass. and London: Harvard University Press, 1993), p 19.

Further challenges to biblical authority emerge when people press the point that the biblical writers lived in a culture vastly different from our own. They operated with a world-view long since overthrown by subsequent thinking, and they addressed issues appropriate to their context while remaining inevitably silent about a whole host of issues that concern us. Understanding the world of the biblical writers is far more difficult than many of us think, though it is not totally impossible. It is wise to recognize that truth is largely *relative* to the context in which it is found, but there is no need to accept the fashionable counsel of despair, namely, complete *relativism*. Truth is not *completely* bounded by context. To say: 'You do not understand me because I am a white woman and you are a black man', is the start and not the end of a conversation, a difficult but not impossible encounter of mutual learning in God's plural world. Nevertheless, our attitude towards biblical authority is severely tested when the text presses upon us claims and practices that we have justifiably condemned as false or inappropriate. Any admission that the Bible is wrong about something can easily become the thin end of a broad wedge which ultimately destroys the notion of its authority.

4.   People understandably ask why the Bible should be given such a high status in the church. Why is this set of texts so important? It is far from clear to them why the Bible should be given a status qualitatively different from other secular and religious books. In an era of inter-faith dialogue we have been brought into contact with the sacred texts of other religions. Are we really certain that our scriptures are qualitatively superior to theirs? And, to develop further the question: Why this set of texts?, does not a rigid adherence to biblical authority impose unnecessary limitations upon us? Do not non-biblical resources have an importance in framing certain aspects of our belief and many of our practices?

A great deal of the Bible's importance rests in its ability to take us back to the foundational events which constituted the Christian faith. As we read the New Testament we are returning to the quarry from which we were hewn. This is part of our commitment to be an 'apostolic' church – a body of people who bear witness to Jesus Christ with the apostles, the earliest and foundational witnesses. If we were to sever our relations with that past, we would not only be cutting ourselves off from our roots in antiquity, but also ignoring the early classic models of Christian belief and practice. James Barr, therefore, considers the Bible's importance to lie partly in it being the source of 'the basic foundation myth of Christianity'[43] It provides what he calls 'a classic model of understanding' in that it furnishes for us 'the classic sources for the expression of Jesus and of God'.[44] The church through the ages has returned to these models for edification, enlightenment and correction; it has based its faith and practice on an engagement with them. The Bible therefore has been 'a common resource of life and spirituality, the provider of a unity of feeling among Christian people'.[45] Since it has repeatedly functioned successfully, the Bible has received the status of a religious classic. Its authority is revealed, therefore, in having been granted this status.

---

[43]   James Barr, *The Bible in the Modern World* (London: SCM Press, 1973), p 137.
[44]   Ibid., pp 120, 118.
[45]   Maurice Wiles, *Explorations in Theology 4* (London: SCM Press, 1973), p 81.

5.   The idea that biblical authority rests in its status as the classic text of Christianity is not to say that the accumulative wisdom of the Christian centuries is always inferior to what are the earliest and sometimes the crudest traditions of the church, namely, the various witnesses of the New Testament.   Those who have done their hill-walking on the peat-clad Pennines are not foolish enough to believe that a river is clearest at its source! And how can an acorn be considered to be superior to an oak tree? It is not without significance that the Patristic period largely provided the Reformers with the Golden Era of Christianity that they attempted to recapture; they did not yearn after the first century church at Jerusalem or Corinth.

Time moves on, developments take place and changes occur – sometimes for the better. Often accumulated tradition, personal experience and reason offer a surer guide in important matters than the Bible. When it comes to our understanding of cosmology, biology and anthropology, for example, most of us no more take the Bible to be authoritative than we do Aristotle. We know that both have been wrong in important instances. Nor do we adopt the biblical view concerning usury, slavery or the role of women in the church, since we have seen fit to discard such views as inappropriate and inadequate. By so doing we have set the authority of accumulative wisdom and widespread common sense above that of the plain teaching of Scripture. However loud some shout *sola scriptura,* in practice they cannot avoid altogether bending the knee towards the liberal observation that common experience and reason play a crucial role in theology.

6.   There is a story told about Paul Tillich being confronted by someone offended by what the great theologian had said in a sermon. The young man thrust his Bible into the ageing professor's hands with the words: 'Professor Tillich, do you believe this?' Tillich took the book and thumbed it through thoughtfully. Then he gave it back with the words: 'Yes, I believe this; but remember, my friend, do not grip it, let it grip you!' The Bible is not a textbook or code of law to be rammed down people's throats. John Barton is near the mark when he invites us to regard the authority of the Bible in terms of an analogy with 'a trusted friend, on whose impressions and interpretations of an important event or experience we place reliance'.[46] We relax with friends and enter into conversation with them, but so much use of the Bible in our churches reflects the ethos of the advocate remorselessly establishing a case. Along with Tillich, we need to go forward gripping the Bible less and letting it grip us more.

---

46   John Barton, *People of the Book: The Authority of the Bible in Christianity* (London: SPCK, 1988), p 45.

PART 2

We believe in the one living and true God,
creator, preserver and ruler of all things
in heaven and earth, Father, Son and Holy
Spirit. Him alone we worship and in him
we put our trust.

CENTRAL to the entire theology of the URC is a belief in God, understood as a being who in some sense is distinct from the world. God is the creator, preserver and ruler of all things'. But what is God's precise relationship to the world, and what can we know about God? The URC also stands firmly in a trinitarian tradition, but how are we to understand the claim that God is both One and Three: Father, Son and Holy Spirit? To these and other basic questions concerning God we now turn.

CHAPTER 4

God: Sovereign and Suffering

THE REFORMED ethos is rooted in the central acknowledgement that each and every one of us at all times is living before our Creator, Redeemer and Sustainer. It is with God that we have to do. We are to place our lives at God's disposal; as creatures we are to serve our Creator. God's glory and purpose are of fundamental significance, more important even than our salvation. Religion is not intended simply to satisfy our needs, or to give meaning to our lives; it is primarily the means by which we can acknowledge, praise and serve our Creator. Our lives are meant for God, and to God we must extend our praise. We come before God confident that our sinful lives are at the disposal of One who is gracious and just. It was through reflection upon the contrast between the sovereignty of God and the sinfulness of human beings that the theology of Augustine of Hippo took shape, and John Calvin became an heir to this tradition. We might sum it up in the slogan: The beginning and end of all things lies in *the* fact that God *is* God! The vision which emerges is of an utterly indescribable Majesty, a sovereign Mystery and an immediate and ubiquitous Presence before whom we can only stand with empty hands.

John Calvin

Calvin maintains that, while in principle we can gain a knowledge of God through our human faculties, in practice due to our sin that possibility has become seriously undermined. We each know that there is a God and that God is our maker, but because of our sin we have failed to give God adoration and honour. God has also revealed Godself in the natural world. Not only can Calvin say consequently that 'a sense of divinity is by nature engraven on human hearts',[1] he also speaks of the 'skillful ordering of the universe' being 'a sort of mirror in which we can contemplate God'.[2] God has left human beings therefore without excuse – 'wherever you cast your eyes, there is no spot in the universe wherein you cannot discern at least some sparks of his glory',[3] but through sin they have been blind to the Deity's splendour and have consciously turned away from God. We all stand guilty before God, sinners at the throne of holiness.

We will only gain a true knowledge of God, argues Calvin, when we put our trust in the grace of God who reconciles us in the cross of Christ. Piety is the prerequisite for such knowledge. By 'piety' Calvin means 'reverence joined with love of God which the knowledge of his benefits induces'.[4] So only those who have had their minds renewed by the Christ event, and their hearts turned towards God's self-revelation in Christ, possess a proper knowledge of God. This knowledge,

---

[1]   Calvin, *Institutes* 1,4,4.
[2]   Ibid., 1,5,1.
[3]   Ibid.
[4]   Ibid., 1,2,1.

in principle, had been available to human beings since the foundation of the earth, but now it is 'more intimately and also more vividly revealed in his Word'.[5] And, as we have seen, God's Word has been made available to us in the Bible.

Calvin's understanding of God, therefore, is developed through an investigation of Scripture, though he seldom departs from the classical model of God bequeathed to theology by the likes of Augustine. God is perfect, complete and self-sustained, so in need of nothing. The world is totally dependent upon God for its origin and ongoing life, but God in no way is dependent upon the world. Everything that has happened, is happening, or will happen in the world accords with God's will, all events being willed by the omnipotent Deity. Just what becomes of human freedom in this deterministic picture is rather debatable.

While many have not been wholly convinced by Calvin's argument, few can fail to recognize the stature of the sovereign God he is describing. Supreme in power and might, God rules over sinful subjects who have been found guilty of offending the holiness of God. The relationship between the holy God and our sinful world is wholly asymmetrical, all the power belonging to an omniscient God. The Deity rules so that 'nothing happens except what is knowingly and willingly decreed by him',[6] while 'all things always were, and perpetually remain under his eyes, so that to his knowledge there is nothing future or past, but all things are present'.[7] The idea that God, for example, knew and willed the holocaust will offend even the most hard-hearted; but Calvin insists that 'it pertains to [God's] wisdom to foreknow everything that is to happen', and that 'it pertains to [God's] might to rule and control everything by his hand'.[8] So even the most horrendous things that take place occur for a purpose since they have been freely willed by a righteous God. If we are puzzled how an all-powerful, totally benevolent Deity could ever will the evils of Auschwitz, or a fatal Alpine avalanche, Calvin counsels silence: '. . . if you proceed further to ask why he so willed, you are seeking something greater and higher than God's will, which cannot be found'.[9] But those who choose to stand alongside the poor and disadvantaged in an unequal world will want to rail against such a God.

Calvin places total emphasis upon God's freedom. Bound by nothing God can do what God likes. The Deity is free to shower divine grace on whoever and wherever. The very fact that some people are more fortunate than others does not lead him to question the universality of God's love and generosity. He accepts that 'some mothers have full and abundant breasts, but others are almost dry' and concludes then that 'God wills to feed one more liberally, but another more meagerly'.[10] This becomes evidence for Calvin that 'the very inequality of his grace proves that it is free'.[11] But, an objector may argue, it is one thing for God to be free to be gracious to whoever the Deity wishes, but something else to rule in such an indiscriminate way – if, that is, any content is to remain in the concept of God's universal love.

Calvin follows the view of Greek Fathers who maintained that God is *impassible*, pure act and in no way affected by those upon which the action falls. As in the case of God's power so with the divine love: there is an asymmetrical relationship between the Creator and the creatures.

---

[5]   Ibid., 1,10,1.
[6]   Ibid., 1,16,3.
[7]   Ibid., 3,21,5.
[8]   Ibid., 3,23,7.
[9]   Ibid., 3,23,2.
[10] Ibid., 1,16,3.
[11] Ibid., 3,21,6.

God loves the creatures but in no way is the Deity affected by the response of the creatures; God's love is always active but never passive, an active benevolence which is devoid of the possibility of any passion and pain. The full magnitude of Calvin's doctrine of God is now before us: not only is all the suffering and evil in the world willed by God for a good purpose which only God can fathom, but also the Deity is structurally unaffected by it. Strictly speaking, God is as incapable of sharing our joys as empathising with our sorrows. Nothing, literally nothing, can affect God's life. This concept of God owes more to the idea of Aristotle's 'great unmoved mover' that it does to the vision of God found in the biblical witness or the insights of human experience. To be able to 'suffer' – to be moved by the concerns and suffering of others – is a virtue rather than a defect; and as such it needs predicating as a quality in God.

Both power and love are relational terms. To have all the power is to be a despot who denies power to others. All omnipotence should properly mean is that God has all the power there is to have while other beings (whom God has created) also have power. So God becomes less the autocratic Monarch and more the gifted Ruler who weaves a nation's purpose and destiny out of the contribution of others. On the other hand, God is love-itself, not simply because God is the fountain of benevolence, but also because God is involved with others in such a way as to be moved and affected by them.

Given his dim view of everything human when contrasted with God, it is hardly surprising that Calvin's thought gave rise to polemics against all forms of idolatry. Sinful people have no right to claim too much for themselves, and all exalted claims for human achievement are questioned in a quite iconoclastic manner. Nor can the Infinite be subsumed under the finite. Rooted in classical Reformed theology's awareness of the Creator's contrasting relationship with the creature, we find a resistance to countenance any attempts which try to pin God down in finite and determinate things. So, for example, Calvin is particularly strict about the use of images in churches, while the Reformed ethos is opposed to understandings of Holy Communion which claim that the bread and wine physically become the body and blood of our Lord. The things of heaven must not be fastened to the things of the earth. Nor must there be any attempt to control God by overt identification of God with the church's structures. In all these issues what is at stake is the sovereignty of God.

The focus of attention in the classical Reformed theological ethos has often been upon God's mighty work in creation and redemption, and thereafter in the divine invitation to respond to God in service and discipleship. In this we can trace both positive and negative outcomes. Most certainly the confidence that the Reformers had in being God's elect gave rise to Protestantism's expansionist spirit and the Reformed aim to change societies through preaching, the influence of Christian character and the wholesome nature of the Christian community. Reformed Christians moved ahead in the belief that the Holy Spirit was with them in their mission; but, in their enthusiasm, we now know how brutally the cultures and peoples they encountered on their pilgrimage could sometimes be treated by them.

The clear separation between God and the world also sanctioned the secularization of creation. The earth's magical and mysterious powers were eschewed, and all attempts to endow it with sacred powers were condemned as pagan. This opened up the way for nature to be studied and investigated without fear of 'offending the gods'. Science was born, and with it came all manner of human advancement; but, as with most good things, there was a reciprocal downside. Taking God totally away from the world resulted in nature becoming devalued, the occasion for its abuse appeared, and irresponsibility towards the environment took place. An understanding of God which does justice to God's love of and concern for nature therefore will need to move beyond the God–world dichotomy of Calvin's classical theism. We now turn to consider the work of three twentieth century Reformed theologians who offer us some important insights to further that end: the Congregationalist A E Garvie, the Presbyterian John Oman and the German Jürgen Moltmann.

Alfred Earnest Garvie [12]

A E Garvie (1861-1945) was an eminent Scottish Congregational minister who, after ten years of pastoral ministry in Scotland, had a distinguished career as Professor and then Principal of Hackney and New College, London. His mature theological thought is found in a large three volume constructive theology.[13] Less well known than P T Forsyth, his predecessor at the College, Garvie was more systematic than his fellow Scot, but less charismatic, devoid of Forsyth's memorable, pithy and often colourful turns of phrase, and overall rather more liberal in his theological approach. Garvie attempted to present the Christian Faith to his contemporaries in a way that lost none of its saving significance but made sense in a rapidly changing intellectual climate. Consequently, Christian theology became for him 'an exposition, commendation and appreciation' of the significance of 'the fact of Christ for faith'.[14] Garvie was not only certain that the Christian fact presents an effective challenge to contemporary atheism, but also convinced that modern developments in historiography and science demanded a radical revision of traditional theological claims associated with the fact of Jesus. Indeed, until that revision is made, he believed the apologetic function of Christian theology is deficient.

Garvie's liberalism is clearly displayed in his confidence in the historical critical method 'to interpret the significance and estimate the value of Christ'.[15] He believed that, if we try to learn about God – the Father from God – the Son, we will be duty-bound to affirm God's immanence in the world as strongly as God's transcendence. Human hope does not rest in an aloof Deity, an impassible external bystander, but in a 'fellow-sufferer who is intimately involved with the world's life'.[16]

Equally significant for Garvie was the need to respond to the challenge of modern science. He did not regard science as a threat to theology, believing that science provided theology with an important clue concerning the construction of an adequate concept of God. If cosmic evolution is to be 'interpreted theistically', Garvie believed that theology must not speak of 'a transcendent static but an immanent dynamic God, a God who is present and active in His world'.[17] If reality is processive and the temporal process is consequently all-important, then God's creative and salvific activity must be located in that process and carried out through evolution. The new task for theology, therefore, becomes 'the discovery in the full stream of history of those divine currents that show the direction of the flow' of cosmic evolution.[18] A shift of emphasis had to occur from

---

[12]   This discussion of Garvie is adapted from my 'Alfred Ernest Garvie: Early Scottish Congregational Process Theologian?', *King's Theological Review*, xii, 1 (Spring 1989), pp 18–22.

[13]   The volumes in Garvie's system of constructive theology are *The Christian Doctrine of the Godhead* (London: Hodder and Stoughton Ltd., 1925), *The Christian Ideal of Human Society* (London: Hodder and Stoughton Ltd., 1930) and *The Christian Belief in God* (London: Hodder and Stoughton Ltd., 1932). In his second book of the trilogy, Garvie called the project 'a system of Christian thought, life and work' (p 21), and in the final volume he suggests that 'the last in time should be regarded as the first in order' (p 21).

[14]   Garvie, *The Christian Doctrine of the Godhead*, p 22.

[15]   Ibid., pp 182–3.

[16]   Ibid., p 185.

[17]   Ibid., p 15.

[18]   Ibid.

---

conceiving God in transcendent isolation from the world to viewing Deity as immanently involved in the evolutionary process. The classical picture of God had been under the spell of Greek thinking which conceived perfection in terms of what is static, complete and impassible. Science meanwhile has shown how these qualities are mere abstractions from the reality of an ever changing, developing, dynamic and interactive cosmos.

The adequacy of any concept of God for Garvie, therefore, was located in its ability to reflect the vision of God on display in the Jesus of the Gospels and the understanding of the world that had recently appeared in modern science. He suggested that an appropriate and credible revision of the God–world relationship could be made by putting the idea of divine immanence alongside the notion of divine transcendence in the concept of God. Every effort needs to be taken to ensure that the identity of God does not become lost in the identity of the world; but Garvie believed that the flight from classical theism need not end up in classical pantheism. To get the correct balance between transcendence and immanence he proposed a panentheistic model for the God–world relationship. He attempts to steer 'the straight middle course' between the Scylla of deism and the Charybdis of pantheism to a safe harbour in panentheism.[19] The resulting concept of God distinguishes but does not separate God and the world; it relates God and the world, derived from and dependent on God, so that 'no reality above or beyond God will be possible for our thought'.[20] God includes the world but the world does not exhaust the divine reality. As Garvie puts it, 'the God in and through all' is also 'overall'; therefore the immanence and transcendence of God are held together in one concept as 'complimentary truths'.[21]

A problem of all doctrines of divine immanence is their tendency to make God's relation with the world a matter of necessity rather than free choice, thus undermining the transcendent sovereignty of God. Garvie is fully aware of this. He forthrightly affirms that God is absolute and has no need of the world, as well as recognising that the Absolute is also unchanging. But how then does Garvie do justice to his intention to speak of God's involvement in a world that brings joy and pain to the divine life? Just when the ship he is steering seems to be about to crash on the rocks of classical theism he adjusts the rudder by introducing the ideas of divine *kenosis* (self-emptying) and divine *plerosis* (self-fulfilment).

Building upon the idea of *kenosis* found in the writings of Paul (Phil. 2: 7), Garvie postulates an eternal activity of self-limitation in the Godhead which becomes the necessary condition not only for God's self-revelation in Jesus of Nazareth but also for the activity of God at other points in the cosmic process. God does not create or redeem out of necessity; rather, by free and loving decision, God's purposes are worked out by *kenosis*. Therefore, Garvie argues, 'the incarnation is the supreme instance of an activity of God which is illustrated by all creation; it is only by self-limitation that the Infinite can create within time and space a finite and changing world'.[22] In the creative process what resembles God the least, the Deity controls the most; that which is most akin to Deity, God leaves the most free. The more God enters into the life of the world, the more the Deity lays aside the divine absoluteness. Creatures are therefore endowed with real autonomy, and they may oppose or co-operate with their Creator. Despite sin and evil abounding in the world, Garvie is confident that God is still firmly in control of the creative process. He is a *meliorist*, accepting that the world

---

[19]   A E Garvie, 'The Divine Immanence as the Basis of Theological Statement', *The Christian Certainty and the Modern Perplexity* (London: Hodder and Stoughton, 1910), p 133.

[20]   Garvie, *The Christian Belief in God*, p 437.

[21]   Garvie, *The Christian Doctrine of the Godhead*, p 188.

[22]   Ibid., p 20.

is partly bad, but believing that it is becoming better and will one day be the best.[23] It is significant, however, that the terms in which Garvie speaks of evolution include 'progress' as well as 'process'. Few today share any simplistic optimism after the Holocaust. We live amidst global inequalities that beggar belief, and face possible apocalyptic scenarios due to environmental misuse. However, in fairness to Garvie, he sets his future confidence firmly inside the perspective of the Christian hope.

Using the notion of *plerosis* (Eph. 1: 23), Garvie then argues that the divine self-emptying leads to a form of God's self-expression in creation which in turn becomes God's self-fulfilment. God not only achieves the divine purpose by self-emptying rooted in love; the Deity also derives joy when that love is returned. Garvie is very critical of understandings of love which dismiss the thought that God desires a response in personal relationship from those loved. When love is conceived solely in terms of giving benefits, he prefers to use the term 'goodness', since for him love is a relational term – 'a personal interchange, a giving as well as a receiving, a finding as well as a losing oneself in another'.[24] However, if God desires a loving response from the creatures, it is difficult to see what significance this can have for God, given Garvie's insistence that there is no development or change in God. Why should God desire my love if even an infinite amount of love cannot make a jot of difference to the divine life?

Garvie's insistence upon giving a full account of the divine immanence necessitates him revising some of the classical attributes of God, particularly omnipresence, omniscience and omnipotence. He argues that the first part of each term points to the divine transcendence and the second part refers to the divine immanence. 'Omnipresence' directs us towards a strong sense of immediacy between God and the world, and hence to a sense of God being present in (and hence limited by) earthly conditions. The divine attribute of 'omniscience' refers to God's ability to know all that there is *as it is*. Due to God's self-limitation, therefore, God's fore-knowledge is ruled out. Garvie believes that God can only speculate as to how the future will turn out, therefore the contingency of the world and human freedom has been jealously safeguarded. 'Omnipotence' means that 'God can do and does, within nature and history, all that is possible within the constitution He has given created reality'.[25] The evil in the world must not necessarily be laid at God's door; nor must God be considered limited in any other way than by divine choice. God's activity is perfect given the parameters within which the Deity has decided to work.

At the centre of Garvie's theology lies a sustained attack upon the doctrine of divine impassibility, grounded in his belief that this doctrine undermines our whole understanding of the Incarnation and Atonement. God is present, involved and affected by what takes place: 'What Christ did, God did in Him; what Christ suffered, God suffered in Him'.[26] Garvie considered the idea of a God who is totally aloof to the world's joy and pain as not only sub-Christian but also a total irrelevance in a world torn apart by sin and evil. He prefers to conceive God as 'fellow-sufferer', rejects the notion of divine impassibility and adds to the usual list of divine attributes 'omnipatience'. God is affected by the divine experience of the world's joy and suffering; the Christian God is after all a God of feeling.

---

23   Ibid., p 236.
24   Garvie, *The Christian Ideal of Human Society,* p 204.
25   Garvie, *The Christian Belief in God,* p 448.
26   Garvie, *The Christian Doctrine of the Godhead,* p 212.

In Garvie's work we witness an honest wrestling with the task of setting out an understanding of the Christian witness of faith that is at one and the same time congruent with its roots in Jesus and credible in the modern world. Up in Cambridge, at Westminster College, another sharp Scottish mind was engaged on a similar task. He arrived at some equally trenchant views concerning the theological adequacy of the view of God he had inherited from the classical theological tradition. Since he was a Presbyterian, the target of John Oman's criticism not surprisingly was a fellow John, John Calvin.

John Wood Oman

Stephen Bevans suggests that 'a reading of Oman today is one of the best ways to see the power and importance of an image of God that takes seriously and consistently God's gracious, personal relationship to men and women, calling them to freedom in community and responsibility in love'.[27] Indeed, it is one of Oman's achievements to have reminded us to image God through analogies and insights drawn from what is best rather than what is worst in human experience. He teaches us the value of using the heights of our personal relationships as the clue by which to gain an understanding of God's nature and work.

Calvin leaves us with the picture of an all-powerful God who has predetermined what will happen in this world and the next. An impersonal Monarch rules, an arbitrary Providence reigns and an omniscient Judge condemns those who it turns out could not prevent themselves from committing the capital offence. In short, the picture of God on display in Calvin seems to be modelled upon some of the worst examples of human life; autocratic leadership, jobs for the boys (and girls!) and rigged justice. Surely there must be a way of doing justice to the stature of God and human beings such that neither are robbed of their true dignity?

In *Grace and Personality*, Oman attacks Calvin's idea that we have not done justice to God unless we speak of the divine will totally determining what happens in the world. A God who resorted to such a strategy would not be showing great strength but considerable weakness. Far more noble and grand is the ruler who can make good use of the citizens' gifts, aspirations and needs in the free interchanges of a genuine community. Oman objects to Calvin's 'conception of grace as the irresistible force of omnipotence directed, in an unswerving line, by omniscience', since 'being mechanical and not spiritual' it 'introduces irreconcilable conflict between moral freedom and the succour of God'.[28] In contrast, he provides a picture of God which involves the Deity engaging with us in the way a good parent treats an offspring. Gone in Oman's theology are the edicts one cannot refuse: the Power which is irresistible; the Being who is incapable of being affected by one's joys or sorrows, pleasure or pain; and the One who knows what I will do before I do it. Instead Oman introduces a recognition that the freedom to say, Yes! or No! to God is fundamental; that God respects human autonomy; that we are regarded by God as children of his love rather than merely objects of his benevolence; and that the future is radically open.

At the heart of Oman's analysis of the relationship between Creator and creature lie two principles which need holding firmly together. First, there is our need to recognize our dependency upon God. This is 'the essential quality of a religious person'.[29] But it is the kind of God we are dependent upon which begins to separate Oman's theology from the classical tradition: 'We are

---

[27] Stephen Bevans, *John Oman and His Doctrine of God* (Cambridge: Cambridge University Press, 1992) p 17.

[28] John Oman, *Grace and Personality*, 2nd edn. (Cambridge: Cambridge University Press, 1919), p. 14.

[29] Ibid., p 52.

never . . . mere subjects, and much less mere pawns in God's pre-determined game, but [God's grace] deals with us as children, not indeed as those who are free, but as those whom [God's grace] can only truly bless by helping them to attain freedom'.[30] Then, secondly, there is a requirement for us as moral persons to be independent. The role of the wise parent is the cultivation of the autonomy of the child, rather than seeking to control the child's life or determine the child's destiny. Oman refuses to liken human beings to puppets dancing to whatever tune God decrees when pulling the strings; rather they are autonomous human subjects who must learn to lead their lives: 'To be independent moral persons, legislating for ourselves, is not only not hostile to true knowledge and right service of God, but is the imperative condition without which God can be neither known nor served.'[31] At first glance it might seem that Oman is advocating a commitment to two principles which contradict one another, or at best possess a paradoxical kind of relationship. But that is not the case. As we seek to become increasingly dependent upon God we discover that the personal power, presence and promise of love we meet graciously invites us to take responsibility for ourselves and our world. As we strive for real autonomy, on the other hand, we discover that our final fulfilment rests in a mutual relationship with the same God. God drives us back into reality, and reality sends us back to God.

As with Garvie, a focal point in the alternative to Calvin's theological proposal centres upon a revised understanding of God's omnipotence. Instead of using mechanical and impersonal categories to talk of God's power, Oman turns to human relationships to find more personal modes of description. God has rejected the short, straight, deterministic route to achieve the divine purpose in favour of the winding path of love and patience. What omnipotence means, therefore, is that God possesses the length, breadth, height and depth of love, graciously and patiently seeking to persuade people to respond freely to the divine invitation and calling. Real power is not concerned with controlling people by brute force, but with getting them to the point where they have the desire to change their minds and alter their lives. As Oman says, '. . . we cannot rest content to ascribe our whole life to the direct operation of God, after a fashion that makes God the most overwhelming of all forces, the most destructive of any reality to which the name personality could be given'.[32]

Oman, like Garvie, attempts to respond to the agenda set by his age. He respects the traditions which have been handed down, but, when it is called for, he is prepared to be revisionary. His attempt to locate God in the immediacy of personal experience, within the reach of us all, however, is balanced by his recognition that God remains a Mystery when encountered. As Bevans puts it: 'The genius of his thought was to propose that to image God as personal is to conceive of God as present within the fabric of human life, clearly within the reach of human knowledge and human experience, but whose mystery could never be exhausted by such knowledge and never reduced to that experience'.[33] Garvie and Oman represent the better examples of the liberal tradition in British Reformed theology. They helped open up theological perspectives which others have more recently popularized. To one such theologian we now direct our attention.

---

30   Ibid., pp 64–5.
31   Ibid., p 48.
32   Ibid., p 28.
33   Bevans, *John Oman and His Doctrine of God*, p 32.

Jürgen Moltmann

Moltmann is the most well-known Reformed theologian of recent times. One interpreter of his work is far from exaggerating when he tell us that Moltmann is 'one of the most influential of contemporary German Protestant theologians, in the non-Western as well as the Western world, and in wider church circles as well as in academic theology'.[34] Moltmann's thought has developed as he has responded to new questions and fresh challenges. It has reached a wide audience perhaps due to Moltmann's often highly successful application of biblical themes to contemporary issues and events, and his ability to find new wine in old biblical wineskins. His writings are a treasure store for preachers, but they can become a trough of desolation for those who ask annoying questions like: What do you mean by that? What reasons can you give in support of this claim? or Why have you read that biblical text this way rather than that way? We shall turn to Moltmann's work at several points in this book. Our concern now is to consider what he has to say about God, and particularly about God's relation to the world.

Moltmann's theological position is anchored in two basic convictions that emerged strongly when he was in a British concentration camp: first, the only basis for hope lies in a belief that God is the God of hope; and, secondly, God is present in the suffering of the world. At the heart of Moltmann's theology, therefore, stand the themes of promise and passion. Both are displayed in the death and resurrection of Jesus. God's raising of Jesus from the dead is the sign and anticipation of God's promised future Kingdom, when the dead will be raised and a new world order will break in. Moltmann re-works the great Old Testament eschatological themes, and then sets the cross in the context of Jewish messianic expectation. God's raising of Jesus, therefore, is the final and decisive event in a history which goes back to the Exodus. It gives the suffering and down-trodden grounds for believing that they have a future, just as it provides Jesus' followers with the motivation to engage with a history which is God's as well as their own, and a mission to join in a process of revolution and reform in the world.

> From first to last, and not merely in the epilogue, Christianity is eschatology, is hope, forward looking and forward moving, and therefore also revolutionizing and transforming the present. The eschatological is not one element of Christianity, but it is the medium of Christian faith as such, the key in which everything in it is set, the glow that suffuses everything here in the dawn of an expected new day. For Christian faith lives from the raising of the crucified Christ,and strains after the promises of the universal future of Christ. Eschatology is the passionate suffering and passionate longing kindled by the Messiah. . . . The God spoken of here is no intra-worldly or extra-worldly God, but the 'God of hope' (Rom.15: 13), . . . the God whom we therefore cannot really have in us or over us but always only before us, who encounters us in his promises for the future, and whom we therefore cannot 'have' either, but can only await in active hope.[35]

In comparison with Calvin one cannot help but see a sharp contrast between the rigid determinism of the great Reformer's picture of the God–world relationship and Moltmann's very open-ended view in which God is at the centre of an historical process that is not yet decided let alone complete, and to which God has invited our contribution. Sceptics who are convinced that futurology is a very inexact science might find Moltmann's approach to be little else than a capitulation to an apocalyptic

---

34   Richard Bauckham, *The Theology of Jürgen Moltmann* (Edinburgh: T & T Clark, 1995), p 1. See also his *Moltmann: Messianic Theology in the Making* (Basingstoke: Marshall Pickering, 1987).
35   Jürgen Moltmann, *Theology of Hope* (London: SCM Press, 1967), p 16.

worldview which is thoroughly discredited. For the marginalized members of our world, on the other hand, Moltmann's view may provide positive theological substance to the sombre view of Claudia in Shakespeare's *Measure for Measure*: 'The miserable have no other medicine / But only hope' (Act 3, Scene 1, Line 2). What hope is there for most people other than God's future for them? Moltmann ends *Theology of Hope*, therefore, with the call for the Christian church to disclose to 'a world of lost horizons . . . the horizon of the future of the crucified Christ'.[36]

In addition to the eschatological theme of promise and hope, the cross and resurrection also reveal the second of Moltmann's basic convictions: God's presence in the suffering of the world. Hope has been generated because God raised the *crucified* Jesus. On the cross, an event took place in which Christ identified with the sinners and the sinned-against (whom Moltmann calls 'the godless' and 'the godforsaken') and died for them. God's love is a love which suffers in solidarity with the estranged and abandoned. On the cross, God embraced Jesus' suffering and hence the world's suffering. God's love consequently is not some gratuitous benevolence but voluntary fellow-suffering. Jesus suffers abandonment by the Father, who in turn suffers over the death of his Son.

> God is not greater than he is in this humiliation. God is not more glorious than he is in this self-surrender. God is not more powerful than he is in this helplessness. God is not more divine than he is in this humanity. The nucleus of everything that Christian theology says about 'God' is to be found in this Christ event. The Christ event on the cross is a God event. And conversely, the God event takes place on the cross of the risen Christ. Here God has not just acted externally, in his unattainable glory and eternity. Here he has acted in himself and has gone on to suffer in himself. Here he himself is love with all his being.[37]

Moltmann offers trenchant criticism of the classical ideas of omnipotence and impassibility, against the back-cloth of the horrendous evil we have seen perpetrated during the twentieth century. In the midst of all the suffering we have seen, What kind of God is it that has total power, yet refuses to use it? Certainly not one who is worthy of our belief. What kind of God is it who amidst this evil cannot, let alone will not, feel the pain and have empathy for the grieving? Moltmann refuses to believe that the God of Good Friday and Easter Day is that kind of God, so he rejects the 'God' of classical theism:

> For a God who is incapable of suffering is a being who cannot be involved. Suffering and injustice do not affect him. And because he is so completely insensitive, he cannot be affected or shaken by anything. He cannot weep, for he has no tears. But the one who cannot suffer cannot love either. So he is a loveless being.[38]

Many of us will say, Quite so!, as we also will to Moltmann's observation that the 'God' of classical theism is 'an in incomplete being' who does not warrant our allegiance:

---

36   Ibid., p 338.
37   Jürgen Moltmann, *The Crucified God* (London: SCM Press, 1974), p 205.
38   Ibid., p 222

What sort of being, then, would be a God who was only 'almighty'? He would be a being without experience, a being without destiny and a being who is loved by no one. A man who experiences helplessness, a man who suffers because he loves, a man who can die, is therefore a richer being than an omnipotent God who cannot suffer, cannot love and cannot die. Therefore for a man who is aware of the riches of his own nature in his love, his suffering, his protest and his freedom, such a God is not a necessary and supreme being, but a highly dispensable and superfluous being.[39]

And since God opens the divine self up to the world and then gathers the world into the divine life, there is in Moltmann's theology the same helpful kind of panentheistic God–world relationship that is proposed by Garvie.

---

39   Ibid., p 223.

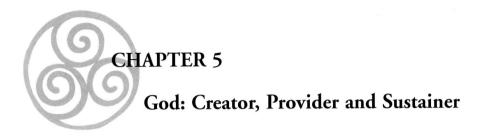

CHAPTER 5

God: Creator, Provider and Sustainer

ONE OF the church's tasks is to generate a respect and reverence for the world in which we live. The God who brought liberation through Jesus Christ is also the 'creator, preserver and ruler of all things'. We interpret the world in the categories of 'creation' and 'providence' because we believe that God is the world's redeemer in the Christ event, just like the Israelites learned to sing the praises of God – the Creator through their deliverance at the Exodus and in the Exile. Our experience of liberation therefore grounds our belief that the world was created by God and forever is in God's providential care. Let us now explore some of the ways in which Reformed theologians have developed the doctrines of creation and providence.

John Calvin

Calvin turns to Genesis to find what he calls 'the history of the creation of the universe',[1] and he follows the Church Fathers in claiming that: ' . . . God by the power of his Word and Spirit created heaven and earth out of nothing'.[2] By insisting upon *creatio ex nihilo* (creation out of nothing) theologians affirm that creation is wholly the product of an act of God, rather than being a natural outpouring or organic development from the divine life, or the result of divine activity on pre-existent matter. Creation is a powerfully personal act by which God chooses to create a universe which reveals within it vestiges of Divinity. Calvin argues, therefore, that creation's beauty reflects God's beauty. He also maintains that God created the universe for our sakes. It has never been plainly apparent to me, though, how a Being who is complete and in need of nothing could be in a position to will anything, let alone a wholly contingent creation. The difference between God and the world, according to the classical tradition, is that God exists necessarily while the world is strictly contingent. But can a wholly necessary God give rise to a contingent creation? How to hold in proper tension the necessity of a loving God to love with the freedom of a sovereign God to act as the Deity pleases is one of theology's trickiest problems.

Calvin does not believe that God has created the world and then left it to its own devices, since God is also the 'everlasting Governor and Preserver'.[3] There can be no chance happenings or random events in the cosmos; everything is strictly determined by God's will; all is governed by the Deity's plan. The sun rises and sets according to God's governance, and every drop of rain that falls does so at God's bidding. According to Calvin, then, God is not just sovereign and free but also completely in control of what goes on in the world: ' . . . God by the bridle of his providence turns every event whatever way he wills'.[4] The Deity wills the evil machinations of Satan as well as the

---

[1]   Calvin, *Institutes*, 1,14,20.
[2]   Ibid.
[3]   Ibid., 1,16,1.
[4]   Ibid., 1,16,9.

loving discipleship of the Saints. Everything that happens is part of God's purposes, even 'whatever our enemy has wickedly committed against us was permitted and sent by God's just dispensation'.[5] Many will find it difficult to view events like the Holocaust as providential, and they will wonder how Calvin can escape having his 'God' indicted for being the cause and prolonger of evil and suffering in the world.

There are two kinds of divine providence according to Calvin's analysis in the *Institutes*. First, *universal* providence, in essence the basic laws of nature, is the means by which God provides us with an orderly world in which to live. Then, secondly, Calvin refers to God's particular care of each creature and the way in which God is constantly intervening in human life. This he calls *special* providence. François Wendel, however, has suggested that there is a third kind of divine providence in Calvin's system, namely, what arises from the work of the Holy Spirit in the elect as they are led to new life. She concludes, therefore, that: 'Thus placed, under the control of the order of nature, of special Providence and of the interior operation of the Holy Spirit, the believer finds himself in a complete and absolute dependence upon God, which, however, he does not feel as a restraint, but as a means to his fulfilment'.[6] We may wonder if the victims of oppression would agree? A very high price is paid when one overrules all chance and randomness in the universe. One has to say with Calvin that '. . . every success is God's blessing, and calamity and adversity his curse . . . '.[7] But might there be rather too much 'calamity and adversity' falling upon innocent people for us to remain comfortable with this idea?

Calvin lived in an age when people had no difficulty in believing in miracles, and they play an important part in his theology. He has no doubt that they happen, whether we think of the whole cosmic process as an entire miracle or individual events within it. Miracles are used by him to prove the authenticity of the gospel. He maintains that they also give authority to Scripture, prove the divinity of Jesus Christ, and are evidence that the natural world is ruled by God rather than impersonal laws. One passage is particularly interesting: 'Then when we read that at Joshua's prayers the sun stood still in one degree for two days [Josh. 10: 13], and that its shadow went back ten degrees for the sake of King Hezekiah [2 Kings 20: 11 or Isa. 38: 8], God has witnessed by those few miracles that the sun does not daily rise and set by a blind instinct of nature but that he himself . . . governs its course'.[8] Joshua 10: 13 became the key passage in the church's opposition to science's undermining of the traditional earth-centred cosmology, but Calvin uses it to establish God's general providence. Some of the greatest challenges and opportunities for theology at the moment come from science. Since the Reformation science has provided the Christian believer with knowledge that cannot be ignored. First, it is now accepted that the earth and planets revolve around the sun in eliptical orbits. The views of Galileo Galilei (1564–1642) challenged the cosmology presupposed in the Bible and affirmed by most theologians of the time, namely that the earth is at the centre of the cosmos. It led to a heated conflict in the church over biblical authority. Secondly, Isaac Newton (1642–1727) developed a mechanistic view of the universe, which suggested that it operated according to fixed laws and without extensive providential intervention from God. While it still seemed possible to suggest that the universe was created by God, there did not appear to be much of a role any longer for the Deity in its ongoing life. If the universe is governed by known laws, the possibility and need for God's miraculous interventions in the cosmic

---

5   Ibid., 1,17,8.

6   François Wendel, *Calvin: The Origins and Development of his Religious Thought* (London Fontana, 1965), 179–180.

7   Calvin, *Institutes*, 1,16,8.

8   Ibid., 1,16,2.

process becomes at best doubtful. Thirdly, the theory of natural selection developed by Darwin (1809–1882), and refined by subsequent biologists, challenges the idea that different species owe their distinctiveness to specific acts of divine creation, and the belief that human beings are somehow special and the pinnacle of God's creation.

Any contemporary doctrine of creation or providence which fails to address these challenges will not be sustainable. Interestingly, the opportunities for theology presented by modern science in some respects may have made science less of a threat to theology today than hitherto; and we must also remember that science was not a complete threat to Calvin. He made certain decisive contributions which enabled the church to develop a positive attitude to science. Alister McGrath notes that Calvin's acknowledgement of the orderliness of the universe led him to encourage people to investigate it. In studying the secrets of the universe he believed that people opened up the possibility of learning more about God's activity. Then, secondly, McGrath argues that Calvin's approach to the Bible freed people from having to support wooden and overtly literalistic readings of Scripture. The Bible, argued Calvin, was not a scientific text book but a witness to Jesus Christ. It 'accommodates' itself in concepts and language appropriate to the context of its audience. The 'science' of Genesis, Calvin argues, may have been appropriate to Israelite nomads, but it is not binding on more sophisticated generations.[9] We now move on to a much more explicit theological attempt to respond to the findings of science.

Alfred Ernest Garvie

Garvie sees some benefit in continuing to assert that God creates *ex nihilo*. The classical doctrine makes a crucial point: 'It is an assertion that God alone is self-subsistent reality; that no other reality exists, underived from or independent of Him; and that it is His causality alone to which all derived and dependent reality is due'.[10] Due attention must be given, therefore, to God's transcendence and hence the essential distinction between Creator and creature. Garvie is very hesitant, however, to join tradition in asserting that the doctrine means that God literally created the world out of nothing. He notes the dictum that *ex nihilo nihil fit* (out of nothing nothing comes) and suggests that it would be wiser to speak of God creating out of nothing *other than what is in God's self*. Garvie's concern to account for God's transcendence over the world is met by his insistence that God does not need this world to meet divine needs: 'We may not ascribe to God any need except love's need of loving and of freely giving of its fullness'.[11] But, in order to affirm the divine immanence, he proposes to 'supplement' the traditional idea of creation with *generation* as affirming immanence, the resemblance of Creator to His creatures'.[12]

Against the charge that this proposal limits God from within and without, Garvie reminds critics that God's whole operation in the evolving creation is by self-limitation (*kenosis*) leading to self-fulfilment (*plerosis*). While God is limited by this world, the Deity is not *necessarily* dependent on this world; it is perfectly possible that God could and may have other worlds in which to express divine love. Just which world God chooses to create and generate, and thus to become partially limited by and dependent upon, is purely a matter for God and God alone to decide. It has been proved demonstrably that the evolutionary principle lies at the heart of the world's development,

---

9   See Alister E McGrath, *Reformation Thought: An Introduction*, 2nd ed. (Oxford: Basil Blackwell, 1993), pp 230–4).
10   Garvie, *The Christian Belief in God*, p 454.
11   Garvie, *The Christian Doctrine of the Godhead*, p 247.
12   Garvie, *The Christian Belief in God*, p 459.

therefore Garvie no longer believed it appropriate to focus the Christian doctrine of creation solely on the universe's origin. Unless the battle with mechanistic science is to be lost at the outset, theologians have to show that God is the chief causative agent at each stage of evolution. To make the universe intelligible, divine creativity has to be seen not only in terms of bringing worlds into being, but particularly as preserving what has come into being through the evolutionary process and participating in the creation of what the process has yet to bring into being.

Just how God works creatively in evolution is a question Garvie never fully answers. The assertion that God is a creative agential force in the world process is often made, but the metaphysical grounds for the assertion are noticeably absent. Using a human analogy, Garvie argues that nature's laws represent God's *habits*. But God might have to resort in certain circumstances to acts which may not conform to divine habits, namely, miracles. Garvie is perfectly clear that we must accept in principle the possibility of divine activity which is not explicable according to contemporary scientific knowledge. However, granted that God will not contradict the habits of a life-time, miracles need examining on the assumption that further scientific knowledge may find a natural explanation for them. And for an interesting and thought provoking discussion of miracles we turn to another outstanding Reformed theologian.

Herbert Henry Farmer

Herbert Farmer stands in the best traditions of liberal theology, and in the years following the Second World War he was one of a very few English theologians who had not come totally under the spell of neo-orthodoxy. At Farmer's feet students discovered that the traditions set in motion by Schleiermacher were not as obsolete as the great Karl Barth had been suggesting. Having been greatly influenced by John Oman, his 'revered teacher',[13] that was hardly surprising. And, like Oman, Farmer's understanding of God was driven by a personalist emphasis.

Farmer maintains that a fully personal relationship between God and persons requires two things. First, there must be a natural and sound environment in which the will of God and the wills of human beings can meet to achieve (or fail to achieve) active co-operation. This space is not circumscribed by God or human beings. It has been created by God and stands over against both God and human beings. It enables men and women to have genuine freedom, but it places certain limitations upon God.

> Stating it from the human side, we may say that it is essential to man's status as a personal being and to his sense of the significance of his moral life, that he should be called upon to make choices and decisions which make a difference and are not merely play-acting; in particular it is essential that he should be able to refuse to do God's will, not merely in the abstract or in imagination, but in such wise that his refusal involves that . . . God's will is not done. If his surrenders or refusals make no difference to the ongoing divine purpose, then he is merely a straw on the stream and has no true standing in a personal world with God . . . Or stating it from the divine side, we might say that if God's purpose in respect of man was to create creators, who should realize themselves by entering into genuine personal co-operation with Himself, then He was under necessity to set man in a world which in a sense was as yet uncreated, a world in which the full working out of His will would depend on the responses and decisions of man.[14]

---

[13]   H H Farmer, *The World of God: A Study of Prayer, Providence and Miracle in Christian Experience,* revised edition (London: Nisbet & Co Ltd., 1936), p xi.

[14]   Ibid., pp 68–9.

The echos of Oman are as clear as is the departure from the iron-will, deterministic world of Calvin. Then, secondly, a genuinely personal relationship between God and persons requires that God acts persuasively rather than coercively. God must elicit a free response of obedience and trust from people.

The natural and social world is the environment in which this meeting of wills takes place. It operates as 'an intrinsic symbol' for God, a symbol 'which is continuous with, and sustained by, the reality which it mediates'.[15] In obedience to 'the sacramental principle', God communicates with human beings in a non-direct way, thus enabling us to respond freely and, hence, grow as persons.[16] Nature and society can therefore both 'veil God' and 'reveal Him'.[17] When God reveals Godself to us through the media of nature and society, we find ourselves in 'an immediate personal relationship to Him as active will and purpose'.[18] Any situation can become disclosive of God's reality, while those that do not are still under God's providential care. Everything in this life is not sweetness and light: ' . . . in God's education of the human spirit into a rich personal sonship to Himself there is a place for darkness and mystery'; but Farmer stipulates, however, that while God may not reveal Godself *in* all situations, the Deity does reveal Godself 'sufficiently *for* all situations'.[19]

Farmer's 'God' is far from being a cosmic tyrant enforcing the divine will on the creation. The Eternal Person weaves the divine purpose out of the activities of humankind, and this places an inevitable limitation on God due to the freedom and power with which God has endowed persons. The divine will is known 'only in so far as it stands in tension with, and is in some sense limited by another will'.[20] God therefore is always involved with the risk that the divine purpose will not come to fruition. How then can we be confident of the providence of God? Farmer tells us that this is one of several mysteries concerning God's relationship with the world.

> That events should be really the result of the interplay of intramundane causes, including the choices of beings who are free to resist God, and yet also be controlled and directed by His manifold wisdom and sovereign will; that God has a purpose which He is working out in history, so that men can have genuine co-operative fellowship with Him here and now, yet which, being God's purpose, transcends history altogether so that man cannot interpret it adequately in terms of this life; that in spite of all the confusion and heartbreak and frustration of life, the sins, follies, accidents, disasters, diseases, so undiscriminating in their incidence, so ruthless in their working out, every individual may, if he will, not in imagination but in fact, rest upon a love which numbers the very hairs of his head – that is a conception before which the intellect sinks down in complete paralysis.[21]

Farmer's vision of God is one in which the total demand that God places upon our lives respects our freedom, and our final wellbeing becomes meaningful when set in the context of God's providential reign. But does it enable us to speak about God's activity in ways that do not run counter to what we know about the world from science?

---

15 Ibid., p 58.
16 Ibid., p 72
17 Ibid., p 73.
18 Ibid., p 76.
19 Ibid., p 90.
20 Ibid., p 98.
21 Ibid., pp 100–1.

Farmer addresses this question by considering the significance of miracles in religion. He notes that 'a miraculous event always enters the religious man's experience as a *revelation* of God'.[22] Miracles disclose the personal power and presence of God to people in such a way that they are called to that trust and obedience we know as faith. They are necessarily connected to revelation. Farmer then draws out four observations from this. He directs us, first, to the supernatural element in miracles, arguing this should be understood in terms of God's personal disclosure, rather than in terms of negating the laws of nature. Secondly, Farmer suggests that when miracles are understood in terms of revelation, we get a true sense of God as an agential force in events. We also, thirdly, do justice to the wonder and awe which constitute people's common response to miracles. And, fourthly, viewing miracles through the lens of revelation reminds us that it is intellectually impossible to demonstrate miracles by reason. God remains a Mystery. The disclosure in a miracle is of the Eternal Person to a human person at a particular time and place; so what may be a miracle for that person may not be to another person whose personal circumstances may be different.

Farmer also notes that miracles are invariably connected with *redemption*: ' . . . a miracle for the religious mind is pre-eminently an event in which God is apprehended as entering succouringly into a situation'.[23] The more personal an awareness of redemption becomes for an individual the more it seems appropriate to speak of God's miraculous activity. This particularly takes place in petitionary prayer when, out of great need or in a tremendous crisis, people turn to God for help and find their prayers miraculously answered. Underlying this is a particular understanding of divine activity: 'The prayer to God for assistance implies the belief that God's will is determined in its activity by its relation with my will, and that it is not imprisoned within the mechanical necessities of the physical universe, but can act freely as an operative cause within them and above them.'[24] Farmer admits that this does not happen very often, since it would be as destructive of a personal relationship with God for there to be 'an adjusting intervention of God at every point' as would 'a complete refusal to intervene at any point'.[25] But can we believe in God initiating events in this way? Does this not contradict science? Farmer thinks not, since he believes that science's findings do not require the elimination of talk about God's providential activity.

Farmer starts his justification for this claim by returning to personal experience. He maintains that at one and the same time we are aware of being bound by the regularities of the world *and* being free to fashion our own destinies. We might say that we are both determined by the world system *and* free to be creative within it. If that is the case for us, by analogy Farmer believes it is also the case for God. He also insists that science does not present a complete account of reality. Science can never lay bare the ultimate reality with which we have to deal. Metaphysics, as the word suggests, is not on the scientific curriculum. Quite clearly, therefore, 'God's initiation of events relevantly to individual situations . . . falls within that area of reality which transcends the scientific interest and method'.[26] But does this not still leave us with a contradiction between the way God initiates events and the way other events before and after then occur? Farmer sets out the challenge facing us as follows: 'Unless we can form some conception, however vague, how it should be possible for events to present themselves truthfully on the one hand as the resultant of the *ad hoc* initiative of will, and on the other hand as the resultant of what appears to be the exact contrary of that, namely necessary determination, the mind is left in a state of dangerous instability.'[27]

22	Ibid., p 109.
23	Ibid., p 116.
24	Ibid., 124.
25	Ibid., p 125.
26	Ibid., p 157.
27	Ibid., p 158.

In order to find such a 'conception' Farmer takes us back to our religious awareness of being in a personal relationship with the ultimate reality we name God. God is disclosed as 'will entering into relation with wills'.[28] The patterns in the natural world should be considered as being at least partially willed by God. The world can only be understood fully in relation to the Ultimate. We live in a processive universe in which our impression of a set pattern in the natural world is really an abstraction from the reality of the rich interaction of events that are ceaselessly taking place. Science formulates highly abstract descriptions of reality which never do justice to the richness of events. In fact, nature is made up of 'an infinite number of entities of a psychical kind in continuous interplay with one another'.[29] Farmer suggests that there are two ways in which God acts in such a process without undermining the fact that its nature was created by God in the first place. Both respect the limits within which God has chosen to operate. First, God has a direct involvement with the sub-personal realm. This is not observable to us. It realigns the relation of particles with our particles, but in doing so it uses 'the routines' of the sub-personal particles.[30] Secondly, God realises the divine purposes by utilizing the co-operation of human beings. God patiently awaits the alignment of our wills with the divine will. We are invited therefore to be 'a personal fellow-worker with the will of God'.[31]

Both of these examples of divine activity take place on the inside of nature, and hence they are invisible. Prayer and miracles belong to this realm. The outward side of nature, however, is what is presented to us by the senses. This is the world in which science works. While the two realms are distinct, they do not contradict each other. So miracles, like all divine activity, take place on the inside of nature, outside the view of science. What is disclosed to individuals through them is One who calls people to faith and obedience, and who promises ultimate security. This is achieved by 'inner rapport and not by external manipulation'.[32] Other theologians may wonder how this view of God measures up to the biblical understanding. A God committed to such a softly, softly approach in the world hardly resembles the One who roars from the skies, moves mountains and scatters enemies. Some will press the question whether Farmer has sacrificed something of the divine transcendence through his stress on the divine immanence. The classical model of God ruling the world in transcendent might and riding roughshod over creation's freedom, however, may have had rather unfortunate spin-offs. If the living God behaves like this, then humankind has a licence to follow suit. And to our shame history is littered with atrocities committed by religious people. There is a danger that in modelling God after a poor example of human relationships we grant credence to patriarchal, autocratic and confrontational behaviour. This is precisely the argument launched by feminist theology at the inherited models of God in Western Christianity; it also flows into the arguments that environmentally concerned Christians have directed at the traditional anthropocentric doctrines of creation.

---

[28] Ibid., p 163.
[29] Ibid., p 171.
[30] Ibid., p 176.
[31] Ibid., p 177.
[32] Ibid., p 178.

Jürgen Moltmann

Arguably the greatest threat to the human race rests in the damage we continue to inflict on our environment. For far too long a carefree attitude has prevailed which has seen us plunder the earth for our benefit, and damage our habitat for the sake of material reward and personal pleasure. The opportunity freely to explore nature has been turned into a selfish licence to exploit it. An intellectual stimulus and under-pinning for this attitude, some have argued, is found in the Christian tradition. Our attention is directed to Genesis 1: 1–2: 3, and in particular God telling newly created human beings to 'fill the earth and subdue it', and to have 'dominion over the fish of the sea and over the birds of the air and over every living thing that moves upon the earth' (1: 28). Given the authoritative status of the Bible, some suggest that its famous creation story has authorized the raping of nature by a culture largely created by Christianity.

Whatever we make of this, Moltmann is convinced that a correct reading of Genesis 1: 1–2: 3 does not sanction the kind of misuse of nature which has given rise to the present environmental crisis. Two fundamental points are basic to his case. First, Gen. 1: 28 is not inviting human beings to seize power over nature, but asserting a dietary law: '. . . human beings and animals alike are to live from the fruits which *the earth* brings forth in the form of plants and trees'.[33] Secondly, Moltmann attempts to undermine views of creation which so elevate the status of human beings that the natural world is both emptied of value for God and only regarded by people to possess a value they themselves can derive from it. He does this by placing the creation story in a theocentric rather than anthropocentric framework. The climax of the story comes with the sabbath and not the creation of human beings. The sabbath is the goal of all God's creative activity, and final eschatological fulfilment involves the whole cosmos, not just human beings. The need for liberation is not confined to people, it is also required by nature (Rom. 8: 22–23). The goal of creation, like that of men and women, is to become an offering to God, redeemed and perfected giving praise to God, and sharing in God's sabbath rest.

> In the resting presence of God all creatures find their sustaining foundation. The sabbath preserves created things from obliteration, and fills their restless existence with the happiness of the presence of the eternal God. On the sabbath all creatures find their own place in the God who is wholly present. The world is created 'out of nothing' and it is created 'for the sabbath'; so on the sabbath it exists 'in' God's presence. This is the sabbath blessing. It does not spring from God's activity; it springs from his rest. It does not come from God's acts; it comes from his present Being.[34]

Moltmann's messianic and eschatological emphases significantly come into play here with a vision of all things being resurrected in a new creation at the End. This will be the messianic, eternal sabbath inaugurated by the life and witness, death and resurrection of Jesus the Christ, the Lord of the sabbath.

A theocentric understanding of creation which emphasises the importance and value of the natural world to God helps strip away from the doctrine of creation some of its less helpful elements. If nature is precious to God, it follows that attitudes rooted in conservation, preservation and stewardship are more in order than the tendency hitherto to exploit and plunder. We must learn

---

[33]   Jürgen Moltmann, *God in Creation: An Ecological Doctrine of Creation* (London: SCM Press, 1985), p 29.
[34]   Ibid., p 282.

the implications of living in an environment in which there is an astonishing degree of relatedness: 'All living things – each in its own specific way – live in one another and with one another, from one another and for one another'.[35] And, given Moltmann's panentheistic model of the God–world relationship, God is no exception. This calls for a different language from that of domination when we are talking of the relationship between living things in our symbiotic world. We need to use language appropriate to living in communities and within relationships.

Moltmann also wishes to move away from an understanding of creation which stresses origins. One of the implications of evolutionary theory has been the need to find a way of conceiving creation as an ongoing event. Nevertheless, what Moltmann says about God creating out of nothing is quite interesting. It would seem that for God freely to create a contingent world there must be some element of contingency in God. But where does that contingency come from? One suggestion would be to say that since 'will' and 'love' are relational terms, there never could be a situation in which God was without some kind of world to will and love. God therefore does not possess *negative* freedom, the freedom to do nothing. By nature God *has* to will and love. But, it can be argued, God does possess *positive* freedom, the freedom to choose what to will and love. So, for example, while God cannot avoid creating, just what is created is purely a matter of divine choice. In this way, necessity and contingency are held together within the divine life as polar rather than contradictory opposites. This strategy is advocated by process theology, but it is rejected by Moltmann. He alleges that process theology has no doctrine of creation, only a doctrine of preservation and ordering of the world.[36] But I am far from convinced that Moltmann has grasped the subtleties and nuances of the process theologians!

One of the features of Moltmann's theological project is that it has been conducted in dialogue with Judaism. And it is to the Yiddish idea of *zimsum* that he turns for a crucial idea in his doctrine of creation: '*Zimsum* means concentration and contraction, and signifies a withdrawing of oneself into oneself'.[37] Moltmann claims that God created contingency and freedom within the divine life, thus producing the space for creation out of nothing to become possible. He asserts that: 'The *nihil* for his *creatio ex nihilo* only comes into being because – and in as far as – the omnipotent and omnipresent God withdraws his presence and restricts his power'.[38] God therefore creates by making room for things to happen. This is another variation on the theme of self-emptying (*kenosis*), and Moltmann makes the interesting suggestion that this 'creative letting-be' is best expressed in 'motherly categories' rather than 'masculine metaphors'.[39] But how does a *wholly* complete and self-sustained Deity get into a position of self-emptying? The mystery remains!

As we have already seen, Moltmann views the world in a radically open-ended way. It is drawn ever onward to its eschatological future by the sustaining and innovative activity of God. His panentheistic doctrine enables him to see God as the transcendent life within which the creation 'lives moves and has its being'. The God who created the world out of nothing, however, is also immanent within the world, driving creation forward to its messianic future and suffering the joys and pain, gains and losses of the cosmic adventure. This is the work of the Creator Spirit who indwells a world made up of a myriad of interconnected events.

---

[35]   Ibid., p 17.
[36]   Ibid., pp 78–9.
[37]   Ibid., p 87.
[38]   Ibid., pp 86–7.
[39]   Ibid., p 88.

> This indwelling Creator Spirit is fundamental for the community of creation. It is not the elementary particles that are basic, as the mechanistic world view maintains, but the overriding harmony of the relations and of the self-transcending movements, in which the longing of the Spirit for a still unattained consummation finds expression. If the cosmic Spirit is the Spirit of God, the universe cannot be viewed as a closed system. It has to be understood as a system that is open – open for God and his future.[40]

The Spirit operates from 'inside' creation, thus her work cannot be distinguished from other causative agencies in the flow of events. The basic scientific model of evolution, therefore, is not contradicted. Indeed, the mode of the Spirit's operation is similar to what Farmer suggested: persuasive, gentle and patient. If the providential work of God in continuing creation by definition is not discernible to the naked eye, and cannot be differentiated from other agency, critics will wonder how in the absence of empirical evidence we can be sure that it actually takes place. Nevertheless, Moltmann, it would seem, does not totally rule out the miraculous.

> Seen in terms of world history, the transforming power of suffering is the basis for the liberating and consummating acts of God . . . . We do not have to expect the accompanying activity of God to take the form merely of supernatural interventions and spectacular disruptions. Any such expectation would actually distort our perception of that accompanying activity. But the pointer to God's still and unobtrusive accompaniment of history by no means excludes experiences of 'signs and wonders'. The discernment of these is only possible at all in the light of the unremitting experience of God's accompanying activity.[41]

At the heart of Moltman's theology of course lies a trinitarian emphasis. He maintains that the concept of panentheism can only be understood fully when it is set in a trinitarian framework. When transcendence is affirmed at the expense of immanence, the result is a deistic view of the God–world relationship in which God has no ongoing involvement in the world; when immanence is affirmed at the expense of transcendence, a pantheistic view of the God–world relationship arises, in which all distinctions and any separation between God and the world are removed. To maintain the correct balance between transcendence and immanence a trinitarian concept of creation is required:

> Creation exists in the Spirit, is moulded by the
> Son and is created by the Father. It is therefore
> from God, through God and in God.[42]

Just what Moltmann's doctrine of the Trinity fully looks like will become apparent in the course of the following discussion of the Trinity.

---

40   Ibid., p 103.
41   Ibid., p 211–12.
42   Ibid., p 98.

CHAPTER 6

God: Three in One and One in Three

THE URC expresses its belief in God in a trinitarian fashion, but there is no explicit and full-blown doctrine of the Trinity which can be read out of the New Testament, even though there is evidence which suggests that the early churches were using trinitarian language in their theology and worship (see Matthew 28: 19; Romans 8: 14–17 and 2 Corinthians 13: 13). Nevertheless, with the doctrine of the Trinity we have an example of the church taking its pattern of orthodoxy from a church council rather than the pages of the New Testament, although some argue that the formulae agreed at the Council of Nicaea were a genuine and appropriate development of the New Testament assertions.

The focus of the Council of Nicaea was a doctrinal dispute between Arius, a presbyter of the Baukalis church in Alexandria, and Alexander, his bishop. Frances Young believes that 'we can reconstruct a picture of a gentle and tolerant bishop gradually forced to move against a popular preacher whose controversial views were finding increased support among considerable sections of the community'.[1] But what were his 'controversial views'? Arius held to a strict monotheism in which the Son makes the Father known by being different. The Father's transcendent divinity is protected by attributing creative activity to the Son who brings time and the world into being. The term 'only-begotten' (*monogenes*) is given to the Son by Arius in order to make it clear that Jesus is neither one of the generated creatures nor akin to the unbegotten God. Arius' position therefore involved him asserting two things: first, the Son is not eternal in the same sense as the Father, since he was born in the era before creation; and, secondly, the Son is wholly superior to other beings because only the Son has been directly produced from the Father.

Arius was charged with propagating heresy on two accounts. First, he was accused of failing to affirm the full divinity of Christ. Secondly, in Arius' scheme, like all other creatures the Son is dependent upon God's grace if he is to carry out the divine will; this led to the charge that Christ was not the Saviour but a mere creature. Arius therefore has been labelled as one of the arch-heretics of Christian history, and the term 'Arianism' has become synonymous with doctrinal views which fail fully to affirm Christ's divinity. However, this would seem to be rather unfair on Arius, since, as recent scholarship has shown, Arius' intentions were quite conservative. His position is thoroughly scriptural, having its roots in texts which portrayed development and weakness in the humanity of Christ, and being confirmed by John 14: 28: '. . . the Father is greater than I'. His intentions perhaps were more concerned with talking about our salvation in Christ rather than working out a precise doctrine of the Trinity. Not for the last time was a Christian theologian to be misinterpreted with devastating results![2]

[1]   Francis Young, *From Nicaea to Chalcedon: A Guide to the Literature and Its Background* (London: SCM Press, 1983), p 59.
[2]   Frances Young regards Arius neither as 'the arch-heretic of tradition, nor even much of an enquirer', but rather as 'a reactionary, a rather literal-minded conservative who appealed to scripture and tradition as the basis of his faith' (ibid., p 64).

Constantine, ever the politician, saw a threat to peace and stability brewing in the dispute between Alexander and Arius, as increasing numbers of people began to take sides. A serious split in the church at this time, of course, was also a fracture in the Roman Empire so, after attempting a softly, softly approach by way of correspondence, Constantine called an ecumenical council to settle the dispute. It opened on 20 May 325 in Nicaea, with over two hundred bishops present and the Emperor in the chair. Amidst glittering pomp and lavish entertainment, the Council arrived at a creed which many regard as the most fundamental statement on the Trinity ever produced by the Church.

THE CREED AND ANATHEMA OF THE COUNCIL OF NICAEA

We believe in one God, the Father Almighty, Maker of all things visible and invisible.

And in one Lord Jesus Christ, the Son of God, begotten of the Father, Only-begotten, that is from the substance (ousia) of the Father; God from God, Light from Light, true God from true God, begotten not made, consubstantial with the Father, by whom all things were made; who for us men and for our salvation came down and was incarnate, was made man, suffered, and rose again the third day, ascended into heaven, and is coming to judge the living and the dead.

And in the Holy Spirit.

And those who say, 'There was when he was not', and 'Before his generation he was not', and 'he came to be from nothing', or those who pretend that the Son of God is of other reality [hypostasis] or being [ousia; some texts add 'or created', probably not original] or alterable or mutable, the Catholic and Apostolic Church anathematizes.

The anathema at the end of the creed quote statements believed to be Arian; but there is good reason to believe that Arius would have been able to defend himself against most of them, with the result that the Arians were able to accept the creed and the anathema, believing that the latter did not apply to them!

A couple of key terms in trinitarian thinking appear in this creed. 'Only-begotten' signifies that Christ was generated from the very essence of God. As the qualification 'begotten not made' makes clear, the comparison is with human reproduction, so the distinction between 'generation' and 'creation' is an attempt to safeguard the divinity of Christ. Then, secondly, the term 'consubstantial' (*homoousios*) further bolsters up Christ's divinity by affirming the identity between Father and Son. However, different people meant different things when they said that the Father and Son are the same. The anti-Arians interpreted it to affirm 'one being or substance of Father, Son and Spirit' while Arians saw it as underwriting the idea that 'the Son is exactly like the Father, and has no other source'. One side therefore could think of *homoousios* in terms of 'a personal and specific identity' – one and the same being – while the other side understood it as 'a much broader, generic identity' – exactly like in being.[3] And, as Henry Chadwick remarks: 'The happy accident of this ambiguity enabled Constantine to secure the assent of everyone except two Libyan bishops.'[4]

---

[3]   See Henry Chadwick, *The Early Church* (Harmondsworth, Middlesex: Penguin Books, 1967), p 130.
[4]   Ibid.

But, inevitably, the trinitarian discussion continued, with the Eastern and Western theologians tending towards different emphases, hence, possible heretical tendencies. In the East, the Greek speaking theologians stressed the 'threeness' of God, thus running the risk of being charged with advocating 'tritheism'; while in the West, the Latin speaking theologians stressed the 'oneness' of God, thereby being prone to 'modalism', the view that Father, Son and Holy Spirit are modes of a monarchical God's operation.

By the end of the Patristic period, there appear to have been two basic types of approach to trinitarian doctrine, the Cappadocian Fathers' *social* model and Augustine's *psychological* model. While the latter has had a considerable influence upon Western theology, it is now felt by some theologians that the contemporary discussion will be best served if we pay greater attention to some of the important features of the Cappadocians' work. Colin E Gunton, URC minister and Professor of Theology at King's College, London, has insisted upon the importance of trinitarian theology for contemporary Christian witness and practice. He firmly believes that the Cappadocians have provided us with a series of conceptual insights that enable us to develop a doctrine of the Trinity which reflects what can be known about God from God's self-revelation to which the Bible is the witness. But what are those insights?

The Cappadocian Fathers

The Cappadocians belong to theology's mystical tradition and its so-called *apophatic* ethos. The more we come to know God through prayer and meditation, the less we realise we know about God theologically. Nevertheless, according to this tradition, God's existence and attributes can be known. Some vestiges of the Creator have been lodged in creation, so nature can become a focus for contemplation, as well as provide the content for knowing what God is not. Since the world is temporal and finite, we can say, for example, that God is eternal and infinite.

Gregory of Nyssa argues that the predicates used of God's relations to us are *analogical*, whereas those describing the inner workings of the Godhead are *essential*. Since he believes that the former are grounded in the latter, what is said about God in scripture can become a basis for theological construction. But he pleads caution since the names of God in scripture can be misleading as well as helpful, and no one name or combination of names will ever be able to define God adequately. Nevertheless, attention to what is said about God, Jesus and the Holy Spirit in the Bible becomes the starting point for a doctrine of the Trinity. As God revealed the divine self in a triune way, so we can know something of the trinitarian nature of God. And, as Gunton says: 'The conceptual and ontological revolution achieved by the Cappadocians is that God is as he is made known by the Son and the Spirit: he is other – distinct – in person, to be sure, but not in being as God – for he is made known *as he is*.'[5]

The standard trinitarian formula of the Cappadocians asserts that God is one *ousia* (being) in three *hypostaseis* (personalities). There is one transcendent being which exists simultaneously in three persons (*prosopa*), each being a unique individual with its own *hypostasis*. So the three persons of the Godhead are consubstantial with each other, with the result that the Deity is a Being-in-communion. Relationality, therefore, is an essential feature of God being God. As Gunton says: 'The persons are not persons who then enter into relations, but are mutually constituted, made what

---

[5]   Colin E Gunton, *The Promise of Trinitarian Theology* (Edinburgh: T & T Clark, 1991), p 54.

they are, by virtue of their relations to one another.'[6] The Cappadocians, with their stress on the unique individuality of Father, Son and Holy Spirit, would be in danger of letting their trinitarian formula lapse into tritheism were it not for their doctrine of co-inherence *(perichoresis)*. This enables them to argue that the Godhead exists undivided in three persons and that there is an identity of nature in each *hypostasis*. As Gregory of Nazianzus makes clear, the three persons are distinguished from each other:

> The Father is father, and without beginning, for he is underived.
> The Son is son, and not without beginning, in that he derives from
> the Father . . . The Spirit is truly holy spirit, as proceeding from
> the Father, not in the manner of the Son, since not by generation
> but by procession . . .[7]

While the nature and activity of the *hypostaseis* are indistinguishable, the Father remains for the Cappadocians the fountain of the Godhead and hence possesses a certain degree of priority. Meanwhile, each divine *hypostasis* is the essence of the Godhead turned towards its unique characteristic in the Godhead.

Augustine of Hippo and John Calvin

Augustine is concerned that Subordinationism, the idea that Son and Spirit are subordinate to the Father in the divine Triad, and Arianism should be rejected. He insists that the whole Trinity lies behind the activity of each of its members. Also, while the Son and Spirit may be said to be posterior to the Father in the process of salvation, Augustine argues that they are co-equal in eternity. This distinction paved the way for the standard trinitarian differentiation between the *economic* and the *essential* Trinity (between God as the divine self operates in creation and redemption, and God as God is within the divine life).

Augustine establishes a place and role for the Holy Spirit within the Trinity. He conceives the Holy Spirit as the love which unites Father and Son, thus prefiguring in the relationship between the two what is made possible for us. The Holy Spirit is the divine gift which unites us to God. Augustine also tried to safeguard the unity of the Trinity by advocating that the Spirit does not proceed from the Father, as the theologians of the East had advocated, but from the Father *and* the Son. So the infamous *filioque* clause was added to the Creed, thereby creating another bone of contention between the churches of East and West. This theological judgement tended to subordinate pneumatology to christology, a move vigorously opposed, as we shall see, by Jürgen Moltmann among others.

The starting point for Augustine's doctrine of the Trinity is the one divine nature or substance, the unity of Father, Son and Holy Spirit, in which the three differ only as eternal relationships. The Father knows himself in the Son and the Son in the Father, and proceeds as Spirit from both Father and Son as personified love. Augustine uses pyschological analogies to develop his trinitarian model. At this point he seems to impose his inherited neoplatonic worldview on his theological proposal. That worldview claimed that the human mind is the apex of humanity; so it

---

[6]   Ibid., p 156.

[7]   Gregory of Nazianzus, *Orations*, 39, 12 found in Henry Bettenson (ed. and trans.), *The Later Christian Fathers: A Selection from the Writings of the Fathers from St.Cyril of Jerusalem to St.Leo the Great* (Oxford: Oxford University Press, 1970), p 119.

was quite natural for Augustine to argue that the theologian should turn to the human mind for traces of the Trinity (*vestigia Trinitatis*). He therefore chooses to conceive God's trinitarian structure by analogy with the inner workings of our minds rather than with personal relationships. Consequently, as Gunton argues powerfully, it is 'a platonizing doctrine of knowledge as recollection' which forms the crucial background to Augustine's doctrine of the Trinity.[8] This opens up the way for him to speak of the triune nature of God as love, beloved and love and in terms of the very individualistic and speculative analogies of the memory, understanding and will. In the process Augustine perhaps lost the crucial insight of the tradition bequeathed to him, namely, that the Trinity is constituted by the relatedness of its three members. Gunton's verdict is somewhat damning: 'Augustine either did not understand the trinitarian theology of his predecessors, both East and West, or looked at their work with spectacles so strongly tinted with neoplatonic assumptions that they have distorted his work.'[9]

There can be no doubting the influence of Augustine on John Calvin, but the Genevan Reformer was no blind camp follower as can be seen particularly in Calvin's discussion of the Trinity, where there is clear evidence of an attempt to move to a more relational view of the members in the Godhead. Calvin's trinitarian views were constructed in reaction to the anti-trinitarianism of disputants like Servetus, who was eventually executed for heresy – an occurrence for which Calvin notoriously was largely responsible. Calvin believed that God had clearly revealed the divine self to be trinitarian on the basis of the witness of the New Testament: 'For he so proclaims himself the sole God as to offer himself to be contemplated clearly in three persons.'[10] It is perfectly legitimate for theologians to express more fully and in a clearer way the teaching of Scripture, and this is precisely what Calvin attempts to do. He is concerned, however, that we should not attempt to know those things which Scripture gives us no grounds for knowing, imploring his readers to 'willingly leave to God the knowledge of himself', thereby making it clear that, while some appreciation of the economic trinity is possible, knowledge of the essential trinity is always ruled out.[11]

Calvin is clearly concerned to counter those who deny the divinity of Christ, as well as those who so construct trinitarian doctrine that they are caught up in modalist views. The unity between Father and Son therefore is emphasized. The Word was 'begotten of the Father before time.'[12] It has 'perpetually resided with him', and as a result Calvin can claim: 'By this, his eternity, his true essence, and his divinity are proved.'[13] Likewise, Calvin asserts that the Holy Spirit is divine, breathing 'essence, life and movement' into all things.[14] While there are three members of the Trinity, there is only one God. However, as Calvin makes clear, there is a clear distinction – though never a division – between them, and they also display an order:

> . . . the observance of an order is not meaningless or superfluous, when the Father is thought of as first, then from him the Son, and finally from both the Spirit. For the mind of each human being is naturally inclined to contemplate God first, then the wisdom coming forth from him, and lastly the power whereby he executes the decrees of his plan. For this reason, the Son is said to come forth from the Father alone; the Spirit, from the Father and the Son at the same time.[15]

---

[8]   Gunton, *The Promise of Trinitarian Theology*, p 45.
[9]   Ibid., pp 38–9.
[10] Calvin, *Institutes* 1,13,2.
[11] Ibid., 1,13,21.
[12] Ibid., 1,13,7.
[13] Ibid., 1,13,8.
[14] Ibid., 1,13,14.
[15] Ibid., 1,13,18.

Calvin plainly follows Augustine by including the controversial addition of the *filioque* clause, 'and from the Son', to the statement about the procession of the Holy Spirit.

In Calvin's account of the Trinity, God is a simple, single essence in which we can differentiate three persons. It is in his understanding of the 'persons' that a departure from Augustine is made in the direction of the more relational understanding of the Cappadocians.

> 'Person', therefore, I call a 'subsistence' in God's essence, which, while related to the others, is distinguished by an incommunicable quality. By the term 'subsistence' we would understand something different from 'essence'. . . Now, of the three subsistences I say that each one, while related to the others, is distinguished by a special quality.[16]

Calvin seems aware of the need to account conceptually for the relations between the persons in the Trinity and the unique personality of each (their 'individuality – in – relation' [Gunton]).[17] However, he does not seem able to avoid 'the characteristic sin of Western trinitarianism, of seeing the persons not as constituting the being of God by their mutual relations but as in some way inhering in being that is in some sense prior to them'.[18] So the path from a psychological to a social doctrine of the Trinity has not been *fully* followed.

Contemporary Social Doctrines of the Trinity:
Jürgen Moltmann and Colin E Gunton

The starting point for Moltmann's doctrine of the Trinity is the New Testament. Trinitarian thinking is not a speculative engagement but an encounter with history. It involves biblical study before an agonising over the adequacy of philosophical concepts. According to Bauckham, Moltmann believes that 'the doctrine of the Trinity is the theological interpretation of the history of Jesus and the Spirit'.[19] In the panentheistic view of God's relationship with the world, God's life is enriched and changed as the world is experienced within the divine life. So the doctrine of the Trinity becomes for Moltmann a theological interpretation of God's history with the world, a history which reached its climax in the cross of Christ.

In *The Crucified God*, Moltmann offers his famous trinitarian understanding of the cross. Jesus dies and the Father suffers his death. In his Son's dereliction, abandonment by the Father is experienced by Jesus. Meanwhile, the Fatherlessness of Jesus is matched by the Sonlessness of the Father. On the cross, Father and Son are at one and the same time totally separated as well as united. And the trinitarian pattern becomes complete when Moltmann tells us that: 'What proceeds from this event between Father and Son is the Spirit which justifies the Godless, fills the forsaken with love and even brings the dead alive, since even the fact that they are dead cannot exclude them from this event of the cross; the death in God also includes them.'[20] This trinitarian understanding is based upon the conception of three divine Subjects existing in mutual loving relationship. There is an inter-subjective relationship between Father, Son and Spirit which is rooted in freedom. The unity

---

[16]   Ibid., 1,13,6.
[17]   Gunton, *The Promise of Trinitarian Theology*, p 170 and passim.
[18]   Ibid., p 170.
[19]   Baukham, *The Theology of Jürgen Moltmann*, p 157.
[20]   Moltmann, *The Crucified God*, p 244.

of the Trinity is protected, and the danger of lapsing into tritheism is averted, Moltmann argues, by introducing the Eastern doctrine of mutual indwelling (*perichoresis*). The divine persons therefore are both one and three in their mutual indwelling.

The unity of the Godhead is further displayed in the common ability of the divine persons not only to open themselves out to one another in love but also to draw the world into their life. Moltmann's eschatological emphasis comes into view when he speaks of the Trinity being open to the world so that we can have fellowship with God and ultimately fellowship in God.[21] The Spirit is sent by the Father through the Son as the agent of "renewal and unification of the whole creation', while 'in the transfiguration of the world through the Spirit all men turn to God, and, moved by the Spirit, come to the Father through Christ the Son'.[22] This outwardgoingness teaches us that God's relationship with the world is a desire for friendship and fellowship rather than simply to rule over us. Familiar themes in Moltmann's theology flow from this observation. God is not 'the omnipotent, universal monarch, who is reflected in earthly rulers'; since God is the Father of the crucified and risen Jesus, the almightiness of the Deity is found in 'his passionate, passible love'.[23] The mutual loving relationships between the persons of the Trinity, therefore, are extended into an open fellowship of love with the whole creation. It follows that God's rule can only be one of love, a love which does not ride roughshod over creaturely freedom. In turn we should model our own behaviour in society upon a non-hierarchical, all-inclusive community of love. This has obvious implications for the way we might deal with others in non-oppressive ways, the manner in which we ought to be treating the natural world with respect, and the creation of communities and churches which reflect the unity and diversity evident in the Trinity.

Colin Gunton is more traditional than Moltmann in his theological judgements. He fears that doctrines of panentheism are overtly prone to stress the immanence of God at the expense of God's transcendence, and that they tend to bring God and the world into too close a relationship. He is also critical of Moltmann's use of the concept of self-emptying *(kenosis)* for God's creative activity, accusing Moltmann of universalizing a concept which has a particular point of reference: 'The point of a concept like *kenosis* is that it enables us to pinpoint the significance of the incarnation, not that it should be applied elsewhere.'[24] Gunton also objects to Moltmann's views concerning the divine suffering, believing that Moltmann is in danger of 'a tritheistic denial of the unity of the divine action' when he speaks of an enmity between God and God in the cross.[25] And Gunton further questions Moltmann's view that God suffers when Jesus dies on the cross, since such language is in danger of 'reducing atonement to theodicy, and thus using the cross chiefly as a means of defending God against responsibility for suffering'.[26] We must not forget, he argues, that a crucial dimension of the crucifixion is an innocent human being offering up his life to God. Following tradition, Gunton argues that the suffering belongs to the Son, but not to the Father, and, in any case, the concept of divine suffering is unbiblical: 'God does not suffer history, he moves it'.[27] But God's activity in salvation, Gunton agrees, is best expressed in a trinitarian way: the Father releases the Son into the world out of boundless love for it, and finally receives back the Son victorious through the work of the Spirit. Divine self-emptying thus leads to divine self-fulfilment.

---

[21]   See Jürgen Moltmann, *The Trinity and the Kingdom of God* (London: SCM Press, 1981), pp 95–6.
[22]   Ibid., p 127.
[23]   Ibid., p 197.
[24]   Colin E Gunton, *Christ and Creation* (Carlisle: The Paternoster Press, 1992), p 85.
[25]   Ibid., p 86.
[26]   Ibid., p 86–7.
[27]   Ibid., p 87.

Gunton's own trinitarian proposals follow closely the Cappadocian Fathers' conclusion that God is being in communion. God is three persons bound together in a unity of inter-relatedness. Gunton argues that this conclusion can be drawn from our own experience of worship and daily life when interpreted by the Bible. We struggle to express the Trinity conceptually because we wish to develop appropriately our reflective awareness of the God we have encountered in the Spirit through Christ. Rather than an attempt to solve a logical puzzle, Gunton claims that the Trinity is 'a given . . . which contains the clue to everything else'.[28] Everything therefore is to be understood in the light of God's self-revelation of the divine self as triune.

Central to Gunton's theology is a belief that God is personal. The Deity is not the Great Unmoved Mover of Aristotle, the great immobile, impassible, passionless Absolute of Greek philosophy; rather God is 'a personal taxis of dynamic and free relations'.[29] As a community of three persons in relation – Father, Son and Holy Spirit – God derives his being from what the three persons 'give to and receive from each other in the freedom of the unknowable eternity'.[30] Once again, the doctrine of *perichoresis* is introduced to ensure that there is such a perfect mutual indwelling and inter-penetration between the three persons that the One is always involved in any action of the Three. This prevents any lurch towards tritheism. Gunton's model, like that of Moltmann's, requires that each member of the Trinity possesses a personal distinctiveness. This leads to a rejection by both of them of the *filioque* doctrine. The Holy Spirit is given a role that is not determined by that of the Son.

According to Gunton, God and the world are ontologically distinct, the latter being the free creation of the former. While the world is clearly dependent upon God for its origin and preservation, God is dependent upon nothing and has no needs or requirements. However, according to Gunton's analysis, the relation between God and the world is a personal one. God has chosen to be related to the world, which as God's creation is essentially good. However, there was no need for God to create the world: 'Because God is, "before" creation took place, already a being-in-relation, there is no need for him to create what is other than himself. He does not need to create, because he is already a *taxis*, order, of loving relations.'[31] Gunton is trying to meet the requirements of giving the God of love an object of love which does not then deny God's absolute self-sufficiency. Only if God's object of love is another person in the divine life can that condition be satisfied. But this all sounds a rather narcissistic way of seeking to resolve the problem of how One who is totally self-sufficient and wholly necessary can be conceived of freely doing anything, let alone creating a wholly contingent universe.

Gunton's trinitrian theology is based upon what is known about God's creative and redeeming activity from the Bible. Following Irenaeus, he claims that the world has been created through the Son, and since the Son also became incarnate, there is continuity to God's work of creation and redemption. 'God the Father is related to the world through the creating and redeeming action of the Son and Spirit who are, in Irenaeus' expression, his two hands.'[32] The way from God to the creatures is via Christ, the Lord of creation; while the way from the creatures to God is also via Christ, the Reconciler and Redeemer.

---

28   Gunton, *The Promise of Trinitarian Theology*, p 28.
29   Ibid., p 150.
30   Ibid., p 164.
31   Ibid., p 147.
32   Ibid.,

While Gunton is confident that we can have a firm understanding of the *economic* Trinity, he is very cautious about what can be known about God's inner life. Nevertheless, he suggests that God's nature ought to provide us with an example of how we should operate as societies and churches. So the world 'echoes the trinitarian being of God in being . . . a dynamic of beings in relation', and Gunton claims that 'the church should echo the dynamic of the relations between the three persons who together constitute the deity'.[33]

The trinitarian approach enables us to have a vision for society in which each individual matters and counts as they contribute to the whole. As Gunton puts it: 'Just as Father, Son and Spirit are what they are by virtue of their otherness-in-relation, so that each *particular* is unique and absolutely necessary to the being of the whole, so it is, in its own way, for our being in society'.[34] Trinitarianism does not support the ideology of the Right which proposes that the idea of society should be abandoned in favour of a brutal individualistic approach to life; nor does it provide a justification for the collectivistic Left who ride roughshod over the lives of individuals. It lands both political extremes in the dock, wanting to affirm the uniqueness of individuals both in their otherness *and* in their relations in community. The trinitarian view also stresses the interpersonal nature of God, whereas many views depersonalize the Deity, and hence provide an ideological support for authoritarian approaches to power and leadership.

Turning to the Church, Gunton correctly laments the fact that the Church's theology has not often been grounded in an adequate understanding of God: '. . . bad ecclesiastical practice is at least in part the outcome of bad theology'.[35] One might wish that churches were genuinely self-critical about their life and witness, since a church that 'echoes' the being of God will be seeking to display a number of things. First, it will be a community in which there is a reflection of the dynamism in the Godhead. The *koinonia* (fellowship or community) of the church should echo the perichoretic interaction between the divine persons, thus ruling out overtly hierarchical models of being church and hence supporting the more congregational and conciliar traditions of the URC. As Gunton correctly says: 'The being of the church consists in the relations of the persons to each other.'[36] Secondly, if the being of the church resides in *koinonia*, it is wrong to seek it in an order of ministry since 'the ecclesiology of community relativizes the whole question of an ordained caste'.[37] This again supports a Reformed view of ministry in which the ordained person exists for the well-being of the church (its *bene esse*) rather than in any way being constitutive of its essence (*esse*). Thirdly, the trinitarian approach provides us with a model that requires a quite flexible approach to Church leadership. Gunton invites us to consider adopting 'an ecclesiology of perichoresis', in which there are no fixed hierarchies of leadership, but instead interchangeability and flexibility 'so that the same person will be sometimes "subordinate" and sometimes "superordinate" according to the gifts and graces being exercised'.[38] Finally, just as the trinitarian model cannot sanction authoritarian and tyrannical leadership in society, the church also ought to be led by people who seek to follow the model of personhood revealed in God's triune life. We shall discuss ecclesiological matters in a later chapter. It will suffice now to note how Gunton helps transform what for many is an obtuse logical puzzle (How can the One be Three and the Three One, and at one and the same time?) into an exploration which provides significant insights for both church and society.

---

[33] Ibid., pp 114, 81.
[34] Ibid., p 13.
[35] Ibid., p 62.
[36] Ibid., p 76.
[37] Ibid., p 80.
[38] Ibid.

Reflections and Observations

1.   Readers have received a brief snapshot of the diversity and creativity in some Reformed theologians' doctrines of God. Each attempt to provide us with a picture of a God worthy of our worship, and in whom it is appropriate to put our trust. From Calvin we get a powerful reminder of what we should never forget, namely, that there is a unique difference between the Creator and the creatures. All too easily we construct a picture of God after our own image, one that cuts the Deity down to our size. What is needed instead is a theological account of the nature of God that produces genuine awe and reverence. God is to be conceived as a profound Mystery who, wholly other than us, elicits our worship and obedience. Our formulation, however, must not compromise the insight flowing from the Incarnation, *viz.* that God has drawn close to us. Therefore in a sound doctrine of God a balance is maintained between God's transcendence and immanence.

All of the twentieth century theologians we have considered try in their own way to move on from Calvin's overt and rather onesided stress on God's transcendent sovereignty. The future discussion may be helped by Colin Gunton's suggestion that we talk of God's otherness and relatedness instead of divine transcendence and immanence. While 'transcendence' and 'immanence' are often conflicting terms 'otherness' and 'relatedness' perhaps are polar opposites which do not suffer from that problem. Nevertheless, the requirement that theology deals with each aspect as complementary parts of a complete picture of God cannot be gainsaid.

2.   Our discussion reveals the importance of finding appropriate conceptuality in which to speak of God. We have seen the danger of modelling God on the basis of the impersonal and mechanistic forces of the natural world, or the autocratic behaviour of all-powerful rulers. The works of Oman and Farmer remind us that the best analogies to assist us in constructing a picture of God are drawn from the world of personal interactions. To be sure, the highest and most eminent examples need choosing, since there is much in our human relationships which is unedifying and bordering on the sub-personal. Gunton, of course, turns the point on its head by arguing that, since God has revealed God's self as a community of persons, united as one being through their perichoretic inter-relatedness, it is the revelation of God which shows us how to depict personhood in the world. Unless we already have some notion of personhood prior to the revelation, however, it is hard to see how we would be able to interpret or understand it in personal categories. The starting point for theological awareness perhaps is neither simply revelation nor simply reason and experience; it is much more a matter of reflecting on the interaction between the two. Be that as it may, unless we want to make God into an object, we need to think of Deity in the categories with which we associate persons and human relationships, and hence do justice to the basic religious experience of encountering God as a personal Thou.

3.   From the classical theism of Calvin, through the panentheism of Garvie and Moltmann, to the social trinitarianism of Gunton, we have encountered difficulties in trying at one and the same time to hold together the concept of God's self-sufficiency with a belief that the contingent world is created by God. How does a necessary Deity produce a contingent world? Perhaps the most intriguing answer we encountered came from Moltmann and involved his use of the idea of *zimsum*. But we still found it difficult to see how a wholly complete divine Person could be in a position to create a world over and against Godself. At this point, one might either invoke the strategy of pleading that we are up against a mystery and say that knowledge about such things is beyond us, or accept that in some sense God is not self-sufficient. Adopting the latter strategy, we can recall a view flagged up earlier, namely, that while God does not need *this* world, the Deity does in fact need *some* world of which to be the ground. The Lover needs a love *beyond the divine life;* but what is chosen to love is the product of God's free choice. This proposition enables freedom and necessity to be held together in tension, but it also means that God can never be said to have been without *some* kind of world. There is neither beginning nor end to God's creative love and God's aesthetic enjoyment of what is other than God; hence, talk of beginnings and endings of creation are necessarily ruled out. That *this* world had a beginning and will have an end of course is beyond dispute; the idea that God is ever devoid of *some* kind of world to ground and love, though, might be a basic theological error.

4.   The recent revival of trinitarian thinking is timely and encouraging. In both Moltmann's and Gunton's social trinities we see the value of returning to old theological quarries, and the benefit of an ecumenical approach to the theological task. The writings of the Cappadocian Fathers are a rich treasure house, while the theology of the East contains great insight.   So there is considerable mileage in adopting the pattern of a social trinity to describe God. But, by way of a caveat, we need to beware of that kind of speculation which owes more to the creative imagination than to what can be discerned from the Bible. Given the problems which exist in biblical interpretation, I wonder whether biblical theology can fully establish the credibility of some of the claims that trinitarian theology makes.

5.   Both Moltmann and Gunton wish to maintain the equality of the persons in the Godhead, and therefore they attribute a more elevated status to God: the Spirit than has been typical of Western theology, burdened as it has been by its acceptance of the *filioque* clause. The time has come perhaps to admit that the churches of Eastern Orthodoxy are correct and to follow Moltmann and Gunton in removing the notorious clause, thus enabling the doctrine of the Holy Spirit to come out of the shadow of the doctrine of Christ. The work of the Holy Spirit needs crediting with activity that is not explicitly associated with and controlled by the work of Christ. The forgotten member of the Trinity can at last be remembered.

6.   Part of the role of the Spirit is to drive history forward into the future. When that   future is conceived in terms of the Christian hope, it becomes a powerful kind of utopia for people to work towards, and it presents a critique of present life and events. We can only welcome the open-ended understandings of the cosmic processes and history that has been evident in some of the theologies we have considered. The idea that God is engaged with creation on a cosmic adventure is attractive and worthy of further exploration. This kind of thinking need not involve us lapsing into the type

of optimism that has bedevilled much theology. We can guarantee that there will be process, but necessary progress is another thing altogether, given recent evidence. Only a thorough recognition of sin and evil prevents our hopes from becoming unworldly and romantic; while a grasp of what we can know about the world from other disciplines needs incorporating in our theology if it is to be credible in the modern world. And might it be that God's joy is not so much in greeting us at a destination already planned for us, but in enabling us to share a creative journey in the divine company?

PART 3

We believe that God, in his infinite love for men,
gave his eternal Son, Jesus Christ our Lord, who
became man, lived on earth in perfect love and
obedience, died upon the cross for our sins,
rose again from the dead and lives for evermore,
saviour, judge and king.

WE NOW start to address those issues and questions which emerge as we attempt to talk about the significance of the life and witness, death and resurrection of Jesus Christ for our individual and communal lives. This directs us to a discussion about the person of Christ (christology) and the work of Christ (soteriology). We will be concerned with what we can know about Jesus from the biblical and non-biblical writings. This historical question naturally leads us to ask whether the Christian Faith is rooted in what we can know historically about Jesus (the so-called 'Jesus of History') or in what the earliest Christians proclaimed about him (the so-called 'Christ of Faith'). Central to Christianity, though, is the claim that Jesus was both human and divine. We will need therefore to explore the ways in which theologians have tried to conceptualize this, starting with the classical two nature view of the Council of Chalcedon before moving to more recent views which have challenged the inherited "orthodoxy". Turning to Christ's work, we will explore how theologians have understood the Cross as the event whereby the world's salvation has been made possible.

But just as answers always presuppose the questions that generate them, christological and soteriological discussions need setting in the context which raises them. We therefore now turn to a consideration of the human condition.

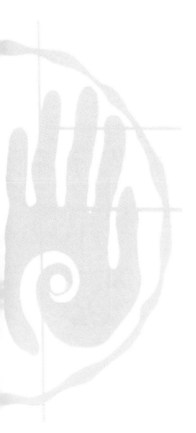

CHAPTER 7

The Human Condition

SCIENTIFIC laws come into being when hypotheses are proven by reference to empirical data. All sustainable theories must fit the facts. One such law is described by the apostle Paul:

> So I find it to be a law that when I want to do what is good, evil lies close to hand. For I delight in the law of God in my inmost self, but I see in my members another law at war with the law of my mind, making me captive to the law of sin that dwells in my members (Romans 7: 21–23).

All honest and reflective people know that there is a phenomenon at work within human life which, to put it crudely, messes everything up.

The Bible offers many helpful insights concerning the nature of sin. Among the many 'pictures' of sin the following stand out. The first belongs to the world of military competition. Soldiers propel arrows or spears at a target, but they do not always hit the bullseye. Sometimes they are off target and wide of the mark, failing to reach the maximum required standard. Using this metaphor Paul can speak of the universality of sin in terms of every human being having fallen short of God's glory (Romans 3: 23). Secondly, there is the metaphor of following a prescribed route. Sometimes the journeyer may deviate from the path, avoiding the straight course and choosing a more tortuous course. So we get the idea of sin as being 'out of line' or 'off route' (Isaiah 53: 6). Thirdly, our eyes are switched to the law courts, from where we get the idea of sin as law breaking (1 John 3: 4). This in turn has given rise to doctrines of salvation which have stressed punishment and the payment of penalties. Fourthly, and closely resembling the metaphor of law breaking, is the understanding of sin in terms of wantonly and knowingly taking a false step or moving off the set route. The well-known word here is 'trespass' (See Ephesians 2: 1–2 and Matthew 6: 14,15). Finally, we move to the medical world to find sin spoken of as disease or pollution. Salvation then is described as being healed or cleansed (Psalm 51: 7 and Mark 7: 21–23).

When theologians consider the nature of the human condition they invariably turn to the account of the Fall in Genesis 3. Two distinct lines of interpretation have emerged which in turn have given rise to two different and competing theological accounts of sin and salvation, associated with Irenaeus and Augustine respectively. Since the Augustinian account has been more influential, we shall deal with it first. However, subsequent theology which has followed the basic patterns of Irenaean thought is no less rooted in Patristic authority than are more Augustinian views.

Augustine and Irenaeus

Augustine argues that everything which God created was essentially good (Genesis 1: 31). Human beings were made in God's image (Genesis 1: 26), and hence they were completely sinless, without fault and immortal. They possessed the ability not to sin. Understanding the serpent in the Genesis 3 story as Satan, a fallen angel, Augustine argues that sin is introduced to the human race through the woman and man succumbing to temptation. It is passed on from generation to generation through the act of sexual intercourse. After the Fall only the ability to sin is left open to human beings. Sin, being hereditary, is unavoidable and only an act of God can get us out of the mess it causes. Christ's redeeming work enables Paradise lost to become Paradise regained as people put their faith in the One Jesus reveals, and by grace receive forgiveness for their sins.

Augustine's theological 'story' has formed the basis upon which a great deal of subsequent theology has been built. And, as we shall see shortly, it was closely followed by Calvin. Augustine's understanding of the human condition was deepened and developed through a confrontational debate with Pelagius, a man whose name has become synonymous with any view which suggests that human beings can by their own efforts free themselves from sin, and hence do what is right in God's eyes without the aid of divine grace. Just as we discovered that the thought of Arius is somewhat different from what became known as Arianism, something similar can be said of Pelagius' ideas and the heresy of Pelagianism. Pelagius certainly had a point in what he was trying to say.

Pelagius, a lay ascetic of British origin who lived in Rome, was rather more confident about human nature than Augustine. Being fearful alike of a lack of hope concerning what is possible for human beings to achieve, and of what Bonhoeffer called 'cheap grace', Pelagius refused to accept that God puts us in a position whereby what we were commanded to do is impossible for us to achieve. His debate with Augustine focussed on four key issues. First, Augustine argued that we never act out of sheer necessity, since we are free to take whatever course of action is open to us. But, as the bishop argued, our free will has been gravely damaged, if not completely destroyed, through sin; so we need God's grace to restore it to its original condition. Pelagius, on the other hand, maintained that our capacity to will a chosen course of action is not destroyed by sin. What God requires, therefore, can be achieved by us, and consequently it is no good people using sin as a feeble excuse for their inability to obey God. God does not ask of us things we were incapable of achieving.

Pelagius' uncompromising requirement that we take responsibility for our actions leads him to a second disagreement with Augustine, this time over the nature of sin. The bishop supports a doctrine of original sin which views the human race as universally held in sin's tight grasp; the layman thinks it always was possible for people to do the right things if they tried hard enough. According to Pelagius, there are no obvious excuses for failure, and he comes close to a highly moralistic attitude in which the state of sinlessness, not just in principle but also in practice, is attainable. Augustine, however, claims that we are all born with an inescapable propensity to sin, and that this basic human flaw can only be overcome by God's grace. Augustine notoriously believes that sin arises in the imbalances caused in human beings when their sexual drives run out of control. Many see here the roots of the church's downgrading of sex, as well as many of its negative and irrational attitudes to it. Augustine does not regard sex itself as evil, however, only the loss of control of our sexual passions. The bishop asserts that newborn infants are not innocents but born sinners. No one – literally no one – can escape what Augustine calls at one point 'the whole mass of perdition'.[1] If anyone wants the reason why the practice of infant baptism spread rapidly in the post New Testament era, they need look no further than the prevailing doctrine of original sin.

Augustine and Pelagius differed, thirdly, over the nature of grace. Pelagius understands it as part of our nature. Our reason and will enable us in principle to avoid sin, but we may need God's further instruction to aid us. Such help, however, is purely educational, and God does not assist us in doing what belongs to us to achieve. For Augustine, on the other hand, grace is a supernatural gift of God. Without any deserving on our part God freely chooses to be concerned about us and to care for us. Grace reflects God's boundless love and generosity. Without it we are lost. It is Christ's saving presence in us, and a power which helps us live rather than merely tell us what we should be doing. According to Augustine's analysis, grace appears in three forms: *prevenient*, active in our lives prior to conversion; *operative*, the means by which we are converted; and *co-operative*, the way God works with us to enable our growth in holiness.[2] Given grace, some will wonder why so many people show no disposition to become Christians. Augustine answers their question by introducing his doctrine of double-predestination, according to which God has decided who will or will not be saved. Just how this doctrine can be made to square with human freedom is a question which must await a later discussion but God's sense of justice is supposed to remain intact: 'Those who receive mercy can only be grateful for grace they had done nothing to deserve. Those who do not receive mercy can have no ground to complain of a justice which all in Adam deserve.'[3] We have good reason, though, to question the moral arbitrariness of such a 'God'.

Finally, the two thinkers disagree over the basis of our salvation. According to Pelagius salvation depends upon merit; basically, we receive what we deserve. Christ is our Saviour only in the sense that he is our perfect role model. Augustine, however, lodges salvation within God's free and unmerited gift of grace. In Jesus Christ, God has given us what we do not deserve, and withheld from us the punishment that we have earned.

It may justifiably be argued that Augustine proposes such an abstract view of grace that he has lost the understanding of it displayed in the New Testament. What essentially belongs to a meeting of wills within the divine–human encounter, has been given a less personal and more mechanical description. God's graciousness is no longer descriptive of God's acceptance of God's wayward children; rather it is akin to someone injecting a life-saving drug into a chronically sick and unconscious patient. In biblical understanding grace is discovered and encountered in a personal relationship between God and persons; God does not bequeath it to us like squeezing toothpaste out of a tube. Irenaeus' understanding of salvation, on the other hand, is read out of Ephesians 1: 10 and centres upon the idea of *recapitulation*. Jesus is the Second Adam, one who sums up afresh the career of Adam. He repeats the life of the first Adam, doing perfectly what had earlier been done badly. Those who believe in Christ receive the Holy Spirit and they are restored to God's likeness. According to Irenaeus, salvation amounts to a progressive education over a long period of time. The purpose of our lives, therefore, is centred in character building, the overcoming of all the difficulties and temptations which lie between us and our eternal rest in God.

---

[1] See Bettenson, ed. and trans., *The Later Christian Fathers*, p 204.
[2] Ibid., pp 204–6.
[3] Henry Chadwick, *Augustine* (Oxford: Oxford University Press, 1986), p 109.

Irenaeus' anthropology sits neatly with what we now know about human beings. We are not confined within fixed bounds; rather we possess the capacity for transcendence, being able to grow and develop in response to changing circumstances and new experiences. However critical we may be of his exegesis of Genesis 1: 26, Irenaeus' basic idea is that post-Fall we possess an inherited potentiality to grow toward God since we are in God's image. This endows human beings with the dignity and responsibility which is necessary if the people are to come into a relationship with a personal God on their own volition. The outlook is less gloomy than Augustine's alternative, but sin is still taken with a healthy degree of seriousness. There is work to be done before we can achieve what Irenaeus understood in company with the rest of the Eastern Fathers as deification. And that would not be achievable were it not for the fact that 'a second Adam to the fight and to the rescue came' (John Henry Newman).

We now move to the views of several Reformed theologians who choose to follow one or other of the two basic 'stories' of sin and salvation that we have just outlined. For a view from the Augustan tradition, we will turn to John Calvin, while Friedrich Schleiermacher provides us with a perspective from the Irenaean viewpoint. The chapter will then conclude by reviewing the insights on the human condition provided by Reinhold Niebuhr, Herbert Farmer and Peter Hodgson.

John Calvin: Total Depravity

Calvin is almost reverential about Augustine, the great bishop of Hippo. He describes him as 'this holy man', and claims that St Augustine is invested by 'the godly . . . with the greatest authority' – that is aside from Scripture.[4] And there is no mistaking the bishop's influence upon Calvin when it comes to understanding the human condition, since Calvin's conclusion reveals an unrelenting negativity about the nature of persons. He is convinced that our only hope is found beyond our lives in the God who has been revealed in the death and resurrection of Christ. He does not convey the bad news gently, but with typical directness.

> . . . whoever is utterly cast down and overwhelmed by the awareness of his calamity, poverty, nakedness, and disgrace has thus advanced farthest in knowledge of himself.[5]

> . . . the mind of man has been so completely estranged from God's righteousness that it conceives, desires and undertakes, only that which is impious, perverted, foul, impure, and infamous. The heart is so steeped in the poison of sin, that it can breathe out nothing but a loathsome stench. But if some men occasionally make a show of good, their minds nevertheless ever remain enveloped in hypocrisy and deceitful craft, and their hearts bound by inner perversity.[6]

This bleak picture has been caused by Adam's unfaithfulness to God in the Garden of Eden (Genesis 3). Calvin regards the incident as an historical event with cosmic implications. Sin entered the world through the disobedience of Adam and that act of unfaithfulness quickly gave rise to 'ambition and pride, together with ungratefulness' among the human race.[7] The rot set in because Adam was not satisfied with being born in God's image and wanted instead equality with God.

---

[4]   Calvin, *Institutes*, 2,3,8.
[5]   Ibid., 2,2,10.
[6]   Ibid., 2,5,19.
[7]   Ibid., 2,1,4.

Adam's sin spread to the whole human race akin to a contagious disease. Following Augustine, Calvin argues that sin is transmitted from generation to generation through the act of procreation. Consequently, sin 'holds all men fast by hereditary right';[8] and hence 'before we saw the light of this life we were soiled and spotted in God's sight'.[9] Many will find it difficult to believe that the nature of a newly born baby is 'a seed of sin', and that 'hence it can be only hateful and abhorrent to God'.[10] But Calvin's belief in original sin is unwavering. He describes it as 'a hereditary depravity and corruption of our nature, diffused into all parts of the soul, which first makes us liable to God's wrath, then also brings forth in us those works which Scripture calls "works of the flesh" [Gal. 5: 19]'.[11] And, along with Augustine, Calvin calls original sin 'concupiscence'. The whole person is affected by it. What Calvin calls 'supernatural gifts' are completely destroyed by sin and these include 'faith, love of God, charity toward the neighbour, zeal for holiness and for righteousness'; but the 'natural gifts' are also corrupted if not destroyed and this involves our 'soundness of mind and uprightness of heart'.[12] So even our rational capabilities have been warped and weakened by sin.

Calvin is quite clear that Paul's law holds good (Romans 7: 21–23). But if we cannot help sinning, how can we be held responsible for what we do? When stress is placed upon the will being completely bounded by sin, how is it possible also to affirm human freedom? This exposes a logical difficulty in Calvin's thinking, which he tries to overcome by saying that we sin of 'necessity' but without 'compulsion'[13]. Whether this distinction holds good is very debatable – unless, that is, we ascribe a meaning to 'necessity' that is somewhat different from the one it usually has. How can we *willingly* do something that we are *bound* to do? At the very least Calvin leaves us with an acute paradox:

> The chief point of this distinction, then, must be that man, as he was corrupted by the Fall, sinned willingly, not unwillingly or by compulsion; by the most eager inclination of his heart, not by forced compulsion; by the prompting of his own lust, not by compulsion from without. Yet, so depraved is his nature that he can be moved or impelled only to evil. But if this is true, then it is clearly expressed that man is surely subject to the necessity of sinning.[14]

Being in such a hapless position human beings can only turn to God for help. Salvation cannot come through our own efforts; it can only take the form of an unmerited gift from a gracious God. Our whole nature has to be changed if we are to progress: 'For it always follows that nothing good can arise out of our will until it has been reformed; and after its reformation, in so far as it is good, it is so from God, not from ourselves.'[15] It is God's grace which sets us free from sin. And that grace comes in two forms; God provides us with the will to act correctly and to do good works (*operating grace*), and with the ability to accomplish our actions and works (*co-operating* grace). The combined effect of these forms of grace is to ensure that God is credited with our salvation. Human beings cannot save themselves; nor do their own efforts have a contribution to make to their salvation; rather the sole author of their salvation is God. Even the faith which leads to our justification has been set in motion by what the Christian tradition has come to call the *prevenient* grace of God.

---

8   Ibid., 2,1,11.
9   Ibid., 2,1,5.
10 Ibid., 2,1,8.
11 Ibid.
12 Ibid., 2,2,12.
13 Ibid., 2,3,5.
14 Ibid.
15 Ibid., 2,3,8.

Friedrich Schleiermacher: The Limiting Deficiency of God-consciousness

Schleiermacher understands religion in terms of 'feeling'; but his subjective emphasis does not involve a simple reduction of religion to human emotions. He argues that we all possess, however dimly, an immediate awareness of God that is simply given to us by being human. We experience the Infinite through the finite, and the Supernatural within the natural. In fact, all human beings are born in such a way that they develop God consciousness, and come to have a 'feeling of absolute dependence'. Reflection upon the nature of this 'feeling' is the starting point for Schleiermacher's theological exploration. But we should not view this as a totally individualistic approach, since he is not making individual selves the focus of investigation; rather he is reflecting on individuals as they exist in relation to other selves, communities, nature and God.

In direct contrast to the Augustinian interpretation of Genesis 3, Schleiermacher denies that humankind originally was created immortal, or that a primordial act of disobedience once and for all radically altered humankind's relationship with God and the rest of reality. Quite different perspectives on the idea of original perfection emerge from his writings. When considering the original perfection of the world, for example, Schleiermacher's sights are not set upon some primordial past event; rather he seeks to uncover the basic condition which makes it possible for people to possess God-consciousness. The world in which we live, he claims, possesses the quality of original perfection because it provides an environment in which God-consciousness can emerge and find expression.[16] But this environment would be worthless were it not that it is part of the basic nature of humankind to possess 'an inner impulse' or 'predisposition' to God consciousness.[17] So, for Schleiermacher, it is an essential aspect of humankind's original perfection that 'in our clear and waking life a continuous God-consciousness as such is possible'.[18]

We would all be acutely aware that our self-consciousness was playing tricks with us if we were to think that our lives were rooted in a uniform development of God-consciousness. Life is not that kind of bed of roses. Pain is always bound up with pleasure in the ambiguities of life. Equally, we always encounter limitations being imposed upon our inner impulse towards God-consciousness. Schleiermacher, therefore, talks about 'arrestments of the disposition to the God-consciousness' or 'a limiting deficiency of the God-consciousness'.[19] This negative factor in life is what traditionally has been called 'sin'. We live in a world that makes human development possible by way of a struggle between our natural impulse towards God-consciousness and the opposition to that created by sin. But how does sin arise? Schleiermacher is quite clear that we are responsible for it. It arises when there is 'an arrestment of the determinative power of the spirit, due to the independence of the sensuous functions'.[20] So, in a somewhat dualistic way, Schleiermacher roots sin in the conflict between our propensity to seek 'worldly' solutions to our problems, rather than ones grounded in the One to whom our God-consciousness would direct us.

One significant feature of the Christian life is that the closer to God people become, the more aware they seem to be of their inadequacies. It would appear that to grow in grace is to become increasingly conscious of our sin. As Schleiermacher says 'we become conscious also of sin as the God-consciousness awakes within us.'[21] Even within the most exalted religious experiences

---

[16]   Friedrich Schleiermacher, *The Christian Faith* (Edinburgh: T & T Clark, 1928), pp 238–44.
[17]   Ibid., p 244.
[18]   Ibid., p 245.
[19]   Ibid., pp 262, 264.
[20]   Ibid., p 273.
[21]   Ibid., p 274.

sin can be found at work. Grace and sin are discovered tooth to jowl throughout our experience, both existing under God's providential hand. We become fully aware of sin's power, however, in proportion to our consciousness of redemption. This comes to a climax in Jesus Christ: '. . . it is only from the absolute sinlessness and the perfect spiritual power of the Redeemer that we gain the full knowledge of sin'.[22]

Schleiermacher draws a clear distinction between 'original sin' and 'actual sin'. The former is 'something received, something we bring with us, prior to any act of our own, yet something in which our own guilt is latent'; while the latter appears 'in the sinful acts which are due to the individual himself, but in which the received element brought with us is revealed'.[23] Original sin is a basic incapacity for good which is anterior to all human activity. It is expressed in all that we do, and we can only be set free from it by redemption. There is a deep solidarity in sin and Schleiermacher warns that a denial of its corporate character usually is accompanied by an impoverished understanding of Christ's redeeming work. Original sin's gravity is captured when it is spoken of as the guilt of the human race, the corruption of human nature, an original defect in humankind, an original disease that renders the race terminally ill, or an original evil which impedes human flourishing. Since sin is rooted in 'the corporate action and the corporate guilt of the whole human race',[24] the redemption we require is one which extends to all humankind. Schleiermacher argues that such a redemption has taken place in Jesus Christ.

When he turns to actual sins, Schleiermacher is a total realist: '. . . throughout the entire range of sinful humanity there is not a single perfectly good action, *i.e.* one that purely expresses the power of the God-consciousness; nor is there one perfectly pure moment, *i.e.* one in which something does not exist in secret antagonism to the God-consciousness'.[25] All have sinned and fallen short since original sin has flowered in their wayward deeds. Schleiermacher is rather wary of some of the traditional divisions which have been made when analysing sin. He does not believe that one can make a clear separation between sin as '*an expression of appetite*' and sin as 'a positive obscuration, i.e. *a vitiation, of the God-consciousness*', since the former invariably generates the latter.[26] Nor is it usually helpful to divide 'outward' and 'inward' sins, or to draw a distinction between 'intential' and 'unintential' sins. And Schleiermacher is equally suspicious of the differentiation between 'mortal' (unpardonable) and 'venial' (pardonable) sins, since we 'must repudiate the suggestion that there may be a sin which, though repented of in view of redemption, yet cannot be forgiven, as setting a limit to the universality of redemption'.[27] No limit should be placed upon Christ's saving power. What could possibly block 'the energy of the God-consciousness' implanted in people 'personally and spontaneously' by the Redeemer?[28]

Schleiermacher's view of the human condition closely follows that of Irenaeus. Human beings were created to develop into God's likeness. They have been provided with the means to do this: an inbuilt impulse towards God-consciousness, as well as an environment in which that 'sense and taste for the Infinite' can emerge and find expression. While Schleiermacher can testify eloquently that human beings cause sin, and, hence that they are their worst enemies, he

---

22   Ibid., p 279.
23   Ibid., p 281.
24   Ibid., p 304.
25   Ibid., p 305.
26   Ibid., p 308.
27   Ibid., p 311.
28   Ibid., p 313.

nevertheless breaks with tradition in suggesting that *ultimately* sin is ordained by God as the necessary precondition for the human quest for redemption. Sin as well as redemption, therefore, is found within the saving purposes of God.

> . . . it is through the commanding will of God present within us that the impotence of the God-consciousness becomes sin for us. By that will, accordingly – though it may be impossible to ascribe any particular act of sin to a divine causality specially pertaining to it – sin has been ordained by God, not indeed sin in and of itself, but sin merely in relation to redemption; for otherwise redemption itself could not have been ordained.[29]

But, critics may argue, this view comes very close to the obnoxious idea that God created sin and evil in order then to have the privilege of liberating people from the results. Many find field-sports particularly abhorrent, not least the practice of breeding creatures with the end-view in mind of shooting them. Is it not equally appalling a view that God inflicts people with a terminal illness in order to have the privilege of curing them? Schleiermacher, of course, does not paint such a picture. All he is saying is that, if human beings are to have an environment in which they are to grow in God-consciousness, then it must contain sin and evil; otherwise, the choice of whether or not to respond to God would be a hollow challenge. But how much sin and evil does there need to be? Surely, there is more in evidence than is warranted by this divine educational process? And, if God does ultimately ordain sin, how can human beings be held responsible for it? We are face to face with one of the most difficult of all theological problems, namely, doing justice to two seemingly undeniable facts: human freedom and the universality of sin. Few in the twentieth century have wrestled with this problem more thoroughly than Reinhold Niebuhr.

Reinhold Niebuhr: The Impossible Possibility

Reinhold Niebuhr's Gifford Lectures, published under the title *The Nature and Destiny of Man*, contain arguably the most important analysis of the human condition from a Christian perspective found in recent Western literature. Reading Niebuhr makes one powerfully aware of the glory and the gravity of being human. What he says often resonates in our experience, while he makes us face up to realities we are prone to forget.

According to Niebuhr we are beset by an acute vulnerability caused by us possessing freedom in a world bounded by finitude. One minute we feel that we can reach for the stars, the next we experience weakness and helplessness. Our quest for unlimited knowledge quickly becomes shipwrecked on the rocks set in our path by the historical and cultural conditionedness of all thought. We have a natural disposition to pursue our personal and social well-being, but we are condemned to do it in conditions which are limiting, frustrating, challenging and, often, painful. Personally, we are temporally, and biologically vulnerable; interpersonally, we never escape the threat of suffering and alienation; socially, we face incompatibility with others and, hence, conflict; while running through all our lives is the threat of death. Amidst all this conflict sin is born.

We experience freedom and boundedness, unlimited possibilities but limited opportunities. This creates anxiety, 'the internal precondition of sin'.[30] Anxiety besets even the most saintly. It is always found alongside human freedom. In each situation we are faced with a choice. We can

---

[29]   Ibid., p 337.
[30]   Reinhold Niebuhr, *The Nature and Destiny of Man*, vol. 1: *Human Nature* (London: Nisbet & Co Ltd., 1941), pp 194–5.

either put our trust in the ultimate security of God, or we can bow down to an idol of our making. In one way or another, temptation directs us to the latter; so, according to Niebuhr's analysis, the root sin which arises out of the decisions we take due to our anxiety is unbelief. This gets expressed in one of two ways. We may deny the contingent character of our existence, treating what is finite as infinite and the provisional as the final. This manifestation of idolatry is usually known as 'pride' and 'self-love'. On the other hand, we may try to escape from our freedom. This form of sin is generally called 'sensuality'. Instead of placing our trust in God, therefore, we are always being deceived into taking up lifestyles rooted in either pride or sensuality.

Niebuhr delineates four types of pride. It can first of all take the form of power. We can either ignore our finitude, and through the development of illusions of self-sufficiency and self-dominion come to believe that we are secure against all threatening eventualities; or, overtly conscious of our insecurities, we seek self-advancement to overcome our sense of inferiority. While the former is the typical sin of the powerful and the established, the latter reveals the blind-spot of an up and coming bourgeois culture which seeks its security in materialism. Whichever form the will to power takes, injustice is involved, as people protect their position by denying rights and goods to others or take over what rightfully belongs to others. Niebuhr describes this form of pride in a typically pithy way: 'Thus man seeks to make himself God because he is betrayed by both his greatness and his weakness; and there is no level of greatness and power in which the lash of fear is not at least one strand in the whip of ambition.'[31] A second form of pride centres upon knowledge, and our tendency to treat finite knowledge as final: 'Each great thinker makes the same mistake', namely, that 'of imagining himself the final thinker.'[32] All knowledge is accompanied by ideology, since either we ignore the finiteness of the human mind, or we obscure the fact that all thinking is partly bounded by social and cultural conditionedness as well as vested with self-interest. We possess the hellish knack of being able to recognize the limitedness of everyone's thinking except our own!

Niebuhr's third type of pride focuses upon morality. We tend to exalt our virtue to the point of presenting it as the final righteousness; while we endow our relative moral preferences with an absolute status. 'Moral pride thus makes virtue the very vehicle of sin.'[33] The self-righteousness of individuals and nations throughout history has led to the most horrific and brutal social and political cruelties. Finally, there is spiritual pride. Niebuhr says that this particular form of 'self-deification' occurs 'when our partial standards and relative attainments are explicitly related to the unconditioned good, and claim divine sanction.'[34] We are apt at putting our self-assertions in a religious or ecclesiastical framework. We equate our churches with the Kingdom and our theologies with the Word of God: 'Religion . . . is the inevitable fruit of the spiritual stature of man; and religious intolerance and pride is the final expression of his sinfulness.'[35]

Sensuality, the second form of sin, is defined by Niebuhr as 'the destruction of harmony within the self, by the self's undue indentification with and devotion to particular impulses and desires within itself.'[36] It is more clearly on display in human behaviour than is pride, generally being associated with vices such as 'sexual licence, gluttony, extravagance, drunkenness and abandonment to various forms of physical desire.'[37] Some branches of Christianity have identified sin totally with

---

[31]   Ibid., p 207.
[32]   Ibid.
[33]   Ibid., p 212.
[34]   Ibid., p 213.
[35]   Ibid., p 216.
[36]   Ibid., p 242.
[37]   Ibid., p 243.

sensuality, often even making our sexual lives the particular location of sensual lust. Other more mainstream traditions, though, have regarded sensuality largely as a derivative consequence of our more basic and fundamental rebellion against God. Niebuhr, however, regards sensuality as *both* a form of idolatry in which we make the self God *and* an alternative idolatry in which the self seeks an escape in some other pseudo god. For example, sex provides people with the opportunity either to assert themselves over their partners in a dominating manner, or to flee from themselves in acts of sheer escapism.

Niebuhr is well aware that many theologians have felt duty bound by the evidence to sacrifice 'logical consistency' by maintaining at one and the same time that 'the will is free in the sense that man is responsible for his sin' and that persons are not free in the sense that of our own will we can do 'nothing but evil'.[38] And he cannot find any reason to do otherwise. Niebuhr is deeply critical of Pelagian forms of argument that seek to remove from the will the bias towards sin that we everywhere experience. He objects to original sin being re-interpreted as merely 'some sloth of nature which man has inherited from his relation to the brute creation', and hence he is very critical of Schleiermacher who he sees as reducing original sin 'to the institutions and traditions of history'.[39] The buck must finally stop with us. Pelagian arguments end up being so overtly moralistic that, while they correctly make us face up to our own responsibility for all our actions, they do not do justice to the sense in which we cannot avoid committing sin. Niebuhr insists, therefore, that the doctrine of original sin serves an important purpose in theology by throwing some light upon the complexity of the human condition. Reflection upon experience suggests that we have less freedom than we think we have when we commit sin, as well as more responsibility for our basic orientation towards wrongdoing than we usually suppose. A certain amount of gloomy logic pervades the discovery that we could not be tempted if we had not already sinned![40]

The path mapped out by Augustine, however, is finally ignored by Niebuhr in his attempt to avoid sin being treated as a necessity. He criticizes the Augustinian tradition for converting the statistical fact that sin is a universal phenomenon in the world into a dogma which asserted that sin had a natural history.[41] Sin is 'inevitable' but not necessary. It is the responsibility of human beings. If it was not, why would we feel remorse or want to repent for what we have done wrong? Even the habitual sinner cannot remove 'the uneasy conscience' and hence totally turn from 'the realm of moral responsibility to the realm of unmoral nature'.[42] While all wrong doing has social beginnings and implications, the fundamental nature of sin must finally be located in the distortion of our relationship with God. All experience of remorse, or feeling the need to repent, is basically religious: 'Against you, you alone, have I sinned, and done what is evil in your sight' (Psalm 51: 4).

Niebuhr leaves us with a paradox based on experience. On the one hand, the existence of feelings of remorse and repentance suggests that deep down we are aware that we are culpable for our wrongdoing; while on the other hand, as we develop spiritual maturity, we discover that we cannot choose good rather than evil. Sin is inevitable but it is also our responsibility. While it is quite easy sometimes to suspect that theologians are too easily tempted to baptise their muddles as divine mysteries and to turn their logical problems into profound paradoxes, Niebuhr here is genuinely trying to do justice to the heart of the matter. He directs us to the fact that our ability to

---

[38]   Ibid., p 259.
[39]   Ibid., p 261.
[40]   Ibid., p 266.
[41]   Ibid., p 276.
[42]   Ibid., p 271.

do what we know to be right is 'an impossible possibility'. Such a paradox can be accepted as 'a rational understanding of the limits of rationality and as an expression of faith that a rationally irresolvable contradiction may point to a truth which logic cannot contain'.[43]

Herbert Farmer: Sin as Insincerity

When reading the work of H H Farmer, one hears many echoes of Schleiermacher. This is particularly true when we consider his approach to sin and reconciliation. Farmer depicts the human condition in terms of a moral struggle between 'instinctive elements in our make up which *are* functions of the immediate environment' and 'God's addressing of Himself to the soul in sacred demand'.[44] The latter seems to function in Farmer's theology like 'sense and taste for the infinite' or 'God-consciousness' in the theology of Schleiermacher. It is something that every person has been given, and one can choose whether or not to lead one's life on the basis of it. We know what the choice should be, but inexplicably we decide upon the lower rather than the higher way. Farmer notes that 'it is psychologically impossible for a man really apprehending "the good and perfect will of God" to choose evil'; but what happens is that we 'weave a web of sophistications and rationalisations and self-deceptions' in order to do just that.[45] Sin therefore is what we do to turn away from God's immediate demand upon our lives; it is rooted in the pretence and deceit which we become engaged in when faced with the obligations of being in a gracious relationship with God; it is an act of 'insincerity' in the context of a personal relationship: 'It is going against the light, such light as one has, not in the sense of snuffing it out as a man might a candle-flame between his fingers, for that no one can do, but in the sense of screening it under a veil of excuse and subterfuge'.[46] Farmer argues that the result of insincerity is an increasing blindness to the call which God places upon our lives. Slowly but surely, insincerity becomes habitual – 'until it ends by being almost a necessity, for the longer this way is persisted in, the more the monitions of God . . . lose their quality of being an invitation to blessedness and become instead a condemnation threatening the whole structure of the life in a way too disturbing to be faced'.[47] And the problem is radically compounded by the further influence of other people's sin upon us. We are not totally responsible for 'the state of darkness' in which we live, since, while it is always partly the result of our insincerity, it is 'in a measure the result of other people's'.[48]

Clearly, according to Farmer's analysis, the human race *qua* race ultimately is responsible for sin. It is a habit that we have fallen into, and individuals cannot avoid picking it up. Any sense that sin is 'original' in the Augustinian sense, though, has been put to one side in favour of the idea that we are all inevitably bound up with sin, because we live in a sinful world and are victims of other people's insincerity. No doubt Niebuhr would condemn Farmer's position as Pelagian. And, indeed, its similarity to Schleiermacher's view becomes quite clear when he discusses the solution to the human predicament. What is required is as follows: 'Somehow the darkness of [man's] mind must be broken through so that he can at least begin to see things as they really are – God as He really is, himself as he really is, his neighbours as they really are, within that whole personal order which

---

[43]   Ibid., p 278.
[44]   H H Farmer, *The World and God: A Study of Prayer, Providence and Miracle in Christian Experience*, p 191.
[45]   Ibid., p 193.
[46]   Ibid.
[47]   Ibid., pp 194–5.
[48]   Ibid., p 195.

underlies all the circumstances of his life and in which it is the divine will that he should find his right place.'[49] Farmer believes that such a breakthrough has been made possible by the revelation of Godself in Christ. What sinful persons should know from God's self-disclosure to them as human beings, they now are 'reminded' of in the Christ event – and in such a way that they can own it anew, and face up to the fact that they have wilfully acted insincerely towards God. In Jesus Christ, the Eternal is revealed as 'holy love'.[50] A divine standard is set by which our lives are judged; a divine forgiveness is offered by which we are reconciled to God. It is *holy* love which condemns us, and holy *love* which embraces us as lost children. Then, in keeping with his personalist emphasis, Farmer argues that God's saving revelation comes in a way which reflects God's commitment to dealing with people as persons. It takes place through a human being who lived like us in this world; it is effected by 'a personality which is completely surrendered to, at one with, indwelt by, that divine holy love by which man, in his darkness, needs to be confronted';[51] and it is given to a community of people, the Church, which universally bears witness to Christ, and in whose members' lives God's reconciling work is operative.

Peter C Hodgson: The Structures of Sin and Evil

In *Winds of the Spirit*, Peter Hodgson provides us with a neat summary of the structures of sin and evil that we find in life. As we come to the end of our discussion of the human condition it will be useful to take note of it.

In keeping with many theologians, Hodgson views sin as 'a disruption of the personal and interpersonal structures of human being'.[52] It manifests itself in three forms or structures: idolatry (or broken faith), flight (or fear) and alienation (or violation). *Idolatry* is rooted in our attempt to defy the finite conditions of existence. Fundamentally, this involves a broken relationship with God. We substitute finite gods and idols for the God of Abraham, Isaac, Jacob and our Lord Jesus Christ, and hence create a break of trust. This involves an act of unbelief as we refuse to believe that God is the ultimate source of our salvation and instead, place our faith in pseudo-gods: 'material possessions, economic security, social status, erotic attachments, political ideologies, religious belief-systems, and so on.'[53] And the idols that we erect are often in competition with those being honoured by others.   We then become possessive and self-securing as we absolutize our chosen ideas and ideals. Ultimately this leads to conflict and broken relationships. This form of sin has classically been called 'concupiscence', i.e. excessive desire. We can and must, however, distinguish between legitimate strivings to gain things, power or worth and their great perversions, e.g. possession, domination and pride. Secondly, *flight* is 'a false, aberrant pursuit of life that not only issues in revolt against God and aggression against neighbour but also constitutes a way that leads to death'.[54] Viewed from the perspective of interpersonal relations, it involves the sin of submission in which we surrender to, rather than resist, oppressive forces and people. This form of sin is common in our contemporary culture as people seek an escape from the realities of life due to fear of vulnerability, difference or change.   Thirdly, *alienation* occurs 'when relations are poisoned by

---

49   Ibid., p 196.
50   Ibid., p 197.
51   Ibid., p 198.
52   Hodgson, *Winds of the Spirit: A Constructive Theology,* p 215.
53   Ibid., pp 216–17.
54   Ibid., p 218.

violation and victimization'.[55] It manifests itself wherever there are inequalities between people, leading to resentment (on the part of the violated) and guilt (for the violator).

Few theologians have been more aware of the corporate dimensions of sin than Reinhold Niebuhr. He was thoroughly conscious of the way in which sin takes on the most heinous forms in its collective manifestations within social and political realities. The morality of groups is fundamentally different from the morality of individuals; consequently, the sinfulness of the collective realm requires addressing in a different way from that of the individual. Niebuhr was convinced that 'the pretensions and claims of a collective or social self exceed those of the individual ego'.[56] This means that the sin of the group is invariably more deep-seated and intractable than that found in the individual. 'In every human group there is less reason to guide and check impulse, less capacity for self-transcendence, less ability to comprehend the needs of others and therefore more unrestrained egoism than the individuals, who compose the group, reveal in their personal relationships.'[57] This means that any serious attack on sin has to take into account the collective as well as the individualistic dimension of the human predicament. We do not change an evil world simply by preaching salvation to individuals, nor do we automatically make better individuals by simply liberating people from socially and politically oppressive systems.

None of this is lost on Hodgson who is very aware of the way in which personal and interpersonal sins became objectified and reinforced in the collective realm. The sins of the individual are not reducible to those of society; nor can the sins of society be reducible to those of individuals. Hodgson, therefore, proposes three forms or structures of sin for the social and cosmic realms: law, death and worldly powers. First, law can designate 'the psychological, political and social structures by which consciousness of guilt is objectified and rationally sublimated.'[58] Something wholly positive, necessary and beneficial for any orderly society can be turned into a code of oppression. The phrase 'law and order' gives rise to sinister as well as benign connotations, while oppressive legalism can lead to institutional alienation in which bureaucracies treat people as objects and evils such as patriarchy can flourish. Secondly, if law is the objectification of alienation, the objectification of flight is death. Death, in the sense of physical perishing, is perfectly natural and on the face of it ought not to lead to bondage. However, according to Hodgson, it 'becomes an oppressive, anxiety-laden event . . . when it becomes the occasion for flight from life and freedom'.[59] Death can cease simply being physical mortally, and take up the form of a binding power: 'There is one death, physical death, which is . . . capable of taking on the quality of "deadliness".'[60] To believe in God, though, is to know that death in fact is not 'deadly'. The truth is not located in mortality, Hodgson affirms, but in death and resurrection, since 'God is the victor over mortal death, transforming and preserving each individual in God's life-giving presence'.[61] Thirdly, idolatry becomes objectified in Worldly Powers, appearing in the ideologies propagated by groups and regimes – 'racism, sexism, classism, naturism, homophobia and xenophobia', as well as the injustices practised by nations – 'political, social, economic and environmental oppression'.[62]

---

55   Ibid., p 219.
56   Niebuhr, *The Nature and Destiny of Man,* vol. 1: *Human Nature,* p 221.
57   Reinhold Niebuhr, *Moral Man and Immoral Society: A Study in Ethics and Politics* (New York: Charles Scribner's Sons, 1960), pp xi-xii.
58   Hodgson, *Winds of the Spirit,* p 223.
59   Ibid., p 224.
60   Ibid.
61   Ibid.
62   Ibid., pp 226, 229.

Hodgson maintains that liberation from the structures of sin and evil is not possible simply by human effort. It is also a serious illusion to think that greater awareness or deeper knowledge will achieve our self-emancipation. The concentration camps and pogroms of the twentieth century leave us in no doubt about the depths to which sin and evil can take human beings. Deception deceives itself and freedom binds itself, so we cannot save ourselves. Hodgson, therefore, is driven to the following conclusion: "What is needed is a new incarnation of God's love, powerful enough to set us free from destructive practices, to break the grip of sin and death, to reconcile alienated groups, to engender justice."[63] Like H H Farmer, Hodgson finds that incarnation in the Christ event.

---

[63]   Ibid., p 230.

CHAPTER 8

The Person of Christ

THE DEVELOPMENT of Christian thought about Jesus Christ has followed a three stage path. First, there was the life of Jesus, whose words and deeds have been given to us in the gospel of the early church. We do not possess a history of Jesus of Nazareth, save that which we can isolate from the New Testament witness to him by methods of historical research. The only 'Jesus' given to us is the Jesus proclaimed by the church, and the basic data about Jesus that we find in the New Testament is already in large measure a second-stage reflection. It is, if you like, primitive christology rather than Jesuology. There then followed a third stage in the process of christological development as the post-biblical churches extended their christological understanding through further reflection upon the biblical witness. And just as there had been intense and divisive debates in the build up to the 'settlement' of the trinitarian problem at Nicaea, similar heated discussions centred around the understanding of the person of Christ. These came to a head and were 'resolved' at the Council of Chalcedon (CE 451).

The Chalcedonian formula became enshrined in the canon law of both the Eastern and Western churches. Its basic principles were not substantially challenged until the Enlightenment, and they were largely taken as read by the Reformers. It is important for our discussion, therefore, to gain some awareness of the Chalcedonian formulae – even if the two-natures christology has been challenged by many recent Reformed theologians. But, however important it is to outline the christology of Chalcedon and the arguments of its more contemporary detractors, the three stage path of development in Christian thinking about Jesus puts our discussion in a proper perspective. What the New Testament tells us about Jesus through what it proclaims him to be and do for us will always be of more fundamental importance to us than the conclusions of Chalcedon or subsequent theologians. In this connection we need to heed the words of John Macquarrie. Writing in a magisterial study of modern christological thinking, Macquarrie tells us: 'It is no disparagement of the patristic writers and indeed of all theologians since them to say that they are writing footnotes on the "gospel" proclaimed by the first generation of Christians.'[1]

The Patristic Discussion: The Chalcedonian Two-Natures Doctrine

New Testament scholars are divided on the question whether Jesus attributed christological titles to himself, but there is no doubt that the earlier Christians did. What made Jesus of decisive importance for them was not that he was simply a great man, one who was impressive because he was wiser than others or due to his powers of healing; rather Jesus was of significance because

---

[1] John Macquarrie, *Jesus Christ in Modern Thought* (London: SPCK Press, 1990), p 147. Macquarrie is developing here the claim of Martin Hengel that more happened in the first two centuries to further christological discussion than in the whole of the next seven centuries.

through him they were put into contact with the gift and demand of God's love. In their reflections about him, therefore, the early Christians had to indicate that Jesus was more than a special human being. So they borrowed titles from existing frameworks of understanding which helped them to depict him as not only human but also in some sense divine, e.g. terms like 'Christ', 'Son of Man', 'Son of God', 'Word', 'Lord' and, as time went on, 'God'.[2] Later theologians described Christ's person using the prevailing philosophical conceptuality of the time, and by the fourth century two rival christologies were evident, centred respectively in the theological schools of Alexandria in the East and Antioch in the West.

The Alexandrians stressed the unity of Christ's person. After their union, Christ's Godhead and Personhood were believed to be indistinguishable; there was one nature of the Logos enfleshed, not two natures. The Alexandrian position is usually entitled 'monophysite', or described as the 'Logos-sarx' (Word-flesh) tradition. It eschews the practice of positing some credal statements to Jesus' divinity and others to his humanity, insisting instead that all such statements concern one divine subject who existed in a pre-incarnate and an incarnate state, but without change. The Antiochene school of theology, on the other hand, stressed the humanity of Christ, arguing that he must have advanced in moral goodness in order to achieve a moral victory for men and women as a human being. It put forward what has come to be known as the 'dyophysite' or 'logos-anthropos' (Word-man) position. The Antiochenes argued that the two natures of Christ, his divinity and humanity, were held together by the fact that the Father and the Son were of 'the same substance'.

Ultimately, the difference between the two schools perhaps centres upon their basically different theological starting points. Alexandrians were driven by a soteriological question: How are we to come to share in the life of God?; so they argued that the Logos assumed human flesh to achieve our divinization. This view involved the idea that prior to the Incarnation the Logos existed without flesh, but that afterwards there was only one nature in Christ since the Logos had united human flesh with itself. Antiochenes, on the other hand, were concerned about the moral issue. The Redeemer came to rescue human beings from the result of sin. So, for Antiochenes, Christ unites humanity and divinity in his two natures. There was a perfect union of those natures, with God 'entering' the heart of the moral problem, namely, our humanity.

The debates between the theologians of the respective schools were often rarefied and complex, with misunderstandings about each other's intentions and conceptuality abounding. At the end of the day, the issue seemed to boil down to whether the Logos had united with a human soul or only human flesh. The Alexandrians of the Word-flesh tradition predictably were able to accuse Antiochenes of teaching two Sons due to their stress on the two natures. Conversely, Antiochenes claimed that the monophysite tradition led to what was termed a 'mingling', and, hence, confusion, between the human and divine natures of Christ. To counter this charge, the Alexandrians argued that God had willed an hypostatic union between the two natures, which increasingly were seen by them as watertight compartments within Christ that never interacted with one another but were held together by God. Some suspected that all this boiled down to a mere moral union, like that between a man and wife, and rather akin to the Logos putting on humanity like we put on clothes. It was rather ironic, however, that the Antiochene requirement that the two natures ought not to be confused led the Alexandrians so to stress their distinctiveness that in the process they undermined their proposal of an hypostatic union.

---

[2]   See ibid., pp 27–47. For a much earlier discussion of the same ground by a Congregationalist see Sydney Cave, *The Doctrine of the Person of Christ* (London: Duckworth, 1925), pp 9-28.

In the end, the Antiochene dyophysite position triumphed. It became the orthodox view of the church and largely went unchallenged up to and including the Reformation. English history has taught us, though, that we can hardly be surprised when a change of political leadership causes an about turn in the church's theological outlook. On the 26 July 450, Emperor Theodosius II fell off his horse. If he had not succumbed to this equine misfortune it is debatable whether christological orthodoxy in the church would have been monophysite and not dyophysite! Be that as it may, Pulcheria, his sister, took over office, and when she married Marcian, her husband became the Emperor. Aware of all the ecclesiastical controversy, Marcian called the Fourth Ecumenical Council. The Council of Chalcedon was a huge affair involving about six hundred bishops and extending over fifteen sessions from 8 October to 10 November 451. The Antiochene two nature christology was made the prevailing orthodoxy, with the Alexandrian monophysite tradition being renounced as heretical [Figure 1]. Christological orthodoxy declared that Christ was 'perfect God and perfect man, of one substance with the Father in his divinity and with us in our humanity'. Jesus Christ has been revealed *in* two natures 'without confusion, change, division, or separation'. What is meant by the word 'in' is further elaborated by further clauses: (1) the union does not undermine the differences between the natures; and (2) each nature's properties are preserved and combine 'to form one person and substance'.

FIGURE 1   The Statement from the Council of Chalcedon[3]

Therefore, following the holy Fathers, we all with one accord teach men to acknowledge one and the same Son, our Lord Jesus Christ, at once complete in Godhead and complete in manhood, truly God and truly man, consisting also of a reasonable soul and body; of one substance . . . with the Father as regards his Godhead, and at the same time of one substance with us as regards his manhood; like us in all respects, apart from sin; as regards his Godhead, begotten of the Father before the ages, but yet as regards his manhood begotten, in the last days, for us men and for our salvation, of Mary the Virgin, the God-bearer . . . ; one and the same Christ, Son, Lord, Only-begotten, recognized IN TWO NATURES, WITHOUT CONFUSION, WITHOUT CHANGE, WITHOUT DIVISION, WITHOUT SEPARATION; the distinction of natures being in no way annulled by the union, but rather the characteristics of each nature being preserved and coming together to form one person and subsistence . . . , not as parted or separated into two persons, but one and the same Son and Only-begotten God the Word, Lord Jesus Christ; even as the Prophets from earliest times spoke of him, and our Lord Jesus Christ himself taught us, and the creed of the Fathers has handed down to us.

Although Chalcedon was to shape the church's christological thinking for almost the next fourteen hundred years, monophysites remained in the church, albeit a reducing minority. The two-natures formula had been the theology of a minority, but, with the support of the Emperor, a minority view triumphed and became mainstream orthodoxy. The Chalcedon settlement was only seriously

---

3   From Henry Bettenson, ed., *Documents of the Christian Church,* 2nd. ed. (Oxford: Oxford University Press, 1963), p 73.

challenged when its conceptuality became incredible to a different age and when theological concerns turned from the question of Christ's nature to what Jesus did in his life – or, to put it more precisely, when functional rather than classical ontological christologies became fashionable.

John Calvin: Prophet, King and Priest.

Calvin's christology is a powerful reminder that, while it may be theologically useful to make a distinction between the person and work of Christ, it is doctrinally unsound to effect a separation between them. For Calvin, who Jesus was clearly had to be determined by what he came to do. In other words, Christ's person had to be such that his work could be achieved. And that work centred upon breaking down the barriers to our relationship with God created by our sin. Jesus Christ, then, must have been the kind of 'person' who could achieve a reconciliation of the broken relationship between God and persons. Calvin asserts, therefore, that, 'no man, unless he belonged to God, could serve as the intermediary to restore peace'.[4] Only One who was both human and divine could be the Redeemer, so God took our nature upon himself, in order to give us what belongs to Godself. He adopted us as his children by meeting us as God's son while also being one of us. Our common humanity with Christ therefore enables us to have fellowship with the Son of God who, on the cross, pays the penalty for our sins by dying for us. As God alone, Christ could not experience death; as simply human, Christ would not have the power to overcome it. Therefore, in keeping with Chalcedon, Calvin insists upon Christ's full humanity and full divinity.

According to Calvin, the Son of God became incarnate in Jesus while not being completely lodged in the confines of a human body: 'Here is something marvellous: the Son of God descended from heaven in such a way that, without leaving heaven, he willed to be borne in the virgin's womb, to go about the earth, and to hang upon the cross; yet he continuously filled the world even as he had done from the beginning.'[5] Calvin's acute awareness of the qualitative difference between the Creator and creatures made it impossible for him to believe that Christ's humanity could hold the whole of the Logos. But detractors might read into this a possible loosening of an emphasis upon the divinity of Christ, even if verbally Calvin was fully committed to it.

Humanity and divinity remain united in Christ while they each possess separate natures. Calvin's christology, therefore, clearly belongs to the Antiochene school. What is spoken about Christ in his redeeming work can be lodged with neither his human nature nor his divine nature, but must apply to his complete person as the Christ. When people object to the humanity of Christ by recoiling from the idea that God has blood, suffers and can be touched with human hands, Calvin suggests that, in his redeeming act on the cross, 'the things that he carried out in his human nature are transferred improperly, although not without reason, to his divinity'.[6] At this point, Calvin relies upon the ancient Patristic doctrine of *communicatio idiomatum* which expresses the idea that there was an interchange of the properties belonging to Christ's human and divine natures in the work of Christ. There are various qualities which would seem to apply solely to one of the two natures, but which also by means of this speculative doctrine can be assigned to the other nature when we talk about Christ's person from the perspective of his work as the Mediator. So Calvin makes the following assertion: 'Let this, then, be our key to right understanding: those things which apply to

---

4   Calvin, *Institutes*, 2,12,I.
5   Ibid., 2,13,4.
6   Ibid., 2,14,2.

the office of the Mediator are not spoken simply either of the divine nature or of the human.[7] Whether the unity of the dyophysite Christ can be fully protected by such a speculative doctrine is debatable, but Calvin is quick to renounce the views of those who either denied the humanity of Christ or so distinguished the human and the divine natures in Christ that in effect they separated them and thus destroyed the unity of Christ's person. Chalcedon's orthodoxy was ever to be affirmed: 'For it is no more permissible to commingle the two natures in Christ than to pull them apart.'[8] In the Incarnation, an hypostatic union between the Logos and human nature took place in Jesus of Nazareth whom his followers called 'Christ'. The one Christ possessed two natures, divine and human, which were united – distinct but never separate.

So much then for Calvin's discussion of Christ's person from the perspective of who he was. Calvin's *ontological* christology is thoroughly traditional, but when he considers Christ's person from the perspective of what Christ did, the resulting analysis is highly original; so much so that his more *functional* christology has had a large following among subsequent Reformed theologians. Calvin's discussion makes creative use of the Scriptures on its way to depicting Christ as 'prophet, king and priest'.[9] The first of Christ's offices involves him being 'the herald and witness of the Father's grace'.[10] Other prophets have come and gone, but the message of Jesus Christ is so perfect that he has brought the curtain down on all prophecy. All that one needs to know for one's salvation has been announced by the man from Nazareth.

With Christ's kingly office we receive assurance of Christ's eternal power. Since Christ is head of the Church, the perpetuity of the Church is assured: 'Hence, amid the violent agitation with which it is continually troubled, amid the grievous and frightful storms that threaten it with unnumbered calamities, it still remains safe.'[11] At a time when the acids of secularism are eating into the fabric of the Western churches, it is important to remember that ultimately the future of the Church is not in our hands. Christ is Lord of the church, Calvin claims, bestowing upon the faithful the happiness of 'the heavenly life', a future spiritual life rather than one which is 'earthly or carnal and hence subject to corruption'.[12] The followers of the kingly Christ will not be guaranteed joy and peace, security and riches in this life. No one could ever underwrite 'a prosperity gospel' with the theology of John Calvin, yet the great Reformer assures us that 'our King will never leave us destitute, but will provide for our needs until, our warfare ended, we are called to triumph'.[13] We must leave behind the lure of this world if we are to enjoy the Kingdom.

The third office of Christ is priestly. Calvin's understanding of the atonement will be considered in a later chapter, but at this point we simply note the way in which he depicts Christ in the fashion of the Epistle to the Hebrews. Christ is our High Priest, the One who makes satisfaction for our sins and removes our guilt through his sacrificial death. After having wiped out our guilt and appeased God's righteous anger over our sin, the Son of God continues as our 'everlasting intercessor: through his pleading we obtain favour'.[14] Therefore, at one and the same time, Christ is both priest and sacrifice.

---

[7] Ibid., 2,14,3.
[8] Ibid., 2,14,4. Calvin is referring to the views of Eutyches and Nestorus respectively.
[9] Ibid., 2,15,1.
[10] Ibid., 2,15,2.
[11] Ibid., 2,15,3.
[12] Ibid., 2,15,4.
[13] Ibid.
[14] Ibid., 2,15,6.

Friedrich Schleiermacher: Absolutely Powerful God-consciousness

Schleiermacher was perhaps the first Reformed theologian to launch a sustained attack on the two-natures doctrine. He found it to be illogical, incoherent and, hence, totally incapable of adequately expressing Christ's significance in a way that reflected the Gospel narratives and was comprehensible to contemporary people. While Schleiermacher provides us with 'a very strong case for a radical rethinking and reformulation of the doctrine of the person of Christ', John Macquarrie thinks that in his own alternative theological proposals 'he tried conscientiously to say *in his own terms* all that the classical christology had said.'[15] We will now consider the reasons why Schleiermacher opposed the Chalcedon definition in more detail.

Schleiermacher's first objection concerns the correctness of using the term 'nature' to describe both the humanity and divinity of Christ. 'Nature' is a term which refers to 'the summary of all finite existence, or . . . the summary of all that is corporeal', and as such it is used inappropriately of God: 'the unconditioned and the absolutely simple'.[16] Schleiermacher rather disparagingly accuses the Church Fathers of using terminology for God that even 'the heathen sages themselves had already risen above', once they had discovered that God should be conceived 'as beyond all existence and being.'[17] A second objection to the Chalcedon formula focuses upon Schleiermacher's claim that the term 'nature' refers to a universal. It can be used to describe many individuals or persons, but one person cannot be said to possess two natures simultaneously. And, of course, the critic of Chalcedon will be quick to observe that two-nature doctrines usually either end up collapsing Christ's humanity into his divinity or cannot avoid losing Christ's divinity in his humanity. Schleiermacher's third objection revolves around his insistence that theological concepts should not be used in an equivocal way. If the terms 'nature' and 'person' are to be employed in theology, they should mean the same thing when used in christology as when they are deployed in trinitarian discussions. But Schleiermcher judges that this is precisely what classical theology has failed to do. It speaks of the Trinity as 'three Persons in one Essence' but then describes Christ as being 'one Person out of two natures'.[18] Is the Son of God then one Person made up of two natures, or is he one of three persons who share a common nature – given that what trinitarian thought means by 'essence' is similar to what Chalcedon means by 'nature'?

On the basis of these objections Schleiermacher leaves Chalcedon in search of a more adequate christology. His quest takes him back to an analysis of the instinctively Christian experience of redemption. We learn about Christ's person through attending to the historical facts about Christ and the redemption which flows from him. It is undoubtedly one of Schleiermacher's legacies that, in the words of Sydney Cave, we try to 'construct theology, not from the presuppositions of an alien philosophy, but from the implicates of the Christian redemption.'[19] Any such theology will insist that Christianity is a distinctive religion, since it is grounded in the salvation effected for men and women by Jesus Christ. The nature of this salvation, Schleiermacher argues, is rooted in an inner change within people as they move from 'God-forgetfulness' to 'God-consciousness'. What is an implicit possibility for them simply as human beings, due to their natural 'sense and taste for the infinite', has become an explicit possibility for them due to Christ's work. Everything needs to be understood in relation to this act of redemption.

---

[15]   Macquarrie, *Jesus Christ in Modern Thought*, pp 209, 192.
[16]   Schleiermacher, *The Christian Faith*, p 392.
[17]   Ibid., p 393.
[18]   Ibid., p 395.
[19]   Cave, *The Doctrine of the Person of Christ*, pp 172–3.

Jesus of Nazareth was born into the world like any other human being. Like us he possessed a propensity towards God-consciousness; but unlike us he was able to lead his life in the ideal way. What it means to be a perfect human being, therefore, is revealed by Jesus. Schleiermacher allows for the fact of human development by saying that Jesus was 'perfect' at each stage of his life: ' . . . He developed in the same way as all others, so that from birth on His powers gradually unfolded, and, from the zero point of His appearance onwards, were developed to completeness in the order natural to the human race'.[20] At every moment of his life, unlike us, Jesus chose the correct option, always being obedient to the way God would have him go. Not only did Jesus develop perfect God-consciousness, but he was also free of sin as we know it. Such purity, Schleiermacher argues, stems completely from his own person as a result of 'the higher God-consciousness implanted in Him originally'.[21] He had been specially selected by God for a purpose and endowed with unique capacity for God-consciousness, and therefore Schleiermacher believes that we can 'attribute to Him an existence of God in Him'.[22] In Schleiermacher's theology, then, Jesus figures as the *archetypal* form of being human; he is more than a distinguished person who through living a good life is an example for everyone to follow; he is the 'ideal' sent from God. We experience redemption as we enter into fellowship with the Redeemer; and when we encounter Jesus the 'existence of God in Him' is decisively represented to us.

Schleiermacher delineates the divine and human in Jesus as follows:

> . . . the existence of God in the Redeemer is posited as the innermost fundamental power within Him, from which every activity proceeds and which holds every element together; everything human (in Him) forms only the organism for this fundamental power, and is related to it as the system which both receives and represents it, just as in us all other powers are related to the intelligence . . . In so far as all human activity of the Redeemer depends, as a connected whole, upon this existence of God in Him and represents it, the expression (that in the Redeemer God became man) is justified as true exclusively of Him; and similarly every moment of His existence, so far as it can be isolated, presents just such a new incarnation and incarnatedness of God, because always and everywhere all that is human in Him springs out of that divine.[23]

The personality of Christ is created by the implantation of the divine in Jesus' human nature. God was the active agent and Jesus the passive receiver in the act of Incarnation. Acts of will were present on both sides. While Schleiermacher agrees that the idea of 'a supernatural conception remains . . . essential and necessary, if the specific pre-eminence of the Redeemer is to remain undiminished', he does not think that it is obligatory to express this in terms of a doctrine of Virgin Birth, and in actual fact considers it 'inadvisable to do so'.[24] Once the personality of Christ has been created, every activity of Christ stems from a common activity embracing both the divine and human elements, so it is possible to 'read' the work of Christ as at one and the same time a human and a divine work. Consequently, what separates Christ from other human beings, namely his absolute perfection and sinlessness, is grounded in a personality whose constitution is marked by nothing other than a union of the divine and the human.

---

[20]   Schleiermacher, *The Christian Faith*, p 381.
[21]   Ibid., p 383.
[22]   Ibid., p 387.
[23]   Ibid., p 397.
[24]   Ibid., pp 405 and 406.

Criticisms of Schleiermacher's christology from those who wish to defend Chalcedon orthodoxy invariably focus upon the accusation that he makes human experience the starting point for christological reflection rather than, say, scripture or tradition, with the alleged result that Christ is reduced to what can be comfortably correlated with human experience. This line of attack upon Schleiermacher's christological project has been made by Karl Barth and other neo-orthodox theologians who argue that theology's proper starting point is God's revelation in Christ rather than human experience, and, hence, suspect that Christian revelation is being made to fit what can be accommodated by sinful, conditioned and, therefore, limited human experience. To a certain degree this criticism is unfair on Schleiermacher, and it also begs the issue of the adequacy of his critics' alternative proposals. The starting-point for Schleiermacher's theology is far more subtle than his opponents would have us believe. It is not simply a matter of reflecting upon our innate, if rudimentary, awareness of God; rather it involves focusing upon the distinctively Christian experience of redemption. Such experience arises from an encounter between persons and Christ's redeeming work. The starting point for theological thinking, therefore, is the life-experience of the Christian, and this includes *both* the general awareness of God universally given with being human *and* the special relation to Christ given with being a Christian. Both implicitly and explicitly the 'experience' which is the starting point for Christian theology has been shaped by divine revelation. When Barth wants to insist that theology must start from revelation, it is difficult to understand how we could be in a position to understand that revelation were it not for a predisposition within us to apprehend that revelation as a revelation from God. That predisposition need not be viewed as a sinful attempt to bring God under human control; it can and should be understood as a God-given ability to be open to God. John Macquarrie wisely warns us that, 'To do justice to the complexity of the problem, it seems necessary . . . to acknowledge – as Schleiermacher does – man's quest for God as well as God's quest for man, and this does not mean that one is denying that God's quest comes before the human one and inspires it.'[25]

Schleiermacher's more functional approach to christology helpfully takes us back to Christ and away from the speculative considerations of the ontological christology inherited from tradition. He invites us to turn to the historical records and rediscover the Jesus whom men and women proclaimed as Christ and experienced as Redeemer. Starting his christology from 'below' rather than 'above', he presents a Jesus with whom we can identify, one of us and yet superlatively different from us, but in 'degree' rather than 'kind'. Four concerns, however, emerge from his proposals. First, can we afford to dispense with ontology in christology? It is important to speak not only about what Jesus *does* but also about what he *is* – even if we must avoid becoming over-speculative. Secondly, has Schleiermacher been historical enough? Many have argued that Schleiermacher's Christ has been watered down into a picture of One whose life was marked by uninterrupted progressive development and faithfulness. The Gospels, however, depict a more human figure in which inner turmoil sometimes was evident. This raises the question whether Schleiermacher actually gets close enough to the historical Jesus. Sydney Cave, for example, presses this very issue: 'The archetypal Christ of whom [Schleiermacher] speaks is a Christ without moral conflict; He is not the Jesus of history whose inner struggle the Gospels do not conceal.'[26] Thirdly, Schleiermacher is wise to seek a basis for Jesus' union with the divine upon a property possessed by all individuals, i.e. their natural God-given gift of a propensity for God-consciousness. Jesus is then set apart from the rest of

---

[25] Macquarrie, *Jesus Christ in Modern Thought*, p 199.
[26] Cave, *The Doctrine of the Person of Christ*, p 171.

humanity by the way in which he perfected that God-consciousness, the difference between them is one of degree rather than kind. But Schleiermacher rather spoils things when he appears to contradict all this by asserting that an additional implantation of God-consciousness was given to Jesus at birth. As Macquarrie observes, this suggestion 'appears no less supernatural than a virgin birth'.[27] Then, fourthly, Schleiermacher's christology, like every christology 'from below', runs the risk of being devoid of evidence to support it. How could one establish, as opposed to merely assert, that Jesus possessed perfect God-consciousness? It is difficult enough to conceive how one would establish that a living person of close acquaintance is of such a nature; it is highly questionable, therefore, how it can be done of one who left behind no personal testimony, save what we can derive from the propaganda put about concerning him by his followers. In principle, as well as in practice, historical information presents a weak defence of psychological claims; but this point in turn raises the wider issue of what we can know about Jesus, and whether knowledge about him, as opposed to knowledge of the claims made about him, is required or even desirable for christology. Before we consider further Reformed christologies, it is appropriate to attend to this much debated issue. Is the Christian faith grounded in what we can know about 'the historical Jesus', the life and witness of Jesus of Nazareth, or is it rooted in 'the Christ of faith', the claims made about Jesus by his followers concerning his saving significance for the world? Or, perhaps, might it be the case that the former is unavoidably bound up in the latter?

The Jesus of History and the Christ of Faith

The advent of historical research on the Bible meant that the Bible could no longer be treated uncritically as a datum for theological work. Theology was faced with coming to terms with what Nietzsche called the discovery of our sixth sense: history. We became aware in the nineteenth century that all thought and experience is to a greater or lesser degree conditioned by our context; and Christianity was not exempted. Creeds and doctrines to a greater or lesser degree are relative to the contexts in which they arise, being partly a product of human history rather than examples of pure inspiration necessarily to be accepted uncritically as authoritative. Perhaps some inherited doctrinal claims – particularly those called into question by the scientific worldview of a post-Enlightenment culture – are not timeless truths, but propositions belonging to a past age which can now be set to one side?

Although the study of history goes back to the Greeks, during the nineteenth century it experienced a revolution through the development of methods which greatly increased its reliability. Nineteenth century theologians, hardly surprisingly, turned to history to find a secure basis for a Christianity under siege from the acids of modernity. They tried to rescue the Christian faith, and its theological expressions, from being a bygone age's final vestiges. The Christian faith was defended against intellectual attack by attempts to ground it in historical evidence that, to use a legal term, was 'safe'. How much better it would be if the significance of Jesus Christ was plainly apparent from the historical information we could have about him, rather than having to defend the ontological claims of two-natures doctrines? Might it not be the case that creeds and Councils have overcomplicated matters that historically we now can know quite clearly? What originally attracted the early Christians to Jesus was the attraction and power of his personality, the argument ran, so let us go back behind the ontological claims to get a historical portrait of him which will serve us now like it did the early Church.

---

[27]   Macquarrie, *Jesus Christ in Modern Thought*, p 208.

The nineteenth century, consequently, spawned a myriad of biographies of Jesus. By and large, the prospects for a new line in apologetics held good until it became clear that the nineteenth century questers for 'the historical Jesus' were just as much at the mercy of the historical conditionedness of thought as the earlier theologians and councils they were seeking to leave behind. Unfortunately, the nineteenth century portraits of Jesus reflected the highest values and virtues of good nineteenth century men and women, so the Christ that the life of Jesus researchers found was, as George Tyrrell famously put it, 'the reflection of a Liberal Protestant face, seen at the bottom of a deep well'.[28] It was more difficult to 'find' the 'historical Jesus' than had been supposed; but for many it merely posted a warning that more care needed taking when trying to reconstruct the life of Jesus. Albert Schweitzer, for example, in his book *The Quest for the Historical Jesus*, does not draw back from joining the quest for 'the historical Jesus' after having pointedly exposed the inadequacies of many in the nineteenth century who had trodden the ground before him.[29] And, needless to say, critics have now found sufficient flaws in Schweitzer's 'Jesus' to prompt further caution about the possibility of writing a life of Jesus.

The reaction to liberal theology from certain neo-orthodox theologians suggested that the quest for the historical Jesus was *historically* impossible as well as *theologically* illegitimate. It was historically impossible because biblical scholarship, it was claimed, has shown conclusively that the Gospels are of such a nature that they do not provide the kind of writings from which we can construct an historical biography of Jesus; but it was also theologically illegitimate because the christological question is: What is the meaning of Christ for us now? and not, Who is Jesus? Also some critics pointed to the impropriety suggested by the doctrine of justification by faith *alone* of the intention to find historical reasons to support or ground faith. Neo-orthodox theologians therefore switched attention from 'the Jesus of history' to 'the Christ of faith', from a concern with the *historical* facts about Jesus to a focus on the *historic* claims made about him. Since the gospel is a personal call to put one's faith in Jesus as the Saviour of world, the thesis went, grubbing around in historical facts to establish its truth is not only beside the point but in a sense an explicit denial of the gospel to which its hearers are called.

No doubt the critics of liberal christologies were perfectly correct to regard those christologies as lacking the essential divinity of Jesus, and hence of being devoid of the sense in which Jesus Christ stands over and against men and women in judgement. Christologies 'from below' always run the risk of projecting on to Jesus a contemporary idealized picture of what is perceived to be best in humanity, and hence of portraying Jesus according to the pattern of our sinful humanity. But to seek to avoid the problem by removing any need to attend to the historical Jesus seems to be akin to taking a sledge-hammer to crack a nut. Many scholars believe that the New Testament message, along with its call to faith, contains essential empirical information about Jesus which anchors the Christ-event in history. They maintain that the question christology seeks to answer does contain an historical element. Unless the *kerygma* is (literally) rooted in the historical Jesus, they say, it 'floats like an unanchored, unstable balloon'.[30]

The suggestion that the writers of the New Testament were solely concerned with 'the Christ of faith', and therefore were not at all concerned with 'the Jesus of history', cannot in the end be substantiated. Käsemann concludes that the writers of the synoptic Gospels intended to make assertions about Jesus in their proclamation of him as the Christ:

---

28   George Tyrell, *Christianity at the Crossroads* (London: Longman's, Green and Co, 1909), p 244.

29   Albert Schweitzer, *The Quest of the Historical Jesus* (London: A & C Black, 1910).

30   C Leslie Mitton, *Jesus: The Fact Behind the Faith* (Oxford: A R Mowbray & Co. Ltd., 1975), p 63.

Doubtless they are dominated by the interests of kerygma. But they express this in the form of gospels, which are essentially not preaching but reporting. Equally certainly, they are not historians in the modern sense and are totally devoid of any claim to scientific method; and this must be held to be true even of Luke. At the same time they supplement the kerygma with historical touches and employ a historicizing mode of presentation.[31]

Graham Stanton accepts, along with most New Testament scholars, that 'no tradition about Jesus was retained *solely* out of historical interest or biographical curiosity, for the traditions are kerygmatic and were used in the service of the preaching of the primitive church'; but he goes on to add that 'the kerygmatic role of the gospel traditions has not smothered interest in the life and character of Jesus'; and he then concludes that the gospel traditions 'intend to proclaim Jesus' but were 'also concerned with his life and character'.[32] There is no reason, therefore, why the kerygmatic aims of the New Testament authors should rule out a concern for history on their part. Jesus is the centre of the kerygma, and it is highly likely that those authors, like us, are interested in what Jesus said and did precisely because of that fact. 'Does what is being proclaimed about him measure up to what he said and did?' seems a natural and reasonable question to want to ask.

But it is one thing to ask a question, something else to answer it. The URC traditions have generated some of the most gifted and respected New Testament scholars of the twentieth century. In my life-time, through their writings and teaching, I have 'known' C H Dodd, John Marsh, T W Manson, G B Caird, C E B Cranfield and, more latterly, Graham Stanton. All of them have seen fit to reject as unwanted scepticism the view that we can know nothing about 'the Jesus of History'; and it follows that those who do not regard historical information about Jesus' personality as christologically relevant might be making a theological virtue out of a self-imposed historical necessity flowing from unfounded scepticism about the historical content of the Gospels. It may well be that it is wise to understand the New Testament as 'the oldest preserved book of sermons of the Church', but that does not rule out, and it perhaps requires, that those sermons carry historical information about Jesus.[33] As the sermons were preached, and as we read them today, it is difficult to believe that something of the Proclaimer was, and is, not heard in the proclamation about him. It is also difficult to explain the church's rise and the development of its theology and traditions by a theory which implies that no information about Jesus was in fact handed down to the early churches. To use an analogy of Humphrey Palmer, while the early witnesses are responsible for some noise on the 'line' to the historical Jesus, it is implausible to suggest that we do not hear the Master's voice through the crackling.[34] To suggest that the Gospels do not tell us anything about the historical Jesus is to take a dim view of the evangelists. If those evangelists thought so much about Jesus that they proclaimed him as Lord and Christ, it is difficult to believe that they did not remember and record certain things he said and did with a high degree of accuracy, or to maintain the idea that they completely mutilated the traditions about him. It is hardly surprising, then, that the vast majority of New Testament

[31]   Ernst Käsemann, 'Blind Alleys in the "Jesus of History Controversy"', in *New Testament Questions of Today* (London: SCM Press, 1969), p 49.

[32]   Graham Stanton, 'The Gospel Traditions and Early Christological Reflection' in S W Sykes and J P Clayton (eds.), *Christ, Faith and History: Cambridge Studies in Christology* (Cambridge: Cambridge University Press, 1972), pp 198–9.

[33]   For the idea of the New Testament being 'the oldest preserved book of sermons of the church' see Willi Marxen, 'The New Testament: A Collection of Sermons, A Contribution to the Discussion of the Canon and to the Question of the Historical Jesus', *The Modern Churchman*,19,4 (Summer 1976), pp 134–43.

[34]   Humphrey Palmer, *The Logic of Gospel Criticism* (London: Macmillan and Co., 1968), p 187.

scholars share the view that a basic kernel of information can be discerned from the Gospels concerning Jesus. They have undermined approaches to biblical scholarship which, in their extreme examples, once gave rise to an overt skepticism now largely left behind.[35]

As a lay-person in the world of biblical scholarship, I feel obliged to introduce a warning, though, at this point. I sometimes get the feeling that certain New Testament scholars, having discovered clear logical fallacies in sceptical approaches to biblical scholarship, then believe that they can continue with their work as if important guidelines for all future biblical work have not been laid down by that scholarship. They tend to forget that any attempt to reconstruct a picture of Jesus from the Gospels is bound to be speculative and inevitably will be governed largely by many of their own presuppositions. This perhaps explains why there is great confidence among New Testament scholars about the possibility of knowing a significant amount of information about 'the historical Jesus', and, *at the same time*, a plethora of books about Jesus written by them which differ in orientation and opinion from one another. The number of opinions often seems to match the number of scholars, and the systematic theologian is entitled to blink in disbelief every time the phrase 'the assured results of biblical criticism' is mentioned by a member of the guild of biblical scholarship. The most that can be said, I suspect, is that we can reconstruct from the Gospels a tentative historical picture of Jesus which is sufficient to authorize the church's proclamation about Jesus in his actual life and teaching. Dennis Nineham is often regarded as an ultra-sceptical New Testament scholar when it comes to historical questions about Jesus, but the following statement actually takes us to the limits of what can and ought to be said on the issue.

> The gospels were not meant to give us an uninterpreted picture of Jesus' ministry so full and detailed that we could interpret its significance for ourselves. They were meant to admit us to that understanding of, and relationship with, Jesus which was vouchsafed to the apostolic church. At the same time they make possible sufficient historical knowledge of the person and ministry of Jesus for us to assure ourselves that the early Christians were not making bricks without straw and also for us to see the sense in which their interpretations were intended and were legitimate and to set about the task of reformulating them in terms of our own needs and experience.[36]

And, as neo-orthodoxy never tired of telling us, the Jesus proclaimed by the church is always more than 'the historical Jesus'. Therefore, the final ground and confirmation of the church's faith can never ultimately lie in historical information. This fact places a logical limit upon what christology from below can achieve, as we can clearly see from a consideration of the christology of C J Cadoux.

Cecil John Cadoux: A Congregationalist Liberal Life of Jesus

C J Cadoux (1883-1947) taught at the Yorkshire United Independent College, Bradford, and Mansfield College, Oxford, and he became an influential figure in Congregationalism during the first part of the twentieth century.[37] He was a died in the wool liberal who on the basis of his biblical scholarship believed that a 'life of Jesus' could be written, and that christology should be woven out of the cloth

---

35   See George B.Caird, 'The Study of the Gospels: From Criticism', *Expository Times*, 87,5 (February 1976), pp 137–41.

36   Dennis Nineham, *Explorations in Theology* 1 (London: SCM Press, 1977), p 60.

37   For a well-crafted and informative biography of Cadoux see Elaine Kaye's, *C.J.Cadoux: Theologian, Scholar and Pacifist* (Edinburgh: Edinburgh University Press, 1988).

provided by the gospels rather than be concerned with the classical two-natures doctrine. His book, *The Life of Jesus*, was a posthumous bestseller, and it is overflowing with opinions about Jesus that reflect the theology of many liberal members of today's URC.[38]

Cadoux had little time for the two-natures christology of Chalcedon. He could agree that it protected 'the central doctrine of the Divinity of Jesus', and thus did justice to 'the conviction that the Divinity which men saw in him was as truly Divine as that of the Creator Himself',[39] but he doubted whether Chalcedon solved the christological problem and suspected that it simply laid down 'the limits and conditions within which it would have to be solved'.[40] And, overall, Chalcedon received from him the somewhat damning verdict that 'instead of synthesizing the historical data, it defies them, and in doing so rules itself out as inadmissible'.[41] He highlights five areas in which he maintains that Chalcedon is at odds with the historical record. First, he argues that 'it is tantamount to a denial of our Lord's real humanity'.[42] Although the humanity of Jesus is affirmed by Chalcedon, its supporters have often suggested that his humanity was *impersonal*. But the picture of Jesus presented by the gospels, Cadoux argues, is one of a genuine person – 'The point is so obvious that it needs no arguing'.[43] Secondly, Chalcedon wrongly presupposed that 'in his earthly life [Jesus] claimed to be God and was recognized by sympathetic contemporaries as being God'.[44] Cadoux denies that the evidence of the New Testament supports such a claim. Thirdly, Cadoux castigates Chalcedon for presenting a portrait of Jesus which, contrary to the historical evidence, does not allow him to have had 'any real personal religion of his own', or to have 'suffered real temptation', or to have 'offered up real prayers to God', or to have 'stood in need of the help of the Holy Spirit'.[45] Fourthly, Cadoux accuses Chalcedon of rejecting the historical fact that 'Jesus during his earthly life was subject to all the normal limitations, physical and intellectual, which are incidental to human life as we know it'.[46] The gospels, for example, are clear about the limitation of Jesus' knowledge, admitting at several points that he was ignorant on certain matters; but Patristic theologians, especially from the East, regarded it as totally unacceptable that Jesus was limited in any way. This prompts Cadoux to thunder: 'Could the weakness of the Chalcedonian Formula be more clearly displayed than by the necessity to which its stoutest champions feel put to play fast and loose with the explicit evidence of the Gospels, and their unabashed willingness to do so?'[47] Finally, Cadoux suggests that Chalcedon's impersonal picture of Christ makes Christ so different from us that he could not possess soteriological significance for us. By ignoring the ethical nature of Jesus' personality, Jesus becomes so abnormal that 'he can be in no real sense an example to us'.[48]

It is interesting that Cadoux's objections to Chalcedon are different from those of Schleiermacher. They are not directed at the metaphysical problems involved in two-natures doctrines but launched from an historical perspective. Taken together, though, the metaphysical and historical points of opposition constitute an accumulative and convincing reason to seek an

---

[38]   Cecil John Cadoux, *The Life of Jesus* (West Drayton, Middlesex: Penguin Books, 1948).
[39]   Cecil John Cadoux, *The Case for Evangelical Modernism: A Study of the Relation between the Christian Faith and Traditional Theology* (London: Hodder and Stoughton, Ltd., 1938), p 90.
[40]   Ibid.
[41]   Ibid., p 91.
[42]   Ibid., p 79.
[43]   Ibid., p 80.
[44]   Ibid., p 83.
[45]   Ibid., p 85.
[46]   Ibid., p 86.
[47]   Ibid., p 89.
[48]   Ibid., p 89.

alternative approach to christology. Cadoux's confidence in being able to know sufficient detail about the personal character of Jesus provided him with his starting point: '. . . tradition must be judged by the historical facts, not the historical facts by tradition'.[49] Unlike some, though, Cadoux had confidence that those facts could be known. He had little sympathy for the claim that the gospels do not provide us with the tools to reconstruct a life of Jesus:

> The suggestion that the strong religious interest of all our evangelists renders it impossible for us to get behind their statements and nearer to the actual facts, pre-supposes a principle of judgment which would – if consistently acted on – bring all historical investigation to a standstill; for every reconstruction of the past rests on our being to some extent able to make allowance for the personal interests and viewpoints of our informants, and so learn something distinctive of the objective facts they profess to be narrating. It is, I hold, quite perverse to argue, on this or on any other ground, that real knowledge of the historical Jesus, in partial distinction from the Christ-picture treasured by Christian devotion, is beyond our reach.[50]

Where the nineteenth-century liberals had failed he was confident that, with care and caution, he could succeed. So, for Cadoux, history provides the basis for faith in the sense that 'the critically-sifted history of Jesus . . . makes explicit and strong that trust in God which is implicitly or tentatively presupposed in all our intellectual, moral, and religious aspirations'.[51]

But what does Cadoux allow to let pass through the sieve? He finds 'good reasons for discarding, or at all events, gravely doubting, on historical grounds'[52] the following: the Virgin Birth – Jesus was 'the legally-born son of Joseph and Mary';[53] Bethlehem as Jesus' birthplace – he was 'probably born . . . at Nazareth, his parents' normal home';[54] the omniscience of Jesus; the nature miracles, e.g. Jesus walking on water, calming a storm, multiplying loaves and fish and causing a fig-tree to wither; Jesus' awareness of being pre-existent; Jesus' claim to forgive sins in his own right; Jesus' awareness that he was 'the sole exception to the rule that all men are in some sense and measure morally imperfect';[55] the idea that Jesus actually said what is attributed to him in John's gospel – 'we have no right to equate its discourses indiscriminately as things actually said by Jesus himself, and so as furnishing direct evidence for his self-consciousness';[56] Christ's physical resurrection and his ascension. This list constitutes 'the less-historical matter' which accompanies the 'historical truth'.[57] But what is dispensable for the liberal is rather more precious to Christians of a more conservative disposition!

This brings us on to what Cadoux regarded as the 'historical' truth. He tells us that 'Jesus lived a life of unbroken, growing, and intimate fellowship with God, and of unrestrained love for man'.[58] His ministry revealed the universal sweep of God's love and the eternal meaning of His will'.[59] Goodness was manifest at every turn – as healer, teacher and preacher. Jesus was supreme among

---

[49]   Ibid., p 111.
[50]   Ibid., pp 114–15.
[51]   Ibid., p 125.
[52]   Ibid., p 128.
[53]   Ibid.
[54]   Ibid., p 130.
[55]   Ibid., p 136.
[56]   Ibid., p 145.
[57]   Cadoux, *The Life of Jesus*, p 19.
[58]   Cadoux, *The Case for Evangelical Modernism*, pp 147–8.
[59]   Ibid., p 148.

men and women, as he possessed 'a genuine and essential uniqueness among the sons of God'.[60] He effected a 'revolutionary salvation' for those who follow him.[61] In his suffering and death, he faced the worst pain and anguish that any human being could ever expect, with the result that the cruxifixion has revealed to men and women 'the cost of human sin to God' and 'God's loving rebuke', such that they have 'been moved by it to respond in penitence' and, consequently 'have been led to receive His forgiveness and be reconciled with Him through His grace'.[62] The resurrection of Jesus, in terms of several post-death appearances to his disciples, provided his followers with the assurance that he was not held captive to death and 'lived on as the Saviour and Lord of as many as would receive him.[63]

Cadoux seeks a working theory of the Person of Christ which can hold together these historical observations. He finds it in Paul's description of Jesus as 'the first born within a large family (Romans 8: 29). A first born holds a unique position in the family, but is nevertheless a part of it. In a certain sense, and to a certain degree, God dwells immanently in each member of the family. But the presence and very self of God is manifested with 'unique clarity and fullness in the overwhelming goodness of Jesus'.[64] The 'firstborn' possesses to the highest degree what with 'less clarity and fullness' is present in the rest of the family, i.e. 'those in whom Jesus himself has called forth a longing to follow him'.[65] Cadoux is confident that this not only safeguards what was not protected by Chalcedon, namely, the humanity of Christ, but also fully affirms 'the unique Divinity of Christ and the qualities wherein he stands apart from all men'.[66]

The time has come to round off our discussion of Cadoux's treatment of the Person of Christ. How adequate is it? Two general lines of criticism can be developed. The first questions the adequacy of Cadoux's historical analysis. Conservatives will find Cadoux's historical conclusions overtly reductionist, suspecting that he reduces 'Jesus' to what can be allowed by the modern worldview. Gone are those aspects of the Jesus story which might be offensive to the contemporary mind – Virgin Birth, nature miracles and empty tomb. Cadoux therefore will be accused of making Jesus into a good citizen of liberal culture. Those who take this line may point to respected New Testament scholars who hold a different view on these features of the gospel tradition. They will then take this as evidence that a more traditional historical portrait of Jesus actually fits the facts. Other more radical spirits, though, might view it as one more reason to doubt the possibility of finding 'the historical Jesus'. What does one do when experts differ? A rather more sophisticated example of this criticism comes from those who believe that Cadoux has left out of his Jesus portrait the ways in which the One who the Church claimed to be God-incarnate stands over and against the human race in judgement. They will argue, therefore, that the God-man is fundamentally different in kind from a fallen human race, and that 'degree' Christologies and the approach 'from below' do justice neither to their intentions nor to the need to hold in place Christ's divinity. In the attempt to avoid docetism, Cadoux, like others who attempt Christology from below, stand accused of making Jesus so superior to us in personal characteristics that he becomes no longer the firstborn member of a family but one who is alien to it. Or, to make the same point in a different way, Gunton says that 'a Christology from below is hard put to avoid being a Christology of a divinized man'.[67]

---

[60]   Ibid.
[61]   Ibid., p 149.
[62]   Ibid.
[63]   Ibid., p 150.
[64]   Ibid., p 156.
[65]   Ibid., p 157.
[66]   Ibid.
[67]   Colin E.Gunton, *Yesterday and Today: A Study of Continuities in Christology* (London: Darton, Longman and Todd, 1983), p 18.

If the first line of criticism focuses upon the tendency to reductionism, and the subsequent removal of many of the essential Godly features from the God-man, the second line is even more radical, since it questions whether it is ever possible to move from historical information about Jesus of Nazareth to the incarnational claim about him which is at the heart of the classical Christian tradition. There are three dimensions to this argument. First, we are not in a position to prove that Jesus was God incarnate by reference to the historical data. As Dennis Nineham says, 'it is impossible to justify any such claim on purely historical grounds, however wide the net for evidence is cast' because the gospel material 'is too scanty, and too largely selected and organized with reference to other considerations to provide the necessary evidence'.[68] And, furthermore, he argues that what we take to be moral perfection in a person most likely is different from what moral perfection meant in Jesus' day. So what passed for 'overwhelming goodness' for Cadoux may well have been different from what it constituted for Jesus and his contemporaries. Unless one is God, it would be impossible to show that a contemporary person, whose life is well known to us, is overwhelmingly good. There is no reason, therefore, to hold out much hope of being able to make a similar judgement about a man concerning whom we have little comparable information and who lived almost two thousand years ago. The second dimension of the argument returns to the point that the Jesus of the gospels is rather more than the historical Jesus. The New Testament does not tell us about a mere man who is on our level, but instead about One who is rather more than us, and in fact on a par with God – even if distinct from God as the decisive re-presentation of God's gift and demand of love. However much *historical* information about Jesus can be gleaned from the gospels – and we can get a good deal – incarnational claims with their *theological* emphasis cannot by definition be warranted by it. Such claims inevitably refer us to God, and as such they cannot be established by information about a historical figure. We are not called to faith *in* the historical Jesus, but *through* him to faith in God. And that in turn takes us away from history and back to ontology! The final dimension of this criticism now comes in view once it is recognized that the kind of incarnational claims Cadoux wants to establish from history are of a logical order which, in principle as well as in practice, cannot be verified by historical enquiry. A historian *qua* historian can never produce the kind of warrants required to establish claims about Jesus which are clearly theological and hence metaphysical in orientation. Even a video recording of Jesus' entire life would not provide the kind of evidence needed to prove that Jesus was God incarnate – even if it could produce evidence which might lead us to doubt it, e.g. if it showed Jesus to be capricious, violent or self-serving.

Peter Taylor Forsyth: Kenosis and Plerosis

It has often been remarked that Forsyth's general approach to theology was formally similar to that of the more famous Karl Barth, although the Scot predated the German by a good few years. The following quotation from Forsyth illustrates the point rather well:

> Do we start from the World or the Word? Are we to demand that Christ shall submit to the standard of certain principles or ideals which we bring to him from our human nature at its heart's highest and its thought's best? Or as our new creator is he his own standard, and not only so but both judge, king, and redeemer of human nature, and the fountain of a new life,

---

[68]   Dennis Nineham, 'Epilogue' in John Hick, ed., *The Myth of God Incarnate* (London: SCM Press, 1977), p 195.

autonomous in him, and for all the rest derived? Is he our spiritual hero, or our Eternal Lord and God? Is he the prophet and champion of man's magnificent resource, or is he the redeemer of man's spiritual poverty and moral wreck? Did he come to transfigure before men the great religious and ethical ideas, or to infuse into men new power, in the thorough, final, and godlike sense of endowing them with a new and ransomed life? Did he refurbish Humanity, or redeem it? Did he release its best powers or bestow them? That is the last issue, however we may blunt its edge, or soften its exigency in particular cases. It is between a rational Christianity and a redemptive.[69]

The language may be different, the rhetorical style that of the preacher-theologian rather than that of the systematic dogmatician, but Forsyth's similarity to Barth is patently obvious. Both were fundamentally opposed to liberal theology.

Forsyth's style leads him to make sharp contrasts between alternative positions. Sometimes one feels that his own preferred side of the polarity might have profited from insights from the side he disowns, but that is the style in which he writes. He offers us choices: between 'theological liberalism', which he perjoratively and unfairly depicts as 'practically unitarian', and 'a free but positive theology, which is essentially evangelical'[70] – as if Schleiermacher had not had evangelical concerns at the forefront of his attempt to write a theology which would win over to the Christian cause 'the cultured despisers' of his age. Or, to give another example, Forsyth invites us to decide between 'the humane Jesus of mere religious liberalism' and 'a far larger Saviour'.[71] And, often, Schleiermacher's proposals are firmly in his sights as the rhetoric flows. He tells us that our Lord was not 'the consummation of a God-consciousness, labouring up through creation, but the invasive source of forgiveness, new creation, and eternal life'; and then he affirms that 'in Christ God did not simply countersign the best intuitions of the heart but He created a new heart within us.'[72] He is wary of the way in which theologians have tried to make Christianity fit an evolutionary worldview, believing that they have lost an appreciation of God's transcendence in their concern to assert the divine immanence. Religion, he tells us, has more to do with God's invasion than with evolution; and, consequently, however much justice ought to be done to 'the evolutionary idea, the progressive idea', Forsyth insists that 'one would like still more to do justice to the redemptive idea, the regenerative, the deepening idea'.[73] The starting point for Forsyth's christology, therefore, is the Saviour's 'salvation' rather than 'his earthly self-consciousness',[74] 'the benefits of Christ' instead of 'the nature of Christ',[75] or 'the whole New Testament Christ and not the humane and residual Christ of much current religion'.[76] Fellow Congregationalists they may have been but there is a world of difference between Cadoux's christological approach 'from below' and Forsyth's alternative approach 'from above'.

Forsyth was clearly opposed to rationalism, the process of using rationality as the supreme test for what is real and truthful. He tells us that there are many important truths which are incapable of rational demonstration. So we have to accept that some of the most vital truths are

---

[69] P T Forsyth, *The Person and Place of Jesus Christ* London: Hodder and Stoughton, 1910), pp 95–6.
[70] Ibid., p 84.
[71] Ibid., p 318.
[72] Ibid., p 58.
[73] Ibid., p 335.
[74] Ibid., p 83.
[75] Ibid., p 278.
[76] Ibid., p 290.

paradoxical in nature. Again the affinity with Barth is quite clear. One of the apparent contradictions facing theology is that Jesus was both God and man, and akin to Barth Forsyth invokes the idea of paradox to resolve the problem. He argues that Chalcedon and the classical approaches to christology have simply lurched to one side or the other of the problem, either asserting divinity at the expense of humanity or vice versa. He objects to the classical tradition's use of 'substance' as a category to depict the nature of the relationship between Father and Son in the Incarnation, believing that it led to materialistic rather than personalistic understandings. What needs describing is a relationship between Father and Son in which forgiveness takes place, mercy is given and guilt is removed. Forsyth proposes to describe the union of humanity and divinity in Christ as 'the mutual involution of two personal movements raised to the whole scale of the human soul and the divine'.[77] He accuses Chalcedon of being metaphysical rather than ethical, but this does not prevent him also accepting that some sort of metaphysics is required to do full justice to a description of Christ's person: 'It is impossible to believe in one who changed the whole relation between the race and God without a metaphysic of the relation between that one and God.'[78] However, and this is the point, the metaphysic required is not 'a metaphysic of mere thought' but 'a metaphysic of faith itself', a 'metaphysic of personality' which does justice to what has to be explained, namely, that which ends in 'God's supreme moral act of redemption' and 'man's supreme moral act of faith'.[79]

Forsyth's starting point for his christology is what we earlier described as the *historic* rather than the *historical* Jesus, but this does not mean that he belittles the historical Jesus, nor that he wishes to cut christology loose from history. While the New Testament never presents us with 'a saint rather than a Redeemer' – the documents always being written in the interest of proclaiming the historic Christ – it always presupposes a continuity between the historical Jesus and the historic Jesus, and, hence, Forsyth states that regarding 'the central things' it is clear that 'the apostolic documents are the prolongation of the message of Jesus'.[80] A recourse to historical investigation, he says, suggests that the Jesus of the synoptic gospels shows a significant degree of congruence with the Johannine Jesus.[81] It also takes us well beyond 'the psychological postulates of a character aesthetically complete' to 'the magnitude, reality, and permanence of his effects in history'.[82] And it is the latter which is crucial for christology. Forsyth argues that the true significance of Jesus is found in what God did through him, rather than in any new ideas or novel teaching that he brought. Through his personality, 'holy, sacrificing, saving love'[83] was revealed. This makes Jesus unique in *kind* when compared to even the greatest saints: 'There is a qualitative difference from any natural passion or affection in the love that loves the Holy with entire holiness, loves a world in arms against it, and loves it so invincibly as to save, loves it from death into life eternal.'[84] What confronts people in Jesus, then, is not someone different in *degree* from them but the living God.

Forsyth suggests that there are two contrasting features in Christ which find their ultimate resolution in the crucifixion. When viewed from the perspective of his life, the judgement of Christ always stands to some extent in contradiction to his mercy, the extent reducing the nearer we approach the cross. We do not know what to expect from Jesus, oscillating between fear and hope

---

[77]   Ibid., p 333, italics removed.
[78]   Ibid., p 355.
[79]   Ibid., p 356.
[80]   Ibid., p 60.
[81]   See ibid., pp 105ff.
[82]   Ibid., p 290.
[83]   Ibid., p 68.
[84]   Ibid., p 69.

– until, from the perspective of the cross, the reconciliation of the seemingly opposite takes place. In the work of Christ, the personality of Christ is revealed to us *and* for us: 'No thought or form can contain the greatness of the personality which it took the eternal act of the cross and resurrection fully to express.'[85] There can be no mistaking that from start to finish Forsyth grounds his christology in soteriology: 'It is from the experience of Christ's salvation that the Church proceeds to the interpretation of the Saviour's person.'[86]

Forsyth believes that it is necessary to affirm the doctrine of Christ's pre-existence if we are to do justice to the Christian experience of salvation. He argues that only our Creator has the power to be our Saviour. If our salvation is to be complete the personality of Jesus must have been grounded in him also being the Son of God. In a most poignant passage, Forsyth spells out the nature of Christ's work:

> His work, consummated on the Cross, is yet larger than a deliverance at a historic point. It is the energy of the whole eternal person who culminated in that act. He does more than release us; he has to uplift and transform us. He does more than inspire the race, he completes it. He brings it to the glory for which it was destined by God. And for this no saintliest man could be enough. Nothing lower than the Holy God could re-hallow the guilty human soul. Only the creator of our destiny could achieve it.[87]

But if Jesus was 'the whole eternal person', in what sense can we meaningfully talk about his humanity? Can a pre-existent Christ be said to be a historical human being without there being a contradiction in terms? Forsyth believes that we can escape the problem if we adopt a doctrine of kenosis which culminates in a doctrine of plerosis.

We have already encountered the ideas of 'kenosis' and 'plerosis' in A E Garvie's discussion of Creation. Garvie most probably was drawing on Forsyth in his exposition. Be that as it may, Forsyth argues that the divine self-limitation which made creation possible and established the divine immanence in the world, is followed by a new creative act of kenosis in the Incarnation. This act is not simply a matter of extending the divine immanence in the world, since Forsyth insists that it is 'a unique, crowning and moral act of self-identification' which actually is 'older than the world'.[88] Some kenotic christologies become problematical when decisions have to be made concerning which attributes are given up by the pre-existent Christ and which are retained. For example, some scholars argue that in the incarnation the pre-existent Christ divested himself of his *relative* divine attributes (e.g. omnipotence, omniscience and omnipresence) in order to become related to the world, while the Logos retained his *immanent* divine attributes (e.g. truth, holiness and love). But if our experience of the pre-existent Christ is solely one of encountering him in the sphere governed by his *relative* attributes, how can we know beyond mere speculation that the Logos actually is not limited as we are and does in fact possess absolute truth, holiness and love? And, in any case, what grounds have we for making the distinction between *relative* and *immanent* attributes in the first place? How do we even know that kenosis takes place at the Incarnation?

Forsyth is alive to such problems. He speaks of kenosis as a 'mystery', accepting the alogical and paradoxical nature of what on rational grounds must be regarded as 'the inconceivability of the self-dispowering of the Eternal Son, and the self-retraction of his glory'.[89] We cannot go beyond the

---

[85]   Ibid., p 74.
[86]   Ibid., p 332.
[87]   Ibid., pp 280–1.
[88]   Ibid., p 316.
[89]   Ibid., p 306.

assertion of this paradox, so presumably all speculation regarding 'immanent' and 'relative' attributes must be ruled out. And it is perhaps with one eye on some of the problems associated with earlier kenotic theories that Forsyth invites us to talk about kenosis involving the attributes taking on 'a new mode of their being' rather than being simply 'renounced'.[90] He tells us that 'the self-reduction', or 'self-retraction', of God might be a better phrase than the 'self-emptying', and then suggests that God's attributes of omniscience and omnipotence are not destroyed at the Incarnation but 'reduced to a potentiality' or 'only concentrated'.[91] God being God possesses the maximum power of self-limitation to further the end of love, so the Logos became a man whose knowledge and power was reduced to a potential which through the life of Jesus slowly flowered until on the Cross and in the Resurrection it was perfected. This means that Christ 'became what he was, and not merely what it was in him possibly to be', and, therefore, that he achieved 'the reintegration of an old state'.[92] In finding his lost sheep, he regained the mode of being that he had left behind at birth. So kenosis gave rise to plerosis, fulfilment for redeemed humanity, who gain what was not theirs by right, and for Christ, who returns to a mode of being he once had by right.

The personality of Christ, according to Forsyth, reflects a twin movement potentially contained within every personality. On the one hand, there is our quest for God; while, on the other hand, there is God's saving quest for us. Forsyth calls these two currents within personal experience 'the two grand actions of spiritual being'.[93] At the centre of the being of Christ they came together like nowhere else 'in final peace and eternal power'.[94] On the one hand, the eternal Logos takes the conditions of this life to become the vehicle for God's revelation and our salvation. The ability of Jesus to sin during his earthly sojourn is rejected by Forsyth, and against those who argue that our Lord's inability to sin would remove him from normal moral tensions, and hence compromise his humanity, Forsyth puts forward three arguments. First, he suggests that Christ ultimately can save because he is God. If, however, he possessed the capacity to sin, his divinity would be thrown into question. Secondly, he argues that moral struggles would have been real enough to Jesus since the kenosis meant that he was not aware of his inability to sin. Then, finally, Forsyth believes that Jesus' special relationship with God was rooted in freedom and not bound by any necessary forces.

The second of the great actions within Christ defines God's movement towards persons. Forsyth argues that there is an essential dynamism within the trinitarian life of God, so the Father always has moved out in a relationship with the eternal Son, in and through whom creation and, hence, humanity came into being. And as the Father creates so the Father saves. God therefore becomes incarnate in a human life as our Redeemer. 'The two grand actions of spiritual being' form two modes of action within the personality of Christ. Forsyth illustrates what this involves: 'It is a polar movement, the reconciliation of two directions, two tendencies, and not the fusion of two quantities, and certainly not of two forces.'[95] One can detect here the kind of distancing from the classical two-natures christology that we might have expected from Forsyth's earlier comments. And, needless to say, he believes that each side of the polarity is protected by the union, the whole purpose of which is the salvation of the world. Kenosis must be complemented by plerosis if we are to do full justice to God-in-Christ.

90   Ibid., p 307.
91   Ibid., p 308.
92   Ibid., p 311.
93   Ibid., p 338.
94   Ibid.
95   Ibid., p 345.

Kenotic christologies were very popular during the latter part of the nineteenth and early twentieth centuries. John Macquarrie sets their importance to the wider theological scene in perspective when he says that kenosis is an important idea in Christian thought but that 'kenotic christologies . . . turned out to be no more than an episode in modern thinking about the person of Jesus Christ'.[96] Why was this so? First, pre-existence, it is argued, is not a central idea in the New Testament. It most likely was absent from the earliest traditions, and therefore it can be set to one side. But if this argument was applied across the board, many more items from the traditional doctrinal corpus would go as well – including, for example, the doctrine of the Trinity. Sometimes the most significant and important ideas have to be drawn out or at least inferred from earlier traditions. Forsyth, though, like other kenotists, relies heavily upon Philippians 2: 1–11, and the inference drawn from that passage that Paul taught the pre-existence of Christ. As is the way in biblical scholarship even that once rock solid conclusion has now been challenged! However, the idea of the pre-existence is clearly present in the New Testament, and increasingly so among the later writings. Whether it is believable of course is another matter. It could be that kenotic christologies are highly speculative theories which are only needed if one accepts the pre-existence of Christ. When incarnational language about God sending his son is understood *metaphorically* rather than literally the pre-existence of Christ is not implied, and the need for speculative kenotic theories (if not the important idea of kenosis) is removed.[97]

A second reason to doubt the adequacy of Forsyth's proposals centres upon his treatment of the sinlessness of Jesus. Can one who is incapable of sinning actually be fully human? Some will not be satisfied with Forsyth's arguments to support the idea that Jesus actually faced the moral dilemmas and ethical predicaments of normal human life. They will see in his christology the problem of all christologies 'from above', namely, the difficulty of safeguarding Christ's full humanity. His heavy commitment to the pre-existence of Christ makes it difficult for Forsyth to avoid repeating the error. One way out, and the way advocated by Macquarrie, is to take leave of the idea of the pre-existence of Christ, and thus completely break free from classical christology. Then the starting point fully becomes Christ's humanity, but problems from the opposite direction then start to loom concerning Christ's divinity.

Thirdly, whatever sympathy we may have with Forsyth's criticisms of the Chalcedon formula, there still needs to be an ontological or metaphysical explanation of what is taking place or exists in the God-man. Forsyth dismisses the ontology of substance so central to the classical view, preferring what he calls a metaphysics of 'personality' or 'conscience'. While his commitment to ontology in christology is perfectly clear,[98] just what is meant by his chosen alternative metaphysics of personality is far from clear, and nowhere in his writings is it fully worked out. The result, as Colin Gunton observes, is that Forsyth falls into the danger of becoming one of those 'who attempt to avoid ontology' only to end up running 'the risk of doing ontology badly'.[99]

Fourthly, the language of self-emptying is theologically helpful if it reminds us of God's true nature rather than in any way underwriting a denial of Christ's full deity. Gunton feels that Forsyth's choice of language unfortunately sometimes suggests that Jesus was less than fully divine. Terms like 'reduction' and 'retraction' are hardly less problematic than 'emptying'. What needs to be said

---

[96]   Macquarrie, *Jesus Christ in Modern Thought,* p 250.
[97]   Ibid., p 56.
[98]   Forsyth, *The Person and Place of Jesus Christ,* pp 354–5.
[99]   Gunton, *Yesterday and Today: A Study of Continuities in Christology,* p 172.

– and Forsyth comes close to saying it – is that in the Incarnation the self-emptying of Christ was the perfect example of God's full nature, rather than the revelation of a diminished Deity. This leads Gunton to the following conclusion:

> It seems thus not inappropriate to speak of a self-emptying of God, but only if it is understood in such a way as to be an expression rather than a 'retraction' of his deity. The self-emptying is part of God's fullness, for the heart of what it means to be God is that he is able to empty himself on behalf of that which is not himself. In other words, it is part of his love, through which he comes among us in our time and history to transform our existence from within.[100]

And, upon that positive note, we end our discussion of Forsyth's kenotic christology. It is an honest and attractive theory which seeks to explain how the Incarnation actually happened in history. We will now draw our discussion of the person of Christ to a close by referring to another interesting christological proposal from the more recent Reformed heritage.

Donald M Baillie: The Paradox of the Incarnation

Donald Baillie's *God was in Christ* remains one of the most important and influential treatments of the person and work of Christ to be written in English in the twentieth century. His theological starting point is the frank admission that some of the most important truths in Christianity are paradoxical in nature. In this respect, Baillie shows a clear affinity to Karl Barth, although there are some major differences between them in their material theological statements. But why is the language of paradox so central to the theological task? Baillie answers this question by saying that paradoxes 'are inevitable . . . because when we "objectify" [divine reality] all our judgments are in some measure falsified, and the higher truth which reconciles them cannot be fully expressed in words, though it is experienced and lived in the "I – and – Thou" relationship of faith towards God.'[101] Consequently, the Christian Faith ends in paradox at very crucial points, including the doctrine of the Incarnation.

Baillie turns to the witness of the New Testament, in general, and I Corinthians 15: 10 in particular, to isolate what he believes to be a universal Christian experience. In some way or another, every Christian knows what Paul is talking about when he says:

> But by the grace of God I am what I am, and his grace toward me has not been in vain. On the contrary, I worked harder than any of them – though it was not I, but the grace of God that is with me.

The Christian knows about what Baillie calls 'the paradox of Grace', namely, '. . . the conviction which a Christian man possesses, that every good thing in him, every good thing he does, is somehow not wrought by himself but by God'.[102] We are aware at one and the same time that we are not only totally responsible for what we have done, but also that whatever good came of it was directly caused by God. It is Baillie's belief that this paradox helps us to understand the mystery of the Incarnation.

---

100   Ibid.
101   Donald M Baillie, *God was in Christ: An Essay on Incarnation and Atonement* (London: Faber and Faber Ltd., 1961), p 109.
102   Ibid., p 114.

The 'God' who is witnessed to in the incarnational language of the New Testament is of a distinctive paradoxical kind. God places absolute demands upon us but gratuitously gives us all that is demanded; the Deity expects total obedience but actually supplies the obedience required; God asks us to work out our salvation but then does the work for us. The God who is encountered in Jesus, therefore, is the One who gives God's very self to us in such a way that by actually choosing to follow a course of action we are forced to attribute what is achieved to God. The Jesus of the Gospels, Baillie tells us, takes nothing as his due as a human being, but invariably attributes all the praise and glory to God: 'The God-Man is the only man who claims nothing for Himself, but all for God.'[103] The work of the Eternal, however, is prevenient in Jesus. He is 'the proto-type of the Christian life', therefore, in so far as to an absolute degree we can say that in his person was present 'the life of a man and yet also, in a deeper and prior sense the very life of God incarnate'.[104] He made human choices but all those choices, though really human, were 'wholly dependent on the divine prevenience'.[105] Baillie argues that when the Incarnation is viewed in this paradoxical way, justice can be done both to the legitimate concerns of those who want to stress the movement from God to humanity through a christology 'from above', and to the equally important concerns of those who want to start their christologies 'from below' with an emphasis upon the humanity of Jesus.

Baillie emphatically wants to avoid any suggestion that Jesus was less than fully human. Docetic tendencies are to be overcome in christology by anchoring all claims in the Jesus of History. And, as we have noted, Baillie believes that the gospels provide us with a clear picture of a man who experienced absolutely the paradox of: 'It was not I, God'. But, Baillie also sees the need to stress the prevenience of the work of God in Jesus' life. This is achieved by setting the Incarnation in a Trinitarian context. From the human life of Jesus we are driven back to his divine origin and place in eternity. If Jesus' life on earth is to be understood as an incarnation rather than as a theophany, attention, therefore, must be paid to the pre-existence of Christ, as well as to the way in which Jesus remains human after he left this world. Baillie suggests that the doctrine of the Trinity enables this to be done. Once again, 'figurative and symbolic' language is required 'to confess that while the life lived by Jesus was wholly human, that which was incarnate in Him was of the essence of God, the very Son of the Father, very God of very God';[106] while only Trinitarian thinking, he argues, can help explain how 'the divine Presence which [Jesus] brought into the world goes on for ever in the hearts of His people through the Holy Spirit'.[107]

Baillie's treatment of the person of Christ is significant for two reasons. First, he invites us to understand Jesus on the basis of a paradox which resonates with our experience, and of which Jesus becomes the prototype in an absolute sense with significant support from the witness of the New Testament. Baillie's proposal connects the Jesus of the Gospels with our experience in such a way that Jesus truly can be spoken of as 'the pioneer and perfecter of our faith', or as Baillie calls him 'the prototype of the Christian life', that is the *representative* man. Secondly, Baillie is alive to the problem which besets all christologies from below, namely, compromising Christ's divinity. Although he suggests that the difference between the paradox besetting us and that besetting Jesus is one of 'absolute degree', he also nevertheless speaks of 'the divine prevenience' in Jesus, and thus of a priority of the 'divine' over the 'human' in him. This makes the difference between us and Jesus

---

[103]   Ibid., p 127.
[104]   Ibid., p 129.
[105]   Ibid., p 131.
[106]   Ibid., p 151.
[107]   Ibid., p 153.

one of 'kind' and not just 'degree' – unless, that is, like many liberal theologians, we believe that, even as sinners, human beings remain in the image of God, and thus to some extent that there is in all of us a divine 'prevenience'. Be that as it may, Baillie helps us see the need to hold together the two christological approaches. While Christology 'from below' has 'chronological priority', as Macquarrie says, christology 'from above' has 'ontological priority'.[108] As is often the case, the truth lies less in an 'either–or' and more in a 'both–and'.

---

[108]   Macquarrie, *Jesus Christ in Modern Thought*, p 373.

CHAPTER 9

The Work of Christ

THE THEOLOGICAL requirement to distinguish between Christ's person and work does not entail their separation, since Christ's person inevitably is viewed through the lens of his work. As J S Whale has said, 'Christology and Soteriology belong together; they are no more separable than are the convex and concave aspects of one and the same curve.'[1] Within the period of the New Testament churches theories to explain Christ's work were well established. Various metaphors drawn from everyday experience were exploited as atonement theologies took shape. From the world of Jewish sacrificial system came the idea that Christ was the perfect sacrifice that wiped out human sin. Experience of military conflict provided the notion that the cross represented Christ's defeat of the Devil. From the slave market came the idea of Christ paying a ransom to set sinful people free. The law-courts provided the further motif of Christ paying the penalty and undergoing the punishment for human sin. Meanwhile the medical world threw up metaphors of healing and restoration. We often encounter these models of atonement operating side by side in theology, and there never has been a time when there was one agreed means of talking about Christ's work. Indeed, such is the monumental nature of that work that it takes a kaleidoscope of metaphors even to get close to doing it justice, and even then we will never fully penetrate the mystery.

There are two general lines of approach taken by theologians in seeking to account for Christ's work. The first views the atonement as a past event through which a transaction took place between God and Christ that in some way achieved reconciliation between God and sinners. According to this approach, the cross of Christ was constitutive for our salvation, and hence its unique bearer – whether we take 'our' to refer to the Elect or, ultimately, to the whole human race. Contrasted with this 'objective' view, we find an alternative model which focuses much more on what happens in the sinner's life when confronted with the life and teaching, death and resurrection of Jesus. This so-called 'subjective' approach sees Christ's work more in keeping with God's ongoing activity in creation rather than a unique and fresh divine initiative. Both approaches are represented in the theologies of the Reformed churches.

John Calvin: Penal Substitution

Calvin's understanding of the Atonement owed a great deal to Anselm who provided us with one of the classical interpretations of Christ's work. The great mediaeval archbishop understood human sin as our failure to give God due honour. The background to this idea lay in the feudal system of the Middle Ages, when society's stability rested in subjects pledging loyalty to their superiors. If due honour was not given, a disorder arose which could only be overcome by the subject paying a debt

---

[1]   J S Whale, *Victor and Victim: The Christian Doctrine of Redemption* (Cambridge: Cambridge University Press, 1960), p 58.

through compensation or by a fine. Making use of this analogy Anselm located the crux of the human problem in God's honour, which had been scorned by sinners; it needed satisfying. Jesus, therefore, according to Anselm's theory, became our penance, an offering given to satisfy God in the wake of our sin. The emphasis was upon what Christ does as a man on our behalf to satisfy a deeply offended Deity.

Calvin's understanding of the Atonement only differs materially from Anselm's satisfaction model. His focus is upon God's justice rather than the divine honour. Human beings have broken God's laws, and if the moral order is to have any real meaning, justice must be effected. An appropriate penalty must be paid if the relationship between God and human beings is to be restored. And that is achieved on the cross, where 'we escape the imputation of our sins to us' since justice has been done through the agency of Christ standing in our stead and receiving the punishment due to us.[2]

Calvin's doctrine of the atonement uses some important and familiar ideas. The cross, for example, is understood in terms of sacrifice. Jesus Christ voluntarily offers himself on our behalf as a vicarious sacrifice. The background may be strange to us, but originally the focus was on expiation of sin and not punishment for it. The blood of the Hebrew sacrificial system was believed to wipe away people's sins, so Christ's death came to be understood as a representative sacrifice on behalf of sinful humanity. The shedding of his blood was the means by which our sins were removed and an atonement for our sin was made. It was not just the means by which 'satisfaction' was achieved, but also it served 'as a laver . . . to wash away our corruption'.[3] The sacrifice satisfied the divine requirement for justice, and thus it appeased God's wrath. Note, however, that, in contrast to Jewish sacrificial ideas, the sacrifice was not just 'expiatory' but also 'propitiatory'. It was certainly an act used by God graciously to forgive sins, but it became for Calvin also an act performed by a Man to get God so to act. God consequently ends up being both the subject and the object of the transaction. The Deity's wrath is appeased and God therefore accepts Christ's self-offering as a substitutionary punishment. Christ takes upon himself the penalty which was really due to us. In the cross, therefore, God wipes out our sin and removes the strangle-hold of death; while, in the resurrection, Calvin claims that 'righteousness was restored and life raised up, so that his death manifested its power and efficacy in us'.[4]

Calvin's understanding of Christ's work has been widely influential in Reformed churches, and it has the undoubted merit of taking human sin absolutely seriously. The focus of salvation is placed well beyond anything that we can achieve for ourselves, being located in a past event which centres upon a transaction between the perfect and sinless Christ and the living God, whereby the punishment due to us is meted out to the One who stood in our stead. Some have major doubts about the adequacy of Calvin's view. Does it not reflect an impoverished view of God? A God who needs the divine justice to be met at all costs seems to reflect some of the worst features of human beings. Why cannot God just simply forgive? Why does the Deity need a sacrifice to force a saving initiative? It might be argued that Calvin has so stressed the theme of 'justice' in his concept of God that he fails to speak adequately of God's mercy. His penal theory has often been criticized, therefore, for the way it makes God seem more vindictive than loving. And, as we shall see later, this objection is central when Calvin's commitment to a doctrine of predestination produces the

---

[2]   Calvin, *Institutes*, 2,16,3.
[3]   Ibid., 2,16,6.
[4]   Ibid., 2,16.13.

unresolved contradiction 'between the conception of a God who foreordained man's fall and in consequence the perdition of the many, and the conception of the God whose holy love Christ's life and death revealed'.[5] An eternal law seems in danger of compromising God being love-itself.

A second criticism of Calvin's position suggests than any understanding of sacrifice in terms of 'propitiation' is inappropriate. Calvin's interpretation of scripture is said to be 'coloured by views of justice at the time', with the result that the idea that a debt can be paid to appease God's wrath becomes central.[6] Most biblical scholars do not believe that the New Testament texts which deal with Christ's sacrifice should be read as implying 'propitiation'. What is involved is 'expiation' – an act in which God takes the initiative rather than responds to a request. The God of wrath does not wait to be appeased but comes in love to forgive, and, of course, the idea that justice can be effected by an innocent receiving the penalty due to the guilty is at best pretty meaningless and at worst plainly abhorrent. It is rather difficult to see how a moral order could be sustained on such a basis, and the possibility of abuse is all too clear.

Thirdly, the argument is pressed that Calvin's theory says a lot about the removal of past guilt but very little about how people are renewed and remade in their present existence. To be sure, his understanding of the Holy Spirit, and its outworking in the Christian church and our individual and corporate lives, must be borne in mind; but, according to Calvin, Christ's benefits are God's gift to the Elect, and, consequently, there is no possibility that everyone can gain them. Paul Fiddes feels that Calvin fails to integrate fully Christ's benefits let loose through the Cross with 'the human response to God, and the healing of human personality here and now'.[7] How to speak meaningfully and convincingly about an event two thousand years ago, and in such a way that it shows how the reality of present day sin and evil are or can be overcome, seems a crucial issue that Calvin has not fully resolved.

Fourthly, we may wonder whether Calvin's emphasis upon the debt sinners owe to God leads to an understanding of Christ which makes him passively rather than actively obedient on the Cross. All that is needed by Calvin's view is that the debt is paid by Christ's merit. But if salvation is to be understood in terms of the healing and restoration of personalities, surely something more is needed than a cold, matter of fact, past transaction? How does the life and example of the Christ who was crucified affect the way we live today? Are we not inspired through Christ's obedience to live better lives? Therefore, as Fiddes remarks: 'Penal substitution simply achieves the wiping of a debt from the pages of a divine ledger', but 'the parable of the Prodigal Son should make us ponder whether such a ledger exists at all.'[8]

Friedrich Schleiermacher: The Satisfying Representative

The second line of approach to Christ's work centres upon the way in which the life and witness, death and resurrection of Jesus effect a vital and salvific moral influence upon our lives. Its roots can be traced back to Abelard, who put forward a view of atonement quite different from that of Anselm, although, it has to be said, he sometimes expressed more traditional 'objective' theories and

---

[5]   Sydney Cave, *The Doctrine of the Work of Christ* (London: University of London Press Ltd, and Hodder and Stoughton Ltd., 1937), p 169.

[6]   Paul S Fiddes, *Past Event and Present Salvation: The Christian Idea of Atonement* (London: Darton, Longman and Todd, 1989), p 98.

[7]   Ibid., p 99.

[8]   Ibid., p 101.

allowed them to sit alongside his 'subjective' alternative. Abelard rejects the idea that the Devil acquired the rights over men and women, and hence sets aside the theory that Christ's work consisted in the overthrow of the Devil and the return of liberated sinners to their rightful owner, the God and Father of our Lord Jesus Christ. Also dismissed is the notion that the sacrifice of God's Son could appease God's wrath over our sin. Abelard focuses instead on God's love, arguing that it is so great that it draws out of us a reciprocating love.

In Christ's sacrifice on the Cross, Abelard argues, we see the selfless culmination of a perfect life that is an example for us to follow. Through his love for us Christ has drawn us to God. As well as speaking about us being reconciled with God through Christ's love, Abelard also focuses upon that love to explain the way in which we are redeemed. The love revealed in Christ's death sets us free from slavery to sin. Abelard therefore places great confidence in the power of that love which was given its supreme incarnation in Christ's suffering and crucifixion. What happened in Jesus' life and death, then, was that all future history was given access to a power which transforms human life: 'No one has greater love than this, to lay down one's life for one's friends' (John 15: 13). Through the love displayed in Jesus a positive change in our lives is drawn out from us. Abelard's approach to the Atonement subsequently provided the basic path to be followed by liberal theology; it will be instructive, therefore, to consider how the theology of Christ's work was advanced by the so-called father of that theology.

Schleiermacher understands Christ's work in terms of the twin themes of redemption and reconciliation. Christ's redemptive activity is a mystical process whereby believers are received into the power of his God-consciousness and hence into his fellowship. What makes that fellowship possible is the way in which Christ's God-consciousness overcomes human sin. In Christ's life and death, the 'person-forming divine influence upon human nature' has not only been continued in an exemplary fashion but also it has been given fresh impetus.[9] Christ does not just affect individuals, since his work is concerned with human nature *per se.* In Christ God-consciousness has been 'implanted as a new vital principle', so his work is also 'world-forming'.[10] The communal dimension of this salvific process, according to Schleiermacher, cannot be over-stressed. Christ draws men and women into a new community, and it is within that community that the full benefits of his work are bestowed. So the precondition for people to experience redemption for themselves is two-fold. First, they should be open to the changes which the influence of God-consciousness can make upon their lives; while, secondly, they should actively seek the power of that God-consciousness, that is to say, the influence of Christ within the community called 'Church'. The Church-centredness and therefore the Christ-centredness of Schleiermacher's theology often has not been fully appreciated.

Christ's reconciling work is a similarly mystical process whereby believers are received into 'the fellowship of His unclouded blessedness'.[11] Again, we note the sense in which reconciliation like redemption involves entering into a personal relationship with Christ: ' . . . the communication of blessedness no less than the communication of perfection is given immediately in the assumption into vital fellowship with Christ.'[12] But this 'vital fellowship' has a communal dimension in so far as Christ's power to effect reconciliation, like that to effect redemption, is mediated through the Church. At the heart of this process of reconciliation is the forgiveness of sins. In the new relationship with

---

9   Schleiermacher, *The Christian Faith,* p 427.
10   Ibid.
11   Ibid., p 431.
12   Ibid., p 432.

Christ, believers encounter 'the general movement contrary to sin' which flows from Christ.[13] While they continue to remain aware of their sin, that awareness stems from 'the corporate life of general sinfulness' which remains with them, rather than has 'its source in [their] new life'.[14] Both personally and corporately those who turn to Christ through the Church experience 'a corporate feeling of blessedness' in which a knowledge of their sin remains, while the once damning crucial connection between sin and evil has been broken.[15] As Schleiermacher puts it: '. . . the redeemed man too, since he has been assumed into the vital fellowship of Christ, is never filled with the consciousness of any evil, for it cannot touch or hinder the life which he shares with Christ.'[16] We may wonder whether Schleiermacher has given significant attention to sin's gravity among believers. Were not German Christians in the post-war period conscious of evil? While in this world, do we ever possess a life which we *completely* share with Christ?

Schleiermacher holds Christ's person and work firmly together. This is plainly apparent when he speaks of Christ's work as a prophet, a priest and a king. He understands Christ's prophetic office, meanwhile, in a fairly conventional fashion as his teaching, prophesying and working miracles show how Christ is the last and final prophet. In his teaching, Christ fully expounded his priestly and kingly offices, since 'He proclaimed His mission to raise men to fellowship with God and to rule spiritually.'[17] What he taught was 'adequate' and 'inexhaustible' since it is the revelation of God, and therefore Christ is the bearer of the final revelation: 'No presentation of our relationship with God can arise outside the sphere in which Christ is recognized, which would not fall short of that revelation; nor can any possible advance within the Christian Church ever bring us to the point either of perceiving anything imperfect in the teaching of Christ Himself, for which we could substitute something better, or of conceiving anything which aids man's understanding of his relation to God more spiritually, more profoundly, or more perfectly than Christ has done.'[18] A more committed affirmation of Christ's uniqueness would be difficult to find. Jesus is the 'climax' and 'end' of prophecy in the further sense that through Christ 'the Spirit has been poured out', and hence 'nothing essential can be thought of which is still lacking to the kingdom of God.'[19] Everything that was prophesied in the past is now fulfilled. Finally, Schleiermacher argues that the significance of Christ's miracles lies in 'their immediate impressiveness',[20] but now there is distance between Christ and us 'our attention is directed away from the individual, more physical, miracles to the general spiritual miracle, which begins with the person of the Redeemer and is completed with the completion of His Kingdom.'[21] Faith in miracles, Schleiermacher opines, belongs to our faith in scripture rather than to our faith in Christ.

Christ's priestly office is described by Schleiermacher as 'His perfect fulfilment of the law (i.e. His active obedience), His atoning death (i.e. His passive obedience), and His intercession with the Father for believers'.[22] Before we consider each element in turn we need to note Schleiermacher's insistence upon the essential connectedness of the first two. He objects to the idea that the 'active'

---

[13]   Ibid., p 433.
[14]   Ibid., p 432.
[15]   Ibid., p 433.
[16]   Ibid., p 432.
[17]   Ibid., p 445.
[18]   Ibid.
[19]   Ibid., p 447.
[20]   Ibid., p 448.
[21]   Ibid., p 449.
[22]   Ibid., p 451.

obedience and 'passive' obedience belong to different phases of Jesus' work – the 'active' from the start of his public life up and until his arrest, with the 'passive' commencing at the arrest. Actually, they are bound up with each other: 'The action of Christ without the suffering could not have been redemptive, nor the suffering without the action reconciling; and on that account redemption cannot be ascribed to the active obedience alone, nor reconciliation to the passive obedience alone, but both to both.'[23]

But what does Schleiermacher mean by the 'active' and 'passive' obedience of Christ? Christ's 'active' obedience consists in the way that his life perfectly matched the divine will for him and fully expressed God-consciousness. This must not be understood as 'the perfect fulfilment of *divine law*', but rather as 'His perfect fulfilment of the *divine will*'. Nor should we speak as if 'Christ fulfilled the divine will *in our place or for our advantage*', thereby implying that we are 'relieved from the necessity of fulfilling it.'[24] Rather, the 'active' obedience of Christ makes it possible for us to be presented as pure before God. He achieves as new Adam what we fail to achieve as old Adam. And, through Christ's life operating within us, we are then also drawn to fulfil God's will, thereby receiving favour in God's sight.

Christ's passive obedience is centred upon his suffering. In order that we come to share in God's fellowship, Christ entered into the fellowship of sinful men and women like us. Incarnate in a world where evil abounds as the result of and hence the punishment for sin, Christ suffered evil which had not been caused by him: '. . . His suffering in this fellowship . . . was suffered for those with whom He stood in fellowship, that is, for the whole human race, to which He belongs, not only because no particular fellowship within the human race can be completely isolated, but also by His own deliberate choice.'[25] Christ, therefore, deliberately sympathizes with our sin, and through his suffering of the evil which arises from sin 'punishment is abolished, because in the fellowship of His blessed life even the evil which is in process of disappearing is no longer at least regarded as punishment.'[26] Christ's passion therefore reveals a completely selfless love, which in turn represents to us God's way with the world.

If we combine the thinking regarding both Christ's 'active' and 'passive' obedience, Schleiermacher believes that it is appropriate to call Christ 'our *satisfying representative*'.[27] Through his 'active' obedience Christ creates the circumstances whereby it is possible that God regards us in Christ as sharers in his act of obedience. Christ, therefore, became for us the source of a blessed life through making satisfaction to God. But Schleiermacher refuses to accept that this satisfaction was vicarious, since the act of Christ does not relieve us of 'the necessity of pursuing this spiritual life by our own endeavour in fellowship with Him'.[28] Turning to the 'passive' obedience of Christ, on the other hand, Schleiermacher is convinced that Christ's suffering was vicarious. He is equally clear, however, that this does not involve satisfaction since 'those who are not yet miserable must first become so in order to be received by Christ', and because Christ's suffering 'does not exclude other suffering of the same sort'.[29] Schleiermacher prefers the term 'satisfying representative' to that of 'vicarious satisfaction', thereby revealing his opposition to traditional atonement ideas like the 'penal

---

23   Ibid., p 453.
24   Ibid., pp 455, 456.
25   Ibid., p 457.
26   Ibid., p 458.
27   Ibid., p 461.
28   Ibid.
29   Ibid.

substitution' theory. He argues that Calvin ignores the connection which needs making between moral evil and punishment when he asserts that God punishes a sinless person instead of those actually responsible for evil. This idea presupposes 'a conception of the divine righteousness which has been transferred to God from the crudest human conditions'.[30]

The third office of Christ refers to his rule over the community of believers. Everything that the Church needs or requires for its life and mission emanates from this office. Christ called the church into being and he will sustain it until the end. Schleiermacher, therefore, affirms that 'among believers there is nowhere any lordship other than His alone'.[31] Christ's kingdom is one of grace: a kingdom of power which knows no limits to the influence that Christ has in the world, and a kingdom of glory which reflects 'the absolute blessedness to be found in Christ alone'.[32] Schleiermacher sees the relationship between church and state very much in the terms set down by Luther. The two kingdoms or 'swords' are to be kept separate from one another, with Christ's kingly power 'beyond all the resources of the civil power', since Christ is 'the climax and end of all spiritual kingship'.[33]

What assessment are we to make of Schleiermacher's proposals? He clearly eschews atonement theories which rest upon ideas of Christ's death satisfying God's honour, or appeasing God's wrath, or paying a price, or being a punishment inflicted by God and undergone on our behalf. Schleiermacher's alternative is to stress the inward change for the better which is brought about in members of the Church through Jesus. We can certainly hear echoes of Abelard in his proposals, but the influence of Irenaeus is also present. Irenaeus creatively employed the Pauline image of Christ as 'the second Adam' who restores sinful men and women to their pre-fallen condition. Christ successfully treads the ground upon which his sisters and brothers have failed; he does well what we have done badly; and he sums up afresh what it truly means to be human. Humankind, therefore, is presented before God perfect in the life and death of Jesus. The Second Adam does not just undo what had been caused by the First Adam, he also brings all things together in a new way. Irenaeus' theory, based upon the idea of 'recapitulation' (Ephesians 1: 10 *anakephalaiosasthai*), involves both the restoration of sinners to communion with God and the summing up of the whole of God's saving purposes in the Incarnation. When Schleiermacher defines 'the Redeemer' as 'the one in Whom the creation of human nature, which up to this point had existed only in a provisional state, was perfected' we certainly can hear the influence of Irenaeus.[34]

Schleiermacher's proposals have undoubted strengths. First, his critique of the traditions he inherited is perceptive and penetrating. He sees the inadequacy of speaking about Christ's work simply in terms of a transaction initiated in an event two thousand years ago; he highlights the way in which 'satisfaction' and 'penal' theories of the atonement often lead to an impoverished and sub-christian view of God and a sense of moral repugnance; and, he raises criticisms that 'might be ignorant' but 'could not easily be answered', for example, concerning the chronological separation of the 'active' and 'passive' obedience of Christ.[35] Following on from this, secondly, Schleiermacher correctly stressed the importance in any account of Christ's work of describing the way in which the life and death of Jesus effects changes in people's present day lives. He brings Jesus from past history

---

[30]   Ibid., p 460.
[31]   Ibid., p 468.
[32]   Ibid., p 470.
[33]   Ibid., p 472.
[34]   Ibid., p 374.
[35]   Cave, *The Doctrine of the Work of Christ*, p 198.

into the experience of the contemporary believer, thereby teaching us that, 'it is as we are in Christ and Christ in us that what He did for us becomes effective in us.'[36] Thirdly, Schleiermacher places both sin and salvation in a corporate context. While his theology is rooted in human experience, that experience is understood in a communal setting. At a time of rampant individualism in the West, Schleiermacher has much to teach us about the social and ecclesial dimensions of both our sin and salvation. Fourthly, Schleiermacher's attempt to locate Christ's work in his life and witness as well as his death reminds us of the need to maintain links between christology and soteriology. His understanding of Christ's redemptive work as the decisive expression of the person-forming divine influence upon human nature also means that he can maintain a proper link between redemption and creation. Fifthly, Schleiermacher does not view Christ totally in exemplarist terms. To be sure, he depicts Jesus as a perfect, human being who is our model to follow; and of course Jesus is the completion of the creation of humanity and a paradigm for a future humanity; nevertheless, Schleiermacher does not end there, since significantly he also speaks of Jesus as the Redeemer and Reconciler. We might say that the influence of Abelard has been complemented by that of Irenaeus.

Negative criticisms of Schleiermacher's proposals are not in short supply, however, particularly from those who wish to defend a more 'objective' emphasis in their atonement theories and hence accuse Schleiermacher's account of Christ's work of being overtly and one-sidedly subjective. This criticism can be understood in different ways. First, some argue that Schleiermacher's soteriology limits salvation to what is experienced in the contemporary Christian community. Redemption and reconciliation then become a present mystical experience which does not get challenged or enhanced by what scripture and tradition has to 'reveal' to us on the subject of our salvation. This raises the question as to whether 'experience' is a sufficient canon of theological adequacy. Secondly, Schleiermacher is accused of producing, in Cave's words, 'a theology of experience instead of a theology of the experienced.'[37] It is a moot point, of course, whether the latter can ever be fully separated from the former, but the gist of the criticism is clear: Schleiermacher ends up talking about humankind, rather than God. Cave suggests that Schleiermacher 'tended to make our poor experience the measure of what God is', and he accuses him of not doing justice to 'God's awful holiness' and 'God's holy love and grace.'[38] Thirdly, Gunton drives home the charge of subjectivity. He believes that Schleiermacher's proposals entail a shift from 'the exposition of doctrine to the articulation of the content of experience', with the result that Schleiermacher is held tightly in the grip of the rationalism of experience.[39] This, in turn, leads Schleiermacher to undervalue the central atonement ideas that 'on the cross Jesus in some way or other underwent the divine judgement on human sin.'[40] For Schleiermacher the cross 'stresses much more strongly the work of the historical Jesus in transmitting to an organic religious community the consciousness of God which he himself possessed in a unique and exemplary manner.'[41] Gunton therefore charges Schleiermacher with playing fast and loose with the Christian tradition: '. . . there can also be little doubt that this theologian has produced a reductionist account of the doctrine [of atonement],

---

[36]   Ibid., p 197.
[37]   Ibid., p 196.
[38]   Ibid., p 197.
[39]   Colin E Gunton, *The Actuality of Atonement: A Study of Metaphor, Rationality and the Christian Tradition* (Edinburgh: T & T Clark Ltd., 1988), p 12.
[40]   Ibid., p 13.
[41]   Ibid.

reductionist in the sense that he changes the meaning of key concepts into something else.'[42] But, in Schleiermacher's defence, we should recognise that erstwhile 'key concepts' sometimes lose their explanatory powers, and that they may need replacing with more meaningful ones if the content of the Christian faith is to be articulated in a coherent and comprehensive way. Why should our understanding of Christ's work be tied to concepts whose original meaning we now can hardly understand in our different culture, let alone find credible and helpful as explanatory aids? But, however much we may feel that Gunton's interpretation does not do justice to Schleiermacher's either intentions or achievement, and however much we may doubt the need to be defensive about the orthodox ways the Christian faith has been expressed, it cannot be gainsaid that Schleiermacher's proposals lose the objective significance of the cross within an account of the subjective effect of the work of the Redeemer upon us now.

The lesson to be learnt from this is the need to hold together what happened in Jesus' death with our contemporary experience of salvation. In many of the classical atonement treatments, the tendency is to emphasize the former at the expense of the latter. With Schleiermacher we are in danger of seeing the trend reversed. However, it is a mistake to think that he had no concern about the objective event. The issue is whether Schleiermacher did justice to it, and in one sense he clearly did not. As both Gunton and Fiddes note, Schleiermacher does not speak about the sense in which Jesus' alienation from God is at the heart of the cross's meaning and significance. The most significant feature of Christ's work, according to Schleiermacher, is the fact that, as Fiddes puts it, 'Christ's communion with God remained undisturbed and unbroken by his suffering and death.'[43] No account is taken of the cry of dereliction from the cross, nor of the sense of God-forsakenness and alienation from God which lay at the heart of the crucifixion. For Schleiermacher, therefore, it is not possible for the cry of dereliction to be what Gunton calls 'an expression of God's oneness with humankind in its alienation from him'.[44] Just as Schleiermacher's confidence that all possess God-consciousness may seem empirically false in a secular world, his refusal to acknowledge any loss of God-consciousness in Jesus may rob him of an important feature of his Redeeming work. Gunton draws the necessary conclusion: 'If it is the God-consciousness which saves, humanity is saved by a kind of christological triumphalism, by successful religiousness rather than by the "failure" of the cross.'[45]

Horace Bushnell and R J Campbell: Love Conquers Everything

We have noted Schleiermacher's heavy but not total reliance upon an exemplarist model to explain Christ's work. What unites Bushnell and Campbell, two Congregationalists, is their almost complete commitment to Abelard's approach.

Bushnell's opposition to Calvinism is as forthright as is his attempt to conceive Christ's work on the basis of the love displayed in his life and death. Love by nature is vicarious since those we love affect our lives. We laugh when our loved-ones laugh; we weep when our loved-ones are in a state of sorrow; and so it is with God. Whether we use the word 'suffer' in its old-fashioned or modern sense, we can say that Christ *suffers* the world. Bushnell completely rejects the notion of God's impassibility, preferring to image God according to God's self-revelation in Jesus rather than

---

42   Ibid., p 15.
43   Fiddes, *Past Event and Present Salvation: The Christian Idea of Atonement*, p 162.
44   Gunton, *Yesterday and Today: A Study of Continuities in Christology*, p 99.
45   Ibid.

the logic of Greek metaphysics. God is love, and the kind of love which is an essential attribute of God is suffering love. The love revealed in the cross, Bushnell argues, is the most powerful example of the suffering and sacrificial love which forever is radiating from God's life. What he has in mind is made clear in this very moving passage:

> Nay, there is a cross in God before the wood is seen upon Calvary; hid in God's own virtue itself, struggling on heavily in burdened feeling through all the previous ages and struggling on heavily now even in the throne of the worlds. This, too, exactly is the cross that our Christ crucified reveals and sets before us. Let us come then not to the wood alone, not to the nails, not to the vinegar and the gall, not to the writhing body of Jesus, but to the very feeling of our God, and there take shelter.[46]

So Christ's suffering is an explicit manifestation of God's suffering. Suffering is inherent in the nature of love.

But does this mean that for Bushnell Jesus' life and death are simply a revelation? No, since the Incarnation brings something new to God. Prior to the Christ, God had what Bushnell calls 'attribute power', from which we get some abstract idea of God; but with the Incarnation came 'cumulative power', a moral power 'gained by Him among men, as truly as they gain it with each other'.[47] So in Jesus' life and death God is encountered as a moral force which alters human lives for the good, a Love which reaches out for a reciprocating love. Bushnell, therefore, argues that Christ's work is an example of God's restoring and renewing love:

> Love is a principle essentially vicarious in its own nature, identifying the subject with others, so as to suffer their adversities and pain, and taking on itself the burden of their evils. It does not come in officiously and abruptly, and propose to be substituted in some formal and literal way that overturns all the moral relations of law and desert, but it clings to the evil and lost man as in feeling, afflicted for him, . . . encountering gladly any loss or suffering for his sake. Approving nothing wrong in him, but faithfully reproving and condemning him in all sin, it is yet made sin – plunged, so to speak, into all the fortunes of sin, by its friendly sympathy.[48]

Bushnell's understanding of atonement, then, is centred upon God's love, a love which suffers over our sinfulness, and a moral power which produces a change for the good in us, thus enabling us to be reconciled to God. As Bushnell says: 'Propitiation is an objective conception, by which that change, taking place in us, is spoken of as occurring representatively in God.'[49]

According to Bushnell, Christ's death should not be understood in terms of 'satisfaction', 'substitution' or as a 'punishment'. Nevertheless, he includes within his proposal a clear sense that sinners deserve and, unless they become penitent, will receive punishment. Justice and mercy are the two sides of God's love. In Bushnell's opinion, however, the responsibility for sin remains with the sinner; so the idea that an individual can take the blame for another's sin is ruled out. Nor does Bushnell interpret Christ's sacrificial death as expiatory. No one can take away our sin for us; the

---

[46] Horace Bushnell, *The Vicarious Sacrifice Grounded in Principles of Universal Obligation* (London: Stanhan and Co., 1871), p 35f.

[47] Ibid., pp 141–3.

[48] Ibid., p 7f. I was moved to read Bushnell's book after reading this quotation in David A Pailin, 'The Doctrine of Atonement: (2) Does it Rest on a Misunderstanding?' *Epworth Review*, 18:3 (September, 1991), pp 68–77.

[49] Ibid., p 450. Also quoted by Pailin in the above article.

buck stops with us. Therefore, it is difficult to argue that Bushnell takes sin lightly, or that his focus upon God's love in Christ leads to sentimentality. The effects of the world's sin are forever felt in God's being, just as the pain involved in Christ's sacrifice was experienced at the centre of God's life.

In the early years of the twentieth century a heated doctrinal debate broke out over the views of R J Campbell, the then minister of the City Temple, London. His liberal theology drew fervent opposition from those of a more orthodox disposition, in whose ranks belonged P T Forsyth. As the debate wore on, Campbell presented his views in *The New Theology* (1907). The doctrine of atonement which he outlined flows out of an essentially revisionist theology which maintains that we are not necessarily obliged to concur with traditional doctrines if they conflict with contemporary thinking. 'It is our duty in religion, as in everything else', he declares, 'to endeavour to express the content of spiritual experience in the forms which best accord with the mental dialect of our own day.'[50]

Campbell has no time for classical atonement theories, since they are based on ideas which are 'unethical', or 'intellectually and morally impossible'.[51] Two rhetorical questions tells us why Campbell dismisses classical atonement theories. 'Why in the world should God require . . . a sacrifice before feeling Himself free to forgive His erring children? And why should it be regarded as in any real sense a substitute for what is due from us, or any equivalent for what we should otherwise have to bear?'[52] How then does Campbell understand atonement? To answer that question he focuses upon the Jewish sacrificial system, in general, and the Day of Atonement, in particular. He argues that two ideas underpin sacrificial worship, namely, that the human race is one and that human beings reach fulfilment in God. Campbell then argues that the basic meaning of atonement is the coming together of God and persons: 'Atonement implies the acting together of God and man, the subordination of the individual will to the universal will, the fulfilment of the unit in the whole.'[53] At another point in his book, he offers a further definition:

> Atonement is the assertion of the fundamental unity of all existence, the unity of the individual with the race and the race with God. The individual can only realise that unity by sacrificing himself to it. To fulfil the self we must give the self to the All. This is the truth presumed in all ancient ideas of Atonement.[54]

So, according to Campbell, atonement does not necessarily involve ideas of 'escaping punishment for transgression' or 'placating a man-like God for offences committed against his dignity.'[55]

What causes the need for atonement is sin. Campbell understands sin as selfishness, the opposite of love. The only way of getting rid of sin is by 'the ministry of love', so the only atonement that is needed is rooted in love's ability 'to share to the uttermost in the painful consequences of sin, and by so doing break their power.'[56] Love can do this because essentially it is grounded in the spirit of self-sacrifice, and in Jesus we find the perfect example of such love. Campbell talks of Calvary as the complete victory over self-interest. But the cross was not the revelation of anything

---

50   R J Campbell, *The New Theology*, (London: Chapman and Hall, 1907), p 128.
51   Ibid., pp 115, 116.
52   Ibid., p 117.
53   Ibid., p 134.
54   Ibid., pp 139–40.
55   Ibid., pp 134, 140.
56   Ibid., pp 165, 169.

new, nor did it make possible a salvation which prior to it was not available. Rather, says Campbell, 'the death of Jesus is the focus and concentrated essence of this age-long atoning process, whereby selfishness is being overcome and the whole race lifted up to its home in God.'[57] Quite clearly this view does not allow for the belief that the Christ event is constitutive for our salvation.

So what role does Jesus play in the atonement? Campbell talks movingly about our Lord's life. His character exhibited a 'disinterested nobleness';[58] his life on earth clearly revealed 'the moral beauty of the faith, courage, and perfect self-devotion' of the man;[59] while 'a perfectly noble and unselfish life was crowned by a perfect sacrificial death.'[60] Both Christ's life and death were needed for there to have been 'a perfect self-offering' which subsequently gave rise to 'the greatest manifestation of the innermost of God that has ever been made to the world', while Jesus' life and death released 'a moral force, a spiritual dynamic greater than any before or since', one which is able to awaken in each one of us 'the true life, the eternal life, within our own souls.'[61] The atonement, therefore, concerns a change which the Christ event creates in our lives. Christ's self-sacrificial life and death provide us with the perfect example of what it means to be human. Campbell is so convinced of Jesus' ability to command reverence, and hence facilitate the necessary change within us, that he tells us: 'Show to the world the real Jesus; tell men how it came about that He had to die, and they cannot help but love Him.'[62]

But the problem is that they do not all love him. Sometimes they have committed the most heinous crimes in his name; often his challenge to change their ways and live less selfishly has gone unheeded. Has the depth of human sin been penetrated by Campbell? Can we so easily be forgiven for our part in the great atrocities of our age? Does Campbell really address the guilt which we feel for what we have done? At one point Campbell says this:

> But then, some one will say, what has the death of Jesus effected in the unseen so as to make it possible for God to forgive us? Nothing whatever, and nothing was ever needed. God is not a fiend, but a Father, the source and sustenance of our being and the goal of all our aspirations. Why should we require to be saved from Him?[63]

Campbell is correctly pointing out by inference some of the less wholesome features of classical atonement theory, but critics will feel that God's judgement has been watered down in this analysis of Christ's work. The cross, they will argue, ends up having no effect on God, and forgiveness is granted at little cost to ourselves. Is Campbell's model of 'Father' adequate? That, at rock bottom, is the issue.

---

57   Ibid., p 166.
58   Ibid., p 122.
59   Ibid.
60   Ibid., p 123.
61   Ibid., pp 123–4; 126, 174.
62   Ibid., p 126.
63   Ibid., p 175.

John McLeod Campbell: Vicarious Repentance and Intercession

History is littered with the names of those whose achievements were not recognized in their life-time. Established orthodoxies are rather difficult to penetrate, and the ancient drive to count as orthodox doctrine only those assertions which can be shown to be congruent with apostolic teaching might lead us to think that originality is the very least expectation within theology. Nevertheless, Christianity has repeatedly thrown up influential figures who have pushed its tradition in new directions, even if they did not live to see it. Occasionally, though, the church has had the grace to admit its fallibility over an earlier judgement. This was the case perhaps in the Church of Scotland when the University of Glasgow conferred an honorary Doctorate of Divinity upon John McLeod Campbell in 1868. At the very least, Campbell went to his grave knowing that his theology was recognized if not universally accepted.

Campbell was minister of the Church of Scotland parish of Rhu in Argyllshire when he was tried and convicted of heresy by the Kirk in 1831. In his preaching he had denied a basic tenet of the Calvinist system by asserting that Christ had made atonement for all sinners and not just the Elect. Setting the doctrine of predestination to one side was bad enough for many members of the Assembly, but when Campbell openly attacked the Westminster Confession, he was clearly heading for trouble – even if he claimed somewhat confusingly that his own teaching was in conformity with it! So a faithful minister, whose theology was not worked out sufficiently to be defended on the floor of the Assembly, was driven out of his pastorate. Friends enabled him to continue a ministry within a building in Glasgow for more than twenty-five years. During this time, Campbell wrote *The Nature of Atonement and its Relation to Remission of Sins and Eternal Life*.[64] It became one of the most influential treatments of Christ's work. Macquarrie has recently described it 'as probably the best theological treatment of atonement to be found in modern writing on the subject'.[65]

Campbell's starting point is Jonathan Edwards's suggestion that, in his atoning work, Christ either could 'endure for sinners an equivalent punishment' or 'experience in reference to their sin, and present to God on their behalf, an adequate sorrow and repentance'[66] Edwards clearly felt that the second alternative was so out of the question that it did not merit further consideration, and as a result he advocated the Calvinist idea that Christ suffered the divine wrath for our sins. But Campbell opposes penal doctrines of the Atonement, especially when they are coupled with a doctrine of election which maintains that Christ only died for a chosen few. As far as he is concerned, love was the cause rather than the consequence of Christ's work, and therefore the atonement was universal and not limited in scope. Christ died for all, not for a favoured pre-ordained few. A limited atonement 'makes the work of Christ to be no longer a revelation of the name of God, no longer a work revealing that God is love.'[67] In fact, Campbell is critical of all accounts which interpret Christ's work via all too human ideas about honour, justice, punishment or even love. We need to view it instead 'by its own light', believing the gospel which maintains that there is forgiveness with God, and that God's love is such that God reaches out towards human beings even though we are hostile to God.[68]

---

[64]   John McLeod Campbell, *The Nature of Atonement and its Relation to the Remission of Sins and Eternal Life* (Cambridge: Macmillan and Co., 1856).

[65]   John Macquarrie, *Jesus Christ in Modern Thought,* p 402.

[66]   Campbell, *The Nature of Atonement,* p 136.

[67]   Ibid., pp 61–2.

[68]   Ibid., p 113.

While Campbell objects to the theory of penal substitution, he is not content with an overtly subjective moral explanation of Christ's work. Christ has achieved something for us on Calvary that we could not do for ourselves. Campbell argues, therefore, that we must do justice to the objective side of the Christ event by focusing upon Christ's self-sacrifice. The suffering of Christ is not a punishment: 'The *sufferer suffers* what he suffers *just through seeing sin and sinners with God's eyes, and feeling in reference to them with God's heart.*'[69] Through this suffering, we have revealed to us both the full scale of human wickedness and the extent of God's love. It tells us what God has done and will still do for us. In other words, Christ's work has both *retrospective* and *prospective* dimensions.

Viewed retrospectively, Christ deals with us on God's behalf by providing a perfect witness of divine love. Campbell is clearly influenced by Ritschl who stresses the value of Christ's life, and the benefit which we can gain from following his display of perfect personhood. Christ's work, therefore, was to show us the Father, to bear witness on behalf of God, and to manifest God's unchanging love – a love which remains the basis of our hope even though we seek to destroy ourselves. In Christ's suffering we encounter the suffering of divine love. So, according to Campbell, Christ honours the Father before human beings with a perfect display of suffering love. But viewed retrospectively, Christ's work also involves Christ dealing with God on our behalf by offering to God a perfect confession of our sins. Vicarious punishment has given way to vicarious repentance. Campbell describes Christ's repentance in the following oft-quoted words: 'This confession . . . must have been *a perfect Amen in humanity to the judgment of God on the sin of man.*'[70] Christ's loving self-sacrifice, the suffering of one without sin for the sins of others, was vicarious and expiatory. It was the voice of the divine love coming from humanity, offering for man a pure intercession according to the will of God, offering that prayer for man which was the utterance alike of love to God and love to man – that prayer which accorded with our need and the Father's glory as seen and felt in the light of the Eternal love by the Son of God and our Brother.'[71]

When he turns to consider the prospective dimension of Christ's work, Campbell first of all argues that Christ's witness on behalf of God not only is 'a light *condemning* our darkness', but also is '*the intended light of life for us*' and hence participation in eternal life.[72] Then, secondly, when he turns to the prospective dimension of Christ dealing with God on our behalf, he argues that Christ not only made confession for our sins but also intercedes for us 'in conscious righteousness as well as conscious compassion and love'[73] By doing this our alienation from God is overcome.

Campbell's treatment of Christ's work develops an interesting and helpful variation upon the classical 'satisfaction' atonement model. The issue of God's righteousness in the face of human sin is met by an equivalent or adequate sorrow and repentance, rather than by an equivalent or adequate punishment. Many will agree that this constitutes a higher, more excellent and spiritual form of satisfaction. Also they will warmly welcome an account of Christ's work which includes our Lord's life as well as his death. And, further, they will support a view which stresses the ongoing fruits of the Christ event as much as its significance as an historic event. The prospective dimension of Christ's work, in which we come to share in Christ's eternal life, is made possible, therefore, by the retrospective tackling of our sins by Christ. However, some will wonder why the idea of vicarious

---

[69]   Ibid., p 116.
[70]   Ibid., p 134.
[71]   Ibid., p 147.
[72]   Ibid., p 151.
[73]   Ibid., 175.

repentance is ultimately free of the problems which beset the idea of vicarious punishment. Should I expect someone else to do for me what I really should be doing for myself? And, as Cunliffe-Jones points out, in the final analysis there seems to be a contradiction at the heart of Campbell's thesis.[74] Campbell argues, as we have seen, that Christ's confession contains 'all the elements of a perfect repentance in humanity for all the sin of man . . . excepting the personal consciousness of sin'.[75] But can someone repent of a sin of which they are unconscious?

P T Forsyth: The Cross As The Great Confessional

The work of Christ lies at the heart of Forsyth's theology. This is not surprising since he maintains that 'some real apostolic belief in the real work of Jesus Christ' is essential to the existence of the church.[76] Forsyth warns against any devaluing of the work of reconciliation: 'If you move faith from that centre you have driven *the* nail into the Church's coffin. The Church is then doomed to death, and it is only a matter of time when she shall expire.'[77] Forsyth was concerned, of course, much less with the Church's survival than with the world's salvation. He believed that God's reconciling work in Jesus Christ was the only basis upon which 'human society can . . . continue to exist in final unity'.[78] Jesus Christ therefore is constitutive of the world's salvation.

Forsyth laments the way in which liberalism 'beclouds' and 'robs' Christianity of 'the power of moral conviction by reducing the idea of sin and dismissing the note of guilt'.[79] We need to recognize, instead, that we stand as sinners before the holiness of God, guilty and at the mercy of divine justice. Forsyth argues that theology must return to a proper stress on God's holiness and recognise that human guilt stirs 'the anger of a holy God' and produces 'separation from Him'.[80] Our sinfulness is described in lurid detail: 'active hostility' to God and 'enmity against God'.[81] Sin so penetrates our human condition that even our ability to respond to Christ had to be created afresh. Since God by nature is holy, sin causes offence; the moral order has been usurped, and, if any sense of justice is to be maintained, a penalty must be paid and God must be satisfied. God's judgement upon human sinfulness cannot be sidestepped; it is just as much part of the divine character as God's love: 'The judgement of God is perfectly compatible with His continued love, just as the father's punishment is perfectly compatible with his love for his children.'[82] Those who consider that the idea of God's judgement is morally repulsive, Forsyth argues, forget that God does not possess the power to overturn the divine nature. God is holy, and if eternal righteousness and holiness is to be set up and maintained, God must exercise judgement over all contrary forces. What else should we expect?

> The holiness of God was God as holy. When that holiness is wounded or defied, could God be content to take us back with a mere censure or other penance and the declaration that He was holy? We could not respect a God like that. Servants despise indulgent masters.[83]

[74] H Cunliffe-Jones, *Christian Theology Since 1600* (London: Gerald Duckworth & Co. Ltd., 1970), pp 91–2.
[75] Campbell, *The Nature of Atonement,* pp 135–6.
[76] P T Forsyth, *The Work of Christ* 2nd. ed. (London: Independent Press Ltd., 1938), p 4.
[77] Ibid., p 53.
[78] Ibid., p 9.
[79] Ibid., p 229.
[80] Ibid., p 80.
[81] Ibid., pp 19, 20.
[82] Ibid., pp 118–19.
[83] Ibid., p 131.

So how is God to be satisfied? How is the penalty for the human race's sin – what Forsyth calls 'solidary sin' – to be met?[84] Where can our pardon be found?

We can clear a way for a description of Forsyth's understanding of Christ's work by noting some of the ideas associated with atonement theories that he rejects. He refuses to accept the notion that the atonement placated an angry God,[85] or that it is 'the touchy honour of a feudal monarch that was to be dealt with at the head of the world'.[86] Nor is reconciliation to be conceived as occurring due 'to some third party coming between us and God, reconciling God on the one hand and us on the other'.[87] Reconciliation is the end for which atonement is the means. Since the atonement was made by God it is therefore 'objective' – 'Any atonement made by man would be subjective, however much it might be made for man by his brother, or by a representative of entire Humanity.'[88] Christ's work was not 'an object-lesson of God's love';[89] it was rather 'the divine initiative as an act' whereby God's justice is met and God's mercy is bestowed in the cross.[90] Forsyth rejects the idea that atonement involves 'a change of affection' in God:

> Reconciliation is not the result of a change in God from wrath to love. It flows from the changeless will of a loving God. No other view could make the reconciliation sure.[91]

Nor does Forsyth sanction the classical substitutionary view of atonement:

> . . . we are not disposed to speak of substitution so much as of representation. But it is representation by One who creates by His act the Humanity He represents, and does not merely sponsor it. The same act as disburdens us of guilt commits us to a new life.[92]

Christ takes 'the penalty of sin', but Forsyth refuses 'to speak of His taking its punishment'.[93] And the notion that Christ suffered an equivalent of the punishment due to the whole collective human race is firmly rejected.[94]

In certain respects, Forsyth follows the path taken by McLeod Campbell, but where Campbell speaks of Christ as a representative who vicariously confesses our sin before God, Forsyth argues that he confesses 'God's holiness in His judgement upon sin'.[95] The context in which this takes place is a meeting between persons, and the act by which reconciliation between the sinner and the holy God is achieved involves change by *both* parties. If the classical theories tend to express an objective change in God, moral influence and exemplarist alternatives tend towards the other extreme by emphasising the subjective change which occurs in the sinner. Forsyth argues that both emphases are required in an adequate doctrine of Christ's work. To be sure, Fiddes suspects that Forsyth ends

84	Ibid., p 189 and *passim*.
85	Ibid., pp 89–90.
86	Ibid., p 231.
87	Ibid., p 88.
88	Ibid., p 93.
89	Ibid., p 101.
90	Ibid., p 69.
91	Ibid., pp 105 and 180.
92	Ibid., p 182.
93	Ibid., p 162.
94	Ibid., pp 181–2.
95	Ibid., p 149.

up stressing the 'one event in the past' at the expense of 'the salvation which we experience', but Forsyth might be forgiven for this when we remember that he was trying to counter what he considered to be mistaken subjective emphases.[96] Not surprisingly he stresses the sense in which 'the moral adjustment of man and God' takes place in one holy, loving, mighty, final and eternal act'.[97] His priorities are quite clear when he argues that Christ's work on God is the prerequisite for his work on persons. He suggests for example that ' . . . we could not have full security except by trust of an objective something, done over our heads, and complete without any reference to our response or our despite.'[98]

But what was the 'objective something' which achieved the reconciliation between God and sinners? What does Forsyth understand by the atonement? The heart of the matter lies in God's act by which the divine judgement on sin fell upon the sinless Eternal Son of God. In essence it was a case of God reconciling God with no third party being involved. In his crucifixion, Christ as 'the representative of the whole race' presented to God 'a perfect racial obedience', that is to say, 'He presented before God a race He created for holiness.'[99] Therefore, the work of redemption is linked, and in a sense made continuous, with the work of creation. But Forsyth not only looks back, he also looks forward. He tells us that Christ 'represents before God not a natural Humanity that produces Him as its spiritual classic, but the new penitent Humanity that His influence creates.'[100] As our representative, through his life and death, in an act of self-sacrifice and obedience, Christ made confession for us. This act saw God making Christ to be sin for us and us righteous in Christ. Therefore, according to Forsyth, 'The real ground of our forgiveness is not our confession of sin, and not even Christ's confession of our sin, but His agonised confession of God's holiness, and its absorbing effect on us.'[101] Christ took our guilt upon himself and 'spread it out as it is before God', thus experiencing the reality of sin 'as only the holy could, as God did'.[102] So, on the cross, Christ secured our liberation as God imposed upon him the penalty for our sin. His obedience involved a penal sacrifice, but Forsyth argues that this was not in the sense that 'God punished Christ' or that 'Christ was in our stead in such a way as to exclude and exempt us'.[103] Rather it was that 'He bore God's penalty upon sin.'[104] Forsyth's approach to Christ's work therefore centres upon 'solidary reparation' rather than the old idea of 'substitutionary expiation'.[105] Christ makes an adequate confession instead of receiving a punishment equivalent to that deserved by the whole human race.

Forsyth understands the atonement as the means by which the whole of humanity was reconciled. A change of relationship takes place, a new sense of community results – the Church is born. Forsyth is very dismissive of individualism in religion. The collective sin of the race calls for 'a collectivist redemption'.[106] Therefore we enter into salvation as we join the body of Christ and become part of what has already been achieved for us: 'What He bought . . . was the Church, and

---

[96]   Fiddes, *Post Event and Present Salvation: The Christian Idea of Atonement*, p 106.

[97]   P T Forsyth, *The Justification of God: Lectures for War-Time on a Christian Theology* (London: Independent Press Ltd, 1948), p 69.

[98]   Forsyth, *The Work of Christ*, p 187.

[99]   Ibid., pp 116 and 129.

[100] Ibid., p 193.

[101] Ibid., pp 214–15.

[102] Ibid., p 159.

[103] Ibid., p 146.

[104] Ibid., p 147.

[105] Ibid., p 164.

[106] Ibid, p 114.

not any aggregate of isolated souls.'[107] The work of Christ, therefore, is final both in nature and effect. What we all discover that we most need has in fact already been done for us. As Forsyth puts it, 'The last judgement is past.'[108]

Forsyth presents us with one of the most important accounts of Christ's work of modern time. He forces us to face up to the depth and gravity of human sin. Before God's holiness we are guilty, and in breach of the moral order. Forsyth then presents the cross in such a way that, as Colin Gunton puts it, it becomes 'a way to express theologically a living relation between God and the world.'[109] But the holy God can only achieve the reconciliation between God and sinners if moral right and wrong is taken seriously, so God's judgement cannot be set to one side if any sense of justice is to prevail. The divine justice is found by Forsyth in God's action of providing the means within history of our redemption. This enables renewed relationships with God and other men and women to be created. However, even such a sympathetic supporter of Forsyth's position as Colin Gunton is forced to admit that Forsyth's proposal 'may appear to lack a grounding in actual human life.'[110] Many think that Forsyth is stronger on rhetoric but weak when it comes to setting out the way by which God's justice becomes real in human life. Indeed, there is something almost mystical, even downright incomprehensible and mysterious, in the way he speaks of us being 'absorbed' into the effects of an event two thousand years ago. And sceptics will press the point that the present state of the world hardly warrants Forsyth's confidence about the 'finality' of Christ's work. They will perhaps want to know how a past event has a bearing on the present, rather than hear assurances that it will be fully effective in some long-awaited future.

D M Baillie: Historical Outcropping of Eternal Atonement

Donald Baillie makes a number of points which rather helpfully enable us to draw this discussion to a close. He reminds us of important issues of principle which we have already encountered. First, Baillie establishes a clear connection between the life and teaching of Jesus and his death. In other words, he holds together Christ's person and work. What took place in the Cross already had been evident in our Lord's ministry. In life as well as in death, Jesus was consciously committed to the love of sinners. This love for them took him to Calvary. Baillie puts it like this:

> . . . His love was bearing their sins at infinite cost as He approached the Cross. That was the passion of Christ: and all this is even more important than the question as to how far He interpreted His coming death. For it is entirely congruous with the whole meaning and method of the Incarnation that He who, on the ultimate interpretation, died 'for the sins of the whole world' should in His own consciousness be mainly concerned with those sinners who were His immediate environment, the 'lost sheep of the house of Israel' in His own time.[111]

So the Atonement is the culmination of the Incarnation.

---

[107] Ibid.
[108] Ibid., p 160.
[109] Gunton, *The Actuality of Atonement*, p 107.
[110] Ibid., p 109.
[111] Baillie, *God Was in Christ*, p 184.

Secondly, it is clear that the first Christians viewed Jesus' life and teaching from the perspective of the significance of his death for them and the whole world. If it had not been for the cross it is doubtful that Jesus would have entered the annals of history; therefore it is quite clear that Christ's work and the Atonement are at Christianity's centre. When the early Christians looked back at Calvary they understood it in terms of God's redeeming purposes for the world. Baillie reminds us that, "in discoursing of the love that was shown in the Cross of Christ the New Testament is never able to stop short of tracing it up-stream to the eternal love of God dealing sacrificially with the sins of the world."[112] However, the church came to express its understanding of Christ's work, it is clear, therefore, that the earliest Christians were confident that it was rooted in an act of God done for them and the whole world.

Thirdly, Baillie reminds us that the act of God in question did not take place in response to anything meritorious that human beings had done, nor does it imply a change of heart on God's part. Baillie insists that the New Testament idea of atonement centres upon the concept of 'expiation' and not 'propitiation'. The Christian doctrine of atonement should not be understood as implying the appeasement of an offended and angry Deity: ' . . . the New Testament does not speak of God being reconciled to man, but of man being reconciled to God, and of God as the Reconciler, taking the initiative in Christ to that end.'[113] Nor should Christ's work be understood as invoking a change of attitude in God towards human beings. As Baillie says: 'Throughout the whole of [the] New Testament material there is no trace of any contrast between the wrath of God and the love of Christ, or of the idea that God's attitude to sinners had to be changed by the sacrifice of Christ from wrath and justice to love and mercy.'[114] God's love and mercy towards sinful humanity must always be understood as the 'cause and source' of the process of reconciliation and not its *result*.[115] It was God who provided the sacrifice for the atonement.

Fourthly, Baillie argues that the so-called 'objective' and 'subjective' interpretations of the atonement are both necessary in any adequate understanding of Christ's work. There is a clear sense in which the Atonement is '"an objective" reality, something done by Christ, something ordained and accepted by God, in "expiation" of human sin, quite apart from our knowledge of it and its effect upon us;' but, equally clear is the way in which it is 'a "subjective" process, a reconciling of us to God through a persuasion in our hearts that there is no obstacle, a realizing of His eternal love'.[116] After years of theological feuding between the advocates of the rival models of interpretation, Baillie reminds us that both are needed and complement each other in a complete picture.

Finally, Baillie offers some important observations about the status of the Atonement, and the sense in which it is a unique event that has a bearing upon our possibility of salvation. He is quite clear that 'the whole Christian life rests upon a doctrine of the forgiveness of sins which implies a redemptive sin-bearing, a costly atonement, in the heart of God.'[117] But he rejects any argument which implies that before Calvary God was unforgiving and merciless. He tells us that 'God's reconciling work cannot be confined to any one moment of history.'[118] God's atoning work was going on before Christ, and it is continuing 'in every age in the lives of sinful men, whose sins

---

[112] Ibid., p 189.
[113] Ibid., p 187.
[114] Ibid., p 186.
[115] Ibid., p 188.
[116] Ibid., pp 197–8.
[117] Ibid., p 190.
[118] Ibid., p 191.

He still bears'.[119] There has never been, nor will there ever be a time when God's reconciling work is absent. Baillie quotes the well-known statement of C A Dinsmore to illustrate his point: 'There was a cross in the heart of God before there was one planted on the green hill outside Jerusalem.'[120] Nor is 'the sacrificial death of Christ on the Cross . . . the end of His atoning work', since it 'makes possible His entry into the heavenly sphere where His self-offering goes on for ever.'[121] The cross of Christ is that historical point at which we have revealed to us 'the actual outcropping of the divine Atonement'.[122] It is not the case that in the cross God does something new, but rather that we encounter the eternal nature of God's forgiveness and mercy in an historical event. What was and is *always* in God's heart has been *clearly* displayed and *decisively* made clear. To use some alternative language, we might say that Jesus did not so much constitute salvation's possibility as decisively re-present it to us.[123]

119	Ibid.
120	Ibid., p 194.
121	Ibid., p 196.
122	Ibid., p 201.
123	The term 'decisively re-represent' is borrowed from Schubert M Ogden.

Reflections and Observations

The previous discussion has displayed something of the range and richness of Reformed theology. It has also reflected the wider and more ecumenical theological scene – not least because some of the Reformed theologians that we have considered have been principal contributors to it. As we have proceeded, I have raised critical comments and offered judgements about the theological ideas we have been discussing. Part 3 will now be brought to a close by making four points, each of which builds on insights that have already been flagged up in the discussion.

1.   All the classical views of sin tend to view it in overtly individualistic ways through masculine eyes. During the last quarter of the twentieth century, we have been made to see that these were inadequate by liberation and feminist theologians. To some extent, the criticisms of the liberation theologians were already anticipated by Reinhold Niebuhr, and with hindsight it may well be that Niebuhr had already presented a more balanced, realistic and empirically grounded understanding of the Christian doctrine of sin than is evident in their own alternatives. Nevertheless, it cannot be gainsaid that Latin American liberation theologians are absolutely right to criticize views of sin which consider it, in the words of Gustavo Gutierrez, 'as an individual, private, or merely interior reality – asserted just enough to necessitate a "spiritual" redemption which does not challenge the order in which we live.'[1] There is a need to develop a more corporate and collective view of the phenomenon. In another book, Gutierrez makes it very clear what he has in mind:

> Sin is present in the denial that a human being is sister or brother to me. It is present in structures of oppression, created for the benefit of a few. It is present in the spoliation of people's, cultures, and social classes. Sin is the basic alienation. For that very reason, sin cannot be touched in itself, in the abstract. It can be attacked only in concrete historical situations – in particular instances of alienation. Apart from particular, concrete alienation, sin is meaningless and incomprehensible.[2]

Therefore, as far as liberation theology is concerned, any true liberation will need to be radical and possess a social and political dimension. Such a liberation, Gutierrez tells us 'is the gift which Christ offers us'.[3] Without in any way disputing this – after all we should all know from experience that the world is not changed by simply changing individuals – the much needed thrust of liberation theologians is somewhat blunted by their tendency so to allocate sin to the oppressors in social conflicts that it leaves the oppressed as seeming paragons of virtue. One only needs to be a casual

---

[1]   Gustavo Gutierrez, *A Theology of Liberation: History, Politics and Salvation* (Maryknoll, NY: Orbis Books, 1973), p 175.

[2]   Gustavo Gutierrez, *The Power of the Poor in History: Selected Writings* (Maryknoll, NY: Orbis Books, 1983), p 62.

[3]   Gutierrez, *A Theology of Liberation: History, Politics and Salvation,* p 176.

reader of history to know that there is an unfortunate tendency for yesterday's oppressed to become tomorrow's oppressors. And, further, a whole vast area of personal ethics can so easily be sidelined as unimportant if an unfortunate stress upon individual sin is overcome by an opposite and equally unfortunate emphasis upon collective sin. While the former cannot be fully understood outside the context of the latter, it is equally true that any credible concern to be ethical has not finished when it has worked out a viable social ethic.

The feminist challenge to classical views of sin is somewhat different but no less powerful. Daphne Hampson notes that sin has classically been interpreted as pride: 'The major tradition from Augustine through Luther . . . sees sin primarily as pride; sin is that self-centredness whereby the creature in his *hubris* pretends to be adequate of himself, and so sets himself up in the place of God, refusing to be dependent.'[4] In Reinhold Niebuhr's analysis there is a second form of sin, namely 'sensuality', the retreat from the self to become taken up within the world. Hampson points out that Kierkegaard viewed 'pride' and 'sensuality' as gender specific. Pride is 'the manly form of despair', by which we try to be self-sufficient, while sensuality is the 'womanly' form of it – 'the despair of not willing to be yourself.'[5] In Kierkegaard's opinion, then, there would seem to be a form of sin appropriate to each of the sexes, and it is the charge of some feminist theologians that the classical theological tradition in its understanding of sin has presented an overview that is inapplicable to everyone's situation. It has been structured for the temptations which beset the male individual:

> Much theology has indeed been written by men divorced from the daily round of chores, from the human lifecycle of caring and nurturing; theology has been a pre-occupation of monks, bishops and professors. No wonder that the human being whom they take as the norm is the isolated male.[6]

The classical tradition has 'spoken' to men, but women's context and concerns have been largely left out of account; it has failed to address the typically women's sin, which, quoting Judith Plaskow, Hampson defines as 'the failure to take responsibility for self-actualization.'[7]

My experience suggests that it is overstating the case to argue that the two forms of sin delineated here are completely gender specific. I have come across many men who seem inhibited by so-called women's sin, while *hubris* has not escaped a good few women I know – some of them being card-carrying feminists to boot! Nevertheless this should not diminish the importance of the point being made, namely, that the classical doctrine of sin has suffered from a onesidedness which has failed to address the concerns and needs of large numbers of people, many of them women. An adequate doctrine of sin – and, hence, of salvation – must do justice to people like the following woman (even if this 'woman' does not speak for all women and addresses the concerns of some men):

---

4   Daphne Hampson, 'Reinhold Niebuhr on Sin: A Critique', in R Harries ed., *Reinhold Niebuhr and the Issues of Our Time* (London: Mowbrays, 1986), p 46. The gist of this article is taken up in Hampson's widely controversial but extremely challenging, *Theology and Feminism* (Oxford: Basil Blackwell Ltd., 1990), pp 121–6.

5   Hampson, 'Reinhold Niebuhr on Sin: A Critique', p 48.

6   Ibid., pp 51–2.

7   Ibid., p 51.

> For the woman . . . the failure is a failure to come to herself, and so she wishes to be rid of herself by losing herself in another. Far from having an inflated self, she has hardly begun to find herself. Far from being an isolated, self-sufficient individual, she has abnegated responsibility for herself. It is then wide of the mark to prescribe for her that she should forgo her pride, or that she should stop exploiting others and start serving them. Her problem is that she insufficiently values herself.[8]

Some of us, then, are good at finding a place in 'the web of human inter-connectedness which makes for life', but our particular need may be to discover 'that necessary differentiation of the self from others'.[9] Others of us, on the other hand, find ourselves typically thinking 'in terms of hierarchy and are naturally competitive'; we tend to 'keep others at a distance, fearing close relationships'.[10] While some therefore need 'to find *themselves* in relationship', others must learn 'to find themselves *in relationship*'.[11] Therefore, any adequate doctrine of sin must do justice to both sides of the human problem. In keeping with other theologies concerned with liberation, some feminist theology is equally concerned to understand sin in terms of 'the structural sin obtaining in society' rather than primarily as 'a disruption in the relationship between an individual and God (resulting from individual behaviour)'.[12] But, as we have seen, the issue is not a simple matter of either – or.

2.   During our discussion we found ourselves seeking to hold together what some theologians appear to separate. Therefore, at one point, we concluded that it was important to ground our christological claims in 'the Jesus of history' and not just 'the Christ of faith', as well as, at another point, we insisted that we maintain a clear connection between the life and ministry of Jesus and his saving work on the Cross. This causes us to recognize perhaps that the foundational datum of the Christian Faith is a complex and inter-relating sequence of events involving the career of Jesus of Nazareth, the ensuing proclamation of him as the Redeemer and the new way of life which that created for the Christian Church. When we have spoken about 'the Christ event' it is this whole series of events to which we have referred. In the Christ event, according to John Macquarrie, 'there were joined inseparably the career of Jesus and its impact on the believing community, the history of Israel and the history of the church, the tradition of the past and the experience of the participants in the event', and as he says, 'they are inseparably joined because each lends meaning to the other.'[13] Two thousand years on it is inevitable that it may be more difficult than we had supposed, or might like, to separate out into their particular parts the various elements which were 'inseparably joined'. A certain degree of 'agnosticism' about what we know of the life and teaching of Jesus would therefore clearly be in order.

3.   At various points in our discussion, we have used terms like 'model' or 'metaphor' to describe ways of understanding the Incarnation and Atonement. The reasons for this are both positive and negative, in so far as we wish to open up theological awareness in a way that literal language could never do, as well as point to the inevitable limitations of theological language. We will now consider the way in which two radically different yet contemporary URC theologians make use of metaphor.

---

8   Ibid., p 49.
9   Ibid., p 54.
10   Ibid.
11   Ibid., p 55.
12   Hampson, *Theology and Feminism*, p 125.
13   Macquarrie, *Jesus Christ in Modern Thought*, p 20.

Colin E Gunton launches an attack upon a rationalism which he thinks is tearing out the heart of the Christian faith. Rationalism, he tells us, attempts to find a direct relationship between our minds and the world. It seeks to know the world 'directly'. But 'the key to the relation between language and world is . . . its *indirectness*', and therefore 'metaphor is a primary vehicle of human rationality and superior to the pure concept.[14] It is quite appropriate, therefore, for the theologian to deploy metaphorical language when trying to interpret the Christian faith. As Gunton points out, it was ever thus:

> The central focus of the proclamation after Easter was that the events of Jesus' history, and particularly of the Easter period, had changed the status of believers, indeed of the whole world. The metaphors of atonement are ways of expressing the significance of what had happened and was happening. They therefore enable the Christian community to speak of God and he is found in concrete personal relationship with human beings and their world.[15]

It is central to Gunton's thesis that we must take the metaphors of the tradition and then seek to discover the extent to which they still 'work' today. And in Gunton's hands metaphors of victory, justice and sacrifice are penetrated to reveal deeper and more important meanings for the atonement than the literal interpretation would at face value warrant. The result is the provision of a basis upon which to conceive 'a living tradition of worship and praise, centred on the cross and resurrection of Jesus' which is largely traditional in scope and content.[16]

By way of a contrast, John Hick's intention in focusing upon the metaphorical nature of theological language would largely seem to undermine many of the orthodox claims Gunton wishes to defend. The main conclusion of his *The Metaphor of God Incarnate* is that 'the idea of the divine incarnation in its standard Christian form, in which both genuine humanity and genuine deity are insisted upon, has never been given a satisfactory literal sense; but that on the other hand it makes excellent metaphorical sense.'[17] What this metaphorical idea entails is as follows:

> We see in Jesus a human being extraordinarily open to God's influence and thus living to an extraordinary extent as God's agent on earth, 'incarnating' the divine purpose for human life. He thus embodied within the circumstances of his time and place the idea of humanity living in openness and response to God, and in doing so he 'incarnated' a love that reflects the divine love. This epoch-making life became the inspiration of a vast tradition which has for many centuries provided intellectual and moral guidance to Western civilization. Today many aspects of that tradition have lost their gravitas and plausibility, and Western civilization has itself entered a post-Christian phase. But the original inspiration of one who fully trusted in God, though within a human setting very different from our own, is no less powerful than in earlier centuries. If it can be liberated from the network of theories – about Incarnation, Trinity and Atonement – which served once to focus but now serve only to obscure its significance, that lived teaching can continue to be a major source of inspiration for human life.[18]

---

[14]   Gunton, *The Actuality of Atonement*, pp 37 and 39.

[15]   Ibid., p 46. For another tradional exploration of metaphor in atonement theology see J S Whale, *Victor and Victim: The Christian Doctrine of Redemption*.

[16]   Ibid., xi.

[17]   John Hick, *The Metaphor of God Incarnate* (London: SCM Press, 1993), p 12.

[18]   Ibid., pp 12–13.

Hick admits that the ensuing Christianity will be 'non-traditional'; but to many it will be little more than blatant reductionism, the watering down of the Faith to what a sceptical modern might believe – the very result Gunton attributes to rationalism. Nevertheless, at the root of Hick's theology lie some observations which command widespread if not complete support. We may note the following. First, 'such evidence as there is has led the historians of the period to conclude with an impressive degree of unanimity, that Jesus did not claim to be God incarnate.'[19] Secondly, in view of the 'elasticity of the idea of divinity in the ancient world', when clearly there was 'the widespread honorific divinising of outstanding religious figures', it is hardly surprising that metaphorical titles which implied divinity were applied to Jesus.[20] Problems arose, Hick believes, when titles like 'son of God' were applied to him literally. Thirdly, the two natures doctrine of Chalcedon 'merely asserted that Jesus was "truly God and truly man" without attempting to say how such a paradox is possible.'[21] Hick thinks that Chalcedon 'is incapable of being explicated in any religiously acceptable way'.[22] The incarnation of God's life in Jesus is a metaphorical statement which illumines the idea that God was acting through Jesus during his life, a life lived 'in a startling degree of awareness of God and of response to God's presence'.[23] Hick, in fact, turns to Donald Baillie's 'paradox of grace' to explain the basis for this. Fourthly, when discussing the ransom theory for the atonement, Hick claims that 'the idea of an actual human fall resulting in a universal inherited depravity and guilt is totally unbelievable for educated Christians', and that 'the idea of an inherited guilt for being born as the kind of being that we are is a moral absurdity.'[24] Fifthly, with regards to the satisfaction model for the atonement, Hick says that 'in our more democratic age it is virtually impossible to share Anselm's medieval sense of wrongdoing as a slight upon God's honour which requires a satisfaction to assuage the divine dignity before even the truly penitent can receive forgiveness.'[25] Ideas from a by-gone age can be safely set to one side. Sixthly, concerning the penal substitution model for the atonement, Hick tells us that 'the idea that guilt can be removed from a wrongdoer by someone else being punished instead is morally grotesque', and even if we say that 'God punished Godself . . . in order to be able justly to forgive sinners, we are still dealing with the religious absurdity of a moral law which God can and must satisfy by punishing the innocent in place of the guilty.'[26] Seventhly, on the subject of the work of Christ, Hick reckons that it is historically probable that 'Jesus saw himself as the final prophet precipitating the coming of God's rule on earth' rather than viewed himself 'in anything like the terms developed by the church's later atonement theories'.[27] Eighthly, Hick argues that ' . . . a forgiveness that has to be brought by the bearing of a just punishment, or the giving of an adequate satisfaction, or the offering of a sufficient sacrifice, is not forgiveness, but merely an acknowledgement that the debt has been paid in full.'[28] He argues that 'the recorded teaching of Jesus suggests that 'there is, in contrast, genuine divine forgiveness for those who are truly penitent and vividly conscious of their utter unworthiness'.[29] This leads Hick to eschew an idea

---

[19]   Ibid., p 27.
[20]   Ibid., pp 41, 42.
[21]   Ibid., p 48.
[22]   Ibid., p 45.
[23]   Ibid., p 106.
[24]   Ibid., pp 116, 117.
[25]   Ibid., p 118.
[26]   Ibid., p 119.
[27]   Ibid., p 125.
[28]   Ibid., p 127.
[29]   Ibid.

of salvation which is grounded in 'an atoning transaction that enables God to forgive the fallen race', and to favour instead one rooted in 'the gradual transformation of human beings, who already exist in the "image" of God, into what the Hellenistic fathers . . . called the "likeness" of God.'[30] And, of course, it is Irenaeus rather than Augustine who is Hick's guide.

What we find in both Gunton and Hick is the laudable view that major theological doctrines should be understood as metaphorical in character. Both thinkers regard this as a move which will reveal fundamental truths. Hick, for example, says that 'as religious metaphor or myth the idea of incarnation communicates something of momentous importance about Jesus, something that forms the basis of distinctively Christian experience and faith.'[31] However, what Gunton and Hick read out of the metaphors is fundamentally different, and the difference between the two thinkers reflects the theological diversity abroad in the URC. Readers can do little better than weigh up the arguments of these two thinkers as they develop their own theological outlooks.

4.   Several times during our discussion we have counselled a both/and approach, and therefore the reconciliation of contrary views, rather than always seeking the elimination of one of them. When it came to christology, we suggested with Gunton that the approach must be both from 'above', at the risk of abstracting Christ from history 'by eternalizing him', as well as from 'below', at the risk of abstracting Jesus from eternity 'by making his temporality absolute'.[32] Both ways of addressing the christology issue are needed and one model which goes somewhere near to fulfilling the requirement is found in Donald Baillie's idea of 'the paradox of grace'. Then, secondly, we saw a need to hold to an 'objective' and 'transactional' view of atonement as the ground and basis upon which a 'subjective' and 'transformational' understanding can be established. But how can a particular act have universal redeeming purposes? It may be because the Cross provides God with an experience which then can for ever after be offered as a saving opportunity for men and women. This is the line taken by the Anglican Vernon White:

> God in Christ takes into his own divine experience that which qualifies him to reconcile, redeem, and sanctify in his relationship with all people everywhere. To adapt one of Fiddes' pictures: it is something like the mountain guide who first crosses a difficult terrain himself, in order to equip himself to take across all who will follow him. It is a journey we could not make apart from him, yet must make. It is, of course, the journey of dying to self and living wholly to God – through temptation, suffering and death itself.[33]

But is the Christ event 'constitutive of God's saving action for all people in, and beyond, the whole world of space and time', as White seems to imply?[34] Or can sufficient emphasis upon the particularity of the Christ event be maintained if we say something akin to Donald Baillie, namely, that the Christ event is the decisive re-presentation of 'God's saving action for all people'? In order to fully protect the universality of that saving action the ground mapped out by Baillie may prove to be the most fruitful to follow.

---

30   Ibid., p 129–30.
31   Ibid., p 106.
32   Gunton, *Yesterday and Today*, p 53.
33   Vernon White, *Atonement and Incarnation: An Essay in Universalism and Particularity* (Cambridge: Cambridge University Press, 1991), p 53.
34   Ibid., p 115.

PART 4

We believe that, by the Holy Spirit, this glorious gospel is made effective so that through faith we receive the forgiveness of sins, newness of life as children of God and strength in this present world to do his will.

OUR CONSIDERATION of the URC Statement of Faith now takes us to the work of the Holy Spirit, and we are directed to the way in which God effects our salvation through justification and sanctification. We touch here some central themes in Reformed theologies, and in the doctrine of the Holy Spirit we find a principle point of antagonism between Protestants and Catholics at the time of the Reformation. As Geoffrey Nuttall says, '. . . in the doctrine of the Holy Spirit lay the fundamental difference between Protestantism and Roman Catholicism, a difference deeper than that over Scripture, for which in fact it was the basis.'[1] In some Reformed theologies, however, the Holy Spirit's work is only ultimately influential on the favoured few. So, after a consideration of the Holy Spirit and the Christian experience of salvation, we will look at the idea of predestination, and this inevitably involves a discussion of the debate between Calvinism and Arminianism. The notion that Christ's atonement is limited reminds us that life is a very uneven experience, with some folk being more fortunate than others and countless millions dying before they have had time to grow old. This will lead us quite naturally into a discussion of the so-called problem of evil.

---

[1]   Geoffrey F Nuttall, *The Holy Spirit in Puritan Faith and Experience* (Oxford: Basil Backwell, 1949), p 5.

CHAPTER 10

The Holy Spirit the Giver of Life

DURING the second half of the twentieth century Western Christian churches were challenged by three movements which have had subsequent impact upon their theology. Two of them have already been referred to: feminism and the various liberation struggles. The third now provides the back-cloth to this chapter since the Charismatic Renewal Movement has brought with it an emphasis upon religious experience as the touchstone of orthodoxy and a subsequent reawakening of interest in the Holy Spirit.

It is nothing new that people should want to appeal to experience to defend their opinions, and thus implicitly tend towards an anti-intellectual approach in which, to put it rather crudely, 'Spirit' is exalted over 'Word'. As Nuttall has shown, the conflict over the authoritative priority of 'Spirit' or 'Word' was rife in the Puritan era: 'Throughout the years from 1650 onwards there is a perpetual controversy, whether the Word is to be tried by the Spirit, or the spirit by the Word.'[2] While the mainstream Puritan view was to maintain a clear relationship between the two, the radical wing so elevated 'Spirit' over 'Word' that they came to suspect learning and had no time for liturgies or read prayers. More recently, similar differences of opinion have appeared within the churches. While the inherited tradition has very much been akin to the central Puritan position: 'The Spirit speaks in, by, or through the Word,'[3] the Charismatic Renewal Movement has re-emphasized the role of the Holy Spirit and given birth to examples of 'Spirit' being given priority over 'Word'. The temptation to move in this direction is strong when the intellectual challenges to believing are very demanding, as they are at the moment; however, the appeal to experience is not of itself damaging, since believers who do not earth their faith in experience merely end up with a faith that never moves beyond theoretical appeal.

It is easy to see why experience has become so central for Reformed Christians. Our emphasis upon the Word, with its cerebral attachment to preaching and teaching, has in many cases failed to capture the hearts of people who have been unfulfilled by society's love affair with rationalism. It is significant that spiritual traditions beyond the established churches have been sought out by many people, with the influence of Iona, Taizé and Celtic traditions to the fore. While this is a positive development, an emphasis upon spiritual experience on its own is fraught with dangers. 'Spirit' without 'Word' can so easily lead to escapism and a religious outlook that provides a rationalization for our culture's love affair with individualism. Theology should flow out from and then back into experience, as we not only experience God but also witness in God's name. The Charismatic Renewal Movement, though, has brought a renewed emphasis upon personal experience of the Holy Spirit as a fundamental pre-requisite for being a Christian. Displaying a

---

[2] Ibid., p 28.
[3] Ibid., p 33.

pentecostalist background, the Movement tends to stress baptism in the Spirit as a separate work of grace following baptism by water. Also emphasized is the way in which believers receive spiritual gifts to enable them to witness and minister. As in the Puritan period, the more emphasis is placed on a personal reception of the Spirit, the greater the tendency is to become anti-clerical and suspicious of established church order and structure. In fact, a growing number of URC congregations appear, on the surface at least, to have more in common with Pentecostalism than with the Reformed ethos, while many new Christians come to our churches with the emphases of Charismatic Renewal because they have responded to the call of Christ at one of the Movement's ecumenical events. These 'emphases' are directly associated with the sense of freedom and new life the Spirit brings: healing, adult baptism with re-baptism the accepted norm, arm gestures in worship, and simple songs on acetate sheets via the overhead projector rather than the cerebral hymns and four-square tunes of *Rejoice and Sing*. Some URC ministers now believe that the Charismatic Movement promises the most likelihood of renewal in the URC, while others view it as a betrayal of our ethos.

When there is a renewed emphasis upon personal experience grounded in the Spirit's work, certain positive features emerge. First, people's confidence in Christian believing is enhanced. Religious experience carries with it a clear cognitive importance, since, if there were no experiences reported of God, theistic belief and understanding would be vacuous. For many, experience provides evidence for belief. Secondly, some claim that the experiential emphasis has enlivened their worship and spirituality with its informality, movement, freedom and 'modern' musical idioms. This has led, thirdly, to a renewal of congregational life as worshippers have been drawn together in a newly found sense of fellowship. Fourthly, many acknowledge that the emphasis upon lay-leadership and ministries has been long overdue. They may also point, fifthly, to the ecumenical fellowship which has emerged among charismatics as being a very positive development.

We all must give thanks for the way the Spirit breaks into people's lives in transforming ways. And, yet, we all know of upheavals and schisms in congregations caused by disputes over polity and order between the long-established church members and newly-awakened charismatics. The roots of these disputes are theological. For example, the theology of the Charismatic Renewal Movement often supports somewhat 'fundamentalist' approaches to scripture. But can such approaches be sustained in the light of biblical scholarship? Secondly, many view with grave concern the way in which charismatic church leaders often seem to take up authoritarian roles within their fellowships, and they note with despair the subservient role that women are often expected to play in them. Thirdly, the mainstream Reformed view on baptism denies a two-stage work of the Spirit, and it cannot sanction re-baptism. While it acknowledges and affirms charismatic gifts for ministry in the church, the proviso is that this must not devalue the role of ordained ministers. Calvin, of course, viewed the extraordinary charismatic gifts mentioned in I Corinthians 12–14 and Romans 12 as 'temporary', and he restricted the Holy Spirit's activity in ministry to the pastors (who he says the Bible synonymously calls bishops, presbyters and pastors).[4] Fourthly, major problems arise when the church becomes more concerned to feed spiritual experience than seek out the Word or engage in mission in obedience to the Word. We can so easily become introverted and self-satisfied. Bernard Lord Manning puts his finger on the heart of the matter:

---

[4]   Calvin, *Institutes*, 4,3,6–8.

> The argument from experience is a weapon that in careless hands can be used to cut both ways . . . It is not sufficient to say that a thing works or succeeds. We want to know how it works and what follows its success. Tares grow as well as wheat, or better . . . It is not enough to know that a belief satisfies. We want to know if it is true; we want to know what sort of people it satisfies.[5]

We need the Word to test the spirits.   Finally, there always lurks the danger of confusing the experience itself with the One who has possibly caused it, or to whom it might point. It is easy to make the experience matter rather than God, to make authentic Christianity conditional upon having certain religious experiences. We should also beware of adopting absolute convictions based on our religious experiences since, to a greater or lesser degree, 'the content of our experiences is also formed by the ways of understanding available in our culture.'[6] It may well be that it is not the case that some have religious experiences while others do not. Perhaps we all have similar experiences but interpret them differently – some theistically, others non-theistically? We certainly interpret our experiences largely on the basis of the worldview we posses when we have them. Nevertheless, as Pailin says, 'while theology based on experience cannot claim to express an unmediated perception of ultimate reality, it need not be dismissed as nothing more than the explication of the contents of our minds.'[7] A theology of the Spirit which was not rooted in experience clearly would be deficient. For Calvin, though, as Nuttall points out, 'the Holy Spirit is a necessity of thought rather than something known in experience.'[8] So the English Puritan tradition's more experiential emphasis was a welcome corrective to many arid Reformed theologies.

John Calvin: The Holy Spirit and the Creation of Faith

We have already discovered that in his trinitarian theology Calvin regards the Holy Spirit as divine, breathing 'essence, life and movement into all things'. We also observed the way in which for Calvin 'the testimony of the Spirit' is the means whereby Scripture's words 'speak' God's word to us. When he discusses the Holy Spirit in the *Institutes* he defines the Holy Spirit as 'the bond by which Christ effectually unites us to himself'.[9] This bond occurs as faith is generated in us. Without the Spirit's work we would not be led to faith; otherwise, faith would be merely another self-seeking, all too human, work. For Calvin, therefore, the Spirit's fundamental role is to engender faith.

Calvin defines faith as 'a firm and certain knowledge of God's benevolence toward us, founded upon the truth of the freely given promise in Christ, both revealed to our minds and sealed upon our hearts through the Holy Spirit'.[10] But this 'knowledge' is not a matter of giving assent to doctrinal propositions; rather it is a more existential matter. Calvin tells us that the assent involved in faith 'is more of the heart than of the brain, and more of the disposition than of the understanding'.[11] But lest we might think that Calvin is reducing faith to a mere subjective inner impulse, it is important to observe the 'permanent relationship' between faith and Word everywhere

---

[5]   Bernard Lord Manning, *Essays in Orthodox Dissent* (London: Independent Press Ltd., 1953), pp 31–2.

[6]   David A Pailin, *The Anthropological Character of Theology: Conditioning Theological Understanding* (Cambridge: Cambridge University Press, 1990), p 96.

[7]   Ibid., p 86.

[8]   Nuttall, *The Holy Spirit in Puritan Faith and Experience,* p 6 n 5.

[9]   Calvin, *Institutes,* 3,I,I.

[10]   Ibid., 3,2,7.

[11]   Ibid., 3,2,8.

assumed in his theology.[12] The Word is the ground upon which faith is built and developed; take that foundation away and faith's whole edifice collapses. Nevertheless, Calvin reminds us that God's word is not fully received when it merely 'flits about in the top of the brain', since it must be established 'in the depth of the heart that it may be an invincible defense to withstand and drive off all the stratagems of temptation.'[13]

This emphasis upon faith's existential rootedness leads Calvin to argue that 'the knowledge of faith consists in assurance rather than in comprehension.'[14] He accuses the medieval theologians of identifying faith with mere assent to doctrinal propositions, insisting that both heart and mind are involved in faith. The Holy Spirit certainly illumines the mind, but faith also involves the heart being 'strengthened and supported by his power'.[15] Religious certainty arises when we posses an inner confidence earthed in 'a sure confidence in divine benevolence and salvation'.[16] Calvin therefore defines the true believer as a person 'who, convinced by a firm conviction that God is a kindly and well-disposed Father toward him, promises himself all things on the basis of his generosity; who, relying upon the promises of divine benevolence toward him, lays hold on an undoubted expectation of salvation.'[17] Such people know the promise of God's mercy at the bottom of their hearts, and not just off the top of their minds. Ultimately, it is a knowledge of a merciful Father which provides the initial basis for Christian hope; faith and hope therefore are inseparably joined. The Spirit's work, therefore, generates both faith and hope in the believer.

The Holy Spirit clearly plays an influential part in the Christian life. It is the cause of regeneration insofar as faith gives birth to repentance, the means by which we take a new direction in our lives. Calvin defines repentance as 'the true turning of our life to God, a turning that arises from a pure and earnest fear of him'.[18] This first involves what he calls 'a transformation, not only in outward works, but in the soul itself'.[19] A basic and radical about-turn, therefore, is the fundamental starting-point of repentance. Secondly, the very idea of repentance presupposes that we see the need to change our ways. Calvin suggests that this is only prompted by thoughts of divine judgement; fear of God, therefore, induces repentance.[20] Calvin isolates two components within the act of repentance. The first is a basic attitude of contrition which Calvin calls 'mortification of the flesh'. We die to an old way of life. The severity involved is explained by Calvin as follows: 'For from "mortification" we infer that we are not conformed to the fear of God and do not learn the rudiments of piety, unless we are violently slain by the sword of the Spirit and brought to nought.'[21] Once again we are faced with Calvin's very pessimistic understanding of the human condition. The second component of repentance is the restoration in us of God's image which was lost in the Fall. Calvin calls this 'vivification of the Spirit'. It is less the instantaneous product of our turning to Christ than an ongoing process: 'And indeed, this restoration does not take place in one moment or one day or one year; but through continual and sometimes even slow advances God wipes out in his elect the corruptions of the flesh, cleanses them of guilt, consecrates them to

---

[12]	Ibid., 3,2,6.
[13]	Ibid., 3,2,36.
[14]	Ibid., 3,2,14.
[15]	Ibid., 3,2,33.
[16]	Ibid., 3,2,15.
[17]	Ibid., 3,2,16.
[18]	Ibid., 3,3,5.
[19]	Ibid., 3,3,6.
[20]	Ibid., 3,3,7.
[21]	Ibid., 3,3,8.

himself as temples renewing all their minds to true purity that they may practice repentance throughout their lives and know that this warfare will end only at death.'[22]

Calvin's belief that 'vivification of the Spirit' is an ongoing process during our lives has implication for his understanding of sin. He does not hold with the idea that we can be free of sin this side of eternity, since 'there remains in a regenerate man a smoldering cinder of evil, from which desires continually leap forth to allure and spur him to commit sin', and therefore 'the saints are as yet so bound by that disease of concupiscence that they cannot withstand being at times tickled and incited either to lust or to avarice or to ambition, or to other vices.'[23] While believers are liberated from sin's power, sin besets them all their days on earth. In this life, we witness the fruits of repentance, 'the duties of piety toward God, of charity toward men, and in the whole of life, holiness and purity;' but they are never perfected this side of the grave.[24]

Puritanism and the Doctrine of the Holy Spirit

One of the most significant features of Calvin's pneumatology is the way in which the faith generated by the Spirit is existentially rooted in a believer's life. What theologians say as a matter of principle, however, is sometimes not reflected in their theological statements. In one sense, Calvin is the great theologian of the Holy Spirit. The very possibility of salvation, according to Calvin, is the Spirit's work. Nevertheless, the Spirit's role is played down by him when he talks about the role of charismatic gifts in the post-biblical Church. One suspects that he always expects the Spirit's activity to conform to certain patterns definitively established in God's self-revelation in Christ. Calvin's doctrine of the Spirit, therefore, is heavily bounded by his understanding of Christ's person and work. As a result, there is little scope for contemporary experience in the believing community becoming the starting point for our understanding of the Spirit – or, indeed, for 'doing theology'. Calvin's pneumatology never escapes the shadow cast over history by the Word. We might be forgiven for also suspecting that a lawyer and systemizer like Calvin, one so concerned with due order and discipline in the Christian life, is not the kind of person to do full justice to the One who blows where she wills, who disturbs settled routines, and who leads people into new ways and towards fresh experiences. It is hardly surprising that Calvin has been accused of treating the Spirit as 'a necessity of thought rather than something known in experience.'[25]

It is important to remember that the theological traditions which flow into the URC do not all stem directly from the Continental Reformers; some come from the Puritan, Independent and Dissenting traditions which disseminated the ideas of the Reformers in different social and political contexts from those over the Channel. And within these traditions there occurred a renewed emphasis upon the Spirit's work. The Spirit hitherto had been very much the Cinderella of the Trinity. Nuttall suggests that, prior to the seventeenth century, 'there had been latterly so little orthodox teaching about the doctrine of the Holy Spirit that what influences there were must have come largely by heretical channels, subterranean tributaries of the hidden stream . . . so suddenly breaking forth into the light of the day.'[26] What made this epiphany of pneumatology possible was the acceptance in Puritanism of experience as a primary authority.

---

[22]   Ibid.
[23]   Ibid., 3,3,10.
[24]   Ibid., 3,3,16.
[25]   See n 8.
[26]   Nuttall, *The Holy Spirit in Puritan Faith and Experience*, p 15.

During the seventeenth century many people felt that they were living in a radically new era in which they could confidently expect 'more light and truth to break forth from [God's] word'.[27] The English Puritans were confident that the Spirit would open up new vistas and create new opportunities. There was a general view that the Christian community was being empowered by the Spirit in a decisively fresh way. As Nuttall says: 'Accompanying this dynamic principle of pressing on, through and beyond all outward and imprisoning forms, to attain to the full liberty of the Holy Spirit, was a powerful eschatological consciousness.'[28] The Puritan age then was one of confidence and certainty based upon an expectation that the Spirit was leading folk to perfect freedom. The Puritans were convinced that the Spirit's activity was the fundamental feature of the faith, conduct and witness of the first Christians, and that something similar was now taking place in their lives and era.

One way of understanding the change which occurred during this period is to focus on the Puritan's rediscovery of God as a personal 'Thou' who meets us experientially in the act of believing. The medievals had tended to speak about God in somewhat abstract terms through the conceptuality of Greek philosophy, but, based upon their experience of God, the Puritans felt bound to understand God 'as at least not less than personal, as not abstract, ideal or a principle of coherence or perfection, as not 'it' but "he" (if not always "thou")'.[29] This, in turn, led them to conceive the Spirit in personal categories. Pneumatology for the Puritans therefore involved 'a personal God, revealed in a Person and present in personal relationship with persons'.[30]

Radical Puritans like George Fox, of course, insisted that the Spirit not only indwelled contemporary Christians in the same way that she had been present with the Apostles, but also that God's Spirit actually is in every person – sinners as well as saints. In Nuttall's opinion, Fox and the Quakers were correct to understand the Spirit's work in this way; but, quoting from Richard Baxter, he also remarks that 'where they erred was in identifying this bestowal of "the Spirit of God as Creator, or of the Father" with the fuller bestowal of "the Spirit of Christ the Redeemer" granted in and through Christ.'[31] For Baxter, the Spirit's work enables us to have a confident faith in God and a relationship with God akin to a child's relationship with a parent. This then flows out into our everyday lives as 'the Spirit of adoption . . . becomes the Spirit of sanctification', and 'the Spirit's witness "that we are children of God"' is manifest in 'the fruits of the Spirit' taking root in us.[32]

Although there was an increasing emphasis upon personal experience of the Spirit during the Puritan period, it needs to be borne in mind that mainstream Puritans never wanted to separate Spirit and Word. To be sure, the whole era – and other periods within the Christian centuries – is littered with examples of Christians who have set their spiritual experiences against what was commonly understood as God's revealed Word. Nuttall notes that 'cause for sorrow arose from the Quaker's tendency to contrast and (as it seemed) even to oppose the Spirit in themselves to the Spirit in the Word, and to treat the former, not the latter, as the criterion.'[33] But, as he says, 'the central position of Puritanism' was that the Spirit 'speaks in, by, or through the Word.'[34] This leads him to conclude that, 'Puritan piety admits no attempt to seek communion with God's Holy Spirit except as within the bounds of the revelation through Christ.'[35]

---

27   John Robinson's words to the Pilgrim Fathers (and Sisters!) found in George Rawson's hymn, 'We limit not the truth of God'.
28   Nuttall, *The Holy Spirit in Puritan Faith and Experience*, p 108.
29   Ibid., p 172.
30   Ibid., p 171.
31   Ibid., p 174.
32   Ibid., p 59. Nuttall quoting from Richard Baxter.
33   Ibid., p 30.
34   Ibid., p 33.
35   Ibid., p 146.

The Puritans refused to define the Spirit's work in terms which equated it with human reason and conscience; it cannot be fully defined by either. For the radical Puritan, of course, the Spirit was likened to 'a spiritual perception analogous to the physical perception of the senses and given in "experience" as a whole'.[36] Such 'a spiritual perception' was considered superior to reason and conscience. This quite naturally led to a suspicion of education and learning, and even to downright opposition to them. In Baxter's writings, however, we find a more balanced approach, a synthesis of 'the rational and the spiritual principles, both of which were strongly marked in his own temperament'.[37] He believed that education is a means by which God can convey grace to us. He did not fall into some of the common traps associated with those who emphasize the importance of the Spirit, since by insisting that the Spirit works primarily through our reason and conscience, Baxter avoids exaggerating abnormal occurrences in human life when he talks about the Spirit's work. He also could not follow his more radical contemporaries when it came to what is permissible in public worship. The work of the Spirit in a Christian's personal life, he insisted, does not provide sufficient grounds for removing liturgy or read prayers from worship.

Our discussion of Puritan understandings of the Spirit reveals three areas in which the rediscovery of a focus on the Spirit led to significant developments of which today we are still the heirs. First, an approach to the Bible was established which placed scripture in the hands of every believer. It became the means by which the Spirit changed people's lives. The Puritans found that when people read the Bible the Spirit illuminated the text and opened up their minds to understand it. Without the role of the Spirit, the scriptures do not impart 'saving' knowledge. This, in turn, raised the question whether it is the Word or the Spirit that is the criterion by which the adequacy of Christian theology and discipleship is to be judged. As a result, Nuttall notes that 'a contrast, though not necessarily an opposition', is created between Word and Spirit, and that from the Puritan period 'there is a perpetual controversy, whether the Word is to be tried by the Spirit, or the Spirit by the Word'.[38] Secondly, the Puritan discovery of spiritual liberty led to an emphasis upon freedom and toleration in both ecclesiastical and civil contexts. As Nuttall says: 'Toleration in the State, like tolerance in the Church, was a natural outcome of faith in "the liberty of the Spirit"'.[39] Here we find the roots of the idea of 'free churches' and many of the attitudes we simply take for granted in our society. However, it is a moot point how tolerant a tolerant church or society can afford to be. At what point does the opinion or practice of an individual or group have to be opposed in the interests of the wider whole? There is always a tension between 'freedom' and 'order'. Nuttall makes an interesting observation which throws some light upon the emphases which still jostle for supremacy within the life of the URC. He tells us that, in the seventeenth century, 'The Presbyterians . . . did not share the Congregationalists' primary interest in the Holy Spirit', and, as result, 'neither did they share the Congregationalists' spirit of tolerance'.[40] Finally, an emphasis upon the Spirit's importance led to patterns of church government which focused upon the members of a congregation meeting to discern the guidance of the Spirit for their life and work. The centrality of the church meeting clearly rests upon the discernment of the Spirit rather than the democratic means by which we attempt to achieve it. And, when the URC presence is small, and our voice is in danger of being deafened by the larger church battalions, we might be heartened that our

---

[36]   Ibid., p 38.
[37]   Ibid., p 47.
[38]   Ibid., p 28.
[39]   Ibid., p 113.
[40]   Ibid.

Christian forebears were led to a mode of church government which had implications beyond their churches. As Nuttall reminds us, 'it was the church-meeting which gave birth, in England, to political democracy, not *vice versa*.'[41]

At their best the Puritans did justice to both the revealed Word and the experienced Spirit in their theology, making both appropriate starting points for Christian practice and reflection. Reformed theology, however, had to wait until the nineteenth century for a theologian who, with remorseless rigour, worked out theology from human experience.

Friedrich Schleiermacher: The Holy Common Spirit within the Body of Believers

It has sometimes been claimed that Calvin's pneumatology is overtly individualistic, finding its centre in the faith aroused in the believer by the Spirit and, therefore, seemingly strangely at odds with the account of Pentecost which possesses the character of a collective experience and corporate 'happening'. To be sure, Calvin's ecclesiology makes it clear that each believer ultimately is a member of a corporate body, the Church; and there is a real sense in which believers cannot be fully understood apart from such membership. Nevertheless, Calvin moves from the individual to the community, thus reversing what reflection upon the story of Pentecost might suggest.

Schleiermacher's starting point takes him in the opposite direction since he believes that we all possess in our self-consciousness a fundamental, if pre-reflective, sense of the Infinite. As a result, Schleiermacher finds a continuity between the human Spirit and God's Spirit. This has a corporate dimension in so far as reflection upon the Church's life reveals what he calls 'the common Spirit of the new corporate life founded by Christ'.[42] Believers enter into that Spirit when they become part of the Body of Christ; they cannot be fully Christian outside the Church. Schleiermacher argues that 'all informing pictures of the Christian fellowship agree in describing every individual as an integral constituent of the whole, and attributing everything to one spirit moving in, and animating, the whole'.[43] Individual Christians are what they are because of their participation in 'the common Spirit'. This Spirit is 'a true unity through which the multitude of Christians also become a unity and the many individual personalities become a true common life or moral personality'.[44] This unity is formally equivalent to the way in which a nation experiences its unity. A common Spirit is shared by all those who have been brought to faith in Christ. They are united in possessing 'a consciousness of the need to be redeemed that is alike in all, and of the capacity, alike in all, to be taken up into living fellowship with Christ'.[45]

Schleiermacher defines the Spirit as 'the inmost vital power of the Christian Church', and as such is not the same as what is being referred to in other biblical references to 'spirit' in connection with, say, creation, gifts or incarnation.[46] The outpouring of the Spirit at Pentecost is unique: 'In Christ's promises of the Holy Spirit of truth there is nowhere the slightest whisper that this Something had been present earlier and had vanished only temporarily, or indeed that He is anything at all except as He is for the disciples of Christ.'[47] Therefore, the church gains a certain exclusivity due to the gifts and powers granted it by the Spirit. Christians are aware of the Spirit and the Spirit's gifts 'as

---

[41]   Ibid., p 120.
[42]   Schleiermacher, *The Christian Faith*, p 560.
[43]   Ibid.
[44]   Ibid., p 563.
[45]   Ibid., p 565.
[46]   Ibid.
[47]   Ibid., p 570.

something inward', and of the same Spirit endowing people with different gifts.[48] Therefore, a common Spirit animates the church's life, but the new life it brings is forever being challenged by the separations which give rise to the 'old' life. Schleiermacher argues that 'even if someone were actually to reach the point of having the new life diffuse itself over his entire essence, yet the portion of his life spent before his regeneration would still form part of his personality.'[49] There can be no Christian perfection this side of eternity!

When a person through faith enters into fellowship with Christ, the Spirit is bestowed. It follows for Schleiermacher, therefore, that being led into the Christian fellowship, participating in the life of the Spirit and having a living relationship with Christ 'must simply mean one and the same thing'.[50] The leading of the Spirit is nothing other than the enablement of people to follow the life and example set by Jesus. Consequently, 'the fruits of the Spirit are . . . nothing but the virtues of Christ.'[51] When it comes to the miraculous happenings associated with the Spirit's outpouring at Pentecost, Schleiermacher cautiously suggests that 'we do well . . . to regard the miraculous as not of the essence of the matter but as belonging to the circumstances of the time, and leave the whole question to exegesis.'[52] Whatever 'the circumstances', the communication of the Spirit is always experienced as a miracle and 'the more conversion appears to be something sudden, the more are we inclined to regard anomalous accompanying circumstances as miraculous in character.'[53]

When true to its calling the Church represents Christ to the world: "The Christian Church, animated by the Holy Spirit, is in its purity and integrity the perfect image of the Redeemer.'[54] Every church member has a unique part to play in its life. Schleiermacher goes so far as to say of church members that in spite of their 'imperfection and one-sidedness' each nevertheless 'as a subordinate unit in the whole' plays 'a part irreplaceable by any other.'[55] In fact, in a body which owes both its origin and renewal to the Spirit, 'nothing would happen in the Church as it does, unless each individual were what he is.'[56]

Calvin and Schleiermacher clearly offer different starting points for an understanding of the Spirit, the former focusing upon the individual Christian believers, the latter turning to the collective experience of the Church. Both might be accused of domesticating the Spirit's work. The God whose Spirit is an essential feature of divine creative activity (Gen 1: 2) so easily gets robbed of cosmic intent through our overtly selfish attempts to set human concerns and needs at the centre of theological understanding. After all, the climax of the first creation story in the Bible does not center upon human beings but upon God resting on the Sabbath (Gen 2: 2–3). The anthropocentricity of a great deal of Reformed (and Western) theology can be attributed to a failure to understand the full shape and scope of the third person of the Trinity. Similarly, the Spirit who drives us to prophetic commitment and action against social and political injustice (Isa. 61: 1–3 and Luke 4: 16–21) so easily gets shut up inside narrow and introverted ecclesial and ecclesiastical emphases. Whatever might have happened at the first Pentecost, at least we are led to believe by Luke that Peter understood its significance in cosmic and collective ways (Acts 2: 16–21).

---

48 Ibid., pp 571–2.
49 Ibid., pp 573–4.
50 Ibid., p 575.
51 Ibid., p 576.
52 Ibid., p 578.
53 Ibid.
54 Ibid. Italics removed.
55 Ibid., p 580.
56 Ibid., p 581.

In a great deal of Reformed (and Western) theology the doctrine of the Spirit is made subordinate to other doctrines. The reason for this may lie in a doctrinal option taken in the Patristic period, a decision which contributed to the ill-feeling between the Latin and Greek churches that in turn led to the major split in Christianity between West and East. Once more it is necessary to go behind the Reformation in order to shed light on our topic.

The *Filioque* Controversy

The Nicene Creed (CE 381) carries the following clause concerning the Holy Spirit:

> We believe in the Holy Spirit, the Lord, the giver of life,
> who *proceeds from the Father*,
> who with the Father and the Son is worshipped and glorified,
> who has spoken through the prophets.[57]

This statement was accepted by the representatives of both the Eastern and Western churches, but later Western theologians came to teach that the Holy Spirit proceeded not from the Father alone *but also from the Son*. Their intentions were honourable in that they wanted to give no quarter to those who advocated 'modalism', or to those who subordinated the Son and the Spirit to the Father as second or third ranking deities. Like the Fathers at Nicaea the likes of Augustine, Ambrose and Jerome wanted to affirm the Spirit's full divinity, but the addition of the phrase 'and the Son' (*Filioque*) which sought to achieve this was quickly perceived not so much as an interpretive formula but as what Moltmann has called 'a unilateral correction of the common creed'.[58] The Eastern churches were upset about the introduction of the idea of double procession, and, yet, by the time of the Third Council of Toledo in Spain (CE 589) the addition of the word *Filioque* to the creed had been made by the Latin church.

Reformed theologians, until recently, generally have supported the doctrine of double procession. However, as there has been greater opportunity for the churches of East and West to enter into theological dialogue, Eastern insights have started to penetrate Western sensibilities – and vice versa. One example of this that we have already encountered is the way in which Cappadocian theology has influenced contemporary Reformed theologians like Moltmann and Gunton in the construction of their trinitarian theologies; another illustration of the fruit of ecumenical dialogue is found in the way Moltmann and Gunton have also concluded that the addition of the *Filioque* to the creeds is a basic theological error.

But why have these Reformed theologians decided to support the notion of single procession? Several reasons can be given. First, when the Spirit is said to proceed from the Father *and* the Son, it is difficult to see how it is possible to avoid subordinating the Spirit to the Son.[59] The Western view allows christological concerns to dominate, almost reducing the Spirit's work to its focus in Jesus. At a time when there is a greater awareness of the existence and worth of a plurality of world religions it is becoming increasingly implausible to understand the Spirit's work exclusively through the Christ event. Indeed, Jesus' own life would seem to indicate that the Spirit is One who stands over and against him. This suggests, secondly, that the Western view fails to do

---

[57] See Thompson, ed., *Stating the Gospel*, p 9. Italics mine.
[58] Moltmann, *The Trinity and the Kingdom of God*, p 181.
[59] See Jürgen Moltmann, *The Spirit of Life: A Universal Affirmation* (London: SCM Press, 1992), p 293.

justice to the biblical evidence. Moltmann puts it like this: 'If Christ was conceived by the Holy Spirit, baptized with the Spirit, then he presupposes the Spirit, and the Spirit precedes him.'[60] But this cannot be expressed adequately when it is claimed that the Spirit proceeds from the Father *and* the Son. Gunton, meanwhile, also notes that the Gospels show that 'the Spirit is portrayed as over-against Jesus, driving him into the wilderness to be tempted, supporting him through temptation and empowering the ministry that follows.'[61] This evidence of what Gunton calls 'the otherness of the Spirit' requires 'a doctrine of the personal distinctness of the Holy Spirit in relation to both Son and Father', which 'in turn demands an abandonment of the Western *Filioque*.'[62]

Moltmann mentions a third reason why the addition of the *Filioque* should be abandoned, namely, the non-theological factor of clericalism. We have already referred to the way in which Western theology tends to subordinate the Spirit's work to ecclesial activity. Moltmann now drives the point to a conclusion for which there is a great deal of evidence: 'If God is represented by Christ, Christ by the Pope, and the Pope by the bishops and priests, then – by way of the Filioque in the primordial relationships – the Holy Spirit, with all his charismata and energies in salvation history, is tied down to the operative acts of the priesthood.'[63] Before the Free Churches attempt to gain the moral high ground by claiming that this only applies to the 'high' Churches, they should note that clericalism is an inevitable danger that all forms of representative ministry face and also be candid enough to recognize that church councils as well as all types of ordained ministries are just as susceptible to clericalism as popes, bishops and priests. Given that in the Free Churches clericalism will be less obvious, it may well be even more damaging to the church's health.

Moltmann wishes to affirm the unity of the Son and the Spirit. To do this he uses the metaphor of 'the unity of Word and Breath'.[64] There is in salvation history 'the reciprocal co-efficacy of Spirit and Word, Son and Spirit', and, therefore, 'we have to reject the one-sided definition of the Spirit in terms of the Son in the "transcendent primordial ground", and hence the Filioque addition to the Nicene Creed.'[65] But whether it is legitimate to view 'the uttering of the Word and the breathing of the Spirit' as 'complementary, indissoluble activities is doubted by Richard Bauckham, who accuses Moltmann of 'undisciplined speculation' closely linked to 'a degree of hermeneutical irresponsibility'.[66] Bauckham worries about uniting two different metaphors which belong to different stages of the trinitarian discussion, but it is not immediately apparent why such theological creativity must be ruled out. Bauckham is on safer ground, though, when he objects to Moltmann's use of John 15: 26 to support the preference for the Eastern idea of single procession.[67] Most biblical scholars read this passage as referring to the Spirit's temporal mission from the Father rather than referring to 'the pre-temporal origin of the Spirit from the Father'.[68]

When Moltmann affirms that the Spirit proceeds solely from the Father, his reference is to *the Father of the Son*. This means that, 'The Son is the logical presupposition and actual condition for the procession of the Spirit from the Father; but he is not the Spirit's origin, as the Father is.'[69]

---

[60]   Ibid.
[61]   Gunton, *The Promise of Trinitarian Theology*, p 134.
[62]   Ibid.
[63]   Moltmann, *The Spirit of Life: A Universal Affirmation*, p 294.
[64]   Ibid., p 293.
[65]   Ibid.
[66]   Bauckham, *The Theology of Jürgen Moltmann*, pp 167–98.
[67]   For Moltmann's exegesis of John 15: 26 see *The Spirit of Life: A Universal Affirmation*, p 70 and *The Trinity and the Kingdom of God*, p 182ff.
[68]   Bauckham, *The Theology of J?rgen Moltmann*, p 168.
[69]   Moltmann, *The Trinity and the Kingdom of God*, p 184.

Here we see Moltmann trying to find a theological *via media* between East and West. Against the West he denies that the Spirit proceeds from the Father *and* the Son, while against the classical Eastern view he insists that 'the Spirit proceeds from the Father in the eternal presence of the Son, and that therefore the Son is not uninvolved in it.'[70] A further dimension of his attempt to find a rapprochement between East and West appears when, somewhat speculatively, Moltmann not only speaks of the Spirit as proceeding from the Father of the Son, but also as receiving her form from the Father and the Son. At this point, Moltmann is distinguishing between 'the hypostatic procession of the Spirit from the Father' and the Spirit's 'relational, perichoretic form with respect to the Father and the Son'.[71] Regarding the latter, the *Filioque* is an appropriate affirmation. Rather conveniently for ecumenical relationships, therefore, there is a sense in which the Western tradition was correct after all – even if the *Filioque* 'must be kept well away from the procession of the Holy Spirit'.[72]

Moltmann's contribution to our understanding of the Holy Spirit extends well beyond his persuasive arguments against the introduction of the *Filioque*. We will now draw our discussion of the doctrine of the Holy Spirit to a close by highlighting some of the major features of his pneumatology.

Jürgen Moltmann: The Holy Spirit as the Spirit of Life

Moltmann's theology of the Spirit is based upon a sustained attempt to overcome four tendencies which he maintains has bedevilled pneumatology. First, he notes the tendency in Western theology to subordinate pneumatology to christology. Moltmann acknowledges that the Spirit shows forth Christ, but, in order to break out of a christological straightjacket, he also maintains that the Spirit establishes the future. So while life in the Spirit is a matter of entering into fellowship with Jesus, and thereby living from God's offer of salvation in Jesus, it is also an experience of new possibilities and a creative future. Moltmann puts it like this:

> The powers of the Spirit are the powers of life, which determine the present, extending their
> influence forward from the future of the new life. The fruit of the Spirit is the advance payment
> in joy of future blessedness, in spite of the experience of suffering; it is the advance payment
> in love, in spite of the experience of disappointment and hate.[73]

By setting pneumatology in an eschatological as well as christological context, Moltmann tries to overcome what he calls the 'christomonism' of the Western (and Reformed) understandings of the Holy Spirit.[74] But, displaying an admirable ecumenical even-handedness, Moltmann is also critical of Orthodox theology's 'pneumatomonism', and their 'perception of the breadth of the Holy Spirit and the abundance of the Spirit's gifts'.[75] What such theologies need is the development of pneumatology more firmly in the context of what Moltmann calls 'the trinitarian theology of the cross'.[76] Therefore, Moltmann attempts to set pneumatology and christology within a trinitarian pattern which corrects the unfortunate emphases of both Eastern and Western theological traditions.

---

[70] Ibid.
[71] Ibid., p 186.
[72] Ibid., p 187.
[73] Jürgen Moltmann, *The Church in the Power of the Spirit*, (London: SCM Press, 1977), p 34.
[74] Ibid., p 37.
[75] Ibid.
[76] Ibid.

Secondly, Moltmann wishes to cut through the two opposing ways of doing theology represented by liberalism and neo-orthodoxy. Schleiermacher's theological starting-point is our experience of God. This means that 'the Holy Spirit is . . . a modality of our experience of God.'[77] The neo-orthodox tradition, however, takes its theological cue from God's self-revelation in Christ. Our God-consciousness is not given to us in our fundamental humanness, Barth insists, but rather is revealed to us. The Holy Spirit then is not 'a modality of our experience of God' since 'there is a permanent discontinuity between God's Spirit and the spirit of human beings.'[78] Barth therefore replaces 'the theological immanentism' of liberalism with 'a theological transcendentalism'.[79] Moltmann, however, rejects both methodological frameworks. Against Schleiermacher he asks: 'How is a man or woman supposed to be able to talk about God if God does not reveal himself?'; while against Barth he enquires: 'How are men and women supposed to be able to talk about a God of whom there is no experience?'[80] Moltmann's conclusion is that there cannot in principle be any 'fundamental alternative between God's revelation to human beings, and human experience of God.'[81] What he attempts to achieve in his pneumatology, therefore, is an understanding which is grounded in both revelation and experience. As he says: 'Anyone who stylizes revelation and experience into alternatives, ends up with revelations that cannot be experienced, and experiences without revelation.'[82]

Thirdly, Moltmann wishes to move beyond theologies which talk about the Spirit in the context of 'God, faith, the Christian life, the church and prayer' but refuse to find the Spirit at work in connection with 'the body and nature'.[83] He attempts to broaden our pneumatological horizons by putting firmly to one side any residual dualism between body and spirit, in which the latter is affirmed and the former negated, or any Gnostic tendency to undermine the intrinsic value of the created order, or that rugged Western individualism in which life's social dimensions are given minimal status. The Spirit is not confined to certain privileged spheres of life; nor is she alien to the created world, or estranged from the pleasure and pain of daily life. A reductionist anthropocentric understanding of the Spirit's sphere of activity thus makes way for 'a holistic pneumatology', in which Moltmann displays a welcome ecological sensitivity.[84] Life neither begins nor ends with *homo sapiens*, since the Spirit gives life to everything. The work of the life-giving and life-affirming Spirit can be discovered, furthermore, wherever there is even a trace of anything promoting life or resisting injustice and oppression.

Fourthly, Moltmann turns his back on impersonal images of the Spirit. He tells us that 'the Holy Spirit has a wholly unique personhood, not only in the form in which it is experienced, but also in its relationships to the Father and the Son.'[85] What, then, do we make of the extensive biblical imagery which depicts the Spirit in impersonal ways through terms like wind, fire, light or a wide space? At this point Moltman turns once again to the idea of *kenosis*, claiming that metaphors which describe the Spirit in terms of God's power rather than person should be understood as 'the

---

[77]   Moltmann, *The Spirit of Life: A Universal Affirmation*, p 5.
[78]   Ibid.
[79]   Ibid., p 7.
[80]   Ibid., p 6.
[81]   Ibid.
[82]   Ibid., p 7.
[83]   Ibid., p 8.
[84]   Ibid., p xiii.
[85]   Ibid., p 12.

kenotic forms of the Spirit, forms of his self-emptying'.[86] And, as we are about to see, Moltmann's trinitarian emphasis means that he understands the Spirit as well as the Father and Son in a clearly personalist manner.

In keeping with this methodology Moltmann turns to human experience as well as the Bible to construct his pneumatology. But what constitutes an experience of the Spirit? Moltmann answers as follows: 'By experience of the Spirit I mean an awareness of God in, with and beneath the experience of life, which gives us assurance of God's fellowship, friendship and love'.[87] Human experience cannot be fully understood if the assumptions of secularism are accepted; it is shot through with the Divine. Moltmann's *panentheistic* model for the God–world relationship provides the conceptuality for understanding this: 'It is . . . possible to experience God *in, with and beneath* each everyday experience of the world, if God is in all things, and if all things are in God, so that God himself "experiences" all things in his own way'.[88] Consequently, a holistic doctrine of the Spirit comes into view since human beings are to be understood in their totality – body and soul, consciousness and unconsciousness – and in their context – individually and with others, in communities and social institutions. Pneumatology also must embrace 'the wholeness of the community of creation, which is shared by human beings, the earth, and all other created being things'.[89] Moltmann's proposals move us toward an understanding of God which gives intrinsic worth and value to nature, thereby undermining alternative Christian views which have legitimized our habits of exercising destructive power over the non-human realm. In so far as God's Spirit potentially can be experienced in any encounter with what is 'other', Moltmann argues that 'Eternity is found in the depths of the experienced moment, not in the extension of time'.[90] The implications of this for our understanding of the Christian promise and hope will need to be considered in the final chapter.

We turn now to the insights that Moltmann draws from scripture for his understanding of the Spirit. Considering the Old Testament first, he notes that the word *ruach* has usually been translated in the West as 'spirit', meaning 'something immaterial . . . something disembodied, supersensory and supernatural', but the Old Testament uses of *ruach* depict God as 'a tempest, a storm, a force in body and soul, humanity and nature'.[91] The word needs liberating, therefore, from the dualistic thought-world in which 'spirit' is antithetical to 'matter'. Consequently, Moltmann defines *ruach* in a threefold sense as 'the confronting event of the personal presence of God', 'the life force immanent in all the living', and 'the space of freedom in which the living being can unfold'.[92] Israel's judges, prophets and kings are said to have possessed *ruach*, and thereby the nation was endowed with God's Spirit. However, individuals were also spoken of as having an inward experience of the Spirit, thus referring to 'God's commitment to the human person'.[93] *Ruach* enables people to keep God's commandments, which in turn results in a renewed fellowship between people and God. Moltmann further notes that in the Old Testament Spirit (*ruach*) is interchangeable with Wisdom (*hokma*). What is said about Wisdom can also be said of Spirit. In the Patristic period, though, it

---

[86] Ibid.
[87] Ibid., p 17.
[88] Ibid., p 34.
[89] Ibid., p 37.
[90] Ibid., p 40.
[91] Ibid.
[92] Ibid., pp 42, 43.
[93] Ibid., p 45.

was not uncommon for Wisdom to be regarded as a prefiguration of the Spirit. Moltmann suggests, therefore, that the Spirit is 'immanent transcendence', not only 'a kind of counterpart in God himself' but also 'the divine presence in creation and history'.[94]

The description of the Spirit which emerges from Moltmann's exegetical work is then related by him to the Jewish notion of the Shekinah. In doing so he returns to a theme we earlier encountered in his doctrine of creation. The Shekinah, he reminds us, is 'the descent and indwelling of God in space and time, at a particular place and a particular era of earthly beings and in their history'.[95] Kabbalistic thinkers describe 'the radiant brightness' of the Shekinah as the Holy Spirit, so Moltmann suggests that the theology of the Shekinah helps our understanding of the Spirit in three ways. First, it helps draw out 'the personal character of the Spirit'.[96] The Spirit is God as personally present to people and the whole of creation. Secondly, it refers us to 'the sensibility of God the Spirit'.[97] The Spirit is not impassive, but is intimately affected by life. She 'suffers' both the world's joy and pain. Thirdly, it follows that the Shekinah points to 'the kenosis of the Spirit' whereby God empties Godself of impassibility, becoming 'able to suffer because he is willing to love'.[98]

Moltmann also sets the Spirit in the context of Israel's messianic expectations, returning to a familiar eschatological theme in his theology. The expected Messiah will be endowed by *ruach*. He will bring compassion and justice to the poor and wretched, and he will proclaim what Moltmann calls 'the ultimate and eternal sabbath of the End-time'.[99] God's Spirit therefore was responsible for 'the corporate hope' of Israel, and the creation of 'a prophetic people'.[100]

When he turns from the Hebrew Bible to the New Testament, Moltmann emphasises the Spirit's role in Jesus' career: ' . . . the operation of the divine Spirit is the pre-condition or premise for the history of Jesus of Nazareth.'[101] Jesus' ministry was launched at his baptism by John when 'Jesus had his special experience of the Spirit'.[102] The Spirit 'descended' upon Jesus and came to 'rest' upon him. What Jesus was able to do then arose from the Spirit's power which drove him (Mark 1: 12) and led him (Luke 4: 1). Even on the road to the Cross Jesus is accompanied by the Spirit. Moltmann argues, therefore, that the Spirit is 'the transcendent side of Jesus' immanent way of suffering'.[103] He tells us that 'the real controlling agents' in our Lord's passion and death were not the Romans: 'It is Christ himself who is the truly active one, through the operation of the divine Spirit who acts in him.'[104] On the cross, 'the Spirit suffers the suffering and death of the Son, without dying with him.'[105] Picking up his key idea of 'the hidden, absent, even rejecting Father, Moltmann claims that 'in the strength of the indwelling and sym-pathetic divine Spirit, Jesus endures the God-forsakenness vicariously, on behalf of the God-forsaken world; and by doing so he brings the world God's intimate nearness – that is, reconciliation with him.'[106] The Spirit, therefore, plays a key role in Christ's saving work.

---

[94] Ibid., p 47.
[95] Ibid.
[96] Ibid., p 51.
[97] Ibid. Italics removed.
[98] Ibid. Italics removed.
[99] Ibid., p 53.
[100] Ibid., pp 55, 57. Italics removed.
[101] Ibid., p 60.
[102] Ibid.
[103] Ibid., p 62.
[104] Ibid., p 63.
[105] Ibid., p 64.
[106] Ibid., p 65.

Looking beyond the crucifixion, Moltmann highlights how the New Testament attributes the course of the resurrection to the Spirit. There is a close proximity between Easter and Pentecost. Those who saw the risen Christ were aware of 'the life-giving power of the Spirit', while it was the Spirit who enabled them to perceive the risen Christ in the first place.[107] The rise to faith which resulted was the Spirit's work; it was a response to the Word Jesus reveals and is, as well as the start of a new way of living. Moltmann, therefore, tells us that viewed christologically faith is a response, while when viewed eschatologically it is a beginning. It follows, then, that 'it is pneumatology that brings christology and eschatology together'.[108] Meanwhile, the church living from faith in Christ and looking forward in hope finds new gifts and possibilities through the Spirit.

The Holy Spirit brings new life to people in two distinct ways. First, people are set free from 'the obstructions of guilt and the melancholy of death'.[109] Alongside this inward form of liberation, Moltmann speaks secondly of a more outward breaking of 'the compulsions of economic, political and cultural repression'.[110] Perhaps influenced by the liberation theologians he manages to achieve a balance between the redemptive and emancipatory dimensions of God's liberation. Not only is new life affirmed inwardly, but also outwardly new spaces emerge for living. Moltmann is critical of understandings of the Spirit which view her merely as 'the subjective operation of the objective word of God in the hearts of believers', since they fail to give due account of the way the Spirit 'opens new possibilities round about us through the circumstances of history.'[111] He insists that, 'to believe God simply means getting up out of oppression and resignation, and laying hold of our freedom, and living.'[112] And, lest we are to attribute to Moltmann a Pelagian tendency, it is important to bear in mind that he regards the possibility of 'getting up' and 'laying hold' as being created by the Spirit. The great paradigms of liberation are the Exodus and the Resurrection. Moltmann consequently challenges contemporary Christians to become 'radicals' who remember 'the experiences of their own roots'.[113] He asks pointedly:

> Why are the traditions about Israel's Exodus and Christ's resurrection not at the very centre of the Christian churches? Why do the pictures and religious imaginings of the divine majesty resemble earthly potentates rather than the crucified and risen Liberator? Surely these ideas about God's majesty are drawn from the Christian rulers of Byzantium, rather than from the radiance that streams from the face of Jesus Christ?[114]

We always run the risk of constructing 'God' according to our image!

But what does the liberated life opened up by the Spirit entail? Moltmann's answer to this question revolves around three dimensions. First, the freedom which issues forth in faith involves us being taken 'personally captive'.[115] As Moltmann says, 'true freedom . . . means being possessed by the divine energy of life, and participation in that energy.'[116] The Christian life, therefore, involves being

---

[107] Ibid., p 66.
[108] Ibid., p 69.
[109] Ibid., p 99.
[110] Ibid.
[111] Ibid., p 103.
[112] Ibid., p 101.
[113] Ibid., p 109.
[114] Ibid.
[115] Ibid., p 114.
[116] Ibid., p 115.

drawn by the Spirit into God's creativity, as well as grasping the new opportunities and undreamed of potentiality which ensues. In addition to the subjective side of freedom, Moltmann refers secondly to its social side. This is called 'love or solidarity'.[117] What was separated or estranged is brought together: individuals and God, person and person, society and nature, soul and body. Thirdly, Moltmann speaks of freedom as it is aligned to the future – 'the future of the coming God'.[118] He defines it as 'the creative passion for the possible' and 'the creativity in the forecourt of the possible which breaks down frontiers'.[119] Therefore true liberation finds its fullest expression in faith, love – and, finally, hope.

Moltmann makes the point that God endows all those called to faith with gifts: 'This means that every Christian is a charismatic, even if many people never live out their gifts.'[120] And, by and large, Moltmann is more favourably disposed to phenomena associated with the so-called charismatic churches than many other mainline theologians. Commenting about the phenomenon of 'speaking with tongues', he rounds on the mainstream churches:

> It is certainly true that our regular, mainline church services display a wealth of ideas and reflections in their sermons, but are poverty–stricken in their forms of expression, and offer no opportunity at all for spontaneity. They are disciplined and disciplinary assemblies for talking and listening. But does the body of Christ really consist simply of one big mouth and a lot of little ears?[121]

Fearing that 'the mainline churches and the bishops and other leaders may "quench" the Spirit of the "charismatic movement"', Moltmann asks that 'we should all make room for the Spirit, not only in church services, but in our bodies too, since those bodies are, after all, supposed to be "a temple of the Holy Spirit"'.[122] Nevertheless Moltmann's question to the Charismatic Movement should also be voiced: 'Where are the charismata of the "charismatics" in the everyday world, in the peace movement, in the movements for liberation, in the ecology movement?'[123] The question is a valid one, and it will find some 'charismatics' wanting. But, in fairness, it will make many a current URC member uneasy as well, since the de-politicizing of religion is not the sole pastime of 'charismatics'!

Moltmann also displays a quite open attitude to the ministry of healing. He likens healings to signs of new life; they belong to 'the charismatic experience of life' and are a harbinger of resurrection and eternal life.[124] The healing ministry, therefore, is an essential part of the Church's apostolic mission. It carries on Jesus' ministry, and, as a result, Jesus provides the shape of the Church's healing ministry. His healing power resides in 'the power of his suffering', with the effect of healing being the restoration of people to fellowship with God.[125] God assumed humanity to heal it:

> In the passion of Jesus Christ God has assumed sick, weak, helpless and disabled human life and made it part of his own eternal life. God heals the sicknesses and the griefs by making the sicknesses and the griefs his suffering and his grief.[126]

---

[117]   Ibid., p 118.
[118]   Ibid., p 119.
[119]   Ibid. Italics removed.
[120]   Ibid., p 180.
[121]   Ibid., p 185.
[122]   Ibid., p 186.
[123]   Ibid.
[124]   Ibid., p 189.
[125]   Ibid., p 191. Italics removed.
[126]   Ibid.

Moltmann also is insistent that the Spirit's healing power should be understood as working on the whole person. He is critical of modern views of health which mean little more than the restoration of the functions of the body's organs. People need to be treated holistically, and due attention should be given to our being psychosomatic beings, since supposedly physical ailments may well have psychological or spiritual causes. But just where faith-healing and medicine begin and end is never made clear by Moltmann.

Finally, we can note four patterns within which Moltmann sets the Holy Spirit in a Trinitarian text. First, there is the *monarchical* pattern in which 'the One God reveals himself through himself and communicates himself to men and women.'[127] God's work in the world, therefore, stems from the Father, is mediated by the Son, and is completed in the Spirit. 'All activity proceeds from the Father, the Son is always its mediator, and the Holy Spirit the mediation.'[128] It follows that the Spirit simply carries out the work of the Father and Son and has no independent activity. Secondly, there is the *historical* concept in which due notice is taken of 'the sequence of the times of the Father, the Son and the Holy Spirit in salvation history'.[129] This pattern is often linked to the monarchical idea since it can say in a temporal sequence what was expressed monarchically in terms of the vertical relation between eternity and time. The work of sanctification (Spirit) depends upon the work of reconciliation (Son), and both depend upon the work of creation (Father). What is started by the Father finds its culmination in the Spirit. Thirdly, there is the *eucharistic* pattern.[130] While the previous patterns lead naturally to talk of a threefold God, the eucharistic trinitarian concept is best expressed in terms of God's triunity. The work of the Spirit arouses in us thankfulness, adoration and praise. We are moved to respond to God's graciousness through the Son. If the sequence in the monarchical and historical patterns is Father – Son – Spirit, in the eucharistic concept the order is reversed: Spirit – Son – Father.

By attributing the work of glorification to the Spirit, Moltmann gives the third member of the Trinity a function which is not simply a completion of the work of the Father, nor only an activity which ultimately is mediated by the Son. He is able, therefore, to develop a social concept of the Trinity in which the three persons are unique subjects who relate to each other. Fourthly, and finally, Moltmann directs our attention to a pattern which moves beyond the other three. It takes us further than salvation history and places us before 'the eternal essence of God himself'.[131] Moltmann calls this the *trinitarian doxology,* and the basis for the idea is found in the Nicene Creed: 'who with the Father and the Son together is worshipped and glorified.' The emphasis now is upon the equality of Father, Son and Spirit, and the worship and glorification which clearly goes beyond our experience of salvation and the thanksgiving which that in turn generates for us. Turning to the mystical traditions of the church, Moltmann talks of the pattern of eucharistic triunity changing into the pattern of the trinitarian doxology when the point is reached that 'thanksgiving is transformed into prayer, faith into sight and all self-concern is lost in selfless astonishment'.[132] He therefore moves in a typically ecumenical manner to insights and experience outside his own tradition in order to develop his theological perspective. Using ideas from mystical experience he claims that we can arrive at a point through meditation when we can know God *as God is* in the Trinity. This is the

---

[127] Ibid., p 290. See also *The Trinity and the Kingdom of God,* pp 126–8.
[128] Ibid., p 291.
[129] Ibid., p 295.
[130] See ibid., pp 298–301.
[131] Ibid., pp 301–2.
[132] Ibid., p 302.

moment of trinitarian doxology which, Moltmann claims, is 'the sitz im Leben for the concept of the immanent Trinity'.[133] We have moved from 'the linear monarchical movement of God's self-communication to human beings', and 'the eucharistic movement of the self-communication of human beings to God', and now arrived at 'the self-circling and self-reposing movement of *perichoresis*'.[134] But the more empirically-minded may wonder whether we have moved too far and too quickly. Are we ever free in this life of the phenomenon which hinders and distorts our vision of God? Does meditation and contemplation finally remove the corrupting influence of sin? Many of the church's wisest minds have recognized that there comes a time in theological investigation when one responsibly can go no further. When theologians start discussing the nature of the immanent Trinity they perhaps have gone beyond that point.

---

[133] Ibid. Italics removed.
[134] Ibid., p 304.

CHAPTER 11

The Christian Experience of Salvation through Christ

GRANTED that 'all have sinned and fall short of the glory of God' (Rom. 3: 23) how are we to become right with God? The theological battle line at the Reformation centred upon this question, with the standard of the Reformers having emblazoned upon it the slogan *sola fide sola gratia* (by faith alone by grace alone). To gain some understanding of what was involved we will begin with an investigation of the meaning of the major concepts involved in the debate.

Justification

Justification comes from the Latin *justificatio* which was used in the Vulgate to translate *dikaiosis*, a key term of Paul's theology. In Galatians and Romans, Paul talks of the act by which God brings persons into a proper relationship with Godself. This is *dikaiosis*, the occasion when God declares the verdict upon sinners that they are 'righteous' or 'just'. The idea has forensic connotations going back into Judaism: individuals stand in God's court, but are declared innocent; they are *justified* in God's sight. Paul put forward a key alternative to the way he believed the idea functions in Judaism. Instead of adherence to the Jewish law being regarded as the means by which sinners are made right by God, Paul taught a doctrine of righteousness through faith in Christ apart from the Law (Rom. 3: 21–25; 9: 30–31; Gal 2: 15–16). He answered the questions concerning how sinners are made right with God in a forthright and controversial fashion. We are justified by faith through God's free and unmerited act of sending Christ as the atonement for our sin, rather than made righteous before God through merit accrued from our noble efforts and good works. Paul's teaching was both honoured and developed by Augustine. In his debate with Pelagius, Augustine was well aware of the all-pervading influence of sin upon human life. No one can accuse him of forgetting Paul's law (Rom. 7: 21); neither can anyone convict him of condoning boasting about human ability to do what is required in God's eyes. All pretensions to pride were firmly rebutted by him, since, like Paul, he recognized the essential place of God's grace in the search for fulfilment. But whereas for Paul justification seems to have been essentially a forensic term, a declaration that a sinner due to God's grace was in fact righteous after all, with Augustine it also carries a connotation of God actually making the sinner righteous. So Augustine speaks of God's grace effecting 'the healing of the soul from the disorder of sin'.[1] He draws appropriately upon another famous Pauline passage: ' . . . God's love has been poured into our hearts through the Holy Spirit that has been given to us' (Rom. 5: 5). The Christian is enabled to perform good works, but such good works are a product of, and not the pre-condition for, the granting of God's grace; they are not the *cause* of justification but rather the *result* of it.

---

[1]   Found in Bettenson, ed., *The Later Christian Fathers,* p 207.

If the understanding of justification advanced by Augustine had prevailed, Luther's polemic against the prevailing theology of salvation would not have been required. What caused it was the teaching of later Medieval theology that justifying grace had to be earned. But the idea that salvation could be earned was anathema to Luther; while the notion that the eternal penalties, imposed because of sins committed on earth, could be remitted through paying fees to priests (indulgences) added further insult to his theological injury. Originally, of course, indulgences were a thank-offering made by a penitent in a response of gratitude for their forgiveness, but eventually they became what Alister McGrath ruefully calls 'an important source of income for a papacy facing a financial crisis and prepared to be flexible in its theology in order to meet it'.[2] As the material expression of dangerous theological ideas, the practice of indulgences prompted Luther's attack on the church and his championing of justification as it earlier had been understood by Augustine. He proclaimed that God has granted us everything which is necessary for our salvation. All we have to do is to receive God's graciousness as a gift. We are justified by God's grace *through* faith in Christ. Luther thereby eschewed the idea that good works can cause our justification; he asserted instead that they are the result of God's graciousness in counting sinners as righteous.

Sanctification

The root meaning of the term sanctification is found in the Latin *sanctus* which means 'holy'. When employed in Christian theology, sanctification refers to the process by which believers are given new life by the Spirit and thereby are freed from sin's captivity, enabled truly to love God and serve others, and achieve holiness. But the Roman Catholic and Protestant views concerning the way in which we achieve holiness have been a battleground of controversy.

Roman Catholic theology traditionally did not make a radical distinction between justification and santification. According to this theology, divine grace is needed to overcome our original sin and to transmit to our souls a disposition which will lead us to full salvation. Salvation, however, is not the product of faith alone; also involved are the sacramental and penitential rites of the Roman Catholic Church. These are a means by which the ongoing post-baptismal sins of believers are remitted. Special bestowals of grace are needed if all sin is to be eliminated, and since we commit sin to our dying day, forgiveness is only completed at the last rites. This means that, for the classical Roman Catholic view, justification is the equivalent of complete sanctification. Protestants, on the other hand, conceive the relationship between justification and sanctification somewhat differently. For them, faith leads to two outcomes: first, believers receive God's forgiveness of their sin through the Christ event; and, secondly, they commence the process of sanctification through the agency of the Spirit. In contradiction to the Roman position, Protestant theology refused to make the first outcome conditional upon the second. Sanctification flows quite naturally from justification. It is not dependent in any way upon human merit, and therefore it is certainly God's gift rather than our goal.

Paul is quite clear about what distinguishes believers from non-believers. The following passage is representative of his position:

---

[2]   McGrath, *Reformation Thought: An Introduction*, p 103.

> Do you not know that wrongdoers will not inherit the Kingdom of God? Do not be deceived! Fornicators, idolaters, adulterers, male prostitutes, sodomites, thieves, the greedy, drunkards, revilers, robbers – none of these will inherit the kingdom of God. And this is what some of you used to be. But you were washed, you were sanctified, you were justified in the name of the Lord Jesus Christ and in the Spirit of our God (I Cor. 6: 9–11).

The phrases 'were washed', 'were sanctified' and 'were justified' indicate quite clearly that Paul locates salvation's root in something which is done for believers rather than in any purportedly meritorious deeds done by them. But where do deeds fit into the scheme of things? What about James's declaration that 'faith without works is . . . dead' (James 2: 26)? Clearly, good works are an important dimension of the Christian life, and Paul no less than James is clear that the Holy Spirit makes it possible for good works to flourish in believers (Gal. 5: 22–26). Whatever James's theological intentions might have been (and Luther regarded them as sub-Christian), Paul has guided subsequent Protestant theology to the belief that good works are the natural outpourings of a life on the way to a salvation which will be completed at a final judgement. They are not to be seen as the pre-condition of making our salvation possible.

Reformed theologies have also tended to resist the idea that salvation can be fully attained in this life. Calvin is very positive when speaking of what the Holy Spirit can achieve in us. Ever the realist, though, he was unable to take a route later to be mapped out by John Wesley. Wesley argued that salvation was fully possible in this life. Of course, few of Wesley's followers have found themselves able to accept his doctrine of Christian perfection, since, like their Reformed counterparts, Methodists by and large agree that what may be a possibility in principle is far from being a possibility in fact! As Calvin has noted, there are always 'traces of our imperfection' around in everything that we do, and these 'give us occasion for humility'.[3] A person may be justified and involved in the process of sanctification, but that person still remains a sinner – although the sins which occur during a person's life are not counted against faithful people. The believer is at one and the same time justified and a sinner (*simul iustus et peccator*).

John Calvin on Salvation

The classic Reformed understanding of salvation has been provided for us by Calvin. Summarising what he sees as God's benefits which faith bestows, and the effects it brings to individuals, Calvin speaks of sinners receiving 'a double grace', namely, first, 'that being reconciled to God through Christ's blamelessness, we may have in heaven instead of a Judge a gracious Father; and secondly, that sanctified by Christ's spirit we may cultivate blamelessness and purity of life.'[4] The two aspects of the 'double grace' are justification and regeneration. Calvin goes on to call 'justification' 'the main hinge on which religion turns'[5] and 'the sum of all piety'.[6] But what does he understand by the term?

Calvin tells us that the justified are those who have grasped 'the righteousness of Christ through faith' and who then appear before God 'not as a sinner but as a righteous man'.[7] Sinners are justified by God through Christ's intercession to God on our behalf. We are absolved of sin 'not by the confirmation of our own innocence but by the imputation of righteousness, so that we who

---

3   Calvin, *Institutes* 3,14,9.
4   Ibid., 3,11,1.
5   Ibid.
6   Ibid., 3,15,7.
7   Ibid., 3,11,2.

are not righteous in ourselves may be reckoned as such in Christ.'[8] Through faith we enter upon a union with Christ which leads to both our justification and regeneration. Whereas some Reformers view justification as the presupposition of regeneration, claiming that believers start the process of sanctification on account of their justification, Calvin asserts that both justification and regeneration flow from the union of persons with Christ through faith.

Calvin refused to countenance the Roman Catholic view that faith is 'an assurance of conscience in awaiting from God their reward for merits',[9] since sin's all-pervading influence upon our lives means that ultimately we are devoid of the good works which warrant 'reward for merits'. Nor did he accept the interpretation of 'the grace of God . . . as the Spirit helping in the pursuit of holiness', since Calvin understands God's grace as 'the imputation of free righteousness'.[10] He was convinced that his views were supported by the teaching of Scripture on salvation:

> But Scripture . . . leads us . . . to turn aside from the contemplation of our own works and look solely upon God's mercy and Christ's perfection. Indeed, it presents this order of justification: to begin with, God deigns to embrace the sinner with his pure and freely given goodness, finding nothing in him except his miserable condition to prompt Him to mercy, since he sees man utterly void and bare of good works; and so he seeks in himself the reason to benefit man. Then God touches the sinner with a sense of his goodness in order that he, despairing of his own works, may ground the whole of his salvation in God's mercy. This is the experience of faith through which the sinner comes into possession of his salvation when from the teaching of the gospel he acknowledges that he has been reconciled to God: that with Christ's righteousness interceding and forgiveness of sins accomplished he is justified. And although regenerated by the Spirit of God, he ponders the everlasting righteousness laid up for him not in the good works to which he inclines but in the sole righteousness of God.[11]

Essential to Calvin's argument is a recognition that there is nothing within human beings or done by them that merits their righteousness before God. While works clearly have value, since they are the means by which we show our obedience to God, they are not the basis upon which our salvation is based. As Calvin says: '. . . the heart cannot be opened to receive [God's] mercy unless it be utterly empty of all opinion of its own worth.'[12] Indeed, arrogance and complacency regarding our own worth and ability is a fundamental barrier to our salvation: 'For we will never have enough confidence in him unless we become deeply distrustful of ourselves; we will never lift up our hearts enough in him unless they be previously cast down in us; we will never have consolation enough in him unless we have already experienced desolation in ourselves.'[13] We have to learn to place our faith in God – and God alone!

Calvin does not conceive faith in terms of giving assent to beliefs and propositions; instead, he speaks of it in terms of placing our ultimate trust in God:

> For to have faith is not to waver, to vary, to be borne up and down, to hesitate, to be held in suspense, to vacillate – finally, to despair! Rather, to have faith is to strengthen the mind with constant assurance and perfect confidence, to have a place of rest and plant your foot . . .[14]

---

[8]   Ibid., 3,11,3.
[9]   Ibid., 3,11,15.
[10]   Ibid.
[11]   Ibid., 3,11,16.
[12]   Ibid., 3,12,7.
[13]   Ibid., 3,12,8.
[14]   Ibid., 3,13,3.

And the 'place to rest and plant your foot' is found in the good news that without any merit on our part we are justified by God's grace revealed in Christ. If the efficient cause of our salvation resides in the Father's love, the material cause is found in the Son's obedience. Meanwhile, the instrumental cause of our salvation is discovered in the Spirit's engendering of faith in us, while the final cause resides 'in the glory of God's great generosity'.[15] At no point does our salvation reside in any merit of ours. Merit is non-biblical – 'a most prideful term, it can do nothing but obscure God's favor and imbue men with perverse haughtiness.'[16]

Only the regenerate are capable of doing good, and their capacity to do it is entirely the result of the Spirit working with them. Through the regenerate's union with Christ, therefore, they enter upon not only Christ's righteousness but also his sanctification. It follows, therefore, that justification involves good works: ' . . . we are justified not without works yet not through works, since in our sharing in Christ, which justifies us, sanctification is just as much included as righteousness.'[17]

The Protestant–Catholic Debate

Today's ecumenical scene is rather different from Calvin's Geneva. Protestants and Roman Catholics have come to share the view that they are not strangers but fellow pilgrims. On the surface at least, it seems that the doctrinal differences which emerged at the Reformation have been largely overcome. Those differences, of course, centred upon rival visions of God. McGrath defines the competing conceptions as 'a harsh judge who rewards individuals according to their merits' (Roman Catholic) and 'a merciful and gracious God who bestows righteousness upon sinners as a gift' (Protestant).[18] He uses a well-known analogy to remind us of what was at stake in the Reformation debate:

> Let us suppose that you are in prison, and are offered your freedom on condition that you pay a heavy fine. The promise is real – so long as you can meet the pre-condition, the promise will be fulfilled. Pelagius . . . work(s) on the pre-supposition, initially shared by Luther, that you have the necessary money stashed away somewhere. As your freedom is worth far more than the money, you are being offered a bargain. So you pay the fine. But Luther increasingly came to share the view of Augustine that sinful humanity just doesn't have the resources. They work on the assumption that, since you don't have the money, the promise of freedom has little relevance to your situation. For both Augustine and Luther, therefore, the good news of the Gospel is that you have been given the necessary money with which to buy your freedom. In other words, the pre-condition has been met for you by someone else.[19]

And as the Roman Catholic–Protestant debate developed, the respective positions became caricatured. Roman Catholics have tended to view the Protestant view as purely legalistic and forensic, with Christ doing the forgiving and no inner change in the sinner being required at all; while Protestants have tended to regard the Roman Catholic view as being based upon human merit and a somewhat magical understanding of the Roman church's sacramental and penitential rites. While theologians can be found who did or do represent such caricatured positions, neither does

[15]   Ibid., 3,14,21. See also 3,14,17.
[16]   Ibid., 3,15,2.
[17]   Ibid., 3,16,l.
[18]   McGrath, *Reformation Thought: An Introduction*, p 96.
[19]   Ibid.

justice to the view of most theologians on either side in the debate. Calvin's emphasis upon the Spirit's work in our regeneration helps protect him against the charge that the Protestant position does not involve an inner change in the believer in the salvific process. Meanwhile, some Roman Catholics regard what they call 'merit' as a gift from God – hence they conclude that justification is entirely gratuitous!

Sometimes disputes revolve around key terms being understood in different ways, thus creating unnecessary division or unfounded unity. In one respect at least the Roman Catholic–Protestant debate over salvation's meaning is an example of the former. Roman Catholics viewed justification as the event by which a person is made right with God through Christ's atoning work and the process by which that person is made holy through the internal work of the Spirit on that person. Calvin, on the other hand, distinguished between justification – the event whereby we are made righteous through the cross, and sanctification – the process of regeneration effected by the Spirit. The result was that Roman Catholics and Protestants were able to use the word 'justification' to mean quite different things, with Roman Catholics using it in a way that, for Protestants, meant not just justification but also sanctification. A great deal of the Roman Catholic–Protestant debate, therefore, resembled a dialogue of the deaf.

We end this brief chapter by noting the ecumenical convergence which has emerged on this issue. The Report of the Second Phase of the Reformed / Roman Catholic International Dialogue (1984-90)[20] reflects the tremendous advances in inter-denominational understanding which have been made possible due to the Ecumenical Movement. The Report affirms that 'we are justified by the grace which comes from [Christ], by means of faith which is a living and life-giving faith', and it explicitly states that 'our justification is a totally gratuitous work accomplished by God in Christ' (para 77). Persons who are justified can live 'according to righteousness' and they are expected 'to bear fruits worthy of that grace' (para 79). Justification by faith, therefore, brings with it the gift of sanctification which 'can grow continuously as it creates life, justice and liberty' (para 79). And then the Report asserts that 'All justification takes place in the community of believers, or is ordered toward the gathering of such a community' (para 80). Christ is present in the church as both 'a reality of grace' (a typically Protestant view) and 'a concrete community in time and space' (a typically Roman Catholic view) (para 80). This understanding perhaps reflects the Report's concern to hold together two different understandings of the Church: the Reformed idea of the Church as the creation of the Word (*creatura verbi*) and the Roman Catholic notion of the Church as a Sacrament of Grace. Whatever else we make of this Report the very least we can acknowledge is that the Reformed–Roman Catholic debate no longer needs to reflect the polemics of the Reformation and the era which followed it up to the Second Vatican Council.

---

[20]   *Towards a Common Understanding of the Church* (Geneva: World Alliance of Reformed Churches, 1991).

CHAPTER 12

Can All Be Saved?

WHY IS it that some people believe in the Christian gospel while others do not? Does the answer lie in the fact that only a section of humankind find it persuasive? Or might it be the case that God has so arranged it that some will respond to the divine call while others will spurn it? To seek answers to these questions we turn now to consider the ideas of election and predestination. Both concepts have played significant roles in the way many Reformed theologians have sought to answer the question: Can all be saved?

Election

Central to both the Hebrew and Christian scriptures is the idea that God chooses some but not others, to carry out the divine will. Israel is said to be the Elect nation simply on account of the fact that God loved it: 'And because he loved your ancestors, he chose their descendants after them. He brought you out of Egypt with his own presence, by his great power, driving out before you nations greater and mightier than yourselves, to bring you in, giving you their land for a possession, as it is still today' (Deut. 4: 37–39). The skeptical person, of course, will wonder whether the Exodus should be seen as an act of liberation or as the brutal ethnic cleansing of Canaan. Once the idea that persons are 'chosen' over and above other peoples gets established it seems inevitable that those who are not chosen become oppressed by those that are. Nevertheless, the Jewish scriptures claim that Israel was elected by God gratuitously and without any reference to whether or not the nation merited it. Indeed, we are told that Israel did not earn election because of its size (Deut.7: 7) or its righteousness (Deut.9: 4–7); rather the nation was chosen solely by God's sovereign will.

When we turn to the New Testament the same theme is prominent. Jesus chooses his disciples irrespective of their merit: 'For many are called, but few are chosen' (Matt. 22: 14). After Easter, some writers came to view the church, called and chosen by God, as the New Israel. One writer, for example, can describe the church as 'a chosen race, a royal priesthood, a holy nation, God's own people (1 Pet. 2: 9), before going on to illustrate what he means by using a passage which in it is original context refers to Israel rather than the church:

> Once you were not a people,
> but now you are God's people;
> once you had not received mercy,
> but now you have received mercy
> (1 Peter 2: 10; see Hos. 2: 23).

The same theme is found in John's Gospel: 'You did not choose me but I chose you' (John 15: 16); while it is affirmed every time we sing:

Elect from every nation,
yet one o'er all the earth,
her charter of salvation
one Lord, one faith, one birth:
one holy name she blesses,
partakes one holy food,
and to one hope she presses
with every grace endured.
(Samuel J Stone)

But what is the purpose of election? Is being elected as the chosen people an end in itself, so that the elect can glory and laud it over the rest? Or are Israel and the church chosen for a purpose, such that the few are elected to bear witness to the many? The latter answer is most typical of scripture. A universal divine intention is achieved by choosing a particular person or people to fulfill a task. Lesslie Newbigin provides us with some examples:

> [God] chooses one to be the bearer of his blessing for the many. Abraham is chosen to be the pioneer of faith and so to receive the blessing through which all nations will be blessed. Moses is chosen to be the agent of Israel's redemption; Israel is chosen to be a kingdom of priests for the whole earth. The disciples are chosen that they may be 'fishers of men' (Mark 1: 17) or, in another metaphor, that they may 'go and bear fruit' (John 15: 16). The church is a body chosen 'to declare the wonderful deeds' of God (1 Pet. 2: 9).[1]

While the doctrine of election undoubtedly has served as a warrant for some Christians and churches to adopt an elitist and superior attitude towards their fellow human beings, there are countless statements in scripture which would condemn such an understanding. To be chosen by God, the Bible would suggest, carries with it certain clear responsibilities and radical demands. Nor have the elect any grounds for boasting about their status or standing.

> Consider your own call, brothers and sisters: not many of you were wise by human standards, not many were powerful, not many were of noble birth. But God chose what is foolish in the world to shame the wise; God chose what is weak in the world to shame the strong; God chose what is low and despised in the world, things that are not, to reduce to nothing things that are, so that no one might boast in the presence of God (1 Cor 1: 26–29).

Many people find it hard to believe that God chooses some rather than others, and in a totally arbitrary way devoid of all references to whether or not the chosen merit their election. Why should some be favoured and not the others? This question is partially answered when certain features of election are borne in mind. First, election represents the biblical paradigm for the way in which God's universal purpose is worked out. As Newbigin puts it: 'From the beginning of the Bible to its end we are presented with the story of a universal purpose carried out through a continuous series of particular choices.'[2] Secondly, all suggestions that election bestows upon the chosen a privileged status and grounds for elitist attitudes are undercut by the recognition that, according to Newbigin's reading of the Bible, 'God . . . purposes the salvation of all.'[3] The elect's responsibility is

---

[1] Lesslie Newbigin, *The Open Secret: Sketches for a Missionary Theology* (Grand Rapids, Michigan: William B Eerdmans, 1978), p 75.
[2] Ibid.
[3] Ibid., p 80.

to witness to God's offer of the possibility of salvation for all – and that, says Newbigin, is 'a fearful responsibility' rooted in being God's servant.[4] Thirdly, any idea that election involves establishing a contract between God and the elect should be set to one side. The basic idea is not that of people following some commands in order to receive a subsequent benefit, since the key to the relationship between God and the elect is the notion of 'covenant' rather than 'contract'. And, as Newbigin says, 'The covenant is an act of the free grace of God; it is the unconditional promise of blessing to be received by faith.'[5]

The above considerations, however, cannot fully divert our attention away from those who are not chosen. At the end of the day, are some people rejected by God? We all know of people who have decided to reject the gospel. Does this mean that there are some people who have the will to resist the One who 'purposes the salvation of all'? If that is the case, the omnipotence of God is called into question. But, if the saving purpose of God is irresistible, what then becomes of human freedom? To answer these and other related questions Reformed theologians have traditionally turned to the idea of predestination.

Predestination

Vestiges of a doctrine of predestination are found in the New Testament (Rom. 8: 20, 29–30; Eph. 1: 3–4). The doctrine declares that God decrees from eternity who will or will not be saved. It was developed by Augustine who stood resolutely by the principle that the ground upon which God elects people for salvation is not the merit people possess but simply God's inscrutable decision. Holiness is a consequence of election but never its cause.

Augustine's basic argument can be reduced to four claims: (i) everyone is utterly lost due to sin; (ii) only the grace of God can make it possible that individuals adopt the stance of faith; (iii) God's grace is utterly irresistible; and (iv) God's grace is only given to a limited number of people, the others therefore are passed over.[6] Predestination therefore refers to God giving grace to some but not all, and to the divine decision to bestow grace on those who are to be saved. Interestingly, Augustine does not talk of the non-elect being damned, but he does claim that God passes them over. If we begin from the premise that God elects some but not all for salvation, then surely the demands of logic suggest that God must thereby be electing the rest to damnation? Many may be pleased that Augustine's awareness of God's boundless saving love may well have triumphed over the niceties of theological logic at this point! But they will be disappointed to learn that the Reformers were less prepared to hold back from asserting the inevitable, given their starting point of asserting God's sovereign will over any other divine attribute, including love.

Contrary to theological folklore, the doctrine of predestination is not primary in the theology of John Calvin.[7] It is, however, a central doctrine which appears in the Reformer's treatment of salvation. McGrath tells us that 'Calvin's predestinarianism is to be regarded as *a posteriori* reflection

---

[4] Ibid., p 81.

[5] Ibid., p 83.

[6] See Augustine, *On the Predestination of the Saints* in Philip Schaff, ed., *A Select Library of the Nicene and Post-Nicene Fathers of the Christian Church* (Edinburgh: T & T Clark and Grand Rapids, Michigan: Wm B Eerdmans Publishing Company, 1997).

[7] See Alan P F Sell, *The Great Debate: Calvinism, Arminianism and Salvation* (Worthing: H E Walter Ltd., 1982) for a refutation of the popularist view that 'Calvin was a narrow-minded dogmatist, who so exalted his favourite doctrine, predestination, as to expel all real religion from Christianity, and to land us in a remorselessly logical cerebralism from which Augustine's ecclesiastical palliatives were expunged' (p 2).

upon the data of human experience, interpreted in the light of Scripture, rather than something which is deduced *a priori* on the basis of preconceived ideas concerning divine omnipotence.[8] Nevertheless, Calvin does not demur in inviting us to be drawn into the mystery of some people being predestined to respond to God's gracious offer of salvation but not the rest. It is a fact, he argues, that 'God by his secret plan freely chooses whom he pleases, rejecting others.'[9] Of course, Calvin affirms that God's election of the chosen carries with it great responsibilities rather than significant privileges, but unlike Augustine he does not hold back from the seemingly logical outcome:

> We call predestination God's eternal decree, by which he compacted with himself what he willed to become of each man. For all are not created in equal condition; rather, eternal life is foreordained for some, eternal damnation for others. Therefore, as any man has been created to one or the other of these ends, we speak of him as predestined to life or to death.[10]

Once God's absolute will is made central in a theological system and comes to dwarf and control other divine attributes like love, it is difficult to envisage an alternative answer to the question: Can all be saved?

While Calvin argues that God predestines some to 'eternal damnation' or 'death', he speaks very little about the doctrine of reprobation compared with the eternal will that some should be saved; nevertheless, he goes beyond Augustine's idea of God passing some by. Calvin wants to emphasize predestination to life, and the idea that believers can confidently know that they are recipients of God's grace, but he does not draw back from recognizing the awesome nature of a doctrine of *double* predestination, the predestination of some to life and others to death: 'The decree is dreadful indeed, I confess.'[11] His position has appalled as many people as it has impressed. McGrath is sympathetic to the idea of predestination, but he raises the opposing argument to Calvin's position quite neatly: 'Although Calvin specifically repudiates the conception of God as an absolute and *arbitrary* power, his discussion of predestination raises the spectre of a God whose relationship to his creation is whimsical and capricious and whose conception and exercise of power are not bound to any law or order.'[12] Unless the divine love exercises a more controlling role in our understanding of what God does or does not do, we will never reach that concept of God which A N Whitehead believes does justice to 'the Galilean origin of Christianity':

> It does not emphasize the ruling Caesar, or the ruthless moralist, or the unmoved mover. It dwells upon the tender elements of the world, which slowly and in quietness operate by love; and it finds purpose in the present immediacy of a kingdom not of this world. Love neither rules, nor is it unmoved; also it is a little oblivious as to morals. It does not look to the future; for it finds its own reward in the immediate present.[13]

But many of Calvin's followers took us even closer to the model of 'the ruling Caesar' who arbitrarily decides his subjects' fate.

---

8   McGrath, *Reformation Thought: An Introduction*, p 127.
9   Calvin, *Institutes* 3,21,7.
10   Ibid., 3,21,5.
11   Ibid., 3,23,7.
12   McGrath, *Reformation Thought: An Introduction*, p 128.
13   A N Whitehead, *Process and Reality: An Essay in Cosmology*, corrected edn., eds. David Ray Griffin and Donald W Sherburne (London and New York: The Free Press, 1978), p 343.

Calvin's work gave rise to intricate debates between those who maintained that God decided the decrees of election prior to the creation and fall (*supralapsarianism*) and those who argued that God enacted them after that time (*infralapsarianism*). The latter is obviously the less harsh form of the doctrine since it at least attempts to remain consistent with God's love and justice. Surely, the opponents of supralapsarianism argued, God would not condemn some to eternal damnation before they were even created, or had had due time to exercise their freedom? The idea that a person can be found guilty of a crime before they are in existence to commit it is totally repellent. But Theodore Beza thought otherwise as did *The Westminster Confession* (1647) almost a hundred years later.

The Arminian–Calvinist Debate

Jacob Arminius (1560-1609), a gifted student of Theodore Beza and Professor of Theology at Leyden (1606-1609), found supralapsarian doctrine totally abhorrent. He maintained that it could not be authorized by the Bible, the creeds or the accepted Reformed confessional statements. In addition, Arminius believed that supralapsarianism's claim that the divine creative plan included the Fall severely damages the doctrine of creation by attributing the existence of sin and evil ultimately to God. What becomes of human freedom and responsibility when one propounds a doctrine which holds that whether or not a person has saving faith is decided for them before their birth? And, furthermore, what is the point of the church's mission and evangelism if everyone's salvation has already been decided in eternity before the world's foundation? Seldom has a student developed such forceful, trenchant and appropriate criticisms of a revered teacher!

After his death, Arminius' own students and followers formularized their teacher's objections in the so-called *Arminian Remonstrant* of 1610. This provoked heated debates within the Dutch churches. In 1618, a Synod was called to provide guidance on the issue, since it was deeply dividing so-called Arminians and Calvinists. Alan Sell provides us with a helpful snapshot of what was at stake:

> Those on the evangelical Arminian wing never ceased to protest against what they took to be the reduction of the God and Father of our Lord Jesus Christ to an absolute, capricious, inscrutable will, from whose deliberations even the Son is excluded. Those on the Calvinist side were ever concerned to adopt what they considered to be accurate views of man's state – views which required sovereign grace as the only possible remedy – and to ascribe all the glory of salvation to God.[14]

The Synod of Dort ruled in favour of the prevailing Calvinist orthodoxy. It dealt with the *Remonstrant* point by point but it did not finally settle an issue which is as alive today as it was in early seventeenth century Holland.

I suspect that the URC possesses more Arminians than Calvinists! The liberal mindset finds the theology of Beza no more palatable than did John Wesley, for whom 'All have sinned, all can be saved' was considered to be nearer the truth than the alternative Calvinist slogan of 'All have sinned, only some can be saved'. Beza's view was more hard-line than Calvin's who, as we have seen, is suitably reserved about the doctrine of reprobation. Nevertheless, Wesley's protest against

---

[14]   Sell, *The Great Debate: Calvinism, Arminianism and Salvation*, p 18.

predestination and the image of God which underwrites it, according to Alan Sell, is 'a standing challenge to Calvinists to present their case with due care and humility, and, in the interests of morality, to see that the Cross is never far from their thoughts on the matter.'[15]

No understanding of salvation will be 'Christian' which underplays God's nature as we have seen it in Jesus. All too easily, doctrines of predestination present a picture of God as a sub-personal being who can as willingly consign creatures to Hell as to Heaven. Nevertheless, all Arminian approaches to salvation, including the position of Wesley, can be challenged for not taking sin with due seriousness. Given all the evidence before us, can we be confident that all can be saved? Once doubt is thrown on our ability to return a positive answer to that question, it is tempting to turn aside from Arminianism and to adopt what Sell describes as 'an ameliorated Calvinism.'[16] One of the main features of such a stance is that it does justice to Duncan's claim that 'There is a true and a false synergia. That God works half, and man the other half, is false; that God works all, and man does all is true.'[17] However, if we are confident that in an after life even the greatest of reprobates has an opportunity to amend their lives, a positive answer to the question, Can all be saved? opens up – without in any way compromising our awareness of the gravity of sin. This now directs us to consider the possibility that 'All have sinned, all will be saved'.

A Comparison of views on Predestination[18]	
1610 Arminian 'Remonstant'	**1618–9 Calvinist** 'Canons of Dort'.
God's decrees of election and reprobation are conditional upon foreknown faith, or lack of it	God's decrees of election and reprobation are absolute and unconditional
Christ died for all people and for every person so that he merited reconciliation and forgiveness for all. No one actually enjoys the forgiveness of sins except believers in Christ	Although the death of Christ is sufficient to expiate the sins of the whole world, the atonement is strictly limited to the elect, who are therefore certain to be saved
Regeneration by the Holy Spirit is necessary to salvation	The total inability of men and women to will the good necessitates the regenerative work of the Holy Spirit
God's grace is resistable	God's call is effectual, and hence God's grace is irresistible
The final perseverance of believers can neither be denied, nor positively asserted.	Those who are elected and called cannot but be saved, and cannot finally be lost.

15   Ibid., p 76.
16   Ibid., p 98.
17   Quoted by Sell in ibid.
18   Based on ibid, pp 13–14.

Schleiermacher and Barth on Predestination

In many theological systems, the doctrine of predestination is located within discussions of divine providence, thereby giving emphasis to God's sovereign power over and within the created order, as well as providing an underlying reason for the order, beauty and stability of the universe. In Calvin's mature theology, however, the doctrine of predestination is introduced under the heading of soteriology and linked with the doctrine of justification. Instead of providing the background whereby an answer can be given to the question: Why this kind of world?, the doctrine of predestination is used by Calvin to answer a quite different question: Why do some but not others come to faith in Jesus Christ? We now turn to two further Reformed ways of understanding predestination, one which locates the doctrine within ecclesiology, the other which sets it in a christological context.

As Schleiermacher set about constructing an *apologia* for Christianity which addressed the concerns of the 'cultured despisers' of religion, he knew that he had to present theological ideas which did not run counter to the general axioms of an age increasingly dominated by science. Instead of developing a doctrine of providence which took its starting point from the existence of miracles, he asserted that our awareness of God's providence comes when we recognize that we are placed in a closed system of nature which is governed by fixed and identifiable laws. Actual miracles cannot be countenanced in a world which has been created by God, since the intervention into the created order which a miracle presupposes would cast doubt on the competence of God as a creator. Nevertheless, Schleiermacher maintains that everything within the created order stands inside God's providence, the evil as well as the good, since no restrictions should be placed upon God's causality. But the model for understanding God's activity ought not to be that of an individual who performs certain acts in, and over-against, the world; rather, Schleiermacher asks us to embrace an alternative view which rests upon the co-extensiveness of divine and natural causation:

> Thus the divine omnipotence can never in any way enter as a supplement (so to speak) to the natural causes in their sphere . . . Rather everything is and becomes altogether by means of the natural order, so that each takes place through all and all wholly through the divine omnipotence, so that all indivisibly exists through One.[19]

It is the *entire* created order which must be perceived as divinely ordained, rather than any particular part of it. Meanwhile, God's providential care is understood in terms of the entire act by which God has set in motion a creative process, rather than in the more traditional sense of divine interruptions into the general run of things.

Schleiermacher has been widely criticized for collapsing divine activity into the world's natural processes and therefore of advocating pantheism. This is hardly fair since, as Gerrish reminds us, it is 'precisely because the omnipotence of God grounds the entire temporal system of nature' that, in Schleiermacher's theology, 'divine and natural causality cannot be identical', thereby entailing that 'God must be a "cause" in a unique, non-temporal and non-spatial sense.'[20] Schleiermacher attempts to image God in such a way that Deity becomes the ground of the world's activity instead of one activity among many others within the world. This puts his view of 'special providence' at odds with that of Calvin. Gerrish illustrates the differences very clearly:

---

[19]   Schleiermacher, *The Christian Faith*, pp 212.
[20]   Gerrish, *Tradition and the Modern World*, p 107.

For Calvin, it is in his special care for each individual creature that God's fatherly love is known: this is the heart of his doctrine of providence. God's hand is ever present. Nothing takes place without his deliberation. He does not merely watch over the order of nature he has established, but continues to cherish each of his works. He singles out the individual and is immediately, actively present to him. And this Schleiermacher cannot assert without hedging. Talk of God's fatherly care does not spring naturally to his mind. For a God who made ad hoc decisions, like an earthly father, would himself be entangled in the causal nexus of nature.[21]

The question remains, though, whether Schleiermacher maintains a proper sense of God being personal in his attempt to avoid overt anthropomorphic descriptions of Deity.

Schleiermacher sought to overthrow the traditional Christian mythological worldview and provide an account of the Christian witness which is credible in a modern scientific age. God did not at a certain time create the world and human beings, witness a set-back in Adam's fall, and then appear in Jesus to set matters right; nor does God pronounce forgiveness every time sinners come to faith in Christ. Instead of all the different divine activities involved within this framework, Schleiermacher argues that there is a single divine purpose to raise humanity above the rest of nature to full personhood. The creative activity which grounds the whole cosmic process therefore is coterminous with Christ's redemptive activity which gave birth to the church. The church, therefore, is the *unique* historical sphere within which the creation of human beings is brought to completion: '. . . salvation or blessedness is in the Church alone, and . . . since blessedness cannot enter from without, but can be found within the Church only by being brought into existence there, the Church alone saves.'[22] This significant place in God's providence gives the church a clear missionary mandate: 'This organization must increasingly overpower the unorganized mass to which it is opposed.'[23] And, like the rest of creation, the church continues on its course according to immanent laws. This leads Schleiermacher towards what Gerrish describes as 'a brilliant reinterpretation' of the doctrine of predestination.[24]

Schleiermacher argues that, while there is a basic equality in the incapacity of human beings – 'All men for us are in the state of common sinfulness', there seems to be an inequality in the help received to counter it.[25] Why is it that some turn to Christ, while others are unregenerate when they die? Like Calvin, Schleiermacher insists that no answer to this question holds up which compromises the fact that things are as they are because God wills them to be so. He also follows Calvin in setting election within our experience of a world full of diversity and fundamental inequalities. But the two great Reformed theologians differ in their understanding of the referent of election. For Calvin, the divine decree refers to individuals, whereas for Schleiermacher it involves a totality governed by natural laws. Furthermore, for Schleiermacher, the decree is single and not double, it refers to the redemption of humankind in Christ – that and that alone! So Schleiermacher avoids treating election atomistically as referring to individuals; rather, he sees the purpose of predestination as bringing everyone to fellowship in Christ.

There is, then, only one divine decree: the decree to redeem humankind in Christ. Sooner or later all human beings will be taken up into fellowship in Christ. As the historical embodiment of God's election, the Church will eventually reach everyone – even if beyond this life in some cases.

---

21   Ibid., p 110.
22   Schleiermacher, *The Christian Faith*, p 527.
23   Ibid., p 528.
24   Gerrish, *Tradition and the Modern World*, p 112.
25   Schleiermacher, *The Christian Faith*, p 534.

But, while everyone cannot be saved at one and the same time in such an historical phenomenon, all eventually will be saved: ' . . . no divine fore-ordination can be admitted as a result of which the individual would be lost to fellowship with Christ.'[26] A doctrine of predestination which includes a belief in an eternal reprobation, therefore, is a doctrinal error. Given his belief that 'all belonging to the human race are eventually taken up into living fellowship with Christ' and that 'every nation will sooner or later become Christian', Schleiermacher considers the darker side of life to be merely a fleeting phenomenon which cannot hinder God's salvific purposes.[27] After all, the operation of universal grace cannot avoid being set within history's limits.

Gerrish makes the point that Reformed theologians have often highlighted God's sovereignty to affirm the very things which Schleiermacher so resolutely denies, namely, that 'God is the free Lord over the works of his hands and is not irrevocably committed to the natural sequence of events.'[28] Karl Barth, for example, sets out an understanding of election which is as different from the view of Calvin as it is from that of Schleiermacher. He places predestination neither in the context of soteriology (Calvin), nor of ecclesiology (Schleiermacher); instead he provides the doctrine with a 'Christological basis' by expounding it 'in the light of Christology' and thereby understands Christ as its very substance.[29]

The starting point for Barth's investigation of predestination is predictable: 'At no point . . . , and on no pretext, can we afford either to dispense with, or to be turned aside from, the knowledge of Jesus Christ', since what we can know about 'the concept of eternal election' is to be found in Scripture's witness to 'the exhaustive self-revelation of God' in Christ.[30] In fact, Barth maintains that when one pays serious attention to the Bible, the conclusion must be drawn that 'the divine predestination is the election of Jesus Christ', or, to put it another way, that 'God's eternal will is the election of Jesus Christ.'[31] In Jesus Christ, God gave Godself for a world which had been created by, but which had 'fallen' away from, God. It is that gracious gift, willed from eternity, which is, for Barth, the basic content of divine predestination.

The entire dogma of predestination gets summed up by Barth in two statements. First, 'Jesus Christ is the electing God.'[32] This statement addresses the issue surrounding 'the Subject of the eternal election of grace'.[33] Barth objects to the traditional idea that predestination originates in a rather dark, obscure, rigid and distant absolute decree (*decretum absolutum*), since it belongs to a personal power, presence and promise the world has witnessed in Christ. In the beginning God chose to have with Godself the Word which is Jesus (John 1: 1). For Barth, then, the very essence of predestination lies in the fact that Christ was with God from the beginning, and, therefore, Christ's will is also God's will. What we learn about Christ from the Bible's witness to him, directs us therefore towards what predestination universally entails, namely, 'the acceptance and reception of man only by the free grace of God'.[34] Even Jesus' election to a saving relationship with God is not due to any merit or goodness. Jesus, the one who is elected by grace, is also the Elector, since through him we are taken up into eternal life and blessedness.

---

26   Ibid., p 548.
27   Ibid., pp 549, 559.
28   Gerrish, *Tradition and the Modern World*, p 148.
29   Barth, *Church Dogmatics* 11/2 (Edinburgh: T & T Clark, 1957), pp 145, 149.
30   Ibid., p 153.
31   Ibid., pp 103, 146.
32   Ibid., pp 103 and 145.
33   Ibid., p 145.
34   Ibid., p 118.

> In the very foreground of our existence in history we can and should cleave wholly and with full assurance to Him because in the eternal background of history, in the beginning with God, the only decree which was passed, the only Word which was spoken and which prevails, was the decision which was executed by Him. As we believe in Him and hear His Word and hold fast by His decision, we can know with a certainty which nothing can ever shake that we are the elect of God.[35]

The second statement Barth uses to define predestination provides an answer to the question concerning 'the object of the eternal election of grace'.[36] He argues that Jesus Christ is not only the electing God but also 'elected man'.[37] Jesus is not one of the elect; he is *the* elect of God. He does not stand alongside other members of the elect; rather he is 'before and above them as the One who is originally and properly the Elect'.[38] What separates Christ from the rest of the elect is the fact that 'as elected man He is also the electing God, electing them in His own humanity.'[39] Christ's election consequently is totally unique: ' . . . the election of Him who Himself elects'.[40] It contains within it the means by which all divine electing takes place. Barth underscores the point that, as the first-born of all creation, Jesus is 'the beginning of all God's ways and works'.[41] In Jesus' election, God makes a decision to be gracious with creation. Election is always concerned, therefore, with the bestowal of free grace, but Barth does not allow us to forget that Jesus was elected for suffering in order to redeem a fallen creation. The idea that election implies privilege or status is immediately questioned by Jesus' example. 'God from all eternity ordains this obedient One in order that He might bear the suffering which the disobedient have deserved and which for the sake of God's righteousness must necessarily be borne.'[42] While Jesus was predestined to passion and pain, Barth also argues that our election is rooted in his. From all eternity God loves and elects us in Jesus, and God sees us in Jesus as sinners to whom he is gracious. In Jesus, the Judge takes the place of the judged who are relieved of paying sin's penalty.

Barth adopts a strict supralapsarian position: 'With the traditional teaching and the testimony of Scripture, we think of predestination as eternal, preceding time and all the contents of time.'[43] Few theologians have ever stressed the primacy of God's sovereign will as much as Barth: 'We must not allow God to be submerged in His relationship to the universe or think of Him as tied in Himself to the universe.'[44] God has no need of any world other than himself. According to Barth, God could have remained perfectly fulfilled through the divine inner-trinitarian life. What reason, then, is there for God to choose to tie Godself to the world? None – save that God graciously decides to do it: 'The fact that He is not satisfied, but that His inner glory overflows and becomes outward, the fact that He wills the creation, and the man Jesus as the first-born of all creation, is grace, sovereign grace, a condescension inconceivably tender.'[45] We learn about God's eternal plan, and the 'condescension

---

35   Ibid., p 115–16.
36   Ibid., p 145.
37   Ibid., pp 116 & 145.
38   Ibid., p 116.
39   Ibid., p 117.
40   Ibid.
41   Ibid., p 121.
42   Ibid., p 123.
43   Ibid., p 155.
44   Ibid.
45   Ibid., p 121.

inconceivably tender', from God's self-revelation in Christ, since that plan is identical with what God has revealed about Godself in history. Just how we can establish this fact, opposed to merely assert it from the Bible, though, is not clear.

Since Christ is both 'elected man' as well as 'electing God', Barth speaks of God's will involving 'a double predestination'.[46] It quickly becomes clear, however, that Barth does not have in mind the traditional and dualistic understanding which asserts that God has foreordained some to salvation and others to damnation. He claims that from all eternity 'God has elected fellowship with man for Himself' and that in addition 'God has elected fellowship with Himself for man.'[47] These two dimensions of God's eternal will together constitute the double-predestination that Barth has in mind. The first, God's election of Godself as the companion of the human race, Barth refers to as predestination's *negative* side. It is negative because by willing fellowship with us for God's good pleasure, God inevitably has to surrender the divine impassibility to make it possible. This involves on God's part what Barth calls 'severe self-commitment' in that 'God does not merely give Himself up to the risk and menace, but He exposes Himself to the actual onslaught and grasp of evil.'[48] God's commitment extends to the atoning deed whereby God took upon Godself the punishment that should have fallen upon sinful human beings. Barth argues that from all eternity God willed to suffer for us in order that we might be justified and forgiven. This reveals that God is both just and merciful.

> God's eternal decree in the beginning was the decree of the just and merciful God, of the God who was merciful in His justice and just in His mercy. He was just in that He willed to treat evil seriously, to judge it and to sentence it, to reject and to condemn its author, delivering him over to death. But He was merciful in that He took the author of evil to His bosom, and willed that the rejection and condemnation and death should be His own.[49]

The second dimension of God's eternal election involves the fact that God has elected fellowship with Godself for men and women. Barth calls this the *positive* side of predestination, the Yes rather than the No of the eternal election. It entails 'the wonderful exaltation and endowment of man to existence in covenant with Himself', and the fact that persons are 'enriched and saved and glorified in the living fellowship of that covenant'.[50] While, from eternity, we are both the cause and object of God's glory, goodness and favour, Barth is also clear that, simultaneous with positive predestination, 'like a shadow preceding and following', there exists the foreordination of all human beings to 'danger and trouble' as a result of their proneness to temptation and sin.[51] A moral universe must be one in which evil is *permitted:* In this life two phenomena therefore go hand in hand. On the one hand, there is God's *positive* will that everyone should enjoy blessedness and eternal life; on the other hand, there is God's *permissive* will which leads human beings into sin and, hence, guilt before God. Barth firmly believes that the latter is clearly subordinate to the former: 'The first is an authoritative Yes, the second a No which is determined only by the Yes, thus losing its authority from the very outset.'[52]

---

[46] Ibid., p 162.
[47] Ibid.
[48] Ibid., p 164.
[49] Ibid., p 167.
[50] Ibid., p 168.
[51] Ibid., p 169.
[52] Ibid., p 172.

Not surprisingly, Barth has been credited with preaching universalism, the doctrine that all will one day be saved. It is perfectly clear that he holds that God has *intended* the election of everyone: 'The real foreordination of man is to attestation of the divine glory, to blessedness and to eternal life.'[53] In so far as Barth eschews the idea that God eternally willed that some sinners are not saved, Barth could be regarded as turning aside from his Calvinist heritage as resolutely as did Schleiermacher. However, he explicitly denied that his theology entailed universalism: 'What right have we to tell God that in His love, which is certainly quite different from ours, He cannot equally seriously, and from the very beginning, from all eternity, condemn as well as acquit, kill as well as make alive, reject as well as elect?'[54] All that Barth actually claims is that in Christ the world knows that God has elected to be with us. Whether everyone responds positively is perhaps not for us to speculate upon, and Barth was clearly less certain about it than Schleiermacher. Nevertheless, this debate does raise an interesting issue concerning whether some construals of Deity actually present a God who is worthy of our worship. If God is omnipotent, and out of graciousness and goodness wills the salvation of all, why is it that there can be inhabitants in Hell? Is a God whose purposes are finally overcome by sin and evil worthy of belief? And, does not the sheer amount of sin and evil constitute a powerful argument in favour of atheism? To such interesting if vexed questions we turn in the next chapter.

---

[53]   Ibid., p 171. Note also: 'And for this reason, in God's decree at the beginning there is for man only a predestination which corresponds to the perfect being of God Himself; a predestination to His kingdom and to blessedness and life' (ibid., pp 172–3).

[54]   Ibid., p 171.

CHAPTER 13

The Problem of Evil

CONSIDERABLE difficulties arise when we attempt to hold at one and the same time the following three assertions: God is omnipotent; God is omnibenevolent; evil is a reality. For if evil exists – and in the face of the horrors of recent times who is going to question that? – it must mean either that God cannot prevent it, in which case divine omnipotence is denied, or that God actually wills it, in which case God cannot be said to be totally well-meaning towards the creation. We are trapped, therefore, in a trilemma, only ever being able to assert two of the propositions but never the third. This trilemma is the so-called problem of evil.

The presence of deep-seated evil in the world, and the evidence of tremendous amounts and degrees of innocent suffering has prompted some of the sharpest theological analysis and debate. Consider, for example, the famous moment in Dostoyevsky's *The Brothers Karamazov*, when Ivan poses a most searching question to Alyosha in a tense interchange.

> ' . . . imagine that you are creating a fabric of human destiny with the object of making men happy in the end, giving them peace and rest at last, but that it was essential and inevitable to torture to death only one tiny creature – that baby beating its breast with its fist, for instance – and to found that edifice on its unavenged tears, would you consent to be the architect on those conditions? Tell me, and tell the truth'.
>
> 'No, I wouldn't consent', said Alyosha softly.
>
> 'And can you admit the idea that men for whom you are building it would agree to accept their happiness on the foundation of the unexpiated blood of a little victim. And accepting it would remain happy for ever'?
>
> 'No, I can't admit it . . .' said Alyosha . . .[1]

The idea that God's purpose should warrant innocent suffering led to Ivan handing back his entrance ticket to the religious quest for harmony. For many others any kind of theistic commitment beggars belief, or at least provides sufficient evidence to convict God of being less than Jewish and Christian traditions have traditionally claimed.

> In this camp [a sub-camp of Buchenwald] there happened to be a group of particularly learned Jews, several of them rabbis. They had to work six-and a-half days a week, but on Sunday afternoons they were left in relative peace. One such afternoon the learned Jews, in their despair, took up the notion of putting God on trial – not so outrageous as it may seem, for there is a Hebrew term meaning 'to have a legal disputation with the Lord'. So witnesses came

---

[1]   F Dostoyevsky, *The Brothers Karamazov* (Harmondsworth: Penguin Books, 1958), pp 287–8.

forward for the prosecution, there were others for the defence, and there was a bench of rabbis acting as judges.

The case for the prosecution was overwhelming. They had only to look at their condition. Their community was being wiped out; most of their families had already been destroyed; how could a good God permit this to happen? The case having been made and a desperate defence put up, the judges had little difficulty in reaching their verdict: the accused was guilty as charged – guilty of neglecting His chosen people.[2]

We shall return to both those stories at the end of this chapter. But, they will have served us well if they have reminded us that the existence of evil poses severe problems to any belief in an omnipotent and benevolent God.

In fact, the existence of evil is the starting point for a powerful argument for the non-existence of God. This is outlined in the Box 1.

Box 1[3]

1.   God is a perfect reality. (Definition)

2.   A perfect reality is an omnipotent being. (By definition)

3.   An omnipotent being could unilaterally bring about an
        actual world without without any genuine evil. (By definition)

4.   A perfect reality is a morally perfect being. (By definition)

5.   A morally perfect being would want to bring about an actual world
        without any genuine evil. (By definition)

6.   If there is genuine evil in the world, then there is no God.
        (Logical conclusion from 1 through 5)

7.   There is genuine evil in the world. (Factual statement)

8.   Therefore, there is no God. (Logical conclusion from 6 and 7)

It is not just sceptical philosophers who find that the evil in the world prompts them to take an atheistic stance. I well remember as a pastoral minister being unable to 'reach' a one time highly committed church member whose daughter had been swept away by an avalanche when skiing. The fact of evil is more than an intellectual matter; it is rooted in everyday existential experience. Before we outline the way in which some Reformed theologians have tackled the problem of evil, we need to become a little clearer concerning what we mean by 'evil'.

---

[2]   Gerald Priestland, *The Case Against God* (London: Collins, 1984), p 13.

[3]   This particular formulation of the argument is taken from David Ray Griffin, *God, Power and Evil: A Process Theodicy* (Philadelphia: The Westminster Press, 1976), p 9.

The Three Types of Evil

John Hick is one of the most noteworthy (and the more conservative might say notorious!) recent Reformed theologians. Since he has written a classic book on the problem of evil, and developed a distinctive approach which seeks to resolve it, his views will feature several times in this chapter.[4] However, at this point, we turn to him to provide us with a working definition of 'evil'. The term can be divided into three dimensions: moral, natural and metaphysical. *Moral evil* is 'evil that we human beings originate: cruel, unjust, vicious, and perverse thoughts and deeds.'[5] And, once it is accepted that part of God's creative activity is the bestowal of freedom to creatures, then it is plain that it is inappropriate to blame God for how creatures have made use of what essentially is a positive gift. Moral evil is caused by human beings who have been granted the power to be moral or immoral. God ought not then to be credited with the blame for what human beings have freely brought upon themselves and others. This line is generally called 'the free-will defence' in the standard discussions of the problem of evil. It is a helpful line of argument, but, given the evidence, it is questionable whether the amount of evil generated by human beings is a reasonable price to pay for human freedom. Does the time not arrive when the amount of evil produced by the human race at least warrants the intervention of the omnipotent and omnibenevolent God to adjust the balance between good and evil? It was perhaps God's seeming absence and silence in the Nazi concentration camps which was the most powerful prosecution argument in the trial mentioned in the Jewish story told at the start of this chapter.

But we have not finished with evil when we conclude that we have accounted for moral evil. There is a second type of evil which in many ways is more difficult to address. It is called *natural evil* and Hick defines it as 'the evil that originates independently of human actions: in disease bacilli, earthquakes, storms, droughts, tornadoes, etc.'[6] Of course, some of these phenomena may well be brought upon us by our own lifestyle and behaviour. One thinks of the way in which Western habits have caused the prevalence of cardiac diseases and carcinomata of various kinds, and of how global warming has dramatically altered climatic conditions to disastrous effect. Nevertheless, there are some things of a malevolent nature which finally are beyond both our creation and our prevention. This is natural evil. The phenomenon is of even greater magnitude if we adopt a less anthropocentric view of the matter than is usually the case, and if we fully reflect on the waste and destruction endemic to evolution in general and the pain involved for the animal world in particular. The bottom line for Hick is to say that 'natural evil consists in unwelcome experiences brought upon sentient creatures, human or sub-human, by causes other than man himself.'[7] From a scientific perspective, I am not sure where in evolution sentience starts or ends, and my increasing awareness of the way in which the whole of life is intrinsically bound together in an interlocking manner makes me now wonder whether the distinction between sentience and non-sentience is very helpful. But, at this moment, it is sufficient for us to recognize that not every 'unwelcome experience' which befalls us can be attributed to a human cause. At the very best, then, all 'free-will defences' only address part of the evidence.

---

[4]   John Hick, *Evil and the God of Love* (London: Macmillan and Co Ltd., 1966; London: Collins Fontana, 1968).
[5]   Ibid., p 18.
[6]   Ibid.
[7]   Ibid., p 19.

Hick reminds us, thirdly, of *metaphysical evil*: 'the basic fact of the finitude and limitation within the created universe'.[8] In some theology, metaphysical evil is made the cause of both natural and moral evil. Augustine, for example, argues that the existence of all evil derives from within agents rather than from causes outside them. There is no cause of willing before willing. Evil appears, then, when some angels in the first instance, and all human beings thereafter, turn away from God and thereby forsake the possibilities of heaven for the problems of earth – and, ultimately, much worse! It is the fact that they are mutable creatures living in a finite and limited environment, and hence faced by metaphysical evil, which gives rise to physical and moral evil. So all evil is attributed by Augustine to the free-will of beings who were created perfectly good. But would a creature – whether angelic or human – who is so created be capable of 'falling' when faced by metaphysical evil? As Hick powerfully argues: '. . . the idea of an unqualifiedly good creature committing sin is self-contradictory and unintelligible'.[9] And, if such a creature was so capable, would not the very possibility for moral and physical evil then lie in God's hands, since, presumably, the existence of metaphysical evil was made possible by God? Indeed, there is much to commend Hick's view that Augustine's doctrine of predestination, which cannot avoid placing evil's genesis within God's life and purpose, implicitly confirms 'the absurdity of the self-creation of evil *ex nihilo*'.[10]

Augustine and Calvin

Augustine recoils at the possibility that God might be the cause of anything other than what he takes to be commensurate with being omnibenevolent. What does he make, then, of the existence of evil? He adopts a double strategy. The first side of it is to say that evil is not an extant phenomenon which exists alongside other phenomena. Augustine defines it as 'a privation of the good' (*privatio boni*). It is the corruption of something good, the absence of what makes something fully that something; it has no independent existence and amounts to what is missing when something 'falls' from being what God intended it to be. By definition, then, it is impossible for anything to be completely evil. The second side of Augustine's strategy is to say that whatever we might call evil exists only because God can bring good out of it. Hence it is always possible that what we see as life's great negative features are occasions out of which God can weave such good that all the pain and misery within life's warp and weft is shown to be worthwhile. As Job discovered, who are we to question the work of God?

The undoubted merit of Augustine's line of thinking is the way in which it resolutely affirms that evil is not God's creation. It fully endorses the Christian view that what God has created is essentially good. Nothing is outside God's sovereign will. Augustine finds no place for dualistic notions which locate evil's agency in some co-existing being beyond divine control. Also his doctrine of privation goes some way to establishing evil's cause in the wilful turning of creatures away from the good. Augustine does not do justice, however, to those examples of evil which are more physical than moral in nature; all free-will defences end up shipwrecked on the rocks of physical evil. But the major problem with Augustine's scheme goes much deeper and Hick perceptively puts his finger on it. While Augustine's idea of the *privatio boni* helps explain 'metaphysically' that 'evil has not been created by God, and hence that the status of evil within the cosmos is 'secondary and parasitic rather than primary and essential', it is incorrect to say that

---

[8]   Ibid.
[9]   Ibid., pp 68–9.
[10]   Ibid., p 69.

'evil is *empirically* – that is to say, as a fact of experience – accurately describable as a loss or lack of goodness.'[11] For many, including Alyosha in his conversation with Ivan and the rabbis in the death camp, evil has inflicted itself in such a way that it has been experienced less as an absence of the good than as an uncontrollable phenomenon of real existence and intensity. As Hick says, 'It would be an arbitrary and unfruitful amendment of the dictionary, rather than an illuminating way of looking at the facts, to describe moral evils as merely privations of their corresponding moral goods'.[12] Augustine presents us with a classic instance of putting forward a metaphysical account of a problem which ultimately does not do justice to the evidence.

Augustine's theory of predestination, and more so that of Calvin, ends up by calling into question God's omnibenevolence. For both God's sovereign will is supreme. But what morally sensitive Creator would decide from eternity, and before even the birth of any creatures, that some creatures were destined for heaven and others for hell? Nor is it helpful to say that the basis for such an action is made honorable if we remember that God simply foreknows that some will freely choose salvation while others will freely choose hell. All such arguments achieve is the raising of further questions: If God foreknows that some choose hell, what has become of God's will to save? If God is God, should we not entertain the paradox that, if hell exists on account of Love's righteous judgment, then the fact that no one inhabits the place is witness to Love's universal grace? Whatever we make of that – and if we dismiss the purported truth contained in the paradox it may be more to do with a personal problem we have in wishing to assume that, if God accepts us, then God must reject others – huge question marks are placed upon the worshipfulness of Calvinism's 'God'. Therefore Hick concludes: 'Thus in its over-developed doctrine of the divine decrees Calvinism introduces a dogma which restricts God's love and thereby nullifies the attempt to present faithfully the theological structure of the Christian gospel.'[13]

Schleiermacher, Farmer and Hick

We noted earlier the way in which Schleiermacher presents an understanding of the human condition rather different from the one mapped out by Augustine and to a large degree followed by Calvin. Instead of viewing men and women as creatures who have fallen from being in God's image and likeness to their present sinful condition, Schleiermacher argues that they were born in God's image as immature beings who, through their encounters, choices and decisions in an ambiguous world are to grow up into God's likeness. In Schleiermacher's scheme sin and evil are ordained by God as the very precondition for this 'growing up' process and hence their redemption. Hick draws out the difference between Augustine and Schleiermacher as follows:

> For Schleiermacher, then, man has been created at a distance from God, both as regards his own imperfect nature and as regards the circumstances of his life, precisely in order that he may freely come to God, drawn by redemptive grace. Accordingly, sin has occurred as a preparation for grace rather than, as the Augustinian tradition teaches, grace occurring to repair the damage of sin.[14]

---

11   Ibid., p 61. Italics mine.
12   Ibid., p 63.
13   Ibid., p 132.
14   Ibid., p 238.

Theological accounts which take their starting point from Irenaeus rather than Augustine end up saying with Schleiermacher that evil serves God's good purposes. Whether such an instrumental view of evil is as persuasive to evil's victims as it is to theodicy writers who pen their thoughts from inside academia's comforts is a moot point.

Herbert Farmer's approach to the problem of evil largely follows that of Schleiermacher. What he says, however, needs to be set against the backcloth of his recognition that it is one thing to be able to explain why evil exists in a world created by an omnipotent and omnibenevolent Deity and something else to overcome it. Theologians struggle to help us with the former but the latter has already been tackled by Christ. As Farmer notes wisely: 'Christianity has never claimed to take the sting out of evil by explaining it, but rather by giving victory over it, which is a different thing.'[15] Nevertheless, theology can show how evil is not 'necessarily and finally destructive of persons and the highest values of personal life, thereby helping us develop a coherent and cogent account of God which is credible in the face of evil.[16] Farmer argues that for this to happen theologians must develop three lines of approach. First, they need to show that 'the alleged evil fact' is only 'apparent' evil.[17] Once evil is set inside a proper theistic framework, the argument runs, its ultimate power vanishes. Secondly, theologians must show that all the world's evil which defies explanation is dwarfed by more positive features when set within a theistic framework. As Farmer puts it: ' . . . in so far as theism fails to provide a "hundred per cent" positive illumination of alleged evil, it must seek to show that the margin of darkness which is left unillumined does not finally contradict it.'[18] The Irenaen outlook championed by Schleiermacher shines through Farmer's ideas. The world serves as 'a training ground for personalities', in which 'unillumined darkness' can achieve a positive purpose and hence evil has instrumental value.[19] Farmer even claims that theology's inability to explain evil's mysteries ends up being part of the case for theism. Theologians, thirdly, must show that, while theism may leave some problems unsolved, alternative non-theistic ways of understanding reality leave us with even more vexed mysterious and insolvable problems.

When Farmer considers the problem of innocent suffering caused by natural and/or metaphysical evil he asks us to note that pain is a private matter. No one then is in 'a position to evaluate pain in any kind of final way'.[20] Given the nature of his overall argument, Farmer has a vested interest in setting pain in the most positive of lights, since he has to show that it has instrumental value. This perhaps makes him observe that 'it not infrequently happens that suffering seems more of a problem to the observer than to the sufferer himself'; it also may inspire his counsel of caution against allowing our minds to get 'unnecessarily stunned and intimidated by arithmetical magnitudes' of pain and suffering.[21] He argues that our problem does not reside in the amount of suffering in the world. As Alyosha testified, the problem of evil can be adequately posed by the innocent suffering of just *one* child. What does pose *the* problem, rather, is the inference some draw from innocent suffering, namely, that 'the world is in its essential nature ruthlessly indifferent to individuals and their sufferings.'[22] Many will feel, though, that belief in an omnipotent and omnibenevolent God might be a little bit more credible if the amount of evil in the world were a bit less.

---

[15]   Herbert H Farmer, *Towards Belief in God* (London: SCM Press Ltd., 1942), p 231.
[16]   Ibid., p 233.
[17]   Ibid.
[18]   Ibid.
[19]   Ibid., p 234.
[20]   Ibid., p 235.
[21]   Ibid., p 236.
[22]   Ibid., p 237.

Does this 'training ground for personalities' need to be so harsh and cruel in the arbitrary way it inflicts misfortune on those who often seem to be in the least position to bear it? Indeed, creation's evolutionary nature means that there is an inbuilt amount of destruction and waste, since in the cosmic advance lower forms of life give way to higher ones, while the latter become parasitic on the former. In a somewhat anthropocentric way, Farmer asks us to avoid what he calls 'the mistake of reading into lower forms of sentient existence our own highly developed nervous sensitivity, our memories and hopes and fears, our sense of personal dignity, and so on.'[23] I am sure there is much truth in Farmer's analysis at this point, not least at a time when our ecosensitive age has spawned a degree of sentimentality about the non-human realm which is neither practical nor helpful. Nevertheless, whatever we may make of Farmer's unfounded opinion that 'a merciful provision of nature provides that extremes of agony shall not be borne' - Farmer presumably never watched the Westminster College cat catch and 'play' with a mouse! – the stupidity of merely treating the non-human world as if it had only instrumental value and little intrinsic worth has been recently brought home to us with a vengeance.[24] Oddly enough, though, Farmer asks that we consider the problem of suffering 'existentially' and not only 'theoretically' because he believes that this will enable due recognition to be given to the way people accept 'much frustration and difficulty, and even pain' as the necessary price for a fruitful life.[25] To the observer, the price may be considered too high; but for those involved 'it is commonly felt that the overcoming and enduring of such things enhances the value and significance of the whole enterprise.'[26] While in a Cambridge college study, 'suffering can be seen to be an indispensable means to the achievement of personal character', I seriously doubt whether it feels like that, or can be rationalized in that way, when one is the victim, say, of an earthquake, a flood or a drought.[27]

In fairness to Farmer, though, he is fully aware of his position's difficulties, recognizing that we soon arrive at a point where 'suffering and frustration seem to have no relation to the achievement of the values of personal life, or . . . appear to run counter to that achievement'.[28] He asks us to display a somewhat Stoic attitude in the face of 'facts and laws in this mysterious universe which are just given' and therefore to be accepted.[29] Nor are we in a position to say that the apparent waste within the evolutionary process is in fact waste. Farmer is quite content 'to leave the whole thing in mystery' on the basis that his theism is able to uphold the notion that 'there is nothing finally contradictory . . . in the *apparently* unnecessary surplusage of suffering in the sentient world'.[30] To be sure, it is often the case that theologians are apt to baptize their muddles as mysteries, but Farmer is perfectly aware that the plausibility of an instrumental view of evil requires that there is a life beyond this one in which there is some recompense granted to those who have undergone innocent suffering. And, as the New Testament makes clear, death is the final and ultimate evil. Some critics will have little sympathy with a view which seeks to solve the mystery of evil by invoking the even greater mystery of life after death. But, as long as some kind of life after death is a possibility, Farmer can argue that evil in general and death in particular cannot be counted as a conclusive argument against theism.

---

23   Ibid.
24   Ibid.
25   Ibid., p 238.
26   Ibid.
27   Ibid., p 239.
28   Ibid., p 240.
29   Ibid., p 239.
30   Ibid., p 241.

Farmer seeks to uphold 'a theistic view which interprets human life in terms of an eternal personal purpose seeking to bring finite persons to their highest life through co-operation with itself'.[31] Human freedom is essential to this vision, and with its misuse comes moral evil. Moral evil, then, is the price which has to be paid for placing the responsibility upon human beings to lead their lives. Farmer raises the obvious question: 'The essential freedom of persons doubtless requires that wickedness should have some rope, but must it have quite so much rope as it appears always to have had, and not least in this present time of unspeakable brutality and anguish?'[32] He answers by suggesting that 'a principle of judgment upon, and annulment of, evil' can be seen working in history 'in a broad way, though not in the precise and immediate detail we might desire'.[33] Evil is ultimately self-defeating, so its existence does not prove that the world is ultimately immoral or amoral. And, in any case, the presence of moral evil can only be expected if we live in 'a training-ground for personality'.[34] People have to be led to choose good rather than evil for its own sake, and in the absence of any promised rewards or threatening punishment. A world in which sin was absent, or removed as soon as it appeared, would not in Farmer's opinion be an appropriate arena for character building. Also, it has to be appreciated that community development involves individuals being interdependent and hence open to the evil as well as the goodness which comes from others. But does there not come a time when the moral evil around us is out of all proportion to what is needed in 'a training-ground for personality'? Does the Holocaust, for example, not ruin the plausibility of the argument? While it can be argued that 'freedom at such a ghastly price is not worthwhile, and that men should not be left in such uncontrolled and uninterrupted freedom that they can do that kind of thing', Farmer refuses to allow anything to count against belief in God.[35] Once again he plays the 'mystery' card, and remarks that 'a door of possibility is left open by the fact that we have no empirical knowledge of what lies beyond death'.[36] But the sceptic will be quick to observe that that particular argument cuts both ways.

Hick's well known proposed solution to the problem of evil largely follows the tracks already laid down by his teacher, Herbert Farmer. Hick presupposes that a person who has achieved some measure of goodness in life through overcoming temptations and exercising real choices is much more to be admired than a person who was created in a state of virtue. Lying beneath this presupposition is the suggestion that 'it is an ethically reasonable judgement . . . that human goodness slowly built up through personal histories of moral effort has a value in the eyes of the Creator which justifies even the long travail of the soul-making process.'[37] But, once again, critics will wonder whether the journey needs to be so slow and tortuous, and whether the pain of the route is worth it in the end.

In Hick's 'developmental and teleological' proposal, the relationship between God and the world is likened to that between parents and children.[38] Hick claims support from Jesus in likening God's love for us to that of a parent for a child.

---

31   Ibid., p 244.

32   Ibid., p 245.

33   Ibid.

34   Ibid., p 246.

35   Ibid., p 247.

36   Ibid.

37   Hick, *Evil and the God of Love*, p 292.

38   Ibid.

> If, then, there is any true analogy between God's purpose for his human creatures, and the purpose of loving and wise parents for their children, we have to recognize that the presence of pleasure and absence of pain cannot be the supreme and overriding end for which the world exists. Rather, this world must be a place of soul-making. And its value is to be judged, not primarily by the quantity of pleasure and pain occurring in it at any particular moment, but by its fitness for its primary purpose, the purpose of soul-making.[39]

But need Keats's 'vale of soul-making' be so demanding? As David Ray Griffin has remarked: 'Surely God, if perfectly wise, could find some place to strike a balance between the present world, which is somewhat too dangerous for most of God's children, and a world in which moral qualities would not develop at all.'[40]   Many will agree with him that 'Hick's suggested justification of excessive evils' is 'appalling', and reject 'the goodness of God he is attempting to defend'.[41]

The Irenaean view inevitably seeks its ultimate justification in the future: 'The good that outshines all ill is not a paradise long since lost but a kingdom which is yet to come in its full glory and permanence'.[42] That all will be saved from sin in this kingdom is 'a practical certainty'.[43] Indeed, even though Hick can claim that nature has 'permanent significance', it appears that creation's major purpose is to provide an environment for soul-making.[44] The traditional anthropocentric features of Western theology remain pretty well intact, therefore, in Hick's scheme. Griffin correctly complains about this:

> If a history of the planet earth were to be written comparable in length to Barth's twelve-volume Church Dogmatics, with each page covering half a million years, Homo sapiens would show up somewhere on the last page of the last volume. Is it any longer credible to suggest that the rest of the universe was created for the sake of human beings, as Hick does . . .?[45]

Perhaps the truth is that the good which triumphs over evil is to be located neither in a past paradise nor in a future utopia, but in the *present* joy and delight God receives from a processive world which unfolds ever more sophisticated configurations of life? And might it not be the case that redemption is not something achieved in the future, but rather is found in God's ongoing activity, the One who is always receiving what is taking place into the divine life, making dross into gold, and laying down the stuff out of which fresh patterns of creativity can evolve?

Karl Barth: *Das Nichtige*

One strategy that theologians have deployed to wriggle out of the problem of evil is to deny that there is any evil while continuing to hold that God is omnipotent and omnibenevolent. We would not expect Karl Barth to adopt such a strategy, given his stance against arguably the greatest evil of the twentieth century, namely, the work of the Third Reich. As a member of the Confessing Church and the architect of the Barmen Declaration we would have expected him to be decidedly clear-headed concerning the holocaust.

39	Ibid., p 295.
40	Griffin, *God, Power and Evil: A Process Theodicy*, p 189.
41	Ibid., p 190.
42	Hick, *Evil and the God of Love*, p 297.
43	Ibid., p 380.
44	Ibid., p 296.
45	Griffin, *God, Power and Evil: A Process Theodicy*, p 191.

But one of the implications of Barth's doctrine of creation involves him denying the reality of evil. What many of us regard as evil is not really evil at all since it is part of a cosmos which because it is created by an omnipotent and omnibenevolent God is therefore good. Barth even suggests that 'the negative aspect of creation' might be good for men and women: 'For all we can tell, may not His creatures praise Him more mightily in humility than in exaltation, in need than in plenty, in fear than in joy, on the frontier of nothingness than when wholly orientated on God?'[46] A final answer to that question will depend upon the extent of the negativeness being exhibited by creation's negative side. Barth is insistent, however, that even the negative side is God's good creation, and therefore not real evil at all. It follows that everything which we know as evil is caused by either the Creator or the creatures.

Given the empirical evidence, it is not surprising that Barth is not fully content with this view. The nature and amount of evil invites us to posit a cause which in a paradoxical sense is beyond both God's positive will and the work of human beings. As Barth says, '. . . there is that at work which can be explained neither from the side of the Creator nor from that of the creature, neither as the action of the Creator nor as the life-act of the creature, and yet which cannot be overlooked or disowned but must be reckoned with in all its peculiarity.'[47] He calls this *das Nichtige*, translated as 'nothingness'. It is an 'alien factor' which 'can never be considered or mentioned together in the same context as other objects of God's providence.'[48] Nothingness is 'inimical to the creature and its nature and existence, but above all to God Himself and His will and purpose.'[49] Its nature is revealed in Jesus Christ as 'the adversary with whom no compromise is possible, the negative which is more than the mere complement of an antithetical positive, the left which is not counterpoised by any right, the antithesis which is not merely within creation and therefore dialectical but which is primarily and supremely to God Himself and therefore to the totality of the created world.'[50] Nothingness is an absolutely alien force which opposes and contradicts God's purposes in creation. It was envisaged by God from eternity, and God has taken the decisive act to overcome it.

According to Barth, God became human in Jesus in order to challenge the invasion of nothingness. In the Christ-event God 'smote, defeated and destroyed . . . that which primarily opposes and resists God Himself, and therefore all creation.'[51] Viewed from the standpoint of the cross's triumph, nothingness will generate 'fear and trembling'.[52] It is a malign factor in life which God alone can handle, and Christians claim that God has done just that in Christ. Barth tells us that its primary form is human sin. In Jesus Christ, we realize that we are sinners – agents of nothingness, so 'the sickness is disclosed with the cure'.[53]

Barth delineates a further dimension of nothingness in the evil and death which result from sin. Sin lets forces loose in the world which threaten human existence. The ultimate one is death. Death is more than a cessation of existence. It is, as Barth puts it, 'the ultimate irruption and triumph of that alien power which annihilates creaturely existence and thus discredits and disclaims the Creator.'[54] With death human beings are faced with a phenomenon with which they cannot cope, but, in the Incarnation, God has overcome not only sin but also death. Christ is the Victor over sin and death – *das Nichtige!*

---

[46]   Barth, *Church Dogmatics*, 3,3,297.
[47]   Ibid., p 292.
[48]   Ibid., p 289.
[49]   Ibid., p 290.
[50]   Ibid., p 302.
[51]   Ibid., p 304.
[52]   Ibid., p 305.
[53]   Ibid., p 309.
[54]   Ibid., p 310.

Before we critically consider Barth's view, a few clarifications may be in order. First, Barth is clear that 'Nothingness is not nothing'.[55] While much of what we experience as evil is viewed by Barth as only apparent evil, the shadow side of God's good creation, nothingness is to be regarded as genuine evil. Secondly, Barth is not positing the existence of a self-created being who possesses existence independent of God's will. Nothingness has no power except that permitted by God since 'He is the basis and Lord of nothingness too'.[56] Nothingness has its own malignant and evil being, an existence which is not an independent life apart from God but rather one in ongoing 'confrontation with God's non-willing'.[57] Thirdly, Barth speaks of nothingness and hence evil, in familiar terms. Since it is 'what is alien and adverse to grace, and therefore without it', it is a 'privation, the attempt to defraud God of His honour and right and at the same time to rob the creature of its salvation and right'.[58] Fourthly, our understanding of evil should be based upon the Christian story of salvation, which is rooted in the cross and will be culminated at the End-time. What Barth describes as 'the sinister alien factor in the sphere of the fatherly rule of God' has been defeated on the cross; but since God 'still permits us to be a prey to nothingness' we will only fully see this fact in Christ's *parousia*.[59] Therefore, our perspective on evil should be framed by looking back and looking forward to Christ.

At the heart of Barth's theology are two seemingly conflicting claims: (1) God is the omnipotent and omnibenevolent creator of an essentially good world; and (2) evil is a reality. In his typically paradoxical fashion he seeks to hold both of them simultaneously, but he only achieves this by re-interpreting what is usually meant by 'an essentially good world' and 'evil'. For example, what he understands to be 'an essentially good world' necessarily includes what we commonly call evil and he designates as nothingness. Barth also wants to say, however, that God does not positively will the nothingness that stands in opposition to the divine life. Nothingness exists, he tells us, due to God's omnipotent non-willing:

> God elects, and therefore rejects what He does not elect. God wills, and therefore opposes what He does not will. He says Yes, and therefore says No to that to which He has not said Yes. He works according to His purpose, and in so doing rejects and dismisses all that gainsays it. Both of these activities, grounded in His election and decision, are necessary elements in His sovereign action.[60]

The traditional idea that an essentially good world created by an omnipotent God does not include evil is compromised by Barth's admission that nothingness 'exists' in such a world through the non-willing of God. What truly exists, though, is willed by God; so nothingness, which is not willed by God, does not really exist. And yet we all know that evil does exist.

> [Nothingness] is not a second God, not self-created. It has no power save that which is allowed by God. It, too, belongs to God. It 'is' problematically because it is only on the left hand of God, under His No, the object of His jealousy, wrath and judgement. It 'is', not as God and His creation are, but only in its own improper way, as inherent contradiction, as impossible possibility.[61]

There are few better examples of the paradoxical nature of Barth's theology!

---

55   Ibid., p 349.
56   Ibid., p 351.
57   Ibid., p 353.
58   Ibid.
59   Ibid., pp 365, 367.
60   Ibid., p 351.
61   Ibid.

Barth's argument that nothingness arises from the divine decision to choose good and reject evil, and thus possesses the character of non-being as a result of that decision, leaves it with a nature fundamentally similar to that afforded it by Augustine. The argument presupposes the logical principle that to choose to create a good creation necessarily implies the 'existence' of an alternative which is rejected, namely, evil. But, as John Hick has pointed out, it is not necessarily the case that there exists something called 'non-being' just because we can mentally produce that term as a cognate of 'being'.[62] Hick points out a further problem with Barth's argument. Barth presupposes that prior to God choosing to create a good world there existed 'realities which already stand in some way before Him (or within Him)' from which the choice could be made.[63] This seriously threatens the traditional doctrine of creation out of nothing (*creatio ex nihilo*) and takes Barth well down the road to a form of dualism.

Barth has told a story to account for evil's existence: God wills a good creation; by so doing God rejects and excludes certain things which are contrary to what is good; by not willing such things God has granted them a negative status and reality; they then take the form of a power which works against the rest of creation; this power is nothingness. It is an imaginative and interesting story but there is nothing to substantiate its truth. Hick therefore accuses Barth of 'going beyond the data of faith and becoming entangled in the dangers of philosophical construction' – the very thing that Barth is so fond of lambasting other theologians for doing![64] Why cannot we tell a different story from the one which is 'a product of Barth's own fertile and fascinating mind?'[65] What is to rule out the idea, for example, that it is perfectly possible that, if God wished, the Deity could create a cosmos devoid of the *threat* of evil? Such a story is similar to the one told by Barth in only one respect – being largely devoid of biblical support!

From a theoretical point of view, the problem of evil is an interesting and challenging issue. The existence of several competing accounts which claim to solve the problem only adds to the fascination. Barth's discussion of *das Nichtige* sets paradox upon paradox in order to avoid the denial of any of the three elements in the trilemma; Augustine and Calvin's discussion cause us to wonder whether evil is being taken with sufficient seriousness and we have concluded that their theology undermines the omnibenevolence of God; Schleiermacher, Farmer and Hick, meanwhile, try to show how evil can be understood as part of God's purposes, but they leave us concerned whether they have taken seriously the seemingly excessive amount of evil. Does the 'vale of soulmaking' really need to be so challenging? And is God powerless to prevent the excess?

A positive answer to the final question is unthinkable for those theologians who place great emphasis upon the sovereign will of an omnipotent God. And yet there is a minority trend within theology which grants that God's creative act involves a necessary divine self-limitation. Once freedom is granted to a created world, we move to a situation of power-sharing, with the accompanying risk that God's purposes may be delayed or even thwarted. Given that God has made a cosmos which is largely self-developing, there may well be events which God cannot prevent happening since the Deity is not the sole causative agent in the cosmos. According to this model of the God–world relationship, divine agency is not an irresistible force but a persuasive influence. Calvinists will dismiss such a God as a cosmic weakling, but that perhaps undervalues the power of suffering love, and begs the issue concerning the adequacy of the Calvinist model of God.

62   Hick, *Evil and the God of Love*, p 193.
63   Ibid.
64   Ibid., p 142.
65   Ibid., p 149.

The genius of God, perhaps, lies less in God having decreed from eternity everything which will thereafter ever happen, and more in the way the divine purpose is woven out of the warp and woof of the free lives and decisions of others. In such a theology evil's cause is placed firmly within the world. God is not directly responsible for it, but the Deity is actively engaged in seeking to overcome it and in helping those affected by it. There is risk involved. Sometimes God's will may not be followed. The Deity will then suffer the pain and anguish of loss and mistakes. What may often seem to be evil to us, though, turns out to be a required element in the cosmic advance to greater creative complexity. And sometimes we will find it difficult to interpret what is happening to us in a positive and hopeful light. To speak otherwise denies the experience of evil's victims.

At its depth the problem of evil is an existential and practical issue; it is a matter of coping with what has befallen us, rather than seeking theoretically to understand it. However, if what is happening to us can be set within a helpful theoretical framework, we may be helped in our discipleship in an ambiguous world. Might it not be the case that much of the sting (if not the existential challenge) of the problem of evil is removed when it is recognized that omnipotence is a pseudo-concept? Power is relational, since we only have power with or over others who also possess power. No one, not even God, can possess all the power, given that there are other beings who also have power. So the idea of omnipotence makes no sense in its traditional interpretation. At any one time God possesses all the power that is available to the Deity, given that God's creative activity has ensured that there are other beings, subhuman as well as human, who also have power. The implications of this view for the problem of evil are pointed out by Griffin:

> Why, then, can we say that God is good in spite of all the evil within the divine creation? Because all individuals within the creation necessarily have power partially to determine themselves and others; because both intensity and harmony are necessary for intrinsic goodness, so seeking to increase intrinsic goodness means seeking to overcome triviality as well as avoiding discord; because the conditions for the possibilities of greater good are necessarily the conditions for the possibilities of greater suffering; because God does not promote any new level of intensity without being willing to suffer the possible consequences; because God constantly works to overcome evil in the creation with good, and in human experience does this by simultaneously seeking to increase our enjoyment of life and to enlist our support in the effort to overcome evil by maximizing good.[66]

And, of course, the promise that God is willing to suffer the consequences of creating this rather than any other kind of world is located for Christians in the events of Easter. 'God constantly works to overcome evil' is an assertion which is based upon a prior claim concerning the cross of Christ. God's liberating work is always and everywhere operative but decisively re-presented to the world in Jesus' suffering and death. And *that* fact has been for many their only hope in a world torn apart by evil.

We end with the two stories with which we began. Each of them invites us to faith, even when the evidence might suggest atheism. Ivan asked, amidst his abhorrence at the thought that God's good purposes might involve the innocent suffering of one small child, whether there is 'a being in the whole world who would have the right to forgive and could forgive'? Alyosha, 'with flashing eyes' replies that 'there is a Being and He can forgive everything, all and for all, because He gave His innocent blood for all and everything.'[67] In the cross of Christ we know that

---

66 Griffin, *God, Power and Evil: A Process Theodicy*, p 310.
67 See n I.

'neither death, nor life, nor angels, nor rules, nor things present, nor things to come, nor powers, nor height, nor depth, nor anything else in all creation, will be able to separate us from the love of God in Christ Jesus our Lord' (Romans 8: 38–39). And, perhaps, it was faith in One who is not the cause of our suffering but with us in it that drove the elderly rabbi at the end of the trial which had found God guilty to rise to his feet and say: 'Nevertheless . . . let us not forget. It is time for our evening prayers.'[68]

---

[68]   Priestland, *The Case Against God,* p 14.

Reflections and Observations

1.   Reformed churches are renowned for their stress on the Word. They pay great attention to the Bible and preaching, with the pulpit along with hymn singing becoming the major means by which doctrine is taught and theology communicated. The result can be a highly cerebral ecclesial culture. This study, however, has revealed the important part which the Spirit plays in our theology. Calvin's stress on the Word is underpinned by his strong emphasis upon the Spirit's role in discerning God's Word, as the scriptures are read in worship and expounded in preaching, when the sacraments are administered, and during church councils when the mind of Christ is being sought. Word and Spirit operate together, often giving rise to tensions which can be troublesome as well as creative. We might say that Word without Spirit leads to an arid and lifeless Church, while Spirit in the absence of Word takes the Church towards the fanciful and incredible, away from its apologetic task and towards a kind of life-serving insularity. Institutional decline has penetrated Western Christianity in a devastating way, with many congregations appearing to be terminally ill. If ever an injection of the life-giving Spirit was needed, surely now is the time. Where the dead-hand of traditionalism has killed all sense of adventure and enthusiasm, we must seek tradition's living voice which teaches us to sing new songs, leads us into new pathways of obedience and asks that we do new things. The church needs rescuing from those ministers who cannot recognize their church members' giftedness and thereby actually end up suppressing the Spirit. The Apostle maintains that all Christians have been given spiritual gifts to exercise in the church's life: 'To each is given the manifestation of the Spirit for the common good' (1 Cor. 12: 7). So it is not the case that the Spirit is absent from our churches, but more a question of us failing to feed upon the resources she has already bequeathed to us. To focus upon the Spirit at this time, therefore, will be no bad thing.

     Equally important, however, is the need to attend to our age's intellectual demands. While it is true that one great weakness in our churches centres upon them apparently being spiritually dead, it is also the case that another equally significant weakness is clearly evident. This is our failure to convince people that Christianity is credible. Unless we find a rational case for Christianity which grounds our 'spiritual' activity in what is believable and relevant there will be no long-term renewal of the churches. A religion which is based upon warm fellowship, extraordinary spiritual gifts and the heart's inner feelings will not survive without a theology which provides a framework for engagement with society at both an intellectual and a practical level. Spirit needs Word, just as much as Word depends upon Spirit.

2.   Our study has also reminded us that the health of Christian churches is dependent upon their members' spiritual health. If anything is fundamentally wrong with the church, it is likely that we are the major cause. We may feel the need to improve the quality of our worship, to discover more adequate methods of exercising pastoral care, to find ways of engaging in mission with our

society, or to get our congregation on a sounder financial footing. And so we should. But all such needs are dependent finally upon that renewal of personal faith which gives us the energy and wisdom to meet them. The Spirit engenders faith; faith motivates Christians; Christians make churches what they are in their worshipping lives as well as their missionary ventures. It follows that the major focus in any church ought to be centred upon paying serious attention to church members' spiritual lives. We spend a lot of time on activities which center on the church fellowship through a myriad of organizations and activities, but if we heeded our theological heritage, we would recognize that what we engage in is beside the point if it does not lead from 'fellowship in the church' to 'fellowship of the Spirit'. It is worrying, therefore, that prayer and Bible study figure rather far down the list of priorities in some churches.

3.   We need to express a more holistic understanding of salvation than is often found in our churches. The traditional focus has been upon people knowing the truth (orthodoxy) but we also need to challenge people to do the truth (orthopraxis); we have stressed the needs of individuals when we should also have referred to the joys and sorrows of the communities within which they live; the center of our concerns has been with the renewal of persons but it should also have included the renewal of societies, nations and the earth. It is common to run up against polarized attitudes towards salvation. On the one hand, we find those who regard society as an admixture of individuals who need saving, thereby forgetting that the systems and structures which those people inhabit are also in need of renewal. Then, on the other hand, we come across those who substitute community work or social and political engagement for evangelism, thereby seeking to provide space for God to change people's social and political conditions without ever explicitly talking to those people about God and the Deity's self-revelation in Jesus. To attach the usual labels, conservatives argue forcibly that the Church's mission should focus upon God's redemption of people from sin; while liberals argue equally stridently that the Church's mission is to engage with God's emancipating work among the poor, oppressed and sinned against. But surely it is not a question of either/or? An adequate understanding of salvation will be holistic, covering both redemption and emancipation in an integrated concept of God's liberation.

4.   We cannot understand the Christian doctrine of salvation today without recognizing that Christianity is one religion among many, and then considering the question whether there are more ways to salvation than the one prescribed by Christianity. Until recently, of course, Reformed theologians almost universally endorsed the Patristic dictum, 'Outside the Church there is no salvation'. The overtly Christocentric nature of their thinking guaranteed that Christianity was viewed as salvation's sole locus. However, people today, through immigration and travel, have been increasingly made aware of non-Christian religions and their competing truth-claims. Which of the seemingly rival religions is the true one? Discussion of this question has spawned an extensive literature, with scholars providing us with a standard map upon which to plot the rival answers.[1] To the right stand the *exclusivists*, asserting not only that Christianity is the only true religion but also that only the members of the Christian church are in a position to receive salvation. This view is defended by large numbers of conservative evangelical Christians. Even a sophisticated modern

---

[1]   See Alan Race, *Christians and Religious Pluralism: Patterns in the Christian Theology of Religions* (London: SCM Press, 1983); Paul F Knitler, *No Other Name: A Critical Survey of Christian Attitudes Toward the World Religions* (London: SCM Press, 1985); and (for an interesting variation on the standard typology) Schubert M Ogden, *Is There Only One True Religion Or Are There Many?* (Dallas: Southern Methodist University Press, 1992).

apologist like Lesslie Newbigin asserts that 'there is no salvation except one in which we are saved together through the one whom God sends to be the bearer of his salvation.'[2]   As Newbigin's writings make quite clear, however, he is rather more open about who can or cannot be saved than many suppose.[3]   To the left, in direct opposition to exclusivism, stand *pluralists*, arguing that there are many true religions, each being in its own way a way to salvation.   The most well-known advocate of this position is the United Reformed Church's John Hick,[4] who several years ago crossed what Paul Knitter has described as 'a theological Rubicon' when he moved to pluralism.[5]

What reasons lie behind Hick's proposed paradigm-shift in Christian theology? First, many have been impressed by the sincerity, devotion and practice of the members of the non-Christian faiths.   It has become difficult to regard such people as outside salvation simply because they are not Christians.   Many of them live in ways which put Christians to shame.   Secondly, the exclusivist stance conflicts with the biblical witnesses' presentation of Jesus as the decisive re-presentation of a God whose love is universal.   Jesus' openness to people beyond his own religion's confines stands opposed to the narrow attitudes of many Christian exclusivists.   And, thirdly, the exclusivist position denies the possibility of salvation to those who lived before Jesus or outside the stream of witness which has flowed from him.   But, if God wants to save everyone, and if God is powerful enough to do all that needs doing to save them, except what they must do for themselves, then the fact that some have not had, or never will have, the opportunity of even hearing the gospel surely means that exclusivism's God is not a Deity worthy of our worship?   Exclusivism in a sense, then, is ship-wrecked on the rocks of a form of the problem of evil.

While exclusivism and pluralism are the extreme locations on this theological map, other positions lie somewhere between them.   These are called inclusivist and can be divided into two groups.   At centre-right we find *monist inclusivism*.   This is typified by Karl Rahner's idea of 'anonymous Christianity' which asserts that, while there may be salvation outside Christianity, all such salvation has been made possible by the Christ event.   There can be salvation among Buddhists, say, to the extent to which Buddhists act in ways which Christianity would recognize as faithful.   The monist inclusivist attempts to hold together two convictions in tension: the universal operation of God's grace, which makes salvation possible for everyone in whatever religion *as well as* the Christ event as constitutive of salvation's possibility.   At centre – left we find *pluristic inclusivism*.[6]   According to this position, the Christ event is said to be *re-presentative* rather than constitutive of the opportunity of salvation.   While monistic inclusivists grant that non-Christians can be saved outside the visible Church unknowingly and anonymously, they also believe that any religion becomes a means of salvation which has been transformed by Christ. Such religions mediate implicitly and unknowingly what Christianity mediates explicitly and knowingly.

[2]   Lesslie Newbigin, *The Gospel in a Pluralist Society* (London: SPCK, 1991), p 83.

[3]   Newbigin clarifies his position as follows: 'The position which I have outlined is exclusivist in the sense that it affirms the unique truth of the revelation of Jesus Christ, but it is not exclusivist in the sense of denying the possibility of the salvation of the non-Christian.   It is inclusivist in the sense that it refuses to limit the saving grace of God to the members of the Christian Church, but it rejects the inclusivism which regards the non-Christian religions as vehicles of salvation.   It is pluralist in the sense of acknowledging the gracious work of God in the lives of all human beings, but it rejects a pluralism which denies the uniqueness and decisiveness of what God has done in Jesus Christ' (ibid., pp 182–3).

[4]   See John Hick, *God and the Universe of Faiths* (London and Basingstoke: The Macmillan Press, Ltd., 1973) and *God Has Many Names* (London and Basingstoke: The Macmillan Press, Ltd., 1980).

[5]   'Preface' in John Hick and Paul F Knitter, eds., *The Myth of Christian Uniqueness* (London: SCM Press, 1987), p viii.

[6]   For the terms 'monist inclusivism' and 'pluralist inclusivism' see Ogden, *Is There Only One True Religion or Are There Many?*, pp x–xi.

The pluralistic inclusivist, however, argues that 'if the Christian religion itself is true, then any and all other religions can be true in the very same sense, because or insofar as they give expression to substantially the same religions truth'.[7] This position focuses upon God's universal love making salvation possible for everyone, and with its representative christology it allows for the possibility that there are 'as many true religions as there are religions so transformed by God's love as to be constituted by it and representative of it.'[8]

The clear merits of the pluralistic inclusivist position are threefold. First, it joins other inclusivists and pluralists in insisting that the exclusivist option is not theologically viable. Secondly, pluralistic inclusivists along with pluralists, but in opposition to monistic inclusivists, insist that it is possible that there *may be* more than one true religion. Then, thirdly, what separates the pluralistic inclusivist from the pluralist is simply that the former draws back from the latter's assertion that there *is* a constellation of true religions. Only God could substantiate the pluralist claim. We cannot avoid being taken in a pluralist direction, however, if we want to have a theology which does justice both to the witness of Jesus and the religious realities of the twenty-first century.

---

[7] Ibid., p 103.
[8] Ibid., p 104.

PART 5

We believe in the one, holy, catholic, apostolic Church, in heaven and on earth, wherein by the same Spirit, the whole company of believers is made one Body of Christ, to worship God and serve him and all men in his kingdom of righteousness and love.

IN PART 5 our attention focuses upon the Church and the Christian life. We will first consider the traditional teaching concerning the Church as we ask what marks separate the true from the false church? Then we turn to a discussion of preaching and sacraments, the so-called means of grace, before considering the role of ministry and church organisation. We then end with a discussion about the Christian life which centres upon the role of freedom, discipline and worship. It is in this part of the book, perhaps, that many of the distinctive emphases of the Reformed ethos appear.

CHAPTER 14

One, Holy, Catholic and Apostolic Church

THE NEW Testament writers provide us with a wide range of metaphors with which to describe the church. Very often the ones chosen reflect the emphasis each writer was trying to make to a specific readership. So, when the stress is being laid on the Church as a religious community which replaces Israel, metaphors like 'people of God', 'temple' and 'elect' gained fresh meaning. But if the accent was on the unity of a Christian fellowship made up of diverse individuals, then a term like 'body of Christ' became a powerful description. When the emphasis, however, turned to the church as possessing the true teaching concerning the meaning and purpose of all life, the church was called 'the way'. And in a community made up of the faithful, who had not only a desire to build one another up in Christ but also a missionary purpose beyond itself, the metaphor of 'election' came to take on notes of responsibility and service rather than simply privilege. But, amazing as it might seem, there was little systematic reflection on ecclesiology conducted by the early Christians. One of the reasons, perhaps, was that the church was more a reality bound up with a Christian's whole life than something standing apart from daily affairs. Christians were content to know that they belonged to it, were redeemed in it and, as a result, were different kinds of persons from those who led their lives in other religious ways. So we had to wait for the Patristic period and beyond for more developed ecclesiological understanding.

The Patristic theologians made use of many New Testament images but, in particular, they tended to focus on three metaphors which are still in use today.[1] First, the church was viewed as mother. It brings people to new life in baptism and feeds them with eucharistic food at the Lord's Supper. Christians no longer live in the flesh as born of a human mother; they now live in the Spirit having been born anew in the church. Since the Western church increasingly has to work among folk in a secular society, this particular metaphor reminds us of the difference which faith in Jesus Christ and membership of the church makes to people. Secondly, the Fathers used the image of the ark. It gave expression to Cyprian's belief that 'outside the Church there is no salvation' (*extra ecclesiam nulla salus*). The ark contained those saved from sin's chaotic waters; others outside were lost. This theme was also employed by those less enthusiastic about the idea that membership of the visible church guaranteed salvation. Augustine, for example, believed that the ark contained sinners as well as saints, and that, as a result, God will decide who in the ark will be saved. This important ecclesiological insight is of tremendous contemporary relevance when some in their enthusiasm for the Christian cause have a tendency to un-church fellow church members who do not happen to share their theological convictions or liturgical ethos. Then, thirdly, the Fathers employed the metaphor of the virgin-bride. The church is pure, detached from the wicked world and

---

[1] See Boniface Ramsay, *Beginning to Read the Fathers* (London: SCM Press, 1993), pp 95–108.

wedded to Christ. This image stresses the union between Christ and the church as well as the ongoing need to maintain a clear distinction between church and society. Boniface Ramsay remarks, therefore, that, for the Patristic period, 'the mystery of the Church was at heart a paradox: it was virgin and mother; one, yet dispersed in many places and characterized by a diversity of customs; immaculate, yet with sinful members; created before time began, yet having come into time.'[2] We are still having to live with this paradox in our postmodern era.

Reading the Fathers leaves one with a very clear understanding of the principles which guided their churches. Given the diversity, it was hardly surprising that there was a concern for unity. They also wanted to affirm that Christianity had been entrusted with a gospel for all peoples and cultures, and to acknowledge that the universal Church is fully present in the local church. They strove further for that faithfulness which leads to holiness, and thus against the temptation to worship false gods; and they wished to remain in communion with Jesus by following the traditions which had been handed down by the Apostles, thus avoiding being taken over by alternative ideologies and practices. Most of what we read about the early church's life can be subsumed under one or other of the four 'notes' or 'marks' of the church which are expressed in the Nicene Creed. 'We believe in one holy, catholic and apostolic Church.' What today, therefore, does it mean for the church to attempt to be true to the self-identity mapped out for it in the fifth century?

Before we move on to consider each of the marks of the true church, we should note that, while we are in a theoretical position to make a distinction between a 'true' and a 'false' church, we can never in practice give sufficient content to this distinction that a final judgement can be made on whether a church in fact is 'true' or 'false'. The distinction should always be employed from an eschatological perspective, leaving to God any final delineation concerning who belongs to which. Daniel Jenkins reminds us that 'the distinction between a true and false church cannot be drawn by us but can only be recognized by us in faith as one already made by God Himself.'[3] What, then, can we learn about the marks of a true church from those who have gone before us?

The Unity of the Church

I grew up with a popular but false view of church history. It assumed that there was a time when there was a single undivided church which later broke up into the many different denominations. But this picture on inspection proves to be overtly simplistic. From the very beginning there were many diverse congregations. The issue was never one of maintaining unity so much as achieving it. That is why Paul is so concerned about unity when he writes to churches in danger of disintegration. The issue for him was one of striving for unity amidst the diversity of the Body of Christ. Later in the primitive church's life we find a similar emphasis coming from the Johannine community as Jesus prays that his disciples might be one as he and his Father are one (John 17). The problem we face daily is that the church's rich diversity easily spills over into disunity that becomes highlighted by seemingly intractable theological disagreements between different churches and communions. We all too easily start insisting that *our* theology or *our* polity is *the* way, but this is to make final and absolute what can only ever be provisional. Again the eschatological dimension needs emphasising. The truth is only fully known at journey's end, and, as a result, hindsight will show that all Christian thought and practice is impoverished to greater or lesser degrees.

---

[2]   Ibid., p 108.
[3]   Daniel Jenkins, *The Nature of Catholicity* (London: Faber and Faber Ltd. 1942), p 46.

The unity we all seek will be granted by Christ as we strive to be one in him. What we now know only partially awaits us in fullness in the future. And our ever-now-but-always-not-yet experience of unity hinges on our faithfulness in our particular mission context. It will be given as a gift as we try to be holy, catholic and apostolic in our self-identity and self-expressions as a community of God's people. This much sought after unity will transcend both uniformity and pluralism. It will also be far from merely an end in itself, since the divine gift invariably carries with it a divine commission. The unity we receive in Christ, therefore, must be extended beyond the church to encompass the whole *oikoumene*:

> The unity of Christ, which must not be divided, is not only unity with his disciples and the fellowship of believers but, based on that, is also his unity and fellowship with the oppressed, humiliated and forsaken. The church would not witness to the whole Christ if it were not a fellowship of believers with the poor, a fellowship of the hopeful with the sick, and a fellowship of the loving with the oppressed.[4]

The divisions we now face in the churches are not just about doctrine but also about how we perceive the church's missionary task. The question facing the ecumenical movement therefore sometimes takes on a different shape. Moltmann argues, for example, that 'it is no longer merely true that "doctrine divides but services unites"; now it is often the case that "doctrine unites but politics divide".'[5] Where our United Reformed Church stands, and with whom, can therefore become *the* ecumenical question. What guidelines are there? The only trustworthy one is that we should be where Christ is found. This means that the church's unity should be understood *theologically* rather than simply sociologically or organisationally.

Comparisons are said to be odious, but sometimes they can be very revealing. Let us look first of all at the November 1972 edition of *Reform* which covered the URC's inaugural Assembly and service in Westminster Abbey. Ecumenical optimism exudes from almost every page. The front cover picture of Cardinal John Heenan and Archbishop Michael Ramsey reminds readers of the ecumenical commitment they shared with us that day: '. . . I give thanks with you for this union, and share your resolve to seek that wider unity which is Christ's will.' Ramsey is reported as saying that he was glad that 'in the past decade on the Church scene 'the old devilish self-consciousness of our dividing labels had been blown to bits";' while John Huxtable in his sermon reminded us again of the prevailing expectation that 'the union of our two Churches would be but the beginning of a larger coming together.' Now compare this up-beat ecumenical tempor with a 1982 pamphlet. Not only had the 1964 Nottingham conference commitment to covenant together for unity by Easter 1980 not been met, but we now find a gloomy conclusion regarding the failed Covenant proposals, namely, that 'there was a general lack of the enthusiastic heart and will to make the Covenant happen: and so it died.'[6] What happened during the period 1972-82 to cause such a decline in ecumenical endeavour? Even allowing for the Unification with the Reformed Association of the Churches of Christ in 1981, and a great deal of local ecumenical endeavour in Shared Churches and Local Ecumenical Projects and Partnerships, a sea change of opinion about ecumenism had taken place. Why was it that people were tending now to be protective of their ecclesial identity? A number of factors were involved.

---

4   Moltmann, *The Church in the Power of the Spirit*, p 345.

5   Ibid., p 346.

6   'The Failure of the English Covenant: An Assessment of the Experience of the Churches' Council for Covenanting' (BCC pamphlet, 1982), p 25.

First, some people had fundamental objections to the reasons which were being given for the drive towards visible organic union. A picture had been pressed upon our minds that we were trying to repair a divided church, but this picture presupposed that once there had been an organically united church. Given the preponderance of ecumenical theologians to authorise their claims by Scripture, this in turn presupposed a certain picture of the New Testament church which was false. Käsemann points out that 'only fragments of the discussion within primitive Christianity have been preserved for us', and therefore that 'the variability of the primitive Christian kerygma must have been very much greater than a consideration of the state of affairs as revealed in the canon would lead us to suppose.'[7] The New Testament provides evidence of not only continuity but also discontinuity between the early Christians and Jesus. Differing doctrinal views are present in the earliest traditions, so, Käsemann argues, 'the New Testament canon does not, as such, constitute the foundation of the unity of the Church' but, instead, 'provides the basis for the multiplicity of the confessions.'[8] The simple fact is that primitive Christianity was made up of a diversity of churches which, as their writings show, were searching for unity. The New Testament therefore authorizes a more diverse pattern of church unity than the organic model allows.

It was also maintained of course that a divided church was no help in the healing of a divided world. Too often, though, the obvious truth in this, whether at international, national or more local levels, carried with it a demand for a rather more uniform church organisation than many were prepared to contemplate. Was it not the very genius of the churches constantly to be able to reconstitute themselves afresh in ways appropriate to local circumstances? If ecclesial diversity is a precondition of relevant and effective evangelism in different contexts, why was it such a threat to the ecumenical movement? John Huxtable perhaps reflected the spirit of a passing era when he said in his Abbey sermon: 'If the national communions do not unite as soon as possible, the very ecumenical work at the grass-roots will inevitably produce a condition of confused impotence.'[9] Viewed from a postmodern setting, where differences are more likely to be taken as signs of vitality in organisations than manifestations of weakness, Huxtable's remarks now seem wide of the mark.

Secondly, there were quite fundamental theological objections to the basis upon which the goal of visible unity was to be achieved. Central was the unwillingness of many to accept that mutual recognition of ministries is only possible if we introduce episcopacy into our church order. For ex-Congregationalists, the warning-bells sounded by their predecessors could be heard. As hard as one argued that an order of bishops might be of the *bene esse* of the church, friends could remind one of the judgement of Bernard Lord Manning:

> . . . Congregationalists have taken, and may be counted on to take, much that they are told about the value of the 'historic' episcopate with a certain amount of amused scepticism . . . they have seen other men live with the 'historic' episcopate, and have themselves lived without it, too long to have an exaggerated regard for it. They are perfectly prepared to consider it on its merits, but that it is of the esse of the church, or even that it is always of the bene esse of the church, their past experience and their present observation alike prevent their persuading themselves. They have lived too long in the apostolic succession of the faithful, they have enjoyed too certainly the continuity of the Word and the Sacraments and the sacred ministry of the Gospel, to be in any doubt about what continuity and apostolic succession are.[10]

---

[7]   Käsemann, 'The Canon of the New Testament and the Unity of the Church' in *Essays on New Testament Themes*, p 100.

[8]   Ibid., p 103.

[9]   *Reform*, November 1972, p 3.

[10] Manning, *Essays in Orthodox Dissent*, p 169.

Manning's point was not just that the much vaunted episcopal system is not as useful to church order as Anglicans claim. After all he was prepared to say that 'Congregationalists have no particular war-to-the-knife quarrel with the government of the Church by bishops.'[11] Indeed, had not P T Forsyth stated earlier that he had 'no objection to Episcopacy in itself' and admitted that he could do his work happily under a bishop, and 'feel honoured under the episcopate of many'?[12] Manning's actual objection was to 'salvation by bishops, not with government by bishops'.[13] He should be heard again on what remains a fundamental point for Reformed faith:

> We are saved by grace; by grace which comes as God's free gift, not in legally restricted channels controlled by attorneys in episcopal robes. And we are saved by God's full grace: not by some irregular, imperfect, diluted grace, just adequate to cope with the needs of mere Dissenters, but quite inferior to the 100 percent. streams, of which only the attorneys in episcopal robes can manipulate the sluice-gates. Against any such notion of the work of grace, we protest in season and out of season; and no prospect of union can silence our protest.[14]

That the saving efficacy of the Eucharist is dependent upon the celebrant being ordained by a bishop is still the High Church view. This opinion rests upon the self-same pipeline theory of grace so ridiculed by Manning. While Forsyth would most certainly have agreed with Manning, he further questions the Episcopal system by saying that he would see part of his work under the authority of the bishop as being to preach that bishops as we now know them did not exist in the first century. This was his protest 'against an Episcopal . . . monopoly of Church or Gospel, against polity as a condition of Church unity'.[15] In the Covenant debate, many shared this view, stating that they would only accept conciliar authority, but never Episcopal authority or the required mixture of the two.[16]

Intellectual debate never takes place in a vacuum. We must recognise the impact of the culture in which debate takes place upon the intellectual process. By the 1980s the URC was being affected by both congregational and national pressures. Experience had made many somewhat weary with the ecumenical process. The URC's birth had brought a fair amount of pain – the loss of old Congregational friends for some and the upheaval of local patterns of church order. The prospect of further discord and change damped many folk's enthusiasm. Others suspected that the URC's positive approach was not shared by others. There was some evidence that in local ecumenical arrangements it was the Reformed heritage that was likely to be compromised, so resistance was building up at the grass-roots. And wider afield a new cultural climate was emerging as Thatcherism took root. We entered an era of free enterprise, competition and choice. Our culture became increasingly individualistic. Somewhat ironically, as Bernard Thorogood notes, 'the individualism of western culture . . . had a close link with Reformed Christianity,'[17] but its re-assertion in the 1980s was perhaps one of the key reasons why the ecumenical focus turned from the earlier emphasis on 'unity' to an enthusiastic recognition of the validity of 'diversity'. What emerged was a new phase in the ecumenical journey, and, however it will come to be judged, no one can take away from it the achievement of involving the Roman Catholic Church in the British ecumenical pilgrimage.

---

[11]   Ibid., p 142.
[12]   Forsyth, *Lectures on the Church and the Sacraments*, p 42.
[13]   Manning, *Essays in Orthodox Dissent*, p 142.
[14]   Ibid., pp 141–2.
[15]   Forsyth, *Lectures on the Church and Sacraments*, p 42.
[16]   See *Towards Visible Unity: Proposals for a Covenant: The Report of the Churches' Council on Covenanting* (London: BCC, 1980), p 48.
[17]   Bernard Thorogood, *One Wind, Many Flames: Church Unity and the Diversity of the Churches* (Geneva: WCC, 1991), p 14.

What we have therefore witnessed in the URC, perhaps, is not so much a diminishing of our ecumenical urgency but a fresh understanding of it. God seems to have the knack of sending the Spirit of diversity upon the church when its thinking and practice tend towards monolithic uniformity; equally God sends the Spirit of unity to bind together churches who allow their rich diversity to spill over into disunity. The ecumenical pilgrimage started in 1972 was focused upon unity. We have since come to appreciate the need for diversity. As we journey on with others we will be wise to hold both emphases in tension. This is not to make a virtue out of a necessity; rather it is the discovery of an ecumenical ideal to be followed. As Thorogood has said: 'The next reformation to which we are being led by our ecumenical experience is to acknowledge that the diversities which are theological, cultural and geographical are gifts to be welcomed but which need to be balanced by the visible evidence of unity.'[18] In our culture we tend to be better at the acknowledgement than the balancing act!

The change of ecumenical perspective we have witnessed is part of a wider paradigm-shift which has taken place world-wide. Konrad Raiser argues that what Visser't Hooft calls 'Christocentric universalism' was the pre-dominating paradigm of the ecumenical movement until recently, when it has increasingly been seen to be unable to meet contemporary challenges.[19] This paradigm was in operation when the URC was conceived and born. Its emphasis is upon a christology 'from above' which stresses Christ's lordship, while in ecclesiology the 'stress is laid on the true bond and union between Christ and his church as the foundation of the church's visible unity.'[20] The Christ event is then seen as an event of such universal significance that it gives rise to an ecclesiological vision in which Christ's lordship is 'to be empirically visible, verifiable in history'.[21] History thus comes to be viewed as the stage upon which God's saving purposes are taking place: 'The dynamic conception of universal history as realizing God's plan of salvation is thus the decisive link in the chain holding the basic elements of the paradigm together in tension.'[22]

But this theological approach is very problematical. Raiser notes that in the old ecumenical paradigm there was a movement towards 'an uncritical dogmatic christology with its tendency to abstract generalized statements and docetic triumphalism'; also there was a danger 'of turning an ecumenical theology of history into an ideology which plays down the ambiguity of historical processes and the reality of guilt and tragedy, disappointment and death;' and there was the further tendency 'to make exaggerated claims for the church and its place in the divine plan of salvation.'[23] He argues, therefore, that 'the framework of thought which sustained the extraordinary missionary consciousness of the ecumenical movement'[24] no longer gives direction in a world dominated by religious pluralism, injustice caused by 'transnationalization', threats to the planet and emerging novel but diverse ways of being the Church. So he sketches the outline of a new ecumenical paradigm. Three of its main features begin to open up a perspective which enables the URC to be faithful to its ecumenical identity.

---

18   Ibid., p. 70.
19   Konrad Raiser, *Ecumenism in Transition: A Paradigm Shift in the Ecumenical Movement?* (Geneva: WCC, 1991, pp 35–6).
20   Ibid., p 44.
21   Ibid.
22   Ibid., p 45.
23   Ibid., p 53.
24   Ibid.

The new paradigm takes its bearing first of all from the *oikoumene* (the whole inhabited world) viewed as the household of life, created and preserved by God. Being an interrelated whole, this household is the environment in which an interlocking series of relationships takes place, and in it 'the ecological, social, political and ecclesiological dimensions of the *oikoumene* are linked in the closest way possible'.[25] It becomes clear immediately that ecumenism is now concerned with relationships rather than structures, world order and not just church order, and society as well as the church. The ecumenical issue is about how we are to live as Christians and churches in the *oikoumene*.

A second feature of Raiser's new paradigm is the way in which the theological focus shifts from a christological to a Trinitarian emphasis. God is no longer pictured as the ruling monarch but is modelled on a social doctrine of the Trinity. The Trinity then in turn is made a model for the church. Both unity and diversity can therefore be honoured. Church life comes to be thought of 'as a being-in-relationship of those who remain distinct and different'.[26] It makes a lot of difference to ecclesiastical affairs if we model the church on 'that full unity which is in God and that distinctiveness of persons which is also in God'.[27]

Finally, Raiser turns to the idea of 'eucharistic fellowship' for a third area around which a new ecumenical paradigm might emerge. Fellowship becomes a key ecumenical term: its use enables the church to be 'explicitly anchored in its participation in the living, open communion of the triune God'.[28] At the eucharist the many become one, where 'many' refers not just to numbers but also 'to the whole variety of natural and social differences which are represented in the gathered congregations'.[29] In the Spirit the 'many' are brought together in fellowship in each local congregation, and the local congregations in turn are brought into fellowship with other local congregations. Raiser therefore asks us to observe that according to this model 'differences are not signs of a lack of unity, but signs of vitality in the body of Christ – provided that they do not erect exclusive boundaries between one another or infringe the essential inter-relatedness of the Spirit-produced community'.[30] Viewed from the perspective of a fellowship meal, invitation to the Eucharist must be open to at least all the baptised members of the church. It is the refusal of ecumenical hospitality which therefore needs justifying: 'Confession of Jesus Christ and baptism are the visible signs of the fellowship, which is antecedent to all our ecumenical efforts to make visible the unity of the church.'[31] If the churches of the *oikoumene* were only able to accept this!

The Holiness of the Church

Christians are invited to participate in that overwhelming and fascinating Mystery who is the triune God, the One who brings us to sing God's praise in worship and to obedience in God's service. The Deity is holy and God's people are called to reflect fully that same holiness. Until we become holy we are incomplete, but holiness is not something we can grasp or achieve for ourselves; rather it is a state we inherit gradually as we strive to grow up fully into Christ (Ephesians 4: 15).

---

25   Ibid., p 90
26   Ibid., p 96.
27   Thorogood, *One Wind, Many Flames*, p 2.
28   Raiser, *Ecumenism in Transition*, p 97.
29   Ibid., p 98.
30   Ibid., p 100.
31   Ibid., p 116.

It never becomes our possession this side of the grave and like all the other marks of the church holiness must be understood eschatologically. Its fullness always lies before us on the pilgrim journey as we tread the path Jesus mapped out for us. We are to love God with all our heart, mind and strength, and our neighbour as ourself (Matthew 22: 34–40).

We need to beware, however, of viewing holiness in an unnecessarily narrow and distorted way. The church very often has been guilty of spiritualizing it away, thus ending up with the hypocrisy so clearly pointed out by the prophets (Micah 6: 6–8). Holiness is not just about our interior spiritual life, though it is never less than that; it also concerns the way we lead our lives. Holiness is shaped by our duty to love God and the command to love our neighbour; so it will be as concerned with social action as it is with spirituality. It is about politics as much as piety: Have we really taken our stand with the oppressed, struggled for justice and supported the down-trodden? Do we really respond to Christ in the least of the brothers and sisters? (Matthew 25: 31–46). Participation in the Holy does not take place in some separate religious realm; it occurs in the everyday world. There is always the danger of Christians taking the lift to the Eternal while forgetting to press the button marked, 'Earthly reality'. Our holiness should show that we are bothered about everyday struggles and conflicts as well as the hopes and joys of eternal life.

At several points in her life the church has faced the rather obvious problem of her calling to holiness standing in sharp contrast to her members' sinfulness. Two quite distinct approaches to this issue subsequently developed. First, the rigorist approach of the Donatist and Anabaptist churches emphasised the necessity of holiness among their church members. A perfectionist stance led such churches to exclude those who violated what were perceived to be accepted Christian standards. This position is still typical of sectarian churches who play down the forgivability of their fallible members. The second approach takes its point of departure from the wisdom of always setting ecclesiology in an eschatological context. It was developed initially by Augustine, for whom the church is like a threshing floor on which both wheat and chaff lie until separated. Taking his lead from the parable of the wheat and tares (Matthew 13: 24–30), Augustine argued that at the last judgement the righteous will be separated from the sinful. The visible church, therefore, is always simultaneously a community of sinners and saints.

Moltmann emphasises that the church owes its holiness to Christ rather than to any qualities of its own. He insists that 'the church is holy because it is sanctified through Christ's activity in and on it', and therefore holiness is rooted in God's activity.[32] So when it confesses its sin and places its faith in God's offer of salvation in Christ the church is holy. It follows that the holy church is *ecclesia reformata et semper reformanda* since it is always striving for holiness through 'continual new conversion and permanent reformation' as it witnesses to God's kingdom.[33] Moltmann finds signs of the holy church not only in the church's active service but also particularly in its suffering with Christ. The holy church consequently is a community in solidarity with the poor and fighting poverty. The church's mission, therefore, is concerned with people's material as well as spiritual poverty. Its own poverty will witness to its commitment to the poor. This fellowship, Moltmann believes, is of more value than development aid: 'The problem of poverty in the world is not solved by programmes which mobilize "the church for the poor" or try to win "the poor for the church", but only through the church of the poor itself.'[34] One of the foremost challenges the URC faces is that it does not have a widespread record of effectiveness outside its middle-class strongholds.

---

[32] Moltmann, *The Church in the Power of the Spirit*, p 353.
[33] Ibid., p 355.
[34] Ibid., p 357.

It is hardly 'the church of the poor', nor is it very successful in winning 'the poor for the church'. But there is a passionate commitment among many URC members to work for the poor in down-to-earth practical ways.

People do not usually put first things first; we are not radical enough. What concerns us ultimately is not the God decisively revealed to us and for us by Jesus. We turn away from the fount of holiness to the manifold idols we erect through our misplaced ingenuity. What really is needed is that we turn to God in faith and receive the resources to start getting things right. But even our turning to God is impossible without God's grace. As Paul Tillich reminds us: 'We are justified by grace *alone*, because in our relation to God we are dependent on God, on God alone, and in no way on ourselves; we are grasped by grace, and this is only another way of saying that we have faith.'[35] This is the theological centre of Christianity. We must learn, therefore, to put God first; this is the route of holiness. But I sense a reluctance in many of our URC churches to place church life in God's hands. Instead, some churches seem to look to other sources of salvation. There is a living denial of the principle of justification by grace through faith at the ecclesial level. But what idols do our churches erect? I have particularly observed five:

(1) The *Past*. The answers to the church's predicament are assumed to lie in some ecclesiastical golden age. Some see a certain part of the Reformed tradition as a past ideal which, if recaptured, will cure all ills. Would it not be good to return to pre-URC days when, as Churches of Christ, Congregationalists or Presbyterians, everything in the garden was wonderful! People can sometimes be heard making the birth of the URC a scapegoat for their church's numerical decline. Others turn to the Bible, believing that all will be right with the contemporary church if we return to meeting in houses and become like the Christian sect within Judaism mentioned early in Acts. There is a lot of evidence around to suggest that the church is at the forefront of the nostalgia business!

(2) Some churches make *ministers* their idols, and ministers stupidly play up to the status offered them. There are few things ministers like better than being granted omnicompetence. Such idols of course come and go. It is ironic to listen to churches pressing for a new minister immediately the previous one, of whom they often have been so critical, has left. Some churches seem at times more minister-centred than God-centred. And when we have not enough ministers to go round, we invent new types to satisify the churches' craving. In the process, we do little other than further risk clericalizing the church and lowering the standards of the professional ministry. The way ahead lies in using and enhancing the ministry we have – particularly the eldership.

(3) There is growing evidence of the phenomenon of *bibliolatry*, the confusion (made a virtue now in some quarters) of collapsing the distinction which wise theologians have sought to maintain between the Word of God and the Bible. John Barton is correct when he says that '*sola scriptura* is a metaphor' which 'points us . . . to the truth that the gospel is of God's making, and that human words and traditions cannot contain it.'[36] It follows that 'every attempt to identify this gospel with the words of a book, even of the Bible, is to turn it into human tradition and thereby to domesticate it; and this deprives it of its power to stand over against our own thoughts and ideas and to challenge us to revise them.'[37]

---

35   Paul Tillich, *The Protestant Era* (Chicago: The University of Chicago Press, 1948), p xvii.
36   Barton, *People of the Book? The Authority of the Bible in Christianity*, p 86.
37   Ibid.

(4)   *Numerical Growth.* There is no evidence whatsoever that there is a necessary link between a congregation's numerical strength and the quality of its life. Yet one often hears people in an age of competition and quantification running down their own church because it is not as numerically strong as another neighbouring congregation. The quality of a cricket match should not be gauged by the number of spectators who turn out to watch it. Likewise, the test for every congregation is whether or not it is being faithful, a criterion which is applicable to a congregation of five or five hundred. Ecclesiastically, small may turn out to be beautiful!

(5)   *The Institution.* There is abundant evidence that many are more committed to Christianity's institutional dimensions than the One whom the institution should serve. Organizations run by local churches often take on roles out of all proportion to their real significance. Choirs, uniformed organisations and women's meetings all have been known to become the focal point of church life. Then the tail starts wagging the dog. And which church is ever free of the idolatry of worshipping the church building? Both church organisations and buildings have an important part to play in the church's mission; but neither is an adequate centre around which to sustain a church. The church is constituted by the One in whom it believes, and everything else ecclesiastical is there to serve rather than usurp the One to whom that belief points.

The Catholicity of the Church

The word 'catholic' is difficult for Protestants to own given its association with one side in a long-running ecumenical dispute. Many associate it either with the polity and practice of those Christians who stress the role of creeds, sacraments and bishops in transmitting the gospel from age to age, or with the particular church which more than any other exemplifies such an approach, namely, the Roman Catholic Church. This is rather unfortunate because catholicity is one of the marks of the true church. To be true to its calling the URC needs to be not only reformed but also catholic. Indeed, it is as true to say that 'the Church is never reformed but is always in process of reformation', as it is to claim that 'only a reformed Church can hope to be the Catholic Church.'[38] Hans Küng therefore argues that 'constant practical reform in accordance with the norms of [the] gospel' is an essential aspect of 'authentically catholic tradition and breadth'.[39]

In the New Testament, the term *ekklesia* refers to local worshipping communities which, while autonomous, are still associated with one another by a quality which transcends each of them. A local church is not the church in its wholeness or totality, but it does share in that wholeness. The term 'catholic' came to signify this 'wholeness' or 'totality'. So a local church represents the universal church because it possesses a certain quality in its life which is definitive of the universal Church. The universal Church is present throughout the world (*spatial* catholicity) and across the ages (*temporal* catholicity). Not surprisingly, then, catholicity is essentially bound up with the other marks of the true church, particularly with unity. The term catholic came to stand for the true (or orthodox) church when it was being distinguished from false (or heretical) churches. It was clear, therefore, that to be a catholic church the church must be in continuity with the apostolic witness.

---

38   Jenkins, *The Nature of Catholicity,* pp. 50, 51.
39   Hans Küng, *Credo: The Apostles' Creed Explained for Today* (London: SCM Press, 1992), p 138.

Moltmann reminds us that all the marks of the 'true' church have to be understood in an eschatological context. He insists that we should not collapse the crucial distinction between 'church' and 'kingdom'. The church is 'the people of the coming kingdom', but 'it is not yet the new humanity itself'.[40] Nevertheless, the church participates in the kingdom in a provisional way through mission. It may be 'incomplete in its particularity' but its task in the world is to 'represent nothing other than the future universal society'.[41] That society is one in which barriers between people have been broken down. The church's mission, therefore, is shaped by 'Christian partisan support for the oppressed'.[42] It involves mission among, and fellowship with, the poor and outcasts. Catholicity, for Moltmann, therefore, possesses a distinctive social and political dimension: 'The church is related to the whole and is catholic in so far as, in the fragmentation of the whole, it primarily seeks and restores to favour the lost, the rejected and the oppressed'.[43] What Moltmann calls for is anathema to those church members who resolutely maintain an almost schizophrenic separation between their faith and social and political concerns.

Jenkins outlines eight qualities which he sees as essential if the church is to be genuinely catholic. He stresses the unity of the church, reminding us that church unity should be modelled on God's triunity. He insists that 'a Christian unity which is not expressed . . . in the society of the visible church, is a sentimental delusion'.[44] This unity is based upon the church's constant re-constitution under Word and Sacrament. Secondly, Jenkins suggests that a catholic church will possess universality of appeal by including a wide variety of people and seeking to meet the needs of a significant cross section of society. Legitimate attempts to address particular contexts must beware of threatening the church's catholicity. Jenkins warns that the church 'must always ensure that Jesus Christ has the primacy in her own midst and that her people are faithful to her because they are faithful to Jesus Christ and not because of her central place in the social life of the neighbourhood or her unique position as the repository of the national traditions'.[45] It follows, thirdly, that a truly catholic church will have nothing in its constitutional make-up which could compromise her obedience to God. What Jenkins has in mind here is the way state control, class and financial interests, and powerful personalities can be a negative influence upon the church. He is particularly scathing about the state appointment of some ministers of the Church of England. Jenkins then says that, fourthly, the catholic church will 'permit nothing in the form of its intellectual life which hinders it from its obedience to its Lord'.[46] He believes that 'God's Word in Jesus Christ . . . is universally valid, so that all other truths derive from it'.[47] It is a norm of truth which lies outside the relativities of the age. But Jenkins hardly takes account of the fact that 'God's Word in Jesus Christ' is communicated to us via those who first heard it in a very different culture and era from our own. It is difficult to conceive of an account of the Christian gospel which avoids the relativities of *some* age. Fifthly, a truly catholic church 'will try to grasp for herself the whole of the Faith and the relation of all its parts to each other and try to express it in such a way that it lights up the whole of human life'.[48] The URC might do worse than note Jenkins's comment that church members perhaps 'may be permitted to continue to observe the English custom of being inarticulate on the

---

40 Moltmann, *The Church in the Power of the Spirit*, p 349.
41 Ibid.
42 Ibid., p 352.
43 Ibid.
44 Jenkins, *The Nature of Catholicity*, p 127.
45 Ibid., p 132.
46 Ibid., p 136.
47 Ibid., pp 136–7.
48 Ibid., p 140.

subject of one's deepest beliefs', but that 'it is sheer unadulterated laziness on the part of . . . ministers when they try to do the same.'[49] But we need not only a theologically literate ministry, but also a recognition that some English customs are not very healthy! Sixthly, Jenkins maintains that a truly catholic church will possess 'fullness of liturgical life'.[50] He suggests that Reformed services should contain 'confession, absolution, the reading of the Word, intercessions, the preaching of the Word, the reading of the Words of Institution, the Anaphora, the Prayer of Consecration, the Epiklesis, the Communion, in more or less that order and that the service is not a "full" service when any of these are missing.'[51] Reformed churches need particularly to ask whether the Lord's Supper is a central part of their life and whether it is celebrated with sufficient frequency. Seventhly, Jenkins argues that a truly catholic Church will recognize her responsibility for forming a Christian pattern of society.'[52] The Christian life should reflect what is expected of a society transformed by Christ's life and the Spirit's power – the church's missionary mandate. Finally, Jenkins suggests that 'the most distinctive of all the qualities of a truly catholic Church will be her humility.'[53] She lives from the power of the cross rather than her own resources. All forms of Christian triumphalism therefore are suspect.

In ecumenical debate the Reformed churches are often criticised for being deficient in catholicity. We have only ourselves to blame and must acknowledge that there resides in many congregations an unhealthy spirit of independency which tends to shut out the wider church scene. Local identity ends up being everything, with an impression being given that there is nothing to learn from other churches. Many know more about their own congregation's history than either the history of the Reformed traditions or the present life of other churches in the *oikoumene*. There is also a great need to catch the excitement of the world church – the vitality of new expressions of Christianity and the challenge and commitment of the church of the poor and oppressed. We must guard against a life-draining spirit of independency which confuses parochialism with our need for identity. Therefore our congregational life should open out to the wider church as we seek to be an authentic local manifestation of the catholic Church. What do we of the Church know if we only know our own church?

The Apostolicity of the Church

A Christian is one of two kinds of person: either an Apostle or one who bears witness to Jesus after the Apostles, where the word 'after' has qualitative as well as chronological force. When the church loses touch with the Apostolic witness and testimony it ceases to be a true church. We read in Ephesians that the church is 'built on the foundation of the Apostles . . . with Christ Jesus himself as the corner-stone' (2: 20). The Apostles, according to the New Testament writers, are firstly those who were commissioned by Christ to preach the Good News and those who secondly were witnesses to the risen Christ or, like Paul, had Christ reveal himself to them. Reflecting on this Alister E McGrath concludes that by 'declaring the church to be "apostolic", the creeds thus appear to emphasize the historical roots of the gospel, the continuity between the church and Christ through the Apostles whom he appointed, and the continuing evangelistic and missionary tasks of the church.'[54] Let us now look at each of these three emphases.

---

49   Ibid., p 141.
50   Ibid.
51   Ibid., p 143.
52   Ibid., p 145.
53   Ibid., p 146.
54   Alister E McGrath, *Christian Theology: An Introduction* (Oxford: Blackwell Publishers, 1994), p 426.

(a)   There are good reasons to underscore a view of Christianity which eshews addiction to novelty but endorses the quest to root Christianity in an ongoing concern for originality. We should not lose sight of the fact that Christianity as an historical religion takes its life blood from its origin in the Christ event and the earliest Christian witness to it. The apostles are therefore of fundamental importance for our self-identity. As Ogden puts it: 'By its very nature, Christian faith is apostolic faith – faith *with* the apostles in the Jesus to whom they uniquely are the witnesses and who is himself personally present as the Christ in *their* witness of faith.'[55] Apostolic authorship was one of the criteria used by the church to decide upon the make-up of the New Testament canon, while it is quite clear that the unique authority given the apostles in the early church was due to their having been eyewitnesses to the Christ event. We now know, however, that 'none of the New Testament writings in its present form was authored by an apostle or by one of [Jesus'] disciples', and that even Paul's authentic letters 'come from one who was only indirectly in (*sic*) apostle in this sense, in that he was not a witness of Jesus' earthly life, having seen only the risen Lord.'[56] Christianity's historical and hence apostolic grounding, therefore, cannot be located in eye-witness testimony; rather it can only be found in 'the original witness of the apostolic church, of which all the canonical writings are . . . later interpretations.'[57] Ogden draws two conclusions from this. First, if one of the criteria by which Christian thought and practice is authorized is whether or not it is *credible* according to common human experience and reason, the other is whether or not it is *appropriate* to 'the original witness of the apostolic church' as that can be recovered from the New Testament writings by historical research. Coupled with this insight for theological methodology comes a further observation concerning the nature of biblical authority. Scripture is not the primary authority for the faith and conduct of Christians; rather it is the primary *source* of that authority: 'Accordingly, the witness to which theological assertions must be appropriate is not the *scriptural* witness . . . but, rather, the *apostolic* witness, which is to be discerned by critical interpretation of [the] earliest layer of Christian tradition or kerygma.'[58]   When we remember the role played by apostolicity in the production of the New Testament canon, we ought to realise that 'a canon within the canon' is the church's authoritative norm, and also that Scripture's importance as the authoritative primary source of that norm cannot be overstressed. Once historical research showed that the New Testament writings are all influenced to greater or lesser degrees by the decisions and experience of the Christian community from out of which they arose, it became clear that the old Protestant-Catholic battle over *sola scriptura* is beside the point.

> The theological authority of scripture, great as it may be, is nevertheless a limited authority, in that it could conceivably be greater than it is – namely as great as that of the apostolic witness by which it itself is and is to be authorized. Indeed, relative to Christ himself and to the apostolic witness that alone is authorized by him, there is no difference in principle but only in fact between the authority of scripture, on the one hand, and that of the church's tradition and magisterium on the other.[59]

55   Ogden, *On Theology*, p 60.
56   Ibid., p 56.
57   Ibid.
58   Ibid., p 64.
59   Ibid., pp 57–8.

For the Reformers *sola scriptura* was not an independent theological principle since, as Ogden reminds us, 'it must always be understood in relation to the material principle *solus Christus* which implies, in turn, the further material principles *sola gratia* and *sola fide*.'[60] The Reformers tried to free God's Word from being imprisoned in church tradition; today's reformers need to make sure that biblical fundamentalism does not hide the apostolic witness to Jesus inside a theological outlook which imposes upon us a novel but not original (and hence unorthodox) view of the Bible's nature and status.

(b) Secondly, apostolicity focuses upon the need for the church's belief and practice to be *appropriate* to the apostolic witness and therefore maintain through the apostles a link between Christ and the contemporary church. To unloose that link would be to lose touch with the One who makes Christianity Christian. But how is the apostolic succession to be understood? For many the answer is found by claiming that the church has been kept in the truth by an order of ministry. The order of bishops is said to go back serially uninterrupted to the apostles, bringing God's grace to the faithful via what amounts to a 'pipe-line' going back to Christ. But this account of apostolic succession has been widely challenged. It is historically doubtful whether some holders of the episcopal office ever succeeded in handing on the true faith. Popes, bishops, presbyters and elders have sometimes failed to keep the faith, so any theory which makes a ministerial office of ultimate, as opposed to *proximate,* value in maintaining the continuity of Christian tradition is dubious. What is of *ultimate* importance is the apostolic message itself, the earliest kerygma, discovered by historical research from the New Testament. When the ministry – pope, bishops, presbyters and elders – has been the faithful servant of this message then it has been of proximate, if not ultimate, value in keeping the link between Christ and the church.

What was of ultimate significance at the church's foundation was not the apostles themselves but the message they passed on, so, *mutatis mutandis,* it is that message rather than ministry which constitutes the church anew in our time.

> The strict successor of the Apostles is the New Testament, as containing the precipitate of their standard preaching. It is not the ministry that is the successor of the Apostolate, but the ministry plus the true apostolic legacy of the Bible – the ministry of the Word.[61]

This feature of apostolicity perhaps should remind the URC of two things. First, experience suggests that we are somewhat prone to becoming denominational clubs rather than apostolic communities. To what degree do we actually take our bearings from the apostolic witness? Reformed Christians – no less than Roman, Orthodox, Anglican or Pentecostal – so easily idolize their traditions. We search for the right word, or try to discover the correct action, by looking to the denominational tradition in which we stand instead of going back to the authoritative tradition towards which all denominations and churches point, but only ever partially exemplify, namely, the apostolic witness. How else can we account for the lack of serious attention being paid to the Bible by our members privately and our congregations corporately? Many in the URC are simply out of touch with their origins. Secondly, the role of ministers in helping to keep the church in touch with Christ via the apostolic testimony needs to be re-emphasised. This leads to a high view of the professional ministry which will be outlined in a later chapter.

---

[60] Ibid., p 58.
[61] Forsyth, *Lectures on the Church and Sacraments,* p 128.

(c) An apostolic church, thirdly, is a missionary church. The apostles carried the message about Jesus beyond the confines of the believers. Those who bear witness to Jesus after the apostles must do the same. But why is it so many shy away from mission? There are a number of reasons. First, many associate mission with work overseas, something in which they engage to the extent that they give money for others to do it. The fact that a secular society like ours has become a mission field itself has not yet registered in many people's minds, and the way in which all the members of the Council for World Mission are 'partners in mission' has not penetrated some churches. But, secondly, mission will not become a priority for us unless Jesus is accepted by us as the decisive re-presentation in history of the meaning, value and purpose of human life and community. Mission flows spontaneously from people who have taken their perspective on life from the implications of their commitment to Jesus.   A confidence in mission presupposes a confidence that the gospel is of ultimate significance for everyone. For many, though, faith remains a private matter, along with sex and politics not to be discussed in public. However, those who are horrified about the colonialist implications of much of the church's past missionary work, and who recognize the significance of living in a plural, multi-faith society, will not be led to a serious missionary commitment unless, thirdly, they can be convinced of the adequacy of the theology of contemporary mission practice. For many, the barrier to engaging in mission revolves around the fact that 'mission' means for them an activity engaged in by evangelical figures and movements whose theology and methodology they cannot condone. Few things are more needed than the liberation of the church from stereotypical perceptions of mission.

The way we talk about our faith to others will partly depend upon how we came to that faith. The nature of the church's mission will also partly depend upon the context in which the church is called to serve and witness. It is hardly surprising, therefore, that mission produces different theologies and strategies. Richard Jones made a very helpful presentation to the British Council of Churches Standing Committee on Evangelism sometime in the 1980s in which he outlined six main mission types. He admitted, though, that his typology was far from exhaustive, that 'some of the styles suggested will, in practice, overlap with others', and that 'some churches will practice several . . . and therefore experience a tension within their lives.'[62] First, he pointed to the 'Congregation Building' strategy in which experience of 'the warm, accepting, purposeful life of a caring, worshipping congregation' results in the sincere commitment to draw others into the fellowship. Secondly, a 'Christian Presence' model is rooted in people's experience of God 'in quiet, solitude and adoration'. Mission then becomes a matter of gently getting alongside others. Thirdly, some people encounter God through a call to repent and believe in the gospel. An 'Evangelical/Revivalist' approach to mission is the natural outcome of such experiences. The emphasis then is placed on 'mounting suitable occasions when as many people as possible can be given the chance to hear the Gospel message.' Fourthly, God may be experienced 'as He who gives meaning, ground, cohesion, vitality and purpose to the large-scale human community (e.g. the nation) and He who is for ever at work to enrich, deepen, humanise all such community'. The nature of the mission strategy which stems from this Jones calls the 'Baptizing Community into Christ', and he observes that most of Europe was first 'Christianised' by this method. Fifthly, the 'Prophetic Social Action' model of mission reflects people's experience of God in the struggles to eradicate oppression, injustice, poverty and all forms of helplessness. In this approach, 'Mission is to share all God's on-going humanising and hope-building work with him, to point to him as its Author and Sustainer, to call to all to share in this work'.

---

[62]   This discussion is based on what I think is an unpublished paper entitled, 'Methodology in Mission'.

Finally, 'The Spirit-filled Assembly' model is favoured by those who encounter God through charismatic gifts and experiences. In this approach mission tends to become a matter of 'creating occasions when such experience of God can be shared'. Jones ended his paper by saying that (1) we should 'thank God' for each of these approaches; (2) 'we should want all of them to be practised in the UK;' (3) 'we should not expect any one denomination to be able to feature all in its life . . . but a denomination which only features one of these, and has no tension about mission, has become a sect and is dramatically the weaker;' (4) 'we should want all of them to be in constant dialogue, community, togetherness, with all others;' and (5) 'we should want all of the practitioners to be aware of the inherent weaknesses in every method or style.'

I have quoted Jones at length for two reasons. First, I am sure that we can point to examples in the URC of the mission models he delineates. It would be unfortunate if we use our negative experience of one to justify anti-mission approaches to church life. What will be suitable for one person or context may not be appropriate for another. We can rejoice about the plurality of approaches which are necessary to satisfy people of different psychologies and to be applicable in diverse social and cultural communities. Jones's conclusions are basically sound. We have much to learn from one another, not least about the weaknesses of our own favoured approaches. Mention of the word 'dialogue' of course reminds us secondly that the principles established for inter-faith work are also a helpful guide to our mission activity.[63] It is of fundamental importance that we listen to the context in which our mission is set. The gospel we are to flesh out in dialogue with sisters and brothers is holistic. It is rooted in God's gift and demand of liberation, with its twin emphases of redemption and emancipation; it offers 'good news' about the 'bad news' of both personal and corporate sin. Hence, we are left with a message to proclaim which, being appropriate to the biblical witness and credible in the modern world, is the content of mission.

The Location of the True Church

Ignatius, the bishop of early second-century Antioch, bequeathed to the church the following dictum: *ubi Christus, ibi ecclesia* (where Christ is, there is the church). The location of the true church will be where Christ has promised to be. We can note three examples.[64]

First, Christ has promised to be present in the worshipping community as it lives out its missionary mandate. He is present in Word. The key biblical texts here are John 20: 21–23 and Matthew 28: 18–20. Christ's word is present in the church's proclamation. However, the reverse is not necessarily true, because there is often an asymmetric relationship between Christ and the church. Equally, Christ is present in the sacraments of the Lord's Supper and Baptism. Calvin is authoritative on both points: 'Wherever we see the Word of God purely preached and heard, and the sacraments administered according to Christ's institution, there, it is not to be doubted, a church of God exists, since his promise cannot fail: "Wherever two or three are gathered in my name, there am I in the midst of them".'[65] As the text Calvin quotes perhaps indicates, Christ's presence is not just in the proclamation but is also in the body who do the proclaiming (2 Corinthians 4: 10).

---

[63] The four principles of dialogue with people of other faiths are as follows: (i) Dialogue begins when people meet each other. (2) Dialogue depends upon mutual understanding and mutual trust. (3) Dialogue makes it possible to share in service in the community. (4) Dialogue becomes the medium of authentic witness. See *Relations with People of Other Faiths: Guidelines for Dialogue in Britain.* Rev. ed. (London: BCC, 1983).

[64] The following discussion is heavily influenced by Moltmann. See *The Church in the Power of the Spirit,* p 127.

[65] Calvin., 4,1,9.

So we should certainly expect Christ to be present in the church's fellowship, especially when the church, or groups set apart by the church for specific tasks, meet to plan and oversee the church's ministry and mission. Elders' and church meetings, therefore, should be set in the context of the church's ongoing waiting upon the Word. The importance of the church's ministry and mission being owned by the whole church also cannot be over-emphasised. Christ has promised his presence to the whole church and not just to a ministerial order. But such ministers play a crucial role in the church. While not of the church's *esse* it can certainly be argued that they are of her *bene esse*. Contemporary interpretations of the doctrine of 'the priesthood of all believers', which tend to belittle the role of ministers, owe more, perhaps, to expressions of the egalitarian spirit which resides in many of us rather than to sound ecclesiology.

Secondly, Christ has promised to be present in the fellowship of 'the least of these' (Matthew 25: 31–46). According to the parable of the Last Assize, Christ is hidden in the hungry, the thirsty, the strangers, the naked, the sick and the imprisoned. Whatever we do to them, therefore, we do to Christ. Living in a culture which has a long and dubious colonial history behind it, we might wish that Jesus had not had the King in the story saying: 'Truly I tell you: anything you did for one of my brothers and sisters here, however insignificant, you did it for me' (Matthew 25: 40 and 45). We must become Christ to all those who lay a claim upon our lives and love; meanwhile in the dispossessed and disinherited, the shut-outs and the shut-ins, Christ stands before us, the judge of our complicity in rank injustice.

> It is not that the wretched are the object of Christian love or the fulfilment of a moral duty; they are the latent presence of the coming Saviour and Judge in the world, the touch-stone which determines salvation and damnation. The hidden presence of the coming Christ in the poor therefore belongs to ecclesiology first of all, and only after that to ethics.[66]

Moltmann argues that, in addition to being the fellowship of believers, the church is also the fellowship of 'the least of these'. Both must be combined in our ecclesiology. 'The apostolate says what the church is. The least of Christ's brethren say where the church belongs.'[67] We are pointed, therefore, to the church's social and political responsibility. The Judge of the world who confronts us in 'the least of these' challenges the righteous to act.

Thirdly, we are assured that Christ will meet us on the pilgrim way and at journey's end (Matthew 28: 10). This reminds us of two things. First, Christians essentially belong to a tent rather than a temple tradition. We are called to be on the move, alive to the Spirit, settling down only to reconstitute ourselves as a church ever anew. But when we look at our structures and organisation we are lasting testimonies to an age of success from which we have yet to recover. We should equip people for living Christian lives in the world; they need encouragement to enjoy the ecumenical fellowship of fellow Christians as they journey; and we must enter into dialogue with those outside the church and thus avoid becoming hellishly churchy. Far too much church activity is taken up with getting people to church rather than enabling them to be the Church on their pilgrimage through life. Secondly, we must take heed of the eschatological dimension of ecclesiology. The church is the sign, embodiment and foretaste of a future promised us by God. As a result there will always be a provisionality about it. If we treat it as an absolute, or make it our 'ultimate concern'

---

[66]   Moltmann, *The Church in the Power of the Spirit,* p 127.
[67]   Ibid., p 129.

(Tillich), then it becomes an idol. There should be a tentativeness, therefore, about what we say and do, as we are led into the truth which liberates. This theology is rather foreign to many of a rather dogmatic spirit but it is shared by many in the URC like Donald Hilton.

> I stand in the liberal Christian tradition, and rejoice to see it well-affirmed in the United Reformed Church, because our God is so very big, and has called me to journey along a Way which stretches into unseen distances, hold to a Truth who is great beyond my comprehension, and embrace a Life who is calling me to a maturity I do not yet fully understand.[68]

This certainly reflects the tentativeness which should be the hallmark of Christian thought and practice. But do we not know anything about the Way? Are we totally devoid of any perception of the Truth? And are we completely in the dark about Life? No, surely not! It is of prime importance that those of us who stand in the 'liberal Christian tradition' apply our minds to the *content* of our theology. We are rather prone to counter opposing views with eulogies about our *style* of believing. Being liberal should not mean believing nothing; it ought to involve putting forward a systematic understanding of the Christian faith which seeks to be appropriate to the apostolic witness and credible in our postmodern context. To counsel tentativeness is not to advocate silence!

---

[68]   Donald H Hilton, 'To follow truth, and thus . . . An elliptical faith' (URC Pamphlet 1993), p 12.

CHAPTER 15

The Means of Grace:
Preaching and Sacraments

CENTRAL to Reformed ecclesiology lies the belief that where the Word is preached and the sacraments are properly administered the true Church will be found. Through the preacher's words and in the sacramental elements Christ becomes present in the Christian community's life. From the pulpit and around the Communion Table, the gracious gift of God's reconciling love revealed at Calvary is re-presented to the believer. As the sign, expression and anticipation of God's reign of love over all things, the Church is a community to which people can turn to receive that promise of liberation, healing and acceptance which is made audible in preaching and visible in the sacraments.

We now move on to consider the distinctive marks of a Reformed understanding of preaching and the sacraments of baptism and holy communion. Once again we shall have cause to point out the diversity of doctrinal understanding within the Reformed churches in general and the URC in particular.

Preaching

The importance of preaching in the URC is revealed by the emphasis placed upon the sermon in Sunday worship. While the Lord's Table is laid quarterly, monthly and in a small number of churches weekly, URC services invariably centre upon the pulpit – and, given Victorian chapel architecture, often physically as well as liturgically. This reflects a tradition of gathering to listen to the Scriptures being expounded. Through preaching church members expect the Holy Spirit to transform very human and often inadequate words into God's Word for them. And, therefore, preaching is sacramental in character.

The emphasis upon preaching in the URC may suggest a downgrading of the Lord's Table in some congregations. However, in many others, the infrequency of Communion services raises the sacrament's profile. Those of us who possess a more sacramental emphasis in worship never tire of reminding less sacramentally minded congregations that Calvin advocated weekly celebration of the Lord's Supper, and that the most liturgically satisfactory Reformed act of worship is one in which the Word is heard in preaching and made visible at the Lord's Table. Such worship reflects the need and desire of a congregation to lay hold anew of the gospel, and in such a way that they are equipped to live it and share it with others.

A Reformed understanding of preaching admits that its benefits can only be discovered through serious endeavour by the occupants of both pulpit and pew. Preachers in their preparation labour long and hard to find a Word for the congregation from the scripture patiently being explored; while the congregation need an attentiveness which is born out of a serious expectancy that the Spirit will bring a Word for the hour. Both preacher and hearer are part of a community which has been brought into being by One about whom it is called to exercise heart and mind in discovering more. And both lay hold of a faith whose healing and recreative powers can change lives. One preacher puts the matter like this:

> The faith that I proclaim has been given to me. I believe that it demands that I use my mind, and it liberates my imagination. My mind is exercised by the realising of it in my own understanding, and my imagination on the proclamation of it. I do not make it: it makes me![1]

The preacher as well as the hearer embark upon an exploration of faith in order that the Church has a credible and relevant gospel to proclaim. They are certainly involved in constructing a belief system but only in so far as each age needs to provide one to express the gospel which has been given it.

This emphasis upon preaching reminds us of the virtue of putting our intellect in God's service. Good sermons arise from deep intellectual (and, as Alan Gaunt reminded us, imaginative) endeavour. They have an impact when they bring home the gospel to particular people in particular places at particular times. And that usually can only be achieved by hard mental graft. The URC, therefore, is heir to a tradition in which scholarship is affirmed and a learned ministry is expected. It is important that church members know what they believe and the grounds upon which that believing is based. We all need to possess a theology, what Forsyth calls 'a faith which knows what it is about, a positive faith, faith with not only an experience but a content, not glow only but grasp, and mass, and measure.'[2] But lest we are tempted to dismiss this as mere intellectualism – and, in an anti-intellectual church which seeks its *raison d'être* in religious experience or social reform at the first available opportunity, the temptation is very great – we need to remind ourselves that the Reformed way is to hold together learning and piety. In fact, Reformed theologians have a good track record in producing theologies which are strong in the way they address the pragmatic matters in Christian living as well as wider social and political issues.

Books on the art of preaching come and go; hints and tips about the preacher's craft abound. All are useful no doubt, though I cannot help but suspect that the great preachers are born not made. The preacher who ministered to me most effectively, for example, defied most of the lessons in the standard textbooks, but week in week out he brought us face to face with the gift and demand of God's Good News brought down to earth in Jesus. He not only believed in what he was doing, but he worked hard to do it well. He knew that the Church stands or falls on the ability of its members to have a Word to speak in their place at a particular time, and he accepted that the minister's primary duty is to enable people to find that Word. Like Forsyth, he recognized that 'with its preaching Christianity stands or falls.'[3] Consequently, he devoted much of his time to helping church members 'do' theology – even if they didn't realize it! They were prepared to go on such a journey principally because they knew their minister was going there as well. When he addressed us, he was addressing himself. Some words of Oman spring to mind:

> As for preaching, I have not the slightest idea what makes it popular. Perhaps I am constitutionally not responsive, but much of the popular preaching I have heard seems to me trivial in matter and tawdry in form. Yet I think I have now a pretty clear idea of what is edifying in preaching: and it is what a man is saying to his own soul, as well as to the souls of others.[4]

---

[1]   Alan Gaunt, 'P T Forsyth: The Preacher's Theologian' in Alan P F Sell, ed., P T Forsyth: *Theologian for a New Millennium* (London: The United Reformed Church, 1999), p 62.

[2]   Forsyth, *Positive Preaching and the Modern Mind* (London: Independent Press Ltd, 1907), p 135.

[3]   Ibid., p 1.

[4]   John Oman, *The Office of Ministry* (London: Student Christian Movement, 1928), p 11.

Preachers fall under the judgement of the Word they are proclaiming, and the best preachers are those who take time to allow that Word to enter their lives.

Forsyth wrote what arguably was the best book on preaching during the twentieth century. *Positive Preaching and the Modern Mind* does not provide budding preachers with craved after hints and tips; rather it presents them with a sustained argument about the importance of preaching in the church's life and the true nature and proper content of homiletics. It highlights some of the most important features of preaching from a Reformed perspective. Writing at the start of the twentieth century, Forsyth clearly believed that the standard of preaching in Congregationalism was far from satisfactory. His words seem surprisingly apposite as we embark upon the twenty-first century: 'If the preachers have brought preaching down it is the preachers that must save it.'[5] No church will prosper which diverts its attention from its primary responsibility of declaring the gospel, first to itself but then to share it with others. Preaching, therefore, is the prerequisite of an evangelical and missionary congregation.

Forsyth argues that preaching is not simply a form of oratory: 'The orator comes with but an inspiration, the prophet comes with a revelation.'[6] The preacher is more related to the prophet because, while 'the orator stirs men to rally, the preacher invites them to be redeemed.'[7] Through the preacher the gospel of 'God's grace in the shape of forgiveness, redemption, regeneration' is not simply declared but 'prolonged'.[8] Forsyth, therefore, understands preaching in a sacramental sense: 'Every true sermon. . . is a sacramental time and act.'[9] He talks about preaching bestowing 'the real presence of Christ crucified' to the congregation.[10] And, contrary to some Christian traditions, he argues that preaching, 'the Sacrament of the living Word', is 'the sacrament which gives value to all other sacraments.'[11] The understanding of sacraments displayed here by Forsyth corresponds closely to that put forward by Calvin. It leads to a very demanding perception of preachers:

> The preacher's place in the Church is sacramental. It is not sacerdotal, but it is sacramental. He mediates the word to the Church from faith to faith, from his faith to theirs, from one stage of their common faith to another. He does not there speak to un-faith. He is a living element in Christ's hands (broken, if need be) for the distribution and increment of Grace. He is laid on the altar of the Cross. He is not a mere reporter, not a mere lecturer, on sacred things. He is not merely illuminative, he is augmentive. His work is not to enlighten simply, but to empower and enhance. Men as they leave him should be not only clearer but greater, not only surer but stronger, not only interested, nor only instructed, nor only affected, but fed and increased.[12]

Forsyth is convinced that the gospel is the criterion by which all ages are to be judged. Preachers, therefore, should speak to their age a Word of judgement and grace. The problem, according to Forsyth, is the temptation that 'it is our age we preach', and therefore we 'only hold up the mirror to the time.'[13] Preachers are channels of One who 'redeems our worst' rather than 'represents our best'.[14] They are not to follow public opinion, nor pander to the pews, since they are called to proclaim a Word which may question state as well as church, society and congregation.

---

5   Forsyth, *Positive Preaching and the Modern Mind*, p 129.
6   Ibid., p 1.
7   Ibid., p 2.
8   Ibid., p 3.
9   Ibid., p 56.
11   Ibid., p 4.
12   Ibid., pp 53–4.
13   Ibid., p 5.
14   Ibid., p 83.

Churches are prone to assess preachers on the basis of their personalities and their gift with words rather than on their ability to proclaim the gospel faithfully. Like Oman, Forsyth possessed a healthy disrespect for popular preachers, especially those who through their entertaining style or witty utterances or attractive personalities enable people to hide from the gospel's harsh realities. What really counts is the extent to which preachers' lives and personalities become the means through which people hear the gospel of God's holy love. Therefore, those called to be preachers need to remember that 'the Church does not live by its preachers, but by its Word.'[15] The preacher who makes the gospel live is the one who lives by the gospel. It is the gospel which makes the great preacher and the finest sermon. The proper content of preaching, therefore, is God's Good News revealed in Christ. It centres upon 'the self-bestowal of the living God, His self-limitation in the interest of grace';[16] it is rooted in the revelation of God's grace in the Cross. Forsyth declares, therefore, that 'this cross is the message that makes the preacher.'[17] Preaching becomes authentic when the sermon is a re-presentation of God's gracious action on behalf of fallen humankind on Calvary. It places hearers in touch with 'the holy, gracious God of Christ's Cross', and thereby they have access to 'the one creative, authoritative, life-making, life-giving, life-shaping power of the moral soul'.[18]

The Bible is the indispensable companion of preachers who wish to be faithful to their craft. They are called to proclaim God's 'supreme, saving act of grace to mankind in Christ's Cross',[19] and find that very preaching in the New Testament where it is presented as the culmination of 'a long divine act'.[20] So authentic preaching is biblical preaching. Forsyth describes the Bible as 'the greatest sermon in the world . . . It is the preacher's book because it is the preaching book.'[21] The Scriptures are the authoritative source of our knowledge of Christ, since the Gospels proclaim God's grace bestowed on Calvary and the revelation of God's holy love in the Christ event. The Bible, therefore, is the medium of the gospel. The subtlety of Forsyth's understanding of biblical authority is made clear when he opines: 'Biblical preaching preaches the Gospel and uses the Bible, it does not preach the Bible and use the Gospel.'[22] Preachers, though, need to be immersed in the Bible since 'the true ministry must live on it.'[23] And this has clear implications for the way ministers should be prepared for their service and how they ought to be engaged in biblical study in a thoroughgoing way throughout their ministries.

Forsyth argues that Christ inaugurated the Church, a community rather than an order of ministers or preachers. The proclamation of the Word is the 'first charge' laid upon that church.[24] It is therefore the church's responsibility to preach Christ to the world. Preachers (and, here, Forsyth invariably is thinking of ministers of Word and Sacraments) exist to equip church members and, hence, 'to enable the Church to preach'.[25] They preach to the church in order that the church is motivated and equipped to fulfil its missionary obligations. Forsyth provides us with one of the clearest descriptions of the traditional Reformed view of the role of ministers:

---

15   Ibid., p 41.
16   Ibid., p 10.
17   Ibid., p 49.
18   Ibid., p 146.
19   Ibid., p 43.
20   Ibid., p 6.
21   Ibid.
22   Ibid., p 26.
23   Ibid.
24   ibid., p 59.
25   Ibid., p 53.

> The order of obligation for a preacher is first to the Gospel (in its nature, not its particular applications), second to his church, third to the great Church, and then to the public. He is not first a prophet of social righteousness but an apostle of the Gospel. He is not merely an agent of the ethical kingdom. Every Christian is that. But when he adopts the ministry as a life work, he adopts what is an office of the Church.[26]

Ministers, therefore, lead their congregations in mission by enabling them to be a sign, expression and foretaste in society of God's gracious holy love. They 'act at its head, and not in its stead',[27] in a calling which embraces both the minister and the congregation.

Even in the early twentieth century, Forsyth was bewailing the demise of the traditional sermon. Just what he would have made of the sermon's role in our soundbyte culture can perhaps be gleaned from his comment that, 'a Christianity of short sermons is a Christianity of short fibre.'[28] The Reformed ethos, with its emphasis upon preaching, nevertheless faces an acute challenge in a society which receives most of its information in small packages. Ours is a world in which oratory of any kind is at a premium, and the medium tends to be the message. It is not at all surprising that we are tending towards 'a Christianity of short fibre'.

The very thing ailing congregations need most is in a state of crisis in the church. Ministers do not seem to devote as much time as they once did to preaching, perhaps putting more faith in other ministerial functions: pastoral care, community work, social activism or church management. Perhaps we have been witnessing a collusion between pulpit and pew to undermine the centrality of preaching? Be that as it may, there are other reasons why preaching gets undermined. First, good preaching challenges people, inviting them to see old things in new ways, asking them to change their lives, and pushing them on a pilgrimage of faith. This threatens many folk, particularly those who are living comfortable lives. Authentic preaching will never court popularity in a society at ease with itself. Nor is preaching easy in a postmodern context in which all authorities are questioned and everyone can pick their ideas and truths from a supermarket of competing faiths and ideologies. Secondly, and I am sure related to it, preaching has been largely blunted due to church members (not to mention those outside the church) possessing a very impoverished understanding of the Bible. Forsyth advised that 'we adjust our preaching to the people's disuse of the Bible.'[29] He knew that 'preaching can only flourish where there is more than a formal respect for the Bible as distinct from the Church, namely, an active respect, an assiduous personal use of it, especially by the preacher.'[30] And if this was true in 1907, how much more true it is today! It follows that any renaissance in preaching will involve church members rediscovering the Bible's centrality for their lives.

I am interested when I hear senior ministers bemoaning the fact that the standard of preaching has gone down. By and large what they say is true. Pick up a collection of sermons delivered by one of the late nineteenth or early twentieth century pulpit divines and one cannot but be astonished at their great length, complexity of structure and the amount of biblical and theological knowledge they presupposed of their hearers. Such sermons are impossible to preach today because our congregations are different. Most people, due to radio and television, now have very short concentration spans; although, in the interests of our health, it is good to know that the

---

26   Ibid., p 78.
27   Ibid., p 52.
28   Ibid., p 75.
29   Ibid., p 25.
30   Ibid., p 4.

art of listening is teachable. I am afraid to say, though, that the biblical knowledge of many of our church members casts grave doubts upon whether the Bible really is as important to us in practice as we claim it is in theory. In *this* situation it is to be hoped that the standard of preaching has gone down – right down to the level people are at. Lucky indeed today is the preacher who has a more theologically sophisticated congregation. The rest of us need to cultivate one!

Sacraments

Consider the following definition of the church: The church is a fellowship (*koinonia*) of people called out of the world by the grace (*charis*) of God, universally present but definitively re-presented to us in the life and witness, death and resurrection of Jesus Christ, through the Holy Spirit, to live in the world by offering service (*diakonia*) to God and all who place a claim upon their lives. It is a personal definition, but however inadequate, at least it reminds us of some of the church's essential features. For example, the church is a fellowship of people before it is an institution; it is 'in the world but not of the world'; it has a clear purpose – *diakonia* ('service'). But, in particular, the definition makes it clear that the church is God's creation; it is brought into being by God's grace. But what do we mean by 'grace'?

Grace is God's movement toward humankind; it is God's self-offering to people which enables them to know and love God; it is the free, unmerited offer of God's saving love. 'In this is love, not that we loved God but that he loved us and sent his Son . . . ' (1 John 4: 10). God makes Godself available to us so that we are available for God's service. Grace may be one of the smaller words in the Christian vocabulary but it is among the most important. A correct understanding of the term is crucial for an adequate grasp of the meaning of sacraments. Grace is universally present; the Spirit of God cannot be contained. The Bible teaches that God is gracious always and everywhere, but supremely so in Christ. Not only is the Church brought into being by God's grace, however, it is also sustained by it. Preaching and sacraments, traditionally, have been regarded as the Church's definitive and sustaining access points to God's grace. The Word, whether audible in preaching or visible in sacraments, is focused in Jesus Christ who is the Word made flesh (John 1: 14). And, while the Christian fellowship is the context in which preaching and sacraments are set and focused, *koinonia* becomes a means of grace when 'two or three' gather together in the Christ's name. This will be explored in the next chapter when we consider the councils of the Church. But our concern now is with sacraments as a means of grace. Three possible models come into view (see Box 1).

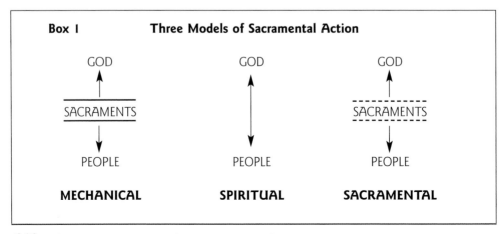

Box 1	**Three Models of Sacramental Action**	
GOD	GOD	GOD
↑	↑	↑
SACRAMENTS		SACRAMENTS
↓	↓	↓
PEOPLE	PEOPLE	PEOPLE
MECHANICAL	**SPIRITUAL**	**SACRAMENTAL**

The mechanical view says, in effect, that God can only reach people via sacraments administered by a priestly order. In various forms this view was predominant in the Medieval church when sacraments became an independent factor between people and God, the spiritual medicine which people sought from priests and required for their salvation. The Church through the priesthood squeezed the sacramental tube and grace was poured out on the faithful. Faced with the unacceptability of making God's access to human beings dependent upon priestly activity, it is tempting to move in the opposite direction and adopt the spiritual view. In effect, this view does away with sacraments and affirms a person's direct spiritual access to God. Divine grace, it is claimed, comes straight to believers without any need for either sacraments or priests. This view clearly has some biblical support, but it fails perhaps to recognise that people tend to get access to the spiritual realm through the physical and material world. We seem to need signs and symbols to approach God (and vice versa). The danger of this view is that people have a tendency to get trapped in the charmed (and not so charmed!) circle of their own selves. But people often need 'physical' and/or 'material' means to take them beyond their egos. While the spiritual view may well be correct in its insistence that sacraments are not necessary for saving faith, as well as in its repudiation of the view that sacraments are the sole deposits of divine grace, a sacramental view, which accepts that sacraments exist for the well-being (*bene esse*) of faith, and are a (if not the only) means of access to God's grace, is the more typical Reformed view.

The Word 'sacrament' comes from a Latin Word (*sacramentum*) which originally referred to a sacred pledge of sincerity or fidelity publicly symbolized by a sign (i.e. a deposit of money or an oath of allegiance). But, in the Christian tradition, sacraments are sometimes also called 'mysteries'. The term 'mystery' stems from a Greek word (*mysterion*) which in Greek religion referred to hidden realities or sacred rites. Augustine defined a sacrament as a sign of a sacred thing, and he regarded as sacraments such diverse entities as baptism, marriage, the bread and wine of Holy Communion, consecrated oil etc. In fact, until the Middle Ages the term 'sacrament' was used for any Church ritual and the symbolic elements used in such rituals.

One very helpful way of understanding sacraments is to view them as 'symbols'. Both 'signs' and 'symbols' point beyond themselves, in the case of sacraments to God's gracious love. But symbols differ from signs in that they participate in that to which they point and grow out of the experience of communities. While signs can be changed somewhat arbitrarily (for example a company logo), symbols (like a monarch's crown or the bread and wine of the Lord's supper) are rather more fixed. The bread and wine of Holy Communion not only point to God's gracious love bestowed in Christ, as symbols they also in some sense 'become' that to which they point for the communicant. But theological problems occur when people take the word 'become' literally and then end up 'worshipping' the sacrament rather than that to which it points. One of the causes of the Reformation lay in the idolatrous fashion with which sacraments had taken the place of the Ultimate in the life of the church.

In 1160, Peter Lombard became the first writer to list the seven sacraments of the pre-Reformation church (See Box 2). The Reformers reduced the seven to the two so-called dominical

```
┌─────────────────────────────────────────────────────────────────────────┐
│                                                                           │
│   Box 2                        The Seven Sacraments                       │
│                                                                           │
│                                Baptism                                    │
│                                                                           │
│                                Confirmation                               │
│                                                                           │
│                                Penance (Confession and Reconciliation)    │
│                                                                           │
│                                Eucharist                                  │
│                                                                           │
│                                Holy Orders                                │
│                                                                           │
│                                Matrimony                                  │
│                                                                           │
│                                Extreme Unction (Anointing of the Sick)    │
│                                                                           │
└─────────────────────────────────────────────────────────────────────────┘
```

sacraments of Baptism and the Lord's Supper (sometimes called Eucharist or Holy Communion as opposed to Mass) due to them being the only sacraments actually instituted by Jesus. Their understanding of sacraments has been helpfully expressed by Nathaniel Micklem (See Box 3).

```
┌─────────────────────────────────────────────────────────────────────────┐
│                                                                           │
│   Box 3                        Principal Features of a Reformed           │
│                                Understanding of Sacraments[31]            │
│                                                                           │
└─────────────────────────────────────────────────────────────────────────┘
```

*   What is vital in a sacrament is not the act of the minister but God's action in Christ. 'It is Christ's act offering himself to men [and women] rather than the act of the Church offering Christ to God'.

*   Sacraments are seals attached to God's promise to people in Jesus Christ.

*   Sacraments are symbols or signs through which God acts. They do more than illustrate since they convey and bring home God's action in Christ to the Church.

*   Sacraments are 'necessary for the Church, but not necessary for individual salvation'. It is the Word which saves; sacraments simply ratify and seal it. The church needs sacraments because its members are 'embodied spirits and not angels'.

*   Protestantism has sacraments of the gospel, not a gospel of sacraments. What is primary is 'the gospel of the grace of God in Christ'. Sacraments are not operative apart from faith in this gospel.

*   '. . . the Sacraments derive their whole meaning from the redeeming work of Christ'. Central to the efficacy of Sacraments is the act of washing (not the water) and the breaking and pouring (not bread and wine).

*   The role of the partaker in a sacrament is quite secondary to the role of God. But what s/he does is still important, since in the sacraments, the church declares her faith in God's redeeming work in Jesus Christ.

---

[31]   Based on 'The Sacraments' in Nathaniel Micklem, ed., *Christian Worship: Studies in its History and Meaning* (Oxford: Oxford University Press, 1936), p 244–6.

When it came to who is authorized to preside at the dominical sacraments, the Reformers again departed from the medieval church, thereby introducing a further ecumenical disagreement into Christian history. Are sacraments valid if they are administered by someone who has been ordained and if the service has been conducted according to set formulae, or are they valid when administered by a person (usually ordained) who is recognized by the Church (where Church can mean a local fellowship or conciliar body)? The question can be put as follows: Is the issue concerning presidency about the president's status giving validity to sacraments or about church order? In the URC, what is at stake is often misunderstood as the former when it is really the latter – the need of the church to ensure that the sacraments are duly administered in an orderly way. It has generally been assumed by Reformed theologians that the required order is best achieved by reserving the right of presidency, *except in cases of pastoral necessity*, to ordained ministers. It is not for nothing that URC ministers are called ministers of Word *and* Sacraments. Whatever may have happened in some URC congregations through bad practice – often on the mistaken assumption that the doctrine of 'the priesthood of all believers' gives anyone the right to do anything in the church – the correct view of the matter is illustrated by Micklem:

> It has been much disputed in the past amongst Congregationalists whether the Sacraments may be administered by the laity. Stress is properly laid upon the universal priesthood of all believers; but the true Congregational principle seems clear that except in cases of necessity it is the minister who should celebrate the Christian sacraments; for our God is a God of order, not of anarchy. Ministers have been called out of the Church under the guidance of the Holy Spirit in virtue of the spiritual gifts entrusted to them; they are ordained to be ministers of the Word and Sacraments. As a matter of order, therefore (not of validity), laymen should not administer the Sacraments unless under exceptional circumstances the Spirit should so direct.[32]

And, presumably, when the church does not have sufficient ministers precisely such an exceptional circumstance has arisen?

The Sacrament of Baptism

Baptism was practised in Palestine long before John the Baptist. The word 'baptism' comes from a Greek word meaning literally 'to dip'. Baptism was a quite common rite at the time of Jesus when many people offered baptism as an act of cleansing and purification. It opened up a new way of life, or signified admission into a religious community or it pointed in the direction of a new relationship with God. When Jesus was baptised, John seems to have used the rite as a token of repentance in preparation for the imminent arrival of God's Reign. Just how Jesus himself interpreted it we shall never know for sure, but there is little doubt that for a first century Jew baptism with water would have carried certain obvious meanings.

It would have possessed important material significance, as well as generated profound symbolic meanings. It was synonymous with washing, and it was employed in a widespread manner for not only physical but also ritual cleansing. Further to this, the Jews possessed an acute awareness of water as a symbol of death from the stories told by those who had been caught in storms on the seas. But, alternatively, water was a symbol of life to those who had experienced its role in agriculture. While water would have generated many ideas for Jesus, having been brought

---

[32]   Ibid., p 254.

up on the Jewish scriptures, he would have regarded it primarily as a symbol of salvation and life. Immediately recalled to mind would have been the cleansing of Naaman in the Jordan (2 Kings 5), the destruction of the sinful world in the Flood (Gen. 7) and the life-giving qualities of the river which flowed out of Eden (Gen 2: 10). And some think that by undergoing John's baptism Jesus would have been consecrating himself to a life-giving death on behalf of his people through an act of vicarious cleansing.

Baptism continued to be used during Jesus' ministry as a symbol of entry into a new life, the old life having been washed away. But the Johannine tradition suggests that while his disciples baptized people, Jesus himself never did (John 4: 2). This might cast doubt in some minds about whether Jesus authorized and commanded his followers to practice baptism. Until recently, of course, Christians accepted that Christ instituted this sacrament on the basis of a familiar text: 'Go therefore and make disciples of all nations, baptizing them in the name of the Father and of the Son and of the Holy Spirit . . .' (Matthew 28: 19). Nowadays, though, biblical scholars have concluded that this key text is splendid evidence that the writer of Matthew's Gospel, and the Christian church or churches in which the Gospel took shape, firmly believed that the practice of baptism was derived from Jesus himself; but they also take the view that the text does not prove that Jesus instituted baptism some fifty or so years earlier. The Gospel story seems to have been edited so that it begins with John's baptism of Jesus in the Jordan, and ends with the Last Supper. Quite possibly these sacraments were uppermost in the Gospel writer's mind when the Gospel was written. The most astute biblical scholars, therefore, authorize the dominical sacraments by reference to our Lord's practice rather than his command. This means that the history of the church's sacramental liturgical practice starts with interpretations of Jesus' own example rather than the following of his clear directives.

The Bible provides evidence that about fifty years after Jesus' death, at the time of the writing of the Acts of the Apostles, baptism was the sole means of entry into the Church. The first Christians were evangelists whose preaching and witness brought people to faith in Jesus. The new converts were baptised, with the ceremony of Christian initiation usually taking place in the open air, by a river or at a lakeside. It was initially reserved for adults, being administered upon the baptismal candidates' confession of past sin and testimony of faith. The convert was dipped into the water three times, in the name of Father, Son and the Holy Spirit respectively. Entry into the church was then marked by 'the laying on of hands' or by the baptised person's head being anointed – or even by both. And when the initiation rite was completed the new Christian went off to celebrate the Lord's Supper with the rest of the church. Needless to say, given the plurality of practice among the early churches, there were variations to the set order, but the above procedure was fairly standard. Often the ceremony was reserved for Easter or Pentecost, with the two weeks preceding it being set aside for the preparation of candidates.

Early Christian baptismal practice reveals a number of key features. First, it incorporated the symbolic gift of the Spirit by 'the laying on of hands' and/or anointing with oil. In this way, baptism was made to resemble as closely as possible John's baptism of Jesus in the Jordan, when it was believed that Jesus received the Spirit. Secondly, baptism was immediately followed by a celebration of the Lord's Supper, thus placing the two dominical sacraments in close proximity. And, thirdly, as the symbolic entry into the Christian community, baptism was rooted in repentance. It signified that a person was making a new start in life. The new convert's sin was washed away sacramentally, and rebirth to a new life within a different community of people took place. Paul can liken it to the experience of Israel at the Exodus (1 Corinthians 10: 1–2). It involved leaving an old life held captive by sin and passing over into a new life full of promise and hope. This feature of early Christian baptismal theology, however, soon started to raise difficulties. It followed from the emphasis on regeneration in baptism that those who had not been baptised would because of their sin be prevented from entering Eternal Life. Many Christians drove home the theological logic of this by delaying their baptism to late in their lives, thus making sure that they would have less time to get infected by post-baptismal sin. Why risk a life-time of sin undermining the regenerative effect of a baptism undergone earlier in life when baptism can be left to one's deathbed?

Regrettably, baptism came to be seen as a type of spiritual insurance policy which protected Christians against sin and opened up for them Eternal Life. And the problem became even more heightened when converts' children were borne in mind. What would happen to them if they died before they were adults and had been baptised? According to the prevailing theology, they would be lost to the torments of hell. What better way to overcome this acute problem than by introducing the practice of infant baptism? It became common then to find whole families being baptized, with parents and church members subsequently making promises on behalf of the children, such promises being later confirmed when the children were of an age to speak for themselves. Infant baptism therefore developed in many churches, becoming the means for the sacramental entry of infants into the church's life. Promises once made by adult candidates came to be placed upon the shoulders of the child's parents, and the church thereby significantly altered primitive baptismal practice and theology.

Three important points emerge from the development of paedo-baptism. First, the sacraments of baptism and Lord's Supper, once closely connected in adult baptismal practice, came to be separated. Except among the Orthodox churches, where newly baptised children were given the consecrated elements and thereby fully integrated into the church's eucharistic celebration, the Lord's Supper took on the role of the sacrament accompanying confirmation or adult baptism. When Christians became knowledgeable members of the church they were able to participate in Holy Communion. Secondly, the development of paedo-baptism led to a vexed theological problem. If infants are not of an age to commit actual sin, from what kind of sin are they delivered by the baptismal waters? The answer was found in the concept of original sin, the idea that because of Adam's misdemeanours we are all born into sin. What happens at infant baptism, therefore, according to this theology, is that children are cleansed of original sin. Thirdly, the advent of paedo-baptism saw a tremendous onus being placed upon the Christian nurture of children in the home and congregation. Remove such nurture and the rug is pulled from underneath the feet of the infant baptist traditions.

Baptism has been one of the main battlegrounds of Christian theology, with Christians of strong conviction setting out their cases for or against the practice of paedo-baptism. In order to explore the issues in greater depth we will now consider views within the Reformed heritage from both sides. First of all, we turn to Calvin who presents a rigorous argument in favour of infant baptism. Then we shall turn to Barth, usually one of Calvin's foremost advocates but on this issue a trenchant opponent. Finally, we shall round off our discussion by noting the way in which contemporary ecumenical endeavour has made it possible within some churches, e.g. the URC, for each side of the argument to be held together in a dual policy which enables both forms of baptism to be made available in each congregation.

John Calvin

Calvin follows Augustine in defining a sacrament as 'an outward sign by which the Lord seals on our consciences the promises of his good will toward us in order to sustain the weakness of our faith.'[33] Through sacraments we attest our faith in him.

They function as seals or confirmation of God's Word, since God has given us a visible means to lead us into the gracious promises granted to us in Christ. While sacraments are not necessary for faith and salvation, they certainly are a means whereby we are made 'more certain of the trustworthiness of God's Word.'[34] In sacraments, God's promises are painted like pictures, displaying graphically and in images the foundation of Christian faith, namely, the Word. And it is the work of the Spirit which makes the sacraments efficacious for us. The Spirit is the 'inward teacher' who enables us to affirm our faith and grow up in the Christian way. Without the Spirit the sacraments are useless. It is the Spirit's work 'to conceive, sustain, nourish, and establish faith.'[35] The Spirit speaks to us by transmitting both the visible Word in preaching and the invisible Word in the sacraments 'from our ears to our soul.'[36] Sacraments are useless without the recipient's faith. Calvin asserts, therefore, that salvation does not depend upon sacraments, but upon faith. Sacraments do not constitute the possibility of salvation, but rather they re-present it. Their role is 'to attest and ratify for us God's good will towards us.'[37] But the sense of the words 'attest' and 'ratify' is genuinely sacramental since Calvin everywhere affirms that God's gracious power is present in sacraments through the work of the Spirit.

Baptism is the sign of Christian initiation. Through baptism we are 'engrafted in Christ' and, hence, 'reckoned among God's children'; it is 'a token and proof' that in Christ our sins have been wiped clean.[38] Drawing on Paul's teaching, Calvin makes it quite clear what baptism means. It does not 'signify that our cleansing and salvation are accompanied by water, or that water contains in itself the power to cleanse, regenerate, and renew'; neither is baptism 'the cause of our salvation'; instead it simply displays 'the knowledge and certainty of such gifts.'[39] And since Christ died once and for all for the world's sins, baptism, which represents that act in the life of the believer and Church, is to be administered once – and once only. Once and for all we become united to the Christ.

While baptism is the confirmation of our liberation from sin in Christ, it also is the means by which we become involved in Christ's death. So the baptised not only receive the benefit of being cleansed from sin, but also they 'feel the effective working of Christ's death in the mortification of their flesh, together with the working of his resurrection in the vivification of the Spirit.'[40] Baptism, therefore, is a sacrament of regeneration and renewal. It is administered in the name of the triune God, reminding us that 'we obtain and, so to speak, clearly discern in the Father the cause, in the Son the matter, and in the Spirit the effect, of our purgation and our regeneration.'[41] At the heart of baptism, therefore, stands the believer's confession of forgiveness and solemn repentance.

---

33   Calvin, *Institutes*, IV,14,i.
34   Ibid., 4,14,6.
35   Ibid., 4,14,9.
36   Ibid., 4,14,10.
37   Ibid., 4,14,17.
38   Ibid., 4,15,1.
39   Ibid., 4,15,2.
40   Ibid., 4,15,5.
41   Ibid., 4,15.6.

It opens up the possibility of new life in Christ. While the Church administers the outward sign which makes such a life possible, Calvin is quite clear that 'Christ is the author of inward grace'.[42] Baptism, however, entails more than 'a mere appearance' of that grace since the sacrament 'effectively performs what is symbolizes'.[43]

Calvin disagrees with the idea that the water in baptism is the supernatural means by which we are liberated from original sin which has corrupted the human race since Adam. Original sin offends God, before whom only 'righteousness, innocence, and purity' is acceptable.[44] As a result, we would stand under the condemnation of God were it not for God's victory over sin in Jesus. In baptism, then, believers are assured that the condemnation has been set aside, and that in the Cross full and complete remission has been made for their sins, all guilt and punishment having been set to one side. As they rise from the baptismal waters they take hold of righteousness – 'such righteousness as the people of God can obtain in this life, that is, by imputation only, since the Lord of his own mercy considers them righteous and innocent'.[45] The baptised must recognize, however, that they will have to struggle continually with sin even though they know that in Christ it can never now overpower them.

Baptism involves a public confession of faith by the candidate in the midst of the Church. The baptized declare their intentions to live in the Christian community, their commitment to worship 'the same God, in one religion with all Christians', and their aim to confess Christ – and Christ alone.[46] Their baptism's efficacy does not depend upon the worthiness of the minister who administers it, since what makes it efficacious is the One into whom the believer is baptised, the triune God. If administered in the name of Father, Son and Holy Spirit a baptism is a valid baptism. Rebaptism is not to be sanctioned, even on the grounds that way back people did not understand what was happening to them when they were baptised. Who at any time can fully understand the meaning of their baptism?

On the practicalities of baptism Calvin has several interesting things to say. For example, he presents us with a clear outline of a baptismal liturgy which stands in sharp contrast to what had become common in the medieval churches.[47] It is noteworthy that Calvin sets Christian baptism firmly in the church's worshipping life, thus eschewing the practice of 'private' baptism. Also useful to note, given contemporary practice, is the centrality of teaching within the process of Christian initiation. And as to the amount of water to be used, Calvin is somewhat agnostic, but he does point out that 'the rite of immersion was observed in the ancient church'.[48]

Calvin maintains that administration of both the dominical sacraments is the province of 'the ecclesiastical ministry'.[49] He also argues against the custom of lay people baptizing those in danger of death if a minister is not to hand. This practice, he holds, confuses the promise with the sign. 'God declares that he adopts our babies as his own before they are born, when he promises that he will be our God and the God of our descendants after us' [Gen 17: 7].[50] It clearly follows that baptism

---

[42]   Ibid., 4,15,8.
[43]   Ibid., 4,15.14.
[44]   Ibid., 4,15,10.
[45]   Ibid.
[46]   Ibid., 4,15,13.
[47]   See ibid., 4,15,19.
[48]   Ibid.
[49]   Ibid., 4,15,20. And Calvin did not permit women to baptize [See ibid., 4,15,21].
[50]   Ibid., 4,15,20.

is not necessary for salvation: '. . . the children of believers are baptized not in order that they who were previously strangers to the church may then for the first time become children of God, but rather that, because by the blessing of the promise they already belonged to the body of Christ, they are received into the church with this solemn sign.'[51]

Calvin's arguments in favour of infant baptism focus upon drawing a clear parallel between the way in which the Israelites were engrafted into the Jewish race and the way in which people are initiated into the Christian church. The Israelites entered the covenant through circumcision, while the children of Christian parents enter the spiritual promise through baptism. A spiritual promise was given to the patriarchs in circumcision such as is given us in baptism, since it represented for them forgiveness of sins and mortification of flesh. Calvin argues that any difference between circumcision and paedo-baptism lies in the outward ceremony rather than the inward meaning which in both cases 'depends upon the promise and the thing signified.'[52] However, it is surely not a minor difference that circumcision is reserved for male children and Christian baptism is offered to both male and female.[53] Nevertheless, baptism should be offered to infants, according to Calvin, since it is 'something owed to them'.[54] They are included in the Covenant promise, so if they participate in what baptism signifies, what right has the church to deny them its sign?

Calvin's entire argument, of course, presupposes that the children being baptized are the children of practising Christians. He argues that 'the children of Christians are considered holy' simply because they share in God's promises.[55] A child who only possessed one Christian parent would be eligible for baptism.[56] But, when Calvin is faced with the objector who argues that, since Christ did not baptize infants, the Church has no right to practise paedo-baptism, he retorts: 'If it is right for infants to be brought to Christ, why not also to be received into baptism, the symbol of our communion and fellowship with Christ?'[57] And against those who argue that Jesus in Matthew 19: 13–15 was referring to young children rather than babies, he says: 'When he commands that infants be allowed to come to him, nothing is clearer than that true infancy is meant.'[58] But what about the argument which rests on the claim that the New Testament is devoid of evidence of the practice of paedo-baptism? Calvin argues that Scripture implicitly (if not explicitly) attests infant baptism, and then, somewhat bullishly, he opines that 'there is no writer, however ancient, who does not regard its origin in the apostolic age as a certainty.'[59]

Earlier in his discussion on baptism, Calvin placed great emphasis upon the persons being baptised confessing their faith before the Church and the world. He also rooted baptism's efficacious nature in the way God's Word creates a change within us. But how can these things meaningfully be said to happen when the one baptized is an infant? Calvin's opponents, the Anabaptists, argue that children should not be baptised, since they are not yet at an age to comprehend the centrality of baptism, namely spiritual regeneration. But Calvin answers this partly by invoking the mystery of

---

[51] Ibid., 4,15,22.

[52] Ibid., 4,16,4,

[53] Calvin's answer to this displays a very hierarchial understanding in which women are ultimately dependent upon men for their value: 'Only the bodies of the males were imprinted with it, which could be imprinted by nature, yet in such a way that the women might be through them, so to speak, companions and partners of circumcision' [ibid., 4,16,16].

[54] Ibid., 4,16,5.

[55] Ibid., 4,16,6.

[56] See ibid. where Calvin bases his argument upon 1 Cor 7: 14.

[57] Ibid., 4,16,7.

[58] Ibid.

[59] Ibid., 4,16,8.

God's ways with men and women and partly by stressing that true knowledge of God is by inward means through the illumination of the Spirit rather than through the cerebral faculties. He suggests that we ought to allow that God will 'shine with a tiny spark' on those 'he will illumine in the future with the full splendour of his light.'[60] But in any case 'infants are baptised into future repentance and faith, and even though these have not yet been formed in them, the seed of both lies hidden within them by the secret working of the Spirit.'[61] Calvin does not fully explain what he is referring to when he uses terms like 'tiny spark' or 'seed' – unlike Luther who asserts that there exists in infants a real if primitive type of faith.

When baptised infants grow up and learn about their baptism, Calvin argues that 'they shall be fired with greater zeal for renewal, from learning that they were given the token of it in their first infancy in order that they might meditate upon it throughout life.'[62] He acknowledges that with adults at baptism 'the sign ought to follow the understanding of the mystery', but infants at baptism are to be regarded as 'following another order'.[63] He accepts that adult baptism presupposes that conversion and faith have been found in the candidate, but in paedo-baptism the covenant with God is simply acknowledged and affirmed, and 'the remaining significance of this sacrament will afterward follow at such time as God himself foresees.'[64] What is common to adult and infant baptism is confession of sin and affirmation of faith, on the one hand, and the baptismal sign, on the other hand; where they differ is in the order in which they occur and the length of time which elapses between them. This understanding enables Calvin to argue that 'if the children of believers are partakers in the covenant without the help of understanding, there is no reason why they should be barred from the sign merely because they cannot swear to the provisions of the covenant.'[65]

While Calvin sets out a powerful argument for infant baptism, he does not go on to sanction the idea that children should be allowed to share in the Lord's Supper: 'A self-examination ought . . . to come first, and it is vain to expect this of infants.'[66]

Karl Barth

Karl Barth wrote two treatises on baptism.[67] Both contain a trenchant argument against the practice of infant baptism, which Barth claims is 'profoundly irregular' and 'an ancient ecclesiastical error'.[68] Paedo-baptism 'can hardly be preserved without exegetical and practical artifices and sophisms.'[69] The two works, however, reveal Barth's fundamental change of mind concerning baptism. In 1967 he announced that he had arrived at a different view of the matter from the one he set out in 1943. So it is to Barth's statements on baptism that we now turn before moving on to consider his polemic against paedo-baptism.

---

60   Ibid., 4,16,19.
61   Ibid., 4,16,20.
62   Ibid., 4,16,21.
63   Ibid.
64   Ibid.
65   Ibid., 4,16,24.
66   Ibid., 4,16,30.
67   Karl Barth, *The Teaching of the Church Regarding Baptism* (London: SCM Press, 1948) and *Church Dogmatics* IV, 4 (Edinburgh: T & T Clark, 1969).
68   Barth, *Church Dogmatics*, IV, 4, p 194.
69   Barth, *The Teaching of the Church Regarding Baptism*, p 49.

In his 1943 pamphlet Barth lays out a view of baptism which is essentially similar to that of Calvin. He regards baptism as a sacramental means whereby God's saving grace in Christ is represented to the recipient. Just what this means starts to emerge when he separates his view from 'Roman and Lutheran and Anglican baptismal teaching' by insisting that 'water-baptism conferred by the Church' is not '*as such* a causative or generative means by which there are imparted to man the forgiveness of sins, the Holy Spirit and even faith – a means by which grace is poured out upon him, so that he is saved and made blessed – a means by which his rebirth is effected, by which he is taken into the covenant by the grace of God and incorporated in the Church.'[70] What is essential for salvation rather is 'the free word and deed of Jesus Christ'.[71] If baptism, then, is not the cause of our reconciliation with God, Barth nevertheless insists that it is a means by which we recognize and gain knowledge of it. He therefore speaks of baptism as a 'sacramental happening in which a real gift comes to man from Jesus Christ'.[72] In baptism, Christ seals the letter he wrote in his person and work, and, hence, baptism 'saves, sanctifies, purifies, mediates and gives the forgiveness of sins and the grace of the Holy Spirit, it effects the new birth, it is the admission of man into the covenant of grace and into the Church.'[73] Barth consequently distances himself from Zwingli's alternative view in which the sacramental dimension is removed and the essence of baptism is located in the baptised person's acknowledgement of God's saving work in Christ. But, as we shall now see, the sea-change in Barth's baptismal understanding revealed in *Church Dogmatics* brought him to a position remarkably similar to that of Zwingli!

Barth's later understanding of baptism strips baptism of its sacramental character. He reserves the term 'sacrament' for Jesus Christ. Nothing is to be allowed to deflect our attention from the centrality of Jesus Christ. We become Christians when God changes our lives. This involves, on the one hand, a power generated by the life, death and, particularly, resurrection of Jesus. The Christ event reveals the fulfilment of God's covenant with men and women in Jesus' obedience to his Father unto death and in his triumph over sin and evil as our Representative and Liberator. Barth, therefore, argues that Christ effected a change in God concerning the divine disposition toward us. We are saved from condemnation and set right with God by an act 'from above'. So Barth concludes that 'the divine change effected in the history of Jesus Christ, in His birth, life and death, becomes . . . the concrete and dynamic relation between God and man, the event of the foundation of the Christian life.'[74] Viewed 'from below', however, the change which makes us no longer strangers but God's friends is the work of the Spirit, who opens us up to receive the Word of our salvation. When drawn together the views 'from above' and 'from below' combine to describe a single divine act in which there is 'the disclosure of His history to all men in the resurrection of Jesus Christ and the opening up of specific men for His history in the work of the Holy Spirit.'[75]

Barth defines the transformation which takes place in persons due to this divine act as their baptism with the Holy Spirit. This baptism is different from water baptism. It involves a number of elements: the recognition that it is Jesus Christ, rather than any sacramental rite or element administered by the church, which is responsible for making us Christians; the realization that the start of the Christian life is made possible through an act of divine grace by which the world is put

---

70   Ibid., p 26.
71   Ibid., p 27.
72   Ibid., p 29.
73   Ibid.
74   Barth, *Church Dogmatics*, IV, 4, p 26.
75   Ibid., p 30.

right with God; the acceptance of this 'omnipotently penetrating and endowing grace' by men and women in gratitude;[76] the admission of new Christians into a new community, the Church; the start of a new life for believers, one which is not perfect or complete but rooted in the company of a pilgrim people. Unlike water-baptism, baptism with the Spirit is genuinely sacramental; it is an 'effective, causative, even creative action on man and in man', and through it lives are cleansed, renewed and changed.[77]

The event whereby individuals become Christians contains two elements: God's movement toward them in baptism with the Spirit, and their movement towards God in baptism with water. Believers ask to be baptised with water, and thereby they respond affirmatively to what God has done for them in Christ. Baptism marks the start of the change in people which corresponds to the divine change in the Christ event. Its basis is to be found in John's baptism of Jesus, where Jesus displayed 'an act of unconditional and irrevocable submission to the will of His Father',[78] where he committed himself unreservedly to his fellow human beings by vicariously taking upon himself their sin and confessing it before God, and where he commenced his calling to be the Messiah and Saviour – 'the first and basic act of His self-proclamation as the Mediator between God and men.'[79] And it is part of the Church's obedience to Jesus that her members emulate him by undergoing baptism with water. In this way, they join those who are called to be his witnesses and who enter into fellowship with him. Baptism's goal, however, is 'God's act of reconciliation in Jesus Christ through the Holy Spirit, God's act of judgement and grace, of salvation and revelation'.[80] Believers ask to be baptised in order to take 'the first step by which they publicly and bindingly confess and commit themselves to their recognised and acknowledged Lord as Mediator of the covenant, and also to the mutual fellowship of Christians.'[81] Baptism, therefore, is rooted in a human work: confession by the new believer, and those in the community they are about to join, of total faith in God as the source of their salvation in Christ.

Both the basis and the goal of baptism, on Barth's analysis, therefore, are rooted in Christ. But, departing from his earlier position, Barth now rejects the idea that baptism is sacramental.

> Baptism takes place in active recognition of the grace of God which justifies, sanctifies and calls. It is not itself, however, the bearer, means, or instrument of grace. Baptism responds to a mystery, the sacrament of the history of Jesus Christ, of His resurrection, of the outpouring of the Holy Spirit. It is not itself, however, a mystery or sacrament.[82]

To support this contention, Barth argues that the Bible does not describe baptism in sacramental terms. Baptism, rather, is 'a true and genuine human action which responds to the divine act and word'.[83] Barth acknowledges that this position can be labelled neo-Zwinglian, although he notes that 'its development does not in fact owe anything to Zwingli's influence.'[84]

---

[76]   Ibid., p 35.
[77]   Ibid., p 34.
[78]   Ibid., p 54.
[79]   Ibid., p 61.
[80]   Ibid., p 72.
[81]   Ibid.
[82]   Ibid., p 102.
[83]   Ibid., p 128.
[84]   Ibid., p 130. Zwingli's understanding of the nature of sacraments will be dealt with later in the chapter.

Baptism is an action of the entire Christian community, as both the church's representative and the baptismal candidate act in God's service. Only those who seek baptism, and who are recognised by the church as ready for baptism, should be baptized. The meaning of baptism, therefore, is grounded in 'the choice, will and action of the participants'.[85] According to Barth, baptism necessarily involves the resolve and decision of the persons being baptized; it follows their conversion. The conversion being referred to here is a turning aside from the pretence that our thoughts and actions are endowed with ultimate value, and the realization that there is but 'the One who is entitled not merely to be called the only Lord but above all to be the only Lord.'[86] Since conversion is of its essence, baptism becomes the first step on a new way of life. As a first step it follows that baptism is only administered once. The baptized, and the community into which they are baptised, thus embark on the narrow path of obedience, a journey which is marked by a renunciation of their sin and guilt and a pledge to render honour and service to the One alone to whom it is due.

Given this understanding of baptism, it is hardly surprising that Barth can find no place for paedo-baptism in the church's life. He attempts to refute all the common arguments in favour of infant baptism. First, he turns to the biblical evidence. Nowhere is infant baptism prohibited by scripture, but nowhere is it either permitted or commanded. Most of the relevant biblical passages contain the sequence of a person's conversion leading to their baptism. Some, however, do suggest that infants were baptized when whole households were baptized (Acts 16: 15, 33; 18: 8; I Cor. 1: 16). Barth refers to these passages as merely the 'thin thread' or 'slender rope' upon which a proof of infant baptism can be established.[87] Nor does the story of Jesus' blessing of the children (Mark 10: 13–16; Matt. 19: 13–15; Luke 18: 15–17) provide biblical evidence for infant baptism. While it most certainly reveals 'a very intimate but for that reason all the more powerful witness to the universal scope of the work and word of Jesus Christ . . . it is not a baptismal text.'[88] Overall, Barth concludes that 'the case for a New Testament proof of infant-baptism is more than weak.'[89]

Secondly, Barth notes that some theologians, for example Calvin, agree that the faith of the baptized is an essential element in a satisfactory understanding of baptism; but, then, they also wish to support infant baptism. To do this they adopt a number of strategies. Reference is often made to the faith of the child's parents and the faith of the Church. But only Jesus Christ is involved in vicarious faith:

> Through His faith we are not only moved but liberated to believe for ourselves. Since we ourselves are freed to believe, believing is something which no one else with his faith can do for us: not even the most believing parents, the strongest Christian brother, the most vital community, the whole Church, the full chorus of believers in every century and country . . . . the personal faith of the candidate is indispensable to baptism.[90]

Nor does Barth have much sympathy with the idea that infants possess a primitive but actual faith (*fides infantilis*). He points out that no one seems to know what such a faith entails. Unlike Luther, Calvin did not posit it, preferring instead to speak of 'a seed of faith' within the infant and thereby

---

85   Ibid., p 135.

86   Ibid., p 142.

87   Barth, *The Teaching of the Church Regarding Baptism*, p 44, and *Church Dogmatics*, IV, 4, p 180.

88   Barth, *Church Dogmatics*, IV, 4, p 182.

89   Barth, *The Teaching of the Church Regarding Baptism*, p 45.

90   Barth, *Church Dogmatics*, IV, 4, p 186.

pointing forward towards 'the faith which will be demonstrated and confessed in later life'.[91] Barth quite rightly observes, therefore, that confirmation is essential if infant baptism is to have credence. But Barth will not award paedo-baptism such credence: 'For what is the point of this action [*viz.* confirmation] which is abstracted from baptism, which follows it fifteen years later, when it really ought to come first, when it ought to be the meaning of baptism as such?'[92]

Thirdly, Barth rejects the argument that paedo-baptism is prefigured in the Jewish practice of circumcision. Col. 2: 11–15 clearly refers to baptism as 'the circumcision of Christ', but Barth argues that 'it noways follows that baptism like circumcision is to be carried out on a babe'.[93] While circumcision 'refers to natural birth', and hence to 'a racial succession', those called to be Church members accept Jesus Christ as their Lord and Saviour, whether or not their parents are also believers.[94] From a New Testament perspective, Barth claims that it is impossible to say that being born into a Christian family means being born into the church.

Fourthly, Barth admits that the strongest argument for infant baptism is that it is a 'remarkably vivid . . . depiction of the free and omnipotent grace of God which is independent of all human thought and will, faith and unbelief'.[95] But he worries that 'this grace is at least set in motion by the minister and is thus transformed into a grace which works automatically and which is simply poured over the person baptised'.[96] His worry here may result from the particular way in which he understands his opponents' theology. But he is correct to notice that, if the Reformation teaching on God's free antecedent grace is used to justify infant baptism, it also follows that infants should be admitted to the Lord's Supper.

Fifthly, Barth dismisses several less weighty arguments. Some, for example, argue that infant baptism must be pleasing to God since God has spiritually blessed those who were baptised in infancy. Barth gives this argument short shrift: 'From the fact that God accompanies and even blesses [the Church] on its erroneous ways, may one conclude that these ways are pleasing to God and that it can and should continue to walk in them?'[97] Others have supported infant baptism on the grounds that, since it delivers a promise and pledge of the Spirit, it can be administered without reference to the candidate's faith. Barth's objection to this is given in a series of rhetorical questions:

> . . . is it not true that the promise and pledge of the Holy Spirit, whose communication is the meaning of baptism, is not given in any case or in advance, let alone generally and intrinsically? Is it not given concretely to specific individuals, to whom it applies not only apart from their faith, but also apart from their baptism? To what extent does this promise and pledge, which is real and valid in itself and hence for these men, stand in need of any actualisation, representation or depiction (through baptism)? What is really needed is . . . that men should come who are ready to hear and grasp the promise, or who are already on the point of doing so.[98]

---

[91] Ibid., p 187.
[92] Ibid., p 189.
[93] Barth, *The Teaching of the Church Regarding Baptism*, p 43.
[94] Ibid., pp 43–4.
[95] Barth, *Church Dogmatics*, IV, 4, p 189.
[96] Ibid., p 190.
[97] Ibid.
[98] Ibid., p 191.

There are yet others who have argued for infant baptism on the ground that adult baptism introduces into the church the possibility of 'hypocritical and imaginary conversions, scrupulosity, the rise of Pharisaical sects of "baptised believers", greater separation between Christians and non-Christians, Church and world, etc'.[99] But, post-Christendom, it is difficult to believe that, as Barth puts it, 'perfectionism' is 'really our greatest worry today'.[100] Far more vexing today is the devaluing of baptism which takes place when infants are baptised indiscriminately, irrespective of whether or not they have Christian (and hence church going) parents. And, quite correctly, Barth will have nothing to do with the argument that infant baptism is needed to assure Christian parents that their children from the beginning 'are within and not without'.[101] The biblical promise of Mark 10: 14 ought to be quite sufficient for such a need. And, as for the argument that infant baptism is necessary 'for the well-being and salvation of the children since it pledges the parents and sponsors and the whole congregation to see to their Christian instruction', is it not the case that this commitment could be made at 'an offering, presenting and commending of new-born infants in the congregation, whereby appropriate assurance could also be given to the parents in respect of their children.'[102] The practice of infant baptism in a church does not guarantee sound Christian nurture in the home nor solid Christian education in the church's life.

URC Baptismal Practice: Focus for Ecumenical Convergence?

Barth's forceful polemic against infant baptism reminds us that inside the Reformed ethos there are disputes over the meaning of baptism. He believes that paedo-baptism is 'a practice which has pushed its way into the Church . . . and in which the character of baptism both as obedience and response is so obscured as to be virtually unrecognisable.'[103] Others, perhaps interpreting the New Testament evidence in a different way and focussing their theology firmly upon the doctrine of God's prevenient grace, take an opposite view. Donald Baillie, for example, supports infant baptism on biblical grounds because he thinks that 'recent study of the thought-world of the New Testament' shows, first, that children were either baptised in New Testament times as infants, or that it was deemed unnecessary to baptize them at all; and, secondly, that 'Christian baptism was administered *without delay* to the children of persons who by baptism came into the Christian Church from paganism.'[104] This leads him to quite the opposite conclusion to that of Barth: 'Thus it is not infant baptism, but the postponement to adult life of the baptism of those who are born of Christian parents, that seems to be inconsistent with the New Testament.'[105] Baillie also rehearses other arguments swept aside by Barth, particularly those which focus upon paedo-baptism being the entrance to a community in which Christian nurture takes place, and which locate a primitive faith in infants that can be developed in a proper Christian environment. Meanwhile, with Calvin, he argues that 'infants are baptized into *future* repentance and faith, the seeds of which are implanted in their hearts by the Holy Spirit; and that according to New Testament teaching "the thing signified" need not precede the sign, but may come after.'[106] However, his central argument in

---

99   Ibid., p 192.
100   Ibid., p 193.
101   Ibid.
102   Ibid., p 194.
103   Ibid., p 195.
104   Donald M Baillie, *The Theology of the Sacraments and Other Papers* (London: Faber and Faber Ltd., 1957), p 84.
105   Ibid.
106   Ibid., p 89.

favour of paedo -baptism centres upon God's gracious initiative which precedes faith. This enables him to conclude that 'it is in *subsequent* faith going on right through a man's life that, above all, the sacrament becomes efficacious and a channel of the grace of God.'[107] If this is so, then, as Baillie recognizes, the profile afforded to confirmation in the church needs to be very high indeed.

Disagreement over the propriety of infant baptism has led to acute divisions in the church. Indeed, the issue is one of the classic battlegrounds of doctrinal dispute. A sympathetic and objective assessment of the contrary arguments – if such a thing is finally possible – perhaps reveals that there are significant points to be conceded to each side. It is the URC's belief that it has found a way to honour both sides in the dispute [Box 4]. The theological basis is located in viewing baptism and confession of faith as twin elements in the process whereby people become part of the church's fellowship. Since, as Calvin argues, what is signified in baptism may follow as well as precede the baptismal sign, the fact that baptism and confession of faith take place in a different order, and over a different length of time, in the two patterns of initiation is not deemed to be ultimately harmful to ecumenical agreement. Indeed, once it is recognized that both patterns are rooted in God's initiative for the world's salvation in Christ, and it is acknowledged that each also requires a response of faith to be made within the Christian community, the differences between

---

Box 4

When the Church observes this sacrament it makes explicit at a particular time and place and for a particular person what God has accomplished in Christ for the whole creation and for all mankind – the forgiveness of sins, the sanctifying power of the Holy Spirit and newness of life in the family of God. In this sacrament the Church affirms its faith in the action of God in Jesus Christ; and takes corporate responsibility for those receiving baptism, promising to support and nourish them as it receives them into its fellowship. Baptism may be administered in infancy or at an age of responsibility. Both forms of baptism shall be made available in the life of every worshipping congregation. In either case the sacrament of baptism is a unique part of the total process of Christian initiation. When baptism is administered at an age of responsibility, upon profession of faith, the baptized person at once enters upon the full privileges and responsibilities of membership. When baptism is administered to an infant, upon profession of faith by his parent(s), he is placed under the nature of the Church that he may be led by the Holy Spirit in due time to make his own profession of faith in Christ as his Saviour and Lord, and enter upon the full privileges and responsibilities of membership. These two patterns of Christian initiation are recognised by the United Reformed Church.[108]

---

infant and so called believer's baptism are significantly blunted. However, within the URC there remain people, to quote *The Basis of Union*, 'whose conviction it is that baptism can only be appropriately administered to a believer and those whose conviction it is that the infant baptism also is in harmony with the mind of Christ.'[109] And, on the basis of the aforementioned theological rationale, the URC honours both convictions believing that God uses each pattern to build up the faith of God's people.

It is tempting to attribute originality to ideas that possess a life before the time in which they finally emerge. When the URC found a way to hold together two quite different patterns of Christian initiation, the achievement was heralded as an ecumenical breakthrough, and as an example for other churches to follow as they seek ecumenical fellowship with other Christian

---

[107] Ibid.
[108] *The Basis of Union*, para. 14, found in Thompson, *Stating the Gospel*, p 251.
[109] Ibid., p 252.

congregations.[110] But what was proposed was far from new, since Forsyth had earlier advocated something essentially similar. He drew out the differences between the two forms of baptism [See Box 5], and then concluded: 'It would be well to accept the historic situation by at least making the

---

Box 5

Clearly the two Baptisms, infant and adult, are psychologically different, though they have in common the main thing – the connection with the Word and its blessings in a faithful Church. In one case the experience precedes the act, in the other it follows (or does not). The one flows from experience, the other seals and commits it. In adult Baptism regard is had to the subject's past experience of the Word; in infant Baptism to a future experience expected and provided for within the Church. Apart from this provision, infant Baptism is a mere beautiful and suggestive ceremony, or, if effective, is so as magic. In adult Baptism the instruction precedes, in infant baptism it must follow. In adult Baptism we are baptized *on* faith, in infant Baptism *unto* faith; but both are justified by faith only. And faith's influence and nurture should be secured always. [111]

---

question an open one in the same Church, with either practice at choice.'[112] When this is done, all manner of tensions and problems emerge, but the ecumenical fellowship it makes possible is the reward which provides the maximum compensation.

Let us now draw our discussion on baptism to a close with some personal observations. First, when infant baptism is practised in an indiscriminate way, it is hardly surprising that churches which practice adult baptism find it difficult, if not even impossible, to acknowledge the validity of infant baptism.[113] All the major treatments on infant baptism by Reformed theologians presuppose that at least one of the infant's parents is a Christian believer – and since the Reformed ethos cannot comprehend Christian believing outside membership of a local church, this means that at least one parent should be an active member of a Christian fellowship. Nathaniel Micklem speaks for them all when he declares that 'Baptism, where it keeps its evangelical meaning, is for the children of the faithful only.'[114] When Micklem continues by saying that Baptism 'is meaningless unless the child is received into, and to be brought up in, the household of faith',[115] my second observation comes into view, namely, that infant baptism will only be efficacious in a Christian congregation which enables children to grow up as an integral part of the church. What passes for Christian nurture and catechetical education in many of our churches is appalling. Forsyth's words are as relevant today:

> . . . the Church's act must not end with the rite. It must make a reality of its care of the baptized child. And that we have failed to do – parents leaving it to the Church, and the Church to the parents.[116]

---

110   See *Baptism, Eucharist and Ministry* (Geneva: World Council of Churches, 1982), p 5.

111   Forsyth, *Lectures on the Church and Sacraments,* p 201.

112   Ibid.

113   *Baptism, Eucharist and Ministry,* p 7.

114   'The Sacraments' in Micklem, ed., *Christian Worship: Studies in its History and Meaning,* p 250. To be sure, some thinkers have argued that since Christ died for the sins of all, baptism must not be denied to any child; the majority view, however, has been to link baptism firmly to the process of Christian initiation, so that apart from the fellowship of the Church infant baptism is completely meaningless.

115   Ibid.

116   Forsyth, *Lectures on the Church and Sacraments,* pp 203–4.

And it might be added that both parents and church then have colluded to pass the responsibility to the State educational system! Christians living in a plural society would gain a whole lot more credibility if they ceased bleating so much about the need to maintain Christian Assemblies and R.E. in our schools and instead attended to the task of making their local churches centres of Christian nurture and learning.

Thirdly, in a post-Christendom world the likelihood is that increasing numbers of people will seek church membership who have not been baptized in infancy. We should expect, as a result, requests for believer's baptism to rise. In our Western missionary context, believer's baptism may become more frequent than hitherto. But whether administered in infancy or at an age of responsibility it is to be administered once – and once only. We ought not to repeat a rite which signifies *a once and for all* gracious act accomplished by God for us in Christ; nor should we repeat something which concerns being initiated into a community – we only join the fellowship of Christ once!

But, fourthly, what of those who are baptised as infants, but who do not stay in the Church, and then are converted in adult life? Should they not be allowed to be re-baptized? While one can appreciate their need to signify publicly their life-changing conversion, what has been said above about re-baptism still applies. And if our services during which people confirm their faith and enter upon church membership were made more significant, incorporating meaningful signs and actions along with the demanding and challenging words, perhaps many of the pastoral problems we face over the issue of re-baptism could be avoided. It remains clear that 'confirmation' or 'the act of becoming a church member' needs to possess a high profile if infant baptism is to gain its proper status in church life.

The Sacrament of the Lord's Supper

When Jesus at the Last Supper took bread before the meal, blessed it, broke it and distributed it around the table, he was not doing anything unusual; when he took the cup after the meal, gave thanks and passed it around those assembled, he was not breaking new ground; rather, he was simply performing rituals expected of hosts at Jewish meals. As a result, we must draw an early conclusion about the context in which the institution of the Lord's Supper ought to be understood, namely, that we cannot gain an adequate understanding of Holy Communion without coming to terms with its roots in Jewish meal practices.

If the model for our celebrations of the Lord's Supper originates in first century Judaism rather than contemporary Western eating etiquette, then the procedural logic and fundamental meaning surrounding Holy Communion must owe a great deal to that Semitic environment. Charles Cranfield describes for us a typical Jewish meal:

> At every Jewish meal, whether private, social or religious, the head of the family or host took bread in his hands, said the berakah or thanksgiving ('Blessed art thou, O Lord our God, King of the world, who bringest forth bread from the earth' was the regular form); the others said 'Amen'; then he broke the bread, ate a fragment of it himself, and then distributed it to the others . . . After the meal followed the final berakah said by the head of house or chief guest. After the invitation 'Let us give thanks', he took the cup and, with his eyes upon it, said the long thanksgiving, then took a sip and handed the cup to others. This cup after the meal had a special name – 'the cup of blessing' . . . [117]

---

[117] 'Thank' in Alan Richardson, *A Theological Word Book of the Bible* (London: SCM Press, 1957), pp 255. The basis of my understanding of the biblical accounts of the Lord's Supper was initially shaped by this article.

A comparison between this standard procedure at Jewish meals in the first century and the four New Testament accounts of the Later Supper (1 Cor. 11: 23–26; Mark 14: 22–25; Matt. 26: 26–29; Luke 22: 14–23) reveals very obvious similarities.

The Hebrew word *berakah* became the technical name for the grace (or blessing) said at every Jewish meal. When it was translated into Greek, two words were used: *eucharisteo* (to give thanks) or *eulogeo* (to bless). In the New Testament accounts of the Lord's Supper, we find the origin of the term 'Eucharist', which some use as a descriptive title for what others have called the Mass, Holy Communion or the Lord's Supper: 'And when he had given thanks (*eucharistesas*) he broke it'. While the Synoptic Gospels suggest that the Last Supper was a Passover meal, John's Gospel indicates that the Passover was on the evening after the Crucifixion. Debates continue about which chronology is correct, but the likelihood of the Synoptics possessing a greater historical reliability suggests that there is a connection between the Last Supper and the Jewish Passover meal. If so, we need to give due weight to an understanding of Holy Communion which is shaped by the Jewish celebration of God's liberation of the Hebrews from Egyptian captivity. At the Passover, Jewish people retell their story and re-enact it around the meal table. They bring the past into the present, piecing it all together (re-membering it) in a narrative which recalls the nation's salvation history. One particular passage of scripture is always used at the Passover celebration: the Hallel (Ps. 115–118, 136). When Mark and Matthew refer to Jesus and the disciples ending the Last Supper with a hymn, in all probability it is the Hallel to which they are referring. The symbolic link between God bringing the Israelites out of bondage under the Pharaoh and God setting people free from sin in Jesus' death and resurrection hardly needs stressing.

The framework of the Last Supper as found in the Synoptic/Pauline tradition is quite clear. The narrative contains a series of events: first, Jesus takes bread, prays, breaks bread and utters a reflective word about it; and, secondly, Jesus takes the cup, prays and says an explanatory word about it. The tradition accredits two formulae concerning the bread and wine respectively – 'This is my body' and 'This is the new covenant in my blood'. At the end of the narrative Jesus then utters an eschatological saying. The Synoptic version runs: 'Truly I say to you I shall not drink again of the fruit of the vine until the day when I drink it new in the Kingdom of God;' while Paul's account has: 'For as often as you eat this bread and drink the cup you proclaim the Lord's death until he comes.' At the Last Supper, an entire meal separated the saying of the two formulae, therefore it is quite unlikely that Jesus was thinking of the two elements which make up a person. The formulae were independent of each other. The bread formula, 'This is my body', in its original Aramaic form would have meant, 'This is me', suggesting that Jesus was indicating he would be with them whenever they broke bread. The breaking of bread, therefore, is a pledge of Jesus' presence with his disciples, followers and friends – a very real but unseen presence during the time of separation between the Last Supper and the final banquet when God's Reign becomes fully manifest. The cup formula, on the other hand, clearly connects 'the cup of blessing' at the end of normal Jewish meals (or the third cup at a Passover meal) with the new covenant God makes with us through the Cross. The cup, therefore, is also a pledge, an assurance of the share which the disciples, followers and friends of Jesus will have in the new covenant. The outcome of Jesus' actions and words at the Last Supper consequently come clearly in view: 'Jesus put new meaning into old familiar usages: the bread and cup of the fellowship meal were henceforward to be the pledges of his real personal presence, till the disciples' fellowship with him should be perfected in the heavenly feast.'[118]

---

[118]   Ibid., p 256.

The early Christians remained attached to the Jewish religion, participating in its worship and rites. But when Jesus' followers met to remember their Lord, the usual Jewish meal soon became transformed into an Agape ('love feast') due to Jesus' actions at the Last Supper. It was not long, however, before the sacrament of Holy Communion began to take shape out of the Agape, as the breaking of bread and sharing of the cup were separated from the fellowship meal and a distinguishing feature of Christian worship was born. Once the bread and wine were brought together, it was quite natural that they became identified with the body and blood of Jesus, and, as the Jesus-sect grew further away from Judaism, the celebration of the Lord's Supper increasingly became an expression of Christian fellowship between those who met to take part. The two commands, 'Do this in remembrance of me' were added to the Last Supper narrative by the Christian community; but these additions only made explicit what was clearly implicit in Jesus' actions.

It is important to have a full grasp of the term 'remembrance' in our understanding of the Lord's Supper. It should not be understood in terms of secular memorial meals (as in pagan mystery religions) or secular occasions when the great events of a nation's history are remembered (e.g. Remembrance Sunday). Instead, we should understand 'remembrance' through Jewish eyes. When Jews meet to celebrate the Passover, they recall God's deliverance of their ancestors from Egypt. They re-enact symbolically what happened, putting the past back together, and thereby enable the past to live again in the present. It is akin to those occasions when we talk about deceased loved ones and get to the point when we feel that they are almost present with us. Remembrance is all about putting the past back together in order to make it a present reality, and as such it is rather more than mere recollection. It is in this sense that the word 'remembrance' should be understood in connection with Holy Communion.

Two observations concerning the New Testament tradition are worthy of particular note. First, there is no trace in the New Testament of the idea that the practice of Holy Communion involves the church offering bread and wine to God or Christ as a sacrifice. All that is being offered – and it is everything! – is the Church's thanksgiving to God for our redemption in Christ. *The sacrifice took place on Calvary, once and for all, and it is not repeated in the church's sacramental life*. Then, secondly, the New Testament is devoid of all mechanical or magical ideas concerning what happens at the Lord's Supper. This needs to be borne in mind when we consider what 'happens' at the Supper; but, alongside this observation, we should also observe that there may be a lack of biblical support for the view that Holy Communion is merely symbolic. As we shall see, many, if not all, in the Reformed churches have viewed the Lord's Supper as bestowing a gift to Christians – a gracious presence which is deeply personal if never mechanical, real and not simply symbolic, the presence of the risen and exalted Jesus.

The Theology of the Lord's Supper in the Reformed Churches

The Church Fathers generally tended to make a strong identification between the bread and wine and the body and blood of Jesus. Christ was understood as both priest and victim, and it was commonplace to understand what was happening at the Lord's Supper as a sacrificial offering of Christ to God, with Christ being represented by the bread and wine as his very body and blood. Indeed, up to the Reformation, the words, 'This is my body' and 'This is my blood' were interpreted completely literally, with those who understood the elements as symbols (*figura*) rather than as realities (*veritas*) being counted among the heretics.

This literal understanding of the Eucharist remained somewhat conceptually imprecise until a philosophical distinction in Aristotle's thought made it possible to nail down the literal view with greater clarity. Aristotle differentiated between an object's essential nature (*substance*) and its outward appearance (*accident*). Armed with this speculative distinction Scholastic theologians argued that, while the *accidents* of the bread and wine (i.e. their appearance, taste, smell etc.) remain unchanged during the Mass, their *substance* (i.e. their essential nature) changes from bread and wine into Christ's body and blood. This gave rise to the objective interpretation of Christ's presence in the eucharistic elements known as *transubstantiation*. God makes it possible that 'the whole substance of one thing be changed into the whole substance of another', and at the point of the prayer of consecration in the Mass 'the whole substance of the bread is changed into the whole substance of Christ's body, and the whole substance of the wine into the whole substance of Christ's blood.'[119] But the change of substance takes place without the bread and wine's appearance, taste or smell altering one iota.

The Reformers firmly rejected the doctrine of transubstantiation. Luther, for example, was opposed to Scholastic attempts to account conceptually for what for him remained a mystery of faith. He thought that the complexity of Aristotelian metaphysics made little sense to the ordinary believer, while he considered faith capable of grasping the Sacrament's truth in a way impossible for the intellect. Nevertheless, Luther wished to hold to the traditional objective understanding which affirms the presence of Christ's body and blood in the consecrated elements. He argued that, as in Origen's analogy of red-hot iron there is present both iron and fire, in the eucharistic elements there exists the simultaneous presence of both bread and wine, body and blood. This view is often called *consubstantiation*, but some Lutheran theologians are at pains to distinguish between, on the one hand, the 'substantial conjunction' of bread and wine plus body and blood (the doctrine of consubstantiation which is 'falsely charged on the Lutheran church') and, on the other hand, that 'sacramental conjunction' whereby the bread and wine are united with the body and blood in a 'mystical mediating relation' (which is the more accurate description of the Lutheran position).[120] For our purposes it is sufficient to know that Luther opposed the doctrine of transubstantiation, while maintaining an objective view of eucharistic action.

Zwingli, however, opposed the objective interpretation of the eucharist advanced in their distinctive ways by both Aquinas and Luther. He perceived that it is an error to believe in a literal corporeal presence of Christ in or under the elements. Zwingli argues, consequently, that the words, 'This is my body' are to be understood metaphorically rather than literally. He notes that, 'If [Christ] is present literally and essentially in the flesh, then he is torn apart by the teeth and perceptibly masticated.'[121] He observes, however, that communicants do not experience doing that, so he concludes that Christ's words cannot refer to physical flesh and blood. Nor is it possible to prove Luther's idea that the body of Christ is somehow present 'under' the bread. Since it cannot be shown that 'his body is eaten literally and perceptibly', the phrase, 'This is my body', therefore, should be taken metaphorically, a conclusion which Zwingli argues is supported by 'the evident teaching of the Word of God', as well as by that section of the Creed which affirms the ascension and exaltation of Christ.[122] When taken metaphorically, '"This is my body", means "The bread

---

[119]   Thomas Aquinas, *Summa Theologica* (London: Burns, Oates and Washburne Ltd, 1914), LXXV, 4.

[120]   See Heinrich Schmid, *Doctrinal Theology of the Evangelical Lutheran Church* (Minneapolis, Minn: Augsburg Publishing House, 1875), p 571.

[121]   Huldrych Zwingli, 'On the Lord's Supper' in G W Bromiley, ed., *The Library of Christian Classics*, XXIV: Zwingli and Bullinger (London: SCM Press, 1953), p 190.

[122]   Ibid., p 199.

signifies my body", or "is a figure of my body"'.[123] The eucharistic bread is a metaphor to remind us that Christ was crucified for us; it is a sign which directs the Christian community to their crucified Lord: '. . . as Christ is broken, that is, put to death for us, so in remembrance of him we offer one another the bread and break it, each representing and communicating with the other, as Christ did for us all.'[124] Meanwhile, the eucharistic wine is 'a sign, a figure, a memorial of the blood of the new testament which was shed for us';[125] it points beyond itself to remind us of Christ's life poured out for the world's salvation. But, in Zwingli's theory, the sign does not appear to contain what it signifies.

Calvin also objects to the objective interpretation of the eucharist and he mounts very similar arguments against it to those put forward by Zwingli.[126] Whereas many of Zwingli's assertions seem to lead him toward a *memorialist* or *commemorative* view of the Lord's Supper, Calvin puts forward a far more *sacramentalist* outlook in which Christ becomes present to the communicant when the bread is eaten and the wine is drunk, due to the work of the Holy Spirit. (See Box 6).

Box 6

Even though it seems unbelievable that Christ's flesh, separated from us by such great distance, penetrates to us, so that it becomes our food, let us remember how far the secret power of the Holy Spirit towers above all our senses, and how foolish it is to wish to measure his immeasureableness by our measure. What, then, our mind does not comprehend, let faith conceive: that the Spirit truly unites things separated in space.

Now, that sacred partaking of his flesh and blood, by which Christ pours his life into us, as if it penetrated into our bones and marrow, he also testifies and seals in the Supper – not by presenting a vain and empty sign, but by manifesting there the effectiveness of his Spirit to fulfil what he promises. And truly he offers and shows the reality there signified to all who sit at that spiritual banquet, although it is received with benefit by believers alone, who accept such great generosity with the true faith and gratefulness of heart.[127]

While Zwingli and Calvin both opposed objective understandings of the eucharist, opinion differs whether they put forward vastly different views on the matter. Against those who sharply contrast their respective views, C J Cadoux argues that, like Calvin, 'Zwingli also asserted that in the Supper the participant does truly, sacramentally, and spiritually receive the Lord's body and blood.'[128] Where perhaps they differed, Cadoux argues, was that 'Calvin laid more stress on the description of the rite as eating and drinking, rather than trusting and being reassured.'[129] Zwingli, no doubt, would have suspected that Calvin had not distanced himself sufficiently from 'the quasi-pagan crudity of Roman literalism'.[130] But we might then ask whether Zwingli's understanding of the Lord's Supper is not bound to involve more than a mere commemorative event, given that the One commemorated is active and present in the Christian fellowship shared by those who meet to break bread and share wine? Whatever the answer to this question, the different emphases of Zwingli and Calvin gave rise to different understandings of the Lord's Supper within Reformed churches. Box 7 contains details

---

[123] Ibid., p 225.
[124] Ibid., p 229.
[125] Ibid.
[126] See Calvin, *Institutes*, 4,17,11-31.
[127] Ibid., 4,17,10.
[128] 'Zwingli' in Micklem, ed., *Christian Worship: Studies in its History and Meaning*, (Oxford: Oxford University Press, 1936), p 147.
[129] Ibid., pp 150–1.
[130] Ibid.

of three different eucharistic theologies which Gerrish has traced in Reformed confessions of faith.[131] It is highly likely, therefore, that at any URC celebration of the Lord's Supper the communicants will bring different interpretive theological frameworks to what they are doing. Not only do we find material differences in URC communion practice, but also there are fundamentally divergent eucharistic theologies apparent as well – both within and across congregations.

Reformed theologians understand the sacrament of Holy Communion differently, but they are united in their opposition to three doctrines commonly attributed to Roman Catholicism. First, they reject the view that the Lord's Supper is an ever repeated sacrifice of Christ to God: a propitiatory sacrifice for the sin of the living and the dead. Reformed theologies hold the contrary view that the cross of Christ is the once and for all sacrifice offered to God for the world's sin. Secondly, Reformed theologians object to the idea that the miracle of 'change' at the consecration can only be performed by the ordained, as well as the further idea which flows from it, namely that a person's salvation is dependent upon receiving the communion elements from a priest. Thirdly, Reformed thinkers renounce the idea that the consecrated elements are efficacious in and of themselves irrespective of the faith of those who receive them (*ex opere operata*: on account of the work which is worked). Calvin, for example, dismisses this idea as 'diabolical', and counsels that those who promise 'a righteousness apart from faith' propel people 'headlong to destruction'.[132]

Box 7   Reformed Understandings of the Lord's Supper

SYMBOLIC MEMORIALISM
 * found in the writings of Huldrych Zwingli
 * elements call to mind what *has* happened - they are signs of a past grace given
 * the Church is the subject of the action: *we* give thanks, *we* make confession, *we* break bread, *we* pour wine.
 * a thansgiving and a commemoration of Christ
 * symbolism is the means by which language can be used in a way that bread and wine are more than bread and wine (i.e. a non-realist way).

SYMBOLIC PARALLELISM
 * found in the writings of Heindrick Bullinger
 * outwardly we consume the elements but inwardly and *at the same time* we feed upon Christ – so not memorialism!
 * outward event does not convey or cause the inward event, but indicates that it is going on – so not instrumentalism!
 * a communication and bestowal of Christ simultaneously *with* the elements
 * symbolism is used in a manner mid-way between memorialism (Zwingli) and instrumentalism (Calvin).

SYMBOLIC INSTRUMENTALISM
 * found in the writings of John Calvin
 * elements call to mind what has happened *and* is happening - they are signs of past *and* present grace given
 * Christ is the subject and not just the author of the sacrament: Christ gives himself to us in bread and wine
 * a communication and bestowal of Christ through the sacrament
 * symbolism is the means we are assured that we receive Christ without having to believe in his localized presence in the elements.

---

[131] See Gerrish, *The Old Protestantism and the New,* pp 118–30.
[132] Calvin, *Institutes*, 4,14,14.

Lack of agreement in eucharistic theology remains a major stumbling block in ecumenical relations, with access to the Table being denied in some churches to those of other traditions. At the point where Christians are invited to meet their Lord in bread and wine deep divisions open up in the Church. A statement from *Baptism, Eucharist and Ministry* points out the damage thereby caused: 'Insofar as Christians cannot unite in full fellowship around the same table to eat the same loaf and drink from the same cup, their missionary witness is weakened at both the individual and corporate levels.'[133] However, despite ongoing disagreements concerning 'the real presence' of Christ in the Lord's Supper, ecumenical discussion has produced a widespread agreement on a number of issues, e.g. (i) the Lord's Supper is a memorial of the Last Supper and Christ's giving of the New Covenant; (ii) the Lord's Supper has a direct link with the Jewish Passover, and consequently it is a celebration of Christ's passing from death (Egypt) to life (Promised Land); (iii) the Lord's Supper is a thanksgiving for the incarnation of God in Christ and our redemption wrought in Christ; (iv) the Lord's Supper signifies the unity of the Christian fellowship in Christ; and (v) the Lord's Supper is a universal feature of the one Church of Jesus Christ – even though, as we regrettably noted, full inter-communion is far from being a reality.

The Practice of Holy Communion in the United Reformed Church

Calvin provided the Reformed churches of his day with a basic outline for the Communion Service (See Box 8). What is striking about it is the flexibility it provides by leaving a great deal to 'the church's discretion' and the similarity it has to contemporary URC practice. Gone, thankfully, is the dark liturgical age when the Service of the Word was separated from the Service of Holy Communion. The two are now integrated into one Act of Worship – and that would have pleased Calvin! Less pleasing to Calvin would be the frequency with which the Lord's Supper is celebrated in URC congregations, since the vast majority have communion monthly or quarterly rather than, as per Churches of Christ practice, weekly as he advocated. However, I sense a clear trend towards greater frequency of eucharistic practice in the denomination as a whole. Also worrying to Calvin would be the resentment which exists in some congregations concerning their need to have lay people authorized to preside at the Lord's Table in cases of pastoral emergency. For Calvin, the invariable rule would have been that presidency was reserved for ordained ministers. And the participation of children in the Lord's Supper in an increasing number of URC congregations would have further bemused the German reformer. Let us now bring the chapter to a close with a brief consideration of the last two issues.

Box 8

But as for the outward ceremony of the action – whether or not the believers take it in their hands, or divide it among themselves, or severally eat what has been given to each; whether they hand the cup back to the deacon or give it to the next person; whether the bread is leavened or unleavened; the wine red or white – it makes no difference. These things are indifferent, and left at the church's discretion . . .

Now . . . the Supper could have been administered most becomingly if it were set before the church very often, and at least once a week. First, then, it should begin with public prayers. After this a sermon should be given. Then, when bread and wine have been placed on the Table, the minister should repeat the

---

133   *Baptism, Eucharist and Ministry,* p 15.

words of institution of the Supper. Next, he should recite the promises which were left to us in it; at the same time, he should excommunicate all who are debarred from it by the Lord's prohibition. Afterwards, he should pray that the Lord, with the kindness wherewith he has bestowed this sacred food upon us, also teach and form us to receive it with faith and thankfulness of heart, and, inasmuch as we are not so of ourselves, by his mercy make us worthy of such a feast. But here either psalms should be sung, or something be read, and in becoming order the believers should partake of the most holy banquet, the ministers breaking the bread and giving the cup. When the Supper is finished, there should be an exhortation to sincere faith and confession of faith, to love and behaviour worthy of Christians. At the last, thanks should be given, and praises sung to God. When these things are ended, the church should be dismissed in peace.[134]

(i) Lay Presidency

The three churches which came to make up the URC each held a different view on lay presidency. However, they were united on a basic principle, namely, that the question of presidency is a matter of order rather than of rights or validity. The idea that a sacrament is efficacious on account of the officiant being ordained was rejected. By and large, the size of Presbyterian churches and their practice of quarterly communion meant that ministers of Word and Sacraments usually presided at the Lord's Table - although it was open in exceptional pastoral circumstances for elders to be authorized to conduct the sacraments. In the larger Congregational churches things were very much the same, with the option of a deacon presiding being available to the Church Meeting when needed. In smaller congregations, however, when ministers of Word and Sacraments were not available, it became commonplace for deacons and lay preachers to preside and often without any formal authorization by the Church Meeting. Meanwhile, in the Churches of Christ, a quite different pattern existed, with local ordained elders presiding at the Sacraments while the ordained ministers focused on preaching and teaching. The URC consequently has had to hammer out a compromise on this matter, one which respects the differences of conviction within URC congregations as well as the ecumenical implications of any sloppy application of lay presidency.

In the URC lay people can be authorized to preside at the sacraments by a District Council. This signifies the way in which responsibility for ministry and sacraments is the final responsibility of the wider rather than the local church. Those appointed need to be in good standing and know what they are doing. While there is a sound theological argument, based on the idea of the priesthood of all believers, which says that at the Lord's Supper everyone is a celebrant, it is still the case that one person – usually a minister or, in cases of pastoral need, an authorized lay person – has to preside and speak on behalf of everyone. The story is told that R W Dale made sure that a lay person always presided once a year at Carr's Lane, Birmingham in order to witness to the doctrine of the priesthood of all believers. And one suspects that he ensured that the persons appointed were so instructed by him that they had a clear understanding of what the Lord's Supper theologically and procedurally involved, and also that he duly sat on the front row to make sure everything was conducted in a fitting and orderly manner! Nevertheless, adherence to the doctrine of the priesthood of all believers does not override the need for the church to have a clear policy on ministry which enables the church to have access to the Word and Sacraments in an orderly manner.

---

[134] Calvin, *Institutes*, 4,17,43.

The 1995 General Assembly set out the following guidelines on presidency in the belief that they are 'true to the spirit of the Basis of Union' and will both 'enable us to be ourselves, and . . . sensitive to our ecumenical context':

> We suggest the following pattern of presidency
>
> (a)   a Minister of Word and Sacraments should preside when available
>
> (b)   in situations of pastoral necessity where no minister is available, the district council should make provision for lay presidency: Moderating Elders and Lay Preachers should be considered first
>
> (c)   authorisation for lay presidency should not cover a period longer than a year without consultation and review of the needs of the congregations concerned.[135]

(ii) Children and Holy Communion

With the advent of all-age worship during the 1960s, some churches began to invite children to attend and in some cases to take part in the Lord's Supper. Thereby they started to do what the Orthodox communion has always done. The illogicality of children being present for part of the church's worship (Word) but not the rest (Lord's Supper) was thus decisively overcome. But others frowned upon the innovation. They insisted that the sacrament is only meaningful when administered to the faithful at an age of understanding. Viewing Holy Communion as a very private and personal act, rather than overtly in terms of an activity of the Christian community, they did not want the importance of the communicant's faith to be undervalued by an understanding of Holy Communion which the Calvinist might perceive as overtly Zwinglian, if not even the Eucharist's dissolution into an Agape meal.

While the issue is far from settled, increasing numbers of churches are opening up the Lord's Table to children. They have recognized that the meaning and significance of the Lord's Supper can be apprehended in various ways, emotionally and communally as well as cerebrally and individually. Just as baptism in infancy precedes an individual's confession of faith and admission to church membership, so the Lord's Supper can be seen as part of the 'growing into belief' process. Children are then enabled to belong to the fellowship by sharing its sacramental life. And, given our Lord's injunctions, might they not in fact be the perfect mentors for many an adult (Matt. 18: 3)?[136]

---

[135]   *Reports to Assembly* (United Reformed Church, 1995), p 125.

[136]   I owe a great deal of my understanding of this issue to Donald Hilton. For an account of many insights on the Lord's Supper which he has offered to me over the years, see his *Table Talk: Looking at the Communion Table from the Outside and the Inside.*

CHAPTER 16

Ministry and Church Order

AT THE heart of the Christian witness of faith lies the belief that everything that was, is or will be ultimately lives before God: Creator, Redeemer and Sustainer. And, further, Christianity holds that, despite the recalcitrance of those who have been born in God's image and likeness (Gen. 1: 26), God has not given up on creation, but rather continues to possess an ongoing mission, rooted and grounded in the divine grace and love, to bring all things into harmony with the divine life. Within this mission lies God's call to everyone to become part of God's people, reconciled to God and liberated from sin's powers. The church has been given a unique role in this mission. She is to bear witness to God's continuing redeeming and emancipatory work in the world as that has been decisively re-presented in Christ. Christ's victory over the powers of sin and death has opened up new possibilities for people, and it is the church's task to lead them to new life. So, empowered by the Spirit, the church is called to be the sign, expression and foretaste of God's reign of righteousness and love; and, as such, she re-presents provisional evidence of a new state of affairs: provisional in the sense that as yet not everyone is part of it, and also because even those who are remain subject to sin. God's mission, and hence Christ's ministry, is therefore continued in and through the church.

From this two things clearly follow. First, the church is not coterminus with the world; rather it is a distinct community, set apart from the world as a witness to God's good news. The ecclesiology of the Reformed churches starts from the church being constituted when Christ's followers gather together and thus make themselves distinct from other people. Sell has noted, therefore, that Congregational ecclesiology rests upon a 'distinction of eternal significance' between the visible saints who belong to a local congregation, 'those who are Christ's', and others in the community who are not!' And the URC, of course, maintains that each locally gathered church contains all the essential marks of the catholic Church. Secondly, the Church does not exist for herself. She is called out of the world to play a fundamental role in God's mission. The ecclesiology displayed in 1 Peter has never been far from the Reformed ethos: 'But you are a chosen race, a royal priesthood, a holy nation, God's own people, in order that you may proclaim the mighty acts of him who called you out of darkness into his marvellous light' (1 Pet. 2: 9). Indeed, this passage directs us immediately not only to a missionary understanding of the church but also to one of Reformed churches' most important doctrines.

The idea that the Church is 'a royal priesthood' underpins the much cherished but often misunderstood doctrine of 'the priesthood of all believers'. This doctrine is primarily concerned with a soteriological rather than ecclesiological issue. To the question: Where must one go to find one's salvation? the Medieval church, in effect, answered: Go to the priest, since he is the custodian of the sacramental means of grace. The Reformers, recapturing the New Testament idea of the church

---

1   Alan P F Sell, *Saints: Visible, Orderly and Catholic* (Geneva: World Alliance of Reformed Churches, 1986), p 58.

as a body which shares in the high priesthood of Christ, gave a different answer: Go to your local church! The thrust of 1 Peter 2: 9 then is to focus priesthood upon the church rather than upon a caste of individuals. As a recent URC statement puts the matter: 'Priesthood is . . . a function of the community of believers, derived from their participation in the high priesthood of Christ.'[2] And it goes on to underscore what has just been said when it states that 'Luther, Zwingli and Calvin were not against the ministry but against a particular view of the priestly office.'[3] The Reformers objected to all forms of sacerdotalism. But while they denied 'a separated priesthood', and, in its place, affirmed the priesthood of all believers, they nevertheless held on to the importance of 'a separated ministry'.[4] Indeed, the idea that designated ministers, appointed, prepared and set apart for their tasks, are crucial to enable and empower the discipleship and vocations of the whole people of God is in no way compromised by the doctrine of the priesthood of all believers. In fact, Daniel Jenkins can go so far as to say that 'the office of the ministry is necessary' for the church's well-being.[5]

All too often, though, the doctrine of the priesthood of all believers has become synonymous with a problematical understanding of ministry which ends up doing justice to neither church members nor ordained ministers. It is used as a licence to authorize anyone to do anything in the church, with scant reference to calling, ability or preparation. The motivation for this lies less in the precedent of the New Testament or Reformed traditions than in a liberal spirit of egalitarianism which rightly is outraged by the hierarchical abuses to which some ministers have succumbed. But one cannot imagine a better way of impoverishing the church than by risking lowering the standard of leadership through diminishing the role of ordained ministers. Those who gave birth to the doctrine of the priesthood of all believers did not thereby endorse what Gordon Rupp, the Methodist historian, calls 'an otiose ministry and an omnicompetent laity'.[6] We do not honour this precious doctrine by undermining the important distinction between the ordained and commissioned ministers of the church (ministers of Word and Sacrament, church-related community workers and elders) and the vocation of the whole people of God. In fact, we encounter as serious a problem when we collapse this distinction as we do when we attribute vocation solely to the ordained and commissioned. Few things are more important, therefore, than the ordained and commissioned being given proper, designated and accountable roles in the church's life, and that those roles are not undermined by any hierarchical and oppressive practice of the ordained and commissioned themselves.

The authorization for the crucial distinction between ministry on the one hand and the discipleship and vocation within the whole people of God on the other comes from the letter to the Ephesians, where the writer acknowledges that the Spirit endows some with particular gifts to be used in the church's ministry (Eph. 4: 11–13). Everyone is not called to be an apostle or prophet or evangelist or pastor or teacher. The Spirit, of course, showers gifts on the whole church, and they are to be used in the church's discipleship and mission. It is the Church's responsibility, then, to identify them and see to it that people can deploy them, thereby engaging in Christ's ongoing work. Nevertheless, from biblical times, it has been the church's policy to set apart those called to specific ministries, and to prepare them for their work within the discipleship and vocation of the whole people of God. Before we consider some of those specific ministries in the URC, we need to develop a basis for the URC's overall understanding of ministry.

---

[2]   'The Priesthood of All Believers', *Reports to the 1995 General Assembly of the URC*, p 139.

[3]   Ibid.

[4]   Ibid., p 140.

[5]   Daniel Jenkins, *The Gift of Ministry* (London: Faber and Faber, 1947), p 41.

[6]   Quoted in 'The Priesthood of All Believers', p 140.

A Reformed Understanding of Ministry

The New Testament abounds with allusions, both direct and indirect, to different types of ministry. The writer of Ephesians speaks of different ministries in the work of apostles, prophets, evangelists and teachers. In other parts of the New Testament we also hear about deacons, presbyters and bishops. The terms are never clearly defined, and in some cases they were interchangeable. During the New Testament period, when the church was expanding and discovering appropriate organisational patterns in a variety of contexts, there was no one pattern of ministry. Indeed, biblical scholarship shows that the bible does not provide any church polity, or understanding of ministry within such polity, with blanket authorization. It is true, of course, that the different Christian communions, whether of Episcopal, Presbyterian or Congregational ethos, have sought to ground their practice in the precedent of scriptural example; but none have in fact established a biblical case for what they are doing without passing over passages which support competing views. Hence a recent URC statement flags up an important conclusion at its outset: 'Few today would wish to argue either that the New Testament provides a single pattern of ministry or that the patterns in the various churches can be evaluated by the extent to which they conform to a single New Testament pattern.'[7] Any ecumenical consensus on matters of church order and ministry, therefore, will not be generated solely by historical considerations.   Far more important will be those theological explorations which seek to discern what forms of church order and ministry are needed today if the church is not only to be credible and effective but also obedient to the pattern of ministry set by Jesus Christ.

But what was 'the pattern of ministry set by Christ'? Jenkins has helpfully offered an answer to this question. He asserts that 'we cannot understand the doctrine of the ministry unless we see how closely it is related to our understanding of the heart of the Gospel, Jesus Christ Himself.'[8] And, as he probes the New Testament, he isolates two clear dimensions to our Lord's ministry. First, he points us to Jesus' servant-hood: 'The whole office of the ministry is to be understood as the expression in the Church of this fundamental paradox – that Jesus Christ, the Son of God, the King of all the earth, comes and establishes His kingly rule among men in the form, not of a king, but of a servant.'[9] The church's ministry is always undermined by those who forget this model of servanthood. Secondly, taking up the other side of the paradox, Jenkins reminds us that Jesus was God's ambassador, the one who spoke with authority, and who reigns with the Father. As Ephesians 4: 11–16 makes clear, ministry should reflect not only our Lord's humiliation through self-emptying (*kenosis*) but also his reign and self-fulfilment (*plerosis*), not just his servanthood, therefore, but also his sonship. Christians, consequently, can speak with an authority given by Christ, but our ministry becomes distorted and demonic when the model of authority followed is not shaped by servanthood. Jenkins utters a much-needed warning to those who judge ministry on terms other than those set by Jesus:

> The crown the King wears is one of thorns and the place from which He reigns, the place where He is lifted up to draw all men unto Him, is the tree of crucifixion. Therefore, while it is right to speak of the pulpit as the throne of the Word of God we must never forget that it is set up, not within the temple at Jerusalem, but on the Hill of the Skull outside the city walls.[10]

---

[7]   'Theology of Ministry', *Reports to the 1995 General Assembly of the URC*, p 41.
[8]   Jenkins, *The Gift of Ministry*, p 17
[9]   Ibid., p 20.
[10]   Ibid., p 27.

We would do well to share Jenkins's basic view that the church's ministry should find its pattern in the *kenosis* and *plerosis* of Christ. Ministry is not 'overt or covert lordship'; nor is it leadership in the accepted secular sense; rather it is *ministry* – an outward disposition towards people which is based upon 'true inwardness'.[11] We are not to come before people with 'lofty words or wisdom', but 'in weakness and in fear and in much trembling' so that faith will be based on 'the power of God' rather than 'human wisdom' (1 Cor. 2: 1–5). The authority for Christian ministry is found in the 'stumbling block' and 'foolishness' of 'Christ crucified' (1 Cor: 1: 23).

Calvin sets Christian ministry within God's purposes. Since God 'does not dwell among us in visible presence . . . he uses the ministry of men to declare openly his will to us by mouth, as a sort of delegated work . . . just as a workman uses a tool to do his work'.[12] Because the Deity could effect the divine mission 'by himself without any sort of aid or instrument, or even by the angels' this chosen pattern is clearly adopted for a number of reasons.[13] By calling ministers God shows us the high regard in which we are held; by using fellow, fickle human beings as the gospel's vehicle, God ensures that the message is heard by humble, teachable spirits rather than forced upon them in a manipulative manner; and, by appointing ministers, those who are entrusted with 'the teaching of salvation and everlasting life', God creates a bond of unity between the minister and congregation.[14] Hence, for Calvin, ministers become 'the chief sinew by which believers are held together in one body'.[15] They are God's instruments whereby the church is governed and sustained. The roots of Jenkins's view that 'the office of ministry is necessary' for the church now comes into view: 'For neither the light and heat of the sun, nor food and drink, are so necessary to nourish and sustain the present life as the apostolic and pastoral office is necessary to preserve the church on earth.'[16] There is no undermining of the importance of ministers in the name of 'the priesthood of all believers' in the writings of the Genevan reformer! In fact, quite the reverse is the case: ' . . . the mode of governing and keeping the church through ministers (a mode established by the Lord forever) may not be ill esteemed among us and through contempt fall out of use.'[17] The notion that one can have a church without a minister is a contradiction in terms.

Calvin takes his views concerning various models of ministry straight from Ephesians 4. He separates them out into two classes. First, there are ministries which 'the Lord raised up . . . at the beginning of his Kingdom, and now and again revives them as the need of the times demands.'[18] These are (1) apostles who God 'sent out to lead the world back from rebellion to true obedience . . . , and to establish his Kingdom everywhere by the preaching of the gospel', that is to say, those who first laid the church's foundations; (2) prophets who 'excelled in a particular revelation'; and (3) evangelists who, 'lower in rank than apostles, were next to them in office and functioned in their place.'[19] Calvin views these three ministerial offices as temporary ones which belonged to the time in which the church was being established 'upon the foundation of the apostles and prophets' (Eph. 2: 20). However, he admits that God is still capable, when the need

---

11   Ibid., p 29.
12   Calvin, *Institutes*, 4,3,1.
13   Ibid.
14   Ibid.
15   Ibid., 4,3,2.
16   Ibid.
17   Ibid., 4,3,3.
18   Ibid., 4,3,4.
19   Ibid.

arises, of raising up people to serve in such offices. Interestingly, Calvin calls Martin Luther, his great mentor, 'a distinguished apostle of Christ',[20] and contemporary members of a post-Christendom church might wonder whether or not the office of evangelist is altogether obsolete.

There are two permanent ministerial offices according to Calvin's analysis, namely, pastor and teacher. The temporary offices of apostle and evangelist were taken up by pastors, while the prophet evolved into the teacher. But what is the difference between the pastor and the teacher, given that in many Reformed churches the office of teacher rightly or wrongly is absent? Calvin answers as follows: '. . . teachers are not put in charge of discipline, or administering the sacraments, or warnings and exhortations, but only of Scriptural interpretation – to keep doctrine whole and pure among believers', whereas 'the pastoral office includes all those functions within itself.'[21] As in the case of evangelists, *mutatis mutandis* there may be compelling reasons to re-establish this office in our anti-intellectual society and in a culture which requires a credible and coherent apology for Christianity if that faith is to gain acceptance. Central to the pastor's office lie three functions: preaching the gospel, administering the sacraments and discipline. And Calvin insists that the minister of one particular church should not interfere in the life of another.

Calvin accepts that the various titles given to 'those who rule the church' in the New Testament are interchangeable.[22] Thereby, he 'affirms a cardinal principle of Presbyterian polity: "bishop" and "presbyter" are names for the same office.'[23] But, after mining various New Testament texts, he comes across other church offices in the epistles which are clearly different from ministers of Word and Sacraments. The gifts of healing and the interpretation of tongues are designated as temporary offices, while two others are considered by Calvin to be permanent: government and caring for the poor. The former task, Calvin claims, belongs to elders. They were elected by the congregation to govern the church with the pastor and thereby they were 'charged with the censure of morals and the exercise of discipline' along with the ministers.[24] So, from earliest times the church possessed 'a senate, chosen from godly, grave, and holy men, which had jurisdiction over the correcting of faults.'[25] This historical precedent is used by Calvin to ground the Reformed understanding of church government by conciliar as opposed to personal oversight (*episcope*), and recently it has been referred to as one of the reasons why the URC should not take episcopacy into its church order. Meanwhile, caring for the poor, Calvin argues, was undertaken by deacons in the early churches, and as with eldership he maintains that the role of deacons has lasting value. Deacons were appointed by the churches 'to distribute alms and take care of the poor, and serve as stewards of the common chest of the poor', and Calvin argues that the church should have such officers.[26]

The understanding of ministry and church order which Calvin laid down was incorporated to varying degrees in the churches which came to make up the URC. Each in their own way dismissed the pattern of ministry which, originating in the third century, had existed in the church until the Reformation. The Medieval pattern of the threefold order of bishop, priest and deacon was decisively rejected by Calvin, largely, one suspects, due to the way those offices had been abused. The traditions of the Churches of Christ, Congregationalism and Presbyterianism followed suit. The Churches of Christ had ministers but, since they were relatively few in number, the major

---

[20]   Ibid., n 4.
[21]   Ibid., 4,3,4.
[22]   Ibid., 4,3,8.
[23]   Ibid., n 8.
[24]   Ibid., 4,3,8.
[25]   Ibid.
[26]   Ibid., 4,3,9.

responsibility for preaching and the conduct of the sacraments fell to elders, while deacons undertook the kind of role carried out by deacons in Congregationalism and elders in Presbyterianism. All ministers were ordained in the three traditions; both elders and deacons were ordained in the Churches of Christ tradition; deacons however were not ordained in Congregationalism. The offices of deacon and elder were clearly similar across many of the churches in each tradition, but the fact there were also differences still comes through in the distinctive ways in which contemporary URC congregations perceive the task of eldership. And, of course, the union of the three traditions meant changes for each of the denominations.

The URC understanding of ministry, therefore, is obviously an attempt to formulate a pattern which gives due recognition to the emphases of each of the three constituting traditions. The *Basis of Union* starts its discussion of ministry with a clear statement on the ministry of the whole people of God, and the role and responsibility of every church member in this 'total ministry' to exercise the gifts God gives them.[27] It then recognizes that God calls some people to exercise their gifts 'in offices duly recognised within his church', particularly going on to refer to elders and ministers. The responsibility for 'the total caring oversight by which [God's] people grow in faith and love' is their 'special concern'.[28] Alongside the two ordained offices in the URC, the *Basis of Union* leaves open the possibility that other designated ministries may be required, and the church has actually introduced one during its life-time, namely, the Church Related Community Worker. We now move on to offer a fuller treatment of the various offices of ministry in the URC.

Ministers of Word and Sacrament

Many different models of ministry are abroad in the Christian church, and the work of individual ministers of Word and Sacraments within the URC reflects this fact. Nevertheless, the Reformed ethos has spawned an understanding of the minister of Word and Sacrament which is distinctive and commendable. Before we tackle some of the particular features of the debate about the contemporary role of ministers in the URC, it will be instructive to note the views of Forsyth and Jenkins on the role and function of the minister of Word and Sacraments. This will provide us with some understanding of what is 'distinctive and commendable' in the URC's view of minister.

Forsyth's discussion of the nature and role of the Christian minister is set within an attack on the ministerial practice of the Congregational churches around the time of the Great War.[29] He recognized the way in which the doctrine of the priesthood of all believers had become diluted and went on to point out how the standard of leadership had declined. If it was true that 'the Church will be what its ministry makes it', then it followed for Forsyth that the church needed a renewed vision of ministry if it was to regain its health and strength.[30] He is caustic about the way in which churches view their ministers:

> There are those who look on the minister simply as one of the members of the Church – the talking or the presiding member. They think anything else spoils him as a brother. They believe a Church could go on without a minister, only not so well, with less decency and order.[31]

27   *The Basis of Union,* para. 20, found in Thompson, ed., *Stating the Gospel,* p 254.
27   Ibid.
29   This material is drawn from my 'P T Forsyth on Ministry: a Model for Our Time?' in Alan P F Sell, ed., *P T Forsyth: Theologian for a New Millennium* (London: URC 1999), pp 171-208.
30   Forsyth, *Lectures on the Church and Sacraments,* p 121.
31   Ibid., p 123.

While ministers must have colluded to some extent in this lowering of their stature, it is the church members who are reminded of the task ministers are called to perform and of the esteem that they should have in the church.

> . . . let the religious public at least have some consideration for its ministry, which it irritates and debases by trivial ethics, and the impatient demand for short sermons and long 'socials'. Let it respect the dignity of the ministry. Let it cease to degrade the ministry into a competitor for public notice, a caterer for public comfort, and a mere waiter upon social convenience or religious decency. Let it make greater demands on the pulpit for power, and grasp, and range, and penetration, and reality. Let it encourage the ministry to do more justice to the mighty matter of the Bible and its burthen, and not only to its beauty, its charm, its sentiment, or its precepts. Let it come in aid to protect the pulpit from that curse of petty sentiment which grows upon the Church, which rolls up from the pew into the pulpit, and from the pulpit rolls down upon the pew in a warm and soaking mist.[32]

It was Forsyth's belief that the churches of his day were desperately in need of rediscovering their roots in the gospel. And ministers were to be a fundamental means by which that came about. They have a sacramental function at the heart of the Church's life; they are called by God and set apart by the church to convey, and not merely declare, God's grace: 'In the sacrament of the Word the ministers are themselves the living elements in Christ's hands – broken and poured out in soul, even unto death; so that they may not only witness Christ, or symbolise Him, but by the sacrament of personality actually convey Him crucified and risen.'[33] Or Forsyth in a more personal vein can say of his calling:

> How solemn our place is! It is a sacramental place. We have not simply to state our case, we have to convey our Christ and to convey Him effectually. We are sacramental elements, broken often, in the Lord's hands, as He dispenses His grace through us.[34]

A 'higher' view of ministry is difficult to imagine.

In Forsyth's analysis of the minister's work he focuses on four primary functions. First, ministers are preachers. Preaching demands 'complete immersion in the Bible', so it follows that 'the ideal ministry is in real touch with the Bible, constant and supreme touch with the Bible.'[35] Forsyth, of course, sees God's saving work in the Easter event as the kernel of the preached message: 'This cross is the message that makes the preacher.'[36] But, as well as being devoted to biblical reading and study, there is also a need for 'deliberate prayer', since without this ministers 'easily become dilettanti not in theology only but in soul, religious amateurs instead of spiritual masters, mere seekers, and experimenters instead of experts of the Gospel and adepts of faith.'[37] The minister's second function is pastoral work. This is a continuation of the preaching function in that it is not merely a matter

---

32   Forsyth, *Positive Preaching and the Modern Mind*, p 100.
33   Forsyth, *Lectures on the Church and the Sacraments*, p 131.
34   From Forsyth, *Revelation Old and New: Sermons and Addresses*, ed. John Huxtable (London: Independent Press Ltd, 1992), p 121.
35   Ibid., pp 102, 113.
36   Forsyth, *Positive Preaching and the Modern Mind*, p 49.
37   Forsyth, *Revelation Old and New*, p 106.

of extending concern and kindliness to people; rather, it is the way the minister takes Christ to people 'not for humane objects only, but for the sake of the Kingdom of God'.[38] Ministers are sacramental in their pastoral endeavour as they become subjects of grace through which the gospel of grace works. The third function of the minister is more priestly than it is prophetic. The minister's conduct of public worship, and especially the leading of a congregation in prayer, is an important part of a minister's responsibilities. When carrying it out the minister is more sacerdotal than sacramental. This prompts Forsyth to make the following observations:

> As priest, the ministry offers to God the Church's soul, as prophet it offers to it the salvation of God. In the minister's one person, the human spirit speaks to God, and the Holy Spirit speaks to men. No wonder he is often rent asunder.[39]

But, as earlier suggested, Forsyth argues that ultimately the minister 'is sacramental . . . more than sacerdotal'.[40] Fourthly, the minister has social and philanthropic functions outside the church. Forsyth was so suspicious of any social gospel strategy that he tended to think that this function was already receiving enough attention by ministers. The more ministers involve themselves in these matters, the less time there is for the preaching, teaching and the liturgical side of ministry. Forsyth also makes the telling point that a social gospel ministerial strategy 'takes work away from the laity'.[41]

Forsyth, therefore, offers us a theology of ministry in which the minister of word and sacraments is essential for the *bene esse* of the church. There is a clear role for people set apart in the church for leadership, particularly through preaching and teaching. Such people should be carefully selected for their office and rigorously prepared to undertake it. Forsyth's view of ministry was demanding. How else, he observed, can we get the heart back into the church? 'If the ministers do not rise to the level of ministry it is for the church to see that they are better selected and trained'.[42] With his emphasis upon preaching and teaching one suspects that Forsyth's view of ministers imposed high theological demands upon them. It was certainly an educated ministry that he was aiming to produce:

> . . . to be true at once to the Gospel and to the age the ministry must be an educated one. I mean as a whole. And by educated I do not mean learned, and I do mean more than merely trained . . . trained in the wisdom and knowledge which is the stored precipitate of past ages of earnest Christian experience.[43]

In modern terms we might say that Forsyth's minister is required to be a practical theologian who enables the whole church to be aware and confident of the faith it holds. Speaking about preachers needing to be rooted and grounded in theology, Forsyth remarks that

> . . . it needs much skill in the treatment of truth to grasp with the right hand the marrow of the Gospel and manipulate with the other the civilization of the time, to stand with one foot on the earth and the other in the infinite sea. Do not think this trained mind, this due knowledge, is a luxury of the literates. It is a necessity for the whole Church . . . [44]

---

38   Forsyth, *Lectures on the Church and Sacraments*, p 135.
39   Ibid., p 136.
40   Ibid.
41   Ibid.
42   Ibid., p 121.
43   Forsyth, *Revelation Old and New*, p 109.
44   Ibid.

While not part of an order, ministers are set apart to maintain church order. They are accountable to the demands which the gospel places upon them rather than the congregation's wishes. Not out to impress people or have people take notice of them, ministers are pneumatics rather than charismatics. They convince by 'the power of the word, the inner nature of the Gospel, the intelligent demonstration of the spirit'.[45] Ministry 'is not a matter of mental or miraculous gifts' as the out and out charismatic would have us believe; rather, it is rooted in 'the gifts of faith, hope and love in the Gospel'.[46]

Jenkins found Forsyth's view of the Christian minister very congenial. He shares Forsyth's high expectation of ministers as well as his view of their unique importance to the church's well-being. Ministers have been granted 'special powers' to be used in their work of exercising oversight of a local church.[47] The first of these, Jenkins argues, is 'the right of preaching the Word and administering the sacraments'.[48] Some will recoil at his use of the word 'right', but, perhaps anticipating such negative reactions, he insists that he is not advocating 'clericalism' so much as applying 'plain common sense'.[49] Ministers are not pastoral counsellors, social workers, community politicians or managers of institutions; they are first and last preachers of the gospel and presidents at baptism and holy communion. Secondly, in the name of the Church, ministers have 'the power of declaring the divine absolution from sin and the protection of the Church's integrity in a fallen world by the exercise of discipline', the so-called 'power of the keys'.[50] But each of these powers is to be exercised in the context of the minister's calling to servanthood.

Ministers stand before God as representatives of the human race. They live normal lives sharing the same difficulties and doubts, hopes and fears, as other people. Jenkins argues, though, that ministers must be committed to doing full-time what others can only do occasionally, namely, wrestling with 'the deep things of God.'[51] Their office sets them apart to stand where human beings are most fully themselves, both in their despair and hope – before God. But Jenkins denies that this setting apart is a licence for 'an improper clerical professionalism' which places the minister in a special caste.[52] What he says about the Congregational minister still applies to ministers in the United Reformed Church: ' . . . he is only one member of the congregation among others and shares with them a common responsibility for the life of the whole.'[53] As a representative figure, however, the minister is called to share 'the representative character of Christ's ministry'.[54] This means that ministers need to be aware of the enormity of the cost borne by Christ for our salvation. To achieve this they must become what the Apostle Paul calls 'a spectacle to the world' (I Cor. 4: 9), experiencing first hand what it means to be rejected. They 'must face as fully as our human frame is able the implications of unbelief', as well as 'a sinful refusal to acknowledge Jesus Christ as Lord and God'.[55] This takes ministers to 'the frontier . . . the hill outside the city where Christ is lifted up upon the Cross', where they watch from afar and count the cost of the world's salvation.[56] Jenkins

---

[45]   Ibid., p 112.
[46]   Ibid., p 111.
[47]   Jenkins, *The Gift of Ministry*, p 45.
[48]   Ibid.
[49]   Ibid.
[50]   Ibid., p 46.
[51]   Ibid., p 60.
[52]   Ibid.
[53]   Ibid., p 61.
[54]   Ibid., p 62.
[55]   Ibid., p 63.
[56]   Ibid., p 64.

believes that authentic ministry takes its shape and power from the cross. Good ministers take seriously their representative character by apprehending 'the tragic nature of man's self-contradictory existence' through their 'self-identification' with their church members and their reflection upon the world's life as it is illuminated by the cross.[57]

But ministers are not only people who take seriously 'what it means to be alone with God and one's sin in the agony and despair of the dereliction', but they are also people of faith.[58] This dimension of the ministerial office has three elements. First, ministers are theologians. They do not rest content with repeating Christian tradition or regurgitating it in the language of the day; rather they 'question the presuppositions on which the tradition works', and then they 'reassert its truth' in terms of their own experience.[59] Reformed ministers appeal to the Bible 'as a living testimony to the voice of God' with whom they have 'personal dealings'.[60] Thereby their theology is given shape and direction. Secondly ministers are preachers. They enable human words to break open and reveal God's Word. This sacramental understanding of preaching is very reminiscent of Forsyth. Through the spiritual nourishment of their preaching ministers can then lead the congregation in their pastoral work: 'The Church, and not merely her minister, is the mother of the faithful who looks after her own with unceasing watchful affection and carries the young and weak by her own resources of faith.'[61] Thirdly, ministers are witnesses. They are called to be living examples of the gospel. This is achieved, Jenkins argues, by ministers aspiring to 'spontaneity, ordinariness, and a single-eyed simplicity of attitude towards other people and life in general'.[62] Good ministers should impress people by their normality – the artists in living who display style in what they do.[63] Ministers, then, are not only those who prophetically point away from themselves to the crucified Christ, but they are also those who must be a living witness to him.

Following the tradition within the Reformed ethos to cultivate a learned and competent ministry, URC stipendiary and non-stipendiary ministers are given extensive training and preparation prior to ordination. But, as the decline in church membership continues, it is debatable how long the URC will be able to maintain its extensive and costly commitment to the theological education of its ministers. This decline, though, has not been matched by an equivalent rate of church closure, with the result that it is proving difficult to find enough ministers to match the need for pastoral oversight. Various Synods have responded to this by preparing selected elders in local churches to act as the Church Leader in their particular congregation. District Councils are involved in their selection, training is given, but Church Leaders are not ordained to their office. As we turn now to consider the ministry of elders, it is interesting to note history repeating itself, since the new URC Local Church Leaders are arguably filling the role of Presiding Elders in the former Churches of Christ tradition.

Elders

The churches of the Reformed heritage display the collaborative nature of ministry in the way that their ordained ministers have usually carried out their responsibilities in partnership with deacons and elders. In Congregationalism, for example, the work of ministers of Word and Sacraments is carried out in close relationship to the diaconate; in the Presbyterian traditions it is set within the

---

[57]   Ibid., p 67.
[58]   Ibid., p 70.
[59]   Ibid., p 75.
[60]   Ibid.
[61]   Ibid., p 83.
[62]   Ibid., p 84.
[63]   Ibid., p 85.

work of the eldership; while in the Churches of Christ tradition it is related to both elders and deacons, the former being more akin to Congregational deacons and Presbyterian elders. In the URC, ministers are expected to work collaboratively with elders while exercising their ministry in the local church, as well as in the District Councils, Synods and General Assembly. Everything that has already been said about the New Testament view of ministry, therefore, applies to elders as well as ministers. The high calling and great expectations which follow have been noticeably absent from many expressions of eldership with the result that the potentiality of this office for the church has not been fully taken up in every URC congregation. The tendency has been for ministers to take on more and more responsibility when it would have been prudent to look to the eldership for help. Most ministers are not well-known for the art of delegation! But, as J M Ross suggested many years ago, the ministry needs the eldership. The church requires lay-people 'to assist in the pastoral and administrative oversight of local congregations and to share with the ministry in the wider government of the Church'.[64] Elders, therefore, set ministers free for 'their primary duties'.[65] And, in principle at least, the office of elder in the Reformed traditions has been revered by many in other church traditions precisely for the way in which it helps focus the conciliar nature of ministry. Some even go so far as to view it as '*the* distinguishing sign of the Reformed tradition'.[66]

We have already concluded that, in Ross's words, ' . . . the fundamental principles of our faith are capable of expression in more than one type of Church Government, and that the type best suited to the infant Church of the first century is not necessarily best for today'.[67] This does not preclude Ross, however, from turning to the Bible to seek some historical background for eldership. Originally the Christian church was a Jewish sect and, consequently, it is hardly surprising that its sense of order and leadership was modelled upon Judaism. In Numbers 11: 10–25 we read of elders being chosen, set apart and commissioned to aid Moses in the leadership of Israel. They were anointed by the spirit for service to the nation, rather than for personal pleasure or honour, and they exercised their office collaboratively with other elders. According to Deuteronomy 25: 5–10, every town had elders who possessed administrative and judicial responsibilities. It was quite natural, then, for the first Christians to base their church order upon what was second nature to them, and, in particular, the example of the synagogue would have been prominent in their minds. However, it is not true that the first Christians simply borrowed an organisational pattern from Judaism, since Jesus' decision to appoint twelve disciples was also crucial in the early developments in church order. Ross, in fact, argues that 'the Twelve were the prototype of the later presbyterate' in the same kind of way that 'the Seven were the prototype of the diaconate' (Acts 6: 1–7).[68] The Apostles appointed deacons, of course, so that they would not be diverted from their primary responsibilities of preaching and teaching.

---

[64]   J M Ross, 'What is an Elder?' Occasional Paper No 5 (London: Presbyterian Church of England, 1949), p 22.

[65]   Ibid.

[66]   Lukas Vischer, 'The Office of the Elders' in *The Ministry of the Elders in the Reformed Churches*, Lukas Vischer, ed. (Bern: Evangelische Arbeitsstelle Oekumene Schweiz, 1992), p 10.

[67]   Ross, 'What is an Elder?', p 2–3. See also *Eldership in the Reformed Churches Today: Report of an International Consultation held at John Knox Centre in Geneva from August 26-31, 1990* (Geneva: World Alliance of Reformed Churches, 1991): 'On the basis of our knowledge of the Bible today, we believe that Scripture does not point to one single church order, and that the effort to impose such an order on Scripture should be abandoned ... One clearly defined church order will be discerned only through selective reading and weighing of some Biblical passages over others' (pp 8–9).

[68]   Ross, 'What is an Elder?', p 4.

The New Testament clearly shows the existence of pastors in charge of local churches. They are given different names: leaders (Heb. 13: 7,17), shepherds (Eph. 4: 11), overseers (1 Pet. 5: 2) and elders (1 Pet. 5: 1). But it is now usual to call them presbyters (from the Greek *presbuteros* which means literally 'elder'). It seems relatively clear that the presbyters worked collaboratively with the apostles (Acts 15: 4; 16: 4) and with one another (1 Tim. 4: 14). They certainly exercised oversight of the congregation (Acts 20: 28–31; 1 Pet. 5: 1–4) and took a leading role in its government (Acts 11: 30; 15: 22ff; 1 Tim. 5: 17). Discipline in the congregation, therefore, was their clear responsibility, and pastoral work (Jas. 5: 14), preaching and teaching was also central to their office. While the functions of the early presbyters tell us a great deal about the work of those set apart by the church for representative ministry, we do not find anywhere in the New Testament examples of what the URC understands by eldership.

It was not long before the separate groups of presbyters found the need to have one of their number exercising leadership within each group. A clear distinction opened up then between presbyters (*presbuteroi*) and bishops (*episcopoi*). In the following decades, the bishops were elevated to an even greater standing and status, such that before the Reformation some bishops were more powerful than many political rulers, while in the Patristic period the term 'presbyter' fell out of use as the classical threefold pattern of ministry evolved and became normative. Stephen Mayor suggests three reasons for this.[69] First, a society in which hierarchical patterns were inbuilt found it more conducive to conceive ministry as a series of offices of different status than a team of equals. Secondly, the development of clericalism led to the advent of the order of bishops, priests and deacons. But, as Mayor notes, 'The development of clericalism was a natural response to the need for an elite who would set a good example.'[70] However, it took the church further away from New Testament views of ministry. Thirdly, the development of priest-craft added to the demise of the presbyter. From Cyprian onwards in the third century, lay people became subordinate to priests. It was widely believed that priests possessed powers, particularly in relation to sacraments, that are absent from those not ordained.

The Reformation challenged the hitherto accepted ministerial pattern of bishop, priest and deacon. Part of the reason for this resided in the abuse which this hierarchical pattern had spawned. The behaviour of many clerics during the church's less seemly periods reminds us of the wise observation of Lord Acton: 'Power tends to corrupt and absolute power corrupts absolutely' (Letter to Mandell Creighton, 5 April 1887). And the practice of many Medieval clerics had little to commend itself to the Reformers. However, there was a deeper theological reason why they moved away from the threefold order. As Elsie Anne McKee reminds us, the Reformers' belief in the priesthood of all believers led them beyond hierarchical understandings of ministry, in which one Christian is superior to another and fundamentally different grades of being Christian are the accepted norm, and this caused them to affirm that lay people are ministers 'not only in private life but also in the leadership of the Christian community'.[71] Of particular importance was the way in which the Reformed churches involved lay leaders in matters of Church discipline, an area the Medieval church hitherto had reserved solely for ordained ministers. And, as McKee notes, 'This was also the most controversial point of the Protestant revision of the doctrine of the ministry because it took power from one group and gave it to another.'[72] So the Reformation led to pattern

---

[69] Stephen H Mayor, *Being an Elder in the United Reformed Church* (London: The United Reformed Church, 1977), p 7.

[70] Ibid.

[71] Elsie Anne McKee, 'The Offices of Elders and Deacons in the Classical Reformed Tradition' in Donald K McKim, ed., *Major Themes in the Reformed Tradition* (Grand Rapids, Michigan: William B Eerdmans Publishing Company, 1992), p 345.

[72] Ibid.

of ministry which included not only pastors, who were responsible for preaching the Word and administering the sacraments, but also lay leaders, who were responsible for all the other duties such as discipline and poor relief. And, as we have seen, Calvin divided the lay leaders into two 'permanent offices': the eldership and diaconate. Ross, however, rather interestingly points to the different way in which elders and deacons found a place in Calvin's Geneva:

> [Elders] owed their existence not really to the dictates of Scripture or Reformed doctrine, but to the necessity for maintaining discipline; and it was only when the office had been found necessary that its institution by Christ was looked for in Scripture. The reverse was the case with the deacon: he had to be appointed because Scripture required it, but there was not a large practical sphere for his activities.[73]

Congregationalists may find it interesting that the diaconate, in the opinion of one learned Presbyterian at least, seems to possess a greater biblical warrant than the eldership!

In Presbyterianism the leadership of a congregation was located in the minister(s) and elders, with certain practical functions to do with property and finance sometimes being delegated to 'managers'. If the deacon was largely absent from Presbyterian churches at the formation of the URC, it was the elder which was found missing from the order of their Congregational counterparts. And yet 'the Congregationalists sided vigorously with the Scottish Presbyterians in the Westminster Assembly in insisting that both doctors (teachers) and ruling elders should be recognised within any Reformed Church of England.'[74] But, eventually, the office of the elder died out in Congregationalism, leaving it with pastors and deacons. Two reasons can be advanced for this, one theological, the other practical. Congregationalism stressed the direct rule of Christ through the entire congregation. As Alan Sell has pointed out,

> . . . the early Congregational Way runs counter to any hierarchical system of church government, whether episcopalian or presbyterian. Ministry is not a matter of priestly caste, but nor is it the case that in the church anyone may do anything. There are gifts, and it is for the church to recognise these . . . All who are called by, and gathered to and under Christ are the Church: hence the reluctance on the part of some later Congregationalists to conceive of a churchly body subsisting between the local church and the Church catholic.[75]

But whatever primacy was attached to the church meeting in principle, many Congregational diaconates in practice functioned in a similar way to elderships, with a good deal of authority being delegated to them and extensive pastoral work being undertaken by individual deacons. A second reason why the office of elder disappeared from Congregationalism may be traced to the fact that its churches were simply too small to support both elders and deacons. The Churches of Christ tradition, however, did manage to maintain ministers, elders and deacons, but only by re-conceiving the roles of ministers and elders. Ministers in this tradition were ordained regionally to exercise a peripatetic ministry of preaching and evangelism, while the elders were set apart to preside at the Lord's Table in local congregations.

---

[73] Ross, 'What is an Elder?', p 11.
[74] Lucas Vischer, 'The Office of the Elders', p 60.
[75] Sell, *Saints: Visible, Orderly and Catholic,* p 53.

The *Basis of Union* attempts to do justice to the roles of both the church meeting and elders' meeting in Congregationalism and Presbyterianism respectively, as well as include within the office of elder the strengths of both Congregationalist deacons and Presbyterian elders. Practice still varies, reflecting the traditions which came together in 1972 and were incorporated at the time of unification with the Churches of Christ in 1981. The functions of the elders' meeting are extensive and demanding, some might call them awesome.[76] Taken as the responsibility of a collective body, they may be deemed achievable by God's grace, but experience suggests that for the well-being of the congregation some of the managerial functions may well be best undertaken by a body delegated by the elders' and church meetings, since there are countless examples of people of great spiritual depth and pastoral sensitivity who are hopeless with finances and building maintenance – and, of course, vice versa! In fact, many URC churches have developed bodies similar to the 'managers' in the Presbyterian tradition in order to achieve greater efficiency and sensible divisions of labour.

By developing eldership to satisfy the cherished emphases of her constituent bodies the URC has simply repeated what has been happening in the Reformed family of churches ever since the Reformation. 'In the centuries following the Reformation, as the Reformed churches spread geographically around the world, they continued to regard the office of elder as essential to the well-being of the Church, but allowed for a remarkable flexibility in developing new patterns appropriate to new contexts.'[77] This means that there is ecumenical discussion about eldership within the Reformed family itself, as well as with non-Reformed churches. What are the issues that are most commonly being raised? We will end our section on eldership by noting five of them.

It is now widely acknowledged that lay people as well as ordained ministers are involved in the church's ministry. So a recent and important ecumenical document makes the following point: 'The word *ministry* in its broadest sense denotes the service to which the whole people of God is called, whether as individuals, as a local community, or as the universal Church.'[78] But disagreement appears when the question is asked about the propriety and validity of an ordained order of elders. The same ecumenical document, for example, nowhere even mentions the office of elder, and when it comes to ministry takes it for granted that the threefold pattern of bishop, priest and deacon is the norm. Given that some Reformed churches do not ordain their elders or lay ministers, preferring to install, induct or commission them, and also that the URC's ecumenical partners find our practice of ordaining elders at best problematical and at worst unacceptable, the question concerning the benefits and drawbacks of ordaining elders is raised. A summary of the cases for and against the ordination of elders is given in Box 1. It is taken from a discussion at a meeting of the URC Doctrine, Prayer and Worship Committee which concluded that the case for ordination is stronger than the case against. Worldwide consultation within the Reformed family has endorsed this judgement.[79]

---

[76]   See the 'Structure of the United Reformed Church', 2. (2) found in *The Manual* (London: URC).
[77]   *Eldership in the Reformed Churches Today*, p 7.
[78]   *Baptism, Eucharist and Ministry* (Geneva: World Council of Churches, 1982), p 21.
[79]   See *Eldership in the Reformed Churches Today*, pp 21–3.

Box I   **Ordination of Elders: The Case for and Against**

FOR   **AGAINST**

* It widens the nature of ministry and   * It devalues the word 'ordination' and the
  expresses the shared nature of ministry   reality behind the word

* It emphasises that the work of elder   * It creates a hierarchy within the membership
  is not simply a job or function

* It has been a valued tradition within   * It devalues other forms of service
  our church

* It links us with the World Reformed   * It confers power and authority in a way
  Church family   which is unhelpful.

* It reflects the importance of 'lay'   * It lacks unambiguous biblical warrant
  authority within the church

* It confers 'responsible' authority   * It places too high a demand on people
  (i.e. under God).

* It maintains 'democracy' in the   * It causes confusion in Local Ecumenical
  leadership of the church   Partnerships and among our ecumenical
                                                partners.

* It places the beginning of an
  Elders' ministry in an act of worship.

* It adds an extra dimension to the elders'
  meeting which is difficult to define.

A second question concerns length of service. Should eldership be for life, or for a fixed term? Historically, elders were ordained for life in the Presbyterian tradition, while deacons in Congregationalism were inducted to fixed terms of service. If a clear distinction is maintained between ordination and induction, a good working compromise is found by maintaining that ordination is for life but that induction is for a fixed period determined by the church meeting. When elders are then re-elected for a further period of service they are not re-ordained. Some churches have found it helpful to limit the number of consecutive periods of service open to elders, while many others, facing a declining leadership pool, have not been able to do this. But what are the benefits of this approach to the elders' length of service?

There are many benefits of a fixed and rotating term of service for elders. The responsibility of eldership is demanding, and a fixed period of service allows individuals relief from the duties of leadership at regular intervals. Fixed terms of service also make possible the participation in leadership of more persons, with a greater variety of gifts and experiences. In this way, too, elders can be chosen whose particular gifts match the particular needs of the community at a given time. Finally, the rotation of elders in and out of active service means that within both the body of elders in service and the community as a whole, there is greater mutual understanding (and hence partnership in ministry).[80]

Thirdly, we turn to the question of how elders are to be chosen. This takes on a significant degree of importance given the somewhat slipshod way in which elders are elected in some URC congregations. At all times, churches ought to be looking for people who possess the gifts and graces appropriate to eldership. The kind of questions which need asking of candidates include: Does this person possess the spiritual gifts for leading and building up the church? Is this a person of mature faith? (And the answer may be affirmative in the case of a seventeen year old, but negative in the case of a seventy year old!) Does this person command respect both inside and outside the congregation? And, perhaps most importantly: Does this person possess a 'call' to serve the church of Christ as an elder? All too often, however, the election of elders in URC congregations becomes little more than a frantic effort to fill vacant places on the eldership, or, equally damaging, a competitive scramble to gain preference.

> In regard to the process of election out of the congregation, it must be remembered that the character of such election ought not to be 'political' or 'democratic' in a divisive or factional way, but rather . . . a collective discerning, through the guidance of the Holy Spirit, of those persons whom God has called and equipped to serve in the leadership of the Christian community. It must also be remembered that individual elders serve not primarily as representatives of particular constituencies or interest groups within the community, but rather in such a way that, collectively, they reflect the diversity of the community and so may provide leadership for the whole community according to the will of God, under the rule and by the example of Christ, and through the guidance of the Holy Spirit.[81]

Fourthly, there is the question of the proper relation of elders to ministers of Word and Sacraments and their fellow church members. Concerning the former Lucas Vischer has a timely word:

> The relationship between pastors and elders can be characterized neither by the word equality nor by the word subordination. If the emphasis lies too heavily on equality, the unique character of each ministry is underrated. To put the office of the pastors before or even to place it above the office of the elders leads to the danger that the office of elder might become secondary or even dispensable. Pastors and elders are rather in a relationship of being assigned to one another. In the differences between their duties they are linked to each other in a cooperative community.[82]

And, of course, where there are no pastors, elders may sometimes have to take upon themselves functions usually assigned to ministers, e.g. being authorized by the District Council to preside at the Lord's Table. Meanwhile, the relation of elder to member is 'a matter of mutual respect and

---

[80]   Ibid., p 24.

[81]   Ibid., p 21.

[82]   Vischer, 'The Office of the Elders', p 83.

support' with the elders empowering the discipleship of the members and upholding the unity of the fellowship, while, through prayerful support, the members are to respect the eldership and look to it for guidance.[83]

Finally, there is the question of preparing elders for their ministries. Given the eldership's high calling and the complex set of responsibilities involved in it, it is a damning indictment of a congregation if it elects a person as an elder and then inducts them to office without any preparation. But that has not been uncommon. It ought to be standard practice for the wider church to prepare those who have been locally elected for their work, and perhaps the District Council should be expected to give concurrence to requests from local churches to ordain elders, thus enforcing rigorous standards of preparation? The content of the preparation should involve biblical and theological study, thorough grounding in the ethos and history of the URC, pastoral studies and any specialist training required to fulfil any particular role within the eldership. It should then be supported by continuing opportunities for in-service training. If the ministry of the elder is to be taken seriously by others, and if there is to be a basis for a genuinely collaborative partnership with ministers of Word and Sacraments, it is essential that eldership preparation be taken with absolute seriousness. Only then will elders be assured of respect and standing within and beyond their home church.

Ordination

Barth maintained his reputation as a controversial theologian when he addressed the question of ordination:

> All those baptised as Christians are eo ipso consecrated, ordained and dedicated to the ministry of the Church. They cannot be consecrated, ordained, or dedicated a second, third or fourth time without devaluation of their baptism. He who has ears to hear, let him hear (and not just in the Roman Catholic world)![84]

Those who object to the idea that the church's ministry belongs to certain individuals rather than the whole body of Christ can be forgiven for agreeing with that statement. Our belief that ministry is debased when set within the context of hierarchical orders may also cause us to conclude that a lot of vexed controversy would have been avoided if Barth's conclusions about ordination had been normative. The fact that they have not reminds us that the issue about ordination is not so simply resolved.

The New Testament makes it clear that early church practice involved certain church members being set apart to exercise distinctive ministries within the discipleship and vocation of the whole people of God. That setting apart is what we have come to know as ordination. It involves the invocation of the Holy Spirit and the laying on of hands (I Tim. 4: 14; 2 Tim. I: 6). Calvin argues that the practice of laying hands on those elected and set apart by the Church for representative ministry owes its origin to Jewish practices. It signifies that a person is being offered to God for service. Calvin tells us that 'it is useful for the dignity of the ministry to be commended to the people by this sort of sign', while the practice of the laying on of hands also serves as a warning to those ordained that they are not laws unto themselves, but 'bound in servitude to God and the church'.[85]

---

83   *Eldership in the Reformed Churches Today,* p 19.
84   Barth, *Church Dogmatics,* 4, 4, p 201.
85   Calvin, *Institutes,* 4,3,16.

The meaning of ordination is spelt out further in *Baptism, Eucharist and Ministry:*

> The act of ordination by those who are appointed for this ministry attests the bond of the Church with Jesus Christ and the apostolic witness, recalling that it is the risen Lord who is the true ordainer and bestows the gift. In ordaining, the Church, under the inspiration of the Holy Spirit, provides for the faithful proclamation of the Gospel and humble service in the name of Christ. The laying on of hands is the sign of the gift of the Spirit, rendering visible the fact that the ministry was instituted in the revelation accomplished in Christ, and reminding the Church to look to him as the source of its commission.[86]

When the statement goes on to develop a sacramental understanding of ordination, alarm bells start ringing for Reformed Christians who accept only two dominical sacraments and are very wary of understandings which underwrite the idea that ordination confers upon people a different kind of being or character. The Reformed heritage has avoided the notion that ordination effects an ontological change. Ontological views of ordination are believed to lead to what Calvin calls 'superstitious abuse'[87] – for example, practices which are based upon the mistaken understanding that certain individuals in the church can bestow upon others almost magical powers and special rights. But are views of ordination which simply understand it in terms of people being entrusted with new responsibilities able to do full justice to what is involved? Perhaps not, since, as every ordained minister knows, post ordination they find themselves in a new relationship with their church members. This change of relationship is based upon 'the burden and opportunity of new authority and responsibility', given to the ordained by the church.[88] A recent URC statement puts the matter like this:

> Public ministry is never completely described by listing the minister's tasks: the relationship to others created by a public recognition of the minister's calling to those tasks itself reshapes the being of the minister, as those who exercise such ministry can testify. The ordinand is therefore different from those not ordained because of the new relationship. Moreover the fact that ordination to a particular ministry is not repeated emphasises the definitiveness of the act.[89]

Ordination takes place in public worship, with representative figures from the wider church being present to emphasise the act's catholicity. Central to these services is the ratification of a person's call to ministry which has been tested before and during their preparation for that ministry, as well as the church's prayer that God in Christ and through the Spirit will empower the ordained to use and develop the gifts given them. Those ordained are 'a pointer to Christ' within the congregation, and the status conferred upon them is that of the 'servant of all, following the example of Christ himself'.[90] From a Reformed perspective, therefore, ordination grants authorisation and, theoretically at least, not power. This explains why in the URC there is not a single ministerial function which must be the sole preserve of the ordained.

---

[86]   *Baptism, Eucharist and Ministry,* para. 39
[87]   Calvin, *Institutes,* 4,3,16.
[88]   *Baptism, Eucharist and Ministry,* para. 44.
[89]   *Reports to the General Assembly of the URC 1995,* Appendix A, para 3,6.
[90]   Ibid., paras. 3.8 and 3.9.

The fact that ordination is understood as primarily a matter of authorisation explains why Congregationalists, Presbyterians and Churches of Christ have all had procedures which enabled those responsibilities entrusted to the ordained to be exercised by those not ordained on occasions. In each tradition the argument for the normal exercise of such responsibilities by the ordained is one of order in the sense of orderliness, not that they have exclusive powers or rights.[91]

As we have seen, the URC ordains people to two ministries, ministry of Word and Sacraments and eldership. But designated ministries within the URC go beyond these.

Other Recognised Ministries in the URC

The *Basis of Union* states that 'the United Reformed Church shall determine from time to time what other ministries may be required and which of them should be recognised as ministries in the whole church' (para 24). Three such ministries have gained widespread significance: lay preachers, church-related community workers (CRCWs) and local church leaders.

(i) On an average Sunday a large number of the worship services which take place in the URC are conducted by the unordained. In a denomination of small churches, it is not possible for ministers of Word and Sacrament always to lead the church's worship. Consequently, the denomination relies heavily on lay worship leaders. Some of these have been accredited and commissioned by the URC following a course of training, others are those a local congregation believes to be competent and appropriate, while yet others are lay preachers in other churches, e.g. Baptists or Methodists. The choice rests with the local church. This will seem strange to those churches which apply as strict rules to the leadership of worship and preaching as they do to presidency at Holy Communion.

As always in the URC the issue here is one of order rather than rights. But it is not immediately obvious why lay presidency should be considered exceptional, allowable in a situation 'where pastoral necessity so requires' (*Basis of Union*, para. 25) and then under the discipline of the District Council, but the regulation of lay preaching left as a matter of local church decision. This situation seems rather odd for at least two reasons. First, different standards of order and discipline are being applied to table and pulpit when at its best the Reformed traditions have tried to hold together preaching and the Lord's Supper. While there is a notable tradition of itinerant preachers which stretches back to the Evangelical Revival, the danger of the standard of worship leadership and preaching falling is an acute problem for those beleaguered congregations hard pressed to find people to conduct their worship. Secondly, it is often pointed out, usually by advocates of lay presidency at the Lord's table and not without a degree of logic, that more harm is likely to be done by an ill-prepared or incompetent preacher than by the lay president who carefully adheres to what is laid out in one of the services of Holy Communion found in the standard URC *Book of Services*. However, while this observation might add weight to the argument for lay presidency put forward by those who regard the matter in terms of rights, those who, in keeping with tradition, are rightly concerned with order might actually see it as a good reason to regulate the conduct of worship as well as presiding as, say, in Methodism. Be that as it may, the church has a responsibility to maintain the highest standards. While this points to the ongoing need for trained and commissioned lay

---

[91]   Ibid., para 3.9.

preachers, many congregations have found that people from within the congregation operating as a worship group under the supervision of a minister provides a good and very appropriate way of covering the vast majority of services when the minister with pastoral oversight is elsewhere.

(ii)   Christians speak passionately about the way in which the rationale for the church's mission should be taken from the gospel rather than from society.   But if only it were so simple! Problems occur as soon as we realise that we do not possess a gospel free from the trappings of a context. What the New Testament provides is a witness set in the cultural framework of the Judaeo-Hellenistic world.   If the gospel had first appeared in another context, presumably it would have taken a different shape. In one sense, therefore, it is impossible to separate faith from culture, even if a distinction between them opens up the possibility for a whole host of contextualizations of the gospel. And, of course, the church has not been slow to put secular insights and practices to work for the Kingdom's sake. Whether we consider post-Constantinian Christianity making use of the organisational patterns of Roman society in its polity and practice, or the quite recent way in which pastoral work has been shaped by psychotherapy and non-directive counselling, it needs recognizing that churches, for better or for worse, have borrowed secular ideas and practices. The ministry of CRCWs provides a further example of church practice being enlarged by essentially worldly theory and practice.

The ministry of church-related community work was recognised by the URC General Assembly in 1980. Several years later the Assembly resolved that in CRCWs 'the Lord Jesus Christ is giving particular gifts for a particular ministry and is calling such individuals to exercise them in an office which is duly recognised within His Church.'[92] Nevertheless, the CRCW programme has been so under-resourced that it has been slow to take off. Twenty years since the creation of CRCWs URC folk are largely oblivious to what is meant by the term CRCW, and few have grasped the potential for mission offered by community work principles:

> Community work is about bringing people together, helping them to identify their own problems and opportunities, mobilising people and resources for change, implementing a programme of action and evaluating and reforming the programme in the light of experience and reflection . . .   Community work is about people taking control of their own lives and stimulating social change.[93]

Such principles can enable the church to become involved in an activity which is 'a vehicle for affirming the Kingdom of God in human affairs'.[94]   Church-related community work is Kingdom orientated because 'it is committed to justice and peace and it is not afraid of costly involvement with people'; and it repeatedly challenges both 'an insular church and an uncaring society' as 'it attempts to find faith in and through action.'[95]   The potential of church-related community work as the churches re-establish themselves at the heart of the communities in which they are set is enormous.

However, the work of CRCWs has often been misunderstood. Sometimes they have been conceived as pseudo-ministers with all the confused expectations which that brings. It is interesting that quite a few of the early CRCWs eventually became ministers of Word and Sacraments. Secondly, CRCWs have been understood as those who are employed to do church-related

---

[92]   *Record of 1987 General Assembly* (London: URC, 1987).
[93]   From the pamphlet 'More about Church-related Community Work Ministry' (London: URC, 1990), p 2.
[94]   Ibid.
[95]   Ibid., p 3.

community work rather than those who are commissioned to enable local churches to engage effectively with their communities. But there are also exciting stories about the way in which community work principles and practitioners have enabled churches to become missiologically effective in urban priority areas, among ethnic minorities and with groups who have special needs, e.g. the elderly, single parent families and the unemployed. Most churches and ministers would benefit from the fresh understanding of being the church-in-the-community which community work theory provides. CRCWs are educated theologically as well as in community work practice.[96]

(iii) At the end of the twentieth century the URC found itself with acute problems in providing ministers for local churches. The effectiveness of spreading available resources ever more thinly over congregations in multi-church pastorates is hardly satisfactory, perhaps accelerating decline rather than initiating renewal. The focus switched in some URC Synods to providing churches with local church leaders (LCL) to fulfil some of the functions hitherto expected of ministers. An elder from a congregation is selected and, after preparation, set apart to serve that congregation. The District Council is involved in the selection process and the Synod concerned usually mounts the required programme of preparation. The General Assembly has given its approval to the creation of LCLs but until they have been in place for a number of years we will not know how their relationship with ordained ministers and their fellow elders will be finally defined. Those with a Churches of Christ background can be forgiven for thinking that the URC would have been spared the need to invent the LCL if it had taken up the concept of the Churches of Christ's Presiding Elder at the Unification in 1981. But sometimes ecclesiological short-sightedness demands the reinvention of the wheel!

Before we move on to consider church order in the URC, it is appropriate to pick up once again the issue of ordination. Why does the URC ordain ministers and elders but not lay preachers, CRCWs or LCLs? This question becomes acute when we remember that ordination grants authorization but does not confer power. While the question historically has been answered pragmatically and traditionally, the following statement offers a quite strong case for the ordination of the other recognised ministries that we have just been describing:

> . . . there is a sense in which ordination has been reserved for those ministries which most closely recall us to the foundational ministry of Christ himself. The ministries of Word and Sacraments are linked because each amplifies the significance of the other. The ministry of oversight and pastoral care is linked to Christ as king and shepherd. The diaconal ministry is linked to Christ as servant. A case could therefore be made for ordaining Church Related Community Workers as deacons. A case could also be made for ordaining lay preachers to the ministry of the Word if they were regular rather than occasional preachers, and in view of the link between Word and Sacraments it would seem logical to ordain those who regularly conduct worship to the ministry of Word and Sacraments, particularly if their ministry is exercised in several congregations.[97]

But it is one thing to establish a case; it is another matter to alter our practice – not least when the URC's practice of ordaining elders (never mind lay preachers, CRCWs and LCLs!) already raises ecumenical eyebrows. Our drive towards ecclesiological consensus with sister denominations undoubtedly will mean that the logic to extend ordination to yet further ministries will be carefully

---

[96] For a person to be accredited and commissioned as a CRCW they must possess both a recognized qualification in theology and one in community work.

[97] *Reports to General Assembly 1995,* Appendix A, para. 3.10.

scrutinized. It is certainly unlikely that the URC ever will act upon what some like Barth see as the even more persuasive case of doing away with the ordination of *some* by insisting that *all* are ordained for Christian ministry simply by being baptised and admitted to church membership!

Church Order in the URC

There are three basic approaches to church order: episcopalian, presbyterian and congregational. The URC has developed an order which seeks to marry together the latter two by holding in tension the centralised framework of presbyterianism with congregationalism's stress upon local church autonomy. Certain functions belong to the Church Meeting, District Council, Synod and General Assembly respectively, while the focus of each council's way of working is located in a conscious attempt to discern Christ's will for the church in respect of the tasks which belong to it.[98] While the attempt to hold together local church autonomy in certain matters with the decision making powers of regional and national councils sometimes creates confusion and disagreement, the URC believes that it is safer and wiser to attempt to run a church by seeking consensus at each level. Sceptics of the system, however, sometimes accuse the URC of having processes which are unnecessarily bureaucratic, inefficient and time consuming, when contemporary society requires instant responses, soundbyte clarity and knockdown answers. Perhaps the truth lies somewhere in the middle, with the Achilles' heel of URC order being the presence of two regional councils, *viz* district council and synod, when, given its size, one might perhaps suffice?

The role of the church meeting is enveloped in precious Congregationalist principles as all the church members gather to seek the mind of Christ for the conduct of their life, witness and mission. Those principles are threatened when few attend or the ethos of the meeting becomes merely that of a democratic assembly. And, perhaps, the church meeting's importance and value in the URC today is being undermined by just such things? It remains a moot point whether the importance of the church meeting can be maintained in a postmodern climate which eschews commitment and belonging. Of course, the church meeting gives expression to 'the priesthood of all believers' by placing the responsibility for a great deal of church government upon all the church members. It is completely misunderstood, though, when it is viewed in terms of the principles of democracy. Jenkins takes us to the heart of the matter:

> Not only does Congregationalism [and hence the URC] insist that a church should be a family, it also gives the church an organ of family responsibility. The church meeting is not a club of the likeminded, who frame the rules to suit their own convenience and according to whims of their own. It is a solemn assembly of the people of God in a particular place, who meet together before God, to consider together, in the light of the Word which is preached and on the basis of their sacramental fellowship with Christ, how they may discern and obey the Lord's will for themselves as His people in that place.[99]

The objective in church meeting is reaching a consensus concerning the mind of Christ rather than gaining consent for actions based upon a show of hands and a majority vote.

---

[98]   For further details about the respective functions of the councils of the URC see *The Manual* B1–B16.

[99]   Daniel Jenkins, *Congregationalism: A Reinstatement* (London: Faber and Faber, 1954), pp 46–47.

To be sure, many of our experiences of church meeting undermine the theory. When the discussion about the church guttering or heating system is in full flow, it is difficult to envisage, let alone believe, that the church meeting is a means of grace. And, yet, it is precisely when God's visible saints meet together to seek God's will for them in their mission that the church comes alive. This was as true for the young churches of the New Testament period as it was for the Puritans from whom so much of the English Reformed ethos flows. And, as the Latin American base-communities recently have shown us, it is still true today. Those who find something fundamentally new in Latin American liberation theology's way of being church have not taken seriously the Congregational principle of gathering together to contextualise the gospel and form the saints for witness and service. If we are to protect the church from the individualism of our era, or the totalitarian tendencies of wider church councils, be they national or regional, the URC will be wise to rediscover God's gift of the local church meeting.

Whether the emphasis is upon the church meeting or the wider councils of the church, the constituent traditions of the URC understand oversight (*episcope*) in a conciliar fashion, with the result that personal episcope has been avoided unless it has been set within a conciliar context. Forsyth's objection to sacerdotal views of ministry was matched by his opposition to the monarchical episcopal system he saw in Roman Catholic and Anglican churches. He describes both episcopacy and priesthood as mere historic growths which are not part of the *esse* of the church. This did not mean, however, that Forsyth denied that there is a sacerdotal emphasis in ministry, or that episcopacy is 'a good polity among others'.[100] His argument was with a system which linked together the priestly and administrative functions of leadership in a ministerial order which then was regarded as a constitutive dimension of the church. No one particular form of church order can ever be said to be of the *esse* of the church. We do not need bishops or priests for our salvation, but rather we must seek that faith which is kindled when God graciously meets us through the Word and Sacraments of the gathered church, the priesthood of all believers.

Jenkins argues that episcopacy is a doctrine which has gained 'immense and portentous significance' in the life of Christianity but without 'serious theological justification'.[101] He admits that it testifies to 'the need for unity and universality in the Church of Christ', but goes on to argue that 'the presence of the ministry in the Church should be a mark of its catholicity and even a symbol of its unity'.[102] This theology clearly requires a very high view of ministry. However, with the Reformed ethos in general, Jenkins objects to the idea that 'the Word and sacraments depend on a ministry which exists prior to them', namely the ministry of bishops, and he maintains instead that all ministry 'depends upon the Word and sacraments for its authority'.[103] A second way in which bishops are said to help us is that they remind us of the apostolic succession. Jenkins accepts the importance of maintaining 'the living bond between ourselves and the apostolic community.[104] The idea that apostolicity is a criterion to judge the church's authenticity is just as much a part of the Reformed ethos as it is in episcopally ordered denominations. However, for the Reformed Christian, true succession is found in 'the whole fellowship of the Church' and 'only secondarily' in 'the ministry'.[105]

---

[100]   Forsyth, *Rome, Reform and Reaction: Four Lectures on the Religious Situation* (London: Hodder and Stoughton, 1899), p 97.

[101]   Jenkins, *The Gift of Ministry*, p 49.

[102]   Ibid., p 50.

[103]   Ibid.

[104]   Ibid., p 51.

[105]   Ibid.

Forsyth put it like this:

> The Apostolic succession has no meaning except as the Evangelical succession. It does not mean, at the one extreme, a historic line of valid ordinations unbroken from the Apostles to the last curate. Nor, at the other end, does it mean merely cultivating the spirit of the Apostles, or their precepts for sanctification. But it is the succession of those who experience and preach the Apostolic Gospel of a regenerating redemption.[106]

The members of the URC ought to have no fundamental problems with the idea of personal episcopacy. The issue for them ought not to be: Do we want personal episcopacy? but rather: What kind of personal episcopacy ought we to have? This is borne out by the fact that the General Assembly's acceptance of the proposals of the Churches' Council for Covenanting in 1981 involved a commitment to embrace the ministry of bishops. However, any such agreement would surely be conditional upon two things. First, the Reformed Christian would want to make it absolutely clear that the episcopate as we have come to know it was not a feature of ecclesiastical life in New Testament times. To insist upon episcopacy as it has developed being a precondition for Christian unity runs close to unchurching all the Christian communities of the first century.[107] It is much more satisfactory to ask the question: What kind of episcopacy does today's ecumenical church require? – always assuming, of course, that certain received patterns of personal episcopacy may be in urgent need of reform. This leads to the second condition which would have to be met if, in a united Church, the URC was to take bishops into its system. There would have to be disestablishment of the Church of England and, thereby, a transfer from the state to the church of the church's ruling authority, with bishops being appointed by the church and becoming the servants of a conciliar rather than monarchical church structure.[108]

There is no authoritative warrant for the style of bishops which has emerged from Patristic times onwards. As Forsyth tells us:

> The original constitution of the Church, whatever it was, was not monarchical. It was corporative; until Cyprianism; and until the black (sic) years when first Constantine and then Charlemagne made it a State Church, and turned its officers into civil servants and its government to a bureaucracy.[109]

And, not surprisingly, Forsyth sees clearly the dangers of an alliance between church and state which could lead to the church's ministry being under state control. He believes that the 'spiritual necessity' in the Reformation will one day require disestablishment, if the Reformation is ever to be considered complete: 'The battle with the world for a free Gospel can only be won by a free Church;

---

[106]   Forsyth, *Lectures on the Church and Sacraments*, p 102.

[107]   The common assumption that the true church must possess a threefold order of ministry: bishop, priest and deacon, is fallacious for similar reasons. See Alan P F Sell, *A Reformed Evangelical Catholic Theology: The Contribution of the World Alliance of Reformed Churches 1875–1982* (Grand Rapids, Michigan: William B Eerdmanns Publishing Company, 1991), p 173.

[108]   Martin H Cressey reminds us of an important ecumenical development when he speaks of 'the fresh approach to understanding apostolic succession, in terms of a corporate succession of the whole church, expressed and focussed, but neither guaranteed nor exhausted, by the succession in the Episcopal sees' ['Three Games in a Long Ecumenical Set' in Peter C Bouteneff and Alan D Falconer, eds., *Episkopé and Episcopacy and the Quest for Visible Unity* (Geneva: WCC, 1999), p 124]. A marriage of the corporate and personal dimensions of *episkopé* such as this has much to commend it from a Reformed perspective.

[109]   Forsyth, *Lectures on the Church and Sacraments*, p 72.

and a free Church is the inevitable effect of a free Gospel, of the freedom of the spiritual power.'[110] Given the history of the English Reformation, the importance of designating the URC with the title 'Free Church' ought not to be gainsaid. Bernard Lord Manning once concluded that, 'It is sometimes hard for a Free Churchman to be sure whether what he dissents from in England is Establishment or Episcopacy.'[111] Equally, it is a matter of conjecture how much of the suspicion about personal episcopacy abroad in the URC is due to real matters of principle – Does the URC not have people already who exercise personal episcopacy? – rather than to an objection to episcopal patterns which have been encountered in the Roman Catholic church and the Established Church in England.

---

[110]   Forsyth, *Rome, Reform and Reaction*, pp 23–4.
[111]   Manning, *Essays in Orthodox Dissent*, p 207.

CHAPTER 17

Worship, Spirituality and Discipline

THE WHOLE of life is to be treated as an offering of obedience and service to God. The Creator, Redeemer and Sanctifier is deserving of our total commitment; God's graciousness towards us has set us free from ourselves and for others. The enacted parable of God's liberation found in Jesus' death and resurrection has become both the basis and driving force for our Christian discipleship. God's holy love flowing from the cross, therefore, is absolutely central to the Reformed way of living. As Isaac Watts reminds us, God's grace demands our complete allegiance:

> Were the whole realm of nature mine,
> That were a present far too small;
> Love so amazing, so divine,
> Demands my soul, my life, my all.

And the gospel's demands are to be met by faithfulness in both private and public worship and rigorous attention being given to leading a holy life. We turn our attention now to some key elements in the offering of 'my soul, my life, my all': corporate worship, personal devotion and spirituality, and discipline.

Worship

Horton Davies defines worship broadly but helpfully as 'the corporate offering of thought, emotion, and decision-making as a response of the Christian churches to the divine saga of Christ and His followers throughout history'.[1] Davies not only reminds us that our worship is a response to God's graciousness and love, but he also betrays his Congregational background in asserting that the corporate decision-making of 'the visible saints' is just as much part of our worship as the preaching of the Word (the audible Word) and the administration of the sacraments (the visible Word). It is salutary to be reminded of worship's multi-faceted nature. Indeed, whenever mind or heart or will is emphasised at the expense of one or the other of its partners, our worship degenerates respectively into mere intellectualism or emotionalism or activism.

Reformed worship originated at various centres in continental Europe during the sixteenth century, but there were sufficient common characteristics in the liturgical life of Zurich, Strasbourg, Basle, Bern and Geneva for people very soon to speak about a single tradition, even if it clearly had several variants. Many of those characteristics still underpin the worshipping life of our contemporary

---

[1] Horton Davies, *Worship and Theology in England: Vol 1 From Cranmer to Hooker 1534–1603* (Princeton University Press, 1970), p xv. Davies prepared for Christian ministry at Yorkshire United College, Bradford, but he has exercised his teaching ministry largely in the U.S.A. and primarily at Princeton University.

Reformed churches. But, before we move on to outline them, it is important to further emphasize the way in which liturgy and work, prayer and practice, are integrated in worship. The roots of this 'seven whole days not one in seven' approach to worship can be found in Puritan times which, according to Gordon Wakefield, revealed 'a common spirituality, founded on personal encounter with the living God, through Scripture and also personal experience of the Holy Spirit, not always without agonising struggles, which governed style of life and political attitudes'.[2] It is hardly surprising that the most customary word which Reformed churches use to describe their acts of worship is 'service' since the idea that we live to serve God through our daily lives and meet Christ as we serve our neighbour reminds us that vocation is part of worship. The common task involves working for God's glory and the benefit of humankind; it is a response to God's gracious promises and not a means of gaining them. Few in our time have seen the link between worship and vocation as clearly as George MacLeod, the founder of the Iona Community. MacLeod encouraged the Iona Community to place worship at the heart of its life, since out of it flows the service of men and women, evangelism and mission. The bread broken at the Lord's Table is for the world and not simply the church.

Over the years the common characteristics of the early Reformed churches' worship have been added to and, in some instances, departed from as churches have responded to various historical and ecumenical pressures. Davies, therefore, has noted that contemporary Free Churches display worship patterns which owe much to the Reformed heritage rooted in the Puritan and Pietist traditions, but also betray more Catholic elements as liturgical forms of worship have been adopted and a deeper appreciation of the sacraments has become evident. As we now move on to outline eight principal features of worship within the URC, we will be wise to remember that the URC believes that its *Basis of Union* embodies 'the essential notes of the Church Catholic and Reformed'.[3] This in turn involves the recognition that at certain times we have lost our sense of Catholicity in our thorough attempts to be seen to be Reformed. The Reformation brought losses as well as gains!

1.   The Bible

Our discussion of biblical authority highlighted the diverse ways in which Reformed theologians have conceived the importance of Scripture, as well as pointed to the limitations imposed upon the use of the Bible by modern critical scholarship, and to the fact that the Bible no longer speaks to our age with the authority it once commanded. Our Puritan forebears turned their backs on Medieval church splendour, favouring the language and imagery of the Bible. Human creations in wood and stone made way for God's word, as worship's form and content were both radically shaped by Scripture. Orders of service were modelled on Biblical accounts of early Christian worship; the Sermon's centrality was sanctioned by the Bible; and the sacraments were reduced from the medieval seven to the dominical two, because the Bible reported only Baptism and the Lord's Supper as being instituted by Jesus. Meanwhile, the content of Puritan worship had at its centre the reading of extensive portions of the Bible as well as lengthy expositions of it through sermons. We cannot help but marvel at the Puritan confidence in being able to contrast the uncertainties and ambiguities of every day life with the clear authority of the Bible.

---

[2]   Gordon Wakefield, *An Outline of Christian Worship* (Edinburgh: T & T Clark, 1998), p 105.
[3]   *Basis of Union*, Schedule D, found in Thompson, *Stating the Gospel*, p 262.

We may no longer totally share that Puritan confidence but the Bible still plays a central role in Reformed worship. Although much shorter, sermons still tend to be based upon the interpretation and application of Biblical passages which have been read in the service. Many churches have adopted lectionaries, and, thereby, they have encouraged exegetical sermons. Further advantages of grounding Reformed worship upon a lectionary are apparent. First, the discipline of the lectionary enables a large amount of biblical material to be used in the course of a year's public worship. This, in turn, secondly, helps a congregation to gain a wider appreciation of the Christian year as the old Reformed practice of continuous reading of biblical books in worship gives way to the selection of passages appropriate for particular Sundays. And, thirdly, lectionaries take the decision about what is to be read in worship away from the whims and fancies of preachers. Many preachers find the discipline of having to preach from texts which have been 'given', rather than personally chosen, a helpful device which prevents them returning *ad nauseam* to pet themes and hobby-horses. While some will agree with James F White's view that 'the rise of the lectionary has probably been the most significant change [in Reformed Worship] in the last two decades',[4] not all will share his enthusiasm for lectionaries. There is a tendency for lectionary passages to be so short that they hardly do justice to their contexts, thus giving rise to a diminished appreciation of Scripture. Most lectionaries, of course, were designed for services where the main emphasis is on the proclamation of the Word through the celebration of the Eucharist rather than preaching. Not surprisingly, therefore, the readings were kept short to ensure worship remained within a reasonable time span. Granted that more recent lectionaries have tended to lengthen the readings, one still suspects, with Gordon Wakefield, that the tendency of lectionary compilers is to pay too much attention to 'half-truths about attention span', as well as to 'a feeling that long lections are due to the desire of clergy and readers to hear their own voices'.[5]

Use of lectionaries in Reformed worship might also have led to two other unfortunate results. My experience of listening to sermons suggests that the modern obsession preachers have with using all the lections as the basis for their pulpit craft often does violence to the passages concerned and usually produces sermons of quite unmemorable generalities. It is debatable whether the standard of Reformed preaching has gone down in recent years, but it is proven that it is hard enough for the preacher to work from one passage let alone focus on three! A second unfortunate result of the use of lectionaries is that they tend to remove Old Testament readings from our worship. When churches that have only two biblical lessons in their worship are faced with dropping a lection it seems standard practice for them to choose the Gospel and Epistle readings from the lectionary and leave out the Old Testament lection. Those who choose the readings for worship need to beware of playing into the hands of the church's Marcionite tendencies!

A basic feature of Reformed worship from the Puritan period and into the Victorian age was the support which was given to public worship by the spiritual discipline of church members in their homes. This was heavily influenced by the attention devoted to biblical study. Such attention is not evident today with the result that preachers can assume very little biblical and theological knowledge from their congregations. A situation lamented by Forsyth has got worse rather than better:

---

4   James F White, *Protestant Worship: Traditions in Transition* (Louisville, Kentucky: Westminster/ John Knox Press. 1989), p 77.
5   Wakefield, *An Outline of Christian Worship*, p 160.

. . . we must use our Bible much more than we do . . . Most people make so little personal use of the Bible that they do not know if an interesting preacher is preaching the Gospel or not. The real strength of a Church is not the amount of its work but the quality of its faith. One man who truly knows his Bible is worth more to a Church's real strength than a crowd of workers who do not . . . Our poverty is not in the amount of our work, but in the quality of our religion.[6]

It is no coincidence that periods of great renewal in the church's life have taken place when people have rediscovered the Bible's significance and relevance for their lives. At a time of rampant decline in Western Christianity it is tempting to look to ministers to turn things round. But this temptation must be resisted – unless, that is, ministers point us to what is truly required, namely, a renewed acquaintance with the gospel. And that, in turn, as Forsyth makes very clear, involves putting the Bible back into the centre of congregational life:

It is not a ministry we need but a Gospel which makes both ministry and Church. The Church will not furnish the ministers the age requires unless it provide them with a Gospel which they will never get from the age, but only from the Bible for the age. But it is from a Bible searched by regenerate men for a Gospel, and not exploited for sermons by preachers anxious to succeed with the public.[7]

A more challenging statement about the importance of the Bible for our contemporary witness is difficult to conceive.

2.   Freedom and Diversity

A few years ago I found myself in two widely contrasting URC congregations on consecutive Sunday mornings. The first congregation followed a fixed liturgy with congregational responses. The minister and gowned choir processed into the sanctuary as the Bible was taken to the lectern and symbolically opened. Candles adorned a communion table which was centrally placed, flanked by a pulpit and lectern. The hymnody was four-square, the preaching demanding and the Lord's Supper was administered with great reverence and dignity. A friend observed that this church's worship was 'higher' than that found in many Anglican churches. The worship on display in the second URC congregation was totally different, seemingly owing much to the Pentecostalist emphases found in the Charismatic Renewal Movement. Central was neither pulpit nor table, but a music group who led the singing of choruses at the start of worship and then accompanied the hymns in a service which focused upon a lengthy didactic sermon that stayed close to a New Testament passage which had been read previously. A long period of prayer after the sermon involved the laying on of hands for healing, while exorcism was offered after the service. The worship was noteworthy for its relaxed style and the high level of congregational participation. Gowns and dog-collars had made way for jeans and sweaters, while the age-range of the congregation made a forty year old feel ancient!

Those two examples remind us of the diversity of worship within the contemporary URC. This diversity has become more pronounced as ecumenical commitments have led to an increased cross-fertilization of traditions within our churches.[8]   As we have learned from other churches,

---

6   Forsyth, *Lectures on the Church and Sacraments*, pp 6–7.

7   Ibid., p 18.

8   The diversity of worship practice in the URC is only partially reflected in the wide range of material found in the URC's hymnbook, *Rejoice and Sing*.

the Reformed have become more Catholic; meanwhile, we have not been afraid to take on board resources and styles which have originated in our sister churches around the world, religious communities like those at Iona and Taizé, and the Charismatic Renewal Movement. The result is the difficulty we now face when we have to describe Reformed worship to others. Unlike other traditions, we cannot in theory or practice point to one rite which is typical of our ethos. Indeed, even before the diversity of our worship patterns was increased by our ecumenical engagements, there never was a time when we could define ourselves by reference to one fixed liturgy.

Reformed worship developed in England against the backcloth of the Dissenters' objection to having their worship determined by what was laid down in the Prayer Book. Davies has captured beautifully what he calls 'the gravamen of the Puritan objection':

> . . . a liturgy can become exceedingly formal, mechanical, and artificial. It can project an idea of God as a remote and utterly transcendent sovereign 'King of Kings and Lord of Lords' and not 'the God and Father of our Lord Jesus Christ'. Its spirit can be exceedingly sober, dignified, even stuffy. It can be singularly lacking in adoration and joy. Familiarity can breed contempt or indifference for its repetitiousness. Above all, the incantatory magic of the words of the Prayer Book and the medieval beauty of the setting may transform worship into a reverie rather than prepare the Christian for a re-entry into life transformed into a deeper commitment to serve God and humanity.[9]

Although fixed liturgies have a tendency to force worship into stereotypes, and often lead to abject staleness, the better ones nevertheless have the power to become so much part of a worshipper's life that well-known phrases and expressions sustain them in the warp and woof of daily life. Some people have found that Cranmer's *Book of Common Prayer* serves such a purpose when more modern liturgies fail them. But, perhaps, their experience is more an acknowledgement of Cranmer's genius, than an argument for one fixed liturgy?

People have different worship needs, largely dependent upon the context in which they find themselves. We are best served by a variety of worship forms which we can use where appropriate, and even when fixed liturgies are offered us, the Reformed spirit will not allow them to be prescribed. This principle was underlined by John Huxtable in the Preface to the 1980 *A Book of Services*:

> . . . the traditions which came together to form the United Reformed Church cherished freedom in worship. The publication of this book does not impugn that freedom. The orders found here are not prescribed. It is not expected that they will be used in our churches to the exclusion of others. Yet we believe most of these services reflect the ethos of our Church and of its inherited traditions.[10]

The key need is to find a healthy tension between, on the one hand, order and form, and, on the other hand, freedom. As Davies has said: 'Form needs freedom to keep it fresh, and freedom needs form to prevent it from turning to irresponsible chaos.'[11] And it is to the URC's credit that it has produced people who have played an outstanding part in the production of liturgical resources for use in our churches.

---

[9]   Horton Davies, *Worship and Theology in England: Vol II From Andrewes to Baxter and Fox 1603–1690* (Princeton: Princeton University Press, 1975), p 529.

[10]   *A Book of Services* (Edinburgh: The Saint Andrew Press, 1980), p 7.

[11]   Davies, *Worship and Theology: Vol 1 From Cranmer to Hooker 1534–1603*, p 75.

3.   Simplicity

Reformed theology is rooted in an acknowledgement that at every moment people stand in God's presence. Their proper response is to confess their sin, accept God's pardon and go forward to live in loving service to God and their neighbours. The divine glory and purposes are of fundamental importance, more important in fact than our salvation.   According to Reformed understanding religion does not simply exist to satisfy our needs or to give meaning and purpose to our lives; it is rather primarily the means by which we can acknowledge, praise and serve the Triune God. We are to act in confidence that life is at the disposal of One who is gracious and just.

Armed with the doctrine of the sovereignty of God, Reformed Christians quickly took a polemical stance against idolatry. Since people ought not to claim too much for themselves, all exalted claims about human achievement were questioned by the Reformers in a quite iconoclastic manner, while they developed a deep resistance to attempts to get control of God by pinning the infinite and indeterminate God down to the realm of the finite and determinate. As a result, they would have nothing to do with images, or with those who made overtly high claims for the church. Then, fuelled by their doctrine of justification by faith through God's grace, the Reformers found it difficult to admit to any practice which might compromise their belief in the sole mediatorship of Christ. The offering of prayers and devotion to the Virgin Mary and the Saints, therefore, are absent from Reformed worship.

Any ceremony or splendour which might get in the way of the worshipper's proper relationship with God was opposed by the early Protestants. Aside from the issue of idolatry, of course, they were not rich enough to build expensive church buildings or to commission high class art. And, in any case, the church's money was deemed to be better spent on the poor. So, as Davies puts it, 'Protestants rejoiced in a simplification of worship and a functionalism which austerity in aesthetics aided.'[12] The Puritan meeting house, with its scrubbed wooden seats and furnishings, clear glass windows and bare white walls, places architecturally central what was at the heart of Puritan liturgical understanding, namely, the audible and visible Word. The streamlining of worship in the direction of greater simplicity, of course, was a direct reaction to the pomp and ceremony of medieval worship. But the Reformers believed that the direction they took reflected the early church practice recorded in the New Testament. Their aim was to rescue Word and Sacraments from the trappings of aesthetic glory and thereby place worshippers before an infinite God's judgement and grace.

The Reformers differed as to how far the reformation in worship should be taken. Zwingli, for example, would not allow music in the Zurich congregation's worshipping life, while Calvin, on the other hand, pioneered the singing of metrical psalms in Geneva. And the two Reformers also had a different basic outlook on the ability of the finite to convey the infinite. Zwingli's dualism between nature and spirit led him to a different sacramental understanding from that of Calvin, who possessed a rich awareness of the way in which God uses material things in order to convey spiritual things. But whatever differences between Zurich and Geneva emerged, both congregations agreed on purging images from their worship. Ornate altars gave way to simple tables around which church members sat for the Lord's Supper, while the prominence of the pulpit reflected the importance Reformed churches placed upon preaching. The effect was that everything done in worship could be seen and heard by all the congregation. Clerical vestments were also abandoned. The Puritans, for example, opposed the wearing of vestments on at least three grounds: (1) It impinges on an

---

[12]   Ibid., p 355.

individual's Christian liberty to enforce the wearing of vestments; (2) it produces an unhelpful identity with the Roman Catholic Church when vestments are worn; and (3) the wearing of vestments is a symbol of the pomp and ceremony which the Puritans so much wanted to avoid.

It is all too easy, though, for the Reformed to have a blind-spot when it comes to the Reformation's negative features. Wakefield reminds us that:

> It is not difficult to see the Reformation as a movement as much political as religious, violently iconoclastic, persecutory, robbing the common people of devotions which were dear to them and sustained their lives in a harsh world, and as bitterly divided within itself, between radicals and the more conservative and not least in liturgy and the understanding of Christ's presence in the Sacrament.[13]

Davies likewise remarks that the move towards simplicity in worship 'must have left many vacant spaces in the affections of the simple believers, as if they had lost their friends.'[14] Few today will look favourably upon a process which saw the destruction of so many art treasures and learned writings in an almost philistine attempt to obey the second injunction of the Ten Commandments. Meanwhile, many in the URC are not far away from a less worthy feature of Puritanism, namely, a 'colour-blind iconoclasm' which has 'few links with tradition or taste.'[15] Or has this writer been going to all the wrong churches?

The idea that the Reformed ethos is against the arts will hardly stand up to scrutiny when one remembers that striving for purity and simplicity in worship does not ultimately depend upon a dislike of art. Even Puritans were not haters of art; they were removers of superstition and idolatry from worship: 'It was not that the Puritans disliked art; it was simply that they loved religion more.'[16] By the time of the twentieth century, a Gothic tradition of church architecture was favoured by Free Churches, stained-glass windows reappeared, organs were installed, gowned choirs were found singing introits, anthems and oratorios and clerical dress was common place. Some of the larger chapels were little short of being local centres for the performing arts! As ecumenical involvement has further increased, and a greater appreciation of aesthetic values has been rekindled in Reformed understanding, practices once condemned as mere popery are now finding a place in many congregations, where colourful banners often adorn the church walls, candles are presented to parents at their children's baptism, and ministers are bedecked in every kind of clerical garb imaginable. When once it could be said of a Dissenting church that it did not possess a tradition of clerical dress, the URC now seems to support *every* tradition of clerical dress! In worship as well as theology, the URC is now both Catholic and Reformed.

At its best the Reformed ethos strives for worship patterns which are simple but not simplistic. Words and music constitute our offering to God and God is worthy of the best, whatever the genre or style. We should search for order and shape but not at the expense of that spontaneity, intimacy and warmth which often is absent from our services. We place central our need to listen for God's Word which addresses us, but perhaps, following other church traditions, we need to cultivate further the contemplative discipline? And, perhaps most of all, we must beware of our focus upon Word making us over-reliant on words. Calvin placed great importance upon signs and

---

13   Wakefield, *An Outline of Christian Worship,* p 70.
14   Davies, *Worship and Theology: Vol 1 From Cranmer to Hooker 1534–1603,* p 21.
15   Horton Davies, *Worship and Theology in England: Vol II From Andrews to Baxter and Fox 1603–1690,* p 207.
16   Ibid., p 204.

symbols as the vehicles God uses to meet us graciously. Hence the words of a sermon, or the bread and wine at the Lord's Table, *become* for us a means of grace through the Spirit's work. But Calvin's heirs have often confused words with Word. They have also belittled sacraments by sloppy practice. We have often become a 'wordy' church which needs to recover the importance of speaking to the heart as well as to the head. And, perhaps, our seeming fear of silence in worship might be overcome if we engaged with the great contemplative spiritual traditions that have graced the Christian churches, not least our sisters and brothers in Dissent, the Society of Friends?

4.   The Centrality of Preaching

The prominence of the pulpit in Reformed church architecture testifies to the important role which preaching plays in our ethos. In the URC, the event at which a minister candidates for a pastorate further underlies this fact: the minister goes to *preach* with a view. The terminology almost suggests that a minister's work is simply the preaching office, while in Free Church traditions the term 'preacher' is often interchangeable with the term 'minister'.

Preaching in the Reformed ethos aims to equip the 'gathered saints' for their Christian vocation. The sermon may be a means of theological education, or guide for people on their spiritual journey, but it is primarily concerned with helping people to be loyal and devout Christians. Preaching therefore is a very practical matter and may be regarded as *kerygmatic* in the widest sense, engaging a person's mind, heart and will. The pattern was established by Calvin in Geneva. White remarks that 'so great was the imperative to teach that each service [in Calvin's church] contains a condensed course in theology and ethics', such that 'this became a lasting characteristic of Reformed worship, contributing to its overwhelmingly cerebral character'.[17] Indeed, Reformed worship is perhaps the most intellectually demanding type of worship in the Western church. The fact that this contributes to its great strength as well as its major weakness is put rather well in Davies's description of nineteenth century Congregational worship:

> . . . Congregational worship lives in the intellect rather than in the heart. Its sobriety and calm
> make it inevitably passionless. It is a type of worship for the sturdy intelligensia, not for the
> multitudes who are unreflective, or trembling in spirit; nor indeed is it suitable even for those
> who feel deeply as well as reason profoundly.[18]

Charismatic Renewal's recent influence has shown the need for worship patterns which address the heart as well as the mind, people's feelings as well as their belief systems. There is no virtue in worship which is theologically rigorous if it leaves people spiritually arid.

At its best, however, Reformed preaching has many virtues. First, in keeping with the Reformed emphasis on the Bible, it represents an attempt to expound the Bible for each age. This involves exegesis, interpretation and application. It presupposes that 'in the ministry of the Word . . . God makes known in each age his saving love, his will for his people and his purpose for the world'.[19] Secondly, the Reformed preacher aims for a plain style and seeks to communicate in a way which is understandable to ordinary folk. Matters of great intellectual importance and penetrating insight

---

[17]   White, *Protestant Worship: Traditions in Transition,* p 65.

[18]   Horton Davies, *Worship and Theology in England: Vol IV From Newman to Martineau* (Princeton: Princeton University Press, 1962), p 216.

[19]   *Basis of Union,* para., 7,13 found in Thompson, *Stating the Gospel,* p 251.

need neither be linguistically incomprehensible nor theologically obtuse. Thirdly, good preaching in the Reformed way demands the preacher's urgent sincerity. Preachers can only convey a message they already have heard and to which they have responded. They preach first to themselves and thereafter to their congregations. Fourthly, Reformed preaching is courageous and prophetic as it tackles difficult issues, addresses the faults and failings of individuals and communities, as well as confronting the evils abroad in society. From a Reformed standpoint, it is difficult to contemplate what 'popular' preaching might be since the gospel says: No! as well as: Yes! – and usually at one and the same time. Fifthly, Reformed preaching is rooted in pastoral experience. As the pastor moves among the congregation, the preacher's agenda is born and the Word is received for the situation.

The importance attached to preaching in many URC congregations has recently reduced as people have come to question the role of lengthy orations in a soundbyte, mainly visual culture. If it is true that the standard of preaching has gone down, we must hope that the more skilful pulpit practitioners have provided others with good models to follow. It is not the case that people are fed up with preaching, since quite lengthy sermons figure in many growing and flourishing churches. But folk *are* fed up with sermons which tell them more about the preacher's prejudices than present a coherent and credible pattern of Christianity for their age. Preaching is an exacting business which many busy ministers are prone to skimp in order to meet the competing demands placed upon them, but people still welcome the well crafted sermon which is carefully delivered. And, as what Davies describes as 'the tyranny of the single ministerial voice' is overcome by more than the minister taking a lead in worship, maybe both ordained and lay will put their minds to developing the art of good preaching.[20]

Preaching's late nineteenth century heyday in the Free Churches is long gone, as it would seem is the day of great orators. During this period there was always a danger that the sermon so dominated the service that all that surrounded it became inconsequential. It might not be such a great loss, then, that we no longer have preachers of such drawing power that their oratory became a substitute for genuine worship. As Davies has noted about the nineteenth century, '. . . preaching removed from the context of a sacred sanctuary and a dedicated people of God and isolated from its necessary connection with the Sacrament was bound to degenerate into the cultivation of tricks and stunts to keep the shallow interested.'[21] Now that the Lord's Table has taken its proper place 'alongside' the pulpit, and no longer either 'above' or 'beneath it', we might hope that, whatever tendencies towards subjectivity occur in preaching, we may have a balanced worship pattern through inclusion of the objectiveness of the Sacrament.

5. The Lord's Table

It is not advisable to base one's view of the importance of sacraments in the Reformed ethos upon an experience of one small part of it. What do they of Church know who only their own congregation know? Those URC congregations who gather round the Lord's Table weekly might be thought to hold the sacrament in higher esteem than, say, a sister church which meets for Holy Communion monthly or quarterly. But anyone who has been present at a quarterly communion service in the Presbyterian tradition will know that infrequency of celebration actually can add to the high status Holy Communion should have in worship. Frequency, conversely, can undermine

20   Davies, *Worship and Theology in England: Vol II From Andrews to Baxter and Fox 1603–1690*, p 534.
21   Davies, *Worship and Theology in England: Vol IV From Newman to Martineau 1850–1900*, p 348.

importance, as well as lead to sloppy practice. It is still the case, however, that in some URC churches the sacrament possesses a low profile, thus lending credence to the view that Reformed churches allow the pulpit to take precedence over the table.

Calvin, of course, advocated a weekly celebration of the Lord's Supper. The congregation gathered around a table set in the midst of the sanctuary. While the Roman Mass tended to be a distant spectacle which brought the worshippers to their knees in adoration, but did not necessarily involve them taking the elements, the Genevan table became the place around which sinners gathered to feed on Christ with thanksgiving. And the English Puritans continued to follow this pattern. Later in the Dissenting tradition, divines like Watts and Doddridge maintained liturgical patterns which clearly showed that the Lord's table had a prominent place. Holy Communion was not an optional extra, tagged on at the end of a preaching service for the dedicated élite; rather it was the climax of the service and the event which, along with preaching, conveyed spiritual nourishment.

By the nineteenth century, however, the high Calvinist sacramental doctrine gave way to a pattern of liberal memorialism which took its lead from the followers of Zwingli. The result was a devaluing of the sacrament in many Free Churches, as the pulpit came to tower above the table. Why did the congregations of this period favour memorialism?[22] First, the prevailing theology tended to affirm God's immanence in the world at the expense of God's transcendence. This favoured an understanding of the Lord's Supper which was rooted in memory and teaching rather than in a supernatural conveyance of spiritual food. Secondly, it was widely believed that Jesus' simple, straightforward beliefs and practice had been transformed by Paul into a complex and institutional religion. So, it was argued, the pattern of Jesus' table-fellowship had been turned into a rite based upon the Greek mystery religions. And, given this belief, it was hardly surprising that Zwinglian emphases were preferred. Thirdly, two highly admired Christian groups, the Salvation Army and the Society of Friends, did not use sacraments to support their life and witness. This led many of those in churches which did have sacraments to adopt a 'low' rather than 'high' view of them. Then, fourthly, the prevailing influence of those whose 'social gospel' theology drove them to build God's kingdom here on earth quite naturally came to understand the Lord's supper as a corporate gathering of God's people under the sovereign God. This again tended to negate Calvin's view, although it need not have done so. The affirmation of Christ's presence in those gathered around the table can be viewed as complementary to, rather than in competition with, Christ's presence to the individual through faith as the elements are taken. Finally, Victorian sensibilities concerning temperance and hygiene led to the use in Free Churches of unfermented wine, small cubes of bread and individual cups. Davies pointedly directs our attention to the devaluation of symbolism which this caused:

> Apart from the historical associations of the chalice, the new custom offended against the symbolical unity of the rite which had been admirably expressed in the shared cup but was shattered in the individual cups. Moreover, the act of lifting these diminutive glasses to the lips was unfortunately reminiscent of drinking a toast. These changes in the administration of the Lord's Supper were aesthetically unfortunate and theologically defective.[23]

---

22   See ibid., pp 83–4.
23   Ibid., p 84.

Here is a very clear example of Free Church theology and practice becoming distorted and diminished by non-theological factors. Once these symbolically detrimental practices had been adopted, though, it was therefore inevitable that sacramental practice was devalued. But, as Davies reminds us: 'The marvel is . . . that the power of the Sacrament itself, with its numinous overtones and hallowed associations, was able to prevail in the popular mind over the implied depreciation of it by the theologians and by the enthusiasts for total abstinence and hygiene who substituted grape-juice for the wine and individual communion cups for the chalice.'[24]

The twentieth century saw a revival in sacramental practice in all the major churches. But what led our churches to restore the visible Word to its rightful place alongside the audible Word? First, they came under the influence of the so-called 'Liturgical Movement' sweeping through Western Christianity. This movement caused many Reformed churches to move in certain clear directions. They started using lectionaries and invited the congregation to take part in responses. Services became less centred upon the minister, with congregational involvement overcoming the 'tyranny of the single ministerial voice'. Visual aids in worship were no longer suspected of being idolatrous, sensual distractions but came to be viewed as vehicles for God's presence. And, following on from this, the Liturgical Movement above everything else placed the Lord's Supper at the centre of Christian worship. The service of Holy Communion increasingly was understood as the source of the Church's life from which all authentic spirituality, mission and evangelism flows. Secondly, and partly influenced by the Liturgical Movement, some important Congregational divines initiated what has been called the Genevan Revival. Nathaniel Micklem, J S Whale and Bernard Lord Manning rediscovered a Calvinistic view of worship which directly countered the prevailing 'low' approaches. Others later added their weight to the movement: John Marsh, H F Lovell Cocks, Hubert Cunliffe-Jones, John Huxtable, Daniel Jenkins and Walter A Whitehouse. While this trend towards a High Genevan sacramental outlook became very influential in Service Books and is an important part of the URC inheritance, it is not acceptable to many ministers and churches who continue to be suspicious of outward symbols in religion and focus more on ethical obedience than on formal sacramental rites. Thirdly, the Ecumenical Movement brought churches closer to one another. This resulted in mutual theological correction and greater understanding of liturgy and worship. And this increasing ecumenical endeavour has tended to elevate the importance of sacraments in worship and the significance of the Lord's Table – not least because it is the scene of much of our disunity!

The current URC scene now reveals an appreciation of the Lord's Supper far deeper than that found in the Victorian chapel tradition where the pulpit princes competed for their congregations. Thankfully, gone are the days when in most of our churches the Lord's Supper was an optional extra after the preaching was over.

6. Prayer

The English Separatists reacted forthrightly against the set liturgical prayers of the Roman Catholic church. They championed the art of free prayer, a practice which has played a very important part in the prayer-life of Reformed congregations. Free prayer is extemporaneous. At its best it is simple, passionate, sincere and moving. But what reasons can be put forward to support an opposition to liturgical prayer?[25] First, liturgical prayers rob people of the need and desire to compose prayers for

---

[24]   Ibid., p 240.
[25]   What follows reveals my indebtedness to Horton Davies's, *Worship and Theology in England*.

themselves. They tend to emasculate the worshipper and worship leader of their liturgical creativity. Anyone who is solely dependent upon set prayers is akin to a person who continues to use a walking stick even though their sprained ankle has long since mended. Secondly, liturgical prayer tends to fail to speak to worshippers' varying needs in different contexts and times. It lacks intimacy and particularity. Meanwhile, the tradition of free prayer enables worship leaders to pray for people and events which have manifested themselves in the course of pastoral work. Hence prayers in public worship become contextually relevant. Thirdly, when liturgical prayer is enforced on the church, a denial of Christian liberty takes place. Human constructions in liturgy are then given the authority of divine revelation, and human decisions take on the power of divine imperatives. Fourthly, the constant use of a set liturgy leads to lip-service being shown to the words, with all the resulting dangers of hypocrisy. By contrast, Davies tells us, 'Free prayer . . . has certain advantages over forms of prayer . . .: in chief, its flexibility, its lively way of exciting the religious affections, and the novelty of thought and expression which retain the attention of congregations.'[26] And, fifthly, the enforcement of a fixed liturgy can bring disharmony to the Body of Christ. When one group imposes its liturgical preferences upon the whole church, the church's unity is threatened; when the state enforces the imposition, the persecution of a section of the church is not far away.

While some Separatists refused even to use the Lord's Prayer, on account of it being part of the Sermon on the Mount and therefore an example of the kind of prayer we should try to use rather than one shamelessly to copy, most Dissenters found a place for worship directories and even liturgies in order that the church's unity and discipline could be maintained. The Puritans, for example, generated an extensive array of prayer books.[27] They recognized the pitfalls of free prayer, five of which are important for us to bear in mind. First, free prayer sometimes merely reveals the superficiality of the prayer leader's mind. Those who do things 'off the cuff' are prone to reveal their mental laziness. Secondly, free prayer sometimes proves to be far from spiritually enriching. There is little that is edifying in glib words or ostentatious turns of phrase. Extempore prayer is a breeding ground for expression of political bias, the inadvertent reference to personal or congregational conflicts, and generally inappropriate particularity. Thirdly, worshippers cannot always fully engage with free prayer because they do not have enough time to take in what is being said. Their minds are fixed on understanding what is said, when what is required is that they 'reach' God through what is said. Fourthly, it is a simple fact that many people are not good at offering extempore prayer. Some of us simply do not possess the gift. And, fifthly, free prayer often leads to a lack of order in worship and a long-windedness that is extremely off-putting.

In the debate concerning the respective merits of liturgical and free prayer there are important points to be observed on both sides. The proponents of liturgical prayer reveal an ecclesiology which stresses 'the corporate nature of the church' and all that is held in common by way of creeds and confessions; the proponents of free prayer, on the other hand, reveal an ecclesiology which stresses 'the need of individuals in a family church'.[28] Free prayer fits the model of the gathered church, the covenant community of visible saints; it belongs, therefore, to the Reformed ethos of worship. Both Reformed ecclesiology and its prayer-life are typified by certain distinguishing marks: '. . . freedom, particularity, flexibility, and the intimacy of fellowship'.[29] However, the URC also strives to be a Catholic body in which 'the corporate nature of the church' is as important as its local, gathered

---

[26]   Davies, *Worship and Theology in England: Vol IV From Newman to Martineau 1850–1900*, p 76.
[27]   See Davies, *Worship and Theology in England: Vol II From Andrews to Baxter and Fox 1603–1690*, pp 405–535.
[28]   Davies, *Worship and Theology in England: Vol 1 From Cranmer to Hooker 1534–1603*, p 270.
[29]   Davies, *Worship and Theology in England: Vol II From Andrews to Baxter and Fox 1603–1690*, p 199.

particularity. It is not surprising, therefore, that contemporary URC worship contains a rich blend of both types of prayer. Indeed, it is quite remarkable that a denomination which has had a noble history of free prayer in worship should also have produced some of the most creative liturgists of the modern era.

7. Hymn Singing

A major feature of the worship in the sixteenth century Genevan Reformed church was the unaccompanied singing of the Ten Commandments and metrical psalms. Calvin believed that Psalms is a book of Christian as well as Jewish praise. He thought that it is inspired by the Holy Spirit and should occupy a central place in Reformed worship. To facilitate this Calvin commissioned tunes to carry French metrical settings of the psalms, and it is fair to say that Calvinistic theology was largely inculcated by the faithful, and spread further afield by evangelists, *via* the period's psalm tunes. Since the Calvinists held that congregational singing had to be of Scripture and Scripture alone, the birth of hymnology actually took place in the Lutheran world, where poetry based upon Scriptural themes and events by the likes of Paul Gerhardt and Luther himself was set to the tunes of a musical genius, J S Bach, and produced some lastingly memorable hymnody.

While German Lutherans were singing quality hymns such as 'O Sacred Head Sore Wounded' to Bach chorales, English Puritans, standing firmly in the Calvinist tradition, were dourly and drearily 'lining out' the Psalms, a practice in which a cantor (often the minister) read or intoned a line of the metrical psalm before it was sung by the congregation. And, with hindsight, what made matters worse was that in English cathedrals the glorious music of Tallis and Byrd was accompanying worship. It was all rather akin to a hungry person having to make do with a greasy-spoon café when the delights of *cordon bleu* cooking were to hand. While the majority of Puritans were not kill-joys when it came to music, many of them must have been tone-deaf when it came to quality church music. But the Puritan resistance to anything other than metrical psalms being sung in worship was not based upon an intrinsic dislike of music; it was anchored in 'the Scripture principle': 'The Puritans . . . demanded a Scriptural warrant for every part of worship, believing it to be a repudiation of the doctrine of original sin for man to assume he was capable of deciding what was appropriate in the service of God, and arrant impudence to legislate for himself when God had already decided for him in the Word of God in the Holy scriptures.'[30] In fairness to the Puritans, however, the advent of the metrical psalms provided worshippers with accessible tunes when many of the musical alternatives on offer were only accessible to the professional musician. But the overriding weakness of the metrical psalm tradition was two-fold: first, it brought monotony into worship and, secondly, it often gave rise to 'divinity couched in the sorriest doggerel'.[31]

While the birth of metrical psalms was an early stage on the journey towards English hymnody, a further decisive step forward came when metrical versions of New Testament passages were prepared to be sung alongside the metrical psalms – 'the creeds and battle-songs of the Puritans.'[32] This was closely followed by combinations and selections of scriptural material being constructed for singing in metrical form, thus paving the way for the English hymn. The English Reformed ethos may have been somewhat slow when it came to the development of hymnody,

30   Ibid., p 254.
31   Davies, *Worship and Theology in England: Vol I From Cranmer to Hooker 1534–1603*, p 387.
32   Davies, *Worship and Theology in England: Vol II From Andrewes to Baxter and Fox 1603–1690*, p 272.

but, as we learn from the parable of the hare and the tortoise, things can pick up after a slow start! And that is precisely what happened after the Congregationalist Isaac Watts had achieved 'the daring transition from psalm to paraphrase to hymn'.[33]

Watts's mastery of the genre of hymnody made it possible for others to contribute to the development of this important aspect of Reformed and Free Church worship. The work of Charles Wesley in the eighteenth century added force to Watts's earlier achievement, and the tradition of hymn singing was thus set in place. In the Free Church tradition hymns have conveyed orthodox theology to our congregations, as well as acted as a counterpoint to a highly cerebral worship pattern largely centred upon the sermon. Hymnody also has ensured that worshippers' emotions are not starved in churches where preaching has been pre-eminent. If the English Reformed heritage can boast the father of hymnody in Watts, it is equally true that the traditions which make up the URC have made a contribution to hymnody well above their size or standing *vis a vis* other denominations. This became particularly apparent during the second half of the twentieth century when the influence of the likes of Eric Thiman and Erik Routley became worldwide, and the work of hymn writers such as Albert Bayly, George Caird, Fred Kaan, Caryl Micklem, Brian Wren and Alan Gaunt gained international recognition.[34] The fruits of the URC contribution to hymnody is immediately apparent in any of the recent mainstream hymnbooks.

8.   The Search for Relevance

Davies has described vividly the type of worship typical of the Free Church and Nonconformist tradition in which the URC stands:

> Such a type of worship presupposes the warmth, spontaneity, intimacy, and even informality of a gathering of friends, of a collection of families each well known to the others. It presupposes a minister who is really the shepherd of his little flock, who has baptized their children, catechized their youth and married them, and admitted them to the fellowship of the Holy Table, and in his visitations 'rejoiced with them that do rejoice and wept with those that weep'. It also assumes that the free and spontaneous Spirit-directed prayers of their minister will not scruple to speak to their peculiar circumstances, even mentioning them by name in his petitions. There is no place for either formality or uniformity in such a conception of prayer; freedom, particularity, and flexibility are its distinguishing marks.[35]

Worship in such churches grows out of the joys and sorrows, offerings and need of 'visible saints'; it is not a system imposed from beyond the context of the congregation. And the first steps on the road to developing such worship were taken by Reformers who made the language of worship the

---

[33]   Davies, *Worship and Theology in England: Vol III From Watts and Wesley to Maurice 1690–1850* (Princeton: Princeton University Press, 1961), p 34. For an assessment of Watts's contribution to hymnody see Bernard Lord Manning, *The Hymns of Wesley and Watts* (London: Epworth Press, 1942) and for a magisterial survey of English hymnody see Richard Watson, *The English Hymn: A Critical and Historical Study* (Oxford: Oxford University Press, 1999).

[34]   For an account of the late twentieth century explosion in hymnody, and the URC's (particularly Mansfield College, Oxford's) central involvement in it, see Horton Davies, *Worship and Theology in England: VI Crisis and Creativity 1965–Present* (Grand Rapids, Michigan: Wm B Eerdmans Publishing Co., 1996), pp 232–60. See also Fred Kaan, *Hymn Texts* (London: Stainer and Bell, 1995); Brian Wren, *Piece Together Praise: A Theological Journey–Poems and Collected Hymns Thematically Arranged* (London: Stainer and Bell, 1996); and Alan Gaunt, *Hymn Texts of Alan Gaunt* (London: Stainer and Bell, 1991) and *Always from Joy: Hymn Texts 1991-96* (London: Stainer and Bell, 1997).

[35]   Davies, *Worship and Theology in England: Vol III From Watts and Wesley to Maurice 1690–1850*, p 27.

vernacular rather than Latin. Christianity, therefore, was presented to people in their own language, with the result that it became fully intelligible, and one-time spectators and listeners at a religious spectacle became full participants. As time has gone, the degree of congregational participation in worship has increased dramatically. As well as making full use of hymnody, most churches invite people to read the lessons, and some ask members of the congregation to lead the intercessory prayers. Nowadays, prayers with said or sung responses are quite commonplace. In really progressive congregations, the structure and content of worship is organised by a worship group which is enabled in its work by the minister.

Just as the move to use the vernacular in sixteenth century Reformed worship led to considerable controversy, so similarly in the twentieth century the transition from addressing God as 'Thou' to 'You', as well as the move towards the use of inclusive language, has been far from straightforward. And, yet, the objectors to these innovations perhaps have been less numerous in the Free Churches than in the Anglican and Roman traditions. Indeed, Reformed liturgists have been in the vanguard of sensitively enabling such transitions. Caryl Micklem, for example, collaborated with several writers to produce an important series of liturgical books;[36] Alan Gaunt has written a vast number of prayers for use in public worship;[37] while Brian Wren has written a perceptive book on inclusive language.[38] Few URC ministers now use archaic language in worship, though, when poetry needed to be protected, the compilers of *Rejoice and Sing* left the archaic language of certain hymns well alone. Some, however, still have great misgivings about the use of inclusive language. Are the terms Creator, Redeemer and Sustainer, for example, equivalent to Father, Son and Holy Spirit? Surely, they argue, the former are functional and not personal terms. Wakefield speaks for many others when he asks:

> Is it possible to have a Christian liturgy which does not call God 'Father', a concept so central to the religion of Jesus, or which abandons language of the Kingdom which some so strongly abominate? . . . To what extent does one yield to the sensitivities of groups and individuals, which may result in objections to what have been regarded as foundation categories of faith and undermine the essential gospel?[39]

The URC answered such questions in a typical 'both-and' fashion when in 1997 it decided not to replace the confession of faith upon which this book is based with an inclusive language version. Many, for example, objected on theological grounds to the clause: 'We worship God . . . whom Jesus called Father.'[40] The Assembly, however, recognized part of the case for inclusive language, and asked for the new version to be made available alongside the 1972 statement, thus hoping to satisfy both sides in the debate.

A further example of the way in which patterns of Reformed worship attempt to be relevant is provided by a consideration of the place of children in worship. The tradition of 'children's sermons' was established in the Victorian and Edwardian Free Churches, and the popularity of

---

[36]   See *Contemporary Prayers for Public Worship* (London: SCM Press, 1967), *More Contemporary Prayers* (London: SCM Press, 1970), and *Contemporary Prayers for Church and School* (London: SCM Press, 1975).

[37]   See *New Prayers for Worship* (Leeds: John Paul the Preacher's Press, 1972) and *Prayers for the Christian Year* (Leeds: John Paul the Preacher's Press, 1979).

[38]   See *What Language shall I Borrow? God Talk in Worship: A Male Response to Feminist Theology* (London: SCM Press, 1989).

[39]   Wakefield, *An Outline of Christian Worship*, p 163.

[40]   *Basis of Union*, para. 18 found in *The Manual* (London: URC, 1998), A5.

Children's Addresses has not waned despite some ministers trying to get rid of them as they have sought to integrate children further into our churches' worshipping life through programmes like 'Family Church' and all-age worship. Objective hearers of such addresses recognize that they seldom escape being patronising. The better ones may offer good entertainment, and even a modicum of education, but invariably they are not conducive to worship. More interesting and significant for the long-term have been the recent attempts to involve children fully at Holy Communion.

Free Church attempts to bring worship to the people by making it intelligible and accessible to the entire church family are wholly laudable. But there can be rather unfortunate spin-offs: the removal of some of the classic prayers of Christian spirituality from public worship; the increase of sociality at the expense of reverence; the loss of liturgical structure due to 'Family Church' patterns which involve children leaving and/or returning to the service at certain points; and the appearance of trite songs and popular music of little contemporary, let alone lasting, merit. Given what passes for worship in some congregations one cannot help but recall Desmond Tutu's oft quoted remark: 'I thank God that I'm not God!'

Spirituality

When people become members of the URC they promise 'to be faithful in private and public worship'.[41] The order of 'private' and 'public' in this promise is significant, since it points to an important truth, namely, that the church's public worship is impoverished if those who participate in it do not bring to it lives rooted in private prayer and biblical exploration. This has two significant implications. First, we are reminded that attendance at public worship once a week is not sufficient to guarantee our spiritual development. We need to recapture the notion that Reformed piety is cultivated in the home as well as the church. But, secondly, the real spiritual battles take place in the context of the daily round. How one handles the great issues of mind and heart largely determines what one brings to corporate worship. True piety is won as we learn through God to handle ourselves. Private and public worship should go hand in hand if we want to become spiritually mature.

Howard L Rice defines spirituality as 'the pattern by which we shape our lives in response to our experience of God as a very real presence in and around us'.[42] When Reformed Christians speak about spirituality, it is often in the context of talking about what Christians outside the Reformed ethos get up to in their devotional life. Some of us do not find it easy to 'own' spirituality; we believe it belongs to the Catholic and Anglican worlds but not to the Reformed ethos. Ordinands seeking a pattern of spiritual discipline to sustain them through their forthcoming ministries often travel outside the Reformed ethos to find one. Why is it, then, that 'spirituality' is not viewed as being Reformed? The reason cannot be that spiritual development and attainment of true piety is not a Reformed concern, since no one can be a Christian without attending to such matters. Nor is it the case that the Reformed heritage is devoid of people who have written about spiritual development. The Puritan period alone produced some of the world's most famous spiritual classics: Baxter's *The Saints Everlasting Rest*, Bunyan's, *The Pilgrim's Progress* and Milton's *Pardise Lost*.

Rice directs us to five reasons why Reformed Christians are wary of spirituality. First, he reminds us that Reformed Christians tend to belong to the middle-classes who are quite self-sufficient by nature and like to be in control of their lives. Many trust reason but are suspicious of

---

41   Ibid., Schedule A found in Thompson, ed., *Stating the Faith*, p 258.
42   Howard L Rice, *Reformed Spirituality: An Introduction for Believers* (Louisville, Kentucky: Westminster/John Knox Press, 1991), p 45.

emotion; they get on with living instead of navel-gazing. People with such a class bias find the whole idea of spirituality very difficult. As Rice remarks: 'Spirituality demands letting go of control, taking the emotions seriously, and emphasizing *being* as of equal value with doing.'[43] It is interesting that non-Western Reformed Christians find the affairs of the Spirit much more easy to attend to, and, without wishing to introduce gender stereotypes into the analysis, it also appears that women are less unhinged by issues of spiritual development than men.

Secondly, the Reformed emphasis upon justification by faith through grace makes it difficult for us to countenance any practice which might suggest that one can work to get oneself right with God. Quite often Reformed Christians have seen patterns of spiritual discipline as illicit attempts to earn God's favour or to get in a position to deserve God's grace. But this may have rested on a basic misunderstanding about what spiritual discipline involves. Baxter, of course, employed Ignatian techniques of spiritual direction in *The Saints Everlasting Rest*. This particular 'meer Catholik', as he liked to be called, was somewhat unusual in incorporating such disciplines in a directive about Puritan vocation. Nevertheless, while the Reformers were hostile to some of the inherited medieval spiritual practices, they still viewed positively the need for daily devotions rooted in prayer and Bible study. They were also open to the idea that people need 'rules' or a discipline to sustain their private worship. But, as Rice points out, 'The great medieval mystics did not claim that one could earn salvation by following their particular way.'[44] He advises us, therefore, to avoid being negative about practices which were never expected to bring grace, and which were viewed as 'a response to God's graciousness, an act of thanksgiving, and an answer to God's invitation to enter into a deeper relationship'.[45]

Thirdly, Reformed Christians have tended to stress the corporate dimensions of the gospel, thereby understanding themselves to be a redeemed community rather than a set of isolated redeemed individuals. The communal dimensions of devotion have often been emphasised above the equally important dimensions of individual piety. A fear of individualism in Christianity has prompted Reformed Christians, therefore, to drive a huge wedge between private and public spirituality, but in fact both are needed for spiritual maturity. When the private dimension is undervalued we come 'obedient and faithful out of a sense of loyalty and duty, but without much joy and enthusiasm'.[46]

Fourthly, Reformed theology's focus on the *audible* Word (often at the expense of the *visible* Word) is always susceptible to a devaluing of the role of the emotions in the Christian life. Our understandable insistence that religion must be credible, and hence rational, not only reminds us that on their own the emotions are never a totally reliable guide for the Christian life, but also can lead us to forget that rationality just as much as the emotions can also distort our devotion and doctrine. Since spirituality is deemed to be a matter of the heart rather than the head, it has tended to be devalued because of the Reformed tradition's stress on the rational. Rice makes the important point:

> The balance between heart and mind is critical. We must test our emotional experiences in the light of what we know, but, at the same time, knowledge without personal experience of the heart is a dead kind of knowing. One can be correct and still without a relationship of trust with God. This knowledge and experience are the parallel necessities for the fullness of Christian faith, and united they prevent us from the false either / or of mind and heart.[47]

43   Ibid., p 49.
44   Ibid., p 51.
45   Ibid.
46   Ibid., p 53.
47   Ibid., p 57.

Fifthly, the Reformed ethos is suspicious of any practice which leads to an overtly otherworldly attitude to the Christian life. Anything which causes us to retreat from our vocation in society must be put to one side – unless, that is, a short period of retreat provides the renewed energy to fulfil our vocation more faithfully. So it is hardly surprising that concerns about spirituality have sometimes been viewed by Reformed Christians as evasions of a Christian's calling in society. As Davies makes clear, 'the Protestant conviction' is that 'God is to be served not *per vacationem* (through a special world – renouncing calling) but *in vocatione* (in one's daily, secular calling)'.[48] We are prone, of course, to take the lift to eternity which does not stop at temporal reality. Nevertheless, Reformed understanding of spirituality is grounded in the integration of piety and daily living. As Rice says: 'One could say that the ideal of Reformed Protestantism was that each Christian home become a little monastery in the world'.[49] Reformed spirituality is far from being other worldly.

It follows that Reformed spirituality is centred upon holding qualities in balance which, when advanced at the expense of their polar opposites, can lead to distortions in the Christian life. Four areas can be noted.[50] First, we need to strike a mutually enriching balance between personal and corporate devotion. The extensive self-scrutiny of a Puritan style of personal devotion needs to be complemented by the gracious Word heard from the pulpit and received around the table: 'Your sins are forgiven, go in peace!' The spiritual discipline of individuals enriches the whole church; while the corporate wisdom of the 'visible saints' is a corrective and challenge to each individual as well as an affirmation of their value and worth. Secondly, we must seek a rapprochement between head and heart, reason and emotion. In a tradition which tends towards an emphasis upon faith's cerebral dimensions, we must remember that faith is more than a matter of giving assent to propositions; it also involves making a personal commitment to One who is worthy of our trust; it is a disposition of mind, heart and will. We are prone to over intellectualize our faith. Thirdly, we should strive for a balance in daily life which holds in tension the fact that, on the one hand, worldly things have been given us by God to be enjoyed and, on the other hand, we must exercise sensitive stewardship of what God has given us and avoid materialistic attitudes which make idols of possessions. Rice points us, therefore, to 'the discipline of frugality'.[51] Exercise of this discipline becomes a life and death matter in a world made up of key non-renewable resources. And, finally, we ought to seek a balance between contemplation and vocation. It is clearly appropriate that we should take the journey inwards to find a deep and lasting relationship with God. Times for quiet meditation and prayer are essential to a holistic Christian life. However, this must be coupled with 'a desire, animated by the presence of Christ, to live out our faith in service to others in the world'.[52] Reformed Christianity leads to responsible and committed citizenship. This vocational emphasis gave rise to the so-called 'Nonconformist conscience', which, according to Davies, produced 'a sturdy questioning, an ethical sensitivity which often manifested itself as a concern for the rights of others and especially of minorities in religion', and was characterized by 'a fear of God but of no man, and an integrity that could not be bought'.[53] It is noteworthy that communities like Taizé and Iona not only place a strong emphasis on personal and public devotion, but also display strong commitments to issues of social and political justice. Their capacity to draw people into their spiritual ethos is due in no small measure to the balance they each display in their spiritual understanding.

---

[48] Davies, *Worship and Theology in England: Vol II From Andrews to Baxter and Fox, 1603–1690*, p 73.

[49] Rice, *Reformed Spirituality: An Introduction for Believers*, p 60.

[50] See ibid., p 67.

[51] Ibid., p 67.

[52] Ibid.

[53] Davies, *Worship and Theology in England: Vol II From Andrews to Baxter and Fox, 1603–1690*, p 454.

Discipline

Reformed Christians are realists who possess a very healthy awareness of their faults and failings, along with a spirited determination to serve God and their neighbours. They try to press on with their vocation, even though they are aware of the ever-present realities of their sinfulness (and the fact that they are often 'sinned-against' by others), and know that they must live with all the perplexities, doubts and sufferings which beset us in daily life. The search for Christian perfection, to use Reinhold Niebuhr's famous phrase, is an 'impossible possibility', something for which we are to strive but will never attain in *this* life. It involves effort on our part: we are to work out our salvation with fear and trembling (Phil. 2: 12); but our effort must be set within a recognition of that internal struggle which takes place between our wish to be Christ's devoted and faithful followers and our honest recognition of our sinfulness. As a result, the Reformed ethos is tempted neither to triumphalism nor to overconfidence. As they follow their Christian vocation Reformed Christians seek to be 'in the world but not of the world'. They attempt to be so involved in culture that their words and deeds are relevant and not un-detached from people's lives and experience, while at the same time they seek to avoid losing their Christian identity. If the Puritans can be said, with hindsight, to have been overzealous in their denial of culture, with all the attendant tendencies to self-righteousness and judgementalism, then the contemporary church surely suffers from a too-easy accommodation to a culture in which there is a breakdown of corporate values and individualism reigns.

Christians should aspire to achieve three things: holiness, righteousness and responsible stewardship of God's gifts. Holiness, the first of these qualities, results from the union of the believer with the triune God. Paul exhorts Timothy to train himself for that godliness (I Tim. 4: 7), which comes from fellowship with God in Christ through the Spirit. Righteousness, the second quality, results from the pursuit of justice. We have been made righteous before God in the cross, and in response we are to seek reconciliation with all those we have wronged as well as those who have wronged us. Responsible stewardship of God's gifts, the third aspiration, involves avoiding the idolatry which comes from clinging to possessions and over-attraction to worldly comforts. What we do with the things we own and how we treat the planet's resources are both crucial to our spirituality; how we use our possessions for the benefit of others and extend charity to the less fortunate is central to our faith. As Christians pursue holiness, righteousness and responsibility in a disciplined way, they become sanctified by the Spirit. There are two dimensions to the discipline involved: one concerns what we attempt as individuals, the other involves what we seek to do through the church.

Personal Discipline

The Christian pilgrimage centres upon our participation in the means of grace. This involves a committed and planned approach to life and work. The question is never whether the Christian life has a discipline to guide it; rather, it is whether the discipline actually being followed is satisfactory. A life-enhancing discipline will involve elements which we attend to ourselves, as we live with ourselves and others away from the church, and those elements which follow from the responsibilities of church membership. The means of grace are accessed by us, therefore, through both *private* and *public* discipline.

Personal discipline in the Christian life involves paying attention to a number of related private matters. First, we should maintain a regular devotional life which includes all the major dimensions of prayer: adoration, confession, thanksgiving, petition, intercession and dedication. Then, secondly, a disciplined Christian life will involve regular and systematic exploration of the Scriptures. Also needed, but often underrated, is ongoing contact with carefully selected individuals who can be mentors for our journey. Far too often, the Christian life is understood in an unnecessarily individualistic fashion. It may be partially true that religion is what we do with our solitude, but it is also the case that religion is something we 'do' with others, and that it is a way of life which can be guided by saints past and present. Fourthly, a disciplined Christian life entails an ethical outlook which is based upon norms and values which sometimes may run counter to those exhibited in the wider culture in which we live.

The public dimension of personal discipline, on the other hand, centres upon those corporate activities which are part of our being Church members.[54] Firstly, we should be faithful in our attendance at worship, where we await with expectancy God's Word speaking to us in preaching. Even if sometimes the sermon does not create the miracle of the Word addressing us through words, we should not rule out the possibility of that miracle ever happening, either by 'switching off' or through absenting ourselves from the congregation. Secondly, we must avail ourselves of the sacraments of Baptism and Holy Communion. They constitute primary means by which God renews us in faithfulness and sustains us for faithfulness. Thirdly, we need to participate fully in the Church's life. This does not mean that we should join all the organisations or attend all the social events. And many of us may feel more blessed when we do not! But it does entail making our gifts available within the congregation, taking part in the decision making processes by attending the church meeting and joining in the church's mission to those around it. Fourthly, we should give to others of our time, money and talents. As Christ gave himself for us, we are to give ourselves for others. When we do so without strings attached and sacrificially, we not only enter into a relationship with the recipients of our giving but we also acknowledge and serve Christ (Matt. 25: 40, 45). Fifthly, the keeping of the Sabbath is a means of grace for us. Unfortunately, the Christian Sabbath has become associated with negatives: for example, refraining from work, recreation, trading, reading (except the Bible), excessive eating and drinking, and social intercourse about 'worldly' rather than 'spiritual' matters. It is possible, however, to treat Sunday observance as a day set apart from other days in a more positive vein. In a busy and time-kept society the Sabbath reminds us that everyone needs rest and it becomes a focus for us having it. It also helps direct our attention away from ourselves and our activities in order to remind us to pay attention to God. It provides us, further, with an opportunity to attend public worship and to become mindful of others. Even in a culture which uses Sunday for sport and recreation, as well as makes the Christian Sabbath just about the busiest shopping-day of the week, time-honoured traditions about Sunday can still carry great importance for Christians.

Personal discipline should be understood as a gift rather than a burden given to the 'visible saints'. We must view it as a wholehearted response to God's graciousness toward us in Christ. It is misunderstood when it takes on the status of law, and we should exercise it freely and joyfully. Its purpose is not to please God to gain a reward but to renew our lives.

---

54   See Rice, *Reformed Spirituality: An Introduction for Believers,* pp 187–99.

Church Discipline

In addition to exercising self-discipline the Reformed Christian is also expected to come under the church's discipline. The pattern was set by Calvin, who believed that discipline should permeate not only the church but also the whole of life. His understanding of church discipline is not only surprisingly gracious but also it continues to inform contemporary Reformed practice.

Calvin raises discipline to a high profile in the church: 'Accordingly, as the saving doctrine of Christ is the soul of the church, so does discipline serve as its sinews, through which the members of the body hold together, each in its own place.'[55] Anyone who said that today no doubt would be dismissed as an oppressive control-freak, but Calvin gives three eminently sensible reasons why church discipline is very important. Its first purpose is to avoid the church being brought into disrepute. Discipline is needed to ensure that there may be no such thing in the church to brand its most sacred name with disgrace.'[56] Calvin argues that the wicked who pollute the name of Christ should be removed from the church family. He is particularly keen that ministers should not distribute the Lord's Supper to unworthy persons. This is in sharp contrast to the recent conclusion of Donald Hilton:

> So throw the table open wide;
> no barriers raised, no fence, no moat.
> It is the Lord's; it is not ours.[57]

If worthiness is the criterion for admission to the Lord's Table then, strictly speaking, no one will be found around it! Secondly, church discipline is needed so 'that the good be not corrupted by the constant company of the wicked'.[58] Calvin is quite clear that 'the wicked' should be excommunicated, and he bases his argument on the New Testament (see I Cor. 5: 1–13). But the reason for excommunication is rehabilitation rather than mere punishment. Consequently, Calvin finds a third purpose for discipline in the fact 'that those overcome by shame for their baseness begin to repent.'[59]

Calvin believes that the church has a clear basis upon which to excommunicate those who commit 'crimes or shameful acts' as opposed to mere 'faults'.[60] Taking his lead from I Cor. 5: 1–13, he argues that the church must exclude 'manifest adulterers, fornicators, thieves, robbers, seditious persons, perjurers, false witnesses, and *the rest of this sort,* as well as the insolent'.[61] This jurisdiction has been given the church by Christ, so the church not only has 'the Word of the Lord to condemn the perverse' but also 'the Word to receive the repentant into grace'.[62] But how far do 'this sort' extend? And who decides who is a member? The risk of arbitrariness and heavy handedness is obvious and thereby one of the difficulties of exercising discipline is revealed. Those one particular age or culture excommunicates are left within the church by another age or culture.

---

55   Calvin, *Institutes,* 4,12,1.
56   Ibid., 4,12,5.
57   Hilton, *Table Talk,* p 132.
58   Calvin, *Institutes,* 4,12,1.
59   Ibid.
60   Ibid., 4,12,4.
61   Ibid. Italics mine
62   Ibid.

Calvin makes a further distinction between *public* (or open) sins and *private* (or secret) sins. Public sins are those observed by many people. Faced with people who commit such sins, the church must summon them to account for what they have done and then correct them according to their fault.[63]   Private sins, on the other hand, are only witnessed by a small number of people. Those who commit them are to be treated, Calvin argues, according to the precedent set down by Jesus (Matt. 18: 15–17).   In such cases the stages of church discipline are as follows: first, the offender is admonished by the minister.   Then, if this has failed to effect a correction of behaviour, the offender is admonished a second time by the minister in the presence of a witness.   Further failure to get offenders to change their ways is followed by taking them to the church elders.   If the elders fail to encourage a change of behaviour then the person(s) involved in the disciplinary action are excommunicated, i.e. deprived of the Lord's Supper.   It is always to be hoped that matters will be resolved by 'verbal chastisement', but the church must be prepared to be severe when the occasion demands.[64]   When excommunication is necessary, Calvin insists that the elders should not take action alone but 'with the knowledge and approval of the church'.[65]   The elders are expected to make the decision, but the whole church is made aware of it 'so that nothing may be done according to the whim of a few'.[66]

Calvin expects discipline, however harsh, to be administered with 'a spirit of gentleness' (Gal. 6: 1), and in such a way that the offender 'be not overwhelmed with sorrow [2I Cor. 2: 7]' lest 'a remedy . . . become destruction'.[67]   One cannot help but admire Calvin's concern to keep the rehabilitation of sinners firmly in view throughout the disciplinary process.   This concern is centred upon his recognition that finality in judgement rests with God rather than the church.   Calvin's confidence in God's forgiveness is great: 'For God, whenever it pleases him, changes the worst men into the best, engrafts the alien, and adopts the stranger into the church'.[68]   He recognises that some of the wayward and intransigent may still be part of the Elect.   Calvin actually looks to Cyprian for support in his advancement of moderation in discipline: 'Let a man mercifully correct what he can; let him patiently bear what he cannot correct, and groan and sorrow over it with love.'[69]

In a way that many contemporary Christians will find alien, Calvin expects ministers, 'according to the need of the times', to 'exhort the people either to fasting or to solemn supplications, or to other acts of humility, repentance, and faith – of which the time, the manner, and the form are not prescribed by God's Word, but left to the judgement of the church.'[70]   Just what kind of 'grave' event would generate such a course of action may not be very clear to us, but Calvin certainly included 'whenever a controversy over religion arises which ought to be settled by either a synod or an ecclesiastical court, whenever there is a question about choosing a minister, whenever, finally, any difficult matter of great importance is to be discussed, or again when there appear the judgements of the Lord's anger (as pestilence, war, and famine) . . . '[71]   Calvin believes that fasting has three purposes.   Private fasting, firstly, seeks 'to weaken and subdue the flesh that it may not act

---

63   Ibid., 4,12,6.
64   Ibid.
65   Ibid., 4,12,7.
66   Ibid.
67   Ibid., 4,12,8.
68   Ibid., 4,12,9.
69   Ibid., 4,12,11.
70   Ibid., 4,12,14.
71   Ibid.

wantonly'.[72]   Private and public fasting, secondly, enables us to 'be better prepared for prayers and holy meditations', and, thirdly, it is 'a testimony of our self-abasement before God when we wish to confess our guilt before him'.[73] Unless we call the likes of '50/50 First World/Third World' meals and sponsored events fasts, the practice of fasting has largely disappeared from Reformed churches, despite Calvin's view that it is 'an excellent aid for believers today (as it always was) and a profitable admonition to arouse them in order that they may not provoke God more and more by their excessive confidence and negligence . . . '.[74] While the great Reformer clearly is aware of the misuses to which fasting can be put, he believes, nevertheless, that it has a part to play in Christian discipline. He insists that when fasting a person's inner disposition should match the outward activity, and he goes on to warn people against understanding fasting as 'a work of merit or a form of divine worship'.[75] Fasting may not be 'one of the chief duties' in a Christian life, but Calvin insists that it plays a helpful role in private and public discipline.[76]

When it comes to the discipline of ministers, Calvin is quite clear that different standards apply from those applicable to church members. As befits their different roles, the weight of discipline falls more heavily upon the church's leaders, who, by virtue of the high profile of their office, possess a greater potential to harm the church's unity or to bring the church into disrepute. Calvin, therefore, suggests that '. . . it is truly fitting that the common people be ruled, so to speak, by a gentler and laxer discipline', while 'the clergy practice harsher censures among themselves and be far less indulgent toward themselves than toward others'.[77] The idea that there should be one law for church members and another for ministers will offend those whose egalitarian view of Christian ministry has caused them to collapse the distinction between church members and ministers on their way to the utopian idea of 'every member ministry', via a somewhat mistaken view that all designated leadership necessarily is hierarchical and, hence, oppressive. The church badly needs well-prepared ministers of high quality to lead it in ministry and mission. We have a right to expect high standards of them, and this involves them coming under a tougher disciplinary regime than that at work in their congregations. Where a conciliar church like the URC might want to disagree with Calvin, however, is in the assumption that the discipline of ministers should be self-regulating. This practice might be likened to putting the lunatics in charge of an asylum, were it not for the high regard in which this writer holds ministers – well most of them! The discipline of ministers is better handled by lay and ordained acting together on behalf of the whole church.

Contemporary discussions about personal and church discipline take place in a turbulent climate. Our culture's postmodern outlook means that many have turned their backs on authority, not least because political, scientific and religious authorities are deemed to have failed us and hence are now no longer worthy of our trust. The philosophy of individualism holds sway, with people largely making up their own values and rules. One is equally hard-pressed when talking about church discipline since, like the society it tends to mirror, the church also is a playground for plural views and attitudes. What price discipline when Christians do not possess a common mind on issues like war, sex before marriage, divorce, IVF, abortion, voluntary euthanasia and homosexuality? For some Christians discipline involves anathematizing those homosexuals who have same-sex

---

[72]   Ibid., 4,12,15.
[73]   Ibid.
[74]   Ibid., 4,12,17.
[75]   Ibid., 4,12,19.
[76]   Ibid.
[77]   Ibid., 4,12,22.

relationships; for others such an understanding is highly oppressive, and viewed as totally incongruent with Christ's inclusivity. In this climate, any corporate body is hard-pressed to maintain norms and values which 'connect' with a wide range of people. But the Christian church and her members cannot rest content with either of the two clear extremes which are abroad in Christianity: *sectarianism*, in which the church's beliefs are set so narrowly that it withdraws from all meaningful contact with society, and *pluralism*, in which any absolute claims for Christianity's truth are eschewed and Christianity simply becomes one of many competing outlooks on life. As the church now struggles to learn afresh what it means to follow Jesus Christ, she and her members will need to develop a fresh understanding of discipline which will enable the 'visible saints' to grow up 'to the measure of the full stature of Christ' (Eph. 4: 13).

Reflections and Observations

'THE CHURCH will be what its ministry makes it.'[1] Forsyth's observation weighs heavily on all who are ministers of Word and Sacraments, a high calling which carries great responsibilities. Ministers certainly attract a great deal of unfair and unwarranted criticism. Like football referees, they become the scape-goats for poor performance. But it was always thus! (2 Cor. 4: 7–12). Sometimes the criticism is justified – after all we are only 'clay jars', and too often our vulnerability shows anything but that 'extraordinary power belongs to God and does not come from us'. It reveals instead superficiality, laziness and abuse of power, with the church resultingly being the poorer. As a theological college teacher I encounter a lot of potential and serving ministers and, perhaps, I may be permitted to round off Part 5 with some comments about designated ministries.

As in any profession, there is a range of ability among ministers, but I believe that ministers display certain collective failings which need exposing to the refiner's fire. The failings I have in mind lead me to think that what the church now requires is a deeper understanding of Christian discipleship and vocation rather than necessarily more ministers. A former colleague in Manchester is worthy of our attention at this point. While a member of staff at Northern Baptist College, Heather Walton observed both ordinands and ordained from the perspective of a lay woman. She accuses the ordained of four things. First, we have failed to enable church members to find God in *their* lives, since we have presented to them a picture of God painted in our clerical image:

> This God operates very much as a 'clergyman' does within the confines of the church. He has a benign patriarchal interest in its members' religious lives and in personal problems, but in little else.
>
> The ministers of religion have not discerned God in what are the core experiences of daily living . . . , those points at which [people] are responsible for naming God's holy power in places where the minister never reaches.[2]

Secondly, Walton accuses the ordained of having failed in our responsibility to keep the faith. The gospel comes alive when it is shared, but we have insisted in entombing it in the institutional church. We are reluctant to let people loose with the stories of faith. *Our* interpretation is made orthodoxy and hence normative. We do not trust our church members with modern hermeneutical methods of Bible study or theological scholarship. All such sacred mysteries are deemed to belong to the professionals. Thirdly, Walton claims that ministers have failed 'to gamble life and lifestyle on the possibility of God'.[3] Most of us share the prevailing consensus on morality and values.

---

[1] Forsyth, *Lectures on the Church and Sacraments*, p 121.
[2] Heather Walton, 'An Abuse of Power 2: Finders, Keepers, Losers, Weepers–A Polemic Concerning the Priests of God and the Ministers of Religion' in *Modern Churchman*, XXXIV,2 (1992), p 23.
[3] Ibid., p 24. Italics removed.

Church members quickly spot the difference between the values ministers preach and those they practise. And when ministers keep their theological views to themselves for fear of confusing and/or upsetting the faithful the maturer members of their congregations pity their naivety and simple-mindedness. This prompts Walton to demand a prophetic degree of honesty and openness which is radical and risky:

> It is time for gay and lesbian clergy to say that they believe they are godly people. Gay and lesbian members of our churches need to hear this. It is time for radical Catholic clergy to affirm that God gave women rights to their own bodies.[4]

Finally, ministers are accused by Walton for having failed to engage with the world's sorrow, only getting close to people when it fits the predominant pastoral methods which now dominate ministerial practice. If a problem cannot be solved in *that* way, we do not get involved. We are unfortunately adept at underestimating 'the agony of creation', while we will only usually face up to 'things that can be cured'.[5] The result is that

> . . . the ministers of religion . . . have shut the doors of our churches against the challenges human beings must make to the God who rules over the pain of our world. They have abolished agony from worship and, instead of the passionate love of God which lives alongside our experience of desolation, we have now only the comforts of religion for hurts too small to really concern us.[6]

Walton concludes that lay people should set themselves free from the captivity inflicted by ministers. They must recognize 'both the duties that they have to support ministers in an isolated and difficult profession, and also the rights that they have to insist that ministers return to their priestly vocation and encourage us in ours.'[7]

Reading Walton's extremely provocative article caused me to return to *God's Frozen People*, a forceful argument for reawaking the vocation of the laity.[8] The message of this classic book is as relevant today as it was in 1964, since the church is still exceedingly dominated by ministers and with concerns about ministers. Eavesdrop on conversations of the so-called laity[9] and you hear them blaming their church's woes on their minister; join the flies on the wall at a ministers' meeting and you will hear the church's ills being attributed to un-committed, or stubborn, or backward church members. The gap between ordained and non-ordained is clear for all to see. No one side can be blamed for the ensuing clericalism, since we all play our part in allowing it to have a stranglehold on the church. But clericalism must be overcome if our churches want to be healthy. The vocation of every church member has to be allowed to flourish. A highly gifted and thoroughly prepared professional ministry, distinct but never separate from lay-people, arguably is the best means there is for enabling and empowering the vocation of the whole church. But one of the URC's problems

---

4   Ibid., pp 24–5.
5   Ibid., p 25.
6   Ibid., p 26.
7   Ibid.
8   Mark Gibbs and T Ralph Morton, *God's Frozen People* (London: Collins, 1964).
9   Strictly speaking the ordained as well as the non-ordained are members of the *laos*, the whole people of God. But while every minister is part of the *laos*, every member of the *laos* is not a minister!

might be that it has far too many ministers who are incapable of the required collaborative style. Nor do all our ministers possess the necessary teaching ability or have the theological acumen needed for their distinctive role of equipping God's people in their discipleship and particular vocations.

The primary locus of vocation in a local church is the congregation itself, with the church members being supported, motivated and prepared for their work by the distinctive ministry of elders under the leadership of a minister of Word and Sacraments. If this pattern is to work, at least three things will be required. First, the standard of eldership in the URC needs to be high. We need to condemn to history the ethos which reduces the elders' ministry to sitting on a church committee. Eldership is a designated ministry in the church for which carefully selected people should be thoroughly prepared. Given that elders are ordained, it would be appropriate that an elder's selection should receive the wider church's blessing, and also fitting that such concurrence is dependent upon candidates for eldership having successfully completed a preparation programme which meets the requirements of the denomination. We will only be able to commend the ministry of elders in the ecumenical dialogue successfully when the eldership is taken with greater seriousness. One way of doing this is to make what happens locally more accountable to the wider church, in this case the District Council. Secondly, the qualities required of ministers of Word and Sacraments must focus upon an ability to collaborate, educate, animate and enable. Gone are the days when we could afford ministers who acted as solo performers whom church members endowed with omnicompetent status. Thirdly, the eldership needs freeing from day to day church management so that it can lead the local church in worship and mission. Far too much time is taken up in URC elders' meetings with matters whose proper importance is best honoured by some sort of finance and property group.

This strategy turns the usual problem about the shortage of ministers into a challenge to develop ministry from the grass roots by way of the distinctive leadership of stipendiary ministers within the eldership. An obsession with ministers is thus turned into seeking greater opportunities for the vocation of everyone in the church. An attempt is thus made to halt clericalism without in any way undermining the need for ministers or their crucial role in the church's life. However, in the interests of strategic planning and justice, there is a strong argument for reversing the present calling-concurrence procedure for stipendiary ministers. The difference between a District Council and a multi-church pastorate is one of degree rather than kind, and since the latter kind of pastorate (or 'clusters' of churches operating together) is increasingly commonplace, stipendiary ministers might now be called to Districts with the pastorates or clusters they serve giving concurrence. There is a good sense also to designate, prepare and authorize one elder in each church to preside at the Sacraments in the absence of the minister and thus to become a focal point of leadership.

When history comes to be written, I suspect that the advent of non-stipendiary ministry within the British churches will be scornfully dismissed as the way ailing churches coped with a ministerial shortage on the cheap. While the concept gave some an opportunity to exercise Christian ministry in their work place after the model of the 'worker priest', the way NSMs have been mainly used to plug gaps in deployment patterns suggests that, in the URC at least, this radical ministerial concept has largely been domesticated. The advent of the NSM further encouraged a culture which seems to say that the only way in which vocation can be effectively exercised is *via* ordination. It has helped turn some very able lay leaders into clerics, aided and abetted by some of them being prepared for ordination on courses where the prevailing understanding of ministry actually runs counter to that in the Reformed heritage. Viewed with hindsight, the production of part-time ordained ministers does not get to the heart of the matter. The temptation for us to interpret issues concerning ministry as a plea for more ordained ministers is alluring, but that is to put the cart before the horse. The real problem involves enabling and supporting people to engage in God's mission; it fundamentally concerns the vocation of every church member; and, as Heather Walton has shown us, that cause has not always been well-served by ministers. The need for ministers able and prepared for such service, however, cannot be gainsaid; but the way to do it is not necessarily to 'convert' all the best Indians into chiefs!

PART 6

We rejoice in the gift of eternal life, and believe that, in the fullness of time, God will renew and gather in one all things in Christ, to whom, with the Father and the Holy Spirit, be glory and majesty, dominion and power, both now and ever.

THE FINAL part of this book opens with a discussion of the meaning of Christian hope. We will particularly focus on the eschatological perspectives found in the Bible. But since a belief in a life beyond death for God's faithful people has been a central feature of traditional Christianity, the following chapter will consider what is involved in 'the gift of eternal life'. Our discussion finally attempts to come to grips with not only eschatology's social and political dimensions but also the cosmic implications of the triumphant claim that 'in the fullness of time, God will renew and gather in one all things in Christ'.

CHAPTER 18

The Christain Hope

CHRISTIAN history is littered with examples of individuals and communities who have been sustained in oppression, and enabled to make remarkably positive contributions to society, due to their confidence that 'in the fullness of time, God will renew and gather in one all things in Christ.' We cannot help but marvel at the faith and hope of the Christian martyrs. Who, for example, can forget Bonhoeffer's parting words to his cell-mate as he was led out to his execution: 'For me this is the end – the beginning of life'? Our earthly pilgrimage may be extremely fraught, but with God's promises we journey on knowing that the End is enveloped in God's gracious judgement in Christ.

Nevertheless, contemporary Western Christian practice hardly displays the same emphasis upon eschatological themes as was once evident. When did we last hear a passionate warning about hell's flames in a sermon? Preachers seldom dwell upon the delights of a heavenly communion with God beyond this life, and the gist of most modern sermons on the Great Assize of Matthew 25: 31–46 centres upon serving Christ through 'the least of these who are members of my family' in the *present* life, rather than upon a consideration of a final judgement in which our destiny *beyond* this life will be decided. Some will find it hard to resist making a similar conclusion about contemporary Christianity to that H Richard Niebuhr made about American Christianity in the middle of the twentieth century: 'A God without wrath brought men without sin into a kingdom without judgement through the ministration of a Christ without a cross.' But there are solid reasons why we tend to eschew overtly eschatological expressions of Christianity as we come to terms with living in a society which has largely lost its sense of transcendence; and, to some extent, these reasons reflect why the Reformers were also to a degree wary of eschatology. In the hands of medieval Catholicism, the doctrine became a vehicle for an unhealthy speculative dimension. Then, as now, there always is a temptation for Christians to speak as if they know 'fully' what they can only know 'in part' (1 Cor. 13: 12). Futurology is a very inexact science, and a reverent agnosticism sometimes can be a theological virtue! The Reformers were also disturbed about a lunatic fringe which used eschatology to make all manner of apocalyptic predictions. Overt emphasis upon 'the last things' has generated some of the most way-out expressions of Christianity. In a secular world which likes to keep its feet on solid ground, it is hardly surprising, therefore, that eschatological themes have been squeezed out of a great deal of contemporary Christianity.

But there is another significant reason to be suspicious of a heavy emphasis upon eschatology. The more we focus upon the future, the less likely it is that we treat the present with significant seriousness. It is a lasting indictment of many versions of Christianity that they can be parodied as offering 'pie in the sky when you die', while the extent to which eschatological emphases take people's minds off earthly realities can be negative as well as positive. A firm hope that ultimately everything is in God's just and gracious hands may inspire those on the underside of history to endure, knowing that they will one day experience liberation, but an eschatological emphasis can equally dull people's interest in improving their lot. Sometimes eternity's greater glory can blind our eyes to the lesser wonders of the temporal realm. It is all too easy to allow ourselves to become unnecessarily other-worldly, thereby losing our commitment to social and political concerns. We not only then start acquiescing in preventable temporal evils, but more widely we press forward to life's end only to miss life itself.[1] John Baillie helps us place our eschatological convictions in a proper perspective:

> If our hope of a fuller life beyond is to be recognized as a fine and manly thing, it must never lead us to be unjust to the values and the demands of the life that now is. It must never lessen our interest in the present life, or make us feel it to be less worth living, or tempt us to hurry through with it. It must never have the effect of taking our minds off our present tasks, so that they shall be done less thoroughly and well; rather should it lead to their more thorough and conscientious performance. And lastly, it must never tempt us to think even for a moment that what particular thing we do does not greatly matter, that our life in time is not worth improving, or our lot bettering, or our health mending, or this whole earthly order of things worth patching up and bringing nearer to heart's desire.[2]

Recent re-evaluations of apocalyptic literature help to maintain the kind of balance between future hope and contemporary commitments advocated by Baillie. It is mistaken to think that the book of *Revelation* provides a warrant for the overt speculation exhibited in some theologies. Nor does apocalyptic literature necessarily underwrite way-out or other-worldly expressions of the Christian world-view.

Christopher Rowland has argued that those who have interpreted *Revelation* (and other examples of apocalyptic literature) in terms of its seemingly future orientation have been guilty of distortion. At the heart of apocalyptic is 'a type of religion whose distinguishing feature is a belief in direct revelation of the things of God which was mediated through dream, vision or divine intermediary.'[3] This revelation of the divine mysteries helps people understand their lives here and now, so any interest in the future is clearly matched by direct reference to the present. The understanding of existence revealed by the apocalyptists, therefore, was dominated by a concern about 'the meaning of existence in the present in the light of God's activity in the past and his hoped for acts in the future', rather than 'the way in which the righteous would spend their time in the kingdom'.[4] Hence, apocalyptic literature seeks to address 'the nature of man and the reason for the desperate straits in which the people of God found themselves'.[5] Through imaginative literary constructions, apocalyptic literature speaks to present needs rather than offers literal descriptions of the End-time. It is the literature of prophetic protest rather than of crystal ball gazers. As Jack McKelvey has said: 'The enduring importance of apocalyptic is its power to confront the dominant culture and offer the faithful an alternative to the world of present experience.'[6] This is important to bear in mind, since some of the more fanciful accounts of the Christian hope have been drawn from an all too literal interpretation of *Revelation*.

---

[1] See Jürgen Moltmann, *The Coming of God: Christian Eschatology* (London: SCM Press, 1996), p xi
[2] John Baillie, *And The Life Everlasting* (London: Oxford University Press, 1934), p 23.
[3] Christopher Rowland, *The Open Heaven* (London: SPCK, 1982), p 21.
[4] Ibid., p 189.
[5] Ibid., p 135.
[6] R J McKelvey, *The Millennium and the Book of Revelation* (Cambridge: The Lutterworth Press, 1999), p 46.

Pilgrimage in Faith and Hope

Christians look back in order to go forwards. But as they fix their sights on God's saving activity in the Christ event, and trust in God's grace alone for the forgiveness of sin, they are given hope to persevere in the earthly pilgrimage until the One who came to earth for their sakes finally completes his work in the transformation of all things. Jesus Christ then is the foundation, guide and goal of Christian hope.

The Bible teaches that the inheritance the faithful receive when they put their trust in God's self-revelation in Christ will only be fully manifest in the future. Meanwhile, as God's adopted sons and daughters, Christians are told to press forward in Christ's earthly service. The promise of an age in which 'death will be no more', and 'mourning and crying and pain will be no more', makes us dissatisfied with our world (Rev. 21: 4); the patience which flows from a hope that all things are being made new (Rev. 21: 5) helps us to endure this life's miseries and mayhem. Through the Holy Spirit we can live with the coming salvation in our hearts, so the earthly pilgrimage can be undertaken confidently.

Calvin uses two major themes to describe the Christian pilgrimage.[7] The first views it as a battle from which Christians emerge victorious (1 Thess. 5: 8; 1 Tim. 6: 12; Eph. 6: 10–20) or as a struggle to make progress in a race (Heb. 12: 1–2; 1 Cor. 9: 24–27); the second sees it from the perspective of the cross, and in three ways. First, we are to share in the sufferings of Christ (2 Cor. 4: 10; Matt. 16: 24; Phil. 3: 10). The more we are given to suffer for the gospels' sake the greater is our fellowship with Christ.[8] As we share in Christ's crucifixion we will come to enjoy the triumph of his resurrection. Bearing Christ's cross leads to a greater knowledge of God and teaches patience and obedience. God brings suffering to us, therefore, 'to free us from the condemnation of the world' rather than 'to ruin or destroy us'.[9] Secondly, as we share in Christ's cross we take part in the process which leads to penitence and sanctification; we participate in Christ's death and our old nature is set to one side. Although our new life with Christ remains hidden in God during our mortal life, we must strive to show evidence of it as we learn our lessons in the school of suffering. Thirdly, the sufferings we endure teach us to hold the present life in contempt, and hence 'to be aroused thereby to meditate upon the future life'.[10] God allows us to be afflicted to ensure that we do not become satisfied by this world's vanities. However, this should not lead to a pessimistic hatred of this life. That would be an act of great ingratitude to our creator. 'Indeed, this life, however crammed with infinite miseries it may be, is still rightly to be counted among those blessings of God which are not to be spurned.'[11] Our aspiration towards the new life, therefore, should not involve a flight from the old world but rather a commitment to live the promised life in this world. Calvin, however, maintains that desire for the future life does involve a longing for death and hence the termination of our sinful mortal life. This should not lead Christians to be overtly morbid. While they aspire to die they also look in confidence to the resurrection. It follows that 'no one has made progress in the school of Christ who does not joyfully await the day of death and final resurrection.'[12]

---

7   See Heinrich Quistorp, *Calvin's Doctrine of the Last Things* (London: Lutterworth Press, 1955), pp 27–51.
8   See Calvin, *Institutes*, 3,8,1.
9   Ibid., 3,8,6.
10   Ibid., 3,9,1.
11   Ibid., 3,9,3.
12   Ibid., 3,9,5.

Biblical Perspectives

Jewish eschatology initially maintained that people pass on to a post-mortem existence in Sheol, an uninviting underground pit where the dead were believed to reside. Sheol was a place from which there would be no return. Its residents were beyond communion with not only the living but also God (Ps. 115: 17). Sheol therefore invited terror rather than rejoicing:

> As the cloud fades and vanishes,
> so those who go down to Sheol do not come up;
> they return no more to their houses,
> nor do their places know them any more
> (Job 7: 9–10).

Sheol's inhabitants 'have no help' and are 'forsaken' – no longer remembered even by God (Ps. 88: 4–5). But, by the time of Jesus, a more positive scenario had emerged. This set future hope in a dual perspective which sought to do justice to both its individual and corporate dimensions. Included was an expectation that there will be a fulfilment of individual lives, as well as a belief in a new social order in which God will reign supreme. And both dimensions are clearly present in Jesus' teaching regarding the Kingdom of God, the concept which formed the framework for his entire teaching. There will be a divinely transformed corporate life as well as the resurrection of individuals when the Kingdom inaugurated by Jesus is fully manifest. Jesus' belief that the faithful would rise from Sheol to participate in God's Kingdom found him siding with the Pharisees against the Sadducees (Mark 12: 18–27). Many Christians maintain, therefore, that the vision of a God who enjoys fellowship with individuals provides a basis for a belief that this same God will restore the faithful to some form of post-mortem existence.

It is clear that the Apostles came to believe that the crucified Jesus was raised from the dead by God. This belief became the very foundation of the Church; it was a central tenet of the earliest Christian theologies (1 Cor. 15: 3–8). The New Testament generally views Jesus' resurrection as God's decisive revelation. It is the supreme vindication of God's sovereignty, the final victory over the powers which oppose him. Sometimes these powers are personified: 'the god of this world' (2 Cor. 4: 4), 'the ruler of this world' (John 12: 31) or 'the ruler of the power of the air' (Eph. 2: 2). But Satan is seldom regarded as operating alone. He is aided and abetted by other demonic 'rulers and authorities in the heavenly places' (Eph. 3: 10) or 'the elemental spirits of the world' (Gal. 4: 3). All these powers, however, are but the envoys of the greatest threat of all: death. And, above everything else, in raising the crucified Jesus, God has triumphed over death.

The Christian tradition has understood death in two quite distinct ways. An Augustinian strand builds upon Paul's idea that death came into the world as a result of the Fall: 'Therefore . . . sin came into the world through one man, and death came through sin, and so death spread to all because all have sinned' (Rom. 5: 12). Human mortality was never intended by the Creator. It has been brought upon the human race due to our sinfulness. According to this theological tradition death is a direct punishment from God. The resurrection, then, is understood in terms of the overcoming of death through an atonement for human sin: 'For since death came through a human being, the resurrection of the dead has also come through a human being; for as all die in Adam, so all will be made alive in Christ' (1 Cor. 15: 21–22). But there is an alternative understanding of human life which leads to a quite different view of death. According to this view, human beings were not created immortal and then punished for their sinfulness by God, and hence rendered mortal. They were created, rather, as immature creatures who have to undergo a process of growth and development. Death, therefore, is a quite natural phenomenon which accompanies creaturehead of all forms; it is not a punishment for sin. At death, of course, human beings complete their earthly pilgrimage. But, given the Christian hope generated by Jesus' resurrection, life's completion can be said to take place beyond the grave. The human pilgrimage, therefore, reaches its end in a post-mortem world created by God for precisely that purpose.

The New Testament contains several different theologies of hope, but upon close inspection there appear to be three distinct but inter-related eschatological dimensions within them.[13] The first centres upon the survival of individuals after death. It has been said that we grow up when we realize that we are mortal. We all die. This is a fact that frightens some and puzzles most. What is life's purpose if it has no permanence? And, set alongside the Christian witness of faith, Paul's judgement appears persuasive: 'If for this life only we have hoped in Christ, we are of all people most to be pitied' (1 Cor. 15: 19). A second feature of the Christian hope flows from the idea of God's Kingdom and is taken up in the notion of the millennium (Rev. 20: 1–6). This envisages a fulfilment of history in which wrongs will be righted and the oppressed set free:

> Blessed are you who are poor,
> for yours is the kingdom of God.
> Blessed are you who are hungry now,
> for you will be filled.
> Blessed are you who weep now,
> for you will laugh.
> (Luke 6: 20–21. See also Matt. 5: 1–12)

The third feature of the Christian hope concerns the cosmos. Paul set his eschatology in the widest terms. A creation which has been 'groaning in labour pains' awaits its final liberation from its 'bondage to decay' (Rom. 8: 21–22). The Seer of Patmos, meanwhile, invites us to expect 'a new heaven and a new earth' with 'all things' made new (Rev. 21: 1 and 5). Both Paul and John point to a need to view the Christian hope in less anthropocentric terms than has often been the case. All three dimensions of the Christian hope are brought together in a single eschatological framework when we turn away from focusing our hope for the future on *ourselves*, *our* history or *our* world: 'The centre has to be God, God's Kingdom and God's glory.'[14]

---

[13] At this point I am following Jürgen Moltmann's analysis in *The Coming of God: Christian Eschatology*.
[14] Ibid., p xv.

CHAPTER 19

The Gift of Eternal Life

WHILE the most frequent means of talking about eternal life undoubtedly involves the concept of resurrection, Paul nevertheless can use the Greek idea of immortality to convey his understanding of the Christian hope for individuals (I Cor. 15: 53–54; Rom. 2: 7; 2 Tim. I: 10). Strictly speaking, 'immortality' usually refers to the continued existence after death of the human soul, and some theologians have regarded the dualistic implications of the term as contrary to the Christian idea of the whole person – body and soul – dying and then being raised to life by God. The Christian doctrine of creation also suggests that creatures cannot by definition be immortal. Nevertheless, as John Hick argues, we perhaps ought not to make too much of these terminological differences:

> . . . if we posit the reality of God the difference between immortality and resurrection, as variations within a theistic picture, becomes quite secondary. For if God has created souls of such a nature that they do not perish with the body, their capacity to survive bodily death is a gift of divine grace. It is as truly a gift of God's grace as would be his recreation of beings whom he had made naturally mortal.[1]

And, as we shall see shortly, some theologians employ both ideas in their eschatologies.

There are three ways in which human beings can be said to 'live' beyond their deaths. The first is called *social* or *hereditary* immortality. It is undoubtedly the case that to lesser or greater degrees we live on in the family, friends and colleagues that we leave behind, with the most able and distinguished among us being more 'immortal' than the less able and undistinguished. J S Whale calls this 'social solidarity of the successive generations' a 'worthless metaphysic',[2] and it certainly does not address the fear and dread which besets those who contemplate their mortality, or explain the seeming purposelessness of the 'perpetual perishing' (A N Whitehead) of all things. Are persons valuable because of the ideas, ideals and example which they bequeath to their fellow human beings? Or are they valuable because they are uniquely precious to God? While social immortality presupposes the former, the Christian hope traditionally has assumed the latter. As John Baillie argues '. . . we have no right to take any *ultimate* comfort from the fact that "my friend's ideals do not die when he dies", or that "the world is a very different place because of those who have left their mark upon us".'[3]

---

[2]   J S Whale, *Christian Doctrine* (London: Fontana Books, 1957), p 168.
[3]   John Baillie, *And the Life Everlasting*, p 169.

The second way in which individuals can be said to live beyond their deaths is called *objective* immortality. It is central to many process theologies. The entire creative process, according to this way of thinking, is enveloped in the 'perpetual perishing' of creatures. But since God is the creator and redeemer of all things, nothing of value is lost. Everything is stored everlastingly in the divine memory. Schubert Ogden helps us develop the understanding of God involved:

> . . . his memory is infallible, and so for him the transience of life is overcome, or, rather, simply does not exist. Because his love of others is literally boundless, whatever comes to be is fully embraced by his love, where it is retained forever without any loss of vividness or intensity. Such value as it has, whether positive or negative, becomes an integral part of his own divine life, and thus is in the strict sense immortal or of everlasting significance.[4]

Every present moment of the many moments in our lives is immortalized in God's perfect memory. Hence, we are not only immortal by being remembered through those we leave behind when we die, but we also receive objective immortality in the divine memory. Our lives are significant to God who, moment by moment, receives us and makes us his own. Not only is *this* life significant for God now, it is also significant for evermore because all that we are, have been or will be is eternally and everlastingly remembered by the Deity. But, significantly, objective immortality does not necessarily entail the continuation of experiencing subjects beyond death.

This understanding of immortality has the merit that it is *theo*centric rather than anthropocentric. It avoids rooting post-mortem existence in a misplaced human assertiveness which negates the qualitative difference between mortal human beings and the immortal God. Also it by-passes some of the common and idolatrous reasons for insisting upon subjective immortality, e.g. the argument which says that if God really loves us he cannot permit us to be lost or destroyed. It is all too easy to make faith conditional upon receiving rewards, instead of living solely from God's love for us. Nevertheless, there are a number of reasons why some find the idea of objective immortality theologically unsatisfactory.[5] They object that objective immortality contradicts the divine impassibility. We saw earlier, however, that in some sense God must be passible if the Deity is to possess real relations with creatures. Secondly, the question is raised whether God's knowledge of the dross in the creative process entails that God gets tainted with the world's imperfections. Hick, for example, notes that according to this theology, 'all the cruelty, hatred and malevolence, all the pain, suffering and misery of the ages', is 'equally perpetuated in the divine consciousness', with the result that 'there is no final resolving of evil in the gradual creation of an ultimate good'.[6] In response to this criticism David Pailin asks us to face up to 'the cost and character of the divine love', as well as recognize that God is not 'polluted by total awareness of the evil in the world'.[7] The divine perfection is displayed precisely in the way that God responds redemptively to every instance of evil. A third objection suggests that objective immortality does not allow God to love us as individuals, since it is our contribution to the divine life which matters to God rather than us as subjects. Pailin counters this by questioning whether 'our continuing being as individuals is of such importance to God that our ceasing to be as subjects would seriously impair the satisfaction of the

---

4   Schubert M Ogden, 'The Meaning of Christian Hope', *Religious Experience and Process Theology: The Pastoral Implications of a Major Modern Movement*, eds. Harry James Cargas and Bernard Lee (New York: Paulist Press, 1976), p 199.

5   See Pailin, *Groundwork of Philosophy of Religion*, pp 193–7 and Hick, *Death and Eternal Life*, pp 217–21.

6   Hick, *Death and Eternal Life*, p 221.

7   Pailin, *Groundwork of Philosophy of Religion*, p 195.

8   Ibid., p 196.

---

divine love.'[8] Whatever we make of this, it is the fourth criticism which is perhaps the most crucial. As Hick opines, ' . . . this is not a doctrine of immortality in the sense of a doctrine about the continuance of human life after bodily death.'[9] He argues that ' . . . to be alive in any ordinary sense of the word is not only to be remembered, but also to be capable of remembering, and of creating fresh and different material for memory.'[10] This is a telling comment for those striving for a theology which does justice to the notes of finality and expectant triumph of the Christian gospel. Pailin presses the issue, though, whether our individual lives are so crucial to God that 'their continuation is a requirement of the rationality and meaningfulness of reality.'[11] We should take seriously his insistence that 'the significance and value of reality does not lie in its contribution to our corporate and individual well-being.'[12] And, yet, when all allowances are made for this radical theocentric approach, the theory of objective immortality falls short of what the New Testament leads us to expect.

This takes us, therefore, to the third sense in which persons may be said to live beyond their deaths: *subjective* immortality. There are two major ways in which theologians have understood the post-mortem existence of experiencing individuals: non-bodily survival and bodily survival, i.e. resurrection.

Non Bodily Survival

Those who make a clear distinction between the human body and an eternal soul argue that at death the body dies and clearly disintegrates but the soul by its very nature lives on.[13] This position is not without merit, since we often talk as if our selves are distinct from our bodies, and we have the impression that we can engage in cerebral activity without necessarily changing our bodily functions. Nevertheless, this dualistic way of understanding the Christian hope is open to serious objections. First, just because we talk as if 'we' are somehow different from our bodies, this in no way establishes that mind and body are distinct entities. Indeed, the entire dualistic argument is rendered questionable by the fact that, when we encounter self-consciousness in others, they are invariably embodied individuals. Secondly, our experience of being ourselves without in any way involving our bodies can be put down to our ability to keep our thoughts to ourselves. Our knowledge of human beings as psychosomatic entities provides evidence which suggests that thinking is a corporeal process. Thirdly, it has been argued that there is nothing incoherent about conceiving ourselves as disembodied after death. But that is not a firm ground upon which to move to the view that upon death we do in fact exist as disembodied souls. Indeed, our whole experience of being alive seems dependent upon having a body, and for us not to have a body beyond death would clearly render impossible most of the things we normally associate as features of everyday living. It is hard to contemplate how bodiless individuals in an after-life could be recognizable as the persons we knew before their deaths. A human being is an extremely complex organism which is largely defined by the fact that it has a body. In what sense, then, would an unbodied individual be continuous with the bodied individual it once was? Fourthly, theologians point out

---

[10]   Ibid.

[11]   Pailin, *Groundwork of Philosophy of Religion,* p 196.

[12]   Ibid.

[13]   The following criticism of the dualist view owes a great deal to Davies, *An Introduction to the Philosophy of Religion,* Pailin, *Groundwork of Philosophy of Religion,* and Baillie, *And the Life Everlasting.*

that the biblical witness does not provide a warrant for non-bodily survival after death. '. . . the original Christian hope was emphatically not a hope of release from embodiment as such, but rather a hope of the revivification of the whole man, soul and body, unto life eternal.'[14]

At its best, Christian theology has resisted the belief that the material world, and hence the human body, is instrinsically bad. Indeed, one of its central doctrines is the resurrection of the body. Richard Baukham draws the following general conclusion: 'Eschatology is emphatically not about the transcendence of immaterial and eternal aspects of creation over the bodily and moral aspects', since what is crucial to it is 'the new creation of the whole of this transient and bodily creation'.[15] Just how theology can speak of the Christian hope in such cosmic terms must await the next chapter. Meanwhile, we turn to Calvin for an example of a Reformed theologian who defends the doctrine of the immortality of the soul. Interestingly, Calvin combines non-bodily and bodily views of Christian hope by arguing that after the final judgement the immortal soul is united in a 'new' body.

John Calvin on the Immortality of the Soul and the General Resurrection of the Dead

Calvin maintains that eternal life involves a belief in the immortality of a soul which, as the term 'immortality' implies, continues to exist after the death and perishing of the body. The body is merely the earthly home of someone eternally precious to God. Calvin asks: 'If souls did not outlive bodies, what is it that has God present when it is separated from the body?'[16] Souls when divested of their earthly vessels have the capacity for eternal fellowship with God. Calvin is rather silent when it comes to the question of 'how?' He only tells us that ' . . . it is neither lawful nor expedient to inquire too curiously concerning our souls' intermediate state.'[17] But he argues that, whereas the body is created through generation and birth, the soul is God's gift to the individual, bestowed in a spiritual event which runs parallel to the normal process of reproduction. Calvin's elevation of soul over body, therefore, is not due to negative perceptions about material bodies *per se*; it is due to its different origin, and the fact that within it lies the elect's divinely given orientation towards God. Even after the Fall, Calvin believes that 'some vestige' of the God-given gravitation to give God honour 'remains imprinted in [our] vices'.[18] In spite of their sin the elect possess a faint idea of being made for eternity, and this is re-presented decisively to them in God's revelation in Christ.

At death our souls enter one of two states. The elect proceed to *provisional* blessedness, the rest to *provisional* damnation. As the elect continue in the interim between death and final judgement to be part of a process of regeneration, they can be confident that what was once merely hoped for is now in sight. Meanwhile, Calvin suggests that the damned will likewise have a foretaste of what is in store for them as their souls await the Second Coming of Christ. At this point, however, we might note the judgement of a very sympathetic interpreter of Calvin's eschatology: 'In spite of his many allusions to the Bible, Calvin fails to convince us that his teaching about immortality and the state after death is consonant with Scripture.'[19] Quistorp reiterates the point noted earlier, namely, that ' . . . the New Testament does not speak about immortality.'[20] And it is

---

[14] Baillie, *And the Life Everlasting,* p 19.
[15] From a discussion of Moltmann's eschatology found in Richard Bauckham ed., *God will be All in All: The Eschatology of Jürgen Moltmann* (Edinburgh: T & T Clark, 1999), p 7.
[16] Calvin, *Institutes,* 3,25,6.
[17] Ibid.
[18] Ibid., 1,15,6.
[19] Quistorp, *Calvin's Doctrine of the Last Things,* p 95.
[20] Ibid., p 96.

certainly the case that '. . . no details are given about [our] state in and after death because the attention of the Biblical witnesses is concentrated on the hope of eternal life.'[21] However much Calvin insists on theology being congruent with the Bible and needing to avoid unnecessary speculation, in practice he has put forward ideas about the soul's provisional post-mortem existence which are unbiblical and thoroughly speculative.

According to Calvin, the fulfilment of Christ's work takes place when at his Second Coming he effects the General Resurrection. The Second Advent and the resurrection of all the dead, whether to salvation or damnation, are one and the same event. Calvin was wary of the apocalyptic fanaticism evident in his day, so his use of the Bible's apocalyptic imagery is quite sparse. The Last Judgement becomes the end of a process rather than a cataclysmic intervention in history.[22] And, unlike the Seer of Patmos in *Revelation*, Calvin casts the Pope and the Roman Catholic Church, rather than Nero and the Roman Empire, in the role of Antichrist. Christ's Parousia, therefore, will be the occasion when the anti-Christian forces in the Roman Catholic Church are defeated and that church's members take their place with the damned. [In our more eirenic ecumenical age, Calvin's theological analysis will be dismissed as inaccurate and misplaced, but then he did not live in an age of open Catholicism!]. Christ's Second Coming then has a two-fold significance: it marks the coming of Christ to judge the godless, and it finalizes Christ's redemption of the faithful.

Calvin is totally convinced that the concept of resurrection is central to Christian belief. He maintains that 'the authority of the gospel would fall not merely in one part but in its entirety' if the dead are not raised.[23] The basis for our resurrection hope is two fold. First, Jesus' resurrection is 'the prototype' and 'the pledge of our coming resurrection'.[24] Even though some treat the resurrection stories as fairy tales, Calvin argues that they are records of historical events: 'To discredit so many authentic evidences is not only disbelief but a depraved and even insane obstinacy.'[25] Secondly, our resurrection hope is based upon divine omnipotence, i.e. 'God's boundless might'.[26] If we can contemplate God creating out of nothing, then we can confidently look forward to the resurrection, since the Word who creates is the same Word that awakens the dead.

Calvin makes three major points about the manner of the resurrection. First, he insists that there is bodily identity between the dead and the raised.[27] This observation underpins the individual's identity in this world and the next. Calvin believes that post-mortem souls will receive the 'same' bodies they had in earthly life. To be sure, our bodies will regain any lost vigour, but the resurrection will be the resurrection of *this* mortal body. Secondly, the risen body while the same will be a *new* body: '. . . we shall be raised again in the same flesh we now bear, but . . . the quality will be different.'[28] Here Calvin makes use of a philosophical distinction between 'substance' (*substantia*) and 'character' (*qualitas*). Although we shall retain 'the substance of our bodies' there will be

---

21   Ibid., p 7.
22   See Quistorp, *op.cit.*, p 95.
23   Calvin, *Institutes*, 3,25,3.
24   Ibid.
25   Ibid.
26   Ibid., 3,25,4.
27   Ibid., 3,25,7.
28   Ibid., 3,25,8.
29   Ibid.

change of character in that 'its condition may be far more excellent.'[29] So the risen body receives new qualities even though its identity with the mortal body remains. Thirdly, the elect who are alive at the *parousia* will not die. It will not be necessary to introduce for them an interval between death and final judgement. Unlike those who have died before the Parousia, and who underwent 'a severing of body and soul', those alive at the Second Advent will undergo a sudden change (1 Cor. 15: 51).[30]

Calvin teaches that at the Second Coming there will be a general resurrection of the dead: '. . . one will be a resurrection of judgement, the other of life [John 5: 29].'[31] The grim situation facing the retrobates is flagged up by the fact that they are raised to face the torment of eternal death. Christ's honour as our supreme Judge has to be respected: 'For to be consumed by death would be a light punishment if they were not brought before the Judge to be punished for their obstinacy, whose vengeance without end and measure they have provoked against themselves.'[32] But the picture of God presented here is profoundly problematical. Not content with deciding who are part of the elect, God is depicted as achieving the resurrection of those he has predestined to damnation for the sole reason that death is not considered by God sufficient punishment. This view lowers our understanding of God to sub-human patterns of justice, and many will find it difficult to equate with the God we have seen in Jesus.

Calvin maintains that at the Second Advent the elect and the reprobate will fall equally under Christ's judgement. While he believes that the latter receive the harshest of penalties, he concentrates what he has to say of those who fall under the judgement of grace. The elect rise to receive 'everlasting blessedness' or 'eternal happiness'.[33] They do not deserve this, since they have been sinners; but eternal life comes to them as a gracious gift. For those who have experienced oppression, injustice and suffering in their lives, the new life will come as a compensation. The retrobate, meanwhile, receive a 'reward' commensurate with their predestined status but confirmed by their sinfulness. They are: '. . . cut off from all fellowship with God', and so 'feel his sovereign power against [them] that [they] cannot escape being pressed by it.'[34]

Objections to Subjective Immortality

It is important to take stock of the arguments of those who do not believe bodily survival actually takes place. First, it is argued that we have no empirical evidence to establish that there is bodily survival after death. No one has returned from death to tell us what happens on 'the other side', it is claimed, so the idea of life after death, in general, and bodily survival, in particular, must be put to one side. Christians, of course, will point to the stories about Jesus' resurrection to counter such scepticism. And there are those who regard the findings of parapsychology and psychical research sufficiently impressive at least to warrant maintaining an open mind on the matter.[35]

A second objection to subjective immortality comes from those who believe that even to contemplate the idea is idolatrous. People who insist upon life after death, the argument runs, are guilty of a misplaced human assertiveness which obscures the qualitative difference between the

29	Ibid.
30	Ibid.
31	Ibid., 3,25,9.
32	Ibid.
33	Ibid., 3,25,10.
34	Ibid., 3,25,12.
35	See Hick, *Death and Eternal Life*, pp 112–46.

eternal and infinite God and temporal and finite human beings. And, further, in wishing for life after death they are displaying a high degree of self-centredness by refusing to live upon the basis of God's love for them *now* rather than on the expectation of a reward beyond this life. This very robust objection to subjective immortality has been forcefully countered by Baillie, who notes that a genuine desire for life after death arises properly when we are concerned about the perishing of our loved ones rather than ourselves:

> Perhaps in certain moods I can contemplate my own death and say, 'I do not care whether that is the end of me or not; the thing does not interest me'. But surely in no mood can I contemplate the death of the most precious soul I know, the death of him whom I most love and reverence, and say. 'I do not care whether that is the end of him or not; the thing does not interest me'. The former might be mistaken for humility; the latter could never be taken for anything but what it is, namely, treason. The man who can see his beloved die, believing that it is for ever, and say, 'I don't care', is a traitor to his beloved and to all that their love has brought them. He has no right not to care.[36]

But, surely, it is one thing 'not to care' and something rather different to refuse to succumb to the collective hubris which results in our failure to accept our finitude? Baillie steps upon much firmer ground, however, when he insists upon a theocentric approach to the spiritual quest. We are to transfer 'the centre of attention and concern from one's self to God', and this will lead us to a recognition that our salvation will be found 'in the knowledge that God alone matters and in the will to do all things for His greater glory', rather than in idle speculation concerning what becomes of us after death.[37] We are never 'deserving of immortality', nor is life after death an 'inalienable right',[38] but it can be viewed appropriately in a non-idolatrous way when understood as God's gift to us rather than as something we achieve. There is nothing basically wrong in God-fearing folk hoping that by God's grace there may be some kind of fulfilment beyond this life – particularly if their lives have been unfulfilled in history.

A third objection to the idea of subjective immortality concerns the difficulty of conceptualising post-mortem existence in a coherent and satisfactory way. So, to give one example, we assume that self-hood by nature involves a process of ongoing development for good or ill. It is difficult, then, to conceive of persons who have endless capacity for life when everything that we know about them informs us that they are fundamentally limited in scope concerning what they can do or achieve. Pailin, therefore, invites us to draw the conclusion that '. . . it makes much more sense of human being to consider that its proper goal is to exploit its capacities to the full before death than to consider there will be an endless series of moments in which to actualise them – to and even beyond the point of bored and boring repetition when nothing novel is possible for us.'[39] Or, to give a second example, there is the difficulty of conceptualising which 'me' is raised to life. Is it the 'me' of youth tearing about the rugby field, the 'me' of middle-age puffing and panting up Lakeland fells with a gammy foot, or the 'me' in my likely senility? If we follow Paul's arguments about 'the spiritual body' (see I Cor. 15: 42–49), though, we might recognize that this difficulty is caused by viewing subjective immortality in an illicitly physical fashion. But the problem then is raised concerning how we conceptualise a physical and earthly body which is identical with the spiritual and risen body.

---

36   Baillie, *And the Life Everlasting*, p 53.
37   Ibid., p 185.
38   Ibid., p 195.

So even if a satisfactory way of understanding how persons can survive the end of their physical bodies can be found, the problem of conceiving *how* that person lives on and *in what kind of way* remains. And those theologians who provide answers might stand accused of going beyond what is given us to know.

A final objection to the idea of subjective immortality simply says that a life beyond death is undesirable. It is certainly the case that many people – secular humanists but also some Christians – live engaging, positive and creative lives without any belief in a life beyond death. And the often trumpeted assertion that human life would be meaningless without the prospect of subjective immortality has been negated by the lives of many an atheist. It also seems perfectly clear that a life beyond death is undesirable if it is merely more of the same but of infinite duration. We need to keep in view the etymological fact that the Greek word we translate as 'eternal' in the phrase 'eternal life (*aionios*) is more concerned with 'quality' and 'depth' than with 'length' or 'duration'. Some ideas of life after death amount to little more than an eternity of idleness, and they are not to be commended as worthy of the Christian hope. But, surely, subjective immortality is desirable if it leads to a life worth living, to an existence which is more than a mere continuation of all the hassles of our present life, and to a fellowship with God and others in which everything which has hindered that fellowship on earth is finally removed. This kind of new life presupposes redemption and transformation; Easter Day always needs Good Friday. Any future life which is desirable, therefore, must involve the removal of all the barriers to a full life which we encounter in this life, as well as provide resources for fulfilment as yet unknown to us. In it we must be relieved of all the burdens of temporality and possess uninterrupted enjoyment with God. A desirable subjective immortality, then, would certainly involve us laying hold of the beatific vision of God, i.e. an immediate and direct transforming experience of God; just as it would imply a sense of fulfilment. Baillie, however, reminds us that 'fruition' is not 'a state of mere passivity'.[40] It is an activity – albeit 'a higher activity than the activity of becoming or of unfulfilled quest'.[41] In the life hereafter, then, we will find 'plenty of room for adventure, and even for social service', but it will be of a kind we have not experienced before, a growing *in* rather than *towards* God.[42] Hick also argues that a desirable life after death will take account of 'the social and interpersonal character of human existence', and, so far from envisaging idleness for us in eternity, he argued in his early writings that after death we go on to 'many successive lives in many worlds', until 'ego-hood is finally transcended in a state of human unity which can be characterized, on the Trinitarian model, as one-in-many and many-in-one.'[43] Some will find it difficult enough to contemplate one life hereafter, let alone many; but the basic idea that there is 'work' for us still to do in eternal life is important. It would seem, therefore, that an attractive and desirable form of post-mortem existence is conceivable, but, as we have already observed, just because we can conceive something does not entail that it exists! We now move on to consider some of the ways in which theologians have justified a belief in subjective immortality.

---

[40]   Baillie, *And the Life Everlasting*, p 231.
[41]   Ibid., p 232.
[42]   Ibid., p 234.
[43]   Hick, *Death and Eternal Life*, p 203. Hick later came to see that it is inappropriate to make speculative assertions about the nature of the final post-mortem state. See *An Interpretation of Religion* (London: Macmillan and New Haven: Yale University Press, 1989), pp 354–55 and *The Rainbow of Faiths*, p 71.

Belief in Bodily Survival

Some theologians have grounded their belief in bodily survival upon their reflections concerning the nature of human beings. Hick, for example, observes that most people do not fulfil their human potential in this life. He paints a realistic picture when he says: 'Most of the earth's inhabitants, in every generation including the present one, have had to live in a condition of chronic malnutrition and under threat of starvation, and very many have always had to dwell in the insecurity of oppression, exploitation and slavery, constantly menaced by the possibility of disasters of both human and natural origin.'[44] If God truly wills the fulfilment of everyone, then God must provide the opportunity for everyone to have a life beyond the present one. Another way of making the same point is to pick up a famous argument put forward by Immanuel Kant. Human beings are moral agents who make choices. For those choices to be real, there must be a state of immortality which enables us to do those things which we found it impossible to do in this life. But how does Hick argue for bodily survival? He starts from the premise that our perceptions after death will be akin to those that we experience in dreams. While our dreams are 'private experiences in which other "people" are only appearances that are not animated by independent centres of consciousness', in the life hereafter there may be 'real communication and interaction with other minds by . . . extrasensory perception.'[45] Hick sees no reason to believe that a post-mortem world (or, as we have seen, worlds) containing such individuals is inconceivable. So, when individuals die they are either immediately, or following an interval of time, recreated in another world. Hick introduces a theory of 'replicas' to explain how this happens:

> A living person ceases to exist at a certain location, and a being exactly similar to him in all respects subsequently comes into existence at another location. And . . . it would be a correct decision, causing far less linguistic and conceptual disruption than the contrary one, to regard the 'replica' as the same person as the original.[46]

This theory is underpinned by a view which regards individuality as 'the pattern or "code" which is exemplified', rather than 'the numerical identity of the ultimate physical constituents of the body'.[47] While identity between the 'earthly' and 'resurrected' bodies is obviously vital in any theory of bodily survival, Hick grants that 'in its new environment' the earthly body is affected by 'processes of healing and repair' which transform it.[48]

    Hick argues that 'the consideration of logically coherent extrapolations can take us as far as the bare ideas of divine reconstitution in another world which is not spatially related to our present world.'[49] Others will be rather more sceptical, believing that Hick's 'extrapolations' are solely the product of 'the creative imagination' which, he tells us, alone can paint pictures of the details of the next world and life within it.[50] And Hick also has recently been led to adopt a greater degree of

---

[44]   Ibid., p 154.
[45]   Ibid., pp 265–66.
[46]   Ibid., p 283.
[47]   Ibid.
[48]   Ibid., p 294.
[49]   Ibid., p 295.
[50]   Ibid.

agnosticism concerning the details of our purported post-mortem existence. It might even be the case that *ultimate* fulfilment for human beings does not depend upon subjective immortality at all, but rather resides in objective immortality and thereby 'the present recognition that we have loved and that God has participated "indestructibly" and "definitively" in the experience of that love.'[51] Meanwhile, those who insist on grounding the Christian hope in bodily survival may feel rather cheated by Hick's idea of 'replicas'. Brian Davies is one such person:

> Knowing that a replica of myself will be wining and dining somewhere is not at all the same as knowing that I shall be wining and dining somewhere. For the continued existence of a person, more is required than replication.[52]

But whatever we make of Hick's arguments, it cannot be doubted that he has made a massive contribution to our understanding of eternal life.

A second way in which theologians have justified a belief in bodily survival is by focusing upon personal experience. Our experience of oneness with God in this life is then said to be a foretaste of a more complete relationship with God beyond death. Baillie reasons that, 'if the promise of *fruition* does not come to us from our experience of the *quest*, it is difficult to see how we can reach it by any more royal road.'[53] It is precisely our experience of God before death which thus kindles our hope for survival beyond death. Through our fellowship with God we come to learn how we are treasured by God. We discover that are intrinsically important to God and thereby is generated the hope that there is life beyond death. As Baillie confidently asserts: 'Because it is a life with God, it is a life that can never die; and it is in proportion to the depth and vividness of our present experience of it that the assurance of its continuance beyond the grave takes root within our souls.'[54] Other theologians, of course, have argued that unity with God does not necessitate subjective immortality, since the required unity can be accounted for either by the self being absorbed into God or by objective immortality.[55]

Arguments from experience are invariably less than fully satisfactory since they often need the support of additional non-experiential reasoning. The aforementioned argument confirms this with its built-in assumption that the God we experience is of such a nature that the Deity will not allow us to be annihilated when we die. This takes us to our third theological argument for life after death in a bodily form, namely, that consideration of God's nature invites such a belief. If God is 'pure unbounded love', it is argued, then an omnipotent God will not allow those with whom a precious relationship has been formed to perish upon death. Baillie calls this 'the only unanswerable argument for immortality that has ever been given, or ever can be given'.[56] He puts his case very succinctly:

> If the individual can commune with God, then he must matter to God; and if he matters to God, he must share God's eternity. For if God really rules, He cannot be conceived as scrapping what is precious in His sight.[57]

---

[51] Pailin, *Groundwork of Philosophy of Religion*, p 188.
[52] Davies, *An Introduction to the Philosophy of Religion*, p 223.
[53] Baillie, *And the Life Everlasting*, p 98.
[54] Ibid., p 210.
[55] See Pailin, *Groundwork of Philosophy of Religion*, p 187.
[56] Baillie, *And the Life Everlasting*, p 137.
[57] Ibid.

Baillie observes that the argument can only be countered if either of its premises is denied. But this is precisely what Pailin does when he suggests that this common argument is over-sentimental. He doubts whether the fact that I matter to God entails that I should share God's eternity: 'While love does imply care for its objects, it does not involve their irreplaceability.'[58] We are always in danger of overstating our importance to God's creative activity in the cosmos. What a loving God requires is that there are *some* creatures to love, not that one of them is 'me' after my death. Just which creatures God chooses to love is for God to decide. But, of course, we cannot rule out the possibility of some of them being individuals to whom God has granted a post-mortem existence.

A final argument bases a belief in bodily survival beyond death upon setting the human story in its relation to God, and especially upon what the biblical faith in Jesus teaches us about God's promises to us. It is certainly the case that Jesus believed that there would be a resurrection of the dead. His earliest followers took up that belief for themselves, with the resurrection of their Lord being understood as a foretaste of their own future resurrection. Baillie agrees with Calvin when he says that 'Christ's followers did not argue from a general resurrection to the Resurrection of their Lord; rather was the Resurrection of their Lord the earnest of their own.'[59] So the faith that God had raised Jesus became the starting point for Christian hope. But Baillie warns us against making 'the disciples' ocular vision of the resurrected body of Christ the sole and sufficient basis of the Church's faith in His (and our) continued life with God'.[60] It is unwise to make faith depend upon the historicity of the biblical accounts of the resurrection appearances, but Baillie nevertheless believes that a belief in the risen Christ (and hence a basis for a belief in our resurrection) is not simply a product of faith:

> . . . to make the vision of the risen Christ conditional upon faith in Him is by no means the same thing as making it the fruit of faith. To say that I cannot see a certain star without lenses does not mean that the lenses create the star.[61]

Other people, however, argue that the apocalyptic worldview within which Jesus and early Christians operated was largely responsible for framing their eschatological outlook. That outlook is now known to be misleading, so we should beware of accepting as credible what the Gospels tell us about resurrection. Even if we are not persuaded about being cautious concerning the credibility of the biblical imagery, we can recognize the problems attached to the overall argument. If we argue from 'Jesus was raised to life by God after his crucifixon' to 'we will be raised to life by God after our deaths', then, we must recognize not just the problem of the historicity of the first claim, but also overcome the further problem of attributing to human beings the same possibility which has been granted to Jesus (who tradition has designated as divine as well as human).

If the above discussion has proved anything, it is that it is impossible to offer a thoroughly satisfactory argument to establish beyond reasonable doubt that there is bodily (or, indeed, non bodily) survival beyond death. As Davies remarks at the end of his philosophical treatment of this subject, ' . . . an attractive form of life after death is not to be dismissed as impossible, though we have seen no compelling reason to believe in life after death in any form.'[62] But to the thoughtful

---

[58]   Pailin, *Groundwork of Philosophy of Religion*, p 189.
[59]   Baillie, *And the Life Everlasting*, p 59.
[60]   Ibid., p 144.
[61]   Ibid., p 152.
[62]   Davies, *An Introduction to the Philosophy of Religion*, p 234.

theological eye this comes as no surprise. The idea that God's relationship with us will not end at death has not been generally understood by Christians as an opinion which needs reasons to establish its credibility; it has been comprehended in the rather different sense of a hope based upon a promise derived from our faith in God's gracious Word in Christ. The fact that we can offer reasons to render the idea of subjective immortality at least a possibility is perhaps all that we can expect; the rest remains 'a mystery' (1 Cor. 15: 51) upon which speculation can be a barrier to true faith. What really matters is our confidence that our lives are always safe with God, since this sets us free for a life of love to God and our neighbours.

Salvation for all or just for some?

There are several ways of understanding what happens to people who are living outside God's fellowship at death. The first is usually described as *conditional immortality* and entails the belief that at death the faithful enjoy life in heaven with God while the rest are simply annihilated. As we saw earlier, though, Calvin thought that this granted too much to all of us, since not only do the faithful need a period beyond death in which to be made ready for heaven, but also the damned need to have placed before them the prospect of the eternal punishment which awaits them in hell. So he argued that everyone at death is raised to a provisional state before moving to their ultimate destination. While the faithful go to heaven and the damned to hell, and, hence, *eternal punishment*, the great Reformer is adamant that the destination of each group was decided before they were born. Nothing they did in their earthly lives could conceivably have altered matters.

Calvin, with customary force, also argues that nothing which occurs in the provisional state *after* death can alter a person's ultimate destination. At death, a pathway is opened up which cannot be altered; the verdict announced before we were born still stands. Calvin is rigorously opposed, therefore, to the Roman Catholic doctrine of *purgatory*. This maintained that all those destined for salvation who die without repentance for venial sins, or who have not received their punishment for that wrongdoing which caused a measure of guilt already removed, go to purgatory where they are prepared for their eventual place in heaven. Calvin rejects the doctrine for two reasons. First, it is unbiblical. Then, secondly, it undermines the all-sufficiency of Christ's work, and hence takes the basis for forgiveness away from the cross. Nothing which can possibly occur in the provisional state following death can alter the fact that Christ has already died for sin on Calvary. Calvin maintains that the doctrine of purgatory seeks 'expiation of sins . . . elsewhere than in the blood of Christ'.[63] It follows that he is equally suspicious of the practice of offering prayers for the dead.

Some Reformed theologians, however, argue that the doctrine of purgatory has a point: 'The gap between the individual's imperfection at the end of this life and the perfect heavenly state in which he is to participate has to be bridged; and purgatory is simply the name given in roman theology to this bridge.'[64] It is even conceivable, if we follow Hick, to argue that 'the gap' may need 'a bridge' which spans several lives. This might be deemed necessary if we adopt an approach which espouses *universal salvation*, and which takes up the idea that one day all will enjoy God's unbroken fellowship. Schemes of salvation marked out by theologians in terms of 'conditional immortality' or 'eternal punishment' tend to make justice rather than forgiveness the primary spiritual attribute. It is therefore not surprising that several Reformed theologians question the role which hell has played in theology. Hick provides us with a catalogue of objections to the idea of hell:

---

[63]   Calvin, *Institutes*, 3,5,6.
[64]   Hick, *Death and Eternal Life*, p 202.

> ... for a conscious creature to undergo physical and mental torture through unending time ... is horrible and disturbing beyond words; and the thought of such torment being deliberately inflicted by divine decree is totally incompatible with the idea of God as infinite love; the absolute contrast of heaven and hell ... does not correspond to the innumerable gradations of human good and evil; justice could never demand for finite human sins the infinite penalty of eternal pain; such unending torment could never serve any positive or reformative purpose precisely because it never ends ... [65]

Doctrines of universal salvation, though, are often dismissed because they do not do justice to an individual's right freely to reject God's offer of salvation. Moltmann counters this objection in two ways. First, he thinks that it is inhumane to maintain the existence of hell on this basis since 'there are not many people who can enjoy free will where their eternal fate in heaven or hell is concerned.'[66] Then, secondly, he notes that the argument elevates human free will over and above God's power and desire to save: 'The logic of hell seems to me not merely inhumane but also extremely atheistic: here the human being in his freedom of choice is his own lord and god.'[67]

While Hick suggests that there are a series of lives in which God has the time and opportunity to draw all people into a lasting relationship with him,[68] Moltmann argues that there is a time between Christ's resurrection and the general resurrection of the dead which is 'filled by the lordship of Christ over the dead and the living, and by the experience of the Spirit, who is the life-giver'.[69] This provides the space in which God's universal salvific intentions materialize. But what becomes of the fate of those who died *before* the Christ event? To answer this very important question Moltmann turns to I Peter's statement that upon death Christ went to make 'a proclamation to the spirits in prison' (3: 19). So not only did Christ experience the hell of Godforsakeness on the Cross, he also went to the dead in order to draw them into fellowship with him. Moltmann's grounds for universalism thus come fully into view: 'It is not the optimistic dream of a purified humanity, it is Christ's descent into hell that is the ground for the confidence that nothing will be lost but that everything will be brought back again and gathered into the eternal kingdom of God.'[70]

Moltmann provides a recent and comprehensive argument for universalism in Reformed theology. Baillie, though, warned that the success of a universalistic soteriology hinges upon its ability to maintain 'the urgency of immediate repentance', and to make 'no promises to the procrastinating sinner'.[71] Whether or not Moltmann has satisfied these criteria for success can be left for the reader to decide. This writer, however, believes that Moltmann's argument carries Barth's soteriology (mentioned in an earlier chapter) to its logical outcome. On this point at least Moltmann has surpassed his mentor's work.

---

[65]   Ibid., pp 200–1.
[66]   Jürgen Moltmann, 'The Logic of Hell' in Richard Bauckham ed., *God Will be All in All: The Eschatology of J?rgen Moltmann*, p 44.
[67]   Ibid., p 45.
[68]   See Hick, *Death and Eternal Life*, pp 242–61.
[69]   Moltmann, *The Coming of God*, p 104.
[70]   Ibid., p 251.
[71]   Baillie, *And the Life Everlasting*, p 245.

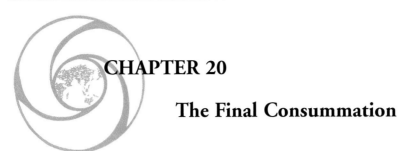

CHAPTER 20

The Final Consummation

THE KINGDOM of God is a central term in Jesus' teaching. Properly understood it refers more to a divine activity than a divine location. It is best thought of as speaking about God's reign or rule over all that is other than God. When used by Jesus the term sometimes possesses a futuristic orientation, thus suggesting that God's reign has yet to become manifest. The disciples are sent out with the warning that the kingdom will have arrived before some of them have died (Mark 9: 1); it is imminent but still awaited in the future. Meanwhile, Joseph of Arimathea is described by the evangelist as one who was 'waiting expectantly for the kingdom of God' (Mark 15: 43). However, there are other passages which suggest that Jesus taught that the kingdom had arrived and was being fulfilled by his life and death. Jesus starts his public ministry in Galilee with the claim that 'the kingdom of God has come near' (Mark 1: 15; note some alternative translations: 'the kingdom of God is upon you' [NEB] or 'the kingdom of God is close at hand' [JB]). He also likens the kingdom to a seed which grows secretly (Mark 4: 26–29), and to a tiny mustard seed which grows into a large shrub (Mark 4: 30–32), thereby suggesting that the kingdom appears mysteriously as well as developing and growing for all to see.

Jesus' teaching about the kingdom as presented by the Gospel writers is clearly very nuanced, so it is not surprising that biblical theologians have interpreted it in three quite different ways. One group, associated with the work of Johannes Weiss and Albert Schweitzer, have argued that Jesus was expecting an immediate and supernatural end of world-history in his lifetime. According to them, therefore, Jesus was teaching an essentially *futuristic* doctrine of the Last Things. Another group, on the other hand, usually associated with C H Dodd, have maintained that the opposite was the case. They suggest that Jesus believed that the kingdom was *realised* in his own life and work. But Jesus' actual statements undermine both theories, since it is quite easy to find passages which defy either interpretation. To do justice to the facts, therefore, most biblical scholars nowadays tend to favour a middle position which regards Jesus' teaching about the kingdom as *proleptic* in orientation. In Jesus' life and work, we are given a sign of God's reign breaking upon the world, but it will only be fully manifest at the end of history.

How one understands Jesus' teaching concerning the kingdom to a certain degree clearly determines how one views the biblical concept of the *parousia*. The Greek word *parousia* can mean either 'presence' or 'coming'. In Christian theology, however, it has become a technical term to depict Christ's second coming to judge people and to bring in the kingdom. The two contrasting ways in which *parousia* can be understood, though, have led to two quite different interpretations of the second coming. The first emphasises Jesus' visible return to earth on a final mission to put an end to our evil world, and, in its place, to establish the thousand years reign of peace (the so-called millennium); while the second interpretation focuses upon Christ's presence in the church, and then, following Christ's reign, the end of this present world history. The former viewpoint stays remarkably close to the New Testament apocalyptic worldview, in general, and the book of *Revelation*, in particular; the latter outlook tends to minimize the cataclysmic end to history envisaged by apocalyptic literature. The debate between the two positions turns upon whether the emphasis is to be put on *temporal* or *eternal* eschatological expectations. And since we find both emphases in Jesus' teaching, we might contemplate the possibility that the two traditional interpretations of the parousia could be offering complementary rather than conflicting 'stories' about Christian hope.

The idea of the millennium, however, has its roots in Jewish Rabbinical literature from where it entered the Christian theological tradition. Its basic idea concerns a temporary golden age on this earth and within our present history that precedes the final eschaton. When taken up by John in *Revelation* the length of this golden age becomes precisely 'a thousand years' (Rev. 20: 6). The idea of the millennium was later adopted by two different traditions within millennialist Christianity: the pre-millennialists and the post-millennialists. Pre-millennialists believe that Christ's Second Coming takes place before the thousand year long golden age. A typical outline of this view begins with the time immediately before Christ's parousia being made up of catastrophes and evils as the Antichrist appears. Then Christ comes to overcome the Antichrist and to raise the faithful from the dead. There follows then a thousand year long period of peace and harmony upon earth when Christ and the faithful reign. At the end of the millennium the world reverts back to 'normal' for a short time, with the forces of evil and death once again in evidence after the wicked have been raised to life. Then follows the Final Judgement when the faithful are left with Christ and the rest are consigned to eternal damnation in hell. Post-millennialists, on the other hand, argue that the Second Coming follows the thousand year reign of the Church on earth, with a conflict between good and evil taking place prior to Christ's Second Coming.

While the pre-millennialists tend to see the Kingdom's dawn as solely a matter for divine agency, the post-millennialists are confident that God makes use of human resources in bringing about the kingdom. Jack McKelvey observes that, 'The former think that the latter underestimate the power of evil, while the latter believe the former take too pessimistic a view of the world.'[1] But to many people outside millennialist Christianity the apocalyptic outlooks of both groups will appear as incredible as they are seemingly irrelevant. People can speculate to their hearts content about when the End will come, what it will be like and whether the millennium precedes or follows the parousia, but by and large we ceased long ago to make pre-critical appeals to the New Testament apocalyptic world view. Unless ideas like 'parousia' and 'millennium' are interpreted 'symbolically' (or 'metaphorically' or 'mythically' – to use different terms for similar ideas) rather than literally, it is difficult to see what sense we can make of them. This is precisely the strategy McKelvey adopts in order to rehabilitate the idea of the millennium. He calls the millennium 'a metaphor' which 'symbolises God's triumph over evil in the person of Jesus Christ and the vindication of the victims of oppression and injustice.'[2] But he then rather spoils his argument by introducing in some of his statements the same kind of literalism he condemns as inappropriate in the older traditions of millennialism. He commends the worthy idea that the millennium 'relates to how we live in the here and now' as well as being 'a transcendent eschatological hope which will not be realised until God consummates all things', but then he surprisingly claims that this hope is 'a promise we are to

---

[1]   McKelvey, *The Millennium and the Book of Revelation*, p 10.
[2]   Ibid, p 92.

expect to see *realised* upon earth', and that, 'it is *in this world* that God's cause will be vindicated and the faithful will experience his blessing.'[3] But claims such as these invite the same kind of 'wrong questions' that McKelvey requests that we avoid: When will this promise be fulfilled? Where will it take place? Who will be included and excluded by it?[4] Given that our planet will one day either be so hot or so cold that it will prevent human life, it is quite difficult to envisage how any this-worldly expressions of Christian hope can possess *lasting* value – even if they can be shown to be credible in the first place. And my reading of history suggests that the oppressed will seek in vain for their *full* vindication in history.

Now that we have gained some insight into the key concepts of parousia, kingdom of God and millennium, it is time to turn our attention to the views of two Reformed theologians who have strikingly different approaches to our topic.

John Calvin: The Eternal Consummation in Christ

Calvin is firmly opposed to millennialism. He describes it as a 'fiction' which is 'too childish either to need or to be worth a refutation.'[5] Christian hope for Calvin is essentially eternal and beyond history. He accuses the millennialists of misinterpreting Rev. 20: 4. The number one thousand in that passage 'does not apply to the eternal blessedness of the church but only to the various disturbances that awaited the church, while still toiling on earth.'[6] Christ's reign is for eternity, not a thousand years, and Calvin fears, therefore that the millennialists are guilty of watering down the Christian hope: 'If their blessedness is to have an end, then Christ's kingdom, on whose firmness it depends, is but temporary.'[7] But one wonders whether Calvin (who follows Augustine at this point) has done justice to Rev. 20: 1–6. Quistorp suggests that Calvin converts the millennium into 'a period in church history' since he interprets it to mean 'the whole time of the church from the epiphany to the parousia.'[8] The text's eschatological thrust is conveniently lost as Calvin spiritualizes and individualizes the Millennium, with the concept merely coming to mean Christ's rule over individuals from birth to their death and the final judgement. Calvin, therefore, largely loses the sense in which the Christian hope concerns this earth as well as a future heaven. As Quistorp says, when the kingdom appears 'it sets up within history a final prefiguring of the consummation because this world must be changed into the new world of God.'[9]

When Christ comes finally to reign, Calvin argues, all worldly powers will be defeated, including the Devil and his cohorts. It also means the end of all those social arrangements which help maintain our earthly lives, e.g. marriage, civil government, and even to a certain extent religion and its ministers. Taking 1 Cor. 15: 24 with the utmost seriousness, Calvin envisages the time when God rather than Christ is central. Christ's purpose is to hand us over to the Father. So at the Last Judgement the faithful enter eternal life, transformed from their sinful nature and re-made in God's image. They receive 'every sort of happiness', and their heavenly reward is a 'measure of glory' suitable for each of them.[10] Along with all the other church members they are also united as a single

---

3   Ibid. (Italics mine).
4   Ibid., p 10.
5   Calvin, *Institutes*, 3,25,5.
6   Ibid.
7   Ibid.
8   Quistorp, *Calvin's Doctrine of the Last Things*, p 160.
9   Ibid., pp 161–2.
10   Calvin, *Institutes*, 3,25,10.

company. So the coming kingdom brings with it the perfecting of both individual Christians and the Church of which they are all a part. And, of course, the anticipated unity of the Body of Christ should be the driving force of our contemporary search for Christian unity. Finally, Calvin believes that Christ's Second Coming will also lead to creation's perfection. Building upon Rom. 8: 8ff, he argues that, just as the Fall had negative implications for the created order, so the Second Coming will have positive ones for it. He avoids too much speculation, but envisages the world's radical transformation. The present age is temporal, but the future age will be eternal. As in the case of the resurrection of the body, the *essence* of the old will remain, but the new will have a change of *character.* Calvin, needless to say, is quite clear about the reason for creation's final consummation; it is to give the Creator praise and glory!

Quistorp argues that, in Calvin's theology there is a tension between 'his loyalty to the biblical message' and 'his humanistic tendency to confine and spiritualise the hope in the direction of the salvation of the individual'.[11] Sometimes Calvin sees the future life as 'a heavenly and spiritual life which definitely begins at death with the liberation of the immortal soul, and which is completed in the immediate vision of God without the mediation of the humanity of Christ'; but, on other occasions, he focuses upon a more biblical view, with 'its concrete hopes, especially in regard to the resurrection of the flesh as the resurrection of this body'.[12] We also face a similar tension: in our case it is between the biblical witness and our scientific worldview. But whatever we make of it, we ought not, in Quistorp's words, to weaken 'the hope of the church . . . to a pale longing for heaven'.[13]

Jürgen Moltmann: God Will Be All In All

Starting with his first major work, *The Theology of Hope,* Moltmann has sought to re-establish eschatology as a pivotal theme in theology. And he has not been content to view Christian hope merely in terms of personal immortality: ' . . . if the Christian hope is reduced to the salvation of the soul in a heaven beyond death, it loses its power to renew life and change the world, and its flame is quenched; it dies away into no more than a gnostic yearning for redemption from the world's vale of tears.'[14] Indeed, his theology's distinguishing mark lies in the way he understands hope to have a profound and prophetic influence upon our contemporary struggles and pilgrimages.

Moltmann defines the eschaton as 'God's coming and his arrival'.[15] God's Advent always beckons, since God is 'on the move and coming towards the world'.[16] And what God brings is 'eternal life and eternal time'.[17] God's future reigns over historical time, and, through our hope for God's coming, we experience transcendence in our lives. This in turn opens up new possibilities, as the eternal is encountered in the temporal and the future breaks into the present. God in the divine coming makes possible a fresh human adventure. Moltmann establishes a clear distinction between, on the one hand, 'future': what will be, and, on the other hand, 'advent': what is coming.[18] Whereas the idea of 'future' cannot give rise to anything *essentially* new, since what emerges out of the cosmic process is already latent in its early stages, the notion of 'advent' carries with it the possibility of *genuine* novelty, what Moltmann calls the *novum.*

---

11   Quistorp, *Calvin's Doctrine of the Last Things*, p 192–3.
12   Ibid., p 193.
13   Ibid., p 194.
14   Moltmann, *The Coming of God*, p xv.
15   Ibid., p 22.
16   Ibid., p 23.
17   Ibid.
18   See ibid., pp 25–6.

Traditionally, the church has spoken of three 'comings' of Christ: in the flesh, in the spirit and in glory. But Moltmann is very critical of understandings of *parousia* which suggest that Christ is coming *again*. Christ has never been absent! Instead, we are to understand the *parousia* as 'Christ's coming presence in glory'.[19] It is an advent hope rather than a future expectation; it ushers in eschatology rather than gets trapped in teleology. The End, therefore, brings something new as the dawn of eternal time replaces historical time. The inbreaking of the *novum*, of course, comes with a note of judgement upon the old. An old order passes away, a new creation appears, and a surprising thing happens which could not have been envisaged. But, on the other hand, Moltmann reminds us that, viewed from a biblical perspective, the advent of the *novum* possesses analogies in the history of God's ways with the world. The 'new' thing which God does is connected with the 'old' things that God has done. But the 'new' can never be contained within the 'old', or fully expected on the basis of it. The new creation, Moltmann reminds us, is 'the new creation of this one, the creation which is perishing from its sin and its injustice'.[20] It is, therefore, 'the quintessence of the wholly other, marvellous thing that the eschatological future brings'.[21]

Moltmann's eschatology seeks a way of speaking about God's involvement in history which frees us from a deterministic outlook that finds little place for divine activity in the world's affairs. Moltmann tries to instil a sense of purpose into history at a time when we are under threat from the power of what he calls *exterminism*: the nuclear threat, the ecological crisis and the impoverishment of the third world.[22] Just as biblical apocalyptic literature sought to lay bare the horrors of Rome, and, thereby, create solidarity and endurance among those who were oppressed by the Empire, so contemporary theology must expose exterminism for the evil that it is, and offer a more hopeful approach to life based upon God's coming reign, when what is transient and mortal will be raised into eternity. This has three dimensions to it. First, as we have seen, we are to await the *parousia*, Christ's coming presence in glory. Then, secondly, we are to expect the earthly reign of Christ in which Christ will rule over history. Finally, the End will come when all things will be consummated. Moltmann seems tied to a quite literal understanding of the key concepts of biblical apocalyptic, *viz.* parousia, millennium, the reign of the Messiah and 'new heaven and new earth'. Nothing that he has written since *The Theology of Hope* has fully countered Hick's early criticism of that book. Hick accused Moltmann of making 'a straight pre-critical appeal to traditional apocalyptic imagery' without acknowledging 'any awareness of the immense critical problems which it involves for the modern Christian'.[23] Moltmann builds his entire theological edifice on the basis of concepts whose meanings need careful analysis and their implications spelt out. However, in refusing to treat these concepts as part of a completely mythological worldview, Moltmann stands exposed to Hick's charge that he has turned his back on 'the task of formulating a coherent and credible Christian expectation concerning the future of the individual and of the race beyond the continuation and termination of their present earthly life'.[24] The problem with Moltmann's theology is that he is in danger of building an intellectual ediface upon imagery which is at best problematical and at worst incredible.

A case in point is Moltmann's treatment of the millennium. He distinguishes between two forms of millenarianism. *Historical* millenarianism conceives the present as the earthly reign of Christ and the saints. Moltmann maintains that this is 'a religious theory used to legitimate political

---

19   Ibid., p 25.
20   Ibid., p 29.
21   Ibid., p 28.
22   Ibid., p 202–18.
23   Hick, *Death and Eternal Life*, p 214.
24   Ibid., p 215.

or ecclesiastical power'.[25]   Examples are found in such diverse events as Constantine's adoption of Christianity as the empire's religion, the American dream, the Medieval Roman Catholic church, and the Enlightenment worldview.[26]   *Eschatological* millenarianism, however, is 'an expectation of the future in the eschatological context of the end, and the new creation of the world'.[27] This is what the Christian tradition has usually understood by millenarianism. It involves the anticipation of an historical transition between this world and the new creation in the form of the rule of Christ and the faithful for a limited period upon earth.   The millennium, therefore, will clearly be an alternative to the present world's evils, and it relates Christ's future reign within history to the final consummation of all things. Moltmann describes it as 'a necessary picture of hope in resistance, in suffering, and in the exiles of this world;'[28] it is based upon the belief that with Christ's coming the new age has dawned in the midst of this age.

Moltmann further argues that eschatology and millenarianism are inseparably connected:

> Millenarianism is the special, this-worldly side of eschatology, the side turned towards experienced history; eschatology is the general side of history, the side turned towards what is beyond history.   Millenarianism looks towards future history, the history of the end; eschatology looks towards the future of history, the end of history. Consequently the two sides of eschatology belong together as goal and end, history's consummation and its rupture.[29]

Moltmann also suggests that the Thousand Year reign of Christ includes not only Christians but also Jews. Reflecting his engagement and dialogue with Jews, Moltmann argues that, while the historical paths of Jews and Christians are different, their eschatological goal is identical and located in the millennium. So the Thousand Year rule is 'the messianic kingdom of Jews and Christians'.[30]

There is no mistaking Moltmann's belief that one day the millennium will take place. It will mark the transition from history to the coming new creation, and be brought about by 'a series of events and the succession of various different phases'.[31] Moltmann, of course, holds that it is not only a necessary theological concept, but also is an historical occurrence which will literally take place. But is it, and will it? Even one of Moltmann's most loyal supporters demurs at this point. Bauckham suggests that Moltmann needs 'to characterize the millennium in such a way as to make it intelligible as transitional rather than final', but in fact, Moltmann fails to justify why it is necessary to make a 'temporal distinction' between the millennium and the new creation.[32]   What *is* theologically required, however, is that we do justice to both the temporal and eternal sides of the Christian hope.   The millennium might then be understood mythically, or metaphorically, as addressing the this-worldly side of that hope.

---

25   Moltmann, *The Coming of God*, p 192.
26   See 'The Millenium' in Baukham, ed., G*od Will be All in All*, pp 126–9.
27   Moltmann, *The Coming of God*, p 192.
28   Ibid.
29   Ibid., p 197.
30   Ibid., p 198.
31   Ibid., p 201.
32   'The Millenium' in Bauckham, ed., *God Will be All in All*, p 142.

Moltmann's statements about cosmic eschatology are very imaginative if no less problematical. We are to hope for 'the perfecting of creation in glory'.[33] The cosmos is a contingent creation in the context of time; it is 'a creation subject to change, and a system open to the future';[34] it is a temporal world looking towards eternity, and a contingent process awaiting a new creation. Cosmic eschatology, therefore, according to Moltmann, represents 'the transition from the temporal creation to the new creation of an eternal "deified" world'.[35] So the 'creation out of nothing' is given its fulfilment in 'the creation out of the old'. Moltmann envisages this final consummation in terms of two Jewish concepts: *sabbath* and *shekinah*:

> Sabbath and Shekinah are related to each other as promise and fulfilment, beginning and completion. In the sabbath, creation holds within itself from the beginning the true promise of its consummation. In the eschatological Skekinah, the new creation takes the whole of the first creation into itself, as its own harbinger and prelude, and completes it. Creation begins with time and is completed in space.[36]

Moltmann thinks that in the new creation everything which has ever been will be brought back. It is not just human beings that are saved from death and decay. All temporal creation will be recreated into an eternal creation, while spatial creation will be transformed into omnipresent creation. There will be a total fulfilment of *all* creative life. All things will be in God: 'All created beings participate directly and without mediation in his indwelling glory, and in it are themselves glorified.'[37] And God will be in all things: 'The innermost heart of the vision of the new Jerusalem and the new creation of heaven and earth is nothing other than the immediate, omnipresent and eternal indwelling of God and of Christ.'[38] Moltmann's panentheistic model for the God–World relationship is once more plainly displayed.

The great merit of Moltmann's cosmic eschatology is that it seeks to do justice to the importance God places upon the *whole* creation. In this theology, nature is precious to God, with the result that Moltmann's ecological concerns receive a theological framework. However, the idea of a consummation in which *every* living thing – presumably viruses as well as plants, animals as well as humans – is brought back is at best mind-blowing and at worst incomprehensible. However attractive this idea might be, and Moltmann insists that God will make *all* things new (Rev. 21: 5), it tends to display a quite sentimental view of nature. Why does the creative purpose of God need to be fulfilled via a 'resurrection' of nature? It is not immediately clear why the pattern which is at the natural world's heart and in which the death of one creature is very much life for another is not as 'perfect' as God wants it or can get it. Once again Moltmann's tendency to use biblical ideas in a literal way, without adequately relating them to what we know about reality, is very much in view.

Our exploration into the meaning of Christian hope has shown us two things very clearly. First, Reformed theologians have attached a great deal of importance to eschatology. Whatever else they think the Christian faith entails, they maintain that faith in Christ gives rise to a promise that there is a meaning and purpose to human life, history and the cosmos which will only be fully

---

33   Moltmann, *The Coming of God*, p 264.
34   Ibid.
35   Ibid., p 265.
36   Ibid., p 266.
37   Ibid., p 307.
38   Ibid., p 315.

discerned in the future. Secondly, as we have reviewed the views of Reformed theologians, we have had reason to doubt the credibility of many of their conclusions regarding the *material* content of the Christian hope. We would be wise to adopt a hopeful attitude to life through trust in God's graciousness towards us, and put to one side fruitless speculations about what it might or might not entail.

CONCLUSION

OUR EXPLORATIONS in the URC's theological traditions must now draw to a close. At the interface of heart and mind, tradition and context, engagement and reflection, we have discovered resources that help us continue our theological journeys. I am now more confident than when I started writing this book that the Reformed theological heritage contains abundant riches that are worthy of extensive exploration. Some have been introduced in this book; others have been excluded through lack of space. As each theological topic has been discussed, I have been mindful that alternative theologians to those chosen could have been introduced to illustrate the various approaches and the options which exist. Some readers, of course, will argue that I could have used better examples to describe certain theological positions. That may be true, not least when one remembers the wealth of continental scholarship which, save for Calvin, Schleiermacher, Barth and Moltmann, has been deliberately omitted from this study due to my decision to make major use of recent British theologians whose work is reasonably accessible. Other readers, however, may complain that the theologians I have called into service are hardly representative of the entire URC world. There is an obvious absence, for example, of significant non-white, non-male, and non-clerical voices. But what does not exist can hardly be represented! It now ought to be a priority on the URC theological agenda to move beyond the white, male and clerical perspectives which hitherto have shaped it. Then, thirdly, some readers may wish that this study had focused more on our traditions' doctrinal statements rather than on our theologians. I take the line, though, that it is more instructive to consider the competing theological issues rather than simply refer to their attempted settlements. My decision to focus on our theologians rather than confessions is largely underpinned by my belief that the church has been driven forward more by charismatic personalities, prophetic voices and original minds than by committees or commissions. The latter's successes are largely dependent upon the personalities, voices and minds of the former!

But what are the principle features of the URC's theological heritage which are of lasting value as we seek to do theology today?[1] First, our emphasis upon the Bible means that the URC follows a theological model which helps to keep us in touch with the quarry from which we are hewn. We acknowledge a clear priority concerning the church's ancient past and apostolic origins. We grant privilege to the primary traditions, but not in any wooden sense. We seek God's mind, Christ's call and the Spirit's leading through the Bible, and thereby we allow our present belief and practice to be reformed anew.

---

[1]   See Brian Gerrish, 'Tradition in the Modern World' in David Willis and Michael Walker, eds., *Toward the Future of Reformed Theology*, pp 3–20.

This leads to a second principal feature of our URC heritage. We fully recognize that tradition is not static. The need for reformation in the church is ongoing. While the URC is a reformed church, it is nevertheless a church which recognizes a need always to be reforming itself – and, by its influence, reforming the society and world in which it lives. A tradition's reception and reformulation is part of the same theological dynamic, and, consequently, it ought to be impossible for any expression of 'fundamentalism' to find a genuine home within the URC.

A third principal feature of the URC theological heritage is its openness to ideas and insight from outside itself. This fact helps ground all our ecumenical commitments. We do not believe that the 'right' way necessarily is the URC way; nor do we un-church those in other churches which do things differently. At our best, we display a willingness to find ways forward which transcend past practices and pursue relevance within each fresh missionary context. Nowadays, this sense of openness is moving well beyond inter-church relations. It has generated 'a wider ecumenism' in which people are increasingly open to receiving insight from non-theological as well as non-Christian sources. When true to itself URC theology is opposed to sectarian attitudes, since we are willing to be challenged as well as informed by voices from beyond our church. There are still those, of course, who feel threatened by dialogue with, say, scientists or the representatives of non-Christian faith communities. As befits the holders of a *public* faith, though, the URC should be supportive of secular learning. It is not without significance that the Reformed ethos provided the soil in which modern science was sown. And, frankly, it is inconceivable to see how the contemporary church can have a role in shaping the future of a plural, multi-cultural world without engaging in extensive dialogue with the representatives of the non-Christian faiths.

Fourthly, URC theology should be thoroughly practical. It seeks to reform individual lives. Since it is rooted in God's gracious gift to the world in Christ, the Christian message invites practical responses to the demands which following Christ lays upon us. But, as Moltmann has made very clear, the reformation involved entails the renewal of social and political structures within society as well as the hearts, minds and wills of individuals: 'Not only the church's proclamation and structure, as well as the life of Christians, but all areas of life are "reformed" according to God's creative, liberating and redeeming Word, for God is God, unbounded and all-encompassing.'[2] While some emphasize God's invitation in Christ to change persons, others stress the injunction that we work for the Kingdom. But both of these aspects of the church's mission hang together and involve 'down to earth' practical commitments and activities.

Finally, Moltmann's statement that 'God is God, unbounded and all-encompassing' reminds us not only about the One in whose service we stand, but also of the One to whom we are finally accountable. The source of grace is also the seat of judgement. And what we are called to do in God's service is not to satisfy ourselves but to please God. We are to take our bearings from what God requires rather than what we want, while the church will be given what it needs and not necessarily what it likes. Reformed theologies therefore have emphasized the way in which both Christians and churches stand under God's Word. They have gone on then to try to understand what that involves for contemporary faith and practice. This book has attempted to sketch the URC traditions' apprehension of that understanding. Whatever its success, we can be totally sure that the interpretation of God's Word remains a task for each new age. As servants of that Word the Reformed should always be reforming!

---

[2]   Jürgen Moltmann, 'Theologia Reformata et Semper Reformanda' in Willis and Welker, eds., *Toward the Future of Reformed Theology*, p 122.

GLOSSARY OF TERMS

ALL FIELDS of human enquiry develop their specialist languages. Words and concepts are employed to explain very complex and often confusing ideas in a shorthand way. For those at home in a particular discipline that discipline's specialist language is as familiar as their mother tongue, but for those new to it there is an inevitable language barrier to be overcome. This is as true for geology as it is for genetics, for anatomy as well as anthropology. Students entering such fields readily accept the need to speak their discipline's language if they are to become skilled in their chosen area of interest. But when it comes to theology, there is an unfortunate tendency for people to complain about theological jargon which they believe is a barrier to advancing their understanding. They expect theology somehow to get by without a specialist language.

This book has been written with the conviction that only mental laziness bars reasonably intelligent people (i.e. most of those who go to church on a Sunday morning) from critically reflecting on faith and, hence, 'doing' theology. As their reflection advances the necessary technical language of theological enquiry can be picked up very quickly. Meanwhile, they will soon learn that it is actually the once seemingly simple words which turn out to be the most vexed. The long technical words in fact are quite easy: demythologizing, eschatology, hermeneutics, etc., but try the short ones! Small words which I once thought I understood now tax my mind, not what theology's detractors perjoratively dismiss as jargon. Christians have gone to theological war over the meaning of words like God, Jesus, sin and so on, not the meaning of sacerdotalism or panentheism!

In this glossary I have defined the technical terms left unexplained in the text. Any I have inadvertently missed can be found fully discussed in one of the many theological dictionaries now readily available. I have found particularly helpful Alan Richardson and John Bowden (eds.), *A New Dictionary of Christian Theology* (London: SCM Press, 1983) and Donald K.McKim (ed.), *Encyclopedia of the Reformed Faith* (Louisville, Kentucky: Westminster/John Knox Press and Edinburgh: Saint Andrew Press, 1992). Also extremely useful for distinguishing the likes of John of the Cross from John of Damascus, and, hence, providing a biographical introduction to all the major theological figures is John Bowden's, *Who's Who in Theology* (London: SCM Press, 1990). Meanwhile, the propensity of some theologians to resort to Latin suggests that, unlike most contemporary people, they have had classical educations. Eugene Ehrlich's, *A Dictionary of Latin Tags and Phrases* (London: Robert Hale, 1985) thankfully has helped me overcome being deprived (if that's the correct word) of Latin at school. And more often than not *The Concise Oxford Dictionary* has been able to come to my aid!

ABSOLUTISM A scheme of philosophical thought which has at its centre a vision of Deity as completely ultimate, unconditioned and self-subsisting, thereby being conceived as totally immutable and hence incapable of any form of change. Absolutism often is associated with the Medieval theology of Thomas Aquinas which was largely dependent upon Aristotelian philosophy. It has been widely challenged in recent times, not least by the various process theologies. (See *process theology, theism* and *relativism*).

ALLEGORY A literary devise in which the plain or surface meaning of a term, phrase or narrative is bypassed in favour of less obvious and more hidden meaning. Sections of the Bible have been considered to be allegorical by some interpreters, so the narratives about Ishmael and Isaac in Genesis are read as referring to two covenants, while other Old Testament passages are not viewed in historical context but taken as speaking about Christ or the Church. The practice of allegorical interpretation was rejected by the Reformers and plays only a minor role in contemporary biblical interpretation.

ANAPHORA From a Greek word which means to take up, or to offer up (as a sacrifice), or to take away (sins), *anaphora* is the technical term for the eucharistic prayer, or prayer of consecration, in the Holy Communion liturgy. Such prayers traditionally include two elements: the *anamnesis*, the commemoration of God's saving acts in biblical history with the Christ event as the focus, and the *epiclesis*, the petitioning of God to continue the divine liberative activity towards humankind. The *epiclesis* may or may not involve the direct invocation of the Holy Spirit. (See *epiclesis*).

APAPHATIC A term from the Eastern Orthodox church which refers to a distinctive way of doing theology dominated by the view that speech appropriately used about human beings is not satisfactory when applied to God. The apaphatic way seeks to avoid unnecessary anthropomorphic descriptions of God by removing from God-talk anything which reflects creaturely qualities. It operates the negative way (*via negativa*) by spurning earthly descriptions of Deity in order to stress God's utter transcendency. But, unless theology is to advocate total silence about God, it must be accepted that all God-talk carries an inevitable anthropological character. As a result, theologians generally agree that the apaphatic way needs complementing by the positive way (*via positiva*) and our stumbling attempt to use the language of finitude to speak about the infinite.

ARIANISM A broad designation for any theological view which fails to affirm the full divinity of Christ. The term is derived from the views of Arius, an Alexandrian priest (c.250–c.336). Arius argued that Jesus in a certain sense was subordinate to God the Father. His views shook the Roman empire and split the church. Emperor Constantine called an ecumenical council to establish a view of God which would unite the churches. At the Council of Nicaea Arius' theology was condemned and an attempt was made to stamp out all supposedly Arian views. Recent historical investigations, however, suggest not only that Arius was far less heretical than Nicaea made out but also that he was far from being an Arian. (See also *subordinationism*).

CANON Coming from an Egyptian word for a reed used for measurement it quickly came to refer to any kind of yardstick for establishing criteria and laws about specific subjects. The church adopted it to designate the list of sacred books it set aside for use in public worship and as an authority to govern or guide its faith and practice. So we speak of the biblical canon, the canon of scripture, canonical authority and, in some ecclesiologies, of canon law.

DIALECTICAL   A term which has had a wide range of meanings in the history of philosophy, but one which is associated with the style of philosophy set in motion by Hegel, who taught that rational enquiry should follow a pattern of positing a thesis against which an antithesis is formulated, with their reconciliation being wrought in a synthesis of the two points of view. In theology, the term describes the neo-orthodox methodology pioneered by Reformed theologians like Karl Barth and Reinhold Niebuhr in which theological insight is achieved by holding seemingly opposite propositions in tension. Dialectical theology acknowledges that life is so complex that it cannot be talked about adequately unless seeming opposites are held together in a paradoxical fashion.

DOCETISM   A term which is now used for theological systems in which Christ's divinity is emphasized in such a way that his humanity is minimized. It comes from a Greek word meaning 'to seem' and originates in early church docetic christologies which suggest that Christ's humanity or suffering was not real but merely apparent. (See also *hypostatic union*).

ENLIGHTENMENT   The title for the dominant intellectual movement in Western culture during the eighteenth century which is often linked with the seventeenth century under the overarching description of 'The Age of Reason'. It was associated with the work of Locke, Leibnitz, Newton and Kant. It possessed certain clear features: a belief that reason must be the final aribiter in every issue; a re-awakened interest in the natural world and the rise of the scientific method; a widespread belief in progress, the view that the present by and large is better than the past; and the rejection of tradition and all deference to the past. While the Enlightenment was influential in giving birth to the *modern* world which spanned the nineteenth and most of the twentieth centuries, a general scepticism about its premises in the light of what it has achieved has generated a negative critique of it which has been the driving force of *postmodern* attitudes. In some ways these build upon the power of the Enlightenment but they also seek to undermine its grand design. In certain theological circles, the Enlightenment is regarded as a wicked witch in need of slaying, since she is deemed responsible for scepticism, rationalism, secularization and all those things which are believed to have led to the general demise of religion. Those who inhabit more liberal theological circles, however, maintain that any attempt to distance ourselves totally from the Enlightenment will merely turn Christianity into a sect which has little or no connection with contemporary life and thought.

EPICLESIS   From a Greek word which means to give a name to someone or to call upon someone for aid, *epiclesis* has become the technical term for that part of the eucharistic prayer (the *anaphora*) which specifically involves the petitioning of God to continue the divine work of redemption and emancipation. (See *anaphora*).

ESCHATOLOGY   Means literally 'words about the last things' and usually refers to a series of theological topics related to the end of human existence, e.g. the second coming of Christ (parousia), the resurrection of the dead, the immortality of the soul, the final judgement, the millennium, heaven and hell etc.

HISTORICAL-CRITICAL METHOD   An approach to the Bible which through historical enquiry seeks: (1) to establish the most reliable and trustworthy texts of biblical books (textual criticism); (2) to discover the relationships between the various biblical books and the sources writers used in their compilation (source criticism); (3) to investigate the preliterary and oral traditions which lie behind the biblical books (form criticism); and (4) to discover what the various texts can tell us about the theology and intentions of their authors (redaction criticism). It employs techniques common in literary criticism and applies them to the biblical canon, but it has often been criticised for its minimalizing tendencies. In contemporary biblical scholarship, attention is often moved from the historical focus generated by this method to concerns about how the Bible is heard today by different groups of people in alternative contexts. This has generated 'readings' of the biblical text from different perspectives, e.g. feminist, black, gay, etc. as the ongoing quest to discover the relevance of the Bible for today is pursued.

HYPOSTATIC UNION   A technical term used in the classical statements concerning the union of humanity and divinity in Jesus Christ. The word 'hypostasis' is a Greek term which eventually was understood in christological discussion as 'individual being'. At the Council of Chalcedon (and beyond) use of the term 'hypostatic union', therefore, stressed the union of the human and divine natures of Jesus as opposed to any merely moral union of the human and divine wills in him. (See also *docetism*).

IMMANENCE   A technical term used to talk about the nearness or presence of God. It is generally used in contrast to transcendence. Any adequate depiction of Deity will show how God is both transcendent and immanent. (See *transcendence, theism, pantheism* and *panentheism*).

JUSTIFICATION   The act by which God brings sinful men and women back into a proper relationship within the divine life. The word 'justification' comes from the Latin *justificatio* which translates a Greek word (*dikaiosis*) that Paul uses to describe the key moment in God's reconciliation of sinners. For both Calvin and Luther, justification involves the forgiveness of sins and the gift of the Holy Spirit. A new and lasting righteousness is thus granted to those who place their complete faith in the mercy of the Father of the crucified, risen and exalted Christ. (See also *sanctification*).

KERYGMA   From a Greek word meaning to proclaim, *kerygma* became the technical term for the original and hence foundational Christian message. Opinion differs, however, about whether it refers to the church's claims about the soteriological significance of Jesus as centred upon his death and resurrection (in which case can it be said that Jesus preached the *kerygma*?) or Jesus' own preaching and teaching (in which case how can we account for the proclaimer becoming the One proclaimed?). Any consideration of this term inevitably leads to the vexed question whether Christianity is founded upon the historical Jesus or the earliest apostolic witness to him, and, hence, to the much discussed 'problem' of the historical Jesus.

MARCIONITE   A term used to describe any Christian outlook which marginalizes the Old Testament in Christian worship or theology. It recalls Marcion, a Christian heretic, who rejected the Old Testament and mistakenly constrasted the God of Jesus (a loving God) with the God of the Old Testament (a cruel, ruthless and vengeful deity). Hence also marcionism.

MODALISM   The system of Trinitarian ideas in which Father, Son and Spirit are understood to be three different modes of divine activity rather than eternal and essential distinctions within the divine life itself. Modalism was an understandable distortion of the Trinitarian concept by Western thinkers who held doggedly to monarchical and hence unitary views of the one sovereign God. By talking of 'modes of being' (thus establishing a contrast with the 'modes of revelation' advocated by modalists who emphasized the unity of the Godhead at the expense of the divine plurality) the Cappadocian Fathers sought to express clear internal relations between the members of the Trinity without sacrificing their unity in the one Godhead. But while the Cappadocians were clearly able to account for plurality in the Trinity, their critics accuse them of lurching in the opposite direction towards tri-theism, notwithstanding the doctrine of co-inherence which they put forward to advance the notion of unity in plurality. (See also *arianism* and *subordinationism*).

ONTOLOGY Literally 'words about being'. Ontology is another name for metaphysics, a reasoned analysis and account of those characteristics which things must display if they are to exist. Due to the efforts of Immanuel Kant, and more recently linguistic philosophers, the attempt to enquire into objects beyond our experience has been shown to be fatally flawed. But when ontology is understood in its most primitive sense as the analysis of the universal structures of human experience, it has an important contribution to make to theology, as has been shown by the work of Paul Tillich.

PANTHEISM The doctrine that God and the world are identical, such that all things are modes of the divine life. Owing its origin to Spinoza, pantheism is usually counted as heresy in Christian circles, but some theologians unfortunately equate the much different idea of panentheism with pantheism. (See also *panentheism, process theology* and *theism*).

PANENTHEISM Literally 'everything-in-God-ism'. Panentheism is a way of conceiving God's relation to the world which is as different from classical pantheism as it is from classical theism, even though it attempts to draw upon the insights of each. In panentheism God includes the world in the divine being analogous to the way our cells are contained within our bodies. God is the unique self of the world whose being and activity is not exhausted by the world's involvement in the divine life. While God acts on and in the world internally and intimately, the Deity is also affected by what is happening in the world. In a panentheistic scheme, therefore, God not only in a certain sense changes but also the future is radically open for God as well as the world. The panentheistic model for the God–world relationship has been adopted by certain Reformed theologians, for example Jürgen Moltmann, but it has been explored with the greatest conceptual clarity by process theologians. (See also *absolutism, pantheism, process theology* and *theism*).

PELAGIANISM An understanding of the relationship between God's grace and human freewill in which too much confidence is placed in our capacities in the scheme of salvation. The term stems from the teachings of Pelagius, a British monk who denied the doctrine of original sin in the belief that God would never ask men and women to do what in principle as well as in practice they cannot do. Augustine objected to what he (perhaps mistakenly) saw as a claim that men and women can save themselves without divine grace. It is now widely accepted that Pelagius had a point. Augustine's tendency to view sin as necessary, rather than merely an inevitable occurrence for people born into the customs and habits of an imperfect world, turns out to be as problematic as Pelagius' seemingly over-confidence in the capacity of freewill.

PERICHORESIS   A technical term which comes from the Eastern church, and particularly the Cappodocian fathers. It arises in trinitarian discussions to account for the way in which each member of the Trinity is present in the other two members. Sometimes called the doctrine of coinherence, *perichoresis* thus establishes the mutual indwelling of the three Persons and functions in Eastern trinitarian models like homoousios does in the Western theology. It protects the unity of the Godhead while strongly affirming its plurality.

PLATONISM and NEOPLATONISM   *Platonism* is the philosophical system developed by the Greek philosopher Plato (427–347 BCE) who argued that a realm of forms exists separate from the temporal world. The forms relate to the world like a perfect model does to an imperfect copy. They generate the eternal principles for which we must strive, the 'we' here being our essential souls (pre-existent and surviving death) rather than our temporal selves. *Neoplatonism* is the philosophical system which revived Platonism in later periods. It is particularly associated with Plotinus (205–270 CE) who developed a triadic understanding of reality. At the apex is the One, totally beyond the mind and forms, pure blessedness. From the One comes Mind (*nous*) which understands in a unitary way the entire system of the forms. And then from the Mind proceeds the World Soul which contains the forms in a temporal state. Plotinus thus attempted to conceive how the eternal One gives rise to the temporal Many. His thought was used widely to help conceptualize the doctrine of the Trinity.

PRAXIS   Originating in Marxist philosophy, this term has found its way into Christian theology via the various liberation theologies which insist that the proper subject of theological attention is more than simply the content of Christian belief. Praxis strictly refers to a pattern of social and political activity which is transformative, but when put to theological use it refers to the entire Christian life of belief, worship, discipleship and mission. It reminds us particularly of the social and political dimensions and implications of Christianity. Theory (belief) and practice (worship, discipleship and mission) are inseparably connected and interact with each other.

PROCESS THEOLOGY   A branch of Christian theology which is rooted in the philosophical conviction that, contrary to a classical Greek presupposition subsequently accepted by main-stream Western theology, process or becoming (rather than substance or being) is the fundamental ontological category. If, as science teaches, all things are in motion, anything we perceive as static is merely an abstraction from its true reality. Process theologians, following A N Whitehead, believe that God is not the exception to this metaphysical principle but its chief exemplification. They are panentheists who argue that Deity possesses a di-polar nature being, in certain respects, not only eternal, infinite, unchanging and immutable (as per classical theism) but, in other respects, also temporal, finite, changing and mutable. Significant members of this theological school are the American theologians, John Cobb, Schubert Ogden and David Ray Griffin, with the outstanding British figure being David Pailin. (See also *panentheism*).

RELATIVISM   A scheme of thought which denies that there is any ultimate reality which is unconditional. It claims that truth is completely relative to particular societies and historical periods. All purportedly absolute claims, therefore, are taken to be culturally and historically conditioned. While relativism does not necessitate the view that there are no absolutes (scepticism), it does hold that, since each society gives birth to a set of ideals and truth claims which are understandable only within that particular society, there cannot be any ultimately successful means of assessing rival claims. While it is important for us to recognize the relativity of all thought, thereby adopting attitudes of provisionality and tentativeness which have hardly been typical of the Christian church, the fact that trans-historical and cross-cultural conversations actually do happen suggests that a necessary recognition of the relativity of all thought need not entail the adoption of out and out relativism. (See also *absolutism*).

ROMANTICISM   A system of thought which has its roots in the period between the middles of the eighteenth and nineteenth centuries. Romanticism sought to express and establish religious truths and ideals through artistic and aesthetic values, thus turning its back on the limitations of the developing rationalism of the period. It stresses imagination over reason, turns inwards towards the warmth of subjectivity as it flees from the coldness of objective investigation, and generally reminds people that anything worthwhile has to speak to the heart as well as to the head. Being an understandable reaction to rationalism, romanticism in some form is not hard to trace in some contemporary attitudes and life-styles throughout the West.

SACERDOTALISM   The view that supernatural powers and sacrificial functions in religion are the sole province of ordained priests. Reformed theology counters this outlook via its doctrine of the priesthood of all believers. This places the means of grace within the church rather than an ordained priesthood, without in any way diminishing a high view of the place of ministers within the church's life.

SANCTIFICATION   From the Latin *sanctus* which means 'holy', sanctification is the process by which a person achieves true holiness. It involves new life being imparted by the Holy Spirit, release from the habitual power of sin and an ability to love God and neighbour truly and fully. While some, most notably John Wesley, have argued that sanctification is possible to attain in this life, most theologians believe the completion of the salvific process which begins with justification is achieved in the life hereafter. (See also *justification*).

SUBORDINATIONISM   The heretical view of the Trinity in which the Son (or Logos) is deemed to be subordinate to the Father, and/or that the Spirit is subordinate to both Father and Son. (See also *arianism*).

TELEOLOGY   Derived from two Greek words, *telos* meaning 'end' and *logos* meaning 'word' or 'discourse', it refers to a scheme of thought which is concerned with ends or final causes. The development of the universe is said to be due to the purpose or design invested in it, and therefore any evidence of design will point to a Designer. The vast amount of dysteleological occurrences in the universe (so-called natural evil), however, seem to undermine the so-called teleological arguments for the existence of God, although some cosmologists now suggest that the statisitical probability of the universe developing in the way it has is so low that the most adequate way to account for what happened is in fact to say that it was 'a put up job', the work of a Creator.

THEISM A view of the God–world relationship in which a clear separation between God and the world is maintained. While the world is clearly related to God, being God's creation, God is not really related to the world, except in those moments when God intervenes in the world's life. The extreme form of theism is deism in which God observes the world as an eternal bystander who takes no further part in its life post-creation. Although the interventionist model of God found in less extreme forms of theism became the predominant view of God in Western theology, many contemporary theologians turn to alternative ways of understanding the God–world relationship less vulnerable to the charge that classical theism can only locate a place for God within the gaps in the cosmic story told us by science. (See also *absolutism, panentheism, pantheism* and *process theology*).

TRANSCENDENCE From a Latin word which means 'to surpass' or 'go beyond', the term has a number of meanings in theology. First, it is used to stress the way God stands over and against the world, to assert God's otherness and to stress that God's nature cannot adequately be grasped by human enquiry. Secondly, it is used to describe God's relationship to the world. The Deity is neither identical with nor exhausted by the world. Thirdly, the term is used for the categories which describe any possible being. In scholastic philosophy, for example, there are six transcendentals: reality, being, truth, goodness, being something and unity. (See *immanence, theism, pantheism* and *panentheism*).

TRINITY The central Christian doctrine of God in which it is stated that in the being of God there are three eternal and essential distinctions. Theologians have usually made a distinction between God viewed apart from the divine activity in the world (the so-called *essential* or *immanent* trinity) and God viewed from the perspective of the divine activity in the world (the so-called *economic* trinity). While all trinitarian theologians affirm the economic trinity, some of them infer the essential trinity from the economic trinity, arguing in effect that the inner life of God must correspond to how God has revealed Godself to us. Other less speculative trinitarian thinkers believe that it is empirically impossible, theologically unnecessary and actually idolatrous to seek knowledge of the nature of the inner-life of Deity.

# BIBLIOGRAPHIES

THE BOOKS listed below are intended to help readers continue their theological explorations beyond this book. The list is divided into two sections, the first dealing with texts of a general nature and the second covering the major themes of each chapter. It is both an indication of the ecumenical nature of Reformed theology, as well as an acknowledgement that the issues tackled by Reformed theologians are common to theologians of other Christian traditions, that many of the books in these bibliographies are written by theologians from beyond the Reformed family.

A. General

The work of two theologians directly or indirectly lies behind the major theological debates within the Reformed world: John Calvin and Friedrich Schleiermacher. What follows is a list of significant primary and secondary works concerning them, augmented by some books of general interest about Reformed theology and overviews of Christian doctrine from Reformed theologians.

Barth, Karl. *Church Dogmatics.* 12 vols. Edinburgh: T & T Clark, 1936-69.

Barth, Karl. *Dogmatics in Outline.* London: SCM Press, 1949.

Barth, Karl. *The Theology of John Calvin.* Grand Rapids, Michigan: William B Eerdmans Publishing Company, 1995.

Calvin, John. *Institutes of the Christian Religion.* Edited by J T McNeil and translated by F L Battle. Philadelphia: The Westminster Press, 1960.

Clements, Keith W. ed. *Friedrich Schleiermacher: Pioneer of Modern Thought.* London: Collins, 1987.

Cornick, David. *Under God's Good Hand: A History of the Traditions which have come together in the United Reformed Church in the United Kingdom.* London: The United Reformed Church, 1998.

Cottret, Bernard. *Calvin: A Biography.* Edinburgh: T & T Clark, 2000.

Cunliffe-Jones, Hubert. *Christian Theology Since 1600.* London: Gerald Duckworth & Co. Ltd., 1970.

Cunliffe-Jones, Hubert. ed. assisted by Benjamin Drewery, *A History of Christian Doctrine.* Edinburgh: T & T Clark, 1978.

Garvie, Alfred E. *A Handbook of Christian Apologetics.* New York: Charles Scribner's Sons, 1938.

Gerrish, Brian A. *Tradition and the Modern World: Reformed Theology in the Nineteenth Century.* Chicago: The University of Chicago Press, 1978.

Gerrish, Brian A. *The Old Protestantism and the New: Essays on the Reformation Heritage.* Edinburgh: T & T Clark, 1982.

Gerrish, Brian A. *A Prince of the Church: Schleiermacher and the Beginnings of Modern Theology.* London: SCM Press, 1984.

Gerrish, Brian A. 'Friedrich Schleiermacher'. In *Nineteenth Century Religious Thought in the West.* Vol. 1, pp 123–57. Edited by Ninian Smart, John Clayton, Patrick Sherry and Steven T Kalz. Cambridge: Cambridge University Press, 1985.

Gerrish, Brian A. *Continuing the Reformation: Essays in Modern Religious Thought.* Chicago: The University of Chicago Press, 1993.

Guthrie, Shirley C. *Christian Doctrine: Revised Edition.* Louisville, Kentucky: Westminster/John Knox Press, 1994.

Guthrie, Shirley C. *Always Being Reformed: Faith for a Fragmented World.* Louisville, Kentucky: Westminster/John Knox Press, 1994.

Hodgson, Peter C. *Winds of the Spirit: A Constructive Theology.* London: SCM Press, 1994.

Johnson, William S and Leith, John H ed. *Reformed Reader: A Sourcebook in Christian Theology, Vol. 1: Classical Beginnings 1519–1799.* Louisville, Kentucky: Westminster / John Knox Press, 1993.

Leith, John H. *Introduction to the Reformed Tradition.* Edinburgh: St. Andrew's Press, 1977.

McGrath, Alister E A. *A Life of John Calvin.* Oxford: Basil Blackwell, 1990.

McKin, Donald K ed. *Major Themes in the Reformed Tradition.* Grand Rapids, Michigan: William B Eerdmans Publishing Company, 1992.

Migliore, Daniel L. *Faith Seeking Understanding.* Grand Rapids, Michigan: William B Eerdmans Publishing Company, 1992.

Parker, T H L. *Calvin: An Introduction to His Thought.* London: Geoffrey Chapman, 1995.

Schleiermacher, Friedrich D E. *The Christian Faith.* Edinburgh: T & T Clark, 1928.

Schleiermacher, Friedrich D E. *On Religion: Speeches to its Cultured Despisers.* New York: Harper Torchbooks, 1958.

Stroup, George. *Reformed Reader: A Sourcebook in Christian Theology.* Vol 2: Contemporary Trajectories 1799–Present. Louisville, Kentucky: Westminster/John Knox Press, 1993.

Thompson, David M ed. *Stating the Gospel: Formulations and Declarations of Faith From the Heritage of the United Reformed Church.* Edinburgh: T & T Clark, 1990.

Wendel, François. *Calvin: The Origins and Development of his Religious Thought.* London: William Collins Sons & Co. Ltd., 1963.

Whale, John S. *Christian Doctrine.* London: Fontana Books 1957.

Willis, David and Welker, Michael eds. *Toward the Future of Reformed Theology: Tasks, Topics, Traditions.* Grand Rapids, Michigan and Cambridge, U.K.: William B Eerdmans Publishing Company, 1999.

B.   Specific

Chapter 1

Barr, James. *Fundamentalism.* London: SCM Press, 1977.

Barr, James. *Escaping from Fundamentalism.* London: SCM Press, 1984.

Davie, Grace. *Religion In Britain Since 1945: Believing Without Belonging.* Oxford: Basil Blackwell, 1994.

Gill, Robin. *Beyond Decline: A Challenge to the Churches.* London: SCM Press, 1988.

Gill, Robin. *Moral Communities.* Exeter: Exeter University Press, 1992.

Harvey, David. *The Condition of Postmodernity.* Oxford: Basil Blackwell, 1990.

Middleton, J R and Walsh B J. *Truth is stranger than it used to be: Biblical Faith in a Postmodern Age.* London: SPCK, 1995.

Packer, J I. *'Fundamentalism' and the Word of God.* Leicester: Inter-Varsity Press, 1958.

Steiner, George. *Real Presences: Is There Anything In What We Say?* London: Faber and Faber, 1989.

Chapter 2

Boff, Clodovis. *Theology and Praxis: Epistemological Foundations.* Maryknoll, New York: Orbis Books, 1987.

Boff, Leonardo and Boff, Clodovis. *Introducing Liberation Theology.* Tunbridge Wells, Kent: Burns & Oates, 1988.

Farley, Edward. Theologia: *The Fragmentation and Unity of Theological Education.* Philadelphia: Fortress Press, 1983.

Farley, Edward. *The Fragility of Knowledge: Theological Education in the Church and University.* Philadelphia: Fortress Press, 1988.

Forester, Duncan B. *Truthfulaction: Explorations in Practical Theology.* Edinburgh: T & T Clark, 2000.

Green, Laurie. *Let's Do Theology: A Pastoral Cycle Resource Book.* London: Mowbray, 1990.

Gunton, C, Rae, M and Holmes, S. *The Practice of Theology.* London: SCM Press, 2001.

Kane, Margaret. *What Kind of God? Reflections on Working with People and Churches in North East England.* London: SCM Press, 1986.

Loades, Ann. *Feminist Theology: A Reader.* London: SPCK, 1990.

Ogden, Schubert M. *On Theology.* San Francisco: Harper Row, 1986.

Ogden, Schubert M. *Doing Theology Today.* San Francisco: Harper Row, 1996.

Segundo, Juan Luis. *The Liberation of Theology.* Maryknoll, New York: Orbis Books, 1976.

Wiles, Maurice. *What is Theology?* Oxford: Oxford University Press, 1976.

Chapter 3

Abraham, W J. *The Divine Inspiration of Holy Scripture.* Oxford: Oxford University Press, 1981.

Alter, R and Kermode, F ed. *The Literary Guide to the Bible.* London: Collins, 1987.

Barr, James. *The Bible in the Modern World.* London: SCM Press, 1973.

Barr, James. *Exploration in Theology 7.* London: SCM Press, 1988.

Barr, James. *Holy Scripture: Canon, Authority, Criticism.* Oxford: Oxford University Press, 1983.

Barth, Karl. *Church Dogmatics* 1, 2, Edinburgh: T & T Clark, 1957.

Barton, John. *People of the Book: The Authority of the Bible in Christianity.* London: SPCK, 1988.

Braaten, Carl E and Jenson, Robert W eds. *Reclaiming the Bible for the Church.* Edinburgh: T & T Clark, 1996.

Caird, George B. *The Language and Imagery of the Bible.* London: Duckworth, 1980.

Calvin, John. *Institutes* 1, 6–10.

Carroll, Robert P. *Wolf in the Sheepfold: The Bible as a Problem for Christianity.* London: SPCK, 1991.

Dodd, Charles H. *The Authority of the Bible.* Rev. ed. London: Collins Fontana, 1960.

Evans, Christopher F. *Is 'Holy Scripture' Christian? And Other Questions.* London: SCM Press, 1971.

Forsyth, Peter T. *The Principle of Authority: In Relation to Certainty, Sanctity and Society.* London: Independent Press, 1952.

Goldingay, John. *Models for Scripture.* Carlisle, Cumbria: Paternoster Press, 1987.

Goldingay, John. *Models for Interpretation of Scripture.* Carlisle, Cumbria: Paternoster Press, 1987.

Hanson, A T and Hanson R P C. *The Bible Without Illusions.* London: SCM Press, 1989.

Harvey, Van A. *The Historian and the Believer*. London: Macmillan, 1967.

Hodgson, Peter. *Winds of the Spirit: A Constructive Theology*. London: SCM Press, 1994.

Kelsey, David H. *The Uses of Scripture in Recent Theology*. London: SCM Press, 1975.

Marshall, I Howard. *Biblical Inspiration*. London: Hodder and Stoughton, 1982.

Marxsen, Willi. *The New Testament as the Church's Book*. Philadelphia: Fortress Press, 1972.

Metzger, Bruce M. *The Canon of the New Testament*. Oxford: Oxford University Press, 1987.

Muddiman, John. *The Bible: Fountain and Well of Truth*. Oxford: Basil Blackwell, 1983.

Nineham, Dennis E. *The Use and Abuse of the Bible*. London: SPCK, 1978.

O'Neill, John C. *The Bible's Authority*. Edinburgh: T & T Clark, 1991.

Reventlow, H Graf. *The Authority of the Bible and the Rise of the Modern World*. London: SCM Press, 1984.

Ricoeur, Paul. *Essays on Biblical Interpretation*. London: SPCK, 1981.

Schüssler Fiorenza, Elizabeth. *Bread Not Stone: The Challenge of Feminist Biblical Interpretation*. Edinburgh: T & T Clark, 1990.

von Campenhausen, H. *The Formation of the Christian Bible*. London: A & C Black, 1972.

Wink, Walter. *Transforming Bible Study*. London: SCM Press, 1980.

Chapters 4 and 5

Calvin, John, *Institutes* 1, 1–4, 9–10, 16–18 and 3, 21–24.

Cob, John B and Pinnock, Clark H eds. *Searching for an Adequate God: A Dialogue between Process and Free Will Theists*. Grand Rapids, Michigan and Cambridge, UK: William B Eerdmanns Publishing Company, 2000.

Cone, James. *God of the Oppressed*. London: SPCK, 1977.

Cupitt, Don. *Taking Leave of God*. London: SCM Press, 1980.

Farley, Edward. *Divine Empathy: Theology of God*. Philadelphia: Fortress Press, 1996.

Farmer, Herbert H. *The World and God: A Study of Prayer, Providence and Miracle in Christian Experience*. Rev. ed. London: Nisbet & Co. Ltd., 1936.

Farmer, Herbert H. *Towards Belief in God*. London: SCM Press, 1942.

Fiddes, Paul. *The Creative Suffering of God.* Oxford: Clarendon Press, 1988.

Garvie, Alfred E. *The Christian Doctrine of the Godhead.* London: Hodder and Stoughton Ltd., 1925.

Garvie, Alfred E. *The Christian Ideal of Human Society.* London: Hodder and Stoughton Ltd., 1930.

Garvie, Alfred E. *The Christian Belief in God.* London: Hodder and Stoughton Ltd., 1932.

Gunton, Colin. *Christ and Creation.* Carlisle: The Paternoster Press, 1992.

Gunton, Colin. *The One, the Three and the Many: God, Creation and the Culture of Modernity.* Cambridge: Cambridge University Press, 1993.

Gunton, Colin. *Doctrine of Creation.* Edinburgh: Edinburgh University Press, 1998.

Hartshorne, Charles. *Omnipotence and Other Theological Mistakes.* Albany: State University of New York Press, 1984.

Hick, John. *The Metaphor of God Incarnate.* London: SCM Press, 1993.

Küng, Hans. *Does God Exist? An Answer for Today.* London: Collins, 1980.

Lampe, Geoffrey W H. *God as Spirit.* Oxford: Clarendon Press, 1978.

Mascall, Eric L. *He Who Is? A Study in Traditional Theism.* London: Longmans, Green & Co., 1958.

McFague, Sallie. *Models of God: Theology for an Ecological, Nuclear Age.* London: SCM Press, 1987.

McFague, Sallie. *The Body of God: An Ecological Theology.* London: SCM Press, 1993.

Moltmann, Jürgen, *The Theology of Hope.* London: SCM Press, 1967.

Moltmann, Jürgen, *The Crucified God.* London: SCM Press, 1974.

Moltmann, Jürgen, *God in Creation: An Ecological Doctrine of God.* London: SCM Press, 1985.

Ogden, Schubert H. *The Reality of God and other Essays.* London: SCM Press, 1967.

Oman, John. *Grace and Personality.* 2nd. ed. Cambridge: Cambridge University Press, 1919.

Pailin, David A. *God and the Processes of Reality.* London: Routledge, 1989.

Pittenger, Norman. *Picturing God.* London: SCM Press, 1982.

Polkinghorne, John. *Science and Providence.* London: SPCK, 1989.

Ruether, Rosemary R. *Sexism and God Talk: Towards a Feminist Theology.* London: SCM Press, 1983.

Torrance, Thomas F. *Christian Doctrine of God: One Being Three Persons.* Edinburgh: T & T Clark, 1995.

Vanstone, William H. *Love's Endeavour, Love's Expense.* London: Darton, Longman & Todd, 1977.

Ward, Keith. *Rational Theology and the Creativity of God.* Oxford: Basil Blackwell, 1982.

Ward, Keith. *Divine Action.* London: Collins Flame, 1990.
Ward, Keith. *God, Chance and Necessity.* Oxford: One World, 1996.

Wiles, Maurice F. *Faith and the Mystery of God.* London: SCM Press, 1982.

Wiles, Maurice F. *God's Action in the World.* London: SCM Press, 1986.

Chapter 6

Boff, Leonardo. *Trinity and Society.* Tunbridge Wells, Kent: Burns & Oates, 1988.

British Council of Churches. *The Forgotten Trinity: Study Commission on Trinitarian Doctrine Today.* 3 vols. London: CCBI, 1992.

Brown, David. *Divine Trinity.* La Salle, Illinois: Open Court, 1984.

Calvin, John. *Institutes* 1, 13.

Fiddes, Paul. *Participating in God: A Pastoral Doctrine of the Trinity.* London: Darton, Longman and Todd Ltd., 2000.

Gunton, Colin. *The Promise of Trinitarian Theology.* Edinburgh: T & T Clark, 1991.

Hanson, Richard P C. *The Search for the Christian Doctrine of God.* Edinburgh: T & T Clark, 1988.

Moltmann, Jürgen. *The Crucified God.* London: SCM Press, 1974.

Moltmann, Jürgen. *The Trinity and the Kingdom of God.* London: SCM Press, 1981.

Ogden, Schubert M. 'On the Trinity'. *Theology,* LXXXIII, 692 (March 1980), pp 97–102.

Torrance, Alan. *Persons in Communion: Trinitarian Description and Human Participation.* Edinburgh: T & T Clark, 1996.

Torrance, Thomas F. *The Trinitarian Faith.* Edinburgh: T & T Clark, 1988.

Torrance, Thomas F. *Trinitarian Perspectives.* Edinburgh: T & T Clark, 1994.

Ward, Keith. *A Vision to Pursue: Beyond the Crisis in Christianity.* London: SCM Press, 1991.

Wiles, Maurice F. *Archetypal Heresy: Arianism through the Centuries.* Oxford: Oxford University Press, 1996.

Williams, Rowan. *The Trinity.* Edinburgh: Edinburgh University Press, 1998.

Williams, Rowan. *Arius: Heresy and Tradition.* 2nd. ed. London: SCM Press, 2001.

Chapter 7

Calvin, John. *Institutes* 2, 1-6.

Cave, Sydney. *The Christian Estimate of Man.* London: Duckworth, 1944.

Farley, Edward. *Good and Evil: Interpreting a Human Condition.* Minneapolis: Fortress Press, 1990.

Farmer, Herbert H. *The World and God: A Study of Prayer, Providence and Miracle in Christian Experience.* Rev. ed. London: Nisbet & Co. Ltd., 1936.

Gutierrez, Gustavo. *A Theology of Liberation: History, Politics and Salvation.* Maryknoll, NY: Orbis Books, 1973.

Gutierrez, Gustavo. *The Power of the Poor in History: Selected Writings.* Maryknoll, NY: Orbis Books, 1983.

Hampson, Daphne. 'Reinhold Niebuhr on Sin: A Critique'. In *Reinhold Niebuhr and the Issues of our Time,* pp 46–60. Edited by Richard Harries. London: Mowbrays 1986.

Hampson, Daphne. *Theology and Feminism.* Oxford: Basil Blackwell Ltd., 1990.

Hodgson, Peter C. *Winds of the Spirit: A Constructive Christian Theology.* London: SCM Press, 1994.

Jenkins, David E. *The Contradiction of Christianity.* London: SCM Press, 1976.

Kierkegaard, Søren *The Sickness Unto Death.* Princeton: Princeton University Press, 1941.

Macquarrie, John. *In Search of Humanity: A Theological and Philosophical Approach.* London: SCM Press, 1982.

Miguez-Bonino, José. *Revolutionary Theology Comes of Age.* London: SPCK, 1975.

Niebuhr, Reinhold. *The Nature and Destiny of Man.* 2 vols. London: Nisbet & Co. Ltd., 1941.

Niebuhr, Reinhold. *The Children of Light and the Children of Darkness.* London: Nisbet & Co. Ltd., 1945.

Niebuhr, Reinhold. *Moral Man and Immoral Society: A Study in Ethics and Politics.* New York: Charles Scribner's Sons, 1960.

Pittenger, Norman. *Cosmic Love and Human Wrong: The Reconception of the Meaning of Sin, in the Light of Process Theology.* New York: Paulist Press, 1978.

Schleiermacher, Frederick D E. *The Christian Faith,* pp 233–354.

Segundo, Juan Luis. *Grace and the Human Condition.* Maryknoll, NT: Orbis Books, 1973.

Smith, Ronald Gregor. *The Free Man: Studies in Christian Anthropology.* London: Collins, 1969.

Chapter 8

Baillie, Donald M. *God Was In Christ: An Essay on Incarnation and Atonement.* London: Faber and Faber Ltd., 1961.

Bartsch, Hans-Werner, ed. and Fuller, Reginald H trans. *Kerygma and Myth: A Theological Debate.* London: SPCK, 1972.

Boff, Leonardo. *Jesus Christ Liberator: Critical Christology.* Maryknoll, NY: Orbis Books, 1978.

Bornkamm, G?nther. *Jesus of Nazareth.* London: Hodder and Stoughton, 1960.

Bowden, John. *Jesus: The Unanswered Questions.* London: SCM Press, 1988.

Bultmann, Rudolf. *New Testament and Mythology and Other Basic Writings.* Selected, edited and translated by Schubert M Ogden. London: SCM Press, 1984.

Bultmann, Rudolf. *Jesus and the Word.* London: Fontana Books, 1958.

Cadoux, Cecil J. *The Case for Evangelical Modernism: A Study of the Relation Between the Christian Faith and Traditional Theology.* London: Hodder and Stoughton Ltd., 1938.

Cadoux, Cecil J. *The Life of Jesus.* West Drayton, Middlesex: Penguin Books, 1948.

Calvin, John. *Institutes.* 2, 12–17.

Cave, Sydney. *The Doctrine of the Person of Christ.* London: Duckworth, 1925.

Dodd, Charles H. *The Founder of Christianity.* London: Collins, 1971.

Dunn, James D G. *Christology in the Making: Inquiry into the Origins of the Doctrine of the Incarnation.* London: SCM Press, 1989.

Forsyth, Peter T. *The Person and Place of Jesus Christ.* London: Hodder and Stoughton, 1910.

Gunton, Colin E. *Yesterday and Today: A Study of Continuities in Christology.* London: Darton, Longman and Todd, 1983.

Hebblethwaite, Brian. *Incarnation: Collected Essays in Christology.* Cambridge: Cambridge University Press, 1987.

Hick, John ed. *The Myth of God Incarnate.* London: SCM Press, 1993.

Macquarrie, John. *Jesus Christ in Modern Thought.* London: SCM Press, 1990.

Mackay, James P. *Jesus the Man and the Myth: A Contemporary Christology.* London: SCM Press, 1979.

McIntyre, John. *The Shape of Christology: Studies in the Doctrine of the Person of Christ.* Edinburgh: T & T Clark, 1998.

Miguez-Bonino, José. *Faces of Jesus: Latin American Christologies.* Maryknoll, NY: Orbis Books, 1985.

Mitton, C Leslie. *Jesus: The Fact Behind the Faith.* Oxford: A R Mowbray & Co. Ltd., 1975.

Moule, Charles F D. *The Origin of Christology.* Cambridge: Cambridge University Press, 1978.

Ogden, Schubert M. *Christ Without Myth: A Study Based on the Theology of Rudolf Bultmann.* London: Collins, 1962.

Ogden, Schubert M. *The Point of Christology.* London: SCM Press, 1982.

Robinson, John A T. *The Human Face of God.* London: SCM Press Ltd., 1973.

Schüssler Fiorenza, Elizabeth S. *In Memory of Her: A Feminist Theological Reconstruction of Christian Origins.* London: SCM Press, 1983.

Sobrino, Jan. *Christology at the Crossroads: A Latin American Approach.* Maryknoll, NY: Orbis Books, 1978.

Theissen, G. and Merz A. *The Historical Jesus: A Comprehensive Guide.* London: SCM Press, 1998.

Vermes, Geza. *Jesus the Jew: A Historian's Reading of the Gospels.* London: SCM Press, 1973.

Wright, N Thomas. *Jesus and the Victory of God: Christian Origins and the Question of God.* London: SPCK, 1996.

Chapter 9

Aulén, Gustav. *Christus Victor: An Historical Study of the Three Main Types of the Idea of Atonement.* London: SPCK, 1931.

Baillie, Donald M. *God Was In Christ: An Essay on Incarnation and Atonement.* London: Faber and Faber Ltd.,1961.

Boff, Leonardo. *Passion of Christ, Passion of the World.* Maryknoll, NY: Orbis Books, 1987.

Bushnell, Horace. *The Vicarious Sacrifice Grounded in Principles of Universal Obligation.* London: Stanham and Co., 1871.

Calvin, John. *Institutes*, 2, 15–17.

Campbell, John McLeod. *The Nature of Atonement and its Relation to the Remission of Sins and Eternal Life.* Cambridge: Macmillan and Co., 1856.

Campbell, R J. *The New Theology.* London: Chapman and Hall, 1907.

Cave, Sydney. *The Doctrine of the Work of Christ.* London: University of London Press, Ltd. and Hodder and Stoughton Ltd., 1937.

Dillistone, Frederick W. *The Christian Understanding of Atonement.* Reissue. London: SCM Press, 1984.

Fiddes, Paul S. *Past Event and Present Salvation: The Christian Idea of Atonement.* London: Darton, Longman and Todd, 1989.

Forsyth, Peter T. *The Work of Christ.* 2nd. ed. London: Independent Press Ltd., 1938.

Forsyth, Peter T. *The Justification of God: Lectures for War-Time on a Christian Theology.* London: Independent Press Ltd., 1948.

Forsyth, Peter T. *The Cruciality of the Cross.* Carlisle: Paternoster Press, 1997.

Gunton, Colin E. *The Actuality of Atonement: A Study of Metaphor, Rationality and the Christian Tradition.* Edinburgh: T & T Clark Ltd., 1988.

Hick, John. *The Metaphor of God Incarnate.* London: SCM Press, 1993.

Macquarrie, John. *Jesus Christ in Modern Thought.* London: SCM Press, 1990.

McIntyre, John. *The Shape of Soteriology: Studies in the Doctrine of the Death of Christ.* Edinburgh: T & T Clark, 1995.

Pailin, David A. 'The Doctrine of the Atonement: (2) Does it Rest on a Mistake?' *Epworth Press,* 18, 3 (September 1991), pp 68–77.

Schleiermacher, Frederick D E. *The Christian Faith,* pp 425–75.

Whale, John S. *Victor and Victim: The Christian Doctrine of Redemption.* Cambridge: Cambridge University Press, 1960.

White, Vernon. *Atonement and Incarnation: An Essay in Universalism and Particularity.* Cambridge: Cambridge University Press, 1991.

Young, Frances. *Sacrifice and the Death of Christ.* London: SPCK, 1975.

Chapter 10

Calvin, John. *Institutes* 3, 1–3.

Cox, Harvey. *Fire from Heaven: The Rise of Pentecostal Spirituality and the Reshaping of Religion in the Twenty-first Century.* London: Cassell, 1996.

Doctrine Commission of the Church of England. *We Believe in the Holy Spirit.* London: Church House Publishing, 1991.

Dunn, James D G. *Baptism in the Holy Spirit: A Re-examination of the New Testament Teaching on the Gift of the Spirit in Relation to Pentecostalism Today.* London: SCM Press, 1970.

Dunn, James D G. *Jesus and the Spirit.* London: SCM Press, 1975.

Dunn, James D G. *The Christ and The Spirit.* 2 vols. Edinburgh: T & T Clark, 1998.

Fox, Matthew, *Original Blessing: A Primer in Creation Spirituality.* Sainte Fe: Bear & Co., 1990.

Lampe, Geoffrey W H. *God as Spirit.* Oxford: Clarendon Press, 1978.

Moltmann, Jürgen. *The Trinity and the Kingdom of God: The Doctrine of God.* London: SCM Press, 1981.

Moltmann, Jürgen. *The Spirit of Life: A Universal Affirmation.* London: SCM Press, 1992.

Moltmann, Jürgen. *Source of Life: Holy Spirit and the Theology of Life.* London: SCM Press,1997.

Moule, Charles F D. *The Holy Spirit.* London: Mowbray, 1978.

Nuttall, Geoffrey F. *The Holy Spirit in Puritan Faith and Experience.* Oxford: Basil Blackwell, 1949.

Schleiermacher, Frederick D E. *The Christian Faith,* pp 560–81.

Smail, T, Walker. A and Wright, N. *Charismatic Renewal: The Search for a Theology.* London: SPCK, 1993.

Taylor, John V. *The Go-Between God: The Holy Spirit and the Christian Mission.* London: SCM Press, 1972.

Welker, Michael. *God the Spirit.* Philadelphia: Fortress Press, 1994.

Chapters 11 and 12

Augustine *On the Predestination of the Saints.* In *A Select Library of the Nicene and Post-Nicene Fathers of the Christian Church,* vol. 5, pp 494–519. Edited by Philip Schaff. Edinburgh: T & T Clark and Grand Rapids, Michigan: William B Eerdmans Publishing Company, 1997.

Barth, Karl. *Church Dogmatics* II, 2. Edinburgh: T & T Clark, 1957, pp 3–506.

Braaten, Carl E. *Justification: The Article by which the Church Stands or Falls.* Philadelphia: Fortress Press, 1990.

Calvin, John. *Institutes.* 3, 11–18; 21–24.

Calvin, John. *Concerning the Eternal Predestination of God.* Trans. with an intro. by J K S. Reid. London: James Clark & Co. Ltd., 1961.

D'Costa, Gavin ed. *Christian Uniqueness Reconsidered.* Maryknoll, NT: Orbis Books, 1990.

Dunn, James D G and Suggate, Alan M. *Justice of God: Fresh Look at the Old Doctrine of Justification by Faith.* Carlisle: Paternoster Press, 1993.

Ford, David F. *Self and Salvation: Being Transformed.* Cambridge: Cambridge University Press, 1999.

Gerrish, Brian A. *Tradition in the Modern World: Reformed Theology in the Nineteenth Century.* Chicago: The University of Chicago Press, 1978.

Hick, John. *God and the Universe of Faiths.* London and Basingstoke: The Macmillan Press, 1973.

Hick, John. *God has Many Names.* London and Basingstoke: The Macmillan Press, Ltd., 1980.

Hick, John. *The Rainbow of Faiths: Critical Dialogues on Religious Pluralism.* London: SCM Press Ltd., 1995.

Hick, John and Knitter, Paul F eds. *The Myth of Christian Uniqueness.* London: SCM Press Ltd., 1987.

Knitter, Paul F. *No Other Name: A Critical Survey of Christian Attitudes Toward the World Religions*. London: SCM Press, 1985.

Küng, Hans. *Justification: The Doctrine of Karl Barth and a Catholic Reflection*. London: Burns and Oates, 1964.

Lindström, Harald. *Wesley and Sanctification: A Study in the Doctrine of Salvation*. London: The Epworth Press, 1950.

McGrath, Alister E. *Iustitia Dei: A History of the Christian Doctrine of Justification*. 2 vols. Cambridge: Cambridge University Press, 1986.

McGrath, Alister E. *Justification by Faith: What it means for us today*. London: Marshall Pickering, 1988.

McGrath, Alister E. *Reformation Thought: An Introduction*. 2nd. ed. Oxford: Basil Blackwell Ltd., 1993.

Newbigin, J F Lesslie. *The Open Secret: Sketches for a Missionary Theology*. Grand Rapids, Michigan: William B Eerdmans Publishing Company, 1978.

Newbigin, J F Lesslie. *The Gospel in a Pluralist Society*. London: SPCK, 1991.

Ogden, Schubert M. *Is There Only One True Religion Or Are There Many?* Dallas: Southern Methodist University Press, 1992.

Race, Alan. *Christians and Religious Pluralism: Patterns in the Christian Theology of Religions*. London: SCM Press, 1983.

Schleiermacher, Friedrich D E. *The Christian Faith*, pp 476–560.

Sell, Alan P F. *The Great Debate: Calvinism, Arminianism and Salvation*. Worthing: H E Walter Ltd., 1982.

Wesley, John. *A Plain Account of Christian Perfection*. Works, xi, pp 366–448. London: John Mason, 1830.

Wesley, John. Christian Perfection'. In *Sermons On Several Occasions*. London: The Epworth Press, 1944.

Chapter 13

Barth, Karl. *Church Dogmatics* III, pp 289–368.

Cobb, John B Jnr. and Pinnock, Clark H. *Searching for an Adequate God: A Dialogue between Process and Free Will Theists*. Grand Rapids, Michigan: William B Eerdmans Publishing Company, 2000.

Davis, Stephen T. *Encountering Evil: Live Options in Theodicy*. Edinburgh: T & T Clark Ltd., 1981.

Farmer, Herbert H. *Towards Belief in God*. London: SCM Press Ltd., 1942.

Farrer, Austin. *Love Almighty and Ills Unlimited*. London: Fontana, 1966.

Fiddes, Paul S. *The Creative Suffering of God*. Oxford: Clarendon Press, 1988.

Griffin, David R. *God, Power and Evil: A Process Theodicy*. Philadelphia: The Westminster Press, 1976.

Hick, John. *Evil and the God of Love*. London: Macmillan and Co. Ltd., 1968.

Surrin, Kenneth. *Theology and the Problem of Evil*. Oxford: Basil Blackwell, 1986.

Vardy, Peter. *The Puzzle of Evil*. London: Fount, 1992.

Chapter 14

Boff, Leonardo. *Church, Charism and Power – Liberation Theology and the Institutional Church*. London: SCM Press, 1985.

Calvin, John. *Institutes* IV, 1-2.

Dulles, Avery. *Models of the Church: A Critical Assessment of the Church in all its Aspects*. Dublin: Gill and Macmillan Ltd., 1976.

Forsyth, Peter T. *Lectures on the Church and Sacraments*. London: Longmans, Green and Co., 1917.

Gunton, Colin E and Hardy, Daniel W eds. *On Being the Church: Essays on the Christian Community*. Edinburgh: T & T Clark Ltd., 1993.

Hodgson, Peter C. *Revisioning the Church: Ecclesial Freedom in the New Paradigm*. Philadelphia: Fortress Press, 1988.

Jenkins, Daniel T. *The Nature of Catholicity*. London: Faber and Faber Ltd., 1942.

Küng, Hans. *The Church*. London: Burns and Oates, 1968.

Manning, Bernard L. *Essays in Orthodox Dissent*. London: Independent Press, 1939.

Moltmann, Jürgen. *The Church In the Power of the Spirit*. London: SCM Press, 1977.

Raiser, Konrad. *Ecumenism in Transition: A Paradigm Shift in the Ecumenical Movement*. Geneva: WCC, 1991.

Ogden, Schubert M. 'The Authority of Scripture for Theology'. In *On Theology*. San Francisco: Harper & Row Publishers, 1986.

Thorogood, Bernard. *One Wind, Many Flames: Church Unity and Diversity of the Churches*. Geneva: WCC, 1991.

Chapter 15

Baillie, Donald M. *The Theology of the Sacraments and Other Papers*. London: Faber and Faber Ltd., 1957.

Baillie, John. *Baptism and Conversion*. London: Oxford University Press, 1964.

Barth, Karl. *The Teaching of the Church Regarding Baptism*. London: SCM Press, 1948.

Barth, Karl. *Church Dogmatics.* IV, 4. Edinburgh: T & T Clark, 1969.

Calvin, John. *Institutes.* 4, 14–19.

Durber, Susan and Walton, Heather eds. *Silence in Heaven: A Book of Women's Preaching.* London: SCM Press, 1994.

Forsyth, Peter T. *Positive Preaching and the Modern Mind.* London: Independent Press Ltd., 1907.

Forsyth, Peter T. *Lectures on the Church and Sacraments.* London: Longmans, Green and Co., 1917.

Gerrish, Brian A. *Grace and Gratitude: The Eucharistic Theology of John Calvin.* Edinburgh: T & T Clark, 1992.

Gorringe, Timothy. *The Sign of Love: Reflections on the Eucharist.* London: SPCK, 1977.

Hilton, Donald H. *Table Talk: Looking at the Communion Table from the Outside and the Inside.* London: URC, 1998.

Heron, Alisdair. *Table and Tradition: Towards an Ecumenical Understanding of the Eucharist.* Edinburgh: The Handsal Press, 1983.

Jeremias, Joachim. *The Eucharistic Words of Jesus.* Oxford: Basil Blackwell, 1955.

Kreider Eleanor. *Given For You: A Fresh Look At Communion.* Leicester: Inter Varsity Press, 1998.

Lash, Nicholas. *His Presence in the World: A Study in Eucharistic Worship and Theology.* London: Sheed and Ward, 1974.

Macquarrie, John. *A Guide to the Sacraments.* London: SCM Press, 1997.

Marty, Martin E. *Baptism.* Philadelphia: Fortress Press, 1977.

Migliore, Daniel. 'Reforming the Theology and Practice of Baptism'. In *Toward the Future of Reformed Theology: Tasks, Topics, Traditions,* pp 494–511. Edited by David Willis and Michael Welker. Grand Rapids, Michigan and Cambridge, U.K.: William B Eerdmans Publishing Company, 1999.

Micklem, Nathaniel ed. *Christian Worship: Studies in its History and Meaning.* Oxford: Oxford University Press, 1936.

Moltmann, Jürgen. *The Church in the Power of the Spirit.* London: SCM Press, 1977.

Report of the Faith and Order Commission of the World Council of Churches: *Baptism, Eucharist and Ministry.* Faith and Order Paper III. Geneva: WCC, 1982.

Stott, John R W. *I Believe In Preaching.* London: Hodder and Stoughton, 1998.

Theissen, Gerd. *Sign Language of Faith: Opportunities for Preaching Today.* London: SCM Press, 1995.

White, James F. *Sacraments as God's Self-giving.* Minneapolis, Minn.: Augsburg Press, 1993.

Yates, Arthur S. *Why Baptize Infants? A Study of the Biblical, Traditional and Theological Evidence.* Norwich: The Canterbury Press, 1993.

Zwingli, Huldrych. 'On the Lord's Supper'. In *The Library of Christian Classics* XXIV: Zwingli and Bullinger, pp 176–238. Edited by G W Bromiley. London: SCM Press, 1953.

Chapter 16

Anderson, Ray S. *Thelogical Foundations for Ministry.* Edinburgh: T & T Clark, 1979.

Ballard, Paul. *Issues in Church Related Community Work.* Cardiff: University of Wales College of Cardiff, 1990.

Ballard, Paul. ed. *Voices from the Margins: Nonstipendiary Ministry in the Church in Wales – Contemporary Perceptions, Attitudes and Experiences.* Cardiff: University of Wales College of Cardiff, 1996.

Baxter, Richard. *The Reformed Pastor.* London: The Epworth Press, 1939.

Beasley-Murray, Paul ed. *Anyone for Ordination? A Contribution to the Debate on Ordination.* London: Marc, 1993.

Boff, Leonardo. *Ecclesiogenesis.* Maryknoll, NY: Orbis Books, 1986.

Bouteneff, Peter C and Falconer, Alan D eds. Episkope *and Episcopacy and the Quest for Visible Unity.* Geneva: WCC, 1999.

Calvin, John. *Institutes* 4, 3–11.

Forsyth, Peter T. *Rome, Reform and Reaction: Four Lectures on the Religious Situation.* London: Hodder and Stoughton, 1899.

Forsyth, Peter T. *Positive Preaching and the Modern Mind.* London: Independent Press Ltd., 1907.

Forsyth, Peter T. *Lectures on the Church and Sacraments.* London: Longmans, Green and Co., 1917.

Forsyth, Peter T. *Revelation Old and New: Sermons and Addresses.* Edited by John Huxtable. London: Independent Press Ltd., 1962.

Herrenbrück, Walter. 'Presbytery and Leadership in the Church'. in *Toward the Future of Reformed Theology: Tasks, Topics, Traditions,* pp 283–301. Edited by David Willis and Michael Welker. Grand Rapids, Michigan and Cambridge, UK: William B Eerdmans Publishing Company, 1999.

Jenkins, Daniel T. *The Gift of Ministry.* London: Faber & Faber, 1947.

Jenkins, Daniel T. *Congregationalism: A Restatement.* London: Faber and Faber, 1954.

Manning, Bernard L. *Essays in Orthodox Dissent.* London: Independent Press, 1939.

Mayor, Stephen H. *Being an Elder in the United Reformed Church.* London: URC, 1977.

McKee, Elsie Anne. 'The Offices of Elders and Deacons in the Classical Reformed Tradition in *Major Themes in the Reformed Tradition,* pp 344–53. Edited by Donald K McKinn. Grand Rapids, Michigan: William B Eerdmans Publishing Company, 1992.

Peel, David R. 'P T Forsyth on Ministry: A Model for our Time?' in *P T Forsyth: Theologian for a New Millenium?*, pp 171–208. Edited by Alan P F Sell. London: URC, 1999.

Report of the Faith and Order Commission of the World Council of Churches: *Baptism, Eucharist and Ministry*. Faith and Order Paper III. Geneva: WCC, 1982.

Rowe, Trevor. *Easier Yoke?: Perspectives on Christian Ministry*. London: Epworth Press, 1992.

Samartha, Stanley J. *Between Two Cultures: Ecumenical Work in a Pluralist World*. Geneva: WCC, 1996.

Sell, Alan P F *Saints: Visible, Orderly and Catholic*. Geneva: World Alliance of Reformed Churches, 1986.

Torrance, Thomas F. *Royal Priesthood: Theology of Ordained Ministry*. Edinburgh: T & T Clark, 1993.

Vischer, Lukas. 'The Office of the Elders'. In *The Ministry of the Elders in the Reformed Churches*, pp 9–95. Edited by Lukas Vischer. Bern: Evangelische Arbeitsstelle Oekumene Schweiz, 1992.

Vischer, Lukas. ed. *Eldership in the Reformed Churches Today: Report of an International Consultation*. Geneva: World Alliance of Reformed Churches, 1991.

Walton, Heather. 'And Abuse of Power 2: Finders, Keepers, Loosers, Weepers – A Polemic Concerning the Priests of God and the Ministers of Religion' in *Modern Churchman*, XXXIV, 2 (1992), pp 21–6.

Chapter 17

Calvin, John. *Institutes*. 4, 12.

Davies, Horton. *Worship and Theology in England*. 6 vols. Princeton: Princeton University Press and Grand Rapids, Michigan: William B Eerdmans, 1970–1996.

Jones, Cheslyn, Wainwright, Geoffrey and Yarnald, Edward eds. *The Study of Spirituality*. London: SPCK, 1986.

McGrath, Alister E. *Christian Spirituality*. Oxford: Basil Blackwell, 1999.

Rice, Howard L. *Reformed Spirituality: An Introduction for Believers*. Louisville, Kentucky: Westminster/John Knox Press, 1991.

Underhill, Evelyn. *Worship*. London: Nisbet & Co. Ltd., 1936.

Wakefield, Gordon. *An Outline of Christian Worship*. Edinburgh: T & T Clark, 1998.

Watson, Richard. *The English Hymn: A Critical and Historical Study*. Oxford: Oxford University Press, 1999.

White, James F. *Protestant Worship: Traditions in Transition*. Louisville, Kentucky: Westminster/John Knox Press, 1989.

White, James F. *Introduction to Christian Worship*. Rev. ed. Nashville: Abingdon Press, 1990.

White, Susan J. *Groundwork of Christian Worship*. London: Epworth Press, 1997.

Wren, Brian A. *What Language Shall I Borrow? God Talk In Worship: A Male Response to Feminist Theology*. London: SCM Press, 1989.

Chapters 18, 19 and 20

Badham, Paul and Badham, Linda. *Immortality or Extinction?* London: Macmillan, 1982.

Baillie, John. *And The Life Everlasting.* London: Oxford University Press, 1934.

Baukham, Richard. 'The Millenennium' in *God Will Be All In All: The Eschatology of Jürgen Moltmann,* pp 123–47. Edited by Richard Baukham. Edinburgh: T & T Clark, 1999.

Calvin, John. *Institutes.* 3, 9 and 21–4.

Davies, Brian. *An Introduction to the Philosophy of Religion.* 2nd. ed. pp 212–34. Oxford: Oxford University Press, 1993.

Forsyth, Peter T. *This Life And The Next.* London: Macmillan and Co. Ltd., 1918.

Hick, John. *Death and Eternal Life.* London: Collins, 1976.

Küng, Hans. *Eternal Life?: Life After Death as a Medical, Philosophical and Theological Problem.* London: SCM Press, 1991.

McKelvey, R J. *The Millennium and the Book of Revelation.* Cambridge: The Lutterworth Press, 1999.

Moltmann, Jürgen. *The Theology of Hope: On the Ground and Implications of a Christian Eschatology.* London: SCM Press, 1967.

Moltmann, Jürgen. *The Experiment Hope.* London: SCM Press, 1975.

Moltmann, Jürgen. *The Coming of God: Christian Eschatology.* London: SCM Press, 1996.

Moltmann, Jürgen. 'The Logic of Hell' in *God Will Be All In All: The Eschatology of Jürgen Moltmann,* pp 43–7. Edited by Richard Baukham. Edinburgh: T& T Clark, 1999.

Ogden, Schubert M. 'The Meaning of Christian Hope' in *Religious Experience and Process Theology: The Pastoral Implications of a Major Modern Movement,* pp 195–212. Edited by Harry James Cargas and Bernard Lee. New York: Paulist Press, 1976.

Pailin, David A. *Groundwork of Philosophy of Religion,* pp 181–97. London: Epworth Press, 1986.

Quistorp, Heinrich. *Calvin's Doctrine of the Last Things.* London: Lutterworth Press, 1955.

Rodd, Cyril C. *Is There Life After Death?* London: SCM Press, 1998.

Rowland, Christopher. *The Open Heaven: A Study of Apocalyptic in Judaism and Early Christianity.* London: SPCK, 1982.

INDEX

J

James, 153
Jenkins, Daniel, 190, 199-200, 240, 241, 244, 247-8, 260, 275
Jenkins, David E, 9
Jerome, 140
Jerusalem
  church at 25
  temple at 241
  see also Councils
Jesus Christ
  alienation from God
  ambassador 241
  ascension 92
  Christ event 29, 114, 116, 125, 140, 152, 194, 201, 210, 222
  death on the cross 29, 38, 48, 56, 57, 64, 68, 93, 96, 97, 98, **103-28**, 142, 145, 146,167, 181, 209, 210, 212, 218, 222, 230, 234, 247-8, 265, 283, 295, 297, 312, 313
  descent into hell 313
  divinity 6, 7, 21, 42, 51-3, 55, 80, 82, 84, 88, 91, 93, 95, 98, 99, 101
  first born 93
  healer 92
  holiness and perfection 85, 94, 96, 99
  humanity 51, 82-3, 91, 93, 97, 99, 101
  Jesus of History – Christ of Faith 64, 79, 86, **87-94**, 96, 101, 110, 125
  inclusivity 288
  judge 94, 205, 305, 306
  king 83, 94, 107, 109
  liberator 222
  life and teaching 48, 64, **79-102**, 125, 127, 212, 222, 239
  lord 58, 80, 89, 93, 95, 109
  love 96, 105, 113, 115, 116, 121
  Messiah 145, 223
  obedience 107-8, 109, 119, 155
  omniscience 92
  only-begotten 51-2
  pre-existence 92, 97, 99, 101
  priest 83-4, 107-8, 231
  prophet 83, 95, 107
  reconciler and mediator 58, 82, 97, 106, 110, 223
  redeemer 17, 18, 29, 41, 58, 80, 82, 85, 94, 95, 98, 106, 107, 109, 110, 111, 136, 139, 214, 231, 235, 305

  representative 101, 108, 112, 118, 119, 222
  resurrection 37, 48, 64, 68, 92, 93, 97, 104, 146, 200, 212, 218, 222, 230, 297, 298, 305, 311
  sacrifice 96
  saviour 51, 67, 88, 93, 96, 97, 103, 117, 145, 205, 223, 285
  servant 241
  suffering 93, 106, 108, 111, 116, 118, 128, 145, 181, 297
  uniqueness 107
  victim 231
  virgin birth 6, 85, 87, 92, 93
    see also atonement, christology, crucifixion, incarnation, *kenosis*, logos, *plerosis*, redemption, resurrection, salvation, son of God, Son of man, soteriology, Word of God
John, the Seer of Patmos, 305, 316
John, the writer of John's Gospel, 299
Jones, Richard, 203-4
John the Baptist, 145, 215, 223
Judaism, 49, 103, 151, 220, 231, 249, 255
  Jewish meals 229-30
Judgement, 209, 223, 286, 295, 319, 324
  Last Judgement (End-time) 120, 196, 295, 304, 316, 317
  see also damnation, God, Jesus
justice, 145, 151, 258, 283, 306, 312, 313
justification, 88, 130, 151-6, 197, 270, 281

K

Kaan, Fred, 278
Kant, Immanuel, 309
Kaufman, Gordon, 23
Käsemann, Ernst, 6, 88, 192
Kaye, Elaine, 90n37
Keats, John, 177
kenosis, 33-4, 43, 49, 57, 94-100, 143-4, 145, 210, 241-2
kerygma, kerygmatic, 88-9, 202, 272
Kingdom of God, 73, 83, 107, 153, 196, 199, 230, 246, 258, 274, 279, 295, 296, 298, 299, 313, 315, 317, 324
Kirkegaard, Søren, 18, 124
koinonia, 59, 212, 230, 231, 235
Knitter, Paul, 185
Küng, Hans, 198

L

M